Early Intervention/Early Childhood Special Education

Early Intervention/Early Childhood Special Education

Recommended Practices

Samuel L. Odom
Mary E. McLean

pro·ed
8700 Shoal Creek Boulevard
Austin, Texas 78757-6897

pro·ed

© 1996 by PRO-ED, Inc.
8700 Shoal Creek Boulevard
Austin, Texas 78757-6897

All rights reserved. No part of the material protected by this copyright notice may be reproduced or utilized in any form or by any means, electronic or mechanical, including photocopying, recording, or by any information storage and retrieval system, without the prior written permission of the copyright owner.

Publisher's Note: The Division on Early Childhood of the Council for Exceptional Children will receive all royalties from the sales of this book.

Library of Congress Cataloging-in-Publication Data

Early intervention/early childhood special education : recommended
   practices / [edited by] Samuel L. Odom, Mary E. McLean.
      p.   cm.
   Includes bibliographical references and index.
   ISBN 0-89079-648-3
     1. Handicapped children—Education (Early childhood)—United
States.   2. Handicapped children—Services for—United States.
3. Early childhood education—Parent participation—United States.
4. Special education—United States.   I. Odom, Samuel L.
II. McLean, Mary E.
LC4031.E27   1996
371.9'0472'0973—dc20   95-25823
                                                                                                           CIP

This book is designed in Palatino.

Production Manager: Alan Grimes
Production Coordinator: Karen Swain
Managing Editor: Tracy Sergo
Art Director: Thomas Barkley
Reprints Buyer: Alicia Woods
Editor: Cynthia Woerner Halm
Editorial Assistant: Claudette Landry
Editorial Assistant: Martin Wilson

Printed in the United States of America

1   2   3   4   5   6   7   8   9   10   00   99   98   97   96

Contents

Contributors vii
Preface ix

1. Establishing Recommended Practices in Early Intervention/Early Childhood Special Education 1
   Mary E. McLean and Samuel L. Odom

2. Assessment for Early Intervention: Emerging Themes and Practices 23
   John T. Neisworth and Stephen J. Bagnato

3. Family Participation 59
   Lisbeth J. Vincent and Mary E. McLean

4. Development and Implementation of IFSPs and IEPs: Opportunities for Empowerment 77
   Vicki P. Turbiville, Ann P. Turnbull, Corinne W. Garland, and Ilene M. Lee

5. The Widespread Adoption of Service Delivery Recommendations: A Systems Change Perspective 101
   Phillip S. Strain, Barbara J. Smith, and R. A. McWilliam

6. General Curriculum and Intervention Strategies 125
   Mark Wolery and Diane M. Sainato

7. Promoting the Cognitive Competence of Young Children with or at Risk for Developmental Disabilities 159
   Carl J. Dunst, Gerald Mahoney, and Kristin Buchan

8. Indicators of Quality in Communication Intervention 197
   Howard Goldstein, Louise A. Kaczmarek, and Nancy H. Hepting

9. Strategies for Promoting Social Interaction and Emotional Development of Infants and Young Children with Disabilities and Their Families 223
   Mary A. McEvoy and Samuel L. Odom

10. Intervention Strategies to Promote Motor Skills 245
    Rebecca R. Fewell

11. Interventions to Promote Adaptive Behavior Skills 259
    Eva M. Horn

12. Transition 287
    Mary Beth Bruder and Lynette Chandler

13. Early Childhood Education of Children Who Are Gifted 309
    Stephen W. Stile

14   Personnel Preparation in Early Education and Intervention:
     Recommended Preservice and Inservice Practices   329
     Patricia S. Miller and Vicki D. Stayton

15   Program Evaluation   359
     Scott Snyder and Robert Sheehan

Appendix: DEC Recommended Practices   379

Author Index   415

Subject Index   431

Contributors

Stephen J. Bagnato
Children's Hospital of Pittsburgh
University of Pittsburgh School of Medicine
One Children's Place
3705 5th Avenue at DeSoto Street
Pittsburgh, PA 15213-3417

Mary Beth Bruder
Child and Family Studies
University of Connecticut Health Center
309 Farmington Avenue, Suite A-200
Farmington, CT 06032

Kristin Buchan
Allegheny-Singer Research Institute
320 East North Avenue
Pittsburgh, PA 15212

Lynette Chandler
EPSCE
Graham Hall
Northern Illinois University
DeKalb, IL 60115

Carl Dunst
Allegheny-Singer Research Institute
320 East North Avenue
Pittsburgh, PA 15212

Rebecca R. Fewell
Debbie School
University of Miami
P.O. Box 014621
Miami, FL 33101

Corrine Garland
Child Developmental Resources
P.O. Box 299
Lightfoot, VA 23090

Howard Goldstein
Department of Communication
117 Cathedral of Learning
University of Pittsburgh
Pittsburgh, PA 15260

Nancy H. Hepting
Child Language Intervention Program
3600 Forbes Avenue, #500
Pittsburgh, PA 15213-3418

Eva Horn
Department of Special Education
Box 328, Peabody College
Vanderbilt University
Nashville, TN 37203

Louise A. Kaczmarek
Department of Instruction and Learning
University of Pittsburgh
Pittsburgh, PA 15260

Ilene Lee
Beach Center
3111 Haworth
University of Kansas
Lawrence, KS 66045

Gerald Mahoney
Family and Child Learning Center
143 Northwest Avenue, Building A
Tallmadge, OH 44278

Mary McEvoy
Department of Special Education
University of Minnesota
225 Burton Hall
Minneapolis, MN 55455

Mary E. McLean
Graduate Special Education
    Department
Box 334
Cardinal Stritch College
6801 North Yates Road
Milwaukee, WI 53217-3985

R. A. McWilliam
F.P.G. Child Developmental Center
CB #8180
University of North Carolina
Chapel Hill, NC 27599

Patricia S. Miller
Department of Education
P.O. Box 10548
Salem College
Winston-Salem, NC 27108

John Neisworth
Department of Special Education
Penn State University
University Park, PA 16802

Samuel L. Odom
Department of Special Education
Box 328, Peabody College
Vanderbilt University
Nashville, TN 37203

Diane M. Sainato
Department of Educational
    Services and Research
356 ARPS Hall
Ohio State University
Columbus, OH 43210-1172

Robert Sheehan
Center for Applied Research in
    Education
1983 East 24th Street
Cleveland, OH 44115

Barbara J. Smith
Elephant Corral Building
1444 Wazee Street, Suite 230
Denver, CO 80202

Scott Snyder
Department of Counseling and
    Human Services
College of Education
UAB University Station
University of Alabama
Birmingham, AL 35294

Vicki Stayton
Department of Special Education
Tate Paige Hall
Western Kentucky University
Bowling Green, KY 42101

Steve Stile
Department of Special Education
New Mexico State University
Las Cruces, NM 88003-0001

Phillip S. Strain
Elephant Corral Building
1444 Wazee Street, Suite 230
Denver, CO 80202

Vicki Turbiville
Beach Center
3111 Haworth
University of Kansas
Lawrence, KS 66045

Ann Turnbull
Beach Center
3111 Haworth
University of Kansas
Lawrence, KS 66045

Lisbeth Vincent
Curriculum and Instruction
School of Education
University of Montana
Missoula, MT 59812-1054

Mark Wolery
Allegheny-Singer Research
    Institute
320 Eash North Avenue
Pittsburgh, PA 15212

Preface

During the halftime of the Kansas–North Carolina NCAA basketball game in 1991, a small group of members from the Division of Early Childhood (DEC) Executive Board met to discuss a process for identifying recommended practices in the field. Although our discussion was interrupted by the second half of the game and then the great celebration by the Jayhawk fans in the room, a subsequent discussion ensued and was the origin of this book. The DEC Recommended Practices Task Force was formed, and the editors of this book were appointed to cochair that task force. Other members of that task force were Susan Fowler (the Jayhawk fan), Larry Johnson, Mary McEvoy, Susie Perrett, Chris Salisbury, Barbara Smith, Vicki Stayton, and Daphne Thomas. These individuals spent hours on conference calls during the initial process of identifying recommended practices. The chairpersons of the content areas, or *strands*, identified in Chapter 1, also contributed many hours and much effort in forming initial work groups, revising practices, and writing the strand summaries that appeared in the initial *DEC Recommended Practices* book. Many of these individuals have served as authors of chapters in this book. When the validation study of the recommended practices occurred, Sam Odom received support for the postdoctoral training program at the University of California at Santa Barbara (UCSB), coordinated by Mel Semmel. Gretchen Butera and the students in the Early Childhood Program at UCSB provided great assistance in piloting early drafts of the validation questionnaires. While Mary McLean was at Auburn University, Altamese Stroud-Hill prepared the validation questionnaire, and Toni Locklar and Keren Self organized the multiple mailings to respondents. The staff of the Auburn Intervention Model program also provided assistance in piloting the questionnaires. At the University of North Dakota, Mickey Koerner typed and maintained the lists of all those who participated in the validation process. Larry Johnson and Maggie LaMontagne conducted the data analysis for the validation study. The many DEC members, family members, and higher education personnel who read, evaluated, and commented on the indicators during the validation study provided the much needed "grounding" for these recommended practices. All of these individuals contributed to the process that has resulted in this book.

The authors of chapters that make up this book have taken the next step of contributing an elaboration of the practices originally identified and an examination of how these practices are supported by the literature on early intervention and early childhood special education. We especially appreciate their continued energy and interest in identifying practices and principles that might guide our work with infants and young children with special needs and their families.

CHAPTER 1

Establishing Recommended Practices in Early Intervention/ Early Childhood Special Education

Mary E. McLean
Samuel L. Odom

In a short quarter century, early intervention for children with developmental delays and their families has moved from a primary and major innovation in the field to common practice. In the 1960s and before, families of young children with disabilities had few options for their children. Many parents were advised to send their children to an institution because this placement would be best for the child and for the family. Now, families in many communities have the option of enrolling their children in specialized or inclusive programs and have access to an array of related services designed to meet their children's needs.

As the field has moved from a revolutionary to an established mode of operation, the creative and driving force of professionals has largely changed focus. Whereas the impetus was originally to establish services (in fact, this focus is still true for infant and toddler programs in many states), the impetus now is to refine services offered so that they may represent the highest quality of practice for infants and young children with disabilities and their families. However, in the recent past, a major conundrum existed: Clearly accepted standards of practice for early intervention/early childhood special education (EI/ECSE) did not exist. Our purpose for this chapter is to describe a process for identifying practices that reflect quality in programs for infants and young children with disabilities and their families. This process resulted in a set of practices in 14 areas that served as the basis for the chapters in this book. We begin by briefly examining the concept of "recommended or best practice" and efforts to establish such practices in EI/ECSE. Next we describe the processes followed for identifying recommended practices and for validating those practices. Last, we provide an overview of the chapters presented in this book.

RECOMMENDED PRACTICES IN EI/ECSE

Attempts to identify practices that represent high quality, or best practice, are motivated by several factors. Probably the foremost is the desire to provide the best possible services to infants and young children with disabilities and their families. Professional ethics, advocacy groups, and state mandates push this drive for quality.

A second motivation may well be to ensure that the knowledge gained through research and practical experience serves as the basis for practices that are established as standard for programs and children and their families. Moving research to practice is a strong initiative within the field today.

A further push for the effort to establish identifiable best practice may be related to the maturity of the field. As EI/ECSE has become accepted and even mandated service in most states, it has reached a level of maturity heretofore absent. Reflections of this level of maturity include specialized professional organizations (e.g., Division for Early Childhood, National Center for Clinical Infant Programs), specialized teacher licensure, legislation that services be provided, and specialized professional journals (e.g., *Journal of Early Intervention, Topics in Early Childhood Special Education*). The status of a profession may well push the ideas that an agreed-upon set of practices exists and that identification of these practices could guide the field through self-evaluation and program development (Wolery & Bredekamp, 1995).

A fourth motivation for the specification of practices in EI/ECSE has come from the field of early childhood education. In the 1980s, the National Association for the Education of Young Children (NAEYC) developed a set of practices (Bredekamp, 1987) and standards for the education of young children without disabilities. The need for specificity grew out of the efforts to establish standards for accreditation of early childhood programs (Bredekamp, 1987). The manual on developmentally appropriate practices (Bredekamp, 1987) and the process for a related national organization establishing practices for the field served as a model for the EI/ECSE community.

Best or Recommended Practices

Using the term *best practice* is somewhat problematic. Although one may wish to identify practices that represent the most advanced knowledge of the field, *best* is a relative term. The appropriateness or effectiveness of a practice depends directly on the characteristics of the child and family, the nature of the early intervention setting, and the skills and motivation of the individual employing the practices. Moreover, practices will change with the evolving knowledge base and values in society. Practices identified as best at one point in time may not be superlative later in a decade (Peters & Heron, 1993). In this book, we have avoided the use of the term *best* and, instead, have used the term *recommended* to represent practices that serve as indicators of quality in EI/ECSE.

Identification of Recommended Practices

Efforts to identify recommended practices in EI/ECSE have paralleled efforts in other areas of special education. These processes have involved use of expert opinion, professional consensus, state-level consensus, and national validation.

Expert Opinion

The approaches followed most frequently in determining recommended practices have been based on reviews or syntheses of the literature by experts in the field. In perhaps one of the earliest approaches to establishing recommended practices related specifically to assessment, Smith and Rundall (1982) reviewed the literature on early childhood assessment and generated a set of recommended practices for the field. Using the "criterion of the next setting" as their guide, Vincent, Salisbury, Walter, Brown, Gruenwald, and Powers (1980) identified practices that would likely lead to placement in mainstreamed kindergarten classrooms. In a subsequent article, Vincent, Brown, and Getz-Sheftel (1981) proposed a set of criteria for determining best educational practice for young children, concluding that integrated programs represented such practice.

Conducting a synthesis of the literature, McDonnell and Hardman (1988) proposed the establishment of six guidelines (i.e., integrated, comprehensive, normalized, adaptable, peer- and family-referenced, and outcome-based) for selecting best practices for early childhood services. In a later review of the literature, Bruder (1993) identified eight characteristics for effective service delivery in early childhood education programs: philosophy related to inclusion, family involvement, team planning, cross-agency collaboration, individual education program (IEP) or individual family service plan (IFSP), integrated service delivery, staff development, program evaluation. In their examination of the application of developmentally appropriate practices for young children with disabilities, Carta, Schwartz, Atwater, and McConnell (1991) proposed a set of premises upon which early childhood special education services are based. These premises, derived from the literature and the law, represent guidelines for the selection of appropriate practices for young children with disabilities.

Identification of practices by experts' syntheses of the literature has also appeared in textbooks. In their text on early intervention, Hanson and Lynch (1989) specified best practices in terms of questions to be asked of early intervention programs. The text by Bailey and Wolery (1992) established seven goals for early intervention: support families, promote child engagement, promote development, build social competence, promote generalized use of skills, provide normalized life experiences, and prevent future problems. In later chapters, they identified practices based on the empirical literature that might meet those goals. Wolery, Strain, and Bailey (1992) summarized a range of best practices in a book published by NAEYC. These practices, based on the empirical and professional literature, included individualized assessment, family-centered services, outcome-based services, normalized interventions, regular monitoring of child progress, mainstreamed placement, planned transition, interdisciplinary involvement, and empirical basis for practice.

Professional Consensus

A second strategy for identifying best practices has been to build a consensus across experts, professionals, or individuals in the field. The process NAEYC followed in establishing the developmentally appropriate practices, as reported by Bredekamp and Rosegrant (1992), was for experts or leaders to establish practices or guidelines. These guidelines were then reviewed by practitioners in the field, and their feedback was incorporated into the final document.

The development of recommended practices for IFSPs followed a somewhat different process. To identify recommended practices, the Carolina Institute for Research on Infant Personnel Preparation initially issued a call to those in the field to submit best practices. From this initial response, an interagency IFSP task force took the lead in generating and synthesizing the information, with a small group of experts or leaders in the field writing the final document (McGonigel, Kaufmann, & Johnson, 1991).

Another professional consensus approach was used to establish a model for evaluating early childhood special education programs through identification of best practice. DeStefano, Howe, Horn, and Smith (1991) generated from the research literature an initial set of best practices from a synthesis of the literature. The practices were related to curriculum programming, organization of the learning environment, social skills, use of support services, family involvement, and transition. Leaders in the field then reviewed these practices, and a revised set of practices was developed into a model. The model was then disseminated to practitioners who provided feedback about the usefulness of the model in general, with a subgroup of these practitioners providing a formal evaluation.

State-Level Consensus Building

At the preschool level (and for some states, at the infant level also), state departments of education are responsible for providing EI/ECSE services. This responsibility has motivated some states to take the lead in identifying best or recommended practices that could serve as guidelines for local programs within their states. For example, the state of Arizona developed a set of early intervention quality indicators (Arizona Department of Education, 1987), which describe practices related to screening, placement, instruction, and program management. Arizona also participated with NAEYC in a self-study of an early childhood special needs component addendum to accreditation guidelines used by the National Academy of Early Childhood Program Accreditation (Arizona Department of Education, 1990). In Vermont, Flynn (1991) involved practitioners in the development of initial quality indicators and then conducted field validations across the state. Indicators were identified for family-centered services, transition planning, program evaluation, IEPs, least restrictive environment (LRE), Child Find, evaluation, and curriculum. These practices were developed through an Early Education Program for Children with Disabilities (EECPD) model demonstration project and have been disseminated nationally through an Outreach training project.

National Validation

The identification of quality indicators or recommended practices through expert and consensus approaches and the efforts of state agencies have provided important guidance for the field. The next step in specifying further practices for children and families is to establish a national consensus. A procedure inherent in several of the approaches just described has been to include practitioners in the generation and validation of practices. Another important consumer of EI/ECSE practices is families. Involving families in identifying and validating practices would also be an important part of the indicator-development process. Although not specifically from the area of EI/ECSE, the process that Meyer, Eichenger, and Park-Lee (1987) followed for identification and validation of practices for students with severe disabilities is one model of national validation. The authors first generated a set of program indicators by researching the professional literature and by polling national experts. This initial list was then validated by six groups representing various constituents (e.g., experts in severe disabilities and deaf–blind, researchers in mental retardation, state directors of special education, parents). These ratings served as the basis for the final list of indicators. Subsequent researchers examined the degree to which these practices could be implemented by teachers in five states (Ayres, Meyer, Erevelles, Park-Lee, 1994). The national validation approach has served as a model for establishing DEC Recommended Practices. We describe the process for specifying these practices in the next section.

Procedures for Identifying and Validating Recommended Practices

In the spring of 1991, the Task Force on Recommended Practices was established by the DEC executive board and charged with developing the procedures to be followed in the identification and validation of recommended practices in EI/ECSE. Members of this task force included the following individuals:

Sam Odom and Mary McLean, Cochairpersons

Susan Fowler, President of DEC

Larry Johnson, Chair, DEC Research Committee

Mary McEvoy, Chair, DEC Publications Committee

Susie Perrett, Cochair, DEC Family Concerns Committee

Christine Salisbury, DEC President-Elect

Vicki Stayton, Cochair, DEC Personnel Preparation Committee

Daphne Thomas, Chair, DEC Multicultural Committee

Barbara Smith (ex officio), DEC Executive Director

The task force began its work by identifying the major content areas, called *strands*, which would be covered in the process. For each strand, the task force selected a chairperson or cochairpersons with recognized expertise in the area. Table 1.1 provides a list of the 14 strands identified and the chairpersons for each.

As discussed previously, task force members believed that it was important to provide for a broad base of input into the process, including individuals considered to be experts, practitioners working directly with children and families, and family members of young children with special needs. Representation from all of these groups was sought for the initial strand meetings in which practices were first identified. These meetings were held at the DEC conference in the fall of 1991. The chairpersons for each strand were asked to invite individuals with a strong knowledge base in their areas in order to assure input from experts. An announcement appeared in the *DEC Communicator* prior to the conference, inviting DEC members to attend any of the working groups. Also, the Family Concerns

Table 1.1. Strands Within DEC-Recommended Practices with Strand Chairs

Strand	Strand Chair(s)
Assessment	John Neisworth
Family Participation	Lisbeth Vincent Julie Beckett
IFSPs/IEPs	Ann Turnbull Corrine Garland
Service Delivery Models	Robin McWilliam Phillip Strain
General Curriculum and Intervention Strategies	Mark Wolery
Interventions to Promote Cognitive Skills	Carl Dunst
Interventions to Promote Communication Skills	Howard Goldstein
Interventions to Promote Social Skills and Emotional Development	Mary McEvoy Paul Yoder
Interventions to Promote Adaptive Behavior Skills	Eva Horn
Interventions to Promote Motor Skills	Rebecca Fewell
Transition	Mary Beth Bruder Lynette K. Chandler
Personnel Competence	Pat Miller Vicki Stayton
Program Evaluation	Scott Snyder
Programs for Children Who Are Gifted	Steve Stile

Committee recruited and financially supported family members to attend each of the group meetings. Individuals who were not able to attend the conference meetings were able to provide input into this endeavor by mail or phone communications with the strand chairpersons.

The task force also identified parameters to guide the work of the groups as they drafted the initial lists of recommended practices. Generally, practices were to be appropriate for children with developmental delays, disabilities, or both between birth and six years of age. A separate strand was created for gifted children; this strand was to include all of the areas covered by the other strands but with reference only to young children who are gifted. In addition, the task force identified six philosophical criteria believed to be fundamental to the provision of quality services to young children with special needs and their families. Strand chairs were asked to ensure that each practice written by their group was consistent with (was not in violation of) the following criteria: research based or value based, family centered, multicultural, cross-disciplinary, developmentally and chronologically age appropriate, and normalized (see Table 1.2).

Research Based or Value Based

Recommended practice status was to be substantiated on the basis of current research or literature demonstrating positive effects for infants, young children, and their families. Although empirical validation was the most desirable, the task force recognized that such validation is not always available. When it was not possible to support a practice empirically, recommended practices were to be supported by a strong value base.

Family Centered

Recommended practices were to be consistent with a family-centered philosophy. Recognition of the importance of family-centered intervention has become a major influence in the field through the literature in early intervention and related fields and also through the federal legislation supporting early intervention services.

Many researchers, parents, and advocates have contributed to the evolving concept of family-centered early intervention. From a health care perspective, Brewer, McPherson, Magrab, and Hutchins (1989) defined family-centered care as follows:

> Family-centered care is the focus of philosophy of care in which the pivotal role of the family is recognized and respected in the lives of children with special health needs. Within this philosophy is the idea that families should be supported in their natural care-giving and decision-making roles by building on their unique strengths as people and families. In this philosophy,

Table 1.2. Philosophical Criteria Identified as Fundamental to the Recommended Practices

Research based or value based

Family centered

Multicultural

Cross-disciplinary collaboration

Developmentally and chronologically age appropriate

Normalization

patterns of living at home and in the community are promoted; parents and professionals are seen as equals in a partnership committed to the development of optimal quality in the delivery of all levels of health care. (p. 1055)

Within early intervention, many different terms have been used to describe this philosophy of family centeredness: family focused (Bailey et al., 1986), parent empowerment (Dunst, 1985; Dunst, Trivette, & Deal, 1988), family guided (Slentz & Bricker, 1992), to name a few. Regardless of the terminology used, these statements of philosophy have in common the idea that intervention should be provided in collaboration with family members, in a manner that facilitates the family's decision-making role, and in a manner that conforms with the family's priorities.

The legislation supporting early intervention, the Education of the Handicapped Act Amendments of 1986 (P.L. 99-457) and the Individuals with Disabilities Education Act Amendments of 1991 (P.L. 102-119), also reflects this emphasis on a family-centered philosophy. According to Safer and Hamilton (1993), the ideas embodied in the philosophy of family-centered services were a major tenet of those who initially wrote Part H of the law establishing the infant–toddler program. This philosophy creates a noticeable difference between this program (Part H) and Part B, which governs the preschool and school-age services for children with disabilities. One major difference is in the use of the IFSP rather than the IEP. The IFSP makes the needs of the family as much a focus of intervention efforts as it does the needs of the child. Under Part H, the family also is empowered to decide which services it will accept and which services it will not accept. In other words, the Part H legislation recognizes the very central role played by the family in the life of a young child and attempts to provide support for the family in that role.

One caveat regarding family centeredness as a description of early intervention services is necessary. Recent research by Carl Dunst and his colleagues (Dunst, Johanson, Trivette, & Hamby, 1991) has revealed the very real possibility that early intervention programs may purport to be family centered but still deliver traditional, professionally directed intervention services. In other words, there is a danger that the new term *family centered* is simply being applied to an old program that is still primarily professionally directed with some level of family involvement (Duwa, Wells, & Lalinde, 1993). Moving toward family-centered services will require significant change on the part of most early intervention programs and professionals and is in many ways a process that will be continually ongoing.

Multicultural

Recommended practices were to be compatible with a multicultural perspective. Specifically, the practices were to be adaptable for use with children and families who identified themselves as members of groups that differ ethnically or linguistically from the mainstream in the United States. Attention to the importance of cultural aspects in the area of human services has been increasing due to the changing demographics of the population in the United States. For the past two decades, our country has experienced an increase in the percentage of the population that can be characterized as being of non-European ancestry. Higher birth rates among minority families and increased immigration from countries around the world experiencing poverty and political oppression are changing the nature of the population in the United States who receive medical, educational, and social services.

Within the field of early intervention, concern has been expressed about the ability of early intervention professionals, who continue to be primarily White and of European descent, to provide adequate services to families whose cultural backgrounds may be substantially different (Anderson & Fenichel, 1989; Hanson, 1992). Hanson (1992) provided the analogy of the interventionist as a traveler moving into and out of the homes and lives of families from a variety of cultural backgrounds and thus experiencing cultural differences in a manner similar to that of someone traveling in foreign countries. At a time when families are dealing with the stress of initial diagnosis and the challenges of caring for a young child with a disability, the potential for cultural clashes is great. By setting a multicultural criterion for development of the recommended practices, the task force hoped to ensure that the practices would not contribute to potential problems and in fact would promote the cultural competence of professionals in early intervention.

Cross-Disciplinary Collaboration

Both Part B and Part H of the Individuals with Disabilities Education Act (IDEA) require that evaluation and assessment be multidisciplinary. According to the law, multidisciplinary means "the involvement of two or more disciplines or professions in the provision of integrated and coordinated services" (§ 303,17). The task force's intent was that the recommended practices be consistent with a model of assessment and intervention in which individuals from various disciplines work closely together rather than as independent professionals. Typically, three models of team organization have been described in relation to early intervention: multidisciplinary, interdisciplinary, and transdisciplinary (Foley, 1990; McGonigel, Woodruff, & Roszmann-Millican, 1994; Peterson, 1987). As it is typically defined, the multidisciplinary model involves professionals working almost independently of each other. The potential for conflicting information and suggestions to be given to the family is great with this model. Bagnato and Neisworth (1991) have suggested that a multidisciplinary model is not even actually a model of team functioning. Although it does connote a situation in which two or more disciplines are involved in delivering services to a child and family, integrated and coordinated services, as mentioned in the law, may not be an outcome of this model. The interdisciplinary team model ensures communication among team members so that the team (including the parents) is unified in relation to intervention. This model may involve professionals working together, individually, or in subgroups, but communication among team members is frequent to ensure a unified team. In the transdisciplinary team model, team members must be willing to allow one teammate to take the role of direct service provider. This model requires that other team members be willing to engage in *role release* by allowing the direct service provider to perform functions that typically are part of the responsibility of their professions (Harris & Tada, 1983; Lyon & Lyon, 1980). Regardless of the model of team functioning followed, collaboration among team members (including the family) with information sharing and consensus decision making is critical for quality assessment and intervention services (Bagnato & Neisworth, 1991; Bruder, 1994; Linder, 1993).

Developmentally and Chronologically Age Appropriate

The recommended practices were to be consistent with developmentally appropriate practice (DAP; Bredekamp, 1987; Bredekamp & Rosegrant, 1992) and, at the same time, to ensure chronological age appropriateness for children with disabilities. This criterion combined philosophy from early childhood education and from special education to ensure appropriate intervention services. Through a series of recent publications, NAEYC has attempted to clarify the meaning of the term *developmentally appropriate* in an effort to address the apparently widely divergent views held in the field of early childhood education about developmental appropriateness (Bredekamp, 1987; Bredekamp & Rosegrant, 1992). The definition of developmental appropriateness recommended by NAEYC as a standard for early childhood programs includes two dimensions: age appropriateness and individual appropriateness. Age appropriateness was equated with the application of knowledge about predictable sequences of child development. The concept of individual appropriateness recognizes the individual differences that exist among young children and specifies that early childhood curriculum must also be appropriate to the individual child's needs.

The DEC Task Force on Recommended Practices was concerned that the practices be consistent with NAEYC's definition of developmentally appropriate practice. Recommending developmentally appropriate practices as a context for early intervention services was believed to be important as a means of supporting the inclusion of young children with disabilities in typical early childhood environments. However, there was concern about the potential misinterpretation of age appropriate as "developmentally age appropriate," which might result in children with disabilities being placed in settings with much younger children rather than with their same-age peers. This interpretation violates a strongly held principle of many in the field of special education—the importance of chronological age appropriateness for children with disabilities (Brown et al., 1979). Placements and curricular activities must be chronologically age appropriate for young children with disabilities even when the learning activities do not correspond to the readiness level, or developmental age, of a particular child. Teachers can make adaptations in materials, activities, or designated outcomes of learning activities that will allow for the inclusion of children with disabilities in learning activities with their chronological age peers (Noonan & McCormick, 1993). The second document published by NAEYC on DAP (Bredekamp & Rosegrant, 1992) assisted in correcting this potential misinterpretation. It stresses that knowledge of the sequence of child development is not the only determinant of appropriate practice but, rather, that the continuum of development of all children in a group should be the basis for appropriate practice.

Normalization

Normalization has been defined by Nirje (1985) as "making available to all persons with disabilities . . . patterns of life and conditions of everyday living which are as close as possible to . . . the regular circumstances and ways of life of society" (p. 67). The task force was concerned that all recommended practices be consistent with the philosophy of normalization. Bailey and McWilliam (1990) stated that the normalization principle is not necessarily equivalent to mainstreaming as a model of service delivery. Rather, normalization also involves aspects of the physical environment, teaching strategies, and family involvement. The philosophy of normalization is being followed when the least intrusive and most normal strategies are being implemented to achieve effective intervention for a child. In 1993, DEC adopted a position statement on inclusion that specifies the following: "Inclusion, as a value, supports the right of all children, regardless of their diverse abilities, to participate actively in natural settings within their communities. A natural setting is one in which the child would spend time had he or she not had a disability. . . . DEC values the diversity of families and supports a family-guided process for determining services that are based on the needs and preferences of individual families and children" (p. 4).

This statement on inclusion exemplifies the criteria of normalization that was delineated by the task force. The recommended practices were to be consistent with a philosophy that supports providing early intervention services in a way that makes the life of a young child with disabilities and his or her family as much as possible like the life of a typical child and his or her family.

Validation Procedures

The recommended practices initially identified by the strand work groups were edited by the strand chairs and then edited again by the task force cochairs for redundancy and duplication. The final list of practices was then formatted into a questionnaire for validation. The validation procedures that were followed have been described elsewhere (DEC Task Force on Recommended Practices, 1993; Odom, McLean, Johnson, & LaMontagne, 1995). The reader is referred to these sources for more detailed information on the validation process.

Validation Data

Five hundred individuals, including DEC members, family members, and higher education and administration personnel, completed the questionnaires by rating their agreement as to whether each practice should be considered a recommended practice (ratings were *strongly agree, agree, disagree, strongly disagree, no opinion, do not understand*). The criterion for validation was set at 50% of respondents' ratings of each practice as *strongly agree* or *agree*. All of the practices met the 50% criterion for inclusion as a recommended practice.

Mean ratings were computed for practitioners, family members, and higher education personnel for each strand, in order to determine whether differences in ratings existed across the three groups of respondents. Separate, one-way ANOVAs were then conducted to examine differences across groups. Tukey post hoc analyses were conducted when a significant main effect occurred.

Significant differences occurred for 4 of the 11 strands. Family respondents were significantly more in agreement with the items on the Family Participation strand and the IEP/IFSP strand than were the practitioners. Higher education respondents did not differ significantly from either group on these strands. Practitioners were significantly more in agreement with the items on the Social–Emotional Intervention strand and the Motor Strand than were family members. Again, higher education respondents did not differ significantly from either group on these strands. Table 1.3 provides the data from these tests for significance.

Ratings of Current Use

The validation questionnaire also asked respondents to rate their impression of the level of current use of the practices in intervention programs

Table 1.3. Mean Ratings of Agreement on "Recommended" by Respondent Groups

Strand	Practitioners	Higher Education Personnel	Family Members	Probability
Assessment	1.226	1.227	1.275	N.S
Family Participation	1.410	1.375	1.260	.02[a]
IEP/IFSP	1.529	1.414	1.385	.04[a]
Service Delivery	1.324	1.369	1.4023	N.S.
General Curriculum	1.340	1.369	1.409	N.S.
Cognitive	1.215	1.290	1.300	N.S.
Communication	1.292	1.296	1.391	N.S.
Social–Emotional	1.209	1.303	1.362	.003[a]
Adaptive Behavior	1.262	1.290	1.271	N.S.
Motor	1.185	1.285	1.333	.004[a]
Transition	1.243	1.289	1.216	N.S.

Note. Data based on Tukey post hoc ($p < .05$) analysis. N.S. = not significant.
[a]Differences between practitioner and family ratings.

with which they were familiar. Respondents were asked to rate each practice as *frequently* (rated as 1), *sometimes* (rated as 2), *rarely* (rated as 3), or *never* (rated as 4) used. The resulting data are presented in detail in Odom et al. (1995). Two criteria were applied to the data to analyze current use of the practices. The first criterion was conservative in that it identified items rated by at least 50% of the respondents as occurring frequently in programs (a rating of 1). A second criteria identified practices that were rated by at least 50% of the respondents as occurring frequently or sometimes in programs. As might be expected, many more practices met the second criterion than the first. Table 1.4 presents the number of items within each strand that met each of the criteria for current use. As these data show, 11 of the 14 strands had four or fewer items that met the first criterion (50% rated as frequently). These data suggest that at the time of the validation survey (summer, 1992), most of the identified recommended practices were not being used frequently in programs with which respondents were familiar. It is also evident from Table 1.4, however, that when the second criterion (frequently or sometimes) is applied to the data, most of the items met the criterion. In general, it is fair to conclude that most of the recommended practices were reported to be used at least sometimes. The differ-

Table 1.4. Number of Items Reaching 50% Criteria of Frequently Used and Frequently or Sometimes Used

Strand	Items Rated 50% Frequently/ Total Items	Items Rated 50% Frequently or Sometimes/ Total Items
Assessment	4/24	23/24
Family Participation	2/49	35/49
IEP/IFSP	1/41	28/41
Service Delivery	4/39	36/39
General Curriculum	3/31	29/31
Cognitive	0/8	8/8
Communication	0/13	11/13
Social–Emotional	5/15	15/15
Adaptive Behavior	1/9	8/9
Motor	4/13	13/13
Transition	0/22	22/22
Personnel Competence	8/53	45/53
Program Evaluation	0/23	22/23
Gifted	32/63	55/63

ence in the frequency of use may indicate movement toward the implementation of the recommended practices.

Another interesting aspect of these data is the varying perspectives of the three groups of respondents. Table 1.5 presents the current-use data analyzed according to responses from practitioners, higher education personnel, and families as they rated the current use of practices as occurring *frequently, sometimes, rarely,* or *never.* Significant differences were found between the groups on every strand but the Family Participation strand (the Gifted, Personnel Competence, and Program Evaluation strands could not be included in this analysis because only one group of individuals rated each of those strands). As the data show, practitioners rated items as occurring significantly more often than did higher education or family respondents on the IEP/IFSP, Service Delivery, General Curriculum, Communication, Social–Emotional, Adaptive Behavior, Motor, and Transition strands. Family members rated items as occurring significantly more often

Table 1.5. Mean Ratings of Frequency of Use by Respondent Groups

Strand	Practitioners	Higher Education Personnel	Family Members	Probability
Assessment	1.888	2.110	1.275	.001[a,b]
Family Participation	2.253	2.313	2.366	N.S.
IEP/IFSP	2.264	2.546	2.537	.003[a,b]
Service Delivery	1.780	2.084	2.071	.001[a,b]
General Curriculum	1.721	2.108	1.920	.001[a,b]
Cognitive	1.768	2.074	1.907	.002[b]
Communication	1.839	2.262	2.165	.001[a,b]
Social–Emotional	1.521	1.785	1.701	.001[a,b]
Adaptive Behavior	1.768	2.117	2.081	.001[a,b]
Motor	1.703	1.901	1.918	.005[a,b]
Transition	1.932	2.159	2.281	.001[a,b]

Note. Data based on Tukey post hoc ($p < .05$) analysis. N.S. = not significant.
[a]Differences between practitioner and family ratings.
[b]Differences between practitioner and higher education personnel ratings.

than did practitioners on the Assessment strand, and both family members and practitioners rated Assessment items as occurring more often than did higher education personnel. There was also a significant difference on the Cognitive strand, with practitioners rating practices as occurring more often than did higher education personnel.

CONTENT OF THIS BOOK

The chapters in this book were written, in most instances, by the strand chairs. In these chapters, the authors used the DEC Recommended Practices (see appendix) as one source of guidance but also drew on their own expertise and knowledge of the research literature. Their charge was to describe recommended practices in their content area of EI/ECSE. Throughout the chapters the authors refer to the specific practices as numbered in the appendix. Practice numbers appear in parentheses in text.

Assessment, addressed in Chapter 2, is the foundation of much of our work in EI/ECSE. Over the past decade, acceptable assessment practices have changed markedly, from application of standardized and clinical forms of testing to broader strategies for collecting information about children. In their chapter, Neisworth and Bagnato examine four standards often applied to assessment: treatment utility, social validity, convergent assessment, and consensual validity. All of the recommended practices are subsumed under these four standards. For each standard, they examine the relevance for EI/ECSE and make recommendations for action. They conclude by looking toward the future of assessment practice in EI/ECSE.

The Family Participation strand is in many ways the heart of the DEC Recommended Practices. The group of individuals working to develop this strand first identified 31 values and beliefs critical to building the family–professional partnership. The result of this group's efforts yielded 185 recommended practices covering nine areas; these were eventually reduced to 49 practices due to the overlap with other strands. Vincent and McLean have written Chapter 3 on family participation, providing not only a literature base for the nine areas addressed by the work group but also adding insightful perspective on progress toward implementing the suggested practices in programs serving young children and their families.

The group working on the IFSP/IEP strand identified two principles that guided the development of recommended practices. Family-centered collaboration and the inclusion of the child and family in the natural environment became the basis for 41 practices covering five areas relative to the development of the IFSP or IEP. Turbiville, Turnbull, Garland, and Lee coauthored Chapter 4, which presents strategies that are empowering for the family and for other team members as they collaboratively plan to meet the needs of the young child.

In Chapter 5, Strain, Smith, and McWilliam discuss the recommended practices relating to service delivery models from a social change perspective. The authors first identify steps that may be needed to bring the recommended practices into being in early intervention programs, discussing attitudinal issues, fiscal and regulatory issues, personnel preparation issues, and program-level issues. The authors then present a model of systems change that may be applied to early intervention service delivery systems.

EI/ECSE is an intervention-oriented field, and a considerable proportion of this book is devoted to the examination of interventions that affect children's development and skills acquisition. In Chapter 6, Wolery and Sainato describe the general principles related to curriculum and intervention for infants and young children with disabilities. They begin by defining curriculum and intervention and then discuss how goals for children should relate to outcomes. After proposing their foundational assumptions about curriculum and intervention, they describe curricular and intervention strategies that range on a continuum from low to high adult mediation.

Many early childhood curriculum approaches are designed to promote the cognitive skills of young children. Yet, aside from the theories of Piaget and Vygotsky, there is little definition of cognitive development as it applies to young children with disabilities and EI/ECSE. In Chapter 7,

Dunst, Mahoney, and Buchan contribute an important conceptual definition for this dimension of child development and discuss procedural implications. They propose principles associated with the use of theories of cognitive development and describe an expanded framework for assessing early cognitive competence. Of importance, they identify principles for promoting the acquisition of early cognitive competence.

Professionals and caregivers have identified the development of communication skills as a need for a great percentage of young children with disabilities. In Chapter 8, Goldstein, Kaczmarek, and Hepting identify intervention approaches that promote communication skills. They first examine issues in assessment uniquely related to communication and emphasize that multiple sources of information are useful. The use of this information to select goals is next described and is followed by a detailed description of intervention strategies that promote communication skills. The authors conclude with an examination of strategies for evaluating the impact of these intervention approaches.

In Chapter 9, McEvoy and Odom describe intervention strategies that support emotional development and the acquisition of social competence. They begin by reviewing typical development of infant–caregiver interaction and attachment during the early years and peer interactions and social relationships during the preschool years. The unique developmental paths of some children with disabilities are also described. A discussion of intervention strategies for infants and caregivers includes the acknowledgement of the sensitivity about the decision to intervene, recognition of the impact of cultural values, arrangement of the environment, triadic strategies for social coaching, and attachment interventions. Strategies to promote peer relationships include providing opportunities to interact with peers, supporting interactions directly in the classroom, fostering interactions that are happy and fun, and building social relationships.

As Fewell notes in Chapter 10, motor skills are the basis for early exploration of the environment and are directly linked to learning in other developmental domains. She begins this chapter by reviewing the theoretical constructs that underlie interventions and then identifies techniques for assessing motor development. Intervention techniques for promoting motor development include using adults as facilitators and arranging the environment. Fewell also discusses curricula that might guide intervention efforts. Of importance, she reviews research that supports the use of these techniques for promoting children's development.

Probably more than any other area of skill development, adaptive behavior "puts to use" the skills described in the other developmental domain chapters. In Chapter 11, Horn begins by noting that adaptive behavior refers to skills needed by infants and children to respond to the immediate requirements of the environment. These requirements are related directly to the cultural values of the family and community. She describes the contexts in which intervention may occur and then describes intervention strategies for the specific adaptive behavior subdomains of self-care, community self-sufficiency, personal–social responsibility, and social adjustment.

In Chapter 12, Bruder and Chandler relate the practices in the Transition strand to the literature that supports those practices. Effective practices are discussed relative to four components of successful transitioning: state and local agencies, sending and receiving program providers, families and other caregivers, and the child.

Stile chaired the work group on children who are gifted and has written Chapter 13, which relates the 77 recommended practices to the literature on intervention for young children who are gifted. This chapter addresses 12 areas relative to programs for young children who are gifted, essentially addressing each of the areas addressed by the other strands relating to children with disabilities. As Stile indicates, young gifted children have been identified as an underserved group. This chapter provides a thorough and enlightening discussion of practices recommended for a group of young children who also fall within the stated mission of the Division for Early Childhood.

Miller and Stayton provide the literature base for the recommended practices in personnel preparation in Chapter 14. Fifty-three practices, covering both preservice and in-service, were identified by the work group in this area. The authors relate the practices to federal law, guidelines from professional organizations, and research in personnel preparation. Content, process, field experiences, and graduate preparation are discussed relative to preservice. Content, process, and the context of in-service preparation are also discussed.

In Chapter 15, Snyder and Sheehan provide an in-depth discussion of the recommended practices in program evaluation. The work group identified 23 practices that follow the outline of the Program Evaluation Standards prepared by the Joint Committee on Standards for Educational Evaluation. Discussion of the practices is organized around four fundamental attributes of evaluation: utility, feasibility, propriety, and technical adequacy.

CLOSING

A central goal of EI/ECSE is to enhance the lives of infants and young children with disabilities and their families. By creating, in partnership with families, experiences tailored to the unique needs of children and their families, practitioners try to support child development when there are delays or to build environments that might reduce the impact of a specific disability. At this point in the brief history of EI/ECSE, research, practical experience, and even politics have provided a basis for creating intervention programs.

Our purpose for this chapter has been to describe a process that established parameters for quality practices; involved multiple constituents in the creation, selection, and validation of the practices; and generated specific descriptions of practices that could be recommended for the field. We see this as a first step in an iterative process. As the field, our society, and the political landscape change, these practices will need to be reviewed and perhaps recast. However, this first step puts us well on our way to a systematic "self" examination of quality in EI/ECSE.

REFERENCES

Anderson, P. P., & Fenichel, E. S. (1989). *Serving culturally diverse families of infants and toddlers with disabilities*. Washington, DC: National Center for Clinical Infant Programs.

Arizona State Department of Education. (1987). *Early intervention quality indicators*. Unpublished manuscript.

Arizona Department of Education. (1990). *Early childhood special needs component: An addendum to the National Academy of Early Childhood Programs accreditation*. Phoenix: Arizona Self-Study Project, Arizona Department of Education.

Ayres, B. J., Meyer, L. H., Erevelles, N., & Park-Lee, S. (1994). Easy for you to say: Teachers' perspectives on implementing most promising practices. *Journal of the Association for Persons with Severe Handicaps, 19*, 84–93.

Bagnato. S. J., & Neisworth, J. T. (1991). *Assessment for early intervention: Best practices for professionals*. New York: Guilford Press.

Bailey, D. B., & McWilliam, R. A. (1990). Normalizing early intervention. *Topics in Early Childhood Special Education, 10*(2), 33–47.

Bailey, D. B., Simeonsson, R. J., Winton, P. J., Huntington, G. S., Comfort, M., Isbell, P., O'Donnell, K. J., & Helm, J. M. (1986). Family-focused intervention: A functional model for planning, implementing, and evaluating individualized family services in early intervention. *Journal of the Division for Early Childhood, 10*, 156–171.

Bailey, D. B., & Wolery, M. R. (1992). *Teaching infants and preschoolers with disabilities* (2nd ed.). New York: Merrill.

Bredekamp, S. (Ed.). (1987). *Developmentally appropriate practice in early childhood programs serving children from birth through age 8*. Washington, DC: National Association for the Education of Young Children.

Bredekamp, S., & Rosegrant, T. (1992). *Reaching potentials: Appropriate curriculum and assessment for young children*. Washington, DC: National Association for the Education of Young Children.

Brewer, E. J., McPherson, M., Magrab, P. R., & Hutchins, V. L. (1989). Family-centered, community-based, coordinated care for children with special health care needs. *Pediatrics, 83*, 1055–1060.

Brown, L., Branston, M., Hamre-Nietupski, S., Pumpian, I., Certo, N., & Gruenewald, L. (1979). A strategy for developing chronological age appropriate and functional curricular content for severely handicapped adolescents and young adults. *Journal of Special Education, 13*, 81–90.

Bruder, M. B. (1993). The provision of early intervention and early childhood special education within community early childhood programs: Characteristics of effective service delivery. *Topics in Early Childhood Special Education, 13*, 19–37.

Bruder, M. B. (1994). Working with members of other disciplines: Collaboration for success. In M. Wolery & J. S. Wilbers (Eds.), *Including children with special needs in early childhood programs* (pp. 45–70). Washington, DC: National Association for the Education of Young Children.

Carta, J. J., Schwartz, I. S., Atwater, J. B., & McConnell, S. R. (1991). Developmentally appropriate practice: Appraising its usefulness for young children with disabilities. *Topics in Early Childhood Special Education, 11,* 1–20.

DeStefano, D. M., Howe, A. G., Horn, E. M., & Smith, B. A. (1991). *Best practices: Evaluating early childhood special education programs.* Tucson, AZ: Communication Skill Builders.

Division for Early Childhood. (1993). DEC position statement on inclusion. *DEC Communicator, 19*(4), 4.

Division for Early Childhood Task Force on Recommended Practices (Eds.). (1993). *DEC recommended practices: Indicators of quality in programs for infants and young children with special needs and their families.* Reston, VA: Council for Exceptional Children.

Dunst, C. J. (1985). Rethinking early intervention. *Analysis and Intervention in Developmental Disabilities, 5,* 165–201.

Dunst, C., Johanson, C., Trivette, C., & Hamby, D. (1991). Family-oriented early intervention policies and practices: Family-centered or not? *Exceptional Children, 58*(2), 115–126.

Dunst, C. J., Trivette, C. M., & Deal, A. G. (1988). *Enabling and empowering families: Principles and guidelines for practice.* Cambridge, MA: Brookline Books.

Duwa, S. M., Wells, C., & Lalinde, P. (1993). Creating family-centered programs and policies. In D. M. Bryant & M. A. Graham (Eds.), *Implementing early intervention: From research to effective practice* (pp. 92–123). New York: Guilford Press.

Education of the Handicapped Act Amendments of 1986, 20 U.S.C. § 1400 *et seq.*

Flynn, L. (1991). *Early childhood special education best practices.* Unpublished manuscript, University Affiliated Program of Vermont, Burlington.

Foley, G. M. (1990). Portrait of the arena evaluation: Assessment in the transdisciplinary approach. In E. Gibbs & D. Teti (Eds.), *Interdisciplinary assessment of infants: A guide for early intervention* (pp. 271–286). Baltimore: Brookes.

Hanson, M. J. (1992). Ethnic, cultural, and language diversity in intervention settings. In E. W. Lynch & M. J. Hanson (Eds.), *Developing cross-cultural competence* (pp. 3–18). Baltimore: Brookes.

Hanson, M. J., & Lynch, E. W. (1989). *Early intervention: Implementing child and family services for infants and toddlers who are disabled and at-risk.* Austin, TX: PRO-ED.

Harris, S. R., & Tada, W. L. (1983). Providing developmental therapy services. In S. G. Garwood & R. R. Fewell (Eds.), *Educating handicapped infants: Issues in development and intervention* (pp. 343–368). Rockville, MD: Aspen Systems Corporation.

Individuals with Disabilities Education Act Amendments of 1991, 20 U.S.C. § 1400 *et seq.*

Linder, T. W. (1993). *Transdisciplinary, play-based assessment: A functional approach to working with young children* (rev. ed). Baltimore: Brookes.

Lyon, S., & Lyon, G. (1980). Team functioning and staff development: A role release approach to providing integrated educational services for severely handicapped students. *Journal of the Association for the Severely Handicapped, 5,* 250–263.

McDonnell, A., & Hardman, M. (1988). A synthesis of "best practice" guidelines for early childhood services. *Journal of the Division for Early Childhood, 12,* 328–341.

McGonigel, M. J., Kaufman, R. K., & Johnson, B. H. (Eds.). (1991). *Guidelines and recommended practices for the individualized family service plan* (2nd ed.). Bethesda, MD: Association for the Care of Children's Health.

McGonigel, M. J., Woodruff, G., & Roszmann-Millican, M. (1994). The transdisciplinary team: A model for family-centered early intervention. In L. J. Johnson, R. J. Gallagher, M. J. LaMontagne, J. B. Jordan, J. J. Gallagher, P. L. Hutinger, & M. B. Karnes (Eds.), *Meeting early intervention challenges: Issues from birth to three* (pp. 95–131). Baltimore: Brookes.

Meyer, L. H., Eichenger, J., & Park-Lee, S. (1987). A validation of program quality indicators in educational services for students with severe disabilities. *Journal of the Association for Persons with Severe Handicaps, 12,* 251–263.

Nirje, B. (1985). The basis and logic of the normalization principle. *Australia and New Zealand Journal of Developmental Disabilities, 11*(2), 65–68.

Noonan, M. J., & McCormick, L. (1993). *Early intervention in natural environments: Methods and procedures.* Pacific Grove, CA: Brooks/Cole.

Odom, S. L., McLean, M. E., Johnson, L. J., & LaMontagne, M. J. (1995). Recommended practices in early childhood special education: Validation and current use. *Journal of Early Intervention, 19,* 1–17.

Peters, M. T., & Heron, T. E. (1993). When is best not good enough: An examination of best practice. *Journal of Special Education, 26,* 371–385.

Peterson, N. L. (1987). *Early intervention for handicapped and at-risk children: An introduction for early childhood special education.* Denver, CO: Love.

Safer, N. D., & Hamilton, J. L. (1993). Legislative context for early intervention services. In W. Brown, S. K. Thurman, & L. F. Pearl (Eds.), *Family-centered early intervention with infants and toddlers: Innovative cross-disciplinary approaches* (pp. 1–19). Baltimore: Brookes.

Slentz, K. L., & Bricker, D. B. (1992). Family-guided assessment for IFSP development: Jumping off the family assessment bandwagon. *Journal of Early Intervention, 16,* 11–19.

Smith, S. L., & Rundall, D. (Eds.). (1982). *Early childhood assessment: Recommended practices and selected instruments.* Springfield: Illinois State Board of Education. (ERIC Document Reproduction Service No. ED 336 907)

Vincent, L. J., Brown, L., & Getz-Sheftel, M. (1981). Integrating handicapped and typical children during the preschool years: The definition of best educational practice. *Topics in Early Childhood Special Education, 1*(1), 17–24.

Vincent, L. J., Salisbury, C., Walter, G., Brown, P., Gruenwald, L. J., & Powers, M. (1980). Program evaluation and curriculum development in early childhood programs for handicapped children: Criteria for the next environment. In W. Sailor, B. Wilcox, & L. Brown (Eds.), *Methods of instruction for severely handicapped students* (pp. 303–328). Baltimore: Brookes.

Wolery, M., & Bredekamp, S. (1995). Developmentally appropriate practices and young children with special needs: Contextual issues and a framework for convergence. *Journal of Early Intervention, 18,* 331–341.

Wolery, M. R., Strain, P. S., & Bailey, D. B. (1992). Reaching potentials of children with special needs. In S. Bredekamp & T. Rosegrant (Eds.), *Reaching potentials: Appropriate curriculum and assessment for young children* (pp. 92–111). Washington, DC: National Association for the Education of Young Children.

CHAPTER 2

Assessment for Early Intervention: Emerging Themes and Practices

John T. Neisworth
Stephen J. Bagnato

That assessment practices have become the focus of much debate and concern is understandable: First, assessment is necessary to grant or deny specialized services and placements. Perhaps this eligibility, or "gate-keeping," role of assessment provokes the greatest dispute. Second, program planning and progress monitoring also call for assessment to assist in making important instructional and service delivery decisions. Third, program accountability has become a prominent concern, especially when funding, enrollment, and parent satisfaction may be influenced or determined through assessment practices. Indeed, assessment plays a pivotal role throughout the early intervention enterprise.

In this chapter, we examine some background concerns and perspectives that provide the reasoning for recommended changes in assessment practices. Second, we describe four major concepts or standards for assessment. These standards provide the basis for the specific recommended practices listed in the appendix.

CONCERNS AND PERSPECTIVES

In this section we address certain concerns and perspectives that surround current and unusual practices and the formulation of recommended practices. What is "best" or "recommended" practice must be seen from several perspectives, placed against a social background, and compared to conventional, past, and current practices.

Assessment Purposes and Practices Are Developed and Promoted Within a Societal Context

Fundamental to a discussion of recommended practices is a recognition of the social basis of early intervention. Societal circumstances and social policy factors provide the context for the field's missions and methods. Social events shape the policy and practices that become responsible for shaping social change. A synergistic relationship exists between society and social policy, with each governing the other (see Edgar, 1988; Odom, 1988). Current social contingencies favor the growth of "general" early childhood education and early intervention as important, even critical, social missions. Social policy, through public law and litigation, now mandates and otherwise promotes a national early intervention effort that is beginning to include general early childhood educators (Deiner, 1993). The infant and preschool years are seen not only as a precious time for children in their eventual development but also as "social capital" that must be spent wisely. The social missions of early childhood education and early intervention, however, are not identical (Carta, Atwater, Schwartz, & McConnell, 1993; Carta, Schwartz, Atwater, & McConnell, 1991). General early childhood education policy and practices seem most concerned with promoting (typical) children's development. Early childhood special education or early intervention is concerned with *changing* development for the better. Pratitioners' efforts are solicited or prompted by the presence of children and families who are not thriving as might be expected or desired. *Assessment* practices are part of the social enterprise and cannot be seen as distinct from this context. Although assessment practices are common in both early childhood education and early intervention, they become critical activities for intervention.

A "paradigm shift" is occurring in early intervention, and certainly changes in assessment practices reflect new assumptions, questions, issues, and a new model more suitable to current demands. Conventional assessment is characterized by much clinging to old standards such as standardized intelligence testing, child-centered (rather than family-centered) practices, and preoccupation with quantitative, statistical approaches to decision making. The apparent shift or period of transition is further evidenced by the prevalence of assessment minutia and research of such specificity that it fails to address real issues and problems (Edgar, 1988; Odom, 1988). On the other hand, the emerging emphasis on family-centered practices, collaborative assessment, and team decision making can be seen as reflections of current social policy, social needs, and the edge of a new paradigm. New assessment materials and approaches are emerging to meet the new priorities of society.

Professional Assessment Practices Are Generally a Substitute for More Thorough Familiarity and Observation of the Child

Derived from the Greek, *assidere* means "to sit or sit beside"; thus, the root meaning of *assessment* suggests a process of getting to know someone.

Assessment should help professionals "really know" the child. Introductory texts in assessment usually point out the distinctions between testing and assessment and emphasize the broader informative nature of assessment. As a process, assessment includes an array of data and information-gathering methods: testing, direct observation and recordings, interviews, anecdotal and running records, work samples, and rating scales completed by a professional or someone familiar with the child. Further, approaches such as "arena assessment" (Foley, 1990), team decision making (Moore, Fifield, Spira, & Scarlato, 1989), and systems to monitor typical functioning at home (Bricker, 1993; Bruder, 1993; Walker & Greene, 1991) are increasingly used to capture more reliable and realistic child and family information. Obviously, professionals do not have the time and resources to get to know referred children as well as they do their own. The tools and methods of assessment allow sampling of child functioning to generate descriptions that are then used for several purposes (e.g., eligibility determination, program planning, monitoring, and evaluation; Neisworth & Bagnato, 1988). The goodness of the sampling and corresponding descriptions will depend on a number of factors and are subject to bias and measurement error. The burden on professionals who conduct assessment is to gather, synthesize, and interpret enough information to help make worthwhile decisions regarding the child and family. Assessment decisions can be seen as being "low stake" (e.g., which of three acceptable goals should be worked on first) or "high stake" (e.g., diagnosis of mental retardation and eligibility for specialized treatment; Cronbach, 1988; Messick, 1975, 1988). It is arguable that higher stakes decisions should be based on greater information sampling and include low-inference measures. Direct observation of ongoing behavior in natural environments, performance assessments, and some ethnographic methods provide results that do not demand as much inference but take more time and effort. Advocates of performance assessments in educational measurement point to qualities such as authenticity (Newmann, 1990) and directness (Frederiksen & Collins, 1989) as criteria of greater value than the conceptually narrow psychometric validity basis of conventional, although expeditious, assessment tools (Moss, 1992).

The determination of appropriate assessment materials and methods depends on the *potential social consequences* of the assessment results. Choices of assessment materials and methods in early intervention are expanding and are thus permitting more important decisions to have a wider validity basis. Several implications for practice result from this focus on the social consequences of assessment. First, professionals must strive to obtain the best and closest descriptions of child status when decisions to be made are not trivial. The gravity of the decisions to be made is, of course, to be judged by the participants and will be imbedded in prevailing social policy. The second implication is corollary to the first: Decisions that are not high stake need not be made with the same set of assessment materials, crew of professionals, and expenditures of time. Decisions regarding inclusion, for example, often do not warrant extended, detailed assessment-driven decisions when the child's progress can be monitored once inclusion takes place. In this case, the precision should focus on progress tracking rather than on placement. Finally, we agree with Messick (1989) that the possible use of a given assessment instrument and approach should be pitted against alternative assessment or means to achieve similar outcomes, including no assessment.

Young Children, Especially Those with Physical, Behavioral, or Cultural Differences, Place Unique Demands on Assessment Practices

Parents and professionals who work with young children are well aware that features of early development can make assessment an adventure. The assessment methods used with older children do not match the developmental characteristics of young children—even those who are considered "typical." The assessment situation becomes even more problematic when children with atypical development are considered.

The expectations of most norm-referenced standardized assessments run counter to the realities of the behavior of young children. Developmental, biological, and situational variables act together to produce assessment scenarios that challenge even skilled professionals. The task is often insurmountable when the professional is forced to "fit the child to the test" rather than conduct sensible assessment (Bagnato & Neisworth, 1993).

The problems related to assessing the developmental status and progress of young children include issues that arise during an assessment session and those issues that relate to the developmental process itself. Assessment session difficulties are often cited as major challenges to adequate, even sensible, assessment. A few of the challenges faced by the assessor include the child's distractibility, lack of interest in the standard objects in the test kit, oppositional behavior and noncompliance, lack of endurance, persistence at other competing (more interesting) activities, and frustration with test tasks. Yet, as noted by Bracken (1983), descriptions such as "distractible," "impulsive," "easily frustrated," and "emotionally labile" are often cited as possible indicators of neurological or emotional disorder and can be descriptive of typical young children as well.

We emphasize that even young typical children who do not have special needs should not be assessed by the downward extrapolation of school-age practices. Young children simply do not reliably sit, listen, and perform. Moreover, the presence of special needs—sensory, response, and affective differences or disabilities—create circumstances that often mask or depress performance (Fuchs, Fuchs, Benowitz, & Barringer, 1987). Assessment of "intelligence" in early intervention, for example, is fraught with difficulties, in part related to the issues of atypical as well as to typical early development (Bagnato & Neisworth, 1994; Neisworth & Bagnato, 1992).

Aside from problems of rapport, motivation, and attention at a given assessment session, characteristics of the course and process of early development also create great difficulties for assessment and cast suspicion on conventional test validity. Normal early development is characterized by nonlinear progression and developmental discontinuity (M. Cole & Cole, 1989), which confound prediction and inferences concerning assessment and intervention effect.

Developmental transition, or "oscillation" (Ausubel & Sullivan, 1970), presents yet another challenge to conventional assessment practices. Children may exhibit a more advanced skill, only to return to a former, less sophisticated one. A skill that will later be consolidated may be "previewed," perhaps a month before it is evidenced reliably. Assessment may take place during a transitional phase and capture a less advanced skill or version of the skill that undergoes rapid progress and is displayed and preferred by the child within the next week. Developmental transition, characterized by emerging and fluctuating skills, provides a strong rationale for repeated, or serial, assessment—a recommended practice.

In addition to the implications of nonlinear development and transition periods, the impact of one developmental dimension on another must be recognized. Professionals must remember, too, that separate "developmental domains" were contrived by professionals for convenience in description and measurement. Parallel development across the interrelated and interactive developmental domains cannot be expected. Uneven (nonparallel) development is characteristic of very young children and especially pertinent when a disability exists. As an illustration, assessment of a child's cognitive development may result in misleading, depressed scores when the examiner depends on the child's subnormal language development as an avenue to appraise intellect.

It is arguable, then, that the new assessment issues and questions of early intervention are not addressed by or managed well with conventional materials and approaches. Recommendations for assessment practices are made within the context of the concerns and perspectives just summarized. Amidst the changing demands and perspectives, four major standards are proposed that seem consistent with emerging beliefs, policies, and practices. The standards form the basis for the specific recommended assessment practices in the appendix.

STANDARDS FOR ASSESSMENT

Common themes for early childhood assessment are evident in the published recommendations of several prominent professional organizations, notably the American Speech and Hearing Association (ASHA, 1990), National Association for the Education of Young Children (NAEYC, 1990), National Association of School Psychologists (Bracken, Bragnato, & Barnett, 1991; Schakel, 1987), and Division for Early Childhood of the Council for Exceptional Children (DEC, 1993). Further, common recommendations are stressed in professional texts and position papers (Bailey & Wolery, 1989; Barnett & Carey, 1992; Bracken, 1991b; Bredekamp, 1987; McLean & Odom, 1993; Neisworth & Bagnato, 1992, 1993). It is informative and reassuring that there is substantial agreement among and across diverse experts—professionals who have not always been in accord.

Four major standards that subsume specific practices are described. These four standards include both conceptual and pragmatic themes and were synthesized through a search of assessment theory, models, and practices of several professions.

Standard 1: Treatment Utility

Assessment Must Be Useful for Early Intervention and Education

That assessment should be useful seems obvious and unnecessary to emphasize. Unfortunately, however, much conventional assessment is not useful for helping infants and young children (Bagnato, Neisworth, & Munson, in press). Several factors have contributed to the misalignment between assessment and intervention. Traditionally, assessment materials and procedures have been devised ostensibly to measure traits or theoretical constructs. Global scores of traits (e.g., intelligence) may be of theoretical interest, but they simply do not produce much useful information for practitioners. The absence of appropriate materials and approaches and the misuse of standardized, norm-referenced materials in early intervention have been emphasized and need not be elaborated here. The essential point to highlight is that conventional assessment, especially norm-referenced assessment of traits, constructs, or "underlying conditions," has had little utility for intervention.

The amazing paucity of assessment materials and approaches for guiding education and treatment is certainly not particular to early intervention and education. Indeed, over 30 years ago, Meehl (1959) reviewed clinical assessment in psychology and proposed that there must be a practical criterion on which to judge assessment. More recently, Hayes, Nelson, and Jarrett (1987) proposed the term *treatment utility* to refer to the "sine qua non" of assessment—the extent to which assessment is shown to contribute to beneficial outcomes. Professionals in school psychology (e.g., Rosenfield & Reynolds, 1990), special education (e.g., Fuchs et al., 1987), early intervention (e.g., Bagnato & Neisworth, 1991), and general early childhood education are joining ranks to assert the priority of utility in assessment. The position paper by The National Association for the Education of Young Children and the National Association of Early Childhood Specialists in State Departments of Education (1991) perhaps best illustrates the straightforward, pragmatic focus that assessment must have. For example, 4 of the 18 position statement guidelines are expressions of treatment utility:

- Is the assessment procedure based on the goals and objectives of the specific curriculum used in the program?

- Are the results of assessment used to benefit children (i.e., to plan for individual children, improve instruction, identify children's interests and needs, and individualize instruction, rather than label, track, or fail children)?

- Does assessment provide useful information to teachers to help them do a better job?

- Is there a systematic procedure for collecting assessment data that facilitates its use in planning instruction and communicating with parents? (pp. 92–93)

Intervention or treatment can be seen to include at least three kinds, or levels, of activity (Wolf, 1978): (a) specification of goals and objectives, (b) selection or design of instructional and therapeutic strategies, and (c) evaluation of intervention effects. We use these three levels to discuss the implications of treatment or intervention utility of assessment. Because assessment is a pivotal component of intervention, we specifically focus on issues of assessment utility as they are related to each of the three levels of intervention.

- Does assessment identify feasible goals and objectives for the child and family?

Assessment that specifies characteristics or behaviors amenable to treatment is useful to teachers, therapists, parents, and the child. Practitioners and parents are, indeed, grateful when they are provided with assessment results that have direct and immediate use in their efforts. Teachers and therapists are very busy people and actively seek information to guide decisions regarding goals and objectives for children. When assessment has a high degree of treatment utility, it is low inference and does not require "translation." Reporting conditions, syndromes, categorical labels (e.g., mental retardation, Down syndrome, learning disability) or global scores requires a great amount of inferring and conjecture before feasible instructional objectives can be divined.

As an illustration, specific measures of concept attainment (e.g., knows *bigger, smaller*) are far more useful than intelligence test scores (e.g., IQ of 67). It should be noted that the utility of objectives can be judged according to two criteria. First, the problem or function cited must be *specific* rather than global. Second, assessment must identify characteristics or functions that are *accessible* to change. Findings such as "minimal brain injury," "sensory integration difficulties," or "subnormal IQ" fail to be specific or accessible. Speculations concerning the child's past, ancestral background, and debates about which label or syndrome best describe the child are seldom helpful for specifying child-specific program objectives. Further, there seems little utility in generating assessment findings about which nothing can be done. Measures of attention to task, pincher grasp, or mother–child reciprocity provide useful information; these measures lend themselves to objectives that can be taught and measured. It is no wonder that psychologists, required to use certain formal instruments, and teachers have found difficulty in communicating and that there has been little linkage between assessment and program planning (Bagnato, Neisworth, & Munson, in press). In brief, to have treatment utility, assessment must identify specific needs and characteristics that can be improved through instruction, therapy, or changes in the child's circumstances. Useful assessment helps practitioners, teachers, and parents to decide *what* to teach.

- Does assessment information assist in the selection or use of instructional methods or approaches?

Persons who work with children who have special needs know that instructional activities must often be adapted to accommodate sensory, response, motivational, and other differences. Likewise, the conduct of assessment frequently must involve adaptations of objects and procedures to enable valid detection of a child's skills.

Some assessment instruments are designed to accommodate specific differences (e.g., visual, auditory, fine motor). Other instruments include manuals that offer illustrations and suggestions concerning adjustments to the materials and administration of items. A skilled assessment specialist will adapt materials and procedures to match a child's characteristics, rather than permitting the child's differences to thwart or underestimate performance. The robotic use of standardized procedures—suitable for "standard children"—is, of course, an example of "misassessment" and has been subject to detailed discussions in the literature (see e.g., Bagnato & Neisworth, 1991; Coster & Haley, 1992; Garwood, 1982; Rosenfield & Reynolds, 1990).

When conducted appropriately, assessment can help teachers, parents, and others to know more about changes in materials and methods needed to reconcile differences. Information concerning assessment adaptations used and certain new forms of assessment such as dynamic assessment (Feuerstein, 1979; Lidz, 1992) offer guidance concerning how children learn. Assessment, then, can offer information regarding *how* to teach.

- Does assessment contribute to evaluating intervention effects?

Assessment that fails to provide information regarding specific, accessible change objectives is also seldom useful for evaluating intervention or program effects. In addition to specificity, another important element is *sensitivity*. When assessment includes items that detect small changes, they are more sensitive and, thus, more useful for progress evaluation. Again, global measures of traits and categorical qualities are not sufficiently sensitive to register changes that reflect intervention efforts.

Too few items, too wide of differences in scaled intervals, and lack of articulation between assessment items and intervention goals (curricula) result in assessment of low or no utility at this level. Assessment content becomes more useful and sensitive for gauging change when it includes a full range of items, function- and performance-based samples, and permits graduated scoring for items.

With the increasing demand for accountability, assessment that is sensitive to child progress becomes paramount. Measures that provide feedback are appreciated by interventionists so that materials and tactics can be adjusted accordingly and so that program efforts will be evident. Of course, parents deserve child assessment that is informative and that detects even small progress. Useful assessment at this level can inform teachers when and if they have reached an objective—*how much* they have taught.

Early intervention professionals must begin to examine critically the measures that they use and the extent to which the measures meet standards of utility. Certain types of widely used tests fail to meet any of these standards, of which the most ubiquitous examples are early tests of intelligence. Survey research on the treatment *futility* of early tests of intelligence includes findings that intelligence tests are reported to be unworkable or unacceptable tools nearly 50% of the time, fail to sample functional skills for goal planning, are not disability-sensitive, and do not accommodate typical early childhood behavioral and temperamental styles (Bagnato & Neisworth, 1994). Intelligence tests are insensitive as measures of developmental progress, do not relate to program curricula, and have no convincing field validation with young children with developmental disabilities (Neisworth & Bagnato, 1992). Fundamentally, then, intelligence testing fails to accomplish any early intervention purpose and, arguably, is at odds with the philosophy and missions of early intervention and early childhood professionals (Bredekamp & Rosegrant, 1992; Perrone, 1991). It is best practice when professionals turn away from assessment that is "dead end" or of little utility and turn toward assessment approaches and instruments that are directly helpful.

Recommended Practices in Action: Treatment Utility

Assessment *for* early intervention yields outcomes that offer prescriptions for progress rather than diagnoses that place predetermined (and, too often, erroneous) limits on progress. Assessment measures and procedures used to accomplish early intervention purposes should

- be flexible for use by teams of parents and professionals;
- generate functional and integrated intervention goals;
- circumvent or accommodate the child's sensory, neuromotor, communication, and behavioral deficits;
- match the behavior styles characteristic in early childhood development;
- be sufficiently sensitive to monitor small increments of change in child capabilities during intervention; and
- be "field validated" (i.e., have high reliabilities when used with similar children and have evidence of utility for instruction).

Curriculum-Based Developmental Assessment: High-Utility Assessment

Curriculum-based developmental assessment (CBA) is one form of measurement that meets standards for treatment utility and fulfills the purposes of early intervention. The foundation for CBA is the developmental task analysis, or hierarchical sequence of competencies. Observation of the child's performance of the various competency items enables teams of parents and professionals to establish current functional levels. Performance levels and profiles can then be used to determine program eligibility; to identify teachable, functional, and measurable goals for instruction and therapy; and to chart the child's progress sensitively during intervention in terms of discrete learning (i.e., numbers of curriculum objectives achieved). Further, CBA is a flexible form of measurement that either allows or directs professionals to adapt administration of items to accommodate child sensory and response differences. The best curriculum-based assessment systems provide numerous suggestions for adapting materials and procedures to allow children to show what they know and to do their best. Using a child's own toy, substituting larger objects, and employing an auditory rather than a visual task are examples of sensible alternatives possible in curriculum-based assessment. These changes do not violate the "sanctity" of standardization procedures because such sensible alternative procedures were, indeed, part of the standardization procedures in developing the curriculum-referenced measures.

CBA also enables professionals to conduct the assessment in natural settings and under structured or unstructured (play) circumstances to match the child's unique behavioral or temperamental style. Graduated scoring of capabilities (e.g., pass, emerging, no pass) allows the team to identify clear objectives for instruction. Other items and scoring procedures on several CBA systems allow scoring at several levels of support needed (e.g., performs independently, performs with verbal prompting, performs with manual prompting). Assessing current levels of support needed to perform a competency reveals the conditions under which the child can demonstrate a behavior, information that provides further instructional guidance. Moreover, CBA "scores" capabilities on the basis of multiple sources of information: observation, interview, direct assessment, trial teaching, and judgment. It should be noted that CBA systems vary in quality and should be evaluated critically. For example, some contain task analyses that are not sufficiently dense to accommodate lower functional levels or to chart small increments of change. Also, the field is moving from a strict adherence to developmental milestone measures, which emphasize tasks that are not feasible when certain sensory–motor difficulties are present and are not instructionally meaningful or predictive of later functioning (e.g., stacking blocks, placing pegs in pegboard). There is a shift toward instruments that focus on behaviors that are truly functional and teachable (e.g., moving about, initiating a social interaction with a peer, activating a simple or electromechanical toy).

Five commercially available CBA systems that meet the standards cited here are the *Hawaii Early Learning Profile-Inside Help* (Parks, 1992) and *Help for Special Preschoolers* (Santa Cruze County Office of Education, 1987), *The Carolina Curriculum for Preschoolers with Special Needs* (Johnson-Martin, Attermeier, & Hacker, 1990), *The Carolina Curriculum for Infants and Toddlers with Special Needs* (Johnson-Martin, Jens, Attermeier, & Hacker, 1991), and the *Assessment, Evaluation, and Programming System for Infants and Children* (Bricker, 1993). Other CBA packages are being developed, some for specific domains of development. Two examples of focused CBA systems are the *Social Skills Rating System* (Gresham & Elliott, 1990) and the *Bracken Basic Concepts Scale* (Bracken, 1984) and matching curriculum (Bracken, 1991a). Each of the preceding systems consists of both a measurement scale and an accompanying curriculum, a combination clearly making them of high intervention utility.

Standard 2: Social Validity

Assessment Must Be Judged as Valuable and Acceptable

As professionals, we recognize the importance of designing and tailoring our assessment practices to meet certain standards of social validity (Neisworth & Fewell, 1990) as well as to meet standards of utility. In brief, professionals stress the importance of *socially appropriate assessment*. In the preceding section, we emphasized the sine qua non of assessment—its utility for intervention. Although an assessment instrument may generate *useful* results, there may be differences in opinion regarding the appropriateness or acceptability of goals or objectives generated from assessment results. For example, assessment may identify specific and teachable objectives (utility) that are not deemed worthwhile (social validity). Professionals for some time have pointed out the need for a social or judgmental dimension to assessment (e.g., Iscoe & Payne, 1972). The discussion provided by Wolf (1978) marked the onset of more systematic work on the social dimensions of "objective" assessment.

"Significance," "importance," and "acceptability" are social validity issues that are crucial to treatment programs for at least two reasons. First, intervention may not be effective when clients are uninterested or in opposition to program goals, methods, or actual outcomes. Often getting people to participate in programs, to cooperate, and to use treatments requires a willingness that is evident only when program goals or methods are appreciated. Second, public law now mandates that clients (i.e., families) participate actively in selecting and consenting to their children's individual plans and services. The implications of social validity of assessment for each level of intervention are discussed here. As with treatment utility, the following assessment standards are suggested at each level of intervention.

- Does assessment identify goals and objectives that are judged as worthwhile and appropriate?

Unfortunately, some instructional or therapeutic objectives are of little consequence to a child's future. Tasks found on numerous traditional assessment devices are often not worthwhile as developmental or educational objectives. Parents and teachers must agree that the targets identified through assessment are worthy of including in the child's IFSP or IEP.

When assessment meets the *utility* standard, it specifies objectives for inclusion in children's programs; although such objectives may be specific, measurable, and teachable, they may not be meaningful or deemed acceptable by clients. Because many assessment scales have a developmental milestone basis, the items often become learning objectives (i.e., teachers teach developmental milestones; Sheehan, 1982). Developmental milestones, especially those found on norm-referenced instruments, are not necessarily worthwhile to teach (e.g., stacking blocks, putting pegs in holes, standing on one foot). Many infants and preschoolers with special needs would benefit much more if taught functional skills—skills important to them in their present circumstances. "Getting across the room" is a more suitable objective than, for example, standing on one foot. Proponents of functional assessment highlight the importance of assessment that identifies skills that are important to the child in the child's context (Bruder, 1993). Certainly, the Developmentally Appropriate Practice position (Bredekamp & Rosegrant, 1992) even more strongly supports assessment procedures and objectives that are acceptable to the family and that are relevant to the child's life and context. Assessment that removes the child from his or her familiar context may distort or misrepresent that child's capabilities. Performance is situational, and it is optional in familiar settings. Conventional, standardized, norm-referenced assessment removes the child from the familiar, imposes strange circumstances, and requires performances detached from the situations where learning and practice are occasioned. Further, the interactive nature of learning, development, and disability is not typically addressed by conventional assessment items. Child difficulties do not reside exclusively with the child but are a function of interaction with circumstances (Coster & Haley, 1992). *Assessment content must embrace the situationality of behavior.* Assessment should and can identify skills for IFSP or IEP objectives that are functional and appreciated. Assessment should sample real performance in real situations rather than emphasize decontextualized skill testing.

The acceptability, meaningfulness, and significance of assessment content are issues that require professionals to make real decisions related to family-centered practices. Professionals may sometimes be faced with consumer resistance to goals or objectives deemed important by professionals but deemed objectionable by parents. Assessment, done collaboratively under authentic circumstances, may generate objectives that are more likely to be acceptable to professionals and family members.

- Are assessment methods and materials acceptable to participants?

The concern here is whether the clients involved (parents, teachers, and perhaps children) agree not only to assessment content but also to the assessment devices and approaches used. That consumers accept an assessment and recognize its importance goes a long way in producing the rapport and validity so necessary to accurate assessment. The use of socially approved assessment materials and procedures is consistent with family-centered practices and is fundamental to early intervention, which is, after all, a social enterprise (Bailey & Simeonsson, 1988).

A surge of research on treatment acceptability occurred in the 1980s. Wolf's (1978) article and a series of publications by Kazdin (see Kazdin, 1977, 1980, 1981, 1984) focused professional concern on client and professional preferences and ethics regarding such issues as time out, use of alternating treatments, and aversive procedures. Interview formats and rating scales have been devised to appraise the acceptability of treatments. Research on treatment acceptability in psychology and education has been well reviewed and conceptualized (see Miltenberger, 1990); however, research on the acceptability of intervention in early intervention is sparse and unsystematic. A notable exception is the literature on preschooler social skills (see Odom, McConnell, & Chandler, 1994), where research on social interventions seems well conceptualized and programmatic.

Intervention procedures, in this case, assessment procedures and materials, can be judged on the basis of cost and benefit, family acceptability, and practical considerations. Assessment methods and instruments objectionable to the users (professionals) or clients (families) will not likely yield valid measures and will impede collaborative efforts.

Estimates of acceptability may be gained through observation, interview, and rating scales. Qualitative research methodologies (e.g., Lincoln & Guba, 1985), designs (e.g., Odom & Shuster, 1986), and materials (e.g., Bailey & Simeonsson, 1988; Gresham & Elliott, 1990; Winton & Turnbull, 1981) are providing professionals with information and approaches needed to address the concerns, preferences, and reactions of families, their children, and professionals.

- Does assessment detect social significance of change?

The profession of early intervention is dedicated to changing the developmental destinies of children with special needs—to altering the direction, content, and rate of functional capabilities beyond predicted levels. *Intervention* denotes influencing accessible variables in order to alter probable outcomes. All too often, professionals "objectively" demonstrate child improvement through test-score improvement. Increases in raw scores, percentile ranks, and standard scores are used to document change. Program accountability is assessed with norm-referenced and competency-based child measures, without due consideration of how meaningful, socially detectable, and developmentally appropriate the goals and changes may be (Elkind, 1986).

Some have argued that the interventionist position conflicts with DAP guidelines, which oppose more formal and intense instruction (Carta et al., 1991). The seeming dilemma between developmentally appropriate versus instructionally effective practice may not be soon resolved, but assessment that includes measures of perceived as well as objective progress may help. Parents, professionals, and children may provide important information regarding the social significance of change that may, in turn, relate to program accountability and what is effective *and* appropriate. A simple question that can be addressed through social measures of change might be "Are child improvements evidenced in intense early intervention programs judged to be significant and meaningful by parents and other relevant participants?" Of course, strong evidence of the effectiveness of intervention does exist, but corresponding measures of consumer satisfaction are rare. A number of instruments, especially newer ones, are available for assessing parent concern and satisfaction with objectives and change as well as child status and progress. Such instruments are extremely helpful not only for identifying intervention objectives but also for assessing the perceived value of the objectives and the significance of change.

Early intervention rests on the principle that efficacy and efficiency are related to family priorities and to marshaling the resources and best efforts of professionals and family members. Assessment is fundamentally a social enterprise that requires negotiation and consensus among parents and professionals. "Objective" estimates of the status and progress of the child or family must be corroborated by social perceptions of functioning in natural settings. Judgment-based assessment is not only an important assessment method but also an excellent way for parents and others to express their input regarding acceptability and significance (see Neisworth & Fewell, 1990).

Recommended Practices in Action: Social Validity

Changes in early childhood assessment practices and instruments reflect the increasing importance of social validity. Included here are brief descriptions of two instruments and an assessment method that give prominence to judgments and perceptions of parents and professionals.

The *Social Skills Rating System* (SSRS; Gresham & Elliott, 1990) incorporates multiple sources—parent and teacher—and an observational/rating format to appraise the child's functional social skills. The assessment links directly to a social skills intervention plan—a basic curriculum. The instrument yields ratings not only of the extent to which a child can demonstrate certain social skills but also of the parent's and teacher's perceptions of the importance of each social skill. Thus, the SSRS offers a way to detect conflicting priorities and to reach consensus about shared goals for intervention. The *Family Needs Survey* (Bailey & Simeonsson, 1988) enables families to conduct self-appraisals and to identify and report in simple language their perceived strengths, priorities, and needs, which form the basis for service delivery and social benchmarks for detecting change and service outcomes.

Goal Attainment Scaling (GAS; Kiresuk & Lund, 1978; Kiresuk, Smith, & Cardillo, 1994; Simeonsson, Huntington, & Short, 1982) is a procedure that enables parents and professionals to set and weight child and family goals for early intervention. With this procedure, parent–professional teams can establish a range (+2+1, 0, –1–2) of *expected, less than expected,* and *more than expected* outcomes for their goals. Treatment outcome and efficacy are evaluated on the basis of combinations of socially derived weighted goals. Goal attainment scaling appears to be especially harmonious with family-centered practices. The GAS approach is particularly suited for program evaluation because it provides a way of comparing the importance of goals, their attainment, and the efforts needed to reach them.

Standard 3: Convergent Assessment

Assessment Must Be Based on a Wide Foundation of Information

Important decisions regarding children's lives cannot and should not be made on the basis of meager, singular, and questionable information. Issues of eligibility, program planning, progress monitoring, and program evaluation require evidence that simply does not come easily or instantly. Even screening to detect possible developmental difficulties—once seen as relatively simple and feasible through shortcut methods—is now being treated as more complex and as demanding more than a single source (Meisels, 1990). Certainly, public law now prohibits the use of a single criterion for diagnosis and eligibility decisions. The DAP guidelines on assessment stress the need for information from multiple sources and the rejection of exclusive reliance on standardized instruments. The DAP position specifically calls for the use of an array of assessment tools and approaches (Bredekamp, 1987, p. 91; Bredekamp & Rosegrant, 1992) for decision making. The endorsement of multisource assessment is a point of agreement between the fields of early intervention and early childhood education (Carta et al., 1991; McLean & Odom, 1993).

Most professionals concur on several major reasons for "casting a wide net" to gather information. First, typical early child development is characterized by uneven, nonlinear progress, a fact making single-point assessment suspect even for children without identified special needs. The complexities of developmental difficulties imposed on typical development often produces an irregular developmental trajectory that certainly confounds simplistic assessment. Second, the reliability and validity of any single measure can be challenged in view of the sensory, response, and temperamental differences of children who are most in need of assessment. A third and increasingly prominent reason for expanding assessment gathering relates to ecological issues and validity. New conceptions of validity (e.g., Moss, 1992) force attention on methods of assessment in context (e.g., performance assessment [Stiggins, 1987]), authentic assessment (Newmann, 1990), and "convergent evidence" (Campbell, 1960; Campbell & Fiske, 1959).

Although still formative, the new conceptions of assessment validity clearly depart from former recommendations and portray validity as a function of multiple types of information used to derive inferences and to make decisions. We professionals are witnessing, then, a general movement within psychology and education away from strict psychometric decision making and toward a model of assessment validity that depends on information sources, situations, and the uses (social consequences) of assessment results. *Convergent assessment* "relies upon the confluence of information across multiple measures, domains, sources, settings, and occasions to accomplish multiple purposes" (Bagnato & Neisworth, 1991, p. 57). There are at least two major advantages to wide-based assessment: It provides concurrent information that can be used to confirm or dispute more narrow findings; and it incorporates information across people, settings, and occasions, generating a strong basis (convergent validity) for decisions. Convergent assessment provides a basis for planning goals and methods and for evaluating outcomes with far greater treatment utility and social validity. Comprehensive, convergent assessment involves meeting standards (described next) related to types of information, settings, sources (especially parents), and occasions.

- Are several types of assessment materials and approaches employed?

The rationale for using several *types* of assessment is to broaden the validity of the decisions based on the assessment effort. Various assessment tools and methods generate information that may be redundant, supplemental, or complementary. Benner (1992) referred to seven strands, or dimensions, of assessment methods: (a) formal/informal, (b) normative/criterion referenced, (c) standardized/adaptive to disability, (d) direct/indirect, (e) naturalistic/clinical, (f) product/process, and (g) unidisciplinary/team approaches. These seven dimensions of assessment encompass most of the prevalent materials and approaches available. A typology of assessment measures was described by Neisworth and Bagnato (1988) to organize types of instruments that can provide cross-confirmation information. Their typology describes the characteristics and uses for eight types of measures: (a) curriculum based, (b) adaptive to handicap, (c) process, (d) norm based, (e) judgment based, (f) ecological, (g) interactive, and (h) systematic observation. Other approaches, such as assessment portfolios, anecdotal records, and interviews (Nuttall, 1992), can be informative and add to the convergence of data and perspectives. Although it is not within the scope of this chapter to describe features of the various instrument types, we stress the inclusion of at least four types: norm-based (NBA), curriculum-based (CBA), judgment-based (JBA), and ecological measures (eco-based). The combination of these four approaches offers several perspectives and kinds of information: a crude comparison to peers vis-à-vis norm-referenced benchmarks, status on a program-relevant curriculum, judgments of parents and others on important dimensions, and estimates of circumstances deemed important to the child.

The convergence of information from these four sources provides a much better description of the child × circumstances than any single measure or approach.

Measures of child status should include examination of the child's *whole* functioning. Even when the presenting problem is a single issue (e.g., intellectual functioning), all developmental domains must be appraised. The analysis of development into domains (cognitive, motor, social, self-help, etc.) is an academic and professional convenience but should not dictate measurement of one domain of functioning at the exclusion of others. Development is interactive and codependent on other domains (e.g., cognitive development relates to social–affective, sensorimotor development). Thus, professionals must appraise strengths and weaknesses in all domains for purposes of eligibility as well as for program planning. This "whole child" imperative is, of course, central to the traditional position of child development professionals and current DAP guidelines.

- Is information collected from multiple sources, especially family members?

The performance of children can be very different across situations. Recognition of the contextual basis of behavior is certainly not new (Lewin, 1954), has been the crux of behavior/functional analysis, and is a current emphasis in early intervention (see Arndorfer & Miltenberger, 1993). The work of measurement experts such as Anastasi (1986), N. Cole and Moss (1989), and Cronbach (1988) confirms the importance of contextual, or ecological, variables in assessment validity. Because development and behavior are contextual, assessment must also include ecological, contextual information. Functional assessment involves appraisal of the events surrounding a behavior in real or simulated settings. Methods for functional assessment include informant judgments (rating scales, checklists, interviews), direct-observation techniques, and experimental manipulation of likely variables—all providing differing but convergent information (Lennox & Miltenberger, 1989). Assessment of a child's performance in that child's natural settings is crucial and may be used to confirm or challenge the clinic-based, isolated assessment that characterizes traditional practices. Performance-based, or authentic, assessment (Meyer, 1992) and portfolio assessment (Arter & Spandel, 1991), for example, the *Work Sampling System* (Meisels, 1993), are clear efforts to capture the qualities of child performance and products as they occur in the child's natural contexts.

The preceding discussion focused on the child's behavior in context. Ecological, contextual assessment can also refer to appraisal of the qualities of the child's environment (e.g., the home, day-care, preschool, or other setting). Such assessment often includes ratings or checklists of dimensions thought to be important (e.g., kinds of toys available, exploratory opportunities, level of distractions). Of course, social dimensions are also important to estimate, such as language stimulation, reciprocity, and contingent attention. Instruments and procedures are available for gathering information on both physical and social setting variables. Assessment of contextual aspects is valuable especially when professionals and families agree that circumstances in the home or early childhood setting may be in need of improvement.

Professionals engaged in best practice recognize the centrality of assessment information provided by the family. Not only is the home environment typically the child's natural setting, but parent reactions and appraisals of their children are also important in their own right, and parent–professional comparisons can be illuminating.

There are several major reasons for parent-generated information about the child. First, it gives practitioners "close-up" information concerning the child's functioning in the setting where it really matters. Parents are potentially the richest source of information concerning their own children, and inclusion of their reports is becoming common practice (Bailey & Wolery, 1989). To gather child information, parents can be provided with (and coached to use) rating scales, checklists, or simple observation schedules. Parents also often reveal useful information through questionnaires and open-ended interviews. Videotaping of the child by the parents may be a strong assessment tool, especially when adequate samples of behavior or critical episodes are captured.

The second reason to include parent report is to obtain estimates of parents' reactions and levels of concern. How parents view child strengths and difficulties and how they perceive progress are important information. Measures of parent stress and anxiety, as well as needs for various resources, are available and are recommended for use when indicated. Parent perceptions or judgments are, of course, measures of social validity as well as ecological observations.

A number of researchers have suggested ways to facilitate parent-provided assessment, and professionals are urged to adapt or develop materials and methods that are family friendly. Five recommendations summarized from the literature by Diamond and Squires (1993) include the following:

- Current, rather than retrospective, child functioning should be targeted.

- Frequent, as opposed to low-strength, behavior seems more useful.

- A recognition (check the descriptions that refer to your child) rather than recall (describe how your child has been acting) format yields more reliable results.

- Parents should not have to provide information on demand but be afforded the time and convenience to complete their assessments while observing and considering their children.
- Attention must be given to the knowledge and skills needed to conduct or complete assessments.

We emphasize the importance of adapting materials and demands to suit parent knowledge and skills, and we add the following suggestions for making parent-provided assessment family friendly:

- The language level must be appropriate, especially when parents are expected to complete the appraisals independently.
- The format should be inviting and simple to complete.
- When possible, the content should be positive; to avoid alarm or anxiety, try to avoid negative items that parents must check. (This may not always be possible, e.g., problem behavior checklists).
- The time and effort should be kept to a minimum. Parents often are pushed to do so much that reliability and accuracy are compromised.
- Scoring should be meaningful (e.g., developmental ages communicate better than standard deviations). Graphic displays, now feasible with computer programs, can be easily understood.

Finally, comparisons between parent and professional assessments are, themselves, useful information. When congruence exists, the two perspectives add to the credibility of the findings. Discrepancies in parent–professional assessment findings signal the need for discussion or closer assessment or both. It is recommended practice to use parent–professional differences constructively, instead of focusing on "who is right" (Blacher-Dixon & Simeonsson, 1982; Iscoe & Payne, 1972). Professionals and parents should not be viewed as interchangeable raters (Suen, Lu, & Neisworth, 1993). Professionals recognize that assessment discrepancies can occur from different settings and perspectives, and they have agreed for some time that both sets of information contribute to the validity of assessment (e.g., Diamond & Squires, 1993; Glascoe, MacLean, & Stone, 1991; Gradel, Thompson, & Sheehan, 1981).

- Is assessment done on more than one occasion?

Convergent assessment not only encompasses multiple instruments, sources, and settings, but also must include multiple occasions. Longitudinal or repeated assessment is needed to capture both stability and change in child functioning. Serial assessment can document developmental status and correct for one-shot assessment. The old practice of "brief encounters" must be replaced with regular and periodic assessment over occasions and settings. Certainly, serial, longitudinal assessment is necessary for detecting progress and for making program changes. Eligibility assessment, however, also demands collection of information beyond the single session. Although it can be argued that information collected from parents contributes multiple-occasion assessment, professionals should distribute their assessment encounters over some extended time. In this connection, arena assessment may be suspect, due to its one-session, all-at-once format. Typical arena assessment may also compromise the independence of observations and estimates. Professionals involved in arena assessment, however, often bring their child observations and appraisals from other occasions and settings, which thus result in multioccasional–multisetting findings.

Recommended Practices in Action: Convergent Assessment

Convergent assessment describes the practice of synthesizing information from multiple sources, occasions, instruments, domains, and settings to attain a wide base of corroborative evidence (Bagnato & Neisworth, 1991). Curriculum-based assessment or hybrid-norm/criterion–referenced systems have attributes that promote convergent assessment. For example, the *Battelle Developmental Inventory* (Newborg, Stock, Wnek, Guidubaldi, & Svinicki, 1984) allows parents and professionals to document child capabilities in various ways: natural observation, standardized administration, disability–modifications, parental report, trial teaching, judgment. In addition, several team members contribute to the assessment of multiple domains of functioning.

Convergent assessment should include at least some information concerning the child's home or program circumstances. *Assessment, Evaluation, and Programming System for Infants and Children* (AEPS; Bricker, 1993) enables early interventionists to appraise the quality of physical and social aspects of the early childhood setting. The resulting profile helps staff and administrators make and evaluate needed changes in routines and materials. AEPS offers a sensitive measure of child progress and circumstances.

Generally, then, materials and practices that include multiple sources and occasions contribute to convergent, wide-based assessment. Many new instruments (e.g., the *Social Skills Rating System*) provide separate checklists to be completed by multiple raters (e.g., teacher, parent, and even child). Collecting multiple perspectives also illustrates convergent assessment. Other new materials permit observation and evaluation of child skills in the child's own context, include parent ratings, and even supply norms for flexible, situational assessment. A promising new instrument that is ecological and parent-friendly and that has early childhood norms is the *Developmental Observation Checklist System* (Hresko, Miguel, Sherbenov, & Burton, 1994).

Standard 4: Consensual Validity

Assessment-Based Decisions Must Be Reached Through Team Member Consensus

Tests do not make decisions—people do. From the time a child is identified for screening, decisions are made by parents and professionals. The choice of screening instruments and procedures, assessment approaches and circumstances, and the decisions derived from assessment are all made by people. The social basis of decision making is crucial to emphasize and is consistent with new conceptions of convergent validity. As discussed in previous sections of this chapter, validity, or "truth," does not reside with any given test, observation, interview, or opinion. Rather, validity relates to the decisions and outcomes derived from assessment. Assessment is valid to the extent that it contributes to accurate and useful decisions.

The decision-making process in early intervention assessment includes two distinct phases. First, a given individual forms impressions and tentative decisions based on available information. A single professional may draw on multiple sources when beginning to consider a decision, whether that decision concerns eligibility, placement, program design, or progress evaluation. The professional may have personally interviewed the parents, reviewed prior material concerning the child, conducted a standardized assessment, and gathered information through child observation. The individual professional, then, begins to put things together through a personal convergence of information.

It is not reasonable, however, to expect a given professional personally to gather information systematically across multiple instruments, sources, settings, and occasions. A group or team effort is desirable to make convergent validity feasible, requiring exchange and deliberation.

- Are assessment information and perspectives shared?

Collaborative decision making entails a collective pooling of findings, wherein multiple individuals—including and especially family members—contribute information. Although parents are usually not assessment professionals, they have, of course, a wealth of information that can be of great value. The professional will not reject parental input but be skilled in how best to access the information that parents may have. Independent observations and cross-validation of findings contribute to the overall validity of assessment, and this contribution underscores the need for more than one person involved in the effort. A kind of grand convergence results when informed persons are able to share their relevant information and considerations. Team assessment and decision making are the preferred approach in early intervention for achieving comprehensive and acceptable assessment. The complex and interrelated developmental, medical, mental health, and psychosocial needs of children demand close collaboration among diverse professionals (Ploof & Feldman, 1992) and sensitive partnerships with parents (Dunst, 1991; Turnbull & Turnbull, 1990). Early interventionists report that they need methods that allow them to collaborate in an integral manner across professionals, to integrate parents on the team, to identify and manage joint medical and developmental needs, to plan effective and acceptable programs, and to smooth the inevitable transitions between programs (Bagnato & Feldman, 1989).

The field has responded to the reality of working together in teams by championing the use of various cross-disciplinary models and combinations for conducting team assessments (i.e., multi-, inter-, and transdisciplinary teams [Woodruff & McGonigel, 1988]). These team models stress *the mechanics of teamwork*: how team assessments are conducted, what instruments will be used, what team members will participate, and how results will be reported.

- Does the team collaborate to achieve consensus on assessment decisions?

The necessity for a team approach covers much more than how and who conducts assessments. Sharing information is one thing, but arriving at collaborative decisions is yet another and major goal of teamwork. A most pressing need and neglected feature of early intervention services is the *dynamics of teamwork*: the interpersonal group dynamics and decision-making processes that enable parents and professionals to work together collaboratively and to arrive at consensual decisions. Current practices fail to enable professionals to achieve group unity, work efficiently, involve parents and families as integral partners, reduce disciplinary boundaries, accomplish joint missions, and negotiate collaborative decisions not only about the child's and family's needs but also about the content and mode of delivering services effectively.

Surprisingly little research has been conducted on either the mechanics or dynamics of teamwork to support its general acceptance and acknowledged importance to the early intervention field. The limited available research and conceptual papers agree that few programs and their staffs are skilled in group dynamics, use team procedures consistently, include parents as partners, encourage interagency teamwork, or identify and resolve dysfunctions in team dynamics and consensus decision making (Bailey, 1984; Moore et al., 1989). It is a paradox that interdisciplinary and interagency teamwork are mandated by law and crucial to the effectiveness of early intervention but that few program staff members know how to work as a unified team.

Problems and Solutions in Teamwork. Table 2.1 lists the major problems associated with the process of teamwork and recommended solutions. Parents are often treated as perfunctory members of the team, having little voice in the assessment and treatment decision-making process for their children; they are merely the recipients of predetermined information. Such a style reinforces family dependency on professionals, impedes the growth of personal decision-making power, and fosters conflict and mistrust among parents and professionals. Vehicles are needed to include the parents as fully functioning team decision makers. The use of parent-friendly assessment materials, meetings scheduled at times convenient to the family, and one team member appointed as a point of contact are ways to facilitate parent participation.

Interdisciplinary teams often lack structure and clear missions. These shortcomings are exacerbated by the absence of leadership or by an authoritarian style that inhibits collaborative problem solving and consensus building. A facilitative leadership style and a process mode that establishes clear team missions are critical to team decision making.

Table 2.1. Problems with Interdisciplinary Team Functioning

- Lack of expertise in group dynamics
- Lack of meeting structure and missions
- Absent or authoritarian leadership
- Strong disciplinary boundaries and jargon
- Unequal member influence and power
- Perfunctory or absent parent participation
- Little collaboration
- Decisions by fiat, not consensus
- Preconceived views about child and family
- Lack of resolution for disparate data
- No common assessment tools
- Limited ecological data
- Limited exposure to child and family, unrepresentative data
- Overemphasis on diagnosis and IQ versus service delivery needs

Teams lack a "common language" to facilitate cross-talk and collaboration. Professionals from each discipline use their own jargon that is little understood by other professionals, let alone by families. The language used by teams is sometimes unfriendly and confusing to families. The absence of a mutual assessment tool may seriously complicate effective decision making.

Table 2.2 outlines recommended solutions for teamwork problems. These solutions can be grouped into four categories: (a) mentoring in group dynamics, (b) forming parent–professional partnerships, (c) using common assessment and decision-making language and tools, and (d) ensuring longitudinal progress monitoring and revised decision making.

Assessment is a decision-making process based on a synthesis and translation of convergent information that has utility for service delivery. Decision making among parents and professionals involves several sequential steps: collecting broad-based data, setting priorities, resolving conflicts, writing shared goals and methods, and setting benchmarks to monitor change. Teams of professionals can attain consensual validity by working with parents to arrive at shared decisions based on shared information.

Recommended Practices in Action: Consensual Validity

Curriculum-based assessment (CBA) is a form of appraisal that simultaneously addresses the organizational needs of interdisciplinary teams and the treatment needs of the young children and families that they serve.

Table 2.2. Solutions for Effective Interdisciplinary Team Functioning

- Mentoring for expertise in group dynamics and team process
- Advocacy and mentoring for parent or family on the team
- Coequal partnership arrangement for parents and professionals
- Framework or system for collaborative decision making
- Common "team" assessment tools for parents and professionals
- Facilitative leadership style
- Natural cross-talk among team members
- Discussion by functional domain–service needs versus discipline
- Tolerant debate about discrepancies in judgments
- Building consensus and "team" decisions about needs
- In-depth discussion of service needs versus diagnosis
- Emphasis on single-case progress data

CBA provides a unifying bridge (e.g., the task analysis of objectives within a common instrument) for all professional disciplines and a "mutual language" for parents and professionals.

With minimal training and coaching, professionals and parents can use a good curriculum-based assessment scale to assess child status and progress. Observation in natural settings, performance in simulated circumstances, and ratings of functioning not directly observable are typically involved. With the CBA format, it becomes relatively easy to share interpretations of observations and to reach assessment decisions that have a mutual basis.

The procedures for CBA are straightforward and include the following:

1. Professionals complete at least one scale of the CBA system (e.g., the physical therapist completes the gross motor section). A professional may complete more than one section if he or she is knowledgeable and has the relevant opportunity.

2. Assessment opportunities for CBA include observations and parent interviews conducted separately by discipline-specific professionals. When independent CBA sessions are held, professionals then share their information and views.

3. When teams employ CBA as a common tool in the arena situation, they take a great step toward mutual decision making. Arena assessment typically involves the operation of a cross-disciplinary or transdisciplinary team.

Although CBA provides a common tool and may assist in "bonding" team members, it does not structure the process for reaching mutual decisions. The actual decision-making process or the dynamics of teamwork negotiation and consensus are often left to chance with haphazard and often discouraging results. Summarized below, however, are a few of the recently developed tools and resources available to professionals for systematizing the collaborative process.

COACH. Choosing Options and Accommodations for Children (COACH; Giangreco, Cloninger, & Iverson, 1993) is an administrative format for designing and implementing IEPs for students in inclusive educational settings. COACH includes a variety of forms and organizational formats to help teams set shared goals and make consensual decisions about inclusive educational programming for each student.

The Delphi Technique. Developed originally for the U.S. Air Force in the 1950s, the Delphi technique has been widely used in business and industry. A group of individuals uses the Delphi method to generate ideas or opinions and to arrive at group decisions. The method includes conducting several "probes" (Linstone & Turoff, 1975). First, a major issue or question is raised and, if possible, each group member contributes relevant information, adds any further insight, and so forth.

The second probe is conducted similarly, but now the question relates to members' views on the importance and feasibility of the issue. A third probe is conducted to examine differences (if they exist) and to arrive at some agreements. Finally, the fourth probe is designed to be a final evaluation of agreements or proposed solutions. The Delphi process is predicated on the belief that the combined (converged) insights of several informed persons is "safer" than the views of just one individual. Divergent views are encouraged, there are open opportunities to negotiate differences and consequences, and consensus rather than compromise is sought. The outcome of the Delphi technique is intended to be a "creative synthesis" (Kurth-Schai, 1988).

SPECS. *System to Plan Early Childhood Services* (SPECS; Bagnato & Neisworth, 1990) is a set of materials and procedures explicitly developed to help early childhood assessment teams reach consensus. The system includes three components: Developmental Specs, Team Specs, and Program Specs. Parents and professionals independently and separately use Developmental Specs to rate a child on each of 19 developmental and functional dimensions. The rating scales encourage convergence of information on the part of each team member. Each team member brings his or her "homework" (i.e., Developmental Specs ratings) to the team meeting. At the meeting, the Team Specs materials and procedures focus the agenda and negotiations on discrepancies in ratings across members and the reconciliation of these differences. A team consensus is reached for a rating on each dimension, essentially through a Delphi technique (just described). The child's developmental profile is then drawn and portrays the distilled, converged assessment information across people, materials, settings, and occasions. Program Specs allows the team to designate desirable program options and service delivery intensities. The convergent assessment distilled by the Team Specs component provides a convergent, socially valid basis for the program planning outlines and options presented in Program Specs.

A FUTURE LOOK

Many professionals will already be employing some of the practices recommended in this chapter, but a field survey conducted by DEC yielded results suggesting that although most of the practices are perceived as desirable, they are not currently or reliably implemented (Odom, McLean, Johnson, & LaMontagne, 1995). Future assessment practices will, we hope, begin to resemble the recommendations generated by practitioners and researchers active in early intervention reflected in this chapter. We encourage the reader to examine the specific Recommended Practices in the appendix to see how they relate to the four validity themes and to consider adopting those practices. As the field grows, no doubt other practices based on emerging themes not discussed here will be recommended. We close by mentioning four trends that seem to have promise in making assessment more useful and acceptable as we all look to the future.

Service-Based Eligibility

Eligibility decisions are currently based on documentation of child disability. The child-disability focus relegates family circumstances and does not include children with less dramatic (but perhaps critical) needs. Service delivery is typically driven by child label and available services, not necessarily by needed services. Service-based eligibility is a proposed alternative (Bryant & Graham, 1993; Graham, 1990). The process is based on the premise that practice in early intervention evaluation needs to shift from making judgments about "what people *are*" to collaborating with families to decide specifically what *help* is needed. By emphasizing service needs rather than categories, governmental agencies, professionals, psychologists, and families can work collaboratively with a single focus: determining the best array of services for child and family. The approach is based on the premises that families should be active members of assessment teams, services are more important than educational labels, and child and family needs can be used to determine appropriate services.

The role of assessment in a service-based approach is to appraise type and intensity of needed services, irrespective of categorical labels. The evaluation team (including parents as team members) determines the level of support a child needs to be successful in early childhood environments. This determination might be accomplished by the use of a service-based support rating scale to estimate the level of support that the child and family would need for success in typical early childhood environments (Schneider, Myers, Neisworth, & Rhyner, 1993). Approaches that emphasize level of need, rather than disability, seem consistent with changing social policy and assessment practices.

Use of Technology in Early Intervention Assessment

With the movement toward more naturalistic forms of assessment, videotaping can become a prominent method of obtaining more representative samples of behavior across home, community, and day-care or preschool settings (Glovinsky, 1993). Videotaping can offer a low-intrusive and ecologically sound method for examining child–child and parent–child interactions in play and for constructing intervention plans with goals that are truly transactional in character. Developmental and behavioral progress can be monitored in socially valid ways that are easily understood and unequivocal in terms of scope of change during treatment.

Parallel with the use of videotaping is the greater use of computers by professionals in the assessment process to appraise learning rate and response-contingent learning. Early interventionists are already using computer software and programs that emphasize preacademic skills (color, shape, number, pre-reading, language concepts) and immediate feedback to chart new learning. Accommodations for children with sensory, neuromotor, and behavioral disabilities will become more commonplace with computer modifications such as augmentative communication devices in the assessment process.

Greater Use of Collaborative Decision-Making Formats

Early intervention teams are recognizing that collaboration with parents and family-centered practices require more "friendly" forms of assessment that have immediate utility for programming and broad-based child and family services. Professionals are demanding less use of contrived "tests" and more formats and tools for synthesizing and interpreting diverse information that enables parents and professionals to use a jargon-free, common language to reach joint decisions. More assessment tools will include multiple forms for use by relevant participants who can offer differing perspectives.

Functional Assessment Approaches

Trends in curriculum-based assessment already show a movement away from developmental milestones and toward sequences of skills that have direct implications for the child's everyday functioning. Various systems (Bricker, 1993; Haley, Coster, Ludlow, Holtiwanger, & Andrellos, 1992) emphasize such skills as initiating social interactions, activating simple or electromechanical toys, locomoting by any method, and applying problem-solving tasks rather than decontextualized activities such as peg placement, form-board use, and block stacking. Assessment techniques will place greater stress on blending testing and teaching to determine the conditions under which the child learns best. Process techniques (e.g., dynamic assessment; Lidz, 1992) also offer more integrated whole-child explanations about the extent to which a particular disability or impairment distorts developmental competence in related developmental domains and results in functional deficits.

CLOSING

Assessment *for* early intervention alludes to the social and practical basis for infant and early childhood evaluation. Neglect of the social basis of assessment is a serious mistake—rigid adherence to psychometric properties and preoccupation with statistical cutoffs reduce the necessary flexibility in assessment and trivialize a complex process by reducing it to an actuarial exercise. Test data are of little use and seriously prone to error until they are interpreted and translated with reference to the child's functioning across social contexts and then linked to plans of instruction and therapy. The rationale and the resulting recommended practices for early intervention emphasize the social missions, legal mandates, family perspectives, and transactional basis for assessment and intervention in the early childhood field.

REFERENCES

American Speech and Hearing Association. (1990). *Guidelines for practices in early intervention.* Rockville, MD: Author.

Anastasi, A. (1986). Evolving concepts of test validation. *Annual Review of Psychology, 37,* 1–15.

Arndorfer, R., & Miltenberger, R. (1993). Functional assessment and treatment of challenging behavior: A review with implications for early childhood. *Topics in Early Childhood Special Education, 13*(1), 82–105.

Arter, J. A., & Spandel, V. (1991). *Using portfolios of student work in instruction and assessment.* Portland, OR: Northwest Regional Educational Laboratory.

Ausubel, D. P., & Sullivan, E. V. (1970). The nature of developmental processes. In D. P. Ausubel & E. V. Sullivan (Eds.), *Theory and problems of child development* (2nd ed., pp. 98–132). New York: Grune & Stratton.

Bagnato, S. J., & Feldman, H. (1989). Closed-head injury. *Infants and Young Children, 2*(1), 1–13.

Bagnato, S. J., & Neisworth, J. T. (1990). *System to Plan Early Childhood Services.* Circle Pines, MN: American Guidance Services.

Bagnato, S. J., & Neisworth, J. T. (1991). *Assessment for early intervention: Best practices for professionals.* New York: Guilford Press.

Bagnato, S. J., & Neisworth, J. T. (1993). Sensible assessment. In D. Bryant & M. Graham (Eds.), *Implementing early intervention* (pp. 148–155). New York: Guilford Press.

Bagnato, S. J., & Neisworth, J. T. (1994). A national study of the social and treatment "invalidity" of intelligence testing for early intervention. *School Psychology Quarterly, 9*(2), 81–102.

Bagnato, S. J., Neisworth, J. T., & Munson, S. M. (1989). *Linking developmental assessment and early intervention: Curriculum-based prescriptions.* Rockville, MD: Aspen.

Bagnato, S. J., Neisworth, J. T., & Munson, S. M. (in press). *Linking authentic assessment and early intervention: Advances in curriculum-based evaluation* (3rd ed.). Baltimore: Brookes.

Bailey, D. (1984). A triaxial model of the interdisciplinary team and group process. *Exceptional Children, 51,* 17–25.

Bailey, D. B., & Simeonsson, R. J. (1988). *Family needs survey* (Report No. CB 8180). Chapel Hill: University of North Carolina, Frank Porter Graham Child Development Center.

Bailey, D., & Wolery, M. (1989). *Assessing infants and preschoolers with handicaps.* Columbus, OH: Merrill.

Barnett, D., & Carey, K. T. (1992). *Designing interventions for preschool learning and behavior problems.* San Francisco: Jossey-Bass.

Benner, S. (1992). *Assessing young children with young children.* New York: Longman.

Blacher-Dixon, J., & Simeonsson, R. J. (1982). Consistency and correspondence of mother's and teacher's assessments of young handicapped children. *Journal of the Division for Early Childhood, 3,* 64-71.

Bracken, B. (1983). Observing the assessment behavior of preschool children. In K. Paget & B. Bracken (Eds.), *The psychoeducational assessment of preschool children* (pp. 64-79). New York: Grune & Stratton.

Bracken, B. (1984). *Bracken Basic Concepts Scale.* Chicago: The Psychological Corporation.

Bracken, B. (1991a). *Basic Concepts Curriculum.* Chicago: The Psychological Corporation.

Bracken, B. (1991b). *The psychoeducational assessment of preschool children.* Boston: Allyn & Bacon.

Bracken, B., Bagnato, S. J., & Barnett, D. (1991). *Early childhood assessment* (NASP position statement). Washington, DC: National Association of School Psychologists.

Bredekamp, S. (1987). *Developmentally appropriate practice in early childhood programs serving children from birth through age 8.* Washington, DC: National Association for the Education of Young Children.

Bredekamp, S., & Rosegrant, T. (Eds.). (1992). *Reaching potentials: Appropriate curriculum and assessment for young children.* Washington, DC: National Association for the Education of Young Children.

Bricker, D. (1993). *Assessment, evaluation, and programming system for infants and children* (Vol. 2). Baltimore: Brookes.

Bruder, M. (1993). The provision of early intervention and early childhood special education within community early childhood programs: Characteristics of effective service delivery. *Topics in Early Childhood Special Education, 13,* 19-37.

Bryant, D., & Graham, M. (1993). Models of service delivery. In D. Bryant & M. Graham (Eds.)., *Implementing early intervention* (pp. 183-215). New York: Guilford Press.

Campbell, D. T. (1960). Recommendations for APA test standards regarding construct, trait, or discriminant validity. *The American Psychologist, 15*(8), 546-553.

Campbell, D. T., & Fiske, D. W. (1959). Convergent and disciminant validity in the multitrait–multimethod matrix. *Psychological Bulletin, 56,* 81-105.

Carta, J., Atwater, J. B., Schwartz, I., & McConnell, S. R. (1993). Developmentally appropriate practices and early childhood special education: A reaction to Johnson and McChesney Johnson. *Topics in Early Childhood Special Education, 13,* 243-254.

Carta, J., Schwartz, I., Atwater, J. B., & McConnell, S. R. (1991). Developmentally appropriate practice: Appraising its usefulness for young children with disabilities. *Topics in Early Childhood Special Education, 11*(1), 1-20.

Cole, M., & Cole, S. (1989). *The development of children.* New York: Scientific American Books.

Cole, N. S., & Moss, P. A. (1989). Bias in test use. In R. L. Linn (Ed.), *Educational measurement* (3rd ed., pp. 201-219). Washington, DC: American Council on Education & National Council on Measurement in Education.

Coster, W. J., & Haley, S. M. (1992). Conceptualization and measurement of disablement in infants and young children. *Infants and Young Children, 4,* 11-22.

Cronbach, L. (1988). Five perspectives on validity argument. In H. Wainer (Ed.), *Test validity* (pp. 3–17). Hillsdale, NJ: Erlbaum.

Deiner, P. (1993). *Resources for teaching children with diverse abilities.* New York: Harcourt Brace Jovanovich.

Diamond, K., & Squires, J. (1993). The role of parental report in the screening and assessment of young children. *Journal of Early Intervention, 17,* 107–115.

Division for Early Childhood Task Force on Recommended Practices (Eds.). (1993). *Recommended practices in early intervention.* Reston, VA: CEC.

Dunst, C. (1991, January). *Symposium on family-centered care—from principles to practices.* Paper presented at the Leadership Training Institute for Faculty Involved in the Preparation of Family-Centered Early Interventionists sponsored by the Center for Developmental Disabilities, the University Affiliated Program of Vermont and Parent to Parent of Vermont, Burlington, VT.

Edgar, E. (1988). Policy factors influencing research in early childhood special education. In S. Odom & M. Karnes (Eds.), *Early intervention for infants and children with handicaps: An empirical base* (pp. 63–73). Baltimore: Brookes.

Elkind, D. (1986). Formal education and early childhood education: An essential difference. *Phi Delta Kappan, 67,* 631–636.

Feuerstein, R. (1979). *The dynamic assessment of retarded performers: The learning potential assessment device, theory, instrument, and techniques.* Baltimore: University Park Press.

Foley, G. (1990). Portrait of arena evaluation: Assessment in the transdisciplinary approach. In E. D. Gibbs & D. M. Teti (Eds.), *Interdisciplinary assessment of infants: A guide for early intervention professionals* (pp. 271–286). Baltimore: Brookes.

Frederiksen, J. R., & Collins, A. (1989). A systems approach to educational testing. *Educational Researcher, 18*(9), 27–32.

Fuchs, D., Fuchs, L. S., Benowitz, S., & Barringer, K. (1987). Norm-referenced tests: Are they valid for use with handicapped students? *Exceptional Children, 54*(3), 263–271.

Garwood, S. G. (1982). Conceptualization and measurement of disablement in infants and young children. *Infants and Young Children, 4,* 11–22.

Giangreco, M., Cloninger, C., & Iverson, V. (1993). *Choosing options and accommodations for children.* Baltimore: Brookes.

Glascoe, F., MacLean, W., & Stone, W. (1991). The importance of parents' concerns about their child's behavior. *Clinical Pediatrics, 30,* 8–11.

Glovinsky, I. (1993). The use of videotaping in the evaluation of preschool aged children and their parents. *Infants and Young Children, 6*(2), 60–66.

Gradel, K., Thompson, M., & Sheehan, R. (1981). Parental and professional agreement in early childhood assessment. *Topics in Early Childhood Special Education, 1*(1), 3–40.

Graham, M. (1990). *An early intervention service delivery system.* Tallahassee, FL: Early Development Consulting for the Policy Studies Clinic, Florida State University College of Law.

Gresham, F., & Elliott, S. (1990). *Social Skills Rating System.* Circle Pines, MN: American Guidance Service.

Haley, S., Coster, W., Ludlow, L., Holtiwanger, J., & Andrellos, P. (1992). *Pediatric evaluation of disability intervention.* Boston: New England Medical Center Hospitals, PEDI Research Group, Department of Rehabilitation Medicine.

Hayes, S. C., Nelson, R. O., & Jarrett, R. B. (1987). The treatment utility of assessment: A functional approach to evaluating assessment quality. *American Psychologist, 42,* 963–974.

Hresko, W., Miguel, S., Sherbenov, R., & Burton, S. (1994). *Development Observation Checklist System.* Austin, TX: PRO-ED.

Iscoe, I., & Payne, S. (1972). Development of a revised scale for the functional classification of exceptional children. In E. P. Trapp & P. Himelstein (Eds.), *Readings on the exceptional child: Research and theory* (2nd ed., pp. 7–29). New York: Appleton-Century-Crofts.

Johnson-Martin, N. M., Attermeier, S. M., & Hacker, B. J. (1990). *The Carolina curriculum for preschoolers with special needs.* Baltimore: Brookes.

Johnson-Martin, N. M., Jens, K. G., Attermeier, S. M., & Hacker, B. J. (1991). *The Carolina curriculum for infants and toddlers with special needs* (2nd ed.). Baltimore: Brookes.

Kazdin, A. E. (1977). Assessing the clinical or applied importance of behavior change through social validation. *Behavior Modification, 1,* 427–452.

Kazdin, A. E. (1980). Acceptability of alternative treatments for deviant child behavior. *Journal of Applied Behavior Analysis, 13,* 259–273.

Kazdin, A. E. (1981). Acceptability of child treatment techniques: The influence of treatment efficacy and adverse side effects. *Behavior Therapy, 12,* 493–506.

Kazdin, A. E. (1984). Acceptability of aversive procedures and medication as treatment alternatives for deviant child behavior. *Journal of Abnormal Child Psychology, 12,* 289–302.

Kiresuk, T. J., & Lund, S. H. (1978). Goal attainment scaling. In C. C. Attkisson, W. A. Hargreaves, M. J. Horowitz, & J. E. Sorensen (Eds.), *Evaluation of human service programs* (pp. 341–370). New York: Academic Press.

Kiresuk, T. J., Smith, A., & Cardillo, J. E. (Eds.). (1994). *Goal attainment scaling: Applications, theory, and measurement.* Hillsdale, NJ: Erlbaum.

Kurth-Schai, R. (1988). Collecting the thoughts of children: A delphic approach. *Journal of Research and Development in Education, 21*(3), 53–59.

Lennox, D., & Miltenberger, R. (1989). Conducting a functional assessment of problem behavior in applied settings. *Journal of the Association for Persons with Severe Handicaps, 14,* 304–311.

Lewin, K. (1954). Behavior and development as a function of the total situation. In L. Carmichael (Ed.), *Manual of child psychology* (2nd ed., pp. 918–970). New York: Wiley.

Lidz, C. S. (1992). Dynamic assessment: Some thoughts on the model, the medium, and the message. *Learning and Individual Differences, 4*(2), 125–136.

Lincoln, Y. S., & Guba, E. G. (1985). *Naturalistic inquiry.* Beverly Hills, CA: Sage.

Linstone, H., & Turoff, M. (Eds.). (1975). *The Delphi method: Technique and applications.* Reading, MA: Addison-Wesley.

McLean, M., & Odom, S. (1993). Practices for young children with and without disabilities: A comparison of DEC and NAEYC identified practices. *Topics in Early Childhood Special Education, 13*(3), 274–292.

Meehl, P. (1959). Some ruminations on the validation of clinical procedures. *Canadian Journal of Psychology, 13,* 102–128.

Meisels, S. (1990). *Developmental screening in early childhood: A guide.* Washington, DC: National Association for the Education of Young Children.

Meisels, S. (1993). Remaking classroom assessment with the work sampling system. *Young Children, 48,* 34–40.

Messick, S. (1975). The standard problem: Meaning and values in measurement and evaluation. *American Psychologist, 30*(10), 955–966.

Messick, S. (1988). The once and future issues of validity: Assessing the meaning and consequences of measurement. In H. Wainer (Ed.), *Test validity* (pp. 33–45). Hillsdale, NJ: Erlbaum.

Messick, S. (1989). Meaning and values in test validation: The science and ethics of assessment. *Educational Researcher, 18*(2), 5–11.

Meyer, C. A. (1992). What's the difference between *authentic* and *performance* assessment? *Educational Leadership, 49*(8), 39–40.

Miltenberger, R. (1990). Assessment of treatment acceptability: A review of the literature. *Topics in Early Childhood Special Education, 10*(3), 24–38.

Moore, K. J., Fifield, B., Spira, D. A., & Scarlato, M. (1989). Child study team decision-making in special education: Improving the process. *Remedial and Special Education, 10*(4), 50–57.

Moss, P. (1992). Shifting conceptions of validity in educational measurement: Implications for performance assessment. *Review of Educational Research, 62*, 229–258.

National Association for the Education of Young Children and the National Association of Early Childhood Specialists in State Departments of Education. (1990). *Position statement: Guidelines for appropriate curriculum content and assessment in programs serving children ages 3 through 8* (NAEYC No. 725). Washington, DC: Author.

Neisworth, J. T., & Bagnato, S. J. (1988). Assessment in early childhood special education: A typology of dependent measures. In S. Odom & M. Karnes (Eds.), *Early intervention for infants and children with handicaps: An empirical base* (pp. 23–50). Baltimore: Brookes.

Neisworth, J. T., & Bagnato, S. J. (1992). The case against intelligence testing in early intervention. *Topics in Early Childhood Special Education, 12*(1), 1–20.

Neisworth, J. T., & Bagnato, S. J. (1993). Assessment. In DEC Task Force on Recommended Practices (Eds.), *DEC recommended practices: Indicators of quality in programs for infants and young children with special needs and their families* (pp. 11–18). Reston, VA: The Council for Exceptional Children.

Neisworth, J. T., & Fewell, R. (Eds.). (1990). Judgment based assessment. *Topics in Early Childhood Special Education, 10*(3), iii–vi.

Newborg, J., Stock, J., Wnek, L., Guidubaldi, J., & Svinicki, J. S. (1984). *Battelle Developmental Inventory.* Allen, TX: DLM/Teaching Resources.

Newmann, F. M. (1990). Higher order thinking in teaching social studies: A rationale for the assessment of classroom thoughtfulness. *Journal of Curriculum Studies, 22*(1), 41–56.

Nuttall, D. (1992). Performance assessment: The message from England. *Educational Leadership, 49*(8), 54–57.

Odom, S. L. (1988). Research in early childhood special education: Methodologies and paradigms. In S. Odom & M. Karnes (Eds.), *Early intervention for infants and children with handicaps: An empirical base* (pp. 1–21). Baltimore: Brookes.

Odom, S. L., McConnell, S., & Chandler, L. C. (1994). Acceptability and feasibility of social interaction interventions for young children with disabilities. *Exceptional Children, 60*, 226–236.

Odom, S. L., McLean, M. E., Johnson, L., & LaMontagne, M. (1995). Recommended practices in early childhood special education: Validation and current use. *Journal of Early Intervention, 19*, 1–17.

Odom, S. L., & Shuster, S. (1986). Naturalistic inquiry and the assessment of young handicapped children and their families. *Topics in Early Childhood Special Education, 4*(4), 1–19.

Parks, S. (1992). *Inside help: Hawaii Early Learning Profile.* Palo Alto, CA: Vort.

Perrone, V. (1991). On standardized testing. *Childhood Education.* Spring, 132–142.

Ploof, D., & Feldman, H. (1992). Organizing early intervention services in a hospital setting. *Infants and Young Children, 5*(1), 29–39.

Rosenfield, S., & Reynolds, C. R. (1990). Mainstreaming school psychology: A proposal to develop and evaluate alternative assessment methods and intervention strategies. *School Psychology Quarterly, 5*(1), 55–65.

Santa Cruze County Office of Education. (1987). *Help for special preschoolers.* Palo Alto, CA: Vort.

Schneider, L. A., Myers, M., Neisworth, J. T., & Rhyner, P. (1993, November). *Service-based eligibility.* Paper presented at the annual meeting of The Association for Persons with Severe Handicaps, Chicago, IL.

Shakel, J. (1987). *Position statement on early childhood assessment.* Washington, DC: National Association of School Psychologists.

Sheehan, R. (1982). Infant assessment. In D. D. Bricker (Ed.), *Intervention with at-risk handicapped infants from research to application* (pp. 47–510). Baltimore: University Park Press.

Simeonsson, R. J., Huntington, G., & Short, R. (1982). Individual differences and goals: An approach to the evaluation of child progress. *Topics in Early Childhood Special Education, 1*(4), 71–80.

Stiggins, R. J. (1987). Design and development of performance assessments. *Educational Management: Issues and Practice, 6*(3), 33–42.

Suen, H. K., Lu, C. H., & Neisworth, J. T. (1993). Measurement of team decision-making through generalizability theory. *Journal of Psychoeducational Assessment, 11,* 120–132.

Turnbull, A. P., & Turnbull, H. R., III (1990). *Families, professionals, and exceptionality: A special partnership.* Columbus, OH: Merrill.

Walker, L. S., & Greene, J. W. (1991). The functional disability inventory: Measuring a neglected dimension of child health status. *Journal of Pediatric Psychology, 16,* 39–58.

Winton, P. J., & Turnbull, A. P. (1981). Parent involvement as viewed by parents of preschool handicapped children. *Topics in Early Childhood Special Education, 1,* 11–19.

Wolf, M. M. (1978). Social validity: The case for subjective measurement or how applied behavior analysis is finding its heart. *Journal of Applied Behavior Analysis, 11,* 203–214.

Woodruff, G., & McGonigel, M. J. (1988). Early intervention team approaches: The transdisciplinary model. In J. Jordan, J. J. Gallagher, P. L. Hutinger, & M. B. Karnes (Eds.), *Early childhood special education: Birth to three* (pp. 164–181). Reston, VA: The Council for Exceptional Children.

CHAPTER 3

Family Participation

Lisbeth J. Vincent
Mary E. McLean

Since the 1970s, family participation in a child's early intervention program, whether at the infant, toddler, or preschool level, has been seen as critical for child, family, and program success. The passage of the Education of the Handicapped Act Amendments (P.L. 99-457) in October 1986 confirmed the commitment to active involvement of family members in their child's infant and toddler services. It also advocated for family participation in the development of early intervention systems and services from a statewide and local community perspective (Garwood & Sheehan, 1989). Thus, family participation moved to the new arena of policy making. Family members were viewed as stakeholders and decision makers for more than their individual child. Their perspective, vision, and expertise were as necessary as those of various professionals and agencies in the system's development, implementation, and monitoring process (Dokecki & Heflinger, 1989; Vincent, 1992; Ziegler, 1989). As Cindy Venuto, the mother of a daughter with special needs who resides in the Los Angeles area, pointed out during a staff development session, "Parents want to make decisions, not just give their perspective" (Venuto, 1994).

Family participation is now guided by the vision that a partnership of equals (Turnbull & Winton, 1984; Vincent, 1985; Ziegler, 1989) is being built between the family and the service system. Although initially discussed for infant and toddler services, collaborative partnerships are now recognized as recommended practice for all early childhood programs (see Turbiville, Turnbull, Garland, & Lee in this volume for a full discussion). These partnerships can focus on issues related to an individual child and family or to the early childhood system as a whole. Most families will not choose systems-level involvement. Yet, early childhood professionals and agencies must be prepared to build such collaborative partnerships with families who are interested.

Until recently, preservice training programs had not focused on teaching team-building, collaboration, or partnership skills (D. Bailey, 1989; D. Bailey, Palsha, & Huntington, 1990). Teachers and related service personnel focused on child learning, development, and intervention techniques. The skills necessary to build an effective partnership with families were at best covered in lecture and written material but not directly practiced. McCollum, Rowan, and Thorp (1994) reported on a preservice training practicum for infant service providers that directly focused on the service provider–parent partnership. The purpose of the practicum was to support students' learning of a family-centered perspective to early intervention. Results of a small-scale evaluation of the experience indicated that it was successful, in conjunction with an academic course on families, in increasing the family-centered perspective of students. Ensuring that students from diverse disciplines receive this type of training during their preservice curriculum will greatly increase the likelihood that family participation will be based on a collaborative and equal partnership model. Such training is necessary to take the step from "talking the talk" of family centeredness to "walking the walk."

Increasing attention is also being given in inservice training materials and sessions to family-centered services. Such a focus recognizes that professionals already practicing as early interventionists need to develop new skills as collaborators with parents and with each other. Professionals who received preservice training in building collaborative partnerships with families will also need to be part of an ongoing staff development effort as the field continues to grow and change (D. Bailey, 1989). Two recent newsletters and a curriculum guide intended for personnel already working in the field serve as examples of efforts to bring the field up to speed on collaboration.

Focal Point (1995), a national bulletin on family support and children's mental health published by the Research and Training Center at Portland State University, was devoted to collaboration and family empowerment on the individual family level. Dechillo and Koren (1995) in a column entitled "Just What Is Collaboration?" provided information on how families define collaboration and how collaboration has affected their perception of services. In a survey of 52 parents and professionals who had received training in collaboration, Dechillo and Koren discovered that both parents and professionals reported that their attempts to collaborate were not always positively received by professionals. Families and professionals identified barriers to collaboration related to previous experience and training of professionals and previous experiences of families with the service system. Gaschnig, Johs, and Weaver (1995) summarized principles of collaboration that stressed the relationship-based, dynamic nature of the process. The principles focused on the need for mutual respect and recognition of each other's expertise.

Spiegel and Harper-Whalen (1995) in a curriculum module entitled *Forging Partnerships with Families* addressed five steps teachers can take to build collaborative partnerships with the parents of children in their settings. First is the need to understand the impact that a child's diagnosis has on the family and its individual members. The early years of new terminology, labels, and recommended services can be very stressful to families. The second step is to establish trusting relationships with families. This step requires the professional's commitment to flexible and open systems of communication and an ability to listen to the family's view of their situation. Recognizing and utilizing family expertise is identified as the third step. It requires that teachers see family members as being knowledgeable observers, assessors, and teachers of their children. In order for family participation to be maximized, opportunities for involvement must be individualized and flexible. Individualizing involvement, which is the fourth step, requires that professionals support whatever type and intensity of participation are most comfortable for the family. The last step in forging a partnership is to facilitate family-to-family support. Families can assist each other with the tasks of day-to-day living with a child with special needs in a way that professionals usually cannot. Recognizing the power of emotional support from another parent and facilitating that interaction, professionals send a powerful message that we believe in the capability and competence of families.

A recent issue of *Advances in Family-Centered Care* (1994), which is published by the Institute for Family-Centered Care, provided information on how families and professionals can work together to improve the quality of services received by young children with special needs on the program or systems level. One of the articles, "Involving Families in Advisory Roles," identified eight guidelines that providers can use to increase the participation of family members in policy roles:

> 1) maintain a broad view of collaboration; 2) expand the definition of successful parent involvement; 3) use innovative ways to identify and recruit families to participate; 4) look for opportunities to promote family involvement; 5) provide training and support to both families and professionals; 6) address logistical barriers comprehensively and creatively; 7) be aware of parental burnout; and, 8) believe family participation is essential. (*Advances in Family-Centered Care*, 1994, p. 2)

The need to develop flexible options for involvement in policy making and advisory activities has been stressed by numerous authors (Paget, 1992; Turnbull & Turnbull, 1990; Vincent, Laten, Salisbury, Brown, & Baumgart, 1981; Warren & Warren, 1989). There must be options other than serving on a formal board or committee. For example, asking families to present on an orientation panel for new staff, or to review written materials about the program, or to meet for breakfast to discuss new service options are all policy-level involvement and do not require a long-term commitment by families. Individualizing participation, whether on the single-family, early childhood program, or statewide level, appears to be critical to successful collaboration.

On the basis of experience with model demonstration efforts, such as those described, and the wealth of professional literature on enabling and empowering families, the Family Participation strand members decided that items generated to reflect recommended practice should cover participation from the individual child level through the program level to the system-wide level. This scope would entail examination of family participation in child program planning, in early intervention program implementation, and in state-level policy development. Originally 185 indicators of recommended practice were generated in the Family Participation strand. These items greatly overlapped with those of other strands. Items that dealt with family participation in assessment, goal setting, IEP or IFSP development, instructional methods and technology, and personnel competence were placed in those respective strands for validation. Discussion of these items is included in the appropriate chapters in this volume. Thus, the majority of items in the Family Participation strand are related to participation in systems-level decision making and the collaboration skills required for success in this area.

FAMILY PARTICIPATION: DEFINITION AND VALUES

The following definition of *family participation* guided item development: families are equal members in, can join together with staff, and can take part in all aspects of the early intervention system, including all aspects of their child's care and all levels of decision making. *Early intervention system* here refers to programs and services available to children from birth through 5 years of age.

Before generating the initial items for the strand, the strand members identified values and beliefs they viewed as critical to building the professional–family partnership. The philosophical, theoretical, and research bases of these beliefs are discussed in later sections of this chapter. The beliefs and values covered four broad areas:

• A recognition of the family's primary role with the child and family as a whole: Family is seen as a self-defined unit that provides the primary human attachments and early social relationships for infants. No amount of intervention can take the place of what the family brings to the child. Strand developers believed that the unique knowledge, resources, and experiences of each family must be respected. The family's interaction and decision-making styles are to be accepted and valued.

Family participation is to be self-defined; it can vary along a number of dimensions and levels of intensity. Families bring to the partnership knowledge and information that is reliable and valuable. Family participation is enhanced when families determine what would be helpful for them. Families know what they need to enhance their development. Collaboration will take place only when the family is the final decision maker and when the team is the implementer of decisions.

- A recognition of the need for orientation and training in collaboration and their impact on the success of the partnership: Collaboration as a model requires developing a common language. Parent–professional partnerships can be enhanced when both members of the partnership are provided with training to enhance their common understanding and skills. Getting started in a partnership requires orientation, for example, orientation to players, roles, overt and covert agendas, funding sources, rights, and responsibilities. Both providers and parents will need orientation or training or both to work within the collaborative partnership. Partners must develop a knowledge and appreciation of relationship building. Family participation is likely to be stronger when families are working with confident, well-supported professionals.
- A recognition of each individual person's impact on collaboration and the partnership: Both service providers and the family bring to a relationship their past experiences, personal values, and beliefs that provide unique contexts in which to view early intervention services. Partnership is a process in which partners are nonjudgmental and in which clear, open communication takes place. Skills that families and professionals develop through the collaborative partnership can enhance a program's effectiveness.
- A recognition that flexibility is essential to collaboration: Family participation is essential at all levels of a program, for example, hiring, planning, implementation, evaluation. In order for participation at all levels to be achieved, a variety of ways for families to participate must be available; for example, in the program evaluation area, the family could be interviewed, could complete a checklist, or could participate in a focus group. The options must support participation and representation from diverse members of a community. Conflict between partners needs to be seen as a healthy part of the collaboration process.

Many of these values and beliefs are also discussed in the chapter on development and implementation of IFSPs and IEPs in this volume. These processes reflect a family-centered orientation to service delivery.

INDICATORS OF RECOMMENDED PRACTICE

Forty-nine indicators of recommended practice related to family participation were selected for field validation in this strand. The indicators were grouped into eight areas where family participation should be established. These were family participation in (a) program advising and policy making; (b) staff hiring, training, evaluation; (c) family support; (d) intervention; (e) interagency collaboration; (f) legislative issues; (g) advocacy; (h) procedural safeguards; and (i) leadership training opportunities for parents. The mean rating of agreement as to whether the items represented recommended practice was 1.37 across all items, with 1 indicating *strongly agree;* 2, *agree;* 3, *disagree;* and 4, *strongly disagree.* All items were rated as *strongly agree* or *agree* by at least 50% of the respondents in the validation study. Thus, all items were endorsed by the respondents as representing recommended practices for family participation. (See Chapter 1 for more information on the validation process.) Interestingly, family members who were respondents to the validation survey showed significantly stronger agreement with the indicators than did practitioners who were respondents (Odom, McLean, Johnson, & LaMontagne, 1995).

Respondents were also asked to rate whether a given indicator occurred *frequently, sometimes, rarely,* or *never* in programs with which they were familiar. These ratings gave an estimate of the current use of recommended practices by EI/ECSE programs. Only 2 of the 49 items were rated by at least 50% of the respondents as frequently occurring in programs. An additional 33 out of the 49 indicators were indicated to be occurring sometimes. Fourteen indicators were rated as rarely occurring, even though all 14 were validated as recommended practice. A similar finding was obtained for the indicators in the IFSP and IEP area, most of which have to do with family–staff or family–agency relationships. Only 1 of 41 indicators was rated as frequently occurring; 27 of 41 were rated as sometimes occurring. Thirteen indicators were rated as rarely occurring. Family items in the Assessment, Service Delivery Models, and Personnel Competence strands were also rated by respondents as rarely seen in everyday practice. Translating the "talk" of family-centered, collaborative services to the reality of an equal partnership between families and professionals appears to be a difficult process.

A discussion of the rationale for items from the Family Participation strand follows. For the purposes of discussion, the eight areas have been collapsed into three broad areas of participation. First, intervention, family support, and procedural safeguards are discussed as they relate to the individual child/family level. Then, family participation in program planning and policy making and in staff hiring, training, and evaluation, which relate to program-level participation, are discussed together. Last, family participation on a systems level in advocacy, interagency collaboration, legislation, and leadership are presented.

Intervention, Family Support, and Procedural Safeguards

Family participation in the intervention process has been accepted as recommended practice in the field of EI/ECSE for over 20 years (Slentz,

Walker, & Bricker, 1989; Vincent & Broome, 1977). The role of parents as a child's primary "teacher" and advocate has been well respected. The participation of family members in formulating intervention designs for their individual children was required by the Education of All Handicapped Children Act of 1975 (P.L. 94-142) and has been further delineated and supported in amendments and new legislation since that time. Recommended practices for intervention strategies and techniques are covered by Wolery and Sainato in this volume.

The 18 items that were generated for the Family Participation strand on the individual child/family level (family-to-family support, intervention, and procedural safeguards areas) reflect the role of families as decision makers in determining how their concerns and hopes will be translated into intervention. All items were validated by survey respondents as recommended practice. Programs having clearly specified procedures for recourse or redress of grievances was rated as occurring frequently. The remaining 17 indicators of recommended practice were rated as occurring at least some of the time in early intervention programs. The family's right to choose the types of services that they believed would benefit their child (Family Participation [FP] 20) was supported by survey respondents and seen to be happening at least sometimes. This item was endorsed even when family choice was viewed as "alternative" to mainstream thought (FP 44). This practice is essential when working with families from diverse cultures and backgrounds who may have different experiences with treatment and healing (Lynch & Hanson, 1992; Vincent, 1992; Vincent & Salisbury, 1988; Vincent, Salisbury, Strain, McCormick, & Tessier, 1990).

The family's role in determining both the *place* and *pace* of service delivery was also supported (FP 19, FP 23). Two decades of research have demonstrated that settings that include typical children can be appropriate for children with disabilities (Guralnick, 1990; McLean & Hanline, 1990; Strain, 1990). In fact, children with disabilities have demonstrated "better" progress in language, cognitive, and social skills in integrated settings (Brinker, 1985; Guralnick, 1990). As Strain (1990) pointed out, these gains were also influenced, in all likelihood, by other elements of the service delivery model. Perhaps one of the most important elements is that the family has been provided the opportunity to determine the focus of instruction and the instructional setting (Beckman & Bristol, 1991). The importance of involving families as teachers in their child's home and community settings has been clearly demonstrated (E. Bailey & Bricker, 1985; Guralnick, 1989; Ramey, Bryant, Sparling, & Wasik, 1985). A program design based on the naturally occurring daily routine of the child and family has been suggested as one way to maximize family participation (Rainforth & Salisbury, 1988; Rainforth, York, & MacDonald, 1992). This type of program planning allows intervention to flex as family needs change. As Bruder and

Bologna (1993) pointed out, the success of integrated community-based placements rests with the child's family as well as with the intervention program. In order for families to maximize their commitment, they must be provided with options for service delivery so that services will mesh with the needs of the family.

The Family Participation strand, however, goes a step further than simply recommending family choice in the area of intervention; professional encouragement and support of the family's dreams and visions for the future are also recommended (FP 24). Janice Fialka (1994), the parent of a child with special needs, has written an article for professionals entitled "You Can Make a Difference in Our Lives." In this article, she listed 10 things professionals can do to make a difference in the lives of parents of children with special needs. Items 1–9 include such things as decreasing the sense of loneliness, recognizing victories, reminding parents how far they have come and how much they have accomplished. Item 10, the last item, states that professionals must allow parents to feel *hope*. Fialka pointed out that parents must feel hope "if we are to get to our next appointment or to face the next birthday party or to use the words 'special needs'" (p. 11).

Families' rights to redress of grievance, including the use of impartial mediators, were also supported (FP 42, FP 43). Although such practices are clearly supported by federal and state laws, their implementation needs to be undertaken in the spirit of partnership (Garwood & Sheehan, 1989; Ziegler, 1989). Partners do not always agree. Disagreements do not have to lead to a complete breakdown in the partnership. In fact, differences can bring strength to the partnership as they increase the types and numbers of alternative solutions that are generated when problems arise (Paget, 1992; Walker, 1989). Successful programs to increase communication and problem solving between parents and professionals have been demonstrated (Brinckerhoff & Vincent, 1986; Walker, 1989).

During the 1980s, the field witnessed a dramatic increase in family support services available to families of children with disabilities (Scott & Doyle, 1984; Singer & Irvin, 1989). This increase reinforced the importance of the role that families play in providing the day-to-day support that is needed by families of children with disabilities. Family support services are designed to allow families to remain successful caregivers. Such services recognize that strong marital relationships; supportive social networks of family, friends, neighbors, and coworkers; and public services such as respite care combine to increase family cohesiveness and positive adaptations to the child with a disability (Fewell & Vadasy, 1986; Friedrich, Wilturner, & Cohen, 1985; Hill, Lakin, & Bruininks, 1984; McCubbin et al., 1983). In addition to emotional support, a network of social support that includes other families of children with disabilities provides families linkages to information as well as to agencies and services (Garshelis &

McConnell, 1993; Spiegel & Harper-Whalen, 1995; Stagg & Catron, 1986). Such linkages enable families to be decision makers for themselves and their families (Dunst, Trivette, & Deal, 1988; Dunst, Trivette, Gordon, & Pletcher, 1989; Vincent et al., 1990). This role prevents families from learning to see professionals and agencies as having "all the answers" (Dunst et al., 1989; Taylor, Knoll, Lehr, & Walker, 1989). Instead, families view themselves as being in control, a view that contributes to persistence in solving problems that arise, positive family self-esteem, and a sense of mastery (Brickman et al., 1982; Summers, Behr, & Turnbull, 1989). These are vital to the family's successfully coping with the needs of a child with a disability within the broader context of the family (Summers et al., 1989).

The family support area of the Family Participation strand includes 5 items that were validated as recommended practice. Apparently, the respondents recognized the importance that families can play in each other's lives. Unfortunately, family support is apparently not available to all families of young children as the 5 items in the strand were rated only as sometimes occurring.

Overall, providing early intervention services in natural community settings with families as equal planning partners was validated as recommended practice and rated as occurring at least sometimes for children and families. In light of the ample research on the appropriateness of settings that include typical peers for children with special needs (Guralnick, 1990; Odom & McEvoy, 1990; Strain, 1990), this was a heartening finding. Disheartening is the fact that for many preschool-aged children with disabilities, services are still provided in essentially segregated settings with families not being offered alternatives (McWilliam et al., 1995). The right of families to have options available that reflect their hopes and dreams for their children is recommended practice. As C. Peterson and McConnell (1993) pointed out, the implementation of recommended practices requires commitment to change and the learning of new skills. The field of EI/ECSE would appear to be in the early part of the learning curve in terms of implementing the practice of including parents as equal partners in educational decision making.

Program Advising and Policy Making and Staff Hiring, Training, and Evaluation

The implementation of family-centered services requires professionals to shift from involving families in the approval of professionally determined intervention plans to involving families as partners throughout the entire assessment and intervention process. As we indicated earlier, this partnership can extend beyond an individual child's or family's intervention and support program to the arena of program advising and policy making.

Although not all parents will choose to be involved in policy-development endeavors, the demands being placed on those who do are extraordinary. The definition of family participation that guided the development of recommended practices in this strand affirms the belief that families are equal decision makers when they enter the policy arena. The 13 items that were generated in the areas of program advising and policy making and staff hiring, training, and evaluation clearly state the need for families to receive support in order to be successful as decision makers. Although all were validated as recommended practice, 8 of the 13 items were rated as rarely implemented.

Gilkerson (1994) suggested that parents who are involved in policy making are being asked to be rational and objective (as expected of those involved in policy making) simultaneously in an area closely linked to their personal lives, which can be emotional and subjective. She saw this dual role as the basis of the "incredible power and unique contribution" of parents. At the same time, Gilkerson warned that this dual role can be not only time consuming but also emotionally draining for parents. Professionals are supported in these roles through financial reimbursement, prior education and experience, clerical support, and staff-development activities. As equal members in decision making, parents should have access to equally supportive structures.

There is evidence that although parents are asked to commit considerable time to program advising, the necessary supports have not been provided. Vincent and Perrett (1990) found that family members serving on state interagency coordinating councils on early intervention (ICCs) often contributed more than 20 hours per month to meetings. Additional costs such as childcare were usually not reimbursed. Many parents must take time away from employment responsibilities to attend state meetings without reimbursement for their time. Clearly this situation will severely limit the number of families who can participate in decision making. Furthermore, those who do agree to participate may soon find this participation to be too costly to continue. Parents in the Vincent and Perrett (1990) survey also noted that, in addition to the time and cost demands, rarely were mentoring and training available to family members in order to develop policy-making skills. This lack is also likely to limit who becomes involved and reduce representation from diverse groups of families.

In a sense, a door has been unlocked for family members to participate in program advising and policy making, but the door may be difficult to open without support for families. Failure to open this unlocked door means that early intervention programs will not benefit from the experience and insight of the families they serve.

The paradigm shift from child-centered to family-centered services has been difficult for some professionals because family-centered services differ in orientation from their preservice training and experience (Bailey,

Buysse, Edmonson, & Smith, 1992). One mechanism for facilitating the development of family-centered services is to involve family members in the hiring and evaluation of program staff (FP 8, FP 10–13) and in the preservice and inservice training of professionals (FP 9, Personnel Competence [PC] 1, PC 4). The recommended practices in the area of staff hiring, training, and evaluation describe the involvement of family members in all aspects of staff hiring and evaluation, involvement thus ensuring that input from families (consumers) will guide the review of program effectiveness and therefore guide program changes.

The involvement of family members in inservice training and preservice training is not a particularly new concept; however, it has traditionally been accomplished through rather limited means such as a guest speaker or panel of parents or articles, poems, or books written by families. Efforts have recently increased, particularly in early intervention, to include family members much more extensively in the planning of both preservice and inservice training (D. Bailey, McWilliam, & Winton, 1992; Gilkerson, 1994). One example is co-instruction in higher education, which refers to the practice of "team teaching" a college course through a parent–professional partnership (McBride, Sharp, Hains, & Whitehead, in press). According to Whitehead and Sontag (1993), the primary purpose of co-instruction is to give students the consumer's perspective on intervention efforts. This broader perspective should result in increased sensitivity to the impact of professionals' actions on families. Co-instruction has brought about a new meaning to the term *parent trainer,* which, in the 1960s and 1970s, referred to a professional who taught parents how to teach their child. In the 1990s, parent trainer refers to a parent who has agreed to help professionals understand the family perspective.

Advocacy, Interagency Collaboration, Legislation, and Leadership

As Turnbull and Turnbull (1990) and Spiegel and van den Pol (1993) have so clearly articulated, the birth of a child with special needs begins the family's journey into lifelong advocacy. Even though federal and state laws that support services for individuals with special needs and their families have been in place for over 20 years, obtaining services is still a complex task for many families (Able-Boone, Goodwin, Sandall, Gordon, & Martin, 1992; Able-Boone, Sandall, Loughry, & Fredrick, 1990; McWilliam et al., 1995). Summers et al. (1989), Warren and Warren (1989), and Taylor et al. (1989) pointed out that working with professionals and agencies to obtain needed services was itself a stressful part of raising a child with a disability. Families reported that eligibility requirements and waiting lists were typical for some services, particularly when the individual with a disability became an adult.

The increase in services for young children with special needs and their families has grown out of legislative changes on the federal and individual state levels (Smith, 1995; Trohanis, 1995). Because young children have not been viewed as part of the public educational responsibility, the success of efforts on behalf of young children with special needs is truly noteworthy. All 50 states have now adopted a statewide, comprehensive, coordinated system of early intervention services for young children (from birth to 3 years of age) with disabilities and sometimes with other risk factors. All states, through their local educational agencies, have assumed responsibility for providing educational and related services to all children with disabilities between 3 and 6 years of age. This success has come through the combined advocacy efforts of parent and professional organizations in the field of developmental disabilities (Trohanis, 1995; Warren & Warren, 1989). Over and over, professionals have heard that the voice of family members has been most influential with legislators. The continued involvement of families in the legislative process is essential. Current laws that underlie EI/ECSE efforts are subject to review, and levels of funding can be changed from budget year to budget year.

The recommended practices in the area of legislation suggest that families should be informed of important legislative issues in their states and on the federal level. If families wish to be involved in legislative advocacy, the information they need should be provided (FP 34, FP 35, FP 36). Typically, parents become involved in legislative activity because they find that supports and services that they and their children need are not in place (Warren & Warren, 1989). However, the lack of financial and mentoring support to learn policy-level skills may be limiting the number and diversity of families who can realistically choose this critical type of family participation. If family members do not have training in the system, its operation and idiosyncrasies, being an equal partner is very difficult (Quirk, Fine, & Roberts, 1992).

Partnerships across disciplines and agencies may also be hampered by lack of training and information exchange (Bruder & Bologna, 1993; Quirk et al., 1992). No one agency or discipline can effectively meet the needs of the diverse children and families who require EI/ECSE services (Garwood & Sheehan, 1989). Along with the shift from a child-centered, agency-directed model to a family-centered model of intervention (Dunst et al., 1988; McGonigel, Kaufmann, & Johnson, 1991; Long, Artis, & Dobbins, 1993; Paget, 1992; Turnbull & Turnbull, 1990; Vincent et al., 1990) has come the need to work across community agencies to provide services to meet the concerns and priorities of families. As Bruder and Bologna (1993) and Peck, Furman, and Helmstetter (1993) have detailed, this shift entails building interagency teams and linkages. These teams need to be guided by a vision of future services that is shaped by each individual community (McNulty, 1989). Teams need to identify what changes are needed in their communities and what these changes will mean to individual participants (D. Bailey, McWilliam, Winton, & Simeonsson, 1992). Family members should be integral members of these teams (FP 29). To participate effectively requires orientation and training to the "agency process" and the opportunity for family members to provide systematic feedback on their interagency experiences (FP 30, FP 31).

CLOSING

Family participation in all types and levels of service delivery has been validated as recommended practice in EI/ECSE. The role of families has been recognized as being much broader than just being involved with their individual child. The power of families to effect policy and legislative change has been acknowledged. However, the actual implementation of practices that would support families in moving into this leadership role may not be occurring. As we indicated earlier, only 2 of the 49 items in the Family Participation strand were identified as occurring frequently in programs. This may be due to the interpretation that *all* families should be involved on the leadership level and that *all* staff would be responsible for building these opportunities. The likely reality is that all families will choose to be involved in their individual child's program in ways that match their family's concerns, priorities, and resources, whereas a smaller number of families will also choose to become involved in interagency collaboration and coordination efforts. More families might contribute to the advisory and policy-making process if we professionals create more diverse options for involvement and if we financially reimburse families for their efforts. The voice that family members bring to the policy and legislative level is a different voice, an essential voice if professionals are to continue to move forward in building high quality EI/ECSE services for young children with special needs and their families all across this country.

Nancy Peterson cautioned in 1991 that as a field, we were not clear on the steps in moving from talking about collaboration to implementing collaborative planning and decision making in our early intervention system. Professionals appear to still be struggling with implementation. Apter (1994) summarized some of what professionals have learned about systems change from our experience thus far. She pointed to the role of a shared understanding of how the change will help individual families, professionals, and agencies; the necessity to learn new information and also change attitudes; the power of state-level interagency agreements to create change; the need to see and use resistance to change as a positive force; and the need for visionary leadership that is shared across all levels of program development. Ongoing efforts at systems change must be based on the lessons learned thus far. Ongoing staff-development efforts must continue to focus on assisting service providers to accept the paradigm shift to family-centered services, while providing information and practice on how to translate the talk of collaboration into the "dance" of equal partners.

REFERENCES

Able-Boone, H., Goodwin, L. D., Sandall, S. R., Gordon, N., & Martin, D. G. (1992). Consumer-based early intervention services. *Journal of Early Intervention, 16,* 201–209.

Able-Boone, H., Sandall, S., Loughry, A., & Fredrick, L. (1990). An informed family-centered approach to Public Law 99-457: Parental views. *Topics in Early Childhood Special Education, 10,* 100–111.

Advances in Family-Centered Care (Vol. 1[2]). (1994, Fall). Bethesda, MD: Institute for Family-Centered Care.

Apter, D. S. (1994). From dream to reality: A participant's view of the implementation of Part H of P.L. 99-457. *Journal of Early Intervention, 18,* 131–140.

Bailey, D. (1989). Issues and directions in preparing professionals to work with young handicapped children and their families. In J. Gallagher, P. Trohanis, & R. Clifford (Eds.), *Policy implementation and P.L. 99–457: Planning for young children with special needs* (pp. 97–132). Baltimore: Brookes.

Bailey, D. B., Buysse, J., Edmonson, R., & Smith, T. M. (1992). Creating family-centered services in early intervention: Perceptions of professionals in four states. *Exceptional Children, 58,* 298–308.

Bailey, D. B., McWilliam, P. J., & Winton, P. (1992). Building family-centered practices in early intervention: A team-based model for change. *Infants and Young Children, 5,* 73–82.

Bailey, D. B., McWilliam, P. J., Winton, P. J., & Simeonsson, R. J. (1992). *Implementing family-centered services in early intervention: A team-based model for change.* Cambridge, MA: Brookline Books.

Bailey, D. B., Palsha, S., & Huntington, G. (1990). Preservice preparation of special educators to serve infants with handicaps and their families: Current status and training needs. *Journal of Early Intervention, 14,* 43–54.

Bailey, E. J., & Bricker, D. D. (1985). Evaluation of a three-year early intervention demonstration project. *Topics in Early Childhood Special Education, 5*(2), 52–65.

Beckman, P. J., & Bristol, M. M. (1991). Issues in developing the IFSP: A framework for establishing family outcomes. *Topics in Early Childhood Special Education, 11*(3), 19–31.

Brickman, P., Rabinowitz, V. C., Karusa, J., Coates, D., Cohen, E., & Kidder, L. (1982). Models of coping and helping. *American Psychologist, 37,* 368–384.

Brinckerhoff, J. L., & Vincent, L. J. (1986). Increasing parent decision-making at the individualized educational program meeting. *Journal of the Division for Early Childhood, 11,* 46–58.

Brinker, R. P. (1985). Interactions between severely mentally retarded students and other students in integrated and segregated public school settings. *American Journal of Mental Deficiency, 89,* 587–594.

Bruder, M. B., & Bologna, T. (1993). Collaboration and service coordination for effective early intervention. In W. Brown, S. K. Thurman, & L. Pearl (Eds.), *Family-centered early intervention with infants and toddlers: Innovative cross-disciplinary approaches* (pp. 103–128). Baltimore: Brookes.

Dechillo, N., & Koren, P. E. (1995). Just what is "collaboration?" *Focal Point, 9*(1), 1–6.

Dokecki, P. R., & Heflinger, L. A. (1989). Strengthening families of young children with handicapping conditions: Mapping backward from the "street level." In J. J. Gallagher, P. L. Trohanis, & R. M. Clifford (Eds.), *Policy implementation and P.L. 99-457: Planning for young children with special needs* (pp. 59–84). Baltimore: Brookes.

Dunst, C. J., Trivette, C. M., & Deal, A. G. (1988). *Enabling and empowering families: Principles and guidelines for practice.* Cambridge, MA: Brookline Books.

Dunst, C. J., Trivette, C. M., Gordon, N. J., & Pletcher, L. L. (1989). Building and mobilizing informal family support networks. In G. H. S. Singer & L. K. Irvin (Eds.), *Support for caregiving families* (pp. 121–142). Baltimore: Brookes.

Education for All Handicapped Children Act of 1975, 20 U.S.C. § 1400 *et seq.*

Education of the Handicapped Act Amendments of 1986, 20 U.S.C. § 1400 *et seq.*

Fewell, R. R., & Vadasy, P. F. (1986). *Families of handicapped children: Needs and supports across the lifespan.* Austin, TX: PRO-ED.

Fialka, J. (1994). You can make a difference in our lives. *Early On Michigan, 3*(4), 6–11.

Focal point. (1995). Portland, OR: Research and Training Center, Portland State University.

Friedrich, W. N., Wilturner, L. J., & Cohen, D. S. (1985). Coping resources and parenting mentally retarded children. *American Journal of Mental Deficiency, 90*, 130–139.

Garshelis, J. A., & McConnell, S. R. (1993). Comparison of family needs assessed by mothers, individual professionals, and interdisciplinary teams. *Journal of Early Intervention, 17*, 36–49.

Garwood, S. G., & Sheehan, R. (1989). *Designing a comprehensive early intervention system: The challenge of Public Law 99-457.* Austin, TX: PRO-ED.

Gaschnig, M. A., Johs, J., & Weaver, P. (1995). Family/professional collaboration and strategies for empowerment. *Focal Point, 9*(1), 11–12.

Gilkerson, L. (1994). Supporting parents in leadership roles. *Zero to Three, 14*(4), 23–24.

Guralnick, M. J. (1989). Recent developments in early intervention efficacy research: Implications for family involvement in P.L. 99-457. *Topics in Early Childhood Special Education, 9*(3), 1–17.

Guralnick, M. J. (1990). Social competence and early intervention. *Journal of Early Intervention, 14*, 3–14.

Hill, B. K., Lakin, K. C., & Bruininks, R. H. (1984). Trends in residential services for people who are mentally retarded: 1977–1982. *Journal of the Association for Persons with Severe Handicaps, 9*, 243–250.

Long, C. E., Artis, N. E., & Dobbins, N. J. (1993). The hospital: An important site for family-centered early intervention. *Topics in Early Childhood Special Education, 13*, 106–119.

Lynch, E., & Hanson, M. (1992). *Developing cross cultural competence: A guide for working with young children and their families.* Baltimore: Brookes.

McBride, S., Sharp, L., Hains, A. H., & Whitehead, A. (in press). Parents as co-instructors in pre-service training: A pathway to family-centered practice. *Journal of Early Intervention.*

McCollum, J. A., Rowan, L. R., & Thorp, E. K. (1994). Philosophy as training in infancy personnel preparation. *Journal of Early Intervention, 18*, 216–226.

McCubbin, H. I., McCubbin, M. A., Patterson, J. M., Cauble, A. E., Wilson, L. R., & Warwick, W. (1983). CHIP—Coping Health Inventory for Parents: An assessment of parental coping patterns in the care of the chronically ill child. *Journal of Marriage and the Family, 45*, 359–370.

McGonigel, M. J., Kaufmann, R. K., & Johnson, B. H. (1991). *Guidelines and recommended practices for the individualized family service plan.* Bethesda, MD: Association for the Care of Children's Health.

McLean, M., & Hanline, M. (1990). Providing early intervention services in integrated environments: Challenges and opportunities for the future. *Topics in Early Childhood Special Education, 10*(2), 62–77.

McNulty, B. (1989). Leadership and policy strategies for interagency planning: Meeting the early childhood mandate. In J. J. Gallagher, P. L. Trohanis, & R. M. Clifford (Eds.), *Policy implementation and P.L. 99-457: Planning for young children with special needs* (pp. 147–167). Baltimore: Brookes.

McWilliam, R. A., Lang, L., Vandiviere, P., Ange, U. R., Collins, L., & Underdown, G. (1995). Satisfaction and struggles: Family perceptions of early intervention services. *Journal of Early Intervention, 19,* 43–60.

Odom, S. L., & McEvoy, M. (1990). Mainstreaming at the preschool level: Potential barriers and tasks for the field. *Topics in Early Childhood Special Education, 10*(2), 48–61.

Odom, S. L., McLean, M. E., Johnson, L. J., & LaMontagne, M. J. (1995). Recommended practices in early childhood special education: Validation and current use. *Journal of Early Intervention, 19,* 1–17.

Paget, K. D. (1992). Proactive family–school partnerships in early intervention. In M. J. Fine & C. Carlson (Eds.), *The handbook of family-school intervention* (pp. 119–133). Boston: Allyn & Bacon.

Peck, C. A., Furman, G. C., & Helmstetter, E. (1993). Integrated early childhood programs: Research on the implementation of change in organizational contexts. In C. A. Peck, S. L. Odom, & D. D. Bricker (Eds.), *Integrating young children with disabilities into community programs: Ecological perspectives on research and implementation* (pp. 187–205). Baltimore: Brookes.

Peterson, C. A., & McConnell, S. R. (1993). Factors affecting the impact of social interaction skill interventions in early childhood special education. *Topics in Early Childhood Special Education, 13,* 38–56.

Peterson, N. L. (1991). Interagency collaboration under Part H: The key to comprehensive, multidisciplinary, coordinated infant/toddler intervention services. *Journal of Early Intervention, 15,* 89–105.

Quirk, J. P., Fine, M. J., & Roberts, L. (1992). Professional and ethical issues and problems in family–school systems interventions. In M. J. Fine & C. Carlson (Eds.), *The handbook of family–school intervention* (pp. 414–427). Boston: Allyn & Bacon.

Rainforth, B., & Salisbury, C. L. (1988). Functional home programs: A model for therapists. *Topics in Early Childhood Special Education, 7*(4), 33–45.

Rainforth, B., York, J., & MacDonald, C. (1992). *Collaborative teams for students with severe disabilities.* Baltimore: Brookes.

Ramey, C. T., Bryant, D. M., Sparling, J. J., & Wasik, B. H. (1985). Project CARE: A comparison of two early intervention strategies to prevent retarded development. *Topics in Early Childhood Special Education, 5*(2), 12–25.

Scott, S., & Doyle, P. (1984). Parent-to-parent support. *Exceptional Parent, 14*(1), 15–22.

Singer, G. S., & Irvin, L. K. (1989). Family caregiving, stress and support. In G. H. S. Singer & L. K. Irvin (Eds.), *Support for caregiving parents* (pp. 3–26). Baltimore: Brookes.

Slentz, K. L., Walker, B., & Bricker, D. (1989). Supporting parent involvement in early intervention: A role-taking model. In G. H. S. Singer & L. K. Irvin (Eds.), *Support for caregiving parents* (pp. 221–238). Baltimore: Brookes.

Smith, B. (1995, June). *The current challenges to early intervention*. Paper presented at the Pennsylvania Statewide Early Intervention Conference, Hershey, PA.

Spiegel, J., & Harper-Whalen, S. (1995). Forging partnerships with families. In R. Van den Pol, J. Guichy, & B. Keeley (Eds.), *Creating the inclusive preschool* (pp. 46–62). Tucson, AZ: Communication Skill Builders.

Spiegle, J., & Van den Pol, R. (1993). *Making changes: Family voices on living with disabilities*. Cambridge, MA: Brookline Books.

Stagg, V., & Catron, T. (1986). Networks of social supports for parents of handicapped children. In R. R. Fewell & P. F. Vadasy (Eds.), *Families and handicapped children: Needs and supports across the lifespan*. Austin, TX: PRO-ED.

Strain, P. S. (1990). LRE for preschool children with handicaps: What we know, what we should be doing. *Journal of Early Intervention, 14*, 291–296.

Summers, J. A., Behr, S. K., & Turnbull, A. P. (1989). Positive adaptations and coping strengths of families who have children with disabilities. In G. H. S. Singer & L. K. Irvin (Eds.), *Support for caregiving families* (pp. 27–40). Baltimore: Brookes.

Taylor, S. J., Knoll, J. A., Lehr, S., & Walker, P. M. (1989). Families for all children: Value-based services for children with disabilities and their families. In G. H. S. Singer & L. K. Irvin (Eds.), *Support for caregiving families* (pp. 41–54). Baltimore: Brookes.

Trohanis, P. L. (1995). Progress in providing services to young children with special needs and their families. *NEC*TAS Notes* (Vol. 7). Chapel Hill: University of North Carolina.

Turnbull, A. P., & Turnbull, H. R. (1990). *Families, professionals, and exceptionality: A special partnership*. Columbus, OH: Merrill.

Turnbull, A. P., & Winton, P. J. (1984). Parent involvement policy and practice: Current research and implications for families of young, severely handicapped children. In J. Blacher (Ed.), *Severely handicapped young children and their families: A research review* (pp. 377–400). Orlando, FL: Academic Press.

Venuto, C. (1994). *Parents as decision-makers*. Los Angeles: Los Angeles Countywide Interagency Coordinating Council Staff Development Program.

Vincent, L. J. (1985). Family relationships. In *Equals in the partnership* (pp. 33–34). Washington, DC: National Center for Clinical Infant Programs.

Vincent, L. J. (1992). Families and early intervention: Diversity and competence. *Journal of Early Intervention, 16*, 166–172.

Vincent, L. J., & Broome, K. (1977). A public school service delivery model for handicapped children between birth and five years of age. In E. Sontag, J. Smith, & N. Certo (Eds.), *Educational programming for the severely and profoundly handicapped* (pp. 111–128). Reston, VA: Council for Exceptional Children.

Vincent, L. J., Laten, S., Salisbury, C., Brown, P., & Baumgart, D. (1981). Family involvement in the educational processes of severely handicapped students: State of the art and directions for the future. In B. Wilcox & R. York (Eds.), *Quality educational services for the severely handicapped* (pp. 67–85). Washington, DC: U.S. Department of Education, Office of Special Education, Division of Innovation and Development.

Vincent, L. J., & Perrett, S. (1990, August). *Implementing P.L. 99-457: Parents and ICCs*. Paper presented at the Annual Meeting of Part H–Part B State Coordinators, Washington, DC.

Vincent, L. J., & Salisbury, C. (1988). Changing economic and social influences on family involvement. *Topics in Early Childhood Special Education, 8*(1), 48–59.

Vincent, L. J., Salisbury, C., Strain, P., McCormick, L., & Tessier, A. (1990). A behavioral–ecological approach to early intervention: Focus on cultural diversity. In S.

Meisels & J. Shonkoff (Ed.), *Handbook of early intervention* (pp. 173–195). London: Cambridge University Press.

Walker, B. (1989). Strategies for improving parent–professional cooperation. In G. H. S. Singer & L. K. Irvin (Eds.), *Support for caregiving families* (pp. 103–120). Baltimore: Brookes.

Warren, F., & Warren, S. F. (1989). The role of parents in creating and maintaining quality family support services. In G. H. S. Singer & L. K. Irvin (Eds.), *Support for caregiving families* (pp. 55–68). Baltimore: Brookes.

Whitehead, A., & Sontag, J. (1993). *Co-instruction: A case study.* Madison: University of Wisconsin–Madison, Wisconsin Personnel Development Project.

Ziegler, M. (1989). A parent's perspective: Implementing P.L. 99-457. In J. J. Gallagher, P. L. Trohanis, & R. M. Clifford (Eds.), *Policy implementation and P.L. 99-457: Planning for young children with special needs* (pp. 85–94). Baltimore: Brookes.

CHAPTER 4

Development and Implementation of IFSPs and IEPs: Opportunities for Empowerment

Vicki P. Turbiville
Ann P. Turnbull
Corinne W. Garland
Ilene M. Lee

Ten years ago, as one of the administrators in a small private school for children with learning disabilities or emotional disorders, I was responsible for directing the development of IEPs (individualized education plans) for the 130 students enrolled in the program. Although a philosophy of family centeredness might have been at the street level in some areas at that time, it certainly was not on my "street," and our process of development was agency-centered first and child-centered second.

Conferences were scheduled to accommodate the schedules of the representatives of the seven school districts that were responsible for the students' educational programs. Consequently, families (mothers) were given little choice other than time on a designated day.

The IEP documents to be signed at the conference were developed in a traditionally multidisciplinary manner. The teachers were responsible for the development of the final document with goals and objectives from the related service areas that were submitted on slips of paper by the discipline specialists. A few of the teachers talked with parents about what was going into the IEP, but the majority of the parents saw these documents for the first time while they waited for their meetings to begin. They then attended their hour meeting during which each specialist reported the year's work, including the reciting of the annual test scores.

I know that our process was fairly standard practice for the time. We specialists were working with seven districts and none of them questioned our procedures. Each year, only one or two parents asked to see the IEP beforehand or to have changes made in the document.

VICKI TURBIVILLE

Many changes have occurred in the field during the last decade. One of the most radical changes has occurred with the passage of the Education of the Handicapped Act Amendments of 1986 (P.L. 99-457) Part H, which requires acknowledgement of the importance of the family in service delivery for children who have a disability. The family-centered philosophy of early intervention is not only permeating IFSPs but is also having an impact on IEP development.

In this chapter, we synthesize recommended practices relative to the IEP/IFSP as they were validated by the membership of the Division for Early Childhood (DEC) of the Council for Exceptional Children. We discuss the overarching outcome of the IEP/IFSP process, two guiding principles of the process, and five groups of recommended practice.

OUTCOME OF IEP/IFSP PROCESS

The outcome of family-centered participation in the IFSP and IEP process is the empowerment of all team members—families, friends, and service providers. Empowerment is a process by which an individual or family develops (a) the motivation to act, (b) the resources and skills necessary to act, and (c) an environment or context responsive to actions by the individual (see Table 4.1; Kieffer, 1984; Sprague & Brunk, 1993). For a family to participate actively in family-centered services, the members of the family must perceive their empowerment. Family empowerment can be observed when families act to change the condition of their lives and to acquire control to manage their own family according to their preferences and priorities (Kalyanpur & Rao, 1991). The empowerment of friends and service providers can be observed when they act to enhance the responsiveness of the home, neighborhood, early childhood education, and community contexts to support families to manage their circumstances consistent with their preferences and priorities.

In traditional models, the service providers have held the power of decision making and intervention planning (Schon, 1983). Families were expected to be fairly passive recipients of decisions and information from service providers (Turnbull & Turnbull, 1990). In the current view of family-centered practices, families have moved into the "power" position (Lee, 1993). As the "next step" of empowerment for all team members, a new mold must be cast that provides for the sharing of power and the recognition of the expertise and balanced contributions of all members (Cochran & Dean, 1991; Sokoly & Dokecki, 1992). Here, families are not *given* opportunities by service providers for decision-making or participation. Rather, as situations arise, team members collaborate to examine the available options with the assumption that everyone's skills and resources are vital and that flexible leadership patterns can be matched to intervention priorities and situational availability of time and energy. It is always

Table 4.1. Definition of Family Empowerment

Family empowerment is a developmental process that consists of motivation, the resources and skills needed for effective action, and contexts or environments that are responsive to individuals and families.

recognized, however, that the family will be the ultimate decision maker (McGonigel & Garland, 1988).

An empowering partnership shifts the power from professionals directing the process to synergistic power emanating from the creative sharing and emotional support by the entire group of family members, friends, and service providers (Craig & Craig, 1974; Sokoly & Dokecki, 1992). Synergistic power means "the capacity of an individual or group to increase the satisfactions of all participants by intentionally generating increased energy and creativity, all of which is used to co-create a more rewarding present and future" (Craig & Craig, 1974, p. 62). Synergistic power is generative and "contagious." It promotes a sense of empowerment of individuals, but it also promotes a sense of collective empowerment. Both individual and collective empowerment transform the disenfranchisement that has traditionally been associated with disability to opportunities for full citizenship and the actualization of visions.

PRINCIPLES LINKING INDICATORS TO EMPOWERMENT

With empowerment as the ultimate outcome of the process, two principles guided the development of the recommended practice indicators and linked them to empowerment:

- Family-centered collaboration is basic to the process.
- The natural environment of the child and the family should be the environment for the development and implementation of the IFSP and IEP.

Figure 4.1 depicts the relationship between these principles and the recommended practices.

Family-Centered Collaboration as a Guiding Principle

Nevin, Thousand, Paolucci-Whitcomb, and Villa (1990) defined *collaboration* as a process during which a team of people with differing expertise work

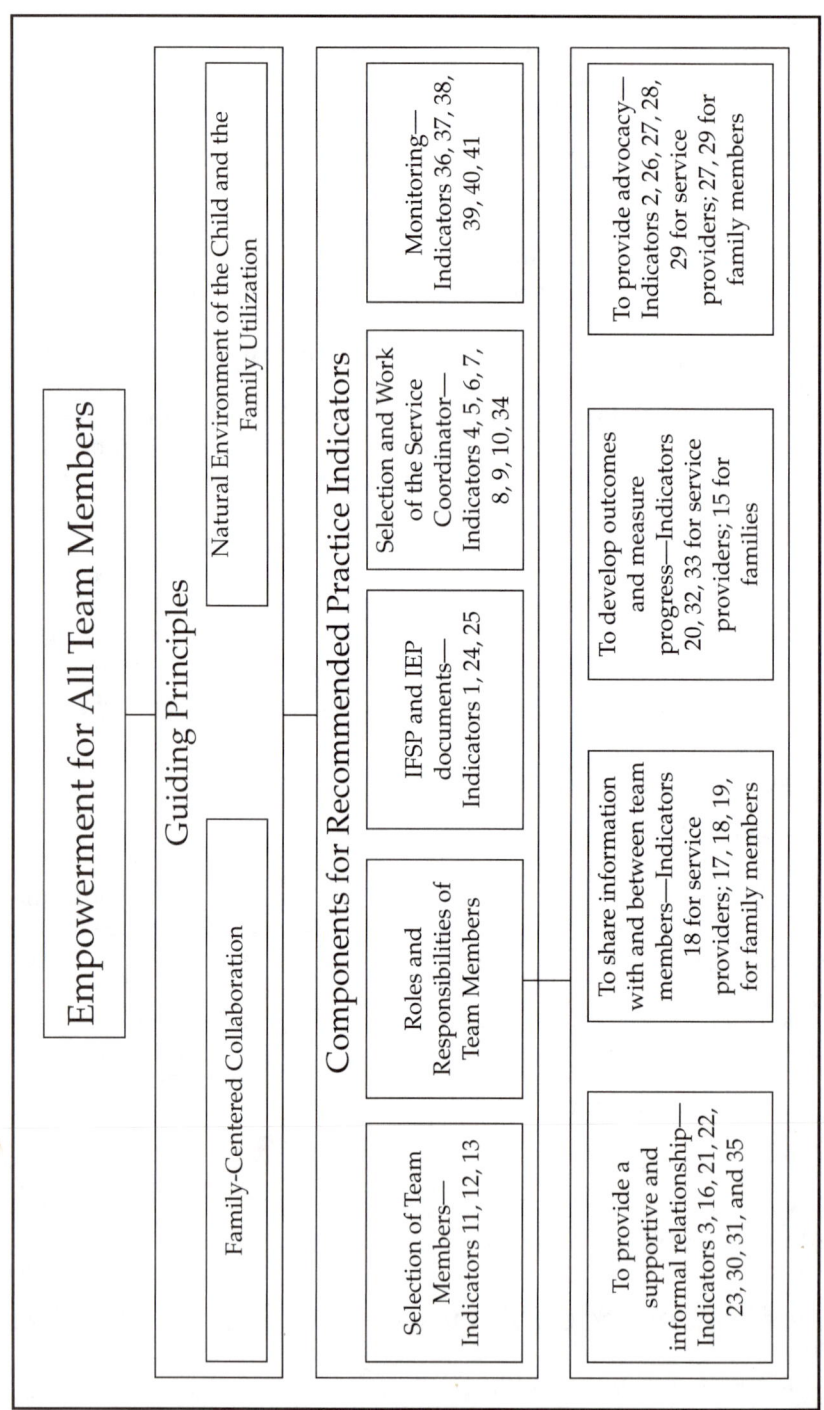

Figure 4.1. Guiding principles and categories for recommended practices for the IFSP and IEP.

together to solve mutually defined problems using the unique abilities and resources of all members to create individualized solutions. Collaboration is multidirectional in response to the strengths and needs of all team members who may at any time be the receivers or givers of information. It is also a process in which the team leadership changes in response to the task.

Family-centered practices have been defined in diverse ways (Lee, 1993). A majority of the definitions describe actions to be taken by the service providers so that families can be more participatory if the families choose. On the basis of these definitions, programs should (a) help determine resources to strengthen a family's formal and informal networks (Dunst, Johnson, Trivette, & Hemby, 1991), (b) attend to family priorities over those of other team members (Bailey, Buysee, Edmondson, & Smith, 1992), and (c) encourage and facilitate parent-to-parent support (Shelton, Jeppson, & Johnson, 1987). For a program to be family centered, it must provide a variety of opportunities for families to participate according to their preferences and priorities.

As defined, family-centered collaboration is a means for advancing the outcome of individual and team empowerment. Collaboration is tied to two definitional elements of empowerment. First, collaboration is a skill and resource that contributes to the process. Second, it is a part of the responsive context, because supportive organizational structures and philosophy must be present for collaboration to exist.

To develop an IFSP or an IEP, team members, whether they are family members, service providers, or friends, must work together to develop the outcomes and the strategies that will address the team's collective concerns, resources, and priorities. Historically, families have been unequal partners in the process; the participation of team members with professional expertise and hard data has been more highly valued (Nash, 1990). Families were the recipients of professionally made decisions (Bailey, Buysee, et al., 1992; Turnbull & Turnbull, 1990). Today, many of the team models most commonly presented are the ones that support a balanced partnership between family members and service providers to identify and achieve outcomes, goals, and objectives (Nash, 1990; Stonestreet, Johnston, & Acton, 1991; Turnbull & Turnbull, 1990). Rather than conceptualized as the dyadic involvement of families and service providers, collaboration should also include friends in the process, particularly in light of the second guiding principle, which emphasizes inclusion in the natural environments. The benefits of collaboration among families, service providers, and friends include better knowledge and understanding of the child's strengths and needs (Campbell & Failey, 1993) and an increased commitment to the outcomes and implementation of the plan by all members of the team (Garland & Linder, 1988).

The collaborative process of IFSP and IEP development includes a recognition of the ultimate decision-making authority of the family. The family's decision may be not to make any decisions, to give the decision-making authority to service providers or friends, or to make decisions that are completely contrary to those recommended by the other team members (McGonigel & Garland, 1988). Decision making should be viewed as a continuum that is based on the family's values, culture, resources, and priorities (Able-Boone, 1993). Any decisions that are made first and foremost affect the family and their child who has a disability. So although we professionals may collaborate as team members, when it comes to the final decision, that decision must be one that works for the family.

Also within the collaborative process, families and service providers must have choices. These choices must reflect the flexibility and creativity of the community and of the team members. Choices must not be limited to the services that are available but must be based on all of the resources that can be identified in a community (Raab, Davis, & Trepanier, 1993). Being familiar with the formal service agency options within a community is not enough. Instead all team members must have information on the range of formal and informal resources and supports that can be drawn upon to meet needs, one of which may be a particular service agency (Raab et al., 1993). When families can see that in most situations they have options and that it is their choice to select the best one for them, they have an opportunity to exercise their empowerment and to lose the sense of anomie or powerlessness that is sometimes felt (Seligman & Darling, 1989).

Inclusion as a Guiding Principle

The second principle supports the inclusion of the child and family in the natural environment. *Inclusion*, as defined by DEC, is "full and successful access to health, social service, education and other supports and services for young children and their families that promote full participation in community life" (Division for Early Childhood, 1993, p. 4). Inclusive environments are responsive environments or, as given in the definition of empowerment, ones that are responsive to the needs and initiatives of individuals. Inclusive environments support the individual or family for full participation in whatever setting is appropriate, typical, or available to others (Brault, 1992). Inclusive environments facilitate empowerment for the individual or family through their responsiveness and through their opportunity for full participation.

The principle of inclusion given here goes beyond the physical setting of the services. The principle that the natural environment of the family and child should be the setting for the development and implementation of the IFSP and IEP expresses the belief that children must be full members of their family, of the family's cultural system, and of its wider community

("Natural Environments," 1993). Full societal inclusion requires (a) physical integration (being where families and children without disabilities are), (b) functional integration (using the same facilities as those families and children), and (c) social integration (participating in interactions with other families from the community and their children whether they have a disability or not) (Demchak & Drinkwater, 1992). Inclusion as used here, then, refers to full citizenship for families and for their children.

Recommended practice indicators for IFSPs and IEPs reflect this principle of inclusion and full citizenship. The indicators guide the development of IFSP and IEP outcomes, goals and objectives, and implementation plans that promote and enhance full participation. During the process of the development of these documents, the team must consider whether the IFSP or IEP promotes the inclusion of the infant or toddler in his or her family, the family in its culture and community, and the toddler or preschooler in the community of childhood—that of children both with and without a disability.

The first critical step in inclusion for some children who have a disability is their integration into the family (Brault, 1992). The IFSPs and IEPs developed according to recommended practices are responsive to all family members, with the child as a member of the family system but not the center of the family system (Turnbull & Summers, 1985). The use of outcomes that are family priorities (Slentz & Bricker, 1992) and routines-based goals and objectives (McWilliams, 1992) helps families include all family members. For some families, inclusion of the child into the family means that parents do not provide interventions beyond normal parenting (LeLaurin, 1992; Turnbull & Turnbull, 1990).

IFSPs and IEPs developed according to these DEC recommended practice indicators help families maintain their place in their community and culture. The development of such an IFSP or IEP requires that service providers listen to families to understand each family's specific cultural background. This listening provides insights into how the family views and approaches the world (Christensen, 1992). The IFSP or IEP developed according to recommended practices is consistent with the views and approaches held by each family.

The principle of inclusive services also includes the full participation of toddlers and preschoolers who have a disability in the natural childhood community. This participation seeks to promote friendship opportunities with children who do not have disabilities as well as with those who do. Though there is much argument about the benefits of inclusion for children with a disability (Lamorey & Bricker, 1993; LeLaurin, 1992; Odom & Brown, 1993), there is no question of the benefits of friendships (Amado, 1993). One of the primary conditions needed for friendships to develop is that the individuals are in the same location and share activities.

RECOMMENDED PRACTICES

Forty-one indicators were validated as recommended practice by DEC. These indicators have been categorized into five groups: (a) selection of team members, (b) roles and responsibilities of team members, (c) service coordination, (d) IFSP and IEP documents, and (e) monitoring of the process and documents.

The use of these indicators alone does not constitute implementation of recommended practices. The empowerment of all team members through the principles of collaboration and inclusion is essential as these indicators are put into practice.

Selection of Team Members

Selection of team members vitally shapes the nature of the IFSP/IEP process. Traditionally, IEP conferences were primarily characterized by a teacher describing a previously developed IEP to the mother (Goldstein, Strickland, Turnbull, & Curry, 1980). Currently, mothers also tend to be the only family member participating in the majority of IFSP conferences (Able-Boone, 1993; Campbell, Strickland, & LaForme, 1992). Although the rhetoric in early intervention literature has changed from *mothers* to *families*, in actual practice, family participation may still be primarily mother participation. One of the greatest challenges in implementing IFSP/IEP recommended practices related to team selection is breaking the mold of the long-standing tradition of having a few professionals and the mother meet and, instead, creating a more collaborative and diverse process for decision making.

The outcome of empowerment and the principles of collaboration and inclusion guide the process for team selection. It is essential that the service coordinator and family determine who will be included on the team and, with family authorization, ensure the participation of relevant team members. In considering the broad range of options for relevant team members, families may select ones who provide emotional support and practical assistance, including service providers, friends, and families of other children with disabilities (IFSP/IEP [I]11, I 12, I 13).

Major issues need to be addressed in ensuring that family members and friends have a meaningful opportunity to participate in IFSP and IEP meetings: (a) scheduling of meetings at times that fathers can attend and ensuring that gender differences, communication, and participation preferences are respected (Levine, 1993; Mahoney, O'Sullivan, & Dennebaum, 1990; Turnbull, 1993); (b) creating opportunities for siblings to share their insights on ways to foster inclusion in sibling, peer, and neighborhood activities

(Powell & Gallagher, 1993); (c) supporting grandparents to understand the nature of their grandchild's disability, to address support, and to offer practical help to the parents and grandchild (Able-Boone, Sandall, Stevens, & Fredrick, 1992; Vadasy, Fewell, & Meyer, 1986; Seligman & Darling, 1989); (d) supporting friends to gain information so that they can provide logistical and emotional support as well as access to inclusive opportunities (Able-Boone et al., 1992); and (e) encouraging connections with veteran parents who "have been there" and have repertoires of invaluable practical insights (Santelli, Turnbull, Lerner, & Marquis, 1993; Smith, 1993).

Excellent models are being developed in person-centered planning, mostly focusing on later life stages, that could be easily adapted and incorporated into model early childhood practices. These person-centered approaches focus on creating circles of support with primary contributions from chronologically aged peers as well as from family friends and community citizens (Stineman, Morningstar, Bishop, & Turnbull, 1993; Vandercook, York, & Forest, 1989).

Service providers as team members are also vital. A recommended practice indicator is that with the consent of the family, the team may also include representatives of agencies in community programs that have previously served, or are likely to serve, the child or family (I 13). With the involvement of previous service providers, particular benefits are likely to be a more intimate knowledge of the child's strengths and needs and of the family's concerns, priorities, and resources. In terms of future service providers, one of the best ways to prepare for transition is to ensure that future providers have necessary information to provide relevant and responsive services. Involving them in meetings 1–2 years prior to transition can help build a solid foundation.

In addition to future providers of educational services, individuals responsible for providing inclusive services in the community such as soccer coaches, religious education teachers, and community recreation staff can also participate in meetings to prepare them to include the child in ongoing community services.

In summary, recommended practices suggest that team selection move from the traditional professional domination with the mother's participation to a broadly constituted group of family members, service providers, and friends, including other families of children with a disability. The definition of collaboration emphasizes the importance of bringing together teams of people with *diverse expertise* to generate *creative solutions* to problems that are mutually defined. One of the great values of IFSP/IEP teams with diverse participants is that the diversity itself creates a broader pool of resources and skills, a prerequisite for empowerment. Diverse participants, particularly ones who can facilitate inclusive experiences, can broaden opportunities in natural settings. We want to reemphasize, however, that parents determine team participation. Some parents will be comfortable with broadly constituted groups and others will not be. This is also a process that may evolve over time. The IFSP/IEP team may start with a smaller group and gradually add people as the synergy of the group expands (Kjerland & Kovach, 1990).

Responsibilities and Work of Team Members

This category, representing the largest number of recommended practice indicators, includes four major subcategories: (a) providing supportive and informal relationships, (b) sharing information with and between team members, (c) developing outcomes and measuring progress for those outcomes, and (d) providing advocacy.

Providing Supportive and Informal Relationships

Respect is fundamental to supportive and informal relationships. Robert Silverstein, director of the Senate's Committee on Disability Policy and crafter of Part H of P.L. 99-457, described the congressional intent for respecting families: "Congress wanted the language of the bill to reflect our utmost respect for the family. The word 'family' must appear ten or fifteen times throughout this legislation; this was intentional. Congress was trying to say: 'do not have professionals come into a family situation and assume that the mom and dad don't know anything. Respect the family'" (Silverstein, 1989, p. A–3).

This congressional intent is clearly an aspect of recommended practices in early intervention programs. A supportive and mutually respectful relationship with families should occur from the time of initial contact (I 3). A critical component of family respect is recognizing that family preferences for participation should pervade the total process (McGonigel & Garland, 1988). Families should receive individualized support and information about their options so that they can participate in the process in the ways they have chosen; other team members can then adjust their roles in response to family preferences (I 16). It is essential for professionals to realize that family preferences vary along many dimensions. Within the family, different members will have different preferences for their individual involvement and, perhaps, for each other's involvement. For example, a mother may prefer to share emotionally sensitive information very openly as a way of garnering emotional support, whereas a father may prefer to retain family privacy and not to share emotionally sensitive information (Tannen, 1990). The father may prefer this reticence not only for himself but also for his wife. Thus, the issue is often not nearly as simple as the family's having a preference but rather that individual family members have different and sometimes conflicting preferences. Additionally, families may prefer to be more involved in some decisions than with other decisions within the same IFSP/IEP meeting, and family preferences will change over time in light of the family's competing responsibilities and their own sense of empowerment. Thus, family preferences are never static but are constantly changing. The IFSP/IEP process should always remain flexible so that it can be responsive to diverse preferences.

In addition to respect for the family, all communications, actions, and written statements of team members should reflect the team members' respect for one another, and all team members should be honest with each other (I 21, I 22). As respect and honesty pervade communications and interactions, team members will be enabled to assert their most creative contributions to the development and implementation of desired child and family outcomes. This respect among team members promotes empowerment by facilitating a partnership for collaboration and a responsive community for inclusion.

Synergistic power emanates from informal relationships characterized by caring and social support (Sokoly & Dokecki, 1992). One of the key characteristics of supportive and informal relationships is a nonjudgmental stance. Kalyanpur and Rao (1991) characterized four supportive and informal communication strategies: (a) being conversational—conversing with mothers on topics of their priorities rather than controlling the conversation through interviews, assessments, or didactics; (b) interpreting—listening and interpreting the situation from mothers' points of view so that strengths rather than deficits are affirmed; (c) sharing—exchanging stories with each other rather than directing or formally teaching the mothers; and (d) accepting—affirming the mothers' skills and competence as parents. Kalyanpur and Rao summarized their approach: "While the expertise of professionals is an integral aspect of the interaction between parents and professionals, the manner in which the expertise is communicated determines the nature of the relationship. Therein lies the essence of empowerment. It involves caring, which builds supportive relationships; respect, which builds reciprocity; and the acceptance of differences, which builds trust" (1991, p. 531).

Sharing Information with and Between Team Members

Both quantitative and qualitative studies have underscored the priority that families place on receiving information about the nature of their child's disability and the availability of services (Able-Boone et al., 1992; Bailey, Blasco, & Simeonsson, 1992). Priority informational needs identified by mothers and fathers include information about (a) future services, (b) present services, (c) how to teach the child, (d) the nature of the child's disability, and (e) the experiences of other parents who have a child with similar needs (Cooper & Allred, 1992). Other high-priority informational needs include ways to deal with the emotional and time demands of parenting, community resources, and legal rights (Gowen, Christy, & Sparling, 1993). The traditional emphasis has been on disseminating research and best practice information to other professionals as contrasted to sharing that information with families and friends. Much greater priority must be placed on the development of accessible, relevant, interesting, and time-efficient resources so that the families and friends have the necessary information to participate in full and equal decision making.

In terms of IFSP/IEP collaboration, families should be invited to participate in any team discussion of their child and family (I 17). This practice contrasts with what happens in some situations, as in our opening scenario in which professionals have premeetings to make preliminary decisions prior to involving families (or to inform families of decisions that have already been made). Synergistic power means that there should not be a distinction between "open" meetings and "closed" meetings; instead, any time issues associated with the child and family are discussed, and the family should have an opportunity to participate. Families should also receive complete copies of all reports concerning them and their children (I 18), and those reports should be written in a way to enhance understanding and comprehension. When technical information must be interpreted and verified, team members should offer this assistance to families (I 18).

One of the critically important areas for sharing information relates to the assessment of the child. In traditional practice, children typically have been assessed by professionals, and then professionals have compiled their results, reported them to each other, and prepared a summary that is shared with parents. Recommended practice in assessment suggests that parents should choose their role and that one of those options includes being a full collaborative partner. Parents can be offered the opportunity to share information in (a) planning assessment, (b) conducting the assessment, and (c) providing feedback. Leviton, Mueller, and Kauffman (1992) provided excellent suggestions for supporting parents to have partnership roles in each of these three assessment phases. With the consent of the parents, these same roles might also be extended to grandparents, brothers and sisters, and friends.

A particularly sensitive area regarding the sharing of information with and between team members is in the area of identifying family concerns, resources, and priorities. Thus, it is essential that families decide what information they wish to share with the team (I 19). A mother explained that it is the parents' responsibility to distinguish between what they may want to share with someone on the team as a confidence and what is IFSP/IEP-relevant information: "The parents should tell you [what to write down]. You just say this is between you and me. You use the same sort of judgment a good friend would have" (Summers et al., 1990, p. 90).

Developing Outcomes and Measuring Progress Toward Those Outcomes

Project Dakota incorporated a process in developing outcomes that begins with asking parents, "What do you want your child to get help with in the next few months?" (Kjerland & Kovach, 1990, p. 294). The team meets within a week to outline specific next steps for action with the parent's preferences guiding the process. Once action steps are identified, emphasis is given to how changes can be made and who is available to help with the changes. Because this kind of team collaboration occurs every 4 months, only a small number of goals are selected so that implementation can occur prior to the next reformulation (Kjerland & Kovach, 1990). A major benefit of having the IFSP/IEP team broadly constituted is to have a wide pool of potential implementers of outcomes.

Family-initiated outcomes, goals, and objectives are given priority in the development of the IFSP/IEP (I 33). As we discuss in greater detail in the section on the IFSP/IEP document, recommended practice also suggests that outcomes should be written in parent language rather than in professional language (Campbell et al., 1992). IFSPs and IEPs differ in their level of specificity. An IFSP, for example, might contain only general outcome statements, or more specific plans of intervention methods and schedules might be added in light of team preferences (Fewell, Snyder, Sexton, & Hockless, 1991). IEPs, on the other hand, may reflect specific program planning with detailed curricular goals (Strickland & Turnbull, 1990).

As we have previously described, it is essential that families have the opportunity to select or change the nature of their role in decision making for each outcome being considered (I 15) because they will have far more experience with some outcomes than with others. This same notion of individualizing roles according to different outcomes should apply to every team member. For example, a brother or sister may have a great amount of participation in suggesting how their sibling might best connect with other children at the soccer field or swimming pool but have far less to offer in designing the best feeding program.

In assessing progress toward outcomes, team members should individualize the criteria for each outcome (I 32). Given assessment results, potential support that can be brought to bear, and outcome priority, team members can make decisions pertaining to the appropriate schedule for updating and revising IFSPs/IEPs in light of family preferences, assessment results, and newly emerging child information (I 20).

Providing Advocacy

To advocate for the child and family means to represent their interests, not just in merely complying, but in dynamically ensuring that services and supports are as meaningful, comprehensive, and individualized as possible.

Advocacy begins with team members being knowledgeable about laws, policies, and recommended practice for the development, implementation, and monitoring of IFSPs/IEPs (I 26). It is startling how many administrators and teachers of school-aged students, 16 years after inception of the IEP, still do not have even a preliminary understanding of their individual and collective legal responsibilities. For example, an elementary teacher recently asked, "Do I have the right to see the IEP of the students in my class?" Obviously, she and the administrators at her school had totally missed the point of the IEP if it is not available for teachers to use as a meaningful instructional document. There continues to be a major need in the field for people with legal expertise to translate the letter and spirit of the law to service providers and families in a way that is understandable and empowering.

Families also need full opportunities for obtaining information about the IFSP/IEP process. The service coordinator or other person(s) responsible for the development of the IFSP/IEP should clearly describe to families the IFSP/IEP process, including their rights and the service coordinator's role (I 2). In addition to service providers' sharing this information with families, families should be put in touch with the Parent Training and Information Center in their locale (Ilott, 1993) as well as the Parent-to-Parent program (Santelli et al., 1993). Both of these family-directed networks provide valuable informational and emotional support to families related to IFSP/IEP issues and are valuable complementary services and supports to early childhood programs. There continues to be a need for written and audiovisual materials for families and friends to provide them with critical information on legal rights and recommended practices related to early childhood services (Cooper & Allred, 1992; Gowen et al., 1993).

As gaps in services and supports are identified by the IFSP/IEP committee, team members need to keep policy makers informed of gaps in community services (I 29). A current need for advocacy is in the area of inclusive supports for families and children. In their discussion of inclusion goals for the next century, Bricker, Peck, and Odom (1993) identified advocacy needs related to the following three areas: (a) addressing conflicts between the elimination of specialized service options and inclusion, with a continuation of emphasis on parental decision making and freedom of choice; (b) shifting focus from a study of the effectiveness of inclusion to discovering ways to make inclusive programs more beneficial for children with and without disabilities and for their families; and (c) conducting research and developing model programs that take into account all potentially relevant variables.

In terms of advocacy, the first point warrants critical attention. As professionals and families work to implement inclusion, it is imperative for professionals to recognize family perspectives. Research trends indicate that parents of children with and without disabilities generally favor inclusion (Bailey & Winton, 1987; Guralnick, in press; Peck, Carlson, &

Helmstetter, 1992; Turnbull, Winton, Blacher, & Salkind, 1983). Many parents, however, have reservations concerning teacher qualifications related to inclusive programs (Bailey & Winton, 1987; Green & Stoneman, 1989). Another parent concern is the likelihood of successful inclusion for children with behavior problems (Guralnick, in press). Thus, advocacy must be individualized to ensure that individual family decision making is respected while new and improved inclusive models of service are being developed and implemented.

The IFSP/IEP Document

The IFSP/IEP document has become the tangible representation of a new understanding of family-centered services as recommended practice. These documents, when developed according to recommended practices, also reflect the collaboration among team members and the inclusion of the child and family in the environments natural to them. In looking at an IFSP/IEP document, one hopes to see a written reflection of the family-centered principles that underlie the process—a form that follows function.

Written statements should reflect the climate of mutual trust, respect, and collaboration in which the IFSP/IEP has been developed. The document should reflect only the information and priorities to which the family has agreed (I 25). The IFSP/IEP should be written in the words and phrases that family members used to describe the outcomes they hope for and the resources they have (Campbell et al., 1992). The outcomes should give clear evidence that the family's observations of child behavior were valued and that their priorities for intervention were honored. If technical terms must be used, explanations should be provided (I 24).

The IFSP/IEP document should be the hopes, priorities, and resources of each child and family rather than being a collection of developmental goals that could apply generically to any child. One IFSP form used at Project Dakota in Eagan, Minnesota, provides a place for a family to draw a picture of how things currently look and how they wish them to look. Each outcome provides a literal picture of family priorities. Even after the IFSP/IEP is written, there should be no doubt that it belongs to the family. At Child Development Resources in Lightfoot, Virginia, outcomes related to child development are in an IFSP section, apart from other outcomes desired by the family. A family can choose to share information related to their child with professionals and agencies with whom they would not necessarily choose to share personal family information. A space for parents' names and signatures precedes the list of other team members to reinforce the family's primacy in developing the plan. The document should be a "living document," able to be easily revised in response to the changing needs of children and priorities of their families.

There are abundant examples of formats that embody the principles of a family-driven, flexible, and individualized IFSP/IEP. The Beach Center on Families and Disability at the University of Kansas in Lawrence clearly links process to document with supplementary forms or worksheets that can be added to the IFSP. The worksheets include a list of helpful names and telephone numbers, to-do lists, a meeting planning guide, a transition planner, and individualized descriptions of family and child information. The IFSP document developed by a parent–professional collaborative effort at the SHARE Center for Excellence in Early Intervention in Los Angeles contains a simple explanation of the purpose of each required section of the IFSP. Each outcome statement is preceded by the question, "What does the family wish to accomplish?" Criteria and timelines begin with the question, "How will we know if we're making progress?" The choice of the language used makes clear that the priorities for intervention are set by the family and that the intervention plan is a collaborative responsibility.

In addition to being collaborative, the IFSP and IEP documents should also be service plans that are inclusive for children and families. IDEA requires that the service included in the IFSP and IEP be provided in the natural environments for the child (and family). When developed according to the recommended practices principle of inclusion, these documents reflect the goals of physical, functional, and social integration for the children and for their families.

Service Coordination

If the IFSP can be understood as a promise on the part of the early intervention community that child and family needs will be addressed through the mobilization of family and community resources and through the delivery of early intervention services, service coordination is the guarantee that the promise will be kept. Although Part H of IDEA specifies service coordination as "the activities carried out . . . to assist and enable a child . . . and the child's family to receive the rights, procedural safeguards, and services that are authorized to be provided under the State's early intervention program" [34 C.F.R. 303.6(a)(1)], service coordination does not stand alone as a required component of state policy planning but also as a support to the IFSP.

Service coordination is a required option under Part H of IDEA. Although service coordination is not required under Part B of the legislation, recommended practices for the development of IEPs should extend its availability to the children and families who are no longer in early intervention. Some states have taken steps toward the adoption of this practice for the preschool-aged population (Brown, 1991). Particularly when goals of inclusion increase the collaboration needed among team members, it is important for professionals to provide assistance to families in the coordination of those services. From the point at which the family enters the service delivery system through successful transition to the next appropriate setting, the service coordinator can be construed as being responsible for (a) the extent to which the family's priorities drive the service system, (b) the extent to which the collaborative intent of the legislation is realized between and among families and providers, and (c) the extent to which the early intervention experience is perceived as a positive one by families.

Although this responsibility is implicit in the legislation, other responsibilities of service coordinators are explicitly defined: (a) coordinating the performance of evaluations and assessments; (b) facilitating and participating in the development, review, and evaluation of IFSPs; (c) helping families identify available service providers; (d) coordinating and monitoring the delivery of available services; (e) informing families of the availability of advocacy services; (f) coordinating with medical and health providers; and (g) facilitating the development of a transition plan to preschool services, if appropriate [IDEA, Part H, 34 C.F.R. 303.6(b)]. This role of service coordination is an expansion of the role described 20 years ago in Part B regulations as *social work services* or the "mobilizing of school and community resources to enable the child to learn as effectively as possible in his or her educational program" [IDEA, Part B, 34 C.F.R. 300.16(b)(12)(ir)].

Of these responsibilities, "the ability to act in a linkage capacity is perhaps the most important role of the service coordinator" (McGonigel, Kaufmann, & Johnson, 1991, p. 72). The service coordinator serves as "the single point of contact in helping parents obtain services and assistance that they need" [IDEA, Part H, 34 C.F.R. 303.6(a)(2)]. Although families may want and need services from a wide array of agencies, the law intends that each family will have one person who, as service coordinator, can bridge the gap between family concerns and a complex service delivery system.

Although the roles and responsibilities of service coordination may "seem straightforward, the process is often complex" (Zipper, Weil, & Rounds, 1991, p. 23). The service coordinator assumes responsibility at the point of referral and continues that responsibility by helping each family to plan for assessment and by determining, on the basis of their individual needs, the family members, and friends, the service protection afforded to them by the law. The service coordinator may need to make logistical arrangements, such as assembling the assessment team at a time and in a place that is convenient for the family. Planning for and participating in evaluation and assessment can be both bewildering and stressful for families. At this time, the real value of the service coordinator to families may be measured by the emotional support he or she can offer.

The service coordinator will participate in the development of the IFSP and, at least during transition to preschool, in the development of the

IEP. Ideally, the service coordinator will understand that the IFSP/IEP process begins with preparing families for that process and with helping them assume their decision-making role to the extent they choose (McGonigel & Garland, 1988). The service coordinator and other persons responsible for the development of the IFSP should clearly describe to families the IFSP process, their rights during the process, and the roles of the family and of the service coordinator (I 2).

Family options in the IFSP/IEP-planning process should be broad and should include choices about time and place of the meeting and team members to be involved, as well as more critical decisions about the content of the plan itself. Once again, the service coordinator must ensure that families are aware of all their options, including the services available and the strengths and disadvantages of each (I 34). It is particularly important that the service coordinator help families to understand their children's rights to be served in natural and inclusive environments and to understand the ways in which services can be provided in those settings.

The service coordinator needs to be knowledgeable about funding sources available and may play a role in helping the family and other members of the IFSP team, and occasionally of the IEP team, identify sources of payment for services. The service coordinator may need to help families understand the role of public and private health insurance coverage in payment for services and the potential consequences of choosing to use family coverage for services. Because of the complex medical needs of some children with disabilities, coordination with medical and health care providers has been singled out in the regulations [IDEA, Part H, 34 C.F.R. 303.6(b)] as a responsibility of the service coordinator. The service coordinator should explore with each family how best to ensure the involvement of the child's primary care physician and other health care specialists as appropriate in order to be certain that concerns and priorities for each child's health and development are fully integrated during assessment and in service planning and implementation.

Although the IDEA Part H requirement for service coordination ends at age 3 of the child, many agencies offer case management to specifically defined populations beyond age 3, even throughout life. The service coordinator will need to work closely with each family during the transition period to determine the extent to which they continue to be interested in having future case management provisions included in the transition plan.

Precisely because the service needs of many persons with disabilities and their families continue long beyond the period of early intervention, recommended practice in service coordination has shifted dramatically. Dunst and Trivette (1989) clearly articulated their support for an approach to service coordination that abstains from controlling and allocating resources but that, instead, enables families to "clarify their concerns and identify their own needs" and ultimately promotes "acquisition of effective behaviors necessary for families to be actively involved in accessing needed resources" (p. 97). Striking this "delicate but important balance of providing a supportive service while promoting parental independence, responsibility, and decision making" (Bailey, 1989, p. 130) is an important goal of service coordination.

The supportive relationship of mutual trust and respect (I 21, I 22, I 23) on which service coordination rests is not built overnight, nor can it be built when the service coordinator sees the family only infrequently. Service coordination is intended to be "an active, ongoing process" [IDEA, Part H, 34 C.F.R. 303.6.(al)(3)] that is flexible and responsive to family needs (McGonigel et al., 1991). If, at any time, changes in family needs or priorities require a change in service coordination, families may request a change in the service coordinator and have that request honored if resources allow (I 7).

The early intervention system makes great demands on service coordinators: Skill in interpersonal as well as in interagency interactions is very important. Statewide systems and local communities should provide competency-based training to ensure that service coordinators, whether family members or professionals, have the skills needed to fill this demanding role (I 5, I 8).

Monitoring

Although the service coordinator is responsible for monitoring service delivery and for identifying any gaps in service for individual children and families, the state system of early intervention has an analogous responsibility for monitoring IFSP/IEP policies and procedures. The purpose of monitoring is to determine the extent to which the intent of the law is being actualized in service delivery. State and local monitoring should lead to identification of any needs for change in service systems, of any service gaps, and of inadequate resources (I 41). If state and local systems of monitoring are to be able to take full measure of the implementation of IFSP/IEP policies and procedures at the local level, they, too, will have to make many of the same kinds of changes that service providers have made. Monitoring will become more collaborative and inclusive simultaneously as it provides for evaluation of collaboration and inclusion.

In order to assess with any accuracy the extent to which systems are responding to the needs of children and families, monitoring teams must expand beyond their traditional professional membership to include families of children receiving services (I 39). Monitoring teams must be skilled in interviewing, must ensure that they speak with families who represent the diversity of the community in which they are working, and must ensure that the teams themselves are representative of local diversity.

Monitoring information should come not only from families whose children are receiving services but also from professionals providing those and other services to children and families (I 38). Families and other team members should be assured that their confidentiality will be protected and should have the opportunity to evaluate their satisfaction with the IFSP/IEP process, document, and degree to which desired outcomes have been reached (I 36, I 37).

On the basis of telephone interviews of Part H coordinators in 30 states (Child Development Resources, 1993), states apparently are still in the process of developing systems to monitor compliance with the basic requirements of IDEA. Monitoring of IEPs for children over the age of 3 seems to have been incorporated into systems already in place within state education agencies. Many states, whether in the stage of design or implementation of their IFSP/IEP monitoring system(s), have embodied innovative strategies, including practices recommended by the DEC.

Some states have begun training parents of children with disabilities to participate in monitoring. The monitoring process includes talking directly with families either through home visits or by telephone. Through Florida's Community Resource Parents Program, parents are trained to communicate with families (including listening to family stories) in homes, centers, and doctor's waiting rooms (Child Development Resources, 1993). Another state plans to hold focus groups made up of families, service providers, and agency representatives to identify successful strategies and barriers (Child Development Resources, 1993). Several states are specifically selecting strategies to measure or assess the degree to which service delivery is family-friendly or family focused (Child Development Resources, 1993).

Several states have developed interagency monitoring plans, an approach consistent with the collaborative nature of interagency state planning and local service delivery. At least four states are planning to involve peer reviews in their monitoring of IFSPs, whereas others are developing self-assessment documents or forms to help providers understand expectations and discover needs for improvement. As states design new systems of monitoring the IFSP/IEP components of IDEA, those systems seem to be as promising as many of the new practices surrounding the IFSP/IEP process itself.

CLOSING

The goal in developing recommended practices for the development of IFSPs and IEPs is to define strategies that, when used, lead to positive changes for the child and are at the same time empowering for the family and other team members (Andrews & Andrews, 1993). The use of a design that includes team empowerment is the difference between the traditional approach to the development of the IFSP and IEP and the recommended practices approach to the development of these documents. The indicators discussed in this chapter evolved from the principles of collaboration between team members and of inclusion of children who have a disability and families in their natural environments. By embedding the use of the indicators within these two principles, all team members, whether family members, service providers, or friends, can experience the development of the motivation, resources and skills, and responsive context that contribute to empowerment for them all.

During the coming decade, recommended practices for the development of IFSPs and IEPs will continue to change. These practices for the most immediate future should promote the continuation and development of synergistic partnerships among family members, service providers, and friends. These partnerships will grow to include the broader community, not just the "disability" community. Possibly the day will come when recommended practice includes an IFSP or IEP to meet the strengths and needs of every child, not just of those whose needs are "special."

REFERENCES

Able-Boone, H. (1993). Family participation in the IFSP process: Family or professional driven? *Infant–Toddler Intervention, 3*(1), 63–72.

Able-Boone, H., Sandall, S. R., Stevens, E., & Fredrick, L. L. (1992). Family support resources and needs: How early intervention can make a difference. *Infant–Toddler Intervention, 2*(2), 93–102.

Amado, R. (1993). Loneliness: Effects and implications. In A. Amado (Ed.), *Friendships and community connections between people with and without developmental disabilities* (pp. 67–85). Baltimore: Brookes.

Andrews, M. A., & Andrews, J. R. (1993). Family-centered techniques: Integrating enablement into the IFSP process. *Journal of Childhood Communication Disorders, 15*(1), 41–46.

Bailey, D. B. (1989). Case management in early intervention. *Journal of Early Intervention, 13*, 120–134.

Bailey, D. B., Blasco, P. M., & Simeonsson, R. J. (1992). Needs expressed by mothers and fathers of young children with disabilities. *American Journal on Mental Retardation, 97*, 1–10.

Bailey, D., Buysee, V., Edmonson, R., & Smith, T. (1992). Creating family-centered services in early intervention: Perceptions of professionals in four states. *Exceptional Children, 58*(4), 298–309.

Bailey, D. B., & Winton, P. J. (1987). Stability and change in parents' expectations about mainstreaming. *Topics in Early Childhood Special Education, 7*(2), 73–88.

Brault, L. (1992). Achieving integration for infants and toddlers with special needs: Recommendations for practice. *Infants and Young Children, 5*(2), 78–85.

Bricker, D. D., Peck, C. A., & Odom, S. L. (1993). Integration: Campaign for the new century. In C. Peck, S. Odom, & D. Bricker (Eds.) *Integrating young children with disabilities into community programs* (pp. 271-276). Baltimore: Brookes.

Brown, C. (1991). IFSP implementation of the fourth year of P.L. 99-457: The year of the paradox. *Topics in Early Childhood Special Education, 11*(3), 1–18.

Campbell, M., & Failey, R. (1993). Teams and teamwork: Parental Perspectives. *ASHA, 35,* 32–33.

Campbell, P., Strickland, B., & La Forme, C. (1992). Enhancing parent participation in the individualized family service plan. *Topics in Early Childhood Special Education, 11*(4), 112–124.

Child Development Resources. (1993). *Monitoring practices for Part H.* Unpublished telephone survey. Lightfoot, VA.

Christensen, C. M. (1992). Multi-cultural competencies in early intervention: Training professionals for a pluralistic society. *Infants and Young Children, 4*(3), 49–63.

Cochran, M., & Dean, C. (1991). Home–school relations and the empowerment process. *The Elementary School Journal, 91*(3), 262–269.

Cooper, C. S., & Allred, K. W. (1992). A comparison of mothers' versus fathers' needs for support in caring for a young child with special needs. *Infant–Toddler Intervention, 2*(2), 205–221.

Craig, J. H., & Craig, M. (1974). *Synergic power: Beyond domination and permissiveness.* Berkeley, CA: Proactive Press.

Demchak, M., & Drinkwater, S. (1992). Preschoolers with severe disabilities: The case against segregation. *Topics in Childhood Special Education, 11*(4), 70–83.

Division for Early Childhood. (1993). DEC position statement on inclusion. *DEC Communicator, 19*(4), 4.

Dunst, C., Johnson, C., Trivette, C. M., & Hemby, D. (1991). Family-oriented early intervention policies and practices: Family centered or not? *Exceptional Children, 58,* 115–126.

Dunst, C. J., & Trivette, C. M. (1989). An enablement and empowerment perspective of case management. *Topics in Early Childhood Special Education, 8*(4), 87–102.

Education of the Handicapped Act Amendments of 1986, 20 U.S.C. § 1400 *et seq.*

Fewell, R. R., Snyder, P., Sexton, D., & Hockless, M. F. (1991). Implementing IFSPs in Louisiana: Different formats for family-centered practices under Part H. *Topics in Early Childhood Special Education, 11*(3), 54–65.

Garland, C., & Linder, T. (1988). Administrative challenges in early intervention. In J. Jordan, J. Gallagher, P. Hutinger, & M. Karnes (Eds.), *Early childhood special education: Birth to three* (pp. 5–28). Reston, VA: Council for Exceptional Children.

Goldstein, S., Strickland, B., Turnbull, A. P., & Curry, L. (1980). An observational analysis of the IEP conference. *Exceptional Children, 46,* 278–286.

Gowen, J. W., Christy, D. S., & Sparling, J. (1993). Informational needs of parents of young children with special needs. *Journal of Early Intervention, 17,* 194–210.

Green, A. L., & Stoneman, Z. (1989). Attitudes of mothers and fathers of nonhandicapped children. *Journal of Early Intervention, 13,* 292–304.

Guralnick, M. J. (in press). Mothers' perceptions of the benefits and drawbacks of early childhood mainstreaming. *Journal of Early Intervention.*

Ilott, B. (1993). *Parent training and information projects* (7th ed.). College Park, GA: Technical Assistance for Parent Programs (TAPP).

Kalyanpur, M., & Rao, S. S. (1991). Empowering low-income black families of handicapped children. *American Journal of Orthopsychiatry, 61,* 523–532.

Kieffer, C. H. (1984). Citizen empowerment: A developmental perspective. *Prevention in Human Services, 3,* 9–35.

Kjerland, L., & Kovach, J. (1990). Family–staff collaboration for tailored infant assessment. In E. P. Gibbs & D. M. Teti (Eds.), *Interdisciplinary assessment of infants: A guide for early intervention professionals* (pp. 287–297). Baltimore: Brookes.

Lamorey, S., & Bricker, D. (1993). Integrated programs: Effects on young children and their parents. In C. Peck, S. Odom, & D. Bricker (Eds.), *Integrating young children with disabilities into community programs* (pp. 249–270). Baltimore: Brookes.

Lee, I. (1993). *A validation study of the family-centered program rating scale.* Unpublished doctoral dissertation, University of Kansas, Lawrence.

LeLaurin, K. (1992). Infant and toddler-models of service delivery: Are they detrimental for some children and families? *Topics in Early Childhood Special Education, 12*(1), 82–104.

Levine, J. (1993). Involving fathers in Head Start: A framework for public policy and program development. *Families in Society, 74*(1), 4–21.

Leviton, A., Mueller, M., & Kauffman, C. (1992). The family-centered consultation model: Practical applications for professionals. *Infants and Young Children, 4*(3), 1–8.

Mahoney, G., O'Sullivan, P., & Dennebaum, J. (1990). Maternal perceptions of early intervention services: A scale for assessing family-focused intervention. *Topics in Early Childhood Special Education, 10*(1), 1–15.

McGonigel, M. J., & Garland, C. W. (1988). The individualized family service plan and the early intervention team: Team and family issues and recommended practices. *Infants and Young Children, 1*(1), 10–21.

McGonigel, M. J., Kaufmann, R. K., & Johnson, B. H. (Eds.). (1991). *Guidelines and recommended practices for the individualized service plan.* Bethesda, MD: Association for the Care of Children's Health.

McWilliams, R. A. (1992). *Family-centered intervention planning: A routines-based approach.* Tucson, AZ: Communication Skill Builders.

Nash, J. K. (1990). Public Law 99–457: Facilitating family participation on the multidisciplinary team. *Journal of Early Intervention, 14,* 318–326.

Natural environments for infants and toddlers. (1993, Fall/Winter). *Coalition Quarterly: Early Childhood Bulletin,* p. 13.

Nevin, A., Thousand, J., Paolucci-Whitcomb, P., & Villa, R. (1990). Collaborative consultation: Empowering public school personnel to provide heterogeneous schooling for all—or, who rang that bell?. *Journal of Educational and Psychological Consultation, 1*(1), 41–67.

Odom, S., & Brown, W. (1993). Social interaction skills intervention for young children with disabilities in integrated settings. In C. Peck, S. Odom, & D. Bricker (Eds.), *Integrating young children with disabilities into community programs* (pp. 39–64). Baltimore: Brookes.

Peck, C. A., Carlson, P., & Helmstetter, E. (1992). Parent and teacher perceptions of outcomes for nonhandicapped children enrolled in integrated early childhood programs: A statewide study. *Journal of Early Intervention, 16,* 53–63.

Powell, T. H., & Gallagher, P. A. (1993). *Brothers and sisters—A special part of exceptional families* (2nd ed.). Baltimore: Brookes.

Raab, M., Davis, M., & Trepanier, A. (1993). Resources versus services: Changing the focus of intervention for infants and young children. *Infants and Young Children, 5*(3), 1–11.

Santelli, B., Turnbull, A., Lerner, E., & Marquis, J. (1993). Parent-to-parent programs: A unique form of mutual support for families of persons with disabilities. In G. Singer & L. Powers (Eds.), *Families, disability, and empowerment* (pp. 27–58). Baltimore: Brookes.

Schon, D. A. (1983). *The reflective practitioner: How professionals think in action.* New York: Basic Books.

Seligman, M., & Darling, R. (1989). *Ordinary families, special children.* New York: Guilford Press.

Shelton, T. L., Jeppson, E. S., & Johnson, B. H. (1987). *Family-centered care for children with special health care needs* (2nd ed.). Washington, DC: Association for the Care of Children's Health.

Silverstein, R. (1989). A window of opportunity. In *The intent and spirit of P.L. 99-457: A sourcebook.* Washington, DC: National Center for Clinical Infant Programs.

Slentz, K. L., & Bricker, D. (1992). Family-guided assessment. *Journal of Early Intervention, 16,* 11–19.

Smith, P. M. (1993). Opening many, many doors: Parent-to-parent support. In P. J. Beckman & G. B. Boyes (Eds.), *Deciphering the system: A guide for families of young children with disabilities* (pp. 130–141). Cambridge, MA: Brookline Books.

Sokoly, M. S., & Dokecki, P. R. (1992). Ethical perspectives on family-centered early intervention. *Infants and Young Children, 4*(4), 23–32.

Sprague, J., & Brunk, G. (1993). *Readiness to act: A model of self-determination.* Unpublished manuscript, Department of Sociology, University of Kansas, Lawrence.

Stineman, R. M., Morningstar, M. E., Bishop, B., & Turnbull, H. (1993). Role of families in transition planning for young adults with disabilities. *Journal of Vocational Rehabilitation, 3*(2), 52–61.

Stonestreet, R. H., Johnston, R. G., & Acton, S. J. (1991). Guidelines or real partnerships with parents. *Infant–Toddler Intervention, 1*(1), 37–46.

Strickland, B., & Turnbull, A. (1990). *Developing and implementing the individualized education plan.* Columbus, OH: Merrill.

Summers, J. A., Dell'Oliver, C., Turnbull, A. P., Benson, H. A., Santelli, B., Campbell, M., & Segal-Causey, E. (1990). Examining the individualized family service plan process: What are family and practitioner preferences? *Topics in Early Childhood Special Education, 10*(1), 78–99.

Tannen, D. (1990). *You just don't understand.* New York: Ballantine.

Turnbull, A. (1993, November). *Fathers as "less apparent" in early childhood special education research and service delivery.* Paper presented at the meeting of the National Reserach Council/Institute of Medicine, Washington, DC.

Turnbull, A., & Summers, J. A. (1985). From parent involvement to family support. In S. Pueschel, C. Tingey, J. Rynders, A. Crocker, & D. Crutcher (Eds.), *New perspectives on Down's syndrome* (pp. 289–306). Baltimore: Brookes.

Turnbull, A., & Turnbull, R. (1990). *Families, professionals, and exceptionality: A special partnership.* Columbus, OH: Merrill.

Turnbull, A. P., Winton, P. J., Blacher, J., & Salkind, N. (1983). Mainstreaming in the kindergarten classroom: Perspectives of parents of handicapped and nonhandicapped children. *Journal of the Division of Early Childhood, 6,* 14–20.

Vadasy, P .F., Fewell, R. R., & Meyer, D.J. (1986). Grandparents of children with special needs: Insights into their experiences and concerns. *Journal of the Division of Early Childhood, 10,* 36–44.

Vandercook, T., York, J., & Forest, M. (1989). The McGill Action Planning System (MAPS): A strategy for building the vision. *The Journal of Association for Persons With Severe Handicaps, 14,* 205–215.

Zipper, I. N., Weil, M., & Rounds, K. (1991). *Service coordination for early intervention parents and professionals.* Chapel Hill: University of North Carolina, Frank Porter Graham Child Development Center.

CHAPTER 5

The Widespread Adoption of Service Delivery Recommendations: A Systems Change Perspective

Phillip S. Strain
Barbara J. Smith
R. A. McWilliam

Service delivery models consist of the overall pattern and location of interventions for young children who have disabilities or who are at risk for disabilities and their families. The recommended practice indicators for service delivery models are organized by common early intervention settings: homes, centers, clinics, and hospitals. A number of practices are grouped together, however, because they should be employed in all settings.

PRINCIPLES

Six general principles guided the selection of recommended practice indicators: normalization, family-centered services, cross-disciplinary service delivery, inclusion of both empirical and value-driven practices, and inclusion of both developmentally and chronologically age-appropriate practices.

Normalization

Optimal services are provided in a way that does not unnecessarily restrict opportunities for children and families. The language in the Individuals with Disabilities Education Act of 1990 (IDEA) states that children should be placed in the least restrictive environment, which is interpreted by many early childhood professionals to mean the most natural setting for young children. Indeed, IDEA presumes that services for a child with a disability will be provided in the most natural environment unless it is shown not to be in the best interest of the child. This is not simply a placement issue, however: The method of providing services, regardless of setting, should allow for maximum participation in the "mainstream." Despite the challenges that a disability might place on a child's and family's ability to lead an ordinary existence, good services promote the potential for "normal" rather than "disabled" routines. Hence, indicators are included that base the nature, delivery, and scope of intervention upon activities of daily living (Service Delivery Model [SDM] 11); that provide fun environments that stimulate children's initiations, choices, and engagement with the social and material ecology (SDM 24); that prepare children for the next, less restrictive environment (SDM 31); and that provide neonatal intensive care unit environments that are appropriate for the neurological status and developmental level of the child (SDM 34).

Family-Centered Service

A second principle was that service delivery models should (a) reflect the recognition that the child is part of a family unit; (b) be responsive to the family's priorities, concerns, and needs; and (c) allow the family to participate in early intervention with their child as much as they desire (Bailey, McWilliam, & Winton, 1992). Services that previously might have been geared almost exclusively toward children must now provide for flexibility, expertise, and resources to meet the needs of other members of the family, as those needs relate to the child's development (IDEA). It is strongly recommended that service providers rethink the concept of "parent involvement" (Foster, Berger, & McLean, 1981). The concept "getting parents more involved in their child's education" presumes that families are not already "involved" and that the opportunities for parent involvement (e.g., parent education classes) are worthwhile for individual families, *compared to their competing priorities*.[1] Thus, the indicators include giving families choices in the nature of services (SDM 3), matching the level of intensity desired by the family (SDM 13), providing center-based services close to where families live (SDM 16), encouraging and supporting families to be with children during clinic-based procedures (SDM 28), and giving families opportunities to participate in hospital-based services (SDM 35).

Cross-Disciplinary Service Delivery

One model for increasing the opportunity for family members to make meaningful decisions and to participate in early intervention as much as

---

[1]Although we agree with the Chinese proverb that it is better to light a candle than to curse the darkness, the need to suggest recommended practice has been clear because of our experiences with services that have violated our values, evidence from research, or families' desires. It is sometimes useful, therefore, to articulate what we in the profession are trying to get away from as well as what we are moving toward.

they want is cross-disciplinary service delivery (Raver, 1991). This model, as described in Chapter 1, involves team members' sharing roles: Each specialist helps other members to acquire skills related to the specialist's area of expertise. This cross-disciplinary sharing requires both *role release* (accepting that others can do what the specialist was trained specifically to do) and *role acceptance* (accepting that one's job can include more than what one was specifically trained to do). Cross-disciplinary service delivery encourages a whole-child and whole-family approach, allows for the efficient use of the primary interventionists (i.e., the child and family do not always need to see many different specialists), and fosters skill development in interventionists. The list of indicators includes only three that are somewhat related to this model: employing pull-out services when routine, activity-based options have failed (SDM 20); providing noncategorical center-based services (SDM 21); and consultants' communicating regularly with center-based staff and families (SDM 26). This small number of indicators probably underrepresents the importance of cross-disciplinary service delivery.

Was such a small number of indicators addressing cross-disciplinary service delivery included because they would be too controversial? Certainly many specialists and their professional associations have stated reservations about the idea that their services could be supplanted by other professionals assuming some of the roles. The most threatening argument against cross-disciplinary service delivery is that it is illegal to practice without a license or to teach without a certificate. This argument reveals a lack of understanding about the judicious use of this model. After all, specialists almost always give families suggestions about how they can do "speech–language therapy," "occupational therapy," "physical therapy," or "special education" with their children. At a time when there are enormous shortages of specialized personnel (Yoder, Coleman, & Gallagher, 1990), when, more than ever, the importance of integrating interventions across developmental domains is recognized, and when early intervention staff roles are being redefined (LeLaurin, 1992), more indicators directly addressing cross-disciplinary service delivery probably should have been included.

Empirically and Value-Driven Practices

For 20 years or so, there has been a steady output of research related to young children with disabilities and their families. Some of these studies are better than others; the most believable findings are those that have been replicated. From this body of work, it was possible to include indicators that are empirically sound, such as adult–children ratios that maximize safety, health, and promotion of identified goals (SDM 19); barrier-free center environments (SDM 22); and environments to promote high levels of engagement (SDM 25). Interestingly, most of the research-based indicators are associated with environments.

A number of indicators address the importance of measuring the effectiveness of services. Most researchers and interventionists would agree that the evaluation of services is haphazard at best. Researchers often find they cannot use the existing data collected by service providers; many of the decisions, both at the individual child and family level and at the program level, are based as much on intuition as on data. More accountable systems are necessary, but they need to be flexible enough to allow for adjustments in families' priorities, children's development, personnel availability, and program resources. Indicators supporting the importance of data collection include measuring effectiveness and communicating results to the family (SDM 2); monitoring service delivery to ensure that agreed-upon procedures and outcomes are achieved in a timely fashion (SDM 4); monitoring interventions frequently and making changes in programming as needed (SDM 9); and continuing clinic-based services only as long as is necessary to reach prearranged goals (SDM 29).

The importance of unproven but highly valued practices must also be acknowledged. Many of these "value-based" indicators emerged from families' and professionals' bad experiences; they stem from a desire to guide services in positive directions and away from practices that violate currently held beliefs and priorities. Considering the enormous diversity of families in early intervention, we professionals cannot be sure that we truly represent all families' values. The most important safeguard against a paternalistic approach, however, is to individualize practices for each child and family. The canon of individualization characterizes early intervention and distinguishes it from other early childhood services; it reflects a strongly held value in our field. Indicators guided by values include having someone available to speak the family's preferred language (SDM 6); basing communication with family members on principles of mutual respect, caring, and sensitivity (SDM 14); making center environments safe and clean (SDM 15); employing clinic-based services only when they are identified as the least restrictive option (SDM 27); and giving opportunities for the family to have access to medical decision making (SDM 36).

Developmentally Appropriate Practice

At the time these indicators are being delineated by the Division for Early Childhood (DEC), the field of early intervention is undergoing examination from within and without as to the developmental appropriateness of its practices. *Developmentally appropriate practice* (DAP) is a term coined by the National Association for the Education of Young Children (NAEYC) to refer to educational methods that are appropriate both for the developmental level of the child as well as for the child's individual needs (Bredekamp, 1987). Early childhood special education (ECSE) has been particularly strong in the practices that address a child's individual characteristics. The strengths of both DAP and the traditional ECSE emphasis on individualization are recognized through indicators such as individualization of services in response to children's characteristics, preferences, interests, abilities, and health status (SDM 7); and curricula that are unbiased and nondiscriminatory with regard to disability, gender, race, religion, and ethnic and cultural origin (SDM 17). As the research base for DAP increases, it is likely that additional recommended practices will be identified.

Some of the recommended practices for service delivery models are stated directly and with no apology (e.g., "Professionals keep appointments in a timely fashion," SDM 33). Some are possibly controversial (e.g., "Programs employ clinic-based services only when they are identified as the least restrictive option," SDM 27). Many, however, will be considered platitudinous; they are little more than common sense and are eminently socially acceptable (e.g., "Environments are safe and clean," SDM 15). These have been included, however, because, unfortunately, they are not universally practiced.

Multicultural

A final guiding principle used to craft these service delivery recommendations was the recognition and appreciation of the rich and diverse cultural backgrounds that make up the U.S. population today. Specific manifestations of this multicultural concern include indicators such as the following: Someone in the program or immediately available to the program speaks the family's preferred language (SDM 6); staff base their communication with family members on principles of mutual respect, caring, and sensitivity (SDM 14); and services ensure an unbiased, nondiscriminatory curriculum with regard to disability, gender, race, religion, and ethnic and cultural origin. Parenthetically, we might add that service programs would likely enhance their probability of achieving these recommended practices by employing staff who reflect the diversity of the client population served.

RECOMMENDED PRACTICE INDICATORS AND SOCIAL CHANGE

The recommended practice guidelines on service delivery models mark an important, necessary, and dramatic departure from past and current practice. The actual content of the guidelines, however, is not the point of radical departure. Rather, what is truly novel here is the implied presumption that there are acceptable ways of conducting the business of service delivery and, therefore, that there are unacceptable practices. In a field that has derived much of its vitality from innovation, entrepreneurial activity, and a decided lack of professional regulatory intrusion, this is indeed a dramatic departure from the past.

Elsewhere (Strain, 1991), the downsides associated with the profession's regulatory-free existence have been chronicled: (a) the promotion of data-less curricula and teaching tactics, (b) the absence of a rational presumption of quality assurance for clients, and (c) training programs that unwittingly serve to perpetuate unproven or even disproven methods. Of course, having a guiding point like the recommended practices document is but the first of a thousand steps needed to create a professional culture in which standards of excellence are widely implemented, valued, and continually reexamined in the light of emerging information and changing societal needs.

In this chapter we hope to take the reader on but a few of the next steps that are likely needed to bring the service delivery recommended practices to fruition. For discussion clarity we refer to these steps according to the following categories: (a) attitudinal issues, (b) fiscal and regulatory issues, (c) personnel preparation issues, and (d) program-level issues. It will also become clear that these categories are quite permeable and interdependent. After examining these four sets of issues, we offer a model of systems change that may be used at multiple organizational levels to move the service delivery recommendations toward widespread adoption and use.

Attitudinal Issues

There can be little doubt that our attitudes and beliefs profoundly color our professional lives (Smith & Rose, 1993). Moreover, it seems abundantly clear that the DEC-recommended-practices document as a whole and the specific service delivery guidelines will elicit many strong reactions. The magnitude of change implied for most programs is reason enough to engender fear and resistance. Moreover, certain elements of the service delivery recommendations (e.g., those supporting developmentally integrated programming) will likely clash with strongly held attitudes and beliefs.

As an example of the role of attitudes, let us explore in some depth the probable impact of our prointegration, inclusion guidelines (e.g., SDM 1, SDM 24, SDM 31, SDM 34) on those who believe in and practice segregated service delivery. Over the last several years, Smith and Rose have done considerable work on attitudinal issues regarding inclusion. Rose and Smith (1993) have conducted a nationwide study of attitudes related to integration that is particularly relevant to this discussion. The types of attitudes reported on their national survey were categorized as follows: turf, teacher preparedness, awareness, "someone will lose," and communication/collaboration/respect.

Turf Attitudes

The pride that the special education community feels related to the provision of services to children with disabilities is powerful and long standing. Survey respondents reported that many special educators are "holding on to the segregated systems of educating children" due to these turf issues.

The location of inclusive preschool services (center based vs. community based) has also contributed to the development of turf issues. As more children with disabilities are placed in community-based preschools, and thus removed from close monitoring by special educators, these individuals report concern about how "their" children are being educated. Special educators believe they have been trained specifically to provide "the best" educational experiences for children with disabilities. They report a loss of control over the very methods, techniques, and curricula presumed to be most effective. Relatedly, special educators also reported concern about the receptivity of community-based programs to technical assistance that they deem critical to ensuring high-quality services. We suspect that where turf issues now exist, when combined with rapidly changing roles for special educators, the prointegration recommendations will initially serve to heighten these attitudes (Smith & Rose, 1993).

Teacher Preparedness Attitudes

In most cases, public school personnel have different teacher certification requirements and varying levels of professional training than do Head Start or community-based preschool teachers. These differences have contributed to public school personnel's harboring some doubts about the expertise of community-based and Head Start teachers. Special educators also reported concern about having children with disabilities placed in community-based preschool settings due to a lack of resources and support personnel available. It was reported that some parents may be reluctant to have their child placed outside of the public school system due to a lack of teacher training related to the needs of children with disabilities.

Community-based providers also expressed concerns about their preparedness to serve children with disabilities, particularly children with severe disabilities or children who are medically fragile. Second, childcare teachers reported that special educators lack basic child development knowledge that childcare teachers believe they have.

Survey respondents reported that the curricula of some prekindergarten and kindergarten programs have too strong an academic focus.

This academic orientation can appear to preclude the placement of children with disabilities in those classrooms (Smith & Rose, 1993).

Awareness

A broad consensus among respondents was the need for more information sharing with respect to children with disabilities. Specific training needs identified by respondents included information on specific disabilities, medical needs, early childhood programming and services, curricula and methods, and integration efforts. Information gathered via other surveys indicates that families very much want and need accurate and up-to-date information about inclusion models, outcomes, and caveats.

Communication/Collaboration/Respect

Parents reported that the people making decisions about their children do not really know the issues because they do not have children with disabilities themselves, and public school personnel believe that community providers are not receptive to technical assistance from the special education community. Communication, collaboration, and respect have been combined here because the attitude barriers related to these issues all seem to stem from the same source, misinformation about other people and programs. This lack of information sharing has been reported to occur at all levels (local, state, and federal). It is difficult to have respect for a program about which little is known and where no relationship with the providers exists.

"Public school officials at the state and local level do not make information available about preschool mainstreaming," was the response from one survey respondent. Similarly, respondents reported that information about specific programs, such as Head Start or childcare programs, was not being effectively communicated (Smith & Rose, 1993).

"Someone Will Lose" Attitudes

Respondents expressed concern about the quality of outcomes for both children with disabilities and typically developing children in integrated settings. Some respondents reported that parents of both typically developing children and children with disabilities were concerned that integration could result in fewer and less appropriate services for their children.

For typically developing children in integrated preschool settings, the concern was that they would not receive a quality preschool experience because the children with disabilities would require an inordinate amount of time and attention from the classroom teacher. Relatedly, fear that the child with a disability would disrupt classroom teaching for the typically developing children was also expressed.

Many survey respondents reported that public school personnel fear a loss of identity and control as a consequence of using community-based preschool placements. Specifically, the public school special education personnel are concerned that they may not be able to supervise the child's IEP adequately in settings outside their traditional administrative purview. Survey respondents reported that parents and public school personnel are reluctant to have children placed in regular education classrooms because they fear that their child will not receive the specialized instruction or intensity of services that may be provided in specialized settings (Smith & Rose, 1993).

The preceding analysis of attitudinal issues with regard to the prointegration recommendations in fact represents what we hope will be a universal second step in the process of creating widespread and lasting change. From a teaching perspective, professionals may equate this attitudinal analysis with collecting baseline information. Professionals are attempting to understand the client (early intervention providers in this case) as thoroughly as possible and, in so doing, to understand the nature, scope, and foci of intervention they must bring to bear if they wish to create change. By way of a simple example, if we in the profession do not know about or attend systematically and respectfully to "someone will lose" attitudes, we will likely not reach our change goals with the clients in question. Notice, also, that individual clients or groups of clients will likely reveal a highly unique pattern of attitudinal issues. It follows then that intervention with and for fellow professionals and paraprofessionals must be as individualized as are the interventions for children and families.

Fiscal and Regulatory Issues

The service delivery recommendations were shared with administrative personnel who were not involved in the recommendation process but who nonetheless have superordinate authority in their administrative capacities to promote or squelch these or any other recommendations. Two predominant themes have emerged. First, these individuals saw and were concerned about the fiscal implications of almost each and every recommendation. Second, these individuals saw that if the recommendations were to have real power and guiding authority they must be translated into existing and occasionally conflicting public policies and regulations.

Consider several examples. Many concerns were voiced regarding the "safe environment" recommendation (SDM 15). Although all administrative personnel fully supported the intent of the recommendation, they enumerated a number of fiscal and regulatory issues. On a fiscal level, the following issues were raised: (a) existing policy and legislative prohibitions regarding the expenditure of capital funds; (b) balancing safety interests and fiscal issues with "conflicting" expenditure interests to improve salaries and benefits and to expand the range and intensity of service delivery; and (c) working within legislated zero-growth budget guidelines. In essence, the common thread here is not simply a complaint about lack of dollars but how one might achieve a high level of safety in buildings and materials within political and fiscal contexts permeated by conflicting interests, "win–lose" decisions across categories of expenditures, and generally constricted budgetary guidelines. Similar kinds of concerns were expressed in regard to recommendations having to do with bringing services as close as possible to families, expanding the array of service options, and providing linguistically diverse staff.

We wish to convey three general principles here. First, many of the service delivery recommendations carry profound fiscal implications. To ignore, downplay, or otherwise fail to highlight this fact is to do a disservice. Second, not every level of service delivery or category of professional or paraprofessional in the field has the authority, leverage, or political power to influence the amount or priorities of funding. Consequently, accountability on practices that require, almost de facto, changes in service delivery expenditures must be reasonably and precisely placed on relevant entities and individuals. Although it may be incumbent on direct service delivery personnel to identify and document unsafe situations, it would be unreasonable to hold these same individuals accountable for proposing a bond issue, reallocating state flow-through dollars, or changing discretionary-dollar priorities. The third principle is implied in the second, namely, that multiple constituents must be a part of any plan to change the level or foci of funding. In the systems change section of this chapter, we detail strategies for constituent input and action planning.

Just as many of the service delivery recommended practices have significant fiscal implications, so do they have significant implications for regulatory policies and procedures that govern the actions of many different service delivery systems. Let us return again to the seemingly straightforward and inarguable recommendation related to safety. In examining this recommendation, several local administrators strongly suggested that clear and consistent language related to safety issues should be included in

- the state's education act dealing specifically with licensure criteria,
- Head Start regulations,
- childcare regulations governing both family-based and center-based services, and
- contract language between legally responsible entities and private providers.

Once again, the necessity for multiple-constituency input and planning is abundantly clear.

In relation to the safety recommendation, these same individuals suggested that in many areas the early intervention program was the safest setting available to families. In these situations, they suggested that safety concerns should also apply to

- people traveling from their home to services,
- people living in unsafe neighborhoods, and
- staff traveling in settings seen as unsafe because of a high incidence of violent crime.

When asked to consider the implications of the prointegration recommendations, the same group of administrative constituents identified the following regulatory needs:

- to simplify contracting regulations to facilitate the use of typical childcare settings,
- to alter some classroom funding formulas incompatible with itinerant service models,
- to alter current agreements with transportation companies to allow more flexible travel to more varied sites, and
- to modify program standards to ensure that high-quality indicators of integrated education are included.

Again, if the foregoing analysis of fiscal and regulatory issues is conceptualized as needed baseline information for designing and implementing strategies that foster the use of the recommendations, three overarching themes emerge. First, the impact of the recommended practices, when taken seriously and thoughtfully, is profound and complex. These practices do not have an impact only on practitioners. They also affect attitudes, values, budgets, and regulatory and statutory language. Second, change toward the adoption of the recommendations in part or as a whole will likely be incremental. Simply put, the diversity of individuals and systems affected will require a change strategy with carefully selected and articulated goals, time lines that take the complexity into account, and goal-monitoring systems that highlight the small causes for celebration along the path to widespread adoption. Third, it seems reasonable to think of the recommendations on service delivery as beginning points in a continuing dialogue with those affected. We acknowledge the legitimate, multiple impacts of any such set of professional recommendations. We also believe that giving due respect to multiple impacts is a necessary step toward faithful adoption and use of the recommendations.

Personnel Preparation Issues

Undoubtedly, the service delivery recommendations, indeed all of the DEC-recommended practices, have profound implications for the *who, what,* and *how* of personnel preparation. Here, we examine several of the issues that are brought into focus by the service delivery recommendations.

The who issue, as alluded to earlier, is nowhere more salient than in the recommended cross-disciplinary model of service delivery (SDM 20). Traditional roles change, people relinquish embedded ways of thinking and doing, and the lines between disciplines become obliterated. When all these things occur, very legitimate questions emerge, such as the following:

- Who should be certified to do what with children and families? Or, does the profession need to revamp the concept of certification?

- How are service delivery systems staffed when multiple paid and nonpaid people conduct overlapping activities?

- Who shall ensure the competence of practitioners when traditional-discipline personnel are removed one step from client contact?

Answering these kinds of who questions at national, state, and local levels will be a key ingredient in moving forward with the recommended practices.

The what issues that emerge from the service delivery recommendations go directly to the scope and sequence of both preservice and inservice training efforts. The long-term objective at the preservice level would involve the installation of specific course work and practical experiences designed to support trainees in acquiring skills to implement the recommendations. Obviously, the recommended practices are not meant as an inclusive and exclusive training content. Neither does it seem likely that one can acquire the relevant competencies without exposure to service systems that are at least attempting to implement the recommendations. Although we are not naive to the often circuitous paths that new courses of study follow in higher education, we can point out a number of historical examples where other disciplines have profoundly influenced courses of study at the university level. Specifically, we are referring to the disciplines of clinical psychology, speech pathology, law, and, to a lesser extent, clinical social work. Each of these disciplines maintain direct regulation and oversight of higher education via the adoption of personnel standards that specify course work, competencies, and ongoing inservice needed to acquire and maintain credentials.

As a content guide, the service delivery recommendations can also aid in the crafting of the scope of inservice activities for professionals, paraprofessionals, and families. From a logistical standpoint the sheer amount of inservice training needed to support just one set of recommendations is enormous. Clearly the task is far beyond the ubiquitous half day in September and in June. Notice also that the recommendations imply action rather than rhetoric. To state the obvious at risk of seeming foolish, training on practices should occur where and when people practice! Therefore, we see functional inservice efforts as occurring on site, focused on real situations, and evaluated via changes in the actions of service providers. Although this concept of the how of inservice training is rarely found in action, the Commonwealth of Pennsylvania has been operating just such a system for 4 years. Some 20 consultants are available on a full-time basis to work directly with providers on issues that providers deem important. Moreover, this training system, known as the Family-Focused Early Intervention System (FFEIS), conducts regional and statewide workshops to enhance provider capacities on issues seen as critical to the Commonwealth, namely inclusion and family-centered services. We would be remiss if we did not mention that this statewide system of technical assistance is supplemented by a comprehensive, multiyear, external evaluation of the quality of early intervention service delivery.

Several lessons learned over the course of the past 4 years on the FFEIS project may be useful for conceptualizing the relevant inservice tasks needed to enact the service delivery recommendations. These lessons include the importance of

- providing predominate training resources to client-driven, field-based consultation;
- providing local teams of providers with the responsibility for helping to define the who, what, and where of training;
- brokering various training topics to local experts, thereby increasing the likely intensity of training available;
- maintaining continuity with sites and trainees via individualized points of contact; and
- publicly recognizing and rewarding outstanding practitioners and programs.

Forging a personnel preparation system that supports the recommended practices is a daunting, nationwide, multiconstituency task. And, it is precisely the job before the profession.

Program-Level Issues

As with the fiscal and regulatory issues, the recommended service delivery practices were shared with early intervention providers who were not a part of the recommendation development process. Their expressed concerns offer a rich database regarding the "street-level" implementation of the recommended practices.

The first set of issues revolves around the question, "How will we know when we are doing things right?" Specific issues emerged:

- the need to define individual recommendations precisely with examples and nonexamples to aid in assessment;
- the need to develop a logistical plan for program assessment, including who will do the assessment, when it will occur, and how the results will be provided to relevant parties; and
- the need to coordinate and correlate program assessment with existing systems for assessing child and family outcomes.

A second set of issues raised by practitioners centered on the question, "Where do we start?" For many of these individuals, their service delivery programs now fall short on numerous recommended practices, and they wondered about a scheme that would allow a logical and orderly process of change. Specific subissues are reflected in this where-to-start theme:

- the need to determine if there is some reasoned developmental ordering of the service delivery recommendations, the intent being to follow such an ordering in changing their systems;
- the need to establish a broadly representative group that would be charged with guiding, monitoring, and institutionalizing change;
- the need to avoid abandoning sound practices in the predicted fervor to overhaul all elements of a program; and
- the need to establish, at the outset, a resources and fiscal plan to parallel and support plans for procedural changes in the program.

A third set of issues raised by practitioners centered on the question, "How do we deal with predictable roadblocks?" The roadblocks identified included

- staff who are habitual naysayers,
- staff feeling threatened or indirectly attacked by the proposed changes,

- convincing now satisfied clients that the changes will be good for them,
- finding the time to plan for orderly change, and
- finding resources outside the organization to help with ongoing training needs.

As a whole, we find the concerns expressed by service providers to be realistic, solution oriented, and supportive of the recommendations. Any hint of trepidation had to do with fear of embarking on an ill-defined, poorly supported venture. A number of respondents recounted prior experiences with "innovations" that ultimately lacked administrative, client, and staff support. They simply and reasonably wished to avoid such a time- and resource-wasteful experience with the recommended practices.

Although the magnitude of the tasks needed to make the recommended practices commonplace is daunting, we believe that planful action can, indeed, bring about such a change. Toward this end, we next describe a model for systems change that incorporates many of the elements needed to effect the recommended practice of service delivery.

SYSTEMS CHANGE MODEL

Data from national surveys, case studies, and work groups conducted between 1989 and 1992 by the Research Institute on Preschool Mainstreaming have suggested a model of systems change with wide applicability for early intervention service delivery (Smith & Rose, 1993). This model was developed on the basis of qualitative research techniques, including compiling descriptive information from case-study interviews and work groups and analyzing for trends. Analyses revealed a high level of consistency in the identification of barriers and recommended systems change strategies across states and localities. Moreover, the face validity of the findings is supported by the fact that all of the change strategies that compose the model have been previously promoted as essential ingredients of a comprehensive systems change approach (Banach, 1991; Champlin, 1991; Finn, 1990; Fullen & Miles, 1992; Garland, 1982; Maeroff, 1993; Servatius, Fellows, & Kelly, 1992; U.S. General Accounting Office, 1993). The strategies reported as effective in changing systems can be organized into the following categories:

- Leadership Commitment
- Team Decision Making

- Vision Setting
- Assessment of Barriers
- Action Planning
- Policy Development and Attitude Change
- Resource Allocation/Technical Assistance
- Evaluation of Process and Outcomes

Figure 5.1 depicts the model with these critical elements of systems change as described by state and local administrators and other stakeholders. Models "give shape to ideas and concepts" (Hazel et al., 1988, p. 7). The ideas, once given "shape" by the model, are then more easily implemented, that is, the systems changed. Although there is a presumption of linear development in the model (i.e., step-by-step progression as indicated by arrows), there is also a recognition that on the basis of the ongoing evaluation and feedback system, any element may need to take priority or be revisited at any time. In light of the circumstances, there may be a desire

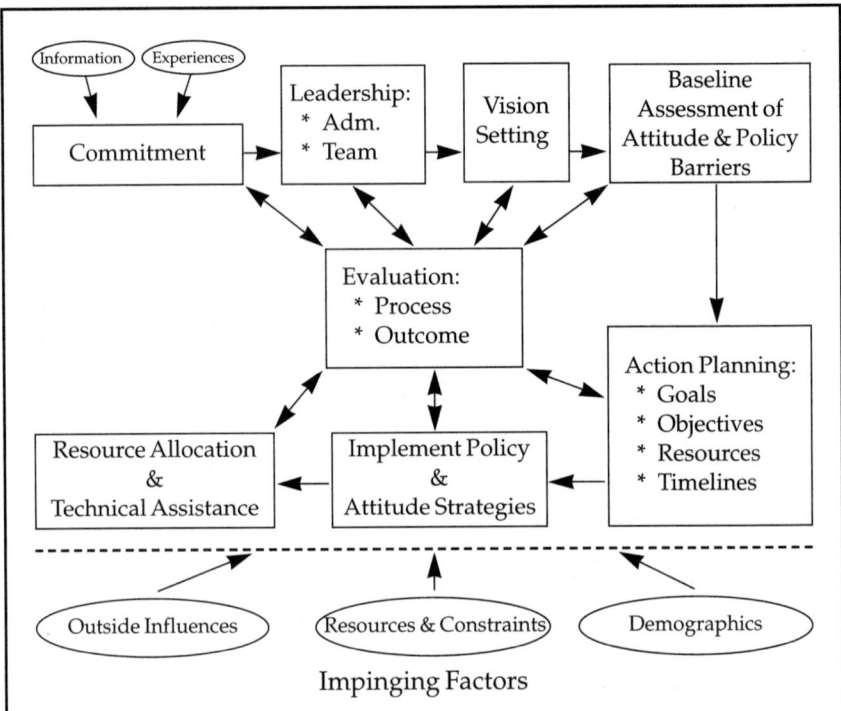

Figure 5.1. Model of systems change for preschool inclusion.

to skip forward to an element, from vision setting to policy development, for instance, in the case of an unexpected legislative window of opportunity. Generally, however, informants recommended a step-by-step, systematic approach to change. The model in Figure 5.1 also reflects the recognition of the role of impinging factors that are outside the particular systems change activities but that often have an impact either positively or negatively on them. Details of the model are presented in the following sections.

Commitment

Key to any systems change effort is the commitment of the leadership and other stakeholders (Meisels, 1985; Morgan, Guetzloe, & Swan, 1991; Smith & Rose, 1993; Striefel, Killoran, & Quinters, 1991). At all levels of service delivery (e.g., local, state, and national), decisions can be made to set the tone of the environment, to allocate resources, and to establish teams of stakeholders. We also know that the commitment on the part of leadership individuals depends on the adequacy and accuracy of the information and experiences available to them (Servatius et al., 1992; Stoneman, 1993). This information will alert them to what change is needed in their system and provide options for change (Kaluzny, 1982; Olson, 1989). In the present case, providing leadership personnel with evidence for the importance of the recommended practices is crucial.

Stakeholder Team

A change process is more likely to succeed if it is implemented by those who will be most affected by the change (Banach, 1991; Champlin, 1991; Hazel et al., 1988; Lambour, Rostetter, Sapir, & Taha, 1980; Smith & Rose, 1993). In our field, the stakeholders are the administrators who have legal responsibility for serving children with disabilities and their families (principals and district staff), parents, teachers, teacher educators, staff representing "natural environments" such as childcare programs or Head Start, and others as appropriate for the local situation. In a recent survey of school administrators, community programs, parents, and others nationwide, local school administrators were ranked as the most influential in setting school policies, parents a close second, and all others (teachers, the public, etc.) less influential. Ownership of the new system and shared vision are critical to the success of the effort (Champlin, 1991; U.S. General Accounting Office, 1993). Success at systems change requires all levels of commitment, from top down to bottom up.

Vision Setting

One of the first steps to changing a system is to define a vision of what the new system should resemble (McNulty, 1989; New Mexico State Department of Education, 1992; Servatius et al., 1992; Smith & Rose, 1993). For instance, a vision statement might be that all young children will be educated in environments that meet the DEC service delivery recommendations. The vision should be developed by the stakeholder team and should be in writing. It will serve as the beacon for the team's subsequent work. The first step to a new vision for an organization is the recognition that there is a discrepancy between the current system and a desired innovation (Kaluzny, 1982; Sava, 1993). The system and the vision needed to obtain the desired innovation should be established by the stakeholders (Champlin, 1991; McNulty, 1989). Again, stakeholders need adequate and accurate information to recognize the discrepancy between the status quo and a new system (Servatius et al. 1992; Stoneman, 1993).

Baseline Assessment of Attitude and Policy Barriers

Based on work conducted by Smith and Rose (1993), we can speculate that the *policy barriers* to implementing the recommendations will include the following categories: policies that govern personnel and program quality, fiscal policies, transportation policies, eligibility policies, and coordination/collaboration policies. (See Figure 5.2 for a description of each policy barrier.)

The *attitudes and beliefs* barriers of likely concern have been previously discussed; they include turf issues, teacher preparedness attitudes, awareness issues, fears that someone will lose, and lack of communication and respect (Rose & Smith, 1993). The term "attitudes and beliefs" is intended to describe existing beliefs and knowledge, however accurate, that affect the behavior of stakeholders and the community. The team of stakeholders should define and describe which barriers are restricting a new system of service delivery for their particular situation.

Because policies define and drive early intervention systems, any systems change effort will have to address current policies that are inadequate for the new vision. Similarly, attitudes of stakeholders will determine their commitment to the vision and subsequently to the new system (Stoneman, 1993).

Action Planning

Once the barriers are identified, the team of stakeholders must decide how to overcome them. Action planning involves setting goals and objectives

> *Program Standards:* restrictive policies related to program or personnel characteristics; supervision of special education implementation; and "approval" policies for non-public school placements.
>
> *Personnel Standards:* restrictive policies related to personnel characteristics.
>
> *Fiscal Policies:* policies primarily governing the use of funds, i.e., limitation on use of certain funding streams for certain personnel or students; or limitations on the use of funds in or for non-public school settings including separation of church and state prohibitions. Also, this category includes how funds are generated, i.e., child count or per "unit"; and amounts available (re: rate-setting, amounts needed for integration, etc.); and how much time and service for which to contract.
>
> *Eligibility Policies:* refers to differences in criteria used to allow children to participate in services. The policy barriers are related to differences in the criteria between special education and integrated entities (Head Start, child care, "at-risk," Chapter 1 [ESEA], kindergarten, etc.).
>
> *Transportation Policies:* policies governing availability, schedules, and prohibitions on non-public school or district use.
>
> *Coordination Policies:* usually the *lack* of policies related to the coordination of procedures, programs, and services critical to the planning and delivery of special education and related services in mainstream settings.

Figure 5.2. Typology of policy barriers.

for changing the policy and attitudes and beliefs barriers, describing strategies for doing so, and identifying the people and resources needed to implement each strategy (Hazel et al., 1988; Olson, 1989; Smith & Rose, 1993). An outcome or evaluation measure should be identified for each objective.

Research in early intervention has substantiated the notion that many barriers, whether related to policy or attitudes, have misinformation as their root cause (Smith & Rose, 1993). Even in the case of perceived policy barriers, what often is described as a policy barrier, after policy analysis, is found not to be. The barrier is often an interpretation or belief of what the written policy actually requires. Thus, accurate and complete information is essential to clarify what the real barriers are and to begin changing attitudes based on fear and false assumptions about systems change. The systems change literature underscores the effect that information has on recognition of the need for change, commitment to change, and the success of systems change efforts (Banach, 1991; McNulty, 1989; Servatius et al., 1992; Stoneman, 1993). Any action plan must address the informational needs of parents, administrators, community program personnel, teachers, and the community at large.

Implementation: Policy Development and Attitudinal Change

Once actual barriers are identified, a set of short- and long-term strategies are required. New policies may be developed and take the form of legislative bills, contracting or other fiscal procedures, program standards criteria, or other documents, on the basis of the actual policy barriers. Similarly, attitudes and beliefs may be addressed through informational strategies (e.g., identifying useful curricula, reviewing data on efficacy of recommended practices, planning for inservice training). The new policies and attitudes will then enable and drive the new system.

Resource Allocation and Technical Assistance

Resources (personnel, fiscal incentives, etc.) and technical assistance are needed to ensure that the systems change process is completed expeditiously and that the new policies, supports, and procedures are implemented faithfully. This resource allocation step is where systems change often breaks down. Many educational innovations are never widely adopted, or they are short-lived, primarily because of inadequate allocation of resources (Fullen & Miles, 1992; Lambour et al., 1980; Strain & Smith, 1993). This step is a major challenge for stakeholders and should be closely monitored by the stakeholder team.

Evaluation

The systems change process must be evaluated both formatively, for ongoing decision making, as well as summatively, to determine if objectives have been met (Garland, 1982; Morgan et al., 1991; Smith & Rose, 1993). For example, the change process should be periodically evaluated to ensure that it is moving toward the vision. Members of the stakeholder team should be asked regularly if they feel enfranchised, whether the vision is still appropriate, and if progress is satisfactory (Fox & Williams, 1991). Careful evaluations of the factors governing the success or failure of each strategy in the action plan should occur.

Impinging Factors

Figure 5.1 shows that systems change strategies can be affected by impinging factors such as state or local budgets, educational reform movements, or changing demographics. Because systems change is conducted in real-life settings, there are always a multitude of uncontrolled variables, inherent both within the process and outside of the process, that can affect the process and outcomes. It is important for stakeholders to be aware of the potential effects of these variables, both positive and negative, throughout the change process.

Cautionary Notes

A conceptual model of systems change is needed so that recommended service delivery at the local community level becomes standard practice. The model proposed in this chapter is based on national surveys, case-study research, focus-group recommendations, and systems change and school-reform literature. However, two areas of new information are needed to ensure the development of new and high-quality service delivery systems. First, the proposed model needs to be evaluated in many different circumstances, such as urban versus rural, state level versus local. Measures on application and modification of each component of the model could yield important information about how well the model applies across different circumstances.

Second, the proposed model is primarily based on research focusing on *implementing* change. Most of the work to date on systems change has focused on initiating and implementing change, but not on *maintaining* change over time. Although theories about conditions necessary to sustain change over time have been proposed (Eisner, 1992; Fullen & Miles, 1992; Murphy, 1993), no information is currently available that systemically assesses what policies, procedures, and resources are necessary to maintain change. Research is needed to report the policies, strategies, and resources identified by state and local stakeholder teams as necessary to address concerns related to maintaining systems change outcomes over time.

CLOSING

We have suggested in this chapter that the adoption of the DEC service delivery recommendations will both require and occasion a fundamental level of change in most service systems. For example, the recommendations may well dictate a shift in a program's personnel, philosophy, client mix, and instructional practices. The sweep and pervasive impact of these recommendations cannot be overstated nor can the likely opposition from some quarters. As a field, we can either shrink from or revel in the great task before us—we believe our clients deserve our most energetic and unfailing efforts.

REFERENCES

Bailey, D. B., McWilliam, P. J., & Winton, P. J. (1992). Building family-centered practices in early intervention: A team-based model for change. *Infants and Young Children*, 5(1), 73–82.

Banach, W. J. (1991). *Creating change in an era of choice: A principal's step-by-step workbook for educational planning and marketing*. Romeo, MI: Banach Associates.

Bredekamp, S. (1987). *Developmentally appropriate practice in early childhood programs serving children from birth through age 8: Expanded edition*. Washington, DC: National Association for the Education of Young Children.

Champlin, J. (1991). Taking stock and moving on. *Quality Outcomes–Driven Education*, 1(1), 7–10.

Eisner, E. W. (1992). Educational reform and the ecology of schooling. *Teachers College Record*, 93, 610–627.

Finn, C. (1990). The biggest reform of all. *Phi Delta Kappan*, 71, 584–615.

Foster, M., Berger, M., & McLean, M. (1981). Rethinking a good idea: A reassessment of parent involvement. *Topics in Early Childhood Special Education*, 1(3), 56–656.

Fox, T. J., & Williams, W. (1991). *Implementing best practices for all students in their local school*. Burlington: University of Vermont.

Fullen, M. G., & Miles, M. B. (1992). Getting reform right: What works and what doesn't. *Phi Delta Kappan*, 73, 745–752.

Garland, C. (1982). Change at a private non-profit agency. In P. L. Trohanis (Ed.), *Strategies for change* (pp. 25–41). Chapel Hill: University of North Carolina.

Hazel, R., Barber, P. A., Roberts, S., Behr, S. K., Hehnstetter, E., & Guess, D. (1988). *A community approach to an integrated service system for children with special needs*. Baltimore: Brookes.

Individuals with Disabilities Education Act of 1990, 20 U.S.C. § 1400 *et seq.*

Kaluzny, A. D. (1982). Change in health-care settings. In P. L. Trohanis (Ed.), *Strategies for change* (pp. 41–65). Chapel Hill: University of North Carolina.

Lambour, G., Rostetter, D., Sapir, S. G., & Taha, A. H. (1980). *A practical guide to institutionalizing educational innovations*. Chapel Hill: University of North Carolina.

LeLaurin, K. (1992). Infant and toddler models of service delivery: Are they detrimental for some children and families? *Topics in Early Childhood Special Education*, 12(1), 82–104.

Maeroff, G. I. (1993). Building teams to rebuild schools. *Phi Delta Kappan, 74,* 512–519.
McNulty, B. (1989). Leadership and policy strategies for interagency planning: Meeting the early childhood mandate. In J. J. Gallagher, P. L. Trohanis, & R. M. Clifford (Eds.), *Policy implementation and P.L. 99-457: Planning for young children* (pp. 147–167). Baltimore: Brookes.
Meisels, S. J. (1985). A functional analysis of the evolution of public policy for handicapped young children. *Educational Evaluation and Policy Analysis, 7,* 115–126.
Morgan, J. L., Guetzloe, E. C., & Swan, W. W. (1991). Leadership for local interagency coordinating councils. *Journal of Early Intervention, 15,* 255–267.
Murphy, J. (1993). Restructuring schools: An overview. *Pennsylvania Reporter, 25*(1), 1–2.
New Mexico State Department of Education. (1992). Vision statement. In B. Smith & D. Rose (Eds.), *Administrator's policy handbook for preschool mainstreaming* (pp. 30–33). Cambridge, MA: Brookline Books.
Olson, J. (1989). Meeting the challenge of change: Implementing P.L. 99-457. *Topics in Early Childhood Special Education, 9*(3), 18–31.
Raver, S.A. (1991). *Strategies for teaching at-risk and handicapped infants and toddlers: A transdisciplinary approach.* New York: Macmillan.
Rose, D. F., & Smith, B. J. (1993). Preschool mainstreaming: Attitude barriers and strategies for addressing them. *Young Children, 48*(4), 59–62.
Sava, S. (1993). Mission: Between dream and reality. *Principal, 73*(2), 64.
Servatius, J. D., Fellows, M., & Kelly, D. (1992). Preparing leaders for inclusive schools, In R. Villa, J. Thousand, W. Stainback, & S. Stainback (Eds.), *Restructuring for caring and effective education* (pp. 267–283). Baltimore: Brookes.
Smith, B. J., & Rose, D. F. (1993). *Administrator's policy handbook for preschool mainstreaming.* Cambridge, MA: Brookline Books.
Stoneman, Z. (1993). The effects of attitude on preschool integration. In C. A. Peck, S. L. Odom, & D. D. Bricker (Eds.), *Integrating young children with disabilities into community programs* (pp. 223–248). Baltimore: Brookes.
Strain, P. S. (1991). Ensuring quality of early intervention for children with severe disabilities. In L. H. Meyer, C. A. Peck, & L. Brown (Eds.), *Critical issues in the lives of people with severe disabilities* (pp. 473–478). Baltimore: Brookes.
Strain, P. S., & Smith, B. J. (1993). Comprehensive educational, social, and policy forces that affect preschool integration. In C. A. Peck, S. L. Odom, & D. D. Bricker (Eds.), *Integrating young children with disabilties into community programs* (pp. 209–222). Baltimore: Brookes.
Striefel, S., Killoran, J., & Quinters, M. (1991). Administrator involvement as a key to integration. In S. Striefel, J. Killoran, & M. Quinters (Eds.), *Functional integration for success: Preschool intervention* (pp. 23–73). Austin, TX: PRO-ED.
Turnbull, A. P., Turnbull, H. R., & Blue-Banning, M. (in press). Enhancing inclusion of infants and toddlers with disabilities and their families: A theoretical and programmatic analysis. *Infants and Young Children.*
U.S. General Accounting Office. (1993). *System-wide Education Reform.* Washington, DC: Author.
Yoder, D. E., Coleman, P. O., & Gallagher, J. J. (1990). *Personnel needs: Allied health personnel meeting the demands of Part H, P.L. 99-457.* Unpublished manuscript, Carolina Institute for Child and Family Policy, University of North Carolina, Chapel Hill.

CHAPTER 6

General Curriculum and Intervention Strategies

Mark Wolery
Diane M. Sainato

This book and this chapter are about practices in which professionals engage when developing and providing services to young children with special needs and their families. "Practices" refer to professionals' performing or putting into action particular principles or assumptions. In early intervention and education, some of these practices are specific to particular types of goals and situations; others can be used to accomplish a range of goals and are applicable to a variety of situations. Because of this chapter's focus, two terms, *curriculum* and *intervention,* are defined. These definitions are followed by a listing of some desired outcomes of early intervention and education, a brief discussion of the contexts in which practices are used, an identification of assumptions that underlie the recommended practices, and a description of a continuum of intervention strategies. We devote a major portion of the chapter to describing those strategies. The final two sections deal with monitoring and adjusting intervention strategies and with areas of future work.

DEFINITION OF CURRICULUM AND INTERVENTION

The early childhood curriculum is quite different from the curricula for older children with or without disabilities. As used in this chapter, curriculum has three elements: (a) the content that can be taught, (b) the methods used to determine what content to teach to each child, and (c) the methods used to ensure the identified content for each child is acquired and used (Dunst, 1981; Wolery & Fleming, 1993).

For infants, toddlers, and preschoolers with special needs, the content of the curriculum is quite broad and includes the behaviors, skills, abilities, and patterns of interaction that are potential targets of intervention.[1] The content is a wide range of skills that would be appropriate for most young children. It includes developmental domains as well as idiosyncratic skills needed to function in unique ecologies. The content also should include some ordering or sequence of those skills. The second element of curriculum is the *methods for identifying the content for each infant or child*. As just noted, the content of the curriculum includes all potential skills that are relevant to young children with special needs. Thus, the curriculum should contain mechanisms for assisting the team (family members and professionals from various disciplines) in determining which skills are most important for an individual infant or child at any given time. This, of course, is accomplished through ongoing instructional program planning assessment that uses multiple measurement strategies to gather information from multiple sources (Bailey & Wolery, 1989; Benner, 1992; Kozloff, 1994; Neisworth & Bagnato, Chapter 2). From this ongoing assessment, the statements of skills that teams believe are important for individual infants and children become the objectives of the intervention. The third element of curriculum is the *methods for teaching the identified content to each individual*. These methods are the purposeful manipulations made in children's environments that are designed to cause them to learn the individually identified content. Some of those methods are the general curriculum and intervention strategies described in this chapter. In early childhood, these strategies are used in various settings (i.e., homes, clinics, childcare programs, schools, and the community), by different individuals (peers, family members, teachers, therapists), and often in the context of children's ongoing daily activities and routines.

Intervention is defined as the act of coming between events or of causing events to change. As used here, intervention refers to those things that professionals do to minimize the potential debilitating effects of children's disabilities on children and their families and to maximize the likelihood that desirable outcomes will result. Professionals do this by causing children to achieve the goals that have been set for them and by supporting families to promote the general well-being of both children and families and to assist them in addressing their concerns. Intervention is a broad term that includes professionals' activities related to changing directly or indirectly children's behaviors in desired ways (Buysse & Wesley, 1993), supporting and strengthening families (Dunst, Trivette, & Deal, 1994), and performing other functions such as prevention (Crocker, 1992) and promo-

---

[1]In this chapter, the term *skills* is used to refer to any behaviors, abilities, and patterns of interactions that are the focus of intervention.

tion (see Dunst, 1993). Curricular interventions are a subset of intervention activities performed by early childhood personnel.

GOALS AND OUTCOMES OF EARLY INTERVENTION AND EDUCATION

Although each child should have high-priority and individualized goals (those things their families and other team members believe are important), some general goals are applicable to most young children with disabilities. The General Curriculum and Intervention Strategies Strand Committee of the Division for Early Childhood Task Force on Recommended Practices identified nine outcomes of the general curriculum and intervention strategies. These outcomes are general goal statements that are applicable to nearly all children and curricular efforts.

First, a major portion of early interventionists' work deals with supporting families in achieving their goals (Bailey, 1994; Dunst, Trivette, & Deal, 1994). When addressing this goal, professionals must take care that they do not recommend and use intervention strategies that will harm children, families, and their relationship (GC 1). Nearly any intervention strategy and many interaction patterns that professionals have with families, if used inappropriately or incorrectly, can be harmful to children, families, and their relationship. For example, expecting families to use a specific teaching or therapy strategy rigidly in a prescribed way in the home at defined times may produce increased stress for families and may decrease positive parent–child interactions. By using appropriate help-giving behaviors (Dunst, Trivette, Davis, & Cornwell, 1994) and by attending to the desired outcomes identified here, the professional can reduce the probability of doing harm.

Second, a primary goal of early intervention is to assist children in interacting with their environments in self-directed and growth-promoting ways (McWilliam & Bailey, 1992). When promoting engagement, the professional must recognize that children's interactions with the environment should lead to mastery of the environment, independence in the environment, and developmental progress across a range of developmental areas (GC 2) (Carta, Atwater, Schwartz, & McConnell, 1993). Similarly, children's initiative, independence, and autonomy should be promoted (GC 3); however, supported participation in routines and activities in which independence is not possible also should occur (GC 6). Active engagement with activities, objects, and people is a means for the child's acquiring and using other skills and can be a means for assisting children in becoming a part of social groups. Promoting children's engagement and ensuring that efficient learning occurs from that engagement compose a major challenge for early childhood personnel (GC 9).

Third, an important goal of early intervention and education is to promote children's development in a number of areas—physical, social, communication, self-care, and cognitive skills (GC 7) (Barnett & Carey, 1992). However, a couple of qualifications are needed. Although we professionals conceptualize children's development in different areas and although some research suggests that unique domains of development exist, children's performance should be viewed as a whole. Performance of many relatively simple skills, in fact, calls on children to use abilities from several domains. Also, emphasis should be placed on providing children with a broad range of skills at their existing development level rather than on only promoting more advanced developmental skills.

Fourth, particular emphasis should be placed on promoting social competence and prosocial behavior (GC 5). Social competence can be defined in a number of ways (cf. Guralnick, 1993; Odom, McConnell, & McEvoy, 1992), but useful definitions focus on children's performance of interpersonal skills. Such abilities are critical to ensuring that children can negotiate the social world in which they live.

Fifth, particular attention in early intervention and education should be placed on ensuring that children use the skills they have acquired. Rapid acquisition of skills by young children with disabilities is important (GC 9), but if they do not use those skills when and wherever necessary, then those skills are of little value (GC 8). As a result, all intervention strategies should be employed with the assumption that the ultimate goal is skill use. This approach also requires an analysis and understanding of the contexts in which children spend time (Haring, 1992).

Sixth, one of the primary goals of early intervention is to assist children in spending their lives with their families and in their communities (Bailey & Wolery, 1992). Thus, professionals must place considerable emphasis on providing intervention in integrated settings and in preparing children to live, learn, recreate, and work in community contexts (GC 4). Such intervention may include assisting children and families in their transition to other programs (Atwater, Orth-Lopes, Elliott, Carta, & Schwartz, 1994). Although a number of barriers exist to widespread, high-quality preschool integration (Odom & McEvoy, 1990), a considerable amount of mainstreaming is occurring (Wolery, Holcombe, et al., 1993), and a large literature exists on how to do it effectively (Peck, Odom, & Britker, 1993; Safford, 1989; Wolery & Wilbers, 1994).

Seventh, another general goal of early intervention is to prevent children from developing future problems and additional disabilities (Bailey & Wolery, 1992). Although the strategies described in this chapter are not specifically designed as prevention activities, they may well have that effect. Specifically, when children acquire means of interacting and mastering their environments and acquiring and using a range of valuable skills, then future problems and disabilities may be minimized or prevented.

CONTEXTS OF EARLY INTERVENTION AND EDUCATION

McWilliam and Strain (1993) suggested that early intervention and education should be characterized by services that are family centered, are devised by a transdisciplinary team, are based on empirical foundations and on shared values, are provided in the least restrictive and most natural environment, and are individually and developmentally appropriate. These characteristics influence how the recommended curricular strategies are implemented.

In terms of the family-centered characteristic, two implications, among many, are noted. First, the early intervention efforts must focus on the entire family rather than on the child only (Bailey 1994; Dunst, Trivette, & Deal, 1994). Many of the strategies in this chapter focus on children, but we readily recognize the need for broader interventions described throughout this text. Second, the selection and implementation of the strategies that are used to address mutually agreed upon skills must be consistent with family values and perceptions (GC 10) (Dunst, Trivette, & Deal, 1994). These two implications require substantial shifts in the roles performed by early intervention staff and call for shifts in the roles of regular early childhood personnel whose charges include children with disabilities.

The need for teams, including transdisciplinary teams, in early intervention and education has been recognized for many years (Allen, Holm, & Schiefelbusch, 1978), and general guidelines for team functioning exist (Bruder, 1994; Bruder & Bologna, 1993). The underlying assumption is that a group of adequately prepared individuals from relevant disciplines working in concert with family members will be able to devise the most appropriate intervention program (GC 12). However, concerns remain about the extent to which members of many disciplines are prepared to work with infants and toddlers, with their families, and with other team members (Bailey, Palsha, & Simeonsson, 1991; Bailey, Simeonsson, Yoder, & Huntington, 1990). Further, enrollment of young children with disabilities in nonpublic programs raises questions about the monitoring of related services (Odom & McEvoy, 1990) and about the general availability of teams in such sites (Wolery, Venn, et al., 1994). In addition, many early childhood special educators are experiencing a redefinition of their roles— from direct service providers to consultants to regular early childhood staff (Buysse & Wesley, 1993). The extent to which curricular interventions are implemented appropriately is undoubtedly influenced by the availability of adequately prepared team members and the degree to which they work as a unit (Bruder, 1994).

In terms of the empirical and value foundations of the curricular interventions described in this chapter, three comments are pertinent. First, the strategies have varying levels of empirical support; however, most of the strategies have some replicable research documenting their effectiveness, and much of that research has occurred in applied, often integrated contexts. Second, as noted by McWilliam and Strain (1993), the values of individuals involved in early intervention and education efforts, including families, may be quite diverse. McWilliam and Strain suggested that individualization and sensitive interactions with families are the primary mechanisms for ensuring that paternalistic practices are avoided. Third, given that sensitivity to cultural and ethnic factors exists, we suspect that many of the value differences that arise will be between nonfamily members of the team (i.e., professionals who hold to differing philosophic assumptions). Reliance on the empirical literature seems to be a reasonable starting point for discussions to resolve such differences.

In terms of the least restrictive and most natural site for services and individually as well as developmentally appropriate practices, several comments are pertinent. For many infants and young children with disabilities, the least restrictive and most natural setting for intervention will be their homes; for many others, it will be some form of group care—or some combination of the two. Regardless of the site of services, the interventions recommended in this chapter are relevant. However, careful planning is required to ensure that these strategies are responsive to children's behavior and interests, are used to promote children's engagement and mastery of the environment, and are used to facilitate acquisition and use of individualized objectives (GC 11, GC 16).

For many young children with disabilities, the least restrictive environment is a program designed and operated primarily for typically developing children (i.e., regular early education and childcare programs). Many of those programs will follow, or attempt to follow, the guidelines of developmentally appropriate practice (Bredekamp, 1987; Bredekamp & Rosegrant, 1992). Since publication of the developmentally appropriate practice guidelines by the National Association for the Education of Young Children (NAEYC), discussion *has* occurred about the relevance of those guidelines for young children with disabilities (Atwater, Carta, Schwartz, & McConnell, 1994; Bredekamp, 1993; Carta et al., 1993; Carta, Schwartz, Atwater, & McConnell, 1991; J. Johnson & Johnson, 1992; K. Johnson & Johnson, 1993; McLean & Odom, 1993; Norris, 1991). From analyses of practices in both general and special early childhood education, the following conclusions have been drawn: Developmentally appropriate practice guidelines are

- generally adequate for young children with disabilities (J. Johnson & Johnson, 1992; Norris, 1991);

- appropriate for young children with disabilities, but some modifications, additional detail, and more emphasis on selected issues are needed for children with disabilities (Bredekamp, 1993; McLean & Odom, 1993);
- necessary but not sufficient (i.e., may require modification) for young children with disabilities (Atwater, Carta, et al., 1994; Carta et al., 1991, 1993); and
- appropriate but not sufficient (i.e., may require modification) for young children with disabilities (Wolery, Strain, & Bailey, 1992).

These statements suggest that it is beneficial for young children with disabilities to be enrolled in programs following the developmentally appropriate practice guidelines. Most of these statements suggest, however, that modifications of the practices will be necessary for some young children with disabilities. Specifically, changes in practices are likely needed to achieve individual appropriateness (Bredekamp, 1993; Wolery & Bredekamp, 1994). When devising those changes, the intervention team should use the strategies described in this chapter; however, it is critical that these strategies be embedded within the ongoing activities of the existing program. Despite guidelines for implementing such modifications (Bricker & Cripe, 1992; Wolery, 1994; Wolery, Werts, & Holcombe, 1994) and defensible research documenting the effectiveness of embedding modifications in ongoing activities (Fox & Hanline, 1993; Losardo & Bricker, 1994; Venn, Wolery, Fleming, et al., 1993; Venn, Wolery, Werts, et al., 1993; Wolery et al., 1994), several formidable barriers may exist. Among others, two salient barriers are philosophic differences and training needs (Odom & McEvoy, 1990). The philosophic disagreements occur over issues such as (a) the extent to which staff believe that children's participation in an early childhood program should result in identifiable outcomes (Wolery, Strain, & Bailey, 1992), (b) what constitutes meaningful engagement (K. Johnson & Johnson, 1993), (c) whether reinforcement is a defensible practice (Wolery & Wilbers, 1994, "Editor's Note," Chapter 6), and (d) whether the staff should use systematic instructional procedures (Copple, 1994). Resolution of these differences is central to providing defensible individualized early childhood programs for young children with disabilities. The training barriers focus on general early educators' learning about providing services to young children with disabilities and their families and special early educators' learning about practices related to typical children and about consultation skills (Kontos & File, 1993; Odom & McEvoy, 1990). The curricular strategies in this chapter are useful in individualizing programs that follow the developmentally appropriate practice guidelines, but the realization of appropriate and individualized intervention may require resolution of difficulties and ongoing staff development.

FOUNDATIONAL ASSUMPTIONS

The practices recommended here are based on several assumptions. First, children's development and learning are influenced by several factors. These factors include their biological and health status and history and their current and past history of interactions with their environment. In short, development and learning are a result of the individual's biological maturation and interaction with changing environments (Anastasiow, 1990). Young children also, of course, influence their environments.

Second, children's development and learning are influenced substantially by experience (i.e., interactions with their environments). Nearly every account of child development ascribes importance to child–environment interactions. For example, Piaget (1952) asserted that children's interactions with the physical and social world, along with equilibration and biological maturation, were the primary forces in the development of children's cognition. Also, Vygotsky (1978) stressed children's interactions with the environment and the role of adults in influencing those exchanges. Similarly, behavioral perspectives (e.g., Bijou, 1993; Bijou & Baer, 1961) argued that children's interactions with the environment are the context in which various behaviors are learned and used. If children's learning and development are influenced by their experiences with the environment, professionals should recognize that all of children's experiences, not just those viewed as interventions, are likely to have an influence. Thus, the totality of children's experiences, in and out of intervention programs, potentially influences how they develop and learn. As a result, interventions must be sensitive to their unique ecologies. In one sense, the curriculum for a child (the child's individualized program) is the sum of that child's interactions (experiences) with the environment.

Third, in light of the importance of child–environment interactions, some of the intervention efforts should focus on those exchanges. Some interventions (e.g., surgery, medications, diet, etc.) are designed primarily to influence children's biological functioning; other interventions (e.g., family support) focus on broader ecological variables (e.g., families' sense of well-being, families' access to needed resources, etc.). However, it is assumed that the outcomes of such interventions influence children's interactions with their environments. Other interventions (e.g., curricular strategies) are designed to focus more directly on child–environment interactions. When designing and implementing such interventions, professionals should recognize that some of those experiences may promote or impede children's development and learning. Thus, some ways of interacting with children, some schedules of daily routines, some activities, some organizations of physical environments facilitate development and learning and others do not. Because no defensible reasons exist for allowing experiences that impede children's development and learning, professionals have a responsibility to ensure that children's experiences promote, not interfere with, development and learning.

CONTINUUM OF CURRICULAR INTERVENTIONS

Many interventions are listed as indicators of high-quality practice in this chapter and other chapters, other interventions exist and may be appropriate, and still other interventions will be devised in the future. All of these interventions cannot and should not be implemented simultaneously. Just as a highly skilled artisan selects the best tool for a particular task, intervention teams must select the most appropriate strategy for the situation at hand. In making such selections, teams must conceptualize intervention strategies in an organized and systematic manner.

Listing of Strategies

A listing of general types of curriculum strategies is presented in Figure 6.1. The strategies are listed on a continuum of teacher directiveness, and the general likelihood that child-initiated behavior and teacher-mediated child behavior will occur is also displayed. Although all curricular interventions are designed to influence child–environment interactions, different strategies are likely to have different influences on those interactions. The strategies on the "low" end of the adult-mediation continuum (left) are designed to encourage children's engagement and to provide children with opportunities for self-initiated and self-directed interactions with the environment. Clearly, some of the strategies on this end of the continuum can result in specific and predictable behavior, but in general, these strategies are designed to promote engagement and child-initiated behavior. The strategies toward the "high" end of the continuum (right) are designed to produce specific child behavior that is teacher selected and initiated. For example, if the teacher wanted a child to learn self-feeding, the strategies on the high end of the continuum would be the more logical choices than those on the low end. However, some of the strategies on the high end of the continuum may increase engagement as well.

We note four cautions for the use of the continuum. First, *listing strategies on a continuum does not imply a sequence by which they should be used.* Because child-initiated and child-directed activity and learning are valued

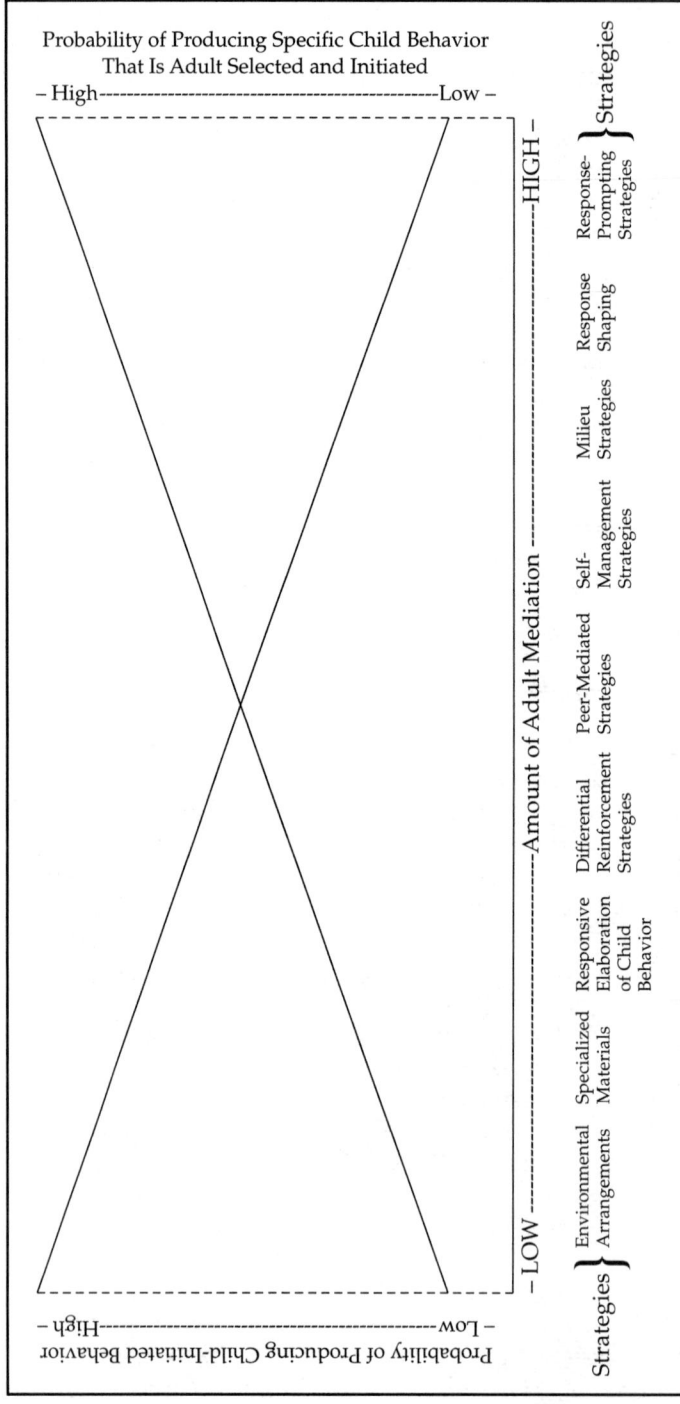

Figure 6.1. A proposed continuum of types of instructional strategies by the amount of adult mediation, by the probability that the strategy will produce child-initiated behavior, and by the probability that the strategy will produce child behavior that is adult selected and initiated. *Note.* From "Instructional Strategies for Teaching Young Children with Special Needs," by M. Wolery, in *Including Children with Special Needs in Early Childhood Programs* (p. 105), edited by M. Wolery and J. S. Wilbers, 1994, Washington, DC: National Association for the Education of Young Children. Copyright 1994 by NAEYC. Adapted with permission.

by families and professionals for many defensible reasons, the strategies on the low end of the continuum are generally preferred. However, this listing and such preferences do not mean that the strategies on the low end should be used and found to fail before those strategies on the high end are employed. When selecting the starting point on the continuum, the team must have substantial information about the child's skills, the child's learning history, the skill that is desired, and the situation in which the strategy will be used. In short, teams should select the strategy (or combination of strategies) that is most likely to produce the desired results and least likely to produce negative results. Second, *the listed strategies can be used in combination.* Some of these strategies (e.g., specialized materials, environmental arrangements, differential reinforcement) may be employed when nearly any of the other strategies are used. Thus, listing these strategies on this continuum does not imply that any of these strategies are used in isolation. In fact, in most cases, multiple strategies will be employed simultaneously. Third, *the amount of learning is independent of a strategy's placement on the continuum.* Children learn from their interactions with the environment, including, of course, observation of others in their environment. Thus, placement of the strategies on the continuum is not designed to imply that learning is more or less likely with one strategy than with another. Rather, we hypothesize that the strategies will exert different influences on the probability that various types of child behavior will occur, a variance that, in turn, may result in different skills being learned. Fourth, *no defensible reason exists for using ineffective strategies.* Some of these strategies may be more appealing than others to teams for a variety of reasons. For example, more normalized strategies often are more appealing to adults than are more intrusive and more restrictive strategies. However, no strategy or combination of strategies should be employed if they do not promote children's engagement and do not assist children in acquiring and using those skills the team has determined to be important.

General Guidelines for Selecting Strategies

Several guidelines have been proposed to help teams in making decisions about which strategy or combination of strategies to use. Nine general indicators of recommended practice are proposed. Early interventionists should devise strategies that support and promote family values and participation rather than strategies that make excessive demands on families (GC 10) (Winton & Turnbull, 1981), that are inconsistent with their cultural practices and belief systems (Lynch & Hanson, 1992), or that interfere with rather than facilitate their participation with their child and the team. Also, the team should select and develop strategies that are based on, follow the lead of, and are responsive to children's behavior (GC 11) (Bredekamp, 1987; Dunst et al., 1987). In selecting strategies, interventionists must consider information from relevant disciplines (GC 12); the extent to which it can be applied in various relevant settings (GC 13); the extent to which multiple goals can be addressed in a single activity; and the extent to which a balance is established between child- and adult-directed learning (GC 14, GC 15). These indicators mean that the intervention strategies should have wide application and promote the types of outcomes mentioned previously. Also, strategies that promote learning in each of its different phases should be selected: learning how to perform new skills (acquisition), learning to use those skills smoothly and easily (fluency), learning to use those skills after intervention has stopped (maintenance), and learning to apply the skills when and wherever they are needed (generalization) (GC 16) (Wolery, Bailey, & Sugai, 1988). Further, if learning is likely to be equal with more than one strategy, then the one strategy that is most normalized (most similar to that used with typically developing children), least restrictive (allows the most child choices and the least imposition on the child's freedom), least intrusive (avoids physical contact and manipulation of the child), and easiest to use should be employed (GC 17, GC 18).

EFFECTIVE CURRICULUM AND INTERVENTION STRATEGIES

Here we provide an overview of several types of intervention strategies. Because space precludes a comprehensive review of these strategies, references are provided for additional information. The strategies are described in the order listed in Figure 6.1—beginning with those that are least directive. We hope early intervention specialists will employ these strategies with attention to the child's level of engagement in the areas of social behavior, communication, cognitive skills, motor performance, interactions with toys and materials, adaptive behavior, and independent performance. McWilliam (1991) has defined engagement as "the amount of time a child spends in developmentally and contextually appropriate behavior" (p. 42). The creation of responsive environments for children helps to ensure optimum opportunities for engagement.

Environmental Arrangements

Home, school, and community environments typically set the occasion for young children to engage in a full range of activities requiring social, physical, communication, and cognitive performance (Peck et al., 1993). The literature in child development, early childhood education, and special education has explored the impact of physical space, the design of physical environments, adult–child ratios, the development of daily schedules, and staff assignments (McEvoy, 1990; Phyfe-Perkins, 1980). Environmental arrangements, created thoughtfully, may enhance effective aspects of the curriculum. Among the findings reported in several excellent reviews, reports of research, and descriptions of ongoing investigations, a consensus appears to exist that the type and arrangement of activities available to children directly impact the level of social behavior (Odom, Peterson, McConnell, & Ostrosky, 1990), observed problem behavior (Nordquist, Twardosz, & McEvoy, 1991), and child engagement (Carta, Atwater, Schwartz, & Miller, 1990; Carta, Sainato, & Greenwood, 1988). For example, in a study in which the environment of two classrooms for young children with autism was systematically altered by adding play materials and by rearranging the room, class schedules, and staff responsibilities, Nordquist and colleagues (1991) demonstrated that environmental reorganization affected not only the children in the room but also the behavior of the teachers. The reorganization of the environment resulted in positive changes in the teachers' affectionate behavior toward the children and in the children's increased use of play materials.

The scheduling of activities and assignment of staff also has been found to influence children's behavior. Suggestions for scheduling of activities include interspersing periods of high activity with periods of quiet activities, for example, following outdoor play with table time or arts and crafts (Krantz & Risley, 1977); reducing the amount of waiting time children may encounter by assigning staff to activity "zones" (LeLaurin & Risley, 1972); and actively planning for transitions between activities (Sainato, 1990).

In addition to the more classroom-based features of environmental arrangement for preschool-aged children, one must also note specific concerns in creating caregiving environments for infants and toddlers. Lubeck and Chandler (1990) noted that health and nutrition safety concerns add an extra dimension to the arrangement of early intervention settings. They suggested that a careful assessment of the caregiving environment is critical and provided a list of environmental assessments and commercially available resources on infant and childcare. Environmental arrangements may have a great impact on both children and teachers. Beyond the numerous recommendations for the design of physical environments for young children (Bailey & Wolery, 1992) comes the recommendation for choosing materials to enhance learning opportunities and child engagement.

Specialized Materials

One of the most visible aspects of the environment for young children is the wide array of toys, materials, and equipment that occupy the physical space. Teachers often choose their materials on the basis of conventional wisdom, standard practices, and intuition (Fernie, 1985). Guidelines for choosing materials and equipment for children with and without disabilities should include attention to children's interests, the responsiveness of the toys or materials to children's actions, the age appropriateness of the material or equipment, and the availability of a continuum of objects for play ranging from those that are very realistic to those that might spark more imaginative play (GC 22) (Bailey & Wolery, 1992; Noonan & McCormick, 1993). Often, early interventionists may find it to their best advantage to offer children choices of toys and materials that promote specific types of fine motor, gross motor, or social behavior and that foster more child-initiated and child-directed play. For example, certain toys such as dress-up clothes, toy housekeeping materials, balls, and toy cars and trucks may prompt more social interaction than do toys such as puzzles, parquetry blocks, and peg boards and pegs (Martin, Brady, & Williams, 1991). An interesting strategy for promoting children's engagement with toys and materials is to systematically rotate some of the toys and materials available in the classroom according to dimensions of size, complexity, developmental level, category, and sensory quality (McGee, Daly, Izeman, Mann, & Risley, 1991). This rotation plan may help to preserve the novelty of the materials and to increase sharing and creative play of children while still offering children opportunities to make choices.

Responsive Elaboration of Infant and Child Behavior

To support child-directed and child-initiated behavior, teachers design classroom environments that contain interesting activities, materials, and toys. However, in addition to planning an interesting and stimulating environment, adults may use a number of other strategies. Common elements across these strategies include (a) providing a responsive environment; (b) promoting children's participation and interaction with the environment by ensuring proximity of materials and people, providing preferred objects and people, responding to children's interactions, encouraging sustained interaction, and encouraging pretend play; (c) responding to and eliciting elaborations of children's play; and (d) providing response-contingent instruction (GC 25, GC 26) (McWilliam & Bailey, 1992). When using these strategies, adults should be aware of children's current skills, be sensitive to children's behavior and the intents of that behavior, and be responsive to the behavior (Mahoney & Powell, 1986). A number of guidelines for implementing these strategies are provided in Table 6.1. Although these strategies are often associated with infants and toddlers, many are also applicable for preschoolers.

Table 6.1. Guidelines for Promoting Elaboration of Children's Behavior

Author(s)	Recommended Strategies
Dunst et al. (1987)	Be aware of and sensitive to the child's behavior and shifts in the child's behavior.
Dunst, Lowe, & Bartholomew (1990)	Consider the child's behavior as purposeful (i.e., as an intent to interact with the physical or social environment).
	Respond contingently to the child's behavior and the assumed intent of that behavior.
	When children are engaged in interactions with the environment, encourage them to continue that engagement.
	Provide models and set up situations that will present children with the need and opportunity to engage in more complex and elaborate behavior.
Mahoney & Powell (1986)	Engage frequently in play with the child.
	Observe the child's behavior and manipulate objects and interactions that are similar to what the child is doing.
	Engage in short rather than long terms when interacting with the child.
	Wait for the child to initiate behavior or to respond to your initiations.
	Observe the child and imitate his or her behavior.
	Avoid using demands that produce the expectation that the child must do particular behaviors.
	Attempt to increase the duration of interactions by taking more turns and looking or waiting expectantly for the child.
	Follow the child's lead in terms of the pace of interactions.
Field (1982)	Use simple and slow responses to children's initiations.

(continues)

Table 6.1. *Continued*

Author(s)	Recommended Strategies
Field (1982) *cont'd*	Promote imitation by imitating the child and responding to the child's approximations of imitation.
	Repeat children's phrases and sounds (particularly for infants and toddlers).
	Observe the child and wait silently for his or her initiations.
	Engage in reciprocal game playing.
MacDonald & Gillette (1988)	Engage in game playing in predictable routines.
	Engage in taking turns with the child.
	Engage in waiting, then acting once, and then waiting and looking expectantly at the child.
	Imitate the child's actions and vocalizations.
	Observe the child, match your response to the child's, and then add an additional behavior.
	Play in a childlike way and attempt to view the play as the child does.
	When interacting, be animated and engaging.
	Accept the child's response to promote longer interactions.
	Display genuine emotions such as affection.

Note. From *Including Children with Special Needs in Early Childhood Programs* (p. 112), by M. Wolery and J. S. Wilbers, 1994, Washington, DC: National Association for the Education of Young Children. Copyright 1994 by NAEYC. Adapted with permission.

Differential Reinforcement Strategies

Positive reinforcement is defined as the contingent delivery, following a behavior, of a stimulus that produces an increased probability that the behavior will maintain or increase in occurrence in the future. The power of positive reinforcement to change the rates of behavior has been demonstrated repeatedly across species. Educators have used positive reinforcement to reduce the frequency of problematic behaviors and to increase the frequency of a wide variety of adaptive and desirable behaviors of many different types of learners (Cooper, Heron, & Heward, 1987). This section includes general comments about positive reinforcement and describes three reinforcement strategies: differential reinforcement, behavioral momentum, and correspondence training.

General Comments

Unfortunately, many individuals view reinforcement only as giving candy and other foods to children. Although food often functions as a reinforcer for some children, so do many other things such as toys, praise, preferred activities, hugs, smiles. Several facts about reinforcers are important to remember. First, what works as a reinforcer for one child may not work for other children. Second, reinforcers that work for a child at one time may not work later. Bailey and Wolery (1992) described procedures for identifying reinforcers for children and for using them. Third, some reinforcers are more easily delivered than are others; if possible, those that are easily used should be employed. Fourth, the reinforcers that are selected and used should be acceptable to family members. Fifth, reinforcers that are found in children's natural environments should be selected and used. Sixth, when it is feasible, teams should structure activities and materials that contain reinforcers or that are reinforcing in their execution or their completion. Often, child-preferred activities have such components.

Differential Reinforcement

Differential reinforcement is a strategy that involves reinforcing particular behaviors when children do them and withholding reinforcers when children do not do those behaviors (GC 28) (Cooper et al., 1987). Differential reinforcement can be used alone or in combination with a variety of other strategies. Several guidelines exist for using differential reinforcement: (a) The reinforcer should be delivered immediately after the behavior occurs; (b) a variety of reinforcers, if known, should be used; (c) natural reinforcers (those found in the natural environment) should be used when possible; and (d) reinforcers that are more difficult to deliver and less normalized should be delivered with stimuli such as praise, hugs, and so on (Bailey & Wolery, 1992).

Behavioral Momentum

Behavioral momentum is a specialized use of differential reinforcement (Davis & Brady, 1993; Mace & Belfiore, 1990; Mace et al., 1988). Behavioral momentum is used primarily for increasing children's compliance with adult requests but can also be used to promote children's engagement in activities. The procedure involves asking children to do a series of behaviors that they are likely to do in rapid succession and quickly reinforcing the performance of each behavior. Children are then asked to do the behavior that they are less likely to do and are given an opportunity to do it. This strategy often results in children's doing things they would not usually do. For example, during a play session, the teacher might say to the child who is reluctant to share, "Jenny, touch the truck," "Say, truck," and "Pick up the truck," immediately prior to requesting, "Give the truck to Susie." Behavioral momentum strategies may have a broad application to communication skills, motor skills, and self-help and adaptive behavior skills.

Correspondence Training

Correspondence training is another specialized use of differential reinforcement (GC 31) (R. Baer, 1990; McEvoy, Odom, & McConnell, 1992; Paniagua, 1990). Although it can be implemented in a variety of ways (see Paniagua, 1990, for a discussion of the various ways to implement it), correspondence training involves reinforcing a correspondence between what the child says and what the child does. For example, a child is asked to say what she or he will do during play (e.g., talk with another child), and at the end of the play period, the child is given reinforcement if she or he did indeed talk with friends during play. Correspondence training has been used effectively with a range of children for supporting their use of selected skills and for facilitating generalization of skills taught with other procedures (Odom & Watts, 1991; Sainato, Goldstein, & Strain, 1992).

Peer-Mediated Strategies

Curriculum intervention strategies often involve the adult as the primary facilitator of children's behavior. Peer-mediated interventions involve the use of the child's peers to encourage children to interact, play, and respond in social situations (GC 24). The teacher is not entirely removed from this activity in that he or she may be providing initial instructions, prompts, or encouragement to the peers. Peer-mediated strategies have been found to be successful in increasing the social and communicative behaviors of young children with disabilities (McEvoy et al., 1992; Strain & Odom, 1986). Odom and Brown (1993) described common components of peer-mediated interventions for social skills, including the following: (a) Children who are viewed as socially competent are selected as peer confederates or interveners; (b) in separate training sessions, these peers are taught social initiations that encourage or support the interactions of the children with poor social skills; and (c) teachers often provide prompts and reinforcement to the peers for making social initiations to their friends (the target students) in play groups outside of the training sessions. It should be noted that teachers' feedback and prompts to peers have been successfully and systematically withdrawn while children maintain their levels of social interaction (Odom, Chandler, Ostrosky, McConnell, & Reaney, 1992). Strategies found to be useful in teaching peers to help engage children with disabilities in play include offering toys, suggesting play ideas, and giving assistance, affection, and compliments (Sainato et al., 1992).

Self-Management Strategies

Along the continuum of intervention strategies, self-management interventions present options for teaching children independent performance skills and for facilitating their interactions with the environment and their peers (GC 30). The importance of helping children become increasingly self-directed and less dependent on teacher prompts cannot be underestimated. The degree of independence displayed by children is a critical aspect of the teacher–child relationship and the teacher's creation of the learning environment (Sainato, Strain, Lefebvre, & Rapp, 1990). In addition, children's ability to manage their own behavior has been found to be an important skill that facilitates task engagement (Higgins-Hains, 1992). Use of self-management strategies with preschool children has received increasing attention in recent years. Various components of self-management include self-assessment, self-monitoring, and self-evaluation. Studies incorporating one or more of these components have focused on target behaviors such as the self-evaluation of independent work skills (Higgins-Hains, 1992; Sainato et al., 1990), social-interaction strategies during play time (Sainato et al., 1992), self-monitoring of on-task behavior with preschool children (DeHaas-Warner, 1992), and appropriate behavior and recruitment of teacher praise during clean-up time (Connell, Carta, & Baer, 1993). Teaching children to use self-management strategies may help children maintain newly acquired skills across settings, teachers, and tasks (D. Baer & Fowler, 1984). Also, the child's ability to engage in the environment independently minimizes the dependence on the presence of the teacher (Burgio, Whitman, & Johnson, 1980). The ability of children to function independently and to self-manage may reduce the amount of time needed for other more adult-directed behavior management activities (Strain & Sainato, 1987).

Several guidelines are recommended for the successful use of self-management strategies in settings for young children with disabilities. Children should be asked to self-assess or self-evaluate only those skills that are already in their repertoire. Teachers should begin introducing self-management strategies by reviewing the expectations and requirements of an activity (e.g., in the case of clean-up or table-time activities) or of a particular routine, such as a transition time. Teachers may need to teach the self-assessment skills by having children indicate whether they are performing a simple task (e.g., "Am I standing or sitting?"), before moving to more complex tasks that have several components (e.g., a table-time activity in which children may be asked if they made a choice of an activity, completed the activity, and returned their materials to the shelves). It is important to remember that self-management activities may require teacher presence and prompting initially but that the teacher direction needs to be faded as children become more skilled or self-directed.

Milieu Strategies

To facilitate children's acquisition and generalization of language skills, in particular, and social-interaction skills, in general, researchers have developed naturalistic approaches that fall under the term *milieu teaching* (Hart & Rogers-Warren, 1978). These strategies, as described by Warren and Kaiser (1988), embed training opportunities within the context of normal conversation by the teacher's following the child's attentional lead during an activity occurring in the child's environment. Milieu teaching strategies encompass a number of more specific procedures including naturalistic time delay (Halle, Baer, & Spradlin, 1981), the mand–model[2] technique (Warren, McQuarter, & Rogers-Warren, 1984), and incidental teaching (Hart & Risley, 1975) (GC 23). General guidelines for using incidental teaching include (a) arranging the environment to encourage the child's initiation of speech; (b) selecting appropriate language skills as the target for intervention prior to the interaction; (c) requesting elaboration of the child's initial communicative attempts; (d) providing models, if needed (i.e., if the child does not produce more complex language); and (e) responding to the child's language attempts and use of targeted language forms by providing adult attention or by giving the child access to the objects or activities in which he or she has expressed an interest (Hart, 1985; Warren & Kaiser, 1988). Although milieu strategies have most often been employed with language skills, Brown, McEvoy, and Bishop (1991) noted success in the application of incidental teaching for peer interactions with young children.

Response Shaping

Response shaping is another specialized use of differential reinforcement (Cooper et al., 1987). The standard definition of response shaping is differential reinforcement of successive approximations of some target behavior

---

[2] A mand is a non-yes/no question or directive that requires a specific response.

(GC 29). Response shaping has been used in a variety of contexts to produce desirable changes in children's skills. In using response shaping, the adult must ensure that a powerful reinforcer is identified and can be delivered immediately and contingently. The adult also must analyze the behavior that will be promoted through response shaping. Specifically, the teacher must identify a series of changes in that behavior that progress from the behavior that the child currently does to the more complex behavior that is desired.

Initially, the adult provides reinforcement to the child for doing the behavior that is currently possible for the child. When this behavior occurs regularly, the teacher provides reinforcement only for a slightly more complex form of the skill. Reinforcement is no longer provided for the behavior the child previously did; it is provided only when the child does the skill in a slightly more complex manner. After the child regularly does this slightly more complex skill, the teacher again changes the rules. Specifically, the previously reinforced, slightly more complex behavior is not now reinforced. Reinforcers are provided only when the child does the skill in an even more complex way. This process of reinforcing a given behavior until it is done regularly and then not reinforcing the behavior unless it is more complex continues until the child performs the behavior at the level and in the manner that is desired. For example, if the teacher is trying to have the child engage in outdoor play and in the use of climbing equipment, the teacher might initially wait until the child approaches the sliding board. The teacher would give praise and encouragement for the child's holding onto the railing of the ladder and taking one step up. If the child climbs down, the teacher then waits until the child once again approaches the sliding board, but praises the child only for climbing up two steps. After the child has increased his or her contact with the sliding board and begins to climb all the way to the top of the slide, the teacher praises the child for climbing and sliding down the slide. In this manner, a teacher shapes small steps toward the desired behavior—going up and down the slide.

The success of response shaping greatly depends on the adult's ability to identify powerful reinforcers, observe the child's behavior carefully, provide the reinforcers contingently, and make judgments about when to stop reinforcing one behavior and begin reinforcing other behaviors. In the hands of a skilled adult, response shaping can be extremely effective in promoting children's engagement with the environment and can lead to the performance of fairly complex and desirable patterns of responding.

Response-Prompting Strategies

Response-prompting strategies, often called "prompting procedures," are interventions with a rich history in teaching useful skills to individuals with disabilities (Billingsley & Romer, 1983; Wolery, Ault, & Doyle, 1992). These strategies include most-to-least prompting (Wolery & Gast, 1984), graduated guidance (Bailey & Wolery, 1984), system of least prompts or increasing assistance (Doyle, Wolery, Ault, & Gast, 1988), simultaneous prompting (Schuster, Griffen, & Wolery, 1992), constant and progressive time delay (Handen & Zane, 1987; Wolery, Holcombe, et al., 1992), transition-based teaching (Wolery, Doyle, Gast, Ault, & Simpson, 1993), and the naturalistic procedures (e.g., incidental teaching, the mand–model procedure; Kaiser, Yoder, & Keetz, 1992) (GC 27). The features of these procedures are provided in Table 6.2. Each strategy is designed to provide learners with adult (sometimes peer) assistance (called "prompts") *and* to fade or withdraw that assistance over time as children learn to perform skills independently (i.e., without assistance). The types of assistance include verbal statements, gestures, models, pictures, partial physical assistance (e.g., nudges), and full physical manipulations (e.g., hand-over-hand guidance). These strategies employ differential reinforcement for the skills being taught.

These procedures have several desirable features: They reduce teachers' material-preparation time, result in effective learning, minimize student failure and errors, often produce desirable interactions between children and teachers, are highly useful across a wide range of skills and learners (on both age and disability status), and are relatively simple to use once the adult has learned them (Wolery, Ault, & Doyle, 1992). Although these strategies have often been used in one-to-one instructional arrangements, considerable research indicates that they can be used in small groups (Collins, Gast, Ault, & Wolery, 1991; Cybriwsky, Wolery, & Gast, 1990). Other research indicates that they can be embedded into low-structure, child-initiated activities such as art (Venn, Wolery, Werts, et al., 1993), mealtimes (Venn, Wolery, Fleming, et al., 1993), free play (Fox & Hanline, 1993), and transitions (Werts, Wolery, Holcombe-Ligon, Vassilaros, & Billings, 1992).

MODIFICATION AND ADJUSTMENT OF STRATEGIES

In considering modifications and adjustments of strategies that have been implemented as a part of any curriculum, one must, of course, consider that as children change and grow so do their needs. Because of the complexity of development and the multiple effects of disabilities on children's development, teams may find the need to revise intervention plans completely and to incorporate the use of different strategies. It also should be noted that the needs and wishes of the child's family may change in the course of an intervention plan, so the curriculum must be recalibrated accordingly (GC 19, GC 21).

Table 6.2. Procedural Parameters of Selected Response Prompting Strategies

Procedure	Description
Error Correction	The teacher provides the target stimulus (discriminative stimulus) and presents an opportunity for the child to respond. Correct responses are differentially reinforced and errors result in more prompts.
Antecedent Prompt and Test	The teacher presents a prompt simultaneously with the target stimulus before the learner responds, presents an opportunity to respond, and reinforces correct responses. In subsequent trials, the prompt is removed and a "test" is given to determine if the behavior occurs when presented with the target stimulus alone. During a test trial, an error response may or may not receive a prompt.
Antecedent Prompt and Fade	The teacher presents a prompt simultaneously with the target stimulus, presents an opportunity to respond, and reinforces correct responses. Over trials, the prompt is systematically faded until the learner responds to the target stimulus alone. Fading may occur on the dimensions of frequency or intensity.
Simultaneous Prompting	The teacher provides a prompt simultaneously with the target stimulus, presents an opportunity to respond, and reinforces correct responses. In daily probe trials, the target stimulus is presented alone.
Most-to-Least Prompting (Decreasing Assistance)	The teacher uses a hierarchy of prompts ordered from most to least intrusive. Initially the most intrusive prompt is presented simultaneously with the target stimulus, and correct responses are reinforced. This process continues until the child attains a specified criterion level of performance. When criterion is reached with the most intrusive prompt, the next, less intrusive prompt is provided until performance meets criterion. This process continues until the child responds to the target stimulus alone.
System of Least Prompts (Increasing Assistance)	The teacher uses a hierarchy of prompts ordered from least to most intrusive. On each trial, the teacher presents the target stimulus alone and provides an

(*continues*)

Table 6.2. *Continued*

Procedure	Description
	opportunity for a response. If no response or an error results, the least intrusive prompt is presented as is an opportunity to respond. Again, if no response is forthcoming or an error occurs, the next most intrusive prompt is presented with an opportunity to respond. This process continues until the child responds correctly. Reinforcement is provided and the trial is terminated when the child responds correctly to any level of the hierarchy.
Constant Time Delay	The teacher initially presents the target stimulus simultaneously with a controlling prompt, which is followed by an opportunity to respond for a specified number of trials. Correct responses are reinforced. For subsequent trials, the interval between the delivery of the target stimulus and the presentation of the prompt is increased for a fixed number of seconds. Correct responses before and after the prompts are usually reinforced.
Progressive Time Delay	The teacher initially presents the target stimulus simultaneously with a controlling prompt, which is followed by an opportunity to respond for a specified number of trials. Correct responses are reinforced. For subsequent trials, the interval between the delivery of the target stimulus and presentation of the prompt is gradually increased. Correct responses before and after the prompt are usually reinforced.
Graduated Guidance	The teacher begins each trial with the types and amount of prompts necessary, and as the child begins to perform the task the prompts are removed immediately. If the child stops or begins to perform incorrectly, the types and amount of prompts needed are immediately applied and withdrawn as appropriate. Reinforcement is provided if the child completes even a minimal amount of the task correctly; reinforcement is not provided if the child resists at the end of the task.
Incidental Teaching	The teacher arranges the environment to cause the child to initiate. When the child initiates, the teacher

(continues)

Table 6.2. *Continued*

Procedure	Description
	asks for an elaboration of the child's language and provides a response interval. If the elaboration is forthcoming, the teacher responds according to the child's initiation (e.g., supplies permission, materials, or information). If the elaboration is not forthcoming, the teacher provides a prompt and another response interval and provides consequences as described here.
Mand–Model Procedure	The teacher observes the child and notes his or her focus of attention. When the focus of attention is determined, the teacher provides a *mand* (a non-yes/no question) and provides a short response interval. If the child responds correctly, the teacher praises the child and terminates the interaction. If the child does not respond correctly, the teacher provides a model, a response interval, and consequences as appropriate.

Note. From *Teaching Infants and Preschoolers with Disabilities* (pp. 170–171), by D. B. Bailey and M. Wolery, 1992, Columbus, OH: Macmillan. Copyright 1992 by Macmillan. Adapted with permission.

Careful program monitoring in terms of children's progress is critical. Early interventionists who engage in quality practices consistently monitor the effects of their programs and often alter intervention plans to increase the probability that learning will occur. In addition to considering the progress of children, early interventionists must pay careful attention to whether or not children are able to maintain and generalize skills targeted for specific intervention across various settings, persons, and tasks (GC 20).

FUTURE WORK RELATED TO CURRICULAR INTERVENTIONS

In the past 25 years, the field has learned a substantial amount about teaching young children with disabilities (Bailey & Wolery, 1992; Barnett & Carey, 1992; Bricker & Cripe, 1992) and about early intervention in general (Meisels & Shonkoff, 1990). This book and the references contained in it are evidence of that accumulation of knowledge. However, few areas of practice are completely developed, and much remains to be learned (Wolery, 1991). In fact, future research and training efforts are needed in each of the three elements of the curriculum noted earlier in this chapter.

In terms of the curriculum content, a number of types of skills remain relatively unexplored with young children who have disabilities. For example, the field of emergent literacy, to date, has focused almost exclusively on young children with typical development, although a small literature has begun to accumulate on young children with disabilities (Katims, 1991). In a highly technical society, the acquisition of survival skills such as literacy is important for nearly all learners; thus, this area is an important research focus for early interventionists. Similarly, several common goals of early childhood education for young children with typical development have been relatively unstudied with children who have disabilities. Examples include skills such as persistence, curiosity, problem solving, flexibility, kindness, and many others. Most individuals agree that these are desirable skills, and literatures exist on some of these skills for older children and for children without disabilities. However, relatively little is known about how to promote these skills with infants and young children who have disabilities. Clearly, one of the future tasks for the field is to learn about these skills and to develop and to evaluate intervention strategies for promoting their use by young children with disabilities. Another area of future research related to the content of the curriculum is a set of skills known as "keystone" behaviors—behaviors that allow children to be more independent and efficient learners.

In terms of identifying the content of the curriculum that should become the targets of intervention for each child, research is needed to evaluate more efficient means of assessing the ecological demands of children's environments and to understand the relationships between various domains of development. In addition, substantial training and staff development activities are needed to assist practitioners in conducting meaningful curricular planning assessments.

In terms of intervention strategies, research is needed to refine the existing strategies, to develop new and more powerful strategies, and to ensure generalization of acquired skills across contexts. Also, despite the fact that individualization has been an oft repeated characteristic of early intervention and education, much remains to be learned about how to individualize environments and interventions for young children with disabilities. Finally, substantial training efforts are needed to ensure that what is known about how to support children's engagement and learning is put into practice. In short, the field has learned a great deal, but we have much to do before that knowledge is reflected in most early childhood programs.

> Preparation of this chapter was supported in part by U.S. Department of Education, Office of Special Education and Rehabilitative Services through a grant (Grant No. H086D20005, Providing Effective Instruction in Inclusive Classrooms) to Allegheny-Singer Research Institute and through a grant (Grant No. H024K30001, Research Institute on Preschool Mainstreaming) to St. Peter's Child Development Centers, Inc., with a subaward to Allegheny-Singer Research Institute. However, the opinions expressed do not necessarily reflect the policy of the U.S. Department of Education, and no official endorsement should be inferred. The authors are grateful for the assistance provided by the individuals of the General Curriculum and Intervention Strategies Strand of the Division for Early Childhood Task Force on Recommended Practices.

REFERENCES

Allen, K. E., Holm, V. A., & Schiefelbusch, R. L. (1978). *Early intervention—A team approach.* Baltimore: University Park Press.

Anastasiow, N. J. (1990). Implications of the neurobiological model for early intervention. In S. J. Meisels & J. P. Shonkoff (Eds.), *Handbook of early childhood intervention* (pp. 196–216). New York: Cambridge University Press.

Atwater, J. B., Carta, J. J., Schwartz, I. S., McConnell, S. R. (1994). Blending developmentally appropriate practices and early childhood special education: Redefining best practice to meet the needs of all young children. In B. L. Mallory & S. R. New (Eds.), *Diversity and developmentally appropriate practices: Challenges for early childhood education* (pp. 185–201). New York: Teachers College Press.

Atwater, J. B., Orth-Lopes, L., Elliott, M., Carta, J. J., & Schwartz, I. S. (1994). Completing the circle: Planning and implementing transitions to other programs. In M. Wolery & J. S. Wilbers (Eds.), *Including young children with special needs in early childhood programs* (pp. 167–200). Washington, DC: National Association for the Education of Young Children.

Baer, D. M., & Fowler, S. A. (1984). How should we measure the potential for self-control procedures for generalized educational outcomes? In W. L. Heward, T. E. Heron, D. S. Hill, & J. Trap-Porter (Eds.), *Focus on behavior analysis in education* (pp. 145–161). Columbus, OH: Charles E. Merrill.

Baer, R. A. (1990). Correspondence training: Review and current issues. *Research in Developmental Disabilities, 11,* 379–393.

Bailey, D. B. (1994). Working with families of children with special needs. In M. Wolery & J. S. Wilbers (Eds.), *Including young children with special needs in early childhood programs* (pp. 23–44). Washington, DC: National Association for the Education of Young Children.

Bailey, D. B., Palsha, S. A., & Simeonsson, R. J. (1991). Professional skills, concerns, and perceived importance of work with families in early intervention. *Exceptional Children, 58,* 156–165.

Bailey, D. B., Simeonsson, R. J., Yoder, D. E., & Huntington, G. S. (1990). Preparing professionals to serve infants and toddlers with handicaps and their families: An integrative analysis across eight disciplines. *Exceptional Children, 57,* 26–35.

Bailey, D. B., & Wolery, M. (1984). *Teaching infants and preschoolers with handicaps.* Columbus, OH: Merrill.

Bailey, D. B., & Wolery, M. (Eds.). (1989). *Assessing infants and preschoolers with handicaps.* Columbus, OH: Merrill.

Bailey, D. B., & Wolery, M. (1992). *Teaching infants and preschoolers with disabilities* (2nd ed.). Columbus, OH: Macmillan.

Barnett, D. W., & Carey, K. T. (1992). *Designing interventions for preschool learning and behavior problems.* San Francisco: Jossey-Bass.

Benner, S. M. (1992). *Assessing young children with special needs: An ecological perspective.* White Plains, NY: Longman.

Bijou, S. W. (1993). *Behavior analysis of child development* (3rd ed.). Reno, NV: Context Press.

Bijou, S. W., & Baer, D. M. (1961). *Child development: A systematic and empirical theory* (Vol. 1). Englewood Cliffs, NJ: Prentice-Hall.

Billingsley, F. F., & Romer, L. (1983). Response prompting and the transfer of stimulus control: Methods, research, and a conceptual framework. *Journal of the Association for the Severely Handicapped, 8*(2), 3–12.

Bredekamp, S. (1987). *Developmentally appropriate practice in early childhood programs serving children from birth through age 8* (rev. ed.). Washington, DC: National Association for the Education of Young Children.

Bredekamp, S. (1993). The relationship between early childhood education and early childhood special education: Healthy marriage or family feud? *Topics in Early Childhood Special Education, 13,* 258–273.

Bredekamp, S., & Rosegrant, T. (1992). *Reaching potentials: Appropriate curriculum and assessment for young children.* Washington, DC: National Association for the Education of Young Children.

Bricker, D., & Cripe, J. J. W. (1992). *An activity-based approach to early intervention.* Baltimore: Brookes.

Brown, W. H., McEvoy, M. A., & Bishop, N. (1991). Incidental teaching or social behavior. *Teaching Exceptional Children, 24,* 35–38.

Bruder, M. B. (1994). Working with members of other disciplines: Collaboration for success. In M. Wolery & J. S. Wilbers (Eds.), *Including young children with special needs in early childhood programs* (pp. 45–70). Washington, DC: National Association for the Education of Young Children.

Bruder, M. B., & Bologna, T. (1993). Collaboration and service coordination for effective early intervention. In W. Brown, S. K. Thurman, & L. F. Pearl (Eds.), *Family-centered early intervention with infants and toddlers: Innovative cross-disciplinary approaches* (pp. 103–137). Baltimore: Brookes.

Burgio, L. D., Whitman, L., & Johnson, M. R. (1980). A self-instructional package for increasing attending behavior in educable mentally retarded children. *Journal of Applied Behavior Analysis, 13,* 443–454.

Buysse, V., & Wesley, P. W. (1993). The identity crisis in early childhood special education: A call for professional role clarification. *Topics in Early Childhood Special Education, 13,* 418–429.

Carta, J. J., Atwater, J. B., Schwartz, I. S., & McConnell, S. R. (1993). Developmentally appropriate practices and early childhood special education: A reaction to Johnson and McChesney Johnson. *Topics in Early Childhood Special Education, 13,* 243–254.

Carta, J. J., Atwater, J. B., Schwartz, I. S., & Miller, P. A. (1990). Applications of ecobehavioral analysis to the study of transitions across early education settings. *Education and Treatment of Children, 13,* 298–315.

Carta, J. J., Sainato, D. M., & Greenwood, C. R. (1988). Advances in the ecological assessment of classroom instruction for young children with handicaps. In S. L. Odom & M. B. Karnes (Eds.), *Early intervention for infants and young children with handicaps: An empirical base* (pp. 217–239). Baltimore: Brookes.

Carta, J. J., Schwartz, I. S., Atwater, J. B., & McConnell, S. R. (1991). Developmentally appropriate practice: Appraising its usefulness for young children with disabilities. *Topics in Early Childhood Special Education, 11*(1), 1–20.

Collins, B. C., Gast, D. L., Ault, M. J., & Wolery, M. (1991). Small group instruction: Guidelines for teachers of students with moderate to severe handicaps. *Education and Training in Mental Retardation, 26,* 18–32.

Connell, M. C., Carta, J. J., & Baer, D. M. (1993). Programming generalization of in-class transition skills: Teaching preschoolers with developmental delays to self-assess and recruit contingent teacher praise. *Journal of Applied Behavior Analysis, 26,* 345–352.

Copple, C. (1994). Foreword. In M. Wolery & J. S. Wilbers (Eds.), *Including young children with special needs in early childhood programs* (p. vi). Washington, DC: National Association for the Education of Young Children.

Cooper, J. O., Heron, T. E., & Heward, W. L. (1987). *Applied behavior analysis.* Columbus, OH: Merrill.

Crocker, A. C. (1992). Data collection for the evaluation of mental retardation prevention activities: The fateful forty-three. *Mental Retardation, 30,* 303–317.

Cybriwsky, C. A., Wolery, M., & Gast, D. L. (1990). Use of a constant time delay procedure in teaching preschoolers in a group format. *Journal of Early Intervention, 14,* 99–116.

Davis, C. A., & Brady, M. P. (1993). Expanding the utility of behavioral momentum with young children: Where we've been and where we need to go. *Journal of Early Intervention, 17,* 211–223.

DeHaas-Warner, S. J. (1992). The utility of self-monitoring for preschool on-task behavior. *Topics in Early Childhood Special Education, 12,* 478–495.

Doyle, P. M., Wolery, M., Ault, M. J., & Gast, D. L. (1988). System of least prompts: A review of procedural parameters. *Journal of the Association for Persons with Severe Handicaps, 13,* 28–40.

Dunst, C. J. (1981). *Infant Learning: A cognitive–linguistic intervention strategy.* Hingham, MA: Teaching Resources.

Dunst, C. J. (1993). Implications of risk and opportunity factors for assessment and intervention. *Topics in Early Childhood Special Education, 13,* 143–153.

Dunst, C. J., Lesko, J. J., Holbert, K. A., Wilson, L. L., Sharpe, K. L., & Liles, R. F. (1987). A systematic approach to infant intervention. *Topics in Early Childhood Special Education, 7*(2), 19–37.

Dunst, C. J., Lowe, L. W., & Bartholomew, P. C. (1990). Contingent social responsiveness, family ecology, and infant communicative competence. *National Student Speech Language Hearing Association Journal, 17,* 39–49.

Dunst, C. J., Trivette, C. M., Davis, M., & Cornwell, J. C. (1994). Characteristics of effective help-giving practices. In C. J. Dunst, C. M. Trivette, & A. G. Deal (Eds.), *Supporting and strengthening families: Volume 1: Methods, strategies and practices* (pp. 171–186). Cambridge, MA: Brookline Books.

Dunst, C. J., Trivette, C. M., & Deal, A. (Eds.). (1994). *Supporting and strengthening families: Vol. 1. Methods, strategies and practices.* Cambridge, MA: Brookline Books.

Fernie, D. E. (1985). The promotion of play in the indoor play environment. In J. Frost & S. Sutherland (Eds.), *When children play: Proceedings of the International Conference on Play and Play Environments* (pp. 285–295). Wheatly, MD: Association for Childhood International.

Field, T. (1982). Interactive coaching for high-risk infants and their parents. In H. A. Moss, R. Hess, & C. Swift (Eds.), *Early intervention programs for infants* (pp. 5–24). New York: Haworth.

Fox, L., & Hanline, M. F. (1993). A preliminary evaluation of learning within developmentally appropriate early childhood settings. *Topics in Early Childhood Special Education, 13,* 308–327.

Guralnick, M. J. (1993). Developmentally appropriate practice in the assessment and intervention of children's peer relations. *Topics in Early Childhood Special Education, 13,* 344–371.

Halle, J. W., Baer, D. M., & Spradlin, J. E. (1981). Teachers' generalized use of delay as a stimulus control procedure to increase language use in handicapped children. *Journal of Applied Behavior Analysis, 14,* 389–409.

Handen, B. L., & Zane, T. (1987). Delayed prompting: A review of procedural variations and results. *Research in Developmental Disabilities, 8,* 307–330.

Haring, T. G. (1992). The context of social competence: Relations, relationships, and generalization. In S. L. Odom, S. R. McConnell, & M. A. McEvoy (Eds.), *Social competence of young children with disabilities: Issues and strategies for intervention* (pp. 307–320). Baltimore: Brookes.

Hart, B. (1985). Naturalistic language training strategies. In S. F. Warren & A. Rogers-Warren (Eds.), *Teaching functional language* (pp. 63–88). Austin, TX: PRO-ED.

Hart, B., & Risley, T. R. (1975). In vivo language training: Unanticipated and general effects. *Journal of Applied Behavior Analysis, 8,* 411–420.

Hart, B., & Rogers-Warren, A. K. (1978). A milieu approach to teaching language. In R. L. Schiefelbusch (Ed.), *Language intervention strategies* (pp. 193–236). Baltimore: University Park Press.

Higgins-Hains, A. (1992). Strategies for preparing preschool children with special needs for the kindergarten mainstream. *Journal of Early Intervention, 16,* 320–333.

Johnson, J. E., & Johnson, K. M. (1992). Clarifying the developmental perspective in response to Carta, Schwartz, Atwater, and McConnell. *Topics in Early Childhood Special Education, 12,* 439–457.

Johnson, K. M., & Johnson, J. E. (1993). Rejoinder to Carta, Atwater, Schwartz, and McConnell. *Topics in Early Childhood Special Education, 13,* 255–257.

Kaiser, A. P., Yoder, P., & Keetz, A. (1992). Evaluating milieu teaching. In S. F. Warren & J. Reichle (Eds.), *Causes and effects in communication and language intervention* (pp. 9–47). Baltimore: Brookes.

Katims, D. S. (1991). Emergent literacy in early childhood special education: Curriculum and instruction. *Topics in Early Childhood Special Education, 11*(1), 69–84.

Kontos, S., & File, N. (1993). Staff development in support of integration. In C. A. Peck, S. L. Odom, & D. D. Bricker (Eds.), *Integrating young children with disabilities into community programs* (pp. 169–186). Baltimore: Brookes.

Kozloff, M. (1994). *Improving educational outcomes for children with disabilities: Principles for assessment, programming, and evaluation.* Baltimore: Brookes.

Krantz, P., & Risley, T. R. (1977). Behavior ecology in the classroom. In K. D. O'Leary & S. G. O'Leary (Eds.), *Classroom management: The successful use of behavior modification* (2nd ed.). New York: Pergamon Press.

LeLaurin, K., & Risley, T. R. (1972). The organization of day care environments: "Zone" vs. "man-to-man" staff assignments. *Journal of Applied Behavior Analysis, 5,* 225–232.

Losardo, A., & Bricker, D. (1994). Activity-based instruction and direct instruction: A comparison study. *American Journal on Mental Retardation, 98.* 744–765.

Lubeck, R., & Chandler, L. (1990). Organizing the home caregiving environment for infants. *Education and Treatment of Children, 13,* 347–363.

Lynch, E. W., & Hanson, M. J. (1992). *Developing cross-cultural competence: A guide for working with young children and their families.* Baltimore: Brookes.

MacDonald, J. D., & Gillette, Y. (1988). Communicating partners: A conversational model for building parent-child relationships with handicapped children. In K. Marfo (Ed.), *Parent–child interaction and developmental disabilities: Theory, research, and intervention* (pp. 220–241). New York: Praeger.

Mace, F. C., & Belfiore, P. (1990). Behavioral momentum in the treatment of escape-motivated stereotypy. *Journal of Applied Behavior Analysis, 23,* 507–514.

Mace, F. C., Hock, M. L., Lalli, J. S., West, B. J., Belfiore, P. J., Pinter, E., & Brown, D. K. (1988). Behavioral momentum in the treatment of noncompliance. *Journal of Applied Behavior Analysis, 21,* 123–141.

Mahoney, G., & Powell, A., (1986). *The transactional intervention program teacher's guide.* Rock Hill, SC: Center for Excellence in Early Childhood Education.

Martin, S. S., Brady, M. P., & Williams, R. E. (1991). Effects of toys on the social behavior of preschool children in integrated and nonintegrated groups: Investigation of a setting event. *Journal of Early Intervention, 15,* 153–161.

McEvoy, M. A. (1990). The organization of caregiving environments: Critical issues and suggestions for future research. *Education and Treatment of Children, 13,* 269–273.

McEvoy, M. A., Odom, S. L., & McConnell, S. R. (1992). Peer social competence interventions for young children with disabilities. In S. L. Odom, S. R. McConnell, & M. A. McEvoy (Eds.), *Social competence of young children with disabilities: Issues and strategies for intervention* (pp. 113–133). Baltimore: Brookes.

McGee, G. G., Daly, T., Izeman, S. G., Mann, L. H., & Risley, T. R. (1991). Use of classroom materials to promote preschool engagement. *Teaching Exceptional Children, 23,* 44–47.

McLean, M. E., & Odom, S. L. (1993). Practices for young children with and without disabilities: A comparison of DEC and NAEYC identified practices. *Topics in Early Childhood Special Education, 13,* 274–292.

McWilliam, R. A. (1991). Targeting teaching at children's use of time. *Teaching Exceptional Children, 23,* 42–43.

McWilliam, R. A., & Bailey, D. B. (1992). Promoting engagement and mastery. In D. B. Bailey & M. Wolery (Eds.), *Teaching infants and preschoolers with disabilities* (2nd ed., pp. 229–255). Columbus, OH: Macmillan.

McWilliam, R. A., & Strain, P. S. (1993). Service delivery models. In DEC Task Force on Recommended Practices (Ed.), *DEC recommended practices: Indicators of quality in programs for infants and young children with special needs and their families.* Reston, VA: Council for Exceptional Children.

Meisels, S. J., & Shonkoff, J. P. (1990). *Handbook of early childhood intervention.* New York: Cambridge University Press.

Noonan, M. J., McCormick, L. (1993). *Early intervention in natural environments.* Belmont, CA: Brookes/Cole.

Nordquist, V. M., Twardosz, S., & McEvoy, M. A. (1991). Effects of environmental reorganization in classrooms for children with autism. *Journal of Early Intervention, 15,* 135–152.

Norris, J. A. (1991). Providing developmentally appropriate intervention to infants and young children with handicaps. *Topics in Early Childhood Special Education, 11*(1), 21–35.

Odom, S. L., & Brown, W. H. (1993). Social interaction skills interventions for young children with disabilities in integrated settings. In C. A. Peck, S. L. Odom, & D. D. Bricker (Eds.), *Integrating young children with disabilities into community programs* (pp. 39–64). Baltimore: Brookes.

Odom, S. L., Chandler, L., Ostrosky, M., McConnell, S. R., & Reaney, S. (1992). Fading teacher prompts from peer-initiation interventions for young children with disabilities. *Journal of Applied Behavior Analysis, 25*, 307–318.

Odom, S. L., McConnell, S. R., & McEvoy, M. A. (1992). *Social competence of young children with disabilities: Issues and strategies for intervention.* Baltimore: Brookes.

Odom, S. L., & McEvoy, M. A. (1990). Mainstreaming at the preschool level: Potential barriers and tasks for the field. *Topics in Early Childhood Special Education, 10*(2), 48–61.

Odom, S. L., Peterson, C., McConnell, S. R., & Ostrosky, M. (1990). Ecobehavioral analysis of early education/specialized classroom settings and peer social interaction. *Education and Treatment of Children, 13*, 316–330.

Odom, S. L., & Watts, E. (1991). Reducing teacher prompts in peer-mediated interventions for young children with autism. *Journal of Special Education, 25*, 7–25.

Paniagua, F. A. (1990). A procedural analysis of correspondence training techniques. *The Behavior Analyst, 13*, 107–119.

Peck, C. A., Odom, S. L., & Bricker, D. (1993). *Integrating young children with disabilities into community programs: Ecological perspectives on research and implementation.* Baltimore: Brookes.

Phyfe-Perkins, E. (1980). Children's behavior in preschool settings: A review of research concerning the influence of the physical environment. In L. Katz (Ed.), *Current topics in early childhood education* (Vol. 3, pp. 91–125). Norwood, NJ: Ablex.

Piaget, J. (1952). *The origins of intelligence in children.* New York: Norton.

Safford, P. L. (1989). *Integrated teaching in early childhood: Starting in the mainstream.* White Plains, NY: Longman.

Sainato, D. M. (1990). Classroom transitions: Organizing environments to promote independent performance in preschool children with disabilities. *Education and Treatment of Children, 12*, 288–297.

Sainato, D. M., Goldstein, H., & Strain, P. S. (1992). Effects of self-evaluation on preschool children's use of social interaction strategies with their classmates with autism. *Journal of Applied Behavior Analysis, 25*, 127–141.

Sainato, D. M., Strain, P. S., Lefebvre, D., Rapp, N. (1990). Effects of self-evaluation on the independent work skills of preschool children with disabilities. *Exceptional Children, 56*, 540–549.

Schuster, J. W., Griffen, A. K., & Wolery, M. (1992). Comparison of the simultaneous prompting and constant time delay procedures in teaching sight words to elementary students with moderate mental retardation. *Journal of Behavioral Education, 2*, 305–325.

Strain, P. S., & Odom, S. L. (1986). Peer social initiations: Effective intervention for social skills development of exceptional children. *Exceptional Children, 52*, 543–551.

Strain, P. S., & Sainato, D. M. (1987). Preventive discipline in early childhood special education. *Teaching Exceptional Children, 19*, 26–30.

Venn, M. L., Wolery, M., Fleming, L. A., DeCesare, L. D., Morris, A., Sigesmund, M. H. (1993). Effects of teaching preschool peers to use the mand–model procedure during snack activities. *American Journal of Speech-Language Pathology, 2*(1), 38–46.

Venn, M. L., Wolery, M., Werts, M. G., Morris, A., DeCesare, L. D., & Cuffs, M. S. (1993). Embedding instruction in art activities to teach preschoolers with disabilities to imitate their peers. *Early Childhood Research Quarterly, 8*, 277–294.

Vygotsky, L. (1978). *Mind in society: The development of psychological processes*. Cambridge, MA: Harvard University Press.

Warren, S. F., & Kaiser, A. (1988). Research in early language intervention. In S. L. Odom & M. B. Karnes (Eds.), *Early intervention for infants and young children with handicaps: An empirical base* (pp. 89–108). Baltimore: Brookes.

Warren, S. F., McQuarter, R. J., & Rogers-Warren, A. K. (1984). The effects of mands and models on the speech of unresponsive, socially isolated children. *Journal of Speech and Hearing Disorders, 47,* 42–52.

Werts, M. G., Wolery, M., Holcombe-Ligon, A., Vassilaros, M. A., & Billings, S. S. (1992). Efficacy of transition-based teaching with instructive feedback. *Education and Treatment of Children, 15,* 320–334.

Winton, P. J., & Turnbull, A. P. (1981). Effective programs for parents of young handicapped children. *Topics in Early Childhood Special Education, 1,* 11–19.

Wolery, M. (1991). Instruction in early childhood special education: "Seeing through a glass darkly... knowing in part." *Exceptional Children, 58,* 127–135.

Wolery, M. (1994). Implementing instruction for young children with special needs in early childhood classrooms. In M. Wolery & J. S. Wilbers (Eds.), *Including young children with special needs in early childhood programs* (pp. 151–166). Washington, DC: National Association for the Education of Young Children.

Wolery, M., Ault, M. J., & Doyle, P. M. (1992). *Teaching students with moderate and severe disabilities: Use of response prompting strategies.* White Plains, NY: Longman.

Wolery, M., Bailey, D. B., & Sugai, G. M. (1988). *Effective teaching: Principles and procedures of applied behavior analysis with exceptional students.* Boston: Allyn & Bacon.

Wolery, M., & Bredekamp, S. (1994). Developmentally appropriate practice and young children with special needs: Contextual issues in the discussion. *Journal of Early Intervention, 18,* 331–341.

Wolery, M., Doyle, P. M., Gast, D. L., Ault, M. J., & Simpson, S. L. (1993). Comparison of progressive time delay and transition-based teaching with preschoolers who have developmental delays. *Journal of Early Intervention, 17,* 160–176.

Wolery, M., & Fleming, L. A. (1993). Implementing individualized curriculum in integrated settings. In C. A. Peck, S. L. Odom, & D. Bricker (Eds.), *Integrating young children with disabilities into community programs: Ecological perspectives on research and implementation* (pp. 109–132). Baltimore: Brookes.

Wolery, M., & Gast, D. L. (1984). Effective and efficient procedures for the transfer of stimulus control. *Topics in Early Childhood Special Education, 4*(3), 55–77.

Wolery, M., Holcombe, A., Brookfield, J., Huffman, K., Schroeder, C., Martin, C. G., Venn, M. L., Werts, M. G., & Fleming, L. A. (1993). The extent and nature of preschool mainstreaming: A survey of general early educators. *Journal of Special Education, 27,* 222–234.

Wolery, M., Holcombe, A., Cybriwsky, C. A., Doyle, P. M., Schuster, J. W., Ault, M. J., & Gast, D. L. (1992). Constant time delay with discrete responses: A review of effectiveness and demographic, procedural, and methodological parameters. *Research in Developmental Disabilities, 13,* 239–266.

Wolery, M., Strain, P. S., & Bailey, D. B. (1992). Reaching the potentials of children with special needs. In S. Bredekamp & T. Rosegrant (Eds.), *Reaching potentials: Appropriate curriculum and assessment for young children* (pp. 92–111). Washington, DC: National Association for the Education of Young Children.

Wolery, M., Venn, M. L., Holcombe, A., Brookfield, J., Martin, C. G., Huffman, K., Schroeder, C., & Fleming, L. A. (1994). Employment of related service personnel in preschool programs: A survey of general early educators. *Exceptional Children, 61,* 25–39.

Wolery, M., Werts, M. G., & Holcombe, A. (1994). Current practices with young children who have disabilities: Issues of placement, assessment, and instruction. *Focus on Exceptional Children, 26*(6), 1–12.

Wolery, M., & Wilbers, J. S. (1994). *Including young children with special needs in early childhood programs.* Washington, DC: National Association for the Education of Young Children.

CHAPTER 7

Promoting the Cognitive Competence of Young Children with or at Risk for Developmental Disabilities

Carl J. Dunst
Gerald Mahoney
Kristin Buchan

Our purpose in this chapter is to describe a set of guidelines and general procedures for promoting the cognitive development of infants, toddlers, and older preschoolers with or at risk for developmental disabilities. Cognitive development entails progressive changes in children's perceptions, knowledge, understanding, reasoning, and judgment, and the use of these competencies in everyday situations and routines as a basis for both acting independently and participating in social interactions with others. Early cognitive intervention enhances children's rates and patterns of developing cognitive competencies and promotes utilization of these competencies in ways that permit children to adapt more effectively and efficiently to a broad range of environmental demands and challenges.

More specifically, the material presented in this chapter for implementing interventions is designed to facilitate children's acquisition of progressively more complex, cognitive interactive competencies. The major intervention goal is the facilitation of conventionalized interactive competencies that reflect a shift in the balance of power toward the developing child (Dunst & McWilliam, 1988). Three key terms in this goal statement deserve comment to place the content of the chapter in proper perspective. The term *conventionalization* refers to socially and culturally defined and recognized behavior that permits a child to become a more competent and socially adaptive member of different settings and contexts. An *interactive competency* is a behavior used by a child that influences and is influenced by environmental events and situations. *Balance of power* refers to the child's ability to exercise control over social and nonsocial environments through increased use of conventionalized, social–adaptive competencies. According to Bronfenbrenner (1979), "there is evidence to suggest that the optimal situation for learning and development is one in which the balance of power gradually shifts in favor of the developing person" (p. 58). In view of this assertion, the emphasis of intervention practices should focus on facilitating the acquisition of cognitive (as well as other kinds of) knowledge and skills that increase the types and forms of interactive competencies that a child can use in response to different demands and challenges. The terms *interactive competency* and *developmental competency* are used interchangeably in this chapter to refer to cognitive knowledge and skills that constitute indexes of intellectual growth during the period from birth to approximately 6 years of age.

Recommendations described in this chapter evolved from a series of discussions involving a number of nationally recognized experts in the early intervention field. These discussions were influenced by a number of factors: (1) consensus among these professionals regarding theoretical notions conceptually useful for achieving the goals and objectives of early cognitive intervention; (2) accumulated evidence from descriptive and experimental studies pointing to the potential value and need for various types of intervention procedures for promoting the acquisition of cognitive competence; and (3) a tradition of clinical practice with young children that has yielded outcome data that are both promising and disappointing (Dunst, Snyder, & Mankinen, 1988). The guidelines reflect current beliefs about best practice and are intended to promote use of procedures that are consistent with principles of family-centered early intervention (McGonigel, 1991). The procedures are proposed, however, with the understanding that there continues to be a critical need to move early cognitive intervention beyond the realm of consensus and conjecture to a level of practical knowledge and understanding that is more firmly grounded in empirical research.

CONCEPTUAL AND PROCEDURAL CONSIDERATIONS

The recommendations delineated in this section were developed within the context of several conceptual and procedural considerations. These include the nature of cognitive competence of the developing child, the characteristics of the cognitive competence of children with disabilities, and the social–ecological context of early cognitive development. Each of these considerations is briefly described next as a backdrop against which early cognitive intervention is best understood.

Nature of Cognitive Competencies of the Developing Child

Taxonomic descriptions of developing cognitive competencies vary enormously across theoretical models (e.g., Appleton, Clifton, & Goldberg,

1975; Case, 1985; Fischer, 1980; Harris, 1983; Horowitz, 1987; Piaget, 1970; Rowland & McGuire, 1971; Uzgiris, 1986b; Uzgiris & Hunt, 1975). Yet, there is general consensus regarding a number of cognitive abilities considered hallmarks of the first 6 years of development. These include, but are not limited to, perception, memory, comprehension, symbolic representation, problem solving, purposeful planning, decision making, discrimination, and idea/intention generation. It is also generally recognized that the attainment of these kinds of competencies is intricately linked to the nature of interactions between a developing child and his or her social and nonsocial environments (Piaget, 1945/1951, 1936/1952, 1937/1954). Furthermore, it has long been acknowledged that the cognitive behaviors of young children bear little, if any, resemblance to the cognitive capabilities of older children and adults (Case, 1985; Fischer, 1980; Piaget, 1970). Not surprisingly, therefore, young children engage in cognitive behaviors that are *quantitatively* and *qualitatively* different from intellectual behavior beyond the preschool years.

The feature that most distinguishes the cognitive competencies of the developing child from those of older children and adults is the *close association between children's activity and their cognitive capabilities.* Older children and adults engage in cognitive behaviors primarily through the use of symbolic rule systems and verbal mediators. That is, cognitive behaviors such as problem solving, reasoning, and judgment are carried out as mental operations that can be conducted independently of actual experiences. In contrast, throughout the first 6 years of life, cognitive behavior is intimately tied closely to children's interactions with people and objects in a variety of different settings and situations.

The kinds of activities that children engage in while interacting with objects and people provide insight into children's understanding and reasoning. For example, children's repeated use of behaviors such as throwing and banging with a variety of objects and materials suggests that their interest in and understanding of their world is closely tied to the kinds of actions they perform with different objects, materials, and people. Rather than learning about their world primarily in terms of perceptual attributes, such as color, shape, or size, young children learn about objects and people in terms of the behavior they perform in interactions with these objects and people. Most of the behaviors children produce while interacting with objects and people reflect their efforts to make sense of the world about them. Activities that may appear to have limited purposefulness, such as exploring, manipulating, and practicing, are nonetheless critical in order for children to develop an awareness and understanding necessary for higher levels of cognitive functioning. In fact, evidence indicates that exploring, manipulating, and practicing are essential characteristics of children's acquisition of interactive competencies (see, e.g., Hunt, 1987; Uzgiris, 1986b; White, 1971).

The close association between children's activity and cognitive functioning underscores the important and central role that different kinds of play contribute to the development of interactive competencies. Information about children's play (e.g., Linder, 1993) not only provides important insights about children's preferences and interests but also helps practitioners understand the development of higher order, critical cognitive functions. Consequently, early cognitive intervention can enhance children's awareness and understanding of their environments by increasing their range of play opportunities that encourage and promote engagement in cognitive-related activities that involve practice, exploration, and problem solving. Play-related behavior, used throughout this chapter in a very broad sense, is therefore considered a very important means for enhancing the acquisition of early cognitive competence.

Cognitive Competencies of Children with Disabilities

A corroborative body of evidence now indicates that the cognitive competencies of young children with disabilities are more alike than different compared to those of typically developing children (for reviews and syntheses of the majority of available evidence, see Dunst, 1984, 1990, in press; Dunst & Lesko, 1988; Dunst & McWilliam, 1988). For example, in a recently completed longitudinal study of different groups of children with disabilities, those at risk for developmental delays, and normally developing children, Dunst and others (Dunst, in press; Dunst, Vance, & Hamby, 1994) found that the sequences and patterns of sensorimotor development (Dunst, 1980; Uzgiris & Hunt, 1975) among children with and without disabilities were nearly identical, although not surprisingly, rates of development were slower among children with disabilities compared to those at risk for poor outcomes or to normally developing infants.

One area of research that has contributed enormously to the understanding of early cognitive competence of children with disabilities is that focusing on the development of play behavior. A considerable amount of investigative effort has been devoted to research on children's play to determine (a) if children with disabilities engage in the same types of interactive competencies as those found among normally developing children and (b) whether play-related interactive competencies show similar relationships to other dimensions of development as has been found with typically developing children. These various studies have been either of two types—those in which children with and without disabilities are the same chronological age and those in which children with and without disabilities are the same developmental age—the results of which suggest different foci of early cognitive intervention practices.

Studies that have compared the play of children with disabilities to that of same-aged typically developing children have consistently found that children with disabilities engage in less frequent play (Li, 1985; Jennings, Connors, & Stegman, 1988; Turner & Small, 1985), less varied play (Beeghly, Weiss-Perry, & Cicchetti, 1990; Parsons, 1986), and lower developmental levels of play (Brophy & Stone-Zukowski, 1984; Jennings et al., 1988; Li, 1985). These findings suggest that cognitive delays associated with developmental disabilities may be attributed, at least in part, to differences in the manner and intensity with which children with disabilities handle, manipulate, and otherwise interact with objects and people. The implications of these findings indicate a need to intervene in ways that directly aim to correct differences. However, an alternative conclusion is suggested by a second set of studies.

Studies that have compared the play behavior of children with disabilities with that of younger typically developing children who are at the same developmental level lead to very different conclusions. Findings from these studies indicate that there are few, if any, differences in most features of children's play, findings that are consistent with evidence for other early cognitive domains (Dunst, in press; Dunst et al., 1994). Not only do children with disabilities display comparable levels and intensity of play when matched on developmental level, they also have been found to progress through the same sequence of developmental play stages as do normally developing children (Beeghly et al., 1990; Brooks-Gunn & Lewis, 1982; Crawley & Chan, 1982; Gowen, Goldman, Johnson-Martin, & Hussey, 1989). Research findings from these studies do not negate the fact that there are delays in the age of onset of play behaviors of children with disabilities or that these children remain at different play levels for longer periods of time. These findings do, however, suggest that the processes in the acquisition of play-related cognitive behaviors of children with disabilities are highly similar to those of typically functioning children who are at similar developmental levels.

Further support for the contention that the cognitive behaviors of children with disabilities emerge in ways similar to those of typically developing children comes from studies examining the relationship between children's play and the acquisition of other developmental competencies. Results from these studies consistently indicate that the characteristics of play displayed by children with disabilities are correlated with their language competence (Beeghly & Cicchetti, 1985), interpersonal skills (Hill & McCune-Nicholich, 1981; Motti, Cicchetti, & Stroufe, 1983), and other aspects of cognitive development (Power & Radcliff, 1989; Hill & McCune-Nicholich, 1981) as has been found in studies of typically developing children. Although the possibility remains that there are fundamental differences in the manner that young children with disabilities think, reason, and engage in different types of cognitive behaviors, these differences have yet to be described reliably, with the exception of delays in the onset of cognitive as well as other developmental competencies.

At this time, therefore, it is reasonable to assume that children with disabilities acquire and display cognitive behaviors in much the same way as do typically developing children who are at the same developmental level. Current knowledge of the cognitive abilities of children with disabilities suggests that recommended practices with these children should parallel what is known about the cognitive development of children without disabilities. Consequently, early cognitive intervention practices for children with disabilities need not differ much from practices used with typically developing children.

Social–Ecological Perspective on Cognitive Development

Highly suggestive evidence also indicates that efforts to promote cognitive competencies are best framed in a human ecology perspective of behavior and development. The term *human ecology* refers to the relations between person and environment characteristics and how these characteristics both independently and in combination influence behavior and development. According to Bronfenbrenner (1979), an "ecological orientation . . . to the study of human development is concerned with the progressive accommodation between a growing human organism and its immediate environment, and the way in which this relation is mediated by forces emanating from more remote regions in the larger physical and social milieu" (p. 13).

An ecological perspective of human development recognizes the fact that behavior and development are multiply determined. A *determinant* is a factor or variable affecting or influencing some aspect of a person's behavior or development (e.g., picking up an infant, which leads to both cessation of crying and infant attentiveness to the caregiver). A determinant may be either a *static* or *dynamic* variable. Gender is an example of a static variable. It is static in the sense that although it may function as a determinant, it cannot be changed or manipulated as an intervention factor. Parenting style is an example of a dynamic variable. It is dynamic in the sense that it can be modified or changed and may function as a determinant. Although an ecological science of behavior and development concerns itself with the identification and study of both static and dynamic variables, dynamic variables primarily are the ones of interest as part of intervention practices. This is the case because dynamic variables can be manipulated as interventions for influencing developmental change.

The determinants, or "interventions," that potentially influence early child development can, for heuristic purposes, be grouped into four broad categories: family, interactional, environmental, and systems influences. The categories are not mutually exclusive, but, rather, are highly intertwined and interdependent. We describe selective examples next to illustrate both the types of factors that influence the acquisitions of interactive competencies and which factors become appropriate as part of early cognitive intervention practices.

Family Determinants

Family determinants refer to the characteristics of individual family members, the family unit, and the developing person himself or herself that account for variations in behavior and development. A number of malleable determinants account for such variability. These include, but are not limited to, the physical and psychological health of family members (Field, McCabe, & Schneiderman, 1988), parental beliefs systems (Sigel, 1985), parental attitudes (Schaefer & Edgerton, 1985), parental expectations and attributions (Segal, 1985), and intraindividual adaptations (Lerner & Busch-Rossnagel, 1981). Dunst, Trivette, Hamby, and Pollock (1990), for example, found that a number of aspects of child behavior characteristics (e.g., child temperament, affect, competence) were influenced by both parent and family well-being and health. Maisto and German (1981) found that infants participating in an early intervention program showed greater progress when their mothers assumed beliefs that reflected an internal locus of control. In a study examining the influences of temperament on operant learning, Dunst and Lingerfelt (1985) found that consistency and predictability in the day-to-day routines of infants 2 through 3 months old related to rates of learning—the more consistent the child's routines, the greater the rate of learning. Taken together, a considerable body of evidence documents the importance of a wide array of intrapersonal family characteristics to the developing competencies of young children.

Interactional Determinants

Interactional determinants refer to caregiver styles that influence the behavior and development of infants and toddlers. Caregiver styles cover a wide range of interpersonal characteristics that shape and direct the course of development of very young children (e.g., Marfo, 1988; Tronick, 1982). The evidence regarding the relationship between interactional determinants and infant and toddler behavior and development is both clear-cut and convincing. Directive and coercive interactional behaviors impede development, whereas responsive, facilitative, and supportive styles promote and enhance development (Dunst, Wortman Lowe, & Bartholomew, 1990; Field, 1977, 1979b; Hanzlik, 1986; Mahoney, 1988a, 1988b; White & Watts, 1973). So important are interactional determinants that they constitute a major focus of recommended practices described later in this chapter.

Environmental Determinants

Environmental determinants refer to the physical and organizational characteristics of environments and how these features influence behavior. A number of investigators have described some, but certainly not all, of the environmental considerations and organizational patterns influencing child development (e.g., Herbert-Jackson, O'Brien, Porterfield, & Risley, 1977; O'Brien, Porterfield, Herbert-Jackson, & Risley, 1979; Olds, 1979; Twardosz, 1984; Twardosz & Risley, 1982; Weinstein & David, 1987). White (1971), in a carefully planned and well-executed series of studies, demonstrated the influences that different types of environmental experiences played in accelerating the age of acquisition of visually directed reaching. Similarly, Hunt and others (Hunt, 1987; Hunt, Mohandessi, Ghodssi, & Akiyama, 1976) carried out a series of investigations that were designed, in part, to determine the effects that different environmental regimens had on rates of development of sensorimotor competencies. Hunt found considerable variations in age of acquisition of progressively more complex developmental competencies as a function of differing conditions of rearing as well as of environmental opportunities within settings. The influences that environmental determinants have on child behavior and development are often neglected as part of early cognitive interaction practices despite the fact that their "interventive" impact is clearly indicated.

Systems Determinants

Systems determinants refer to the range of factors that mediate changes in development vis-à-vis extrafamily experiences and events. Bronfenbrenner (1979), for example, noted that

> whether parents can perform effectively in their child-rearing roles . . . depends on role demands, stresses, and supports emanating from other settings. . . . Parents' evaluations of their capacity to function, as well as their view of their child, are related to such external factors as flexibility of job schedules, adequacy of child care arrangements, the presence of friends and neighbors who can help out in large and small emergencies, the quality of health and social services, and neighborhood safety. The availability of supportive settings is, in turn, a function of their existence and frequency in a given culture or subculture. This frequency can be *enhanced by adoption of . . . practices that create additional settings . . . and (experiences) conducive to family life* [italics added]. (p. 7)

The kinds of social support and resources that Bronfenbrenner (1979) refers to have been found to be major determinants of child behavior and development (see e.g., Boukydis, 1987). Social support includes emotional, psychological, physical, informational, instrumental, and material resources provided by personal network members designed to influence the behavior of the recipient of the help and assistance.

The role that social support plays in affecting caregiver behavior has been discussed by both Bronfenbrenner (1979, 1986) and Cochran and Brassard (1979). According to Cochran and Brassard (1979), social network members potentially influence caregiver behavior in at least three major ways. First, the support that is provided may promote health and well-being, which, in turn, may set the occasion for more positive interactive episodes between caregivers and a developing child. Second, social network members may informally establish standards regarding social expectations about acceptable interactional behavior. Third, social network members may serve as role models that affect parenting practices to the extent that esteemed network members demonstrate effective and nurturing childrearing behavior. Each of these forms of influence may potentially affect caregiving behavior to the extent that social network members provide caregivers different types of support, which, in turn, is likely to directly and indirectly affect both parent and child behavior and development.

Bronfenbrenner (1986) recently reviewed and integrated the majority of evidence regarding the influence of personal–social networks on caregiver interactive behavior. The evidence is beginning to paint a clear picture: Provision of supportive experiences to parents of young children has discernible effects on the styles of interaction parents employ with their offspring, which, in turn, affects child behavior and development. Dunst and Trivette (1988), for example, found that availability of support was positively related to responsive, engaging, and facilitative styles, whereas lack of support was found to interfere with the display of these particular caregiving behaviors. Similarly, Dunst, Vance, and Hamby (1988) found that opportunities to observe and interact with caregivers known to interact with young children in a facilitative and supportive manner enhanced teenaged mothers' use of the same kinds of interactional behaviors. Crnic, Greenberg, and Slough (1986) reported findings that demonstrated the direct and indirect influences of social support on infant behavior and development. Collectively, evidence is being amassed that indicates that social support and resources influence a number of aspects of parental behavior, which, in turn, directly and indirectly influence child behavior and development. Incorporating systems influences into early cognitive intervention practices therefore seems highly warranted.

Overview

The remainder of this chapter is divided into three major sections. The first includes the principles and corollaries associated with the use of theories and models of cognitive development for structuring both assessment and intervention practices. The second describes an expanded framework for assessing early cognitive competencies, with particular emphasis on identifying factors influencing child performance. The third, which makes up the bulk of the chapter, describes eight different principles and associated corollaries for structuring efforts to promote the acquisition of early cognitive competence. Collectively, the material described in all three sections provides a framework for enhancing the early cognitive developmental competence of children with or at risk for developmental disabilities.

As part of the description of the principles and corollaries of early cognitive development and intervention, the principles and corollaries are cross-referenced with the DEC-recommended practices describing interventions to promote cognitive skills (Dunst, 1993) and other relevant DEC-recommended practices (Division for Early Childhood Task Force on Recommended Practices, 1993). The cross-referencing is done according to the DEC Task Force on Recommended Practices coding system for individual practice items so that the reader can easily locate them in that document.

PRINCIPLES FOR GUIDING THE CONDUCT OF EARLY COGNITIVE INTERVENTION

The strategies described next for structuring early intervention practices to promote cognitive competence are based on a rich array of empirical evidence suggesting the conditions best suited for optimizing developmental outcomes in children with and at risk for disabilities. This evidence has been used to generate 10 principles and 20 associated corollaries for guiding the conduct of early cognitive intervention. Each principle and set of associated corollaries addresses one important aspect of cogntively related intervention practices. Collectively, they form a foundation for achieving the goal of early cognitive intervention described previously.

Theories and Models of Cognitive Development

Cognitive development theories and models are crucial for early cognitive intervention because they provide roadmaps for charting the course a child traverses during the genesis of cognitive competence. A number of theories and models describe the development of cognitive competencies from birth through the preschool years and beyond (see, e.g., Case, 1985; Horowitz, 1987; Uzgiris, 1986b). Each describes either or both the quantitative and qualitative changes that occur in one or more domains or branches of cognitive development. Most cognitive development theories characterize change in terms of stagelike progress leading to the acquisition of a broad range of cognitive knowledge and skills. The first principle and its corollaries are derived from an understanding of the kinds of changes that transpire in the early development of cognitive competence.

PRINCIPLE 1. Cognitive assessment and intervention practices are based on theories and models that specify progressive changes that occur in children's acquisition of knowledge and skill acquisition and use (GC 3).

COROLLARY 1.1. Relevant and useful theories and models describe changes in both the social and nonsocial domains of cognitive development.

COROLLARY 1.2. The kinds of theories and models most relevant and useful for guiding assessment and intervention practices are ones that describe the development of cognitive competencies in children's interactions with both objects and people.

Models and theories of cognitive development are useful for promoting the acquisition of cognitive competence because they help identify intervention targets and learning opportunities that can be used to promote a child's progress in ways comparable to that of typically developing children. Piaget's theory of cognitive development, for example, has proven useful for this purpose (e.g., Dunst, 1981). Not all cognitive development theories, however, serve this function. Theories that are useful meet at least three important criteria (Dunst & McWilliam, 1988). First, they describe cognitive competencies involving interactions with both *objects* (psychological competencies) and *people* (psychosocial competencies). Second, they describe the development of *practical* knowledge and skills that children can use to interact with their social and nonsocial environments in a competent manner and to adapt to the many demands and challenges faced in daily living. Third, they are *ecologically based*, thus expanding the meaning of development and the implications of an ecologically oriented definition of development for early cognitive intervention practices.

Meaning of Development

According to Bronfenbrenner (1979), development is "defined ... as a lasting change in the way in which a person perceives and deals with his (or her) environments" (p. 3). More specifically, "development is the process through which the growing person acquires a more extended, differentiated, and valid *conception* of ecological environments, and becomes *motivated* and able to *engage in* activities that *reveal* the properties of, sustain, or restructure the environment at levels of similar or greater complexity in *form and content*" [italics added] (Bronfenbrenner, 1979, p. 27). To say that a person has demonstrated development means that relatively permanent changes in behavior have occurred, that change occurs in both perception and action, and that the person's behavior influences or has the potential to influence persons and events beyond the immediate setting in which change has occurred.

Several examples should help clarify the meaning and dimensions of the term *development* as it is used in this chapter. A 3- or 4-month-old child is said to have developed the capacity to initiate and sustain control over social and nonsocial environments when he or she can use simple, undifferentiated behaviors to produce reinforcing consequences (response-contingent learning; Friedman & Vietze, 1972; Watson, 1972) with different people and objects across settings; "recognizes" his or her own capacity to control different aspects of physical and social environments (contingency awareness; Watson, 1966); "recognizes" the behavioral propensities of others (social expectation; Lamb, 1981); and evokes restructuring and reorganization in the ways in which people interact with the child (Goldberg, 1977). Similarly, a child 14 through 16 months old who learns to use gestures to make wants known (intentional communication; Holdgrafer & Dunst, 1986), who uses a variety of gestures across settings with different people (communicative mastery; Bates, 1976; Harding, 1983), who recognizes and anticipates the effects the gestures will have when used in the presence of others (anticipatory effectiveness; Schoville, 1984), and who evokes reorganizations in the complexity of the form and content of interactional episodes (secondary intersubjectivity; Trevarthen & Hubley, 1978) may be said to have developed the capacity to communicate using socially and culturally defined, recognized, and understood interactive competencies. Both of these examples illustrate the complexity of behavior change and how development manifests itself in "a person's evolving conception of the ecological environment, and his relation to it, as well as the person's growing capacity to discover, sustain, or alter its properties" (Bronfenbrenner, 1979, p. 9). Therefore, it is not simply a matter of whether or not a child can perform certain behaviors, but rather how the production of interactive competencies has second and higher effects on his or her own as well as other people's behavior.

Competence and Performance

Developmental growth is typically described in terms of a person's competence and performance. *Competence* is defined as the *achievement and availability* of a variety of different types and forms of behavior at different levels or stages of development (Davidson & Sternberg, 1985). *Performance* is defined as the *utilization of competence* as a result of experiences that evoke adaptations to different demands and challenges (Davidson & Sternberg, 1985). Performance is what practitioners use to determine that a child is capable of a particular level of competence.

The relationship between competence and performance is an important one and has major implications for early cognitive intervention practices. Although a child might have mastered the capacity to perform at a certain level of competence, the developing child's behavior is typically characterized by engagement in a small number of behaviors at this highest level, a large number of behaviors at the preceding level or stage of development, and even continued engagement in a small number of behaviors at earlier stages (see, e.g., Dunst, 1984). Figure 7.1 illustrates this kind of developmental pattern for the play behavior of two groups of children with disabilities functioning at different developmental levels (Mahoney, 1995). As can be seen, as children begin to manifest higher level play behaviors, they continue engagement in different types and forms of play at lower levels of functioning. Dunst, Holbert, and Wilson (1990) found almost identical patterns of behavior for the manifestation of early cognitive interactive competencies (Dunst & McWilliam, 1988). These kinds of data poignantly illustrate that a developing child will not demonstrate performance at only the highest level of competence but rather will display a broad range of interactive competencies at different levels of functioning. Moreover, these data indicate that children's continued engagement in behavior at levels below their highest competency level does *not* prevent them from acquiring more advanced developmental capabilities.

The findings of the sort just described have one very important implication for early cognitive intervention practices. They indicate that one should not only expect but also support the display of a variety of interactive competencies at different developmental levels if interventions are expected to maintain children's engagement with their social and nonsocial environments in ways that affirm their preferences and interests. Moreover, the extent to which interventions can be done in ways that are developmentally challenging, but not excessively demanding, a child should demonstrate continued success and enjoyment as he or she continues to learn and develop.

Assessment Considerations

An ecologically oriented definition of development suggests an expanded perspective of assessment, especially with regard to the assessment of performance for the purpose of planning interventions to promote early cognitive development. This shift includes efforts not only to determine a child's

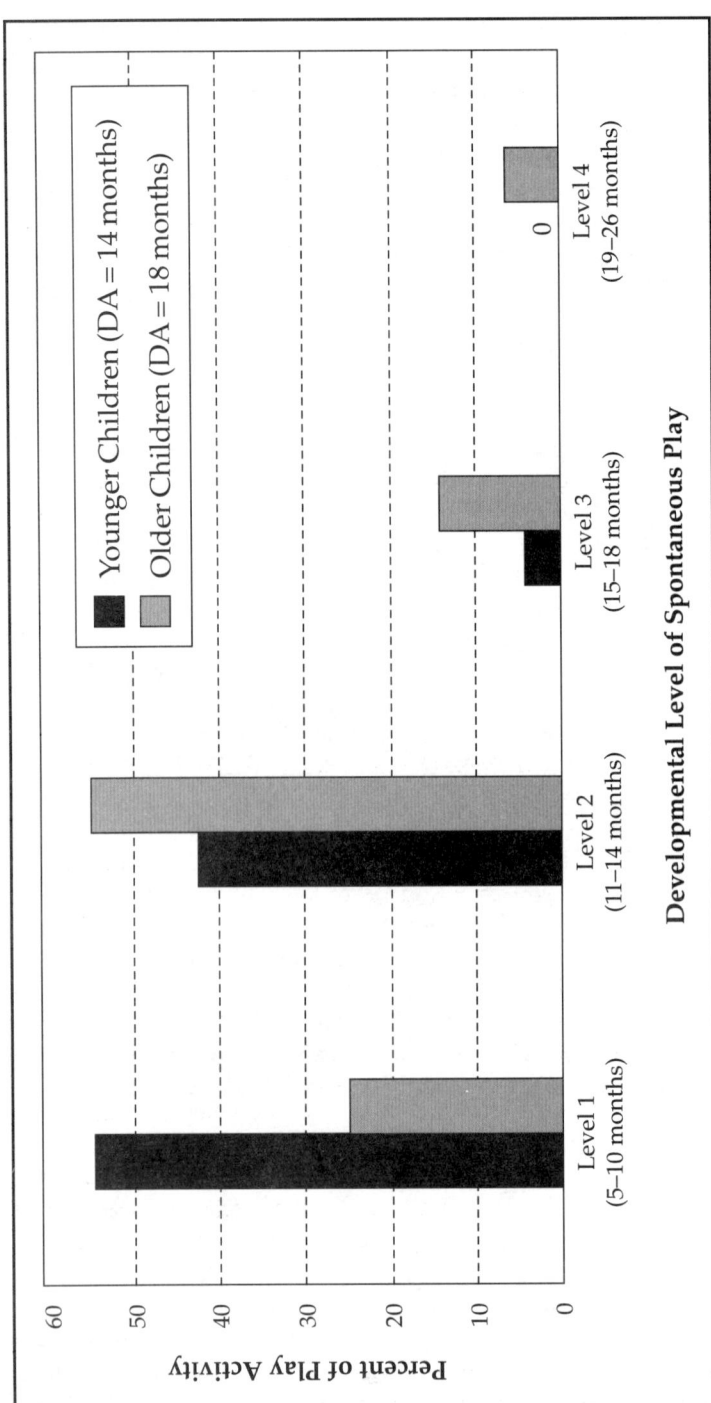

Figure 7.1. Comparisons of the play behavior of developmentally younger (14 months) and older (18 months) children with disabilities 2 through 2½ years old at four levels of spontaneous play. *Note.* From "Developmental Changes in the Spontaneous Play Behavior of Young Children with Disabilities: Implications for Play Based Interviews," by G. Mahoney, in *Family Child Developmental Reports* (Vol. 1), edited by G. Mahoney, 1995, Tallmadge, OH: Family Child Learning Center. Reprinted with permission.

cognitive capabilities but also to identify those intraindividual and environmental factors that influence the acquisition of cognitive interactive competencies. Accordingly, the main purpose of assessment for intervention is to characterize the topography of the child's interactive competencies and to identify factors associated with performance (Dunst, Holbert, & Wilson, 1990; Dunst & McWilliam, 1988). Such information is useful for planning and implementing interventions designed to facilitate acquisition of cognitive competencies. This approach translates into the following principle and corollaries.

PRINCIPLE 2. Cognitive assessment procedures include the identification of person and environmental factors and variables that are related to children's acquisition of cognitive interactive competencies with people, objects, and events (COG 1).

COROLLARY 2.1. Cognitive assessment practices are ongoing and involve a range of formal and informal, and scale-based (norm, ordinal, judgment, etc.) and observational procedures for capturing a child's existing and emerging cognitive competencies (A 6).

COROLLARY 2.2. Cognitive assessment practices are conducted in a variety of settings and under different conditions as a basis for fully understanding the ecological bases of knowledge and skill development and use (COM 2).

A simple but useful way for expanding the meaning and function of assessment may be stated in the form of the relationship, $B = f(A)$, where B is behavior (development, competence, performance, etc.) and A is one or more person and environmental factors (e.g., instructional practices, environmental settings). The relationship between A and B may be stated as follows: B varies as a function (f) of A. The definition proposed by Wachs and Sheehan (1988) for guiding the purposes of assessment with young children reflects this "two-sided" emphasis. According to these investigators, "the assessment of early development means the systematic, purposeful collection of data, reflecting both *patterns of children's emergent abilities* to comprehend and function in their environment and the *factors associated with the emergence of these patterns*" [italics added] (p. viii). This stance toward assessment takes into consideration both the A and B sides of the equation and suggests the need to expand the data-gathering aspects of assessment to include information regarding the determinants of behavior as well as child competence and performance.

This paradigm may be taken one step further and expressed in terms of the *optimization* of behavior and development (Baltes, Reese, & Nesselroade, 1977). It can be written as, Changes in $B = f(A)$, where the emphasis is now on the range of A factors that influence and affect *changes* in behavior and development. Thus, to the extent that assessment is broadened to include identification of those variables responsible for producing variations in behavior and development, practitioners will have gathered information that bears directly on the types of *interventions* that can be used to optimize changes in early cognitive development. An ecological definition of assessment with an emphasis on the optimization of developmental outcomes is easily derived from the $B = f(A)$ paradigm and its change corollary. Assessment may be defined as the systematic gathering of information about both the existing and emerging capabilities of a developing child and the identification of factors that influence and can be used to influence changes in competence and performance.

Intervention Considerations

In this section, we delineate eight principles and their corollaries for structuring intervention practices to promote the acquisition of early cognitive competence. The principles and corollaries derive from a diverse but corroborating body of evidence indicating those aspects of ecologically oriented intervention practices that would be expected to optimize developmental outcomes. The eight principles include (a) the selection of intervention targets, (b) the kinds of environmental settings best suited for promoting competence, (c) the importance of child-initiated learning, (d) the emphasis on high levels of child engagement as a condition for promoting early cognitive development, (e) the use of responsive instructional strategies for supporting and strengthening child competence, (f) the importance of the child–caregiver dyad as one particularly potent context for supporting child development, (g) the use of assistive technology and augmentative devices as environmental supports for promoting competence, and (h) the importance of taking into consideration the broader based social–ecological determinants of development. The principles and corollaries purposely overlap, yet each provides a different vantage point for structuring efforts to promote, enhance, and optimize early cognitive development.

Intervention Targets

The content, or what caregivers teach children, is one of the most important aspects of early cognitive intervention practices. Generally, any behavior that is developmentally and socially appropriate and that reflects both increased conventionalization and a shift in balance of power toward the developing child constitutes an appropriate cognitive intervention target (see Dunst et al., 1987). Additionally, intervention targets include behaviors that permit children to learn about their own capabilities as well as about the propensities of others. The principle and associated corollaries that derive from this position are the following:

PRINCIPLE 3. Cognitive-based intervention methods and strategies are based on processes of human learning and content that progress from awareness to exploration to utilization to inquiry (COG 2).

COROLLARY 3.1. Methods and strategies used to promote cognitive knowledge and skills promote both socially and nonsocially related competencies (SE 10).

COROLLARY 3.2. Effective cognitive-based interventions result in children's awareness and recognition of their own capabilities as well as the propensities of objects, people, and events they interact with and experience in different settings (COG 3).

In contrast to most approaches to early intervention, which organize curricular content according to developmental domains (cognitive, language, motor, etc.), a more useful approach is to think of intervention targets in terms of *behavior functions.* It is possible to distinguish between two major types—engaging and modulating—and two categories—social and nonsocial—of cognitive interactive competencies in terms of such functions (Dunst & McWilliam, 1988).

The term *engaging* refers to behavior that a child uses to elicit or maintain input from the social and nonsocial environments. Engaging behaviors are used to *initiate* and *sustain* interactions with the environment. *Initiating behaviors* are those used by the child to begin or commence an interaction (e.g., picking up a spoon to initiate a feeding episode). *Sustaining behaviors* are those used by the child to maintain or repeat interactive episodes (e.g., an infant's using a spoon, repeating the food-to-mouth sequence, in order to alleviate hunger). The function of initiating and sustaining interactive competencies is to establish and maintain, respectively, interactions with the social and nonsocial environments.

The term *modulating* refers to behaviors that a child uses to modify or accommodate interactions with the social or nonsocial environment or both. Modulating behaviors are used to *regulate* and *adapt* to different environmental conditions and challenges. *Regulating behaviors* are used to terminate input from the environment and to set the occasions for reinitiating interactions (e.g., an infant's using gaze aversion to terminate adult attention and then using fixation on the adult's face to initiate adult responsiveness). *Adapting behaviors* are those used by the child to respond to others' efforts either to establish joint reference or get the child to respond to adult requests or comments (e.g., handing an object to an adult in response to a hand extended in a palm-up gesture). Both regulating and adapting behaviors provide the child with the opportunity to gain balance of power.

In addition to describing behaviors in terms of their types, intervention targets may be broadly classified into two categories: social and nonsocial. *Social behaviors* refer to interactions involving the animate environment, whereas *nonsocial behaviors* refer to interactions with the inanimate environment. By no means are the two categories mutually exclusive. The reason for distinguishing between the two categories of interactive competencies is to broaden the conceptualization of what constitutes appropriate early cognitive intervention targets. Visually attending to an object is one type of attentional capacity, and so is recognition of a familiar person. Making a toy produce an interesting sound is one type of contingency interaction, and so is playing the adult–child game of peek-a-boo. Using a spoon as a tool to eat is one type of differentiated behavior, as is extending the arms to be picked up. Showing foresight in getting an object out of a container (e.g., pouring milk into a glass) is one type of complex interactive behavior, and so is the use of sign language to request help from an adult. Remembering the placement of an object across several hours is one type of symbolic behavior, and so is saying "go play" to request an adult to take the child to the park. Cognitive competencies are manifested in many different ways, and the use of a framework, like the one described here, for identifying appropriate intervention targets is an important step in promoting acquisition of functional, adaptive cognitive competencies.

Intervention Settings

Evidence from a number of sources indicates that the sheer number of learning opportunities are increased and the meaningfulness of what is learned is enhanced when interventions are conducted in the context of *daily routines and situations* (Bricker & Cripe, 1992; Dunst et al., 1987; Dunst & McWilliam, 1988). Thus, to the extent possible, intervention targets should be taught in the context of the child's daily routines in the home (for home-based interventions), daily classroom activities (for classroom-based programs), or community settings (for community-based interventions) if early cognitive intervention is to be optimally effective. This recommendation translates into the following principle and corollaries:

> **PRINCIPLE 4.** Cognitive-based intervention methods and strategies enhance acquisition of knowledge and skills in a variety of different settings and situations (FP 20, AB 2).
>
> COROLLARY 4.1. Acquisition of cognitive skills is optimized when interventions are conducted in the context of daily occurring routines (SDM 11, M 7).
>
> COROLLARY 4.2. Methods and strategies used to promote cognitive knowledge and skills include numerous opportunities to interact with interesting and competency-enhancing people and materials in different settings (SDM 23, GC 4).

Functional knowledge and skills are best learned in the context of daily living rather than in contrived learning situations that do not mirror real-life demands and challenges. Learning by doing in the natural settings strengthens a child's existing capabilities and sets the occasion for developing new competence. Dunst et al. (1987) described this process of promoting competence in the context of normally occurring situations as *routine-based intervention*. Routine-based interventions are best accomplished by use of an intervention target (objectives) × routines matrix as a curricular framework for structuring efforts to promote child competence. Intervention targets are typically broad categories of interactive competencies (e.g., "request" behaviors) that are operationalized by a range of developmental behaviors children might produce to manifest these competencies (e.g., referential looking, gestures, vocalizations). Routines include both daily and occasionally occurring events and situations that constitute potential contexts for promoting competence. A matrix is completed by indicating for each intervention target which contexts provide opportunities for encouraging the child to produce various targets.

The routines that can serve as the context for promoting competence are numerous. These can be distinguished, however, according to three broad types of settings: home, classroom, and community. In home settings, the routines that might be used as contexts for learning include dressing, mealtimes, bathing, nap time and bedtime, toileting, story times, and independent-play times. Potential classroom routines include arrival and departure, nap time, mealtimes, group times, water and sand play, outdoor play, music time, table activities, and social play. Community routines might include shopping, visits to neighbors or friends, eating at restaurants, recreational activities, church activities, and other social events.

Child-Initiated Learning

Most theories of early cognitive development emphasize the importance of child-initiated activity as a mediator of cognitive competence (Horowitz, 1987; Lerner & Busch-Rossnagel, 1981; Piaget, 1936/1952). This position acknowledges that children acquire cognitive behaviors most effectively when they are active participants in the learning process rather than passive observers or responders to adult-directed learning. Therefore, to the greatest extent possible child-directed activity should be used for promoting the development of early cognitive competencies. This approach translates into the following principle and corollaries:

PRINCIPLE 5. Cognitive-based intervention methods and strategies encourage children to initiate and engage in activities related to the general class of behaviors identified as targets for intervention (COG 4).

COROLLARY 5.1. Intervention activities should be planned and implemented so that they complement and encourage child-initiated play and interactions with people and objects (AB 8).

COROLLARY 5.2. Intervention targets should be implemented in ways that promote engaging and modulating behaviors that enhance learning and development.

Child-initiated activity has twofold significance for early cognitive intervention. The first is motivational, and the second is developmental. Activities that are self-initiated reflect motivational features that are highly conducive to enhancing learning and development and, in turn, competence and performance. That is, activities that children self-initiate reflect both their current interests and competence as well as provide children the opportunity to exert control over their environment. Child-development researchers have demonstrated repeatedly that children are more likely to attend to and retain information that relates directly to their interests and that is within their range of competence (Friedman & Vietze, 1972; Harter, 1978; Hunt, 1971; Lamb, 1981; Sameroff & Cavanagh, 1979). Moreover, children enjoy and are more likely to persist at activities that they control (Mahoney, 1988a; Watson, 1972).

The second issue has to do with the use of children's activity as a facilitator of learning. As discussed previously, the more children actively participate or engage in learning opportunities, the greater is the probability that they will benefit from these experiences. Learning activities that are child-directed rather than adult-directed are more likely to enhance learning and development because children tend to participate more actively and intensely in child-directed than in adult-directed activities.

The challenge of utilizing child-initiated activity as a primary context for learning is to do so in ways that ensure that children initiate activities related to the intervention targets. At least two major things can be used to accomplish this objective. The first is to identify intervention targets based on knowledge of children's current levels of competence and interests. Intervention targets that build on what children already do and how they behave in various settings will naturally lead to intervention procedures and strategies that lead to activities that are competence enhancing. The second is to conduct interventions in settings that increase the probability that children will produce a desired class of behaviors. As discussed previously, such settings are those with familiar contexts and routines that are likely to elicit desired behaviors.

Instructional Strategies

A considerable body of evidence now exists indicating that acquisition of both engaging and modulating interactive competencies is best achieved by use of any number of instructional strategies that can be generically termed *responsive teaching* (Raab, Wortman Lowe, & Dunst, 1991). This approach to teaching refers to a wide range of conditional strategies used by caregivers (parents, childcare providers, interventionists, etc.) in which social responsiveness functions as a reinforcer to maintain or evoke further behavior from the child. Contingent responsiveness to child behavior (especially behavior that arises *naturally* during interactions between caregivers and children) has been found to exercise powerful influences on the acquisition of early cognitive competencies. Responsive teaching therefore ought to be the "method of choice" in the majority of cases where the promotion and enhancement of child-initiated developmental competence is the goal of intervention efforts (see especially Wolery & Sainato, Chapter 6). An expanding database indicates that typically developing children as well as children with disabilities are more likely to display competent behavior if caregivers are responsive to and encourage the child's ongoing behavior (e.g., Hanzlik, 1986, 1989; Mahoney, Powell, Finnegan, Fors, & Wood, 1986; Uzgiris, 1986a; Wenar, 1972; White & Watts, 1973). This evidence translates into the following principle and corollaries:

> **PRINCIPLE 6.** Acquisition of cognitive knowledge and skills is maximized by use of a broad range of responsive teaching methods and strategies to enhance acquisition of early cognitive interactive competencies (COG 6).
>
> COROLLARY 6.1. Responsive teaching methods are the instructional strategies of choice when promoting cognitive competence (SE 1).
>
> COROLLARY 6.2. Methods and strategies for promoting cognitive competence emphasize children's ongoing and frequent display of knowledge and skills rather than the production of behaviors at only certain times and only under certain conditions.

An integration and synthesis of the child-development literature reveals a range of instructional strategies best suited for fostering a child's acquisition of cognitive interactive competencies. These strategies are characterized by the following: Paying attention to and focusing on what elicits and maintains a child's interaction with objects and people (Lamb & Easterbrooks, 1981), interpreting and responding to the child's interactive competencies as intentional behavior (Goldberg, 1977), structuring the social and nonsocial environments in ways that produce reinforcing consequences in response to child initiations (Goldberg, 1977; Lamb, 1981), employing "teaching" episodes that emphasize a high level of child-initiated interactions (Appleton et al., 1975), and using interactive episodes that encourage and support a child's attempts to elaborate on his or her competence (Bronfenbrenner, 1979; White & Watts, 1973).

Four sets of studies provide evidence to support the value of responsive teaching as an instructional strategy. The first set of studies demonstrates the value of response-contingent learning episodes as the primary context for infants 1 through 8 months old to learn associations between behavior and its consequences. Studies with both typically developing infants (for reviews, see Hulsebus, 1973; Lipsitt, 1969, 1970; Lipsitt & Werner, 1981; Millar, 1976; Sameroff & Cavanagh, 1979) and children with disabilities (see Dunst & Lesko, 1988) indicate that when a reinforcer follows the child's production of a behavior, the child quickly comes to understand the contingency and the consequences of his or her behavior (e.g., tickling a child's tummy each time the child raises his or her arm above the head, talking to the child each time he or she orients toward the caregiver's face during feeding episodes). Friedman and Vietze (1972) succinctly summarized the significance of response-contingent behaviors when they stated, "the ability to effect change in the environment embodies the concept of competence; the competent infant being one who learns that certain aspects of his (or her) environment are controllable" (p. 318).

A second set of studies by Field (1978, 1979a, 1979b) has demonstrated the importance of reciprocal social responsiveness as the basis for enhancing child learning within the context of parent–infant interactions. She repeatedly found that mutual responsiveness between infants and caregivers is a necessary condition for infants to become competent at influencing the behavior of interactive partners and that social responsiveness on the part of caregivers is a major determinant of the infant's acquisition of early developmental capabilities. In her research, Field (1978) used a set of intervention procedures that she called *interactive coaching*. These procedures are designed to promote the use of contingent social responsiveness, which, in turn, affects an infant's capacity to learn contingencies between behavior and its consequences.

A third body of research from investigations of older, preverbal children provides evidence regarding the importance of contingent social responsiveness (Hanzlik, 1986, 1989; Mahoney 1988b; Mahoney et al., 1986; Uzgiris, 1986; Wenar, 1972; White & Watts, 1973; Yarrow, Rubenstein, & Pederson, 1975). The collective results of these studies demonstrate that when caregivers consistently employ contingent social responsiveness as a technique for supporting and encouraging elaboration in children's behavior, the children's developmental competence is positively enhanced. Mahoney (1988b), for example, concluded from his study of the interactive styles of mothers and their young children with disabilities that "children were more . . . communicatively responsive when their mothers were responsive to children's communication and focused on child-oriented topics" (p. 352). On the basis of the results of other studies conducted by Mahoney (1988a) and his colleagues, Mahoney concluded that "our findings suggest that a responsive, child-oriented style of interaction is related to higher rates of child development than (is) a directive or teacher-oriented" interactive style (p. 216).

A fourth set of studies, aggregated and reviewed by Warren and Kaiser (1986), provides evidence concerning the efficacy of incidental teaching as an intervention strategy for promoting the behavioral skills of young children. *Incidental teaching* refers to interactions between an adult and a child that arise naturally in unstructured or semistructured situations, where child initiations and engagement are followed by (a) adult social contingent responsiveness and (b) requests for elaboration in the child's behavior. The findings of these studies demonstrate that this highly responsive teaching strategy reinforces children's use of language and, more important, sets the occasion for elaboration and expansions in language use. Hart and Risley (1980), for example, found that social contingent responsiveness and requests for elaborations in children's verbal behavior resulted in increases in the frequency of language use, vocabulary growth, and use of new combinations of words. Additionally, the changes associated with the use of incidental teaching were found to be greater compared to changes among comparison groups on children not afforded incidental teaching opportunities.

Collectively, available evidence indicates that caregivers should follow a basic rule of thumb when choosing intervention techniques and teaching procedures for fostering a child's acquisition of early cognitive interactive competencies: *One should use the least intrusive technique possible for fostering the acquisition of early cognitive competence.* The more informal one can be, the more likely one will find a shift in balance of power across successive interactive episodes. This is not to say that other instructional techniques are not effective for producing other kinds of behavior change (see Wolery & Sainato, Chapter 6) but rather that child-initiated learning is best achieved with responsive rather than with directive teaching techniques.

Child Engagement

The extent to which child-initiated learning is likely to occur depends, to a large degree, on whether or not a child is actively engaged with the social or nonsocial environment or both. *Engagement* refers to the *amount of time* children spend interacting with their environments in a manner that is developmentally appropriate. Engagement is important because it provides information about what is interesting and reinforcing to the child, and it sets the occasion for caregivers to use responsive teaching techniques. The following principle and corollaries derive from these contentions:

PRINCIPLE 7. Cognitive-based intervention practices emphasize high levels of child engagement with both social and nonsocial environments (settings, objects, people, etc.) (GC 2).

COROLLARY 7.1. Children's curiosity and desire to learn are maximized when intervention activities are developmentally appropriate and the strategies used to promote children's cognitive capabilities are intrinsically motivating (A 11, SDM 24, GC 11).

COROLLARY 7.2. Intervention practices are most likely to maintain child engagement and interest when methods and procedures are used that emphasize children's integration of previously and newly acquired knowledge and skills (COG 5).

Evidence from a host of studies demonstrates that child engagement with the social and nonsocial environments is increased by a number of factors, including, but not limited to, material availability, arrangement of the physical environment, novelty, consistency of routines, as well as responsive teaching (see, e.g., McWilliam, Trivette, & Dunst, 1985). For example, a classroom schedule that includes movement of a child from one area or "learning zone" to another rather than a child's remaining in the same location throughout the day enhances attention to and interactions with objects and people. This seems to be the case because transitions between areas signal the availability of different kinds of experiences and opportunities. These opportunities increase the likelihood that a child will become engaged in ways that lead to self-initiated activities that make the use of responsive instructional practices possible.

Child–Caregiver Interactions

Evidence from numerous sources now indicates that the child–caregiver dyad is one of the most important and potent interpersonal contexts for promoting early cognitive competence. Child–caregiver interactions provide opportunities for children to learn and practice cognitive skills and for caregivers to respond to and support child behavior. This concept translates into the following principle and corollaries:

PRINCIPLE 8. The child–caregiver (teacher, parent, etc.) dyad is among the most powerful and potent contexts for enhancing and promoting cognitive knowledge and skills.

COROLLARY 8.1. Effective use of child–caregiver dyads as a context for learning emphasizes reciprocity and joint actions between interactive partners as ways of promoting early cognitive competence (COG 7, COM 8, SE 1).

COROLLARY 8.2. Interactive episodes that are competency enhancing are ones in which the balance of power shifts toward the developing child (GC 3, GC 26).

The importance of interactional dyads as the context for learning and development derives from the following rationale: If a child's social behavior elicits or produces consequences in caregiver behavior that is both highly predictable (Lamb, 1981) and effective in producing a positive outcome (Harter, 1978), circumstances are set for enhancement of interactive competencies. Moreover, when interactive competencies produce the same effect across repeated production of the same behavior, there is a high probability that a child will acquire both contingency awareness (Watson, 1966, 1972) and expectations about the behavior of interactive partners (Lamb, 1981). The awareness, or perception, of contingencies and expectations is at least one condition that propels the child to employ his or her competence as a way of producing interesting and desired consequences. Such are the conditions of *competence motivation* (Harter, 1978). Lamb (1981) described this in the following manner:

> In order to recognize that another person's behavior is predictable and controllable, the infant must be capable of learning the association between its behavior and the adults' response; it must be aware of both the contingency and the identity of the respondent; (and) it must remember the repeated occurrences of the contingency so that when it reflects upon the history of interactions with the care(giver), it perceives the characteristic themes that permit it to develop conception of the adult as predictable and itself as efficacious. (p. 160)

In addition to child contributions to the development of competence, caregivers make contributions to the child's acquisition of early cognitive competencies. The role caregivers play in promoting child competence in the context of child–caregiver interactive episodes was described by Goldberg (1977) in the following manner: "As the adult monitors infant behavior, the ability to make decisions about interventions is a joint function of (caregiver) feelings of effectiveness and infant predictability and readability. When infants are highly predictable and readable, (caregivers) are able to arrive at decisions quickly, make decisions early, and have a high probability of making appropriate decisions. Note that this condition enables the (caregiver) to act in precisely the fashion that *provides a high level of contingency experience for the infant*" [italics added] (p. 173).

In instances where the infant is responsive to adult interventions in an expected manner, the caregiver's feelings of efficacy are enhanced and she or he is more likely to sustain ongoing interactions and to initiate other interactions. This, in turn, is likely to increase the infant's contingency awareness and expectancies regarding the propensities of others, which, in turn, lead to a shift in balance of power toward the developing child.

Adaptive Devices and Assistive Technology

Many children with disabilities, and especially those with physical impairments, are often at a disadvantage when it comes to engaging in different types and forms of interactive competencies. When used appropriately, assistive technology and adaptive devices can help enhance children's interactive competencies so that they can gain control and mastery over their social and nonsocial environments. Moreover, evidence indicates that a host of positive consequences are associated with the use of adaptive devices and assistive technology, including increased engagement with people and objects, the acquisition of communicative capabilities, and the ability to become active participants in a variety of social and nonsocial environments (Behrmann, Jones, & Wilds, 1989; Langley, 1990). These conditions translate into the following principle and corollaries:

PRINCIPLE 9. Cognitive-based intervention methods and strategies include, when appropriate, the use of assistive technology (adaptive equipment, augmentative devices, etc.) to promote early cognitive competencies in ways that allow children to actively engage in learning activities (COG 8).

COROLLARY 9.1. Adaptive and augmentative devices and equipment are maximally effective when they serve prosthetic functions permitting children to interact with the social and nonsocial environments in a competent manner (COM 12).

COROLLARY 9.2. Adaptive and augmentative devices and equipment are also maximally effective when they are available to children on an ongoing basis in a variety of settings and situations.

The National Council on Disability (1993) defined an assistive technology device as any item, piece of equipment, or product that is used to increase, maintain, or improve the *functional capabilities* of individuals with disabilities. Assistive technology devices include both "low-tech" and "high-tech" devices such as adapted toys, computers, special seating systems, powered mobility devices, augmentative communication systems, and contingency switches permitting production of reinforcing consequences.

An emerging body of evidence indicates that children with disabilities can and do learn when adaptive toys and equipment are used for enhancing learning (e.g., Behrmann & Lahm, 1984; Behrmann et al., 1989; Burkhart, 1980, 1982; Butler, 1988; Huttinger, 1984, 1987; Langley, 1990; Wacker, Wiggins, Fowler, & Berg, 1988). An analysis of the literature on technology use with preschoolers with disabilities shows that it can be conveniently organized into two groups of studies: those describing technology for use with children having a cognitive understanding of cause–effect relationships (e.g., Bulter, 1988; Douglas, Reeson, & Ryan, 1988; Fazio & Reith, 1986;

Flanagan, 1982) and those describing technology use with children who have not yet mastered cause–effect relationships (e.g., Brinker & Lewis, 1982; Correa, Poulson, & Salzberg, 1984; Friedlander, McCarthy, & Soforonko, 1967). The former, not surprisingly, includes the use of computers as a major form of technology, whereas the latter includes the use of predominantly low-tech devices as "tools" for enhancing learning and development.

Social Systems Context of Development

An important but often neglected feature of early cognitive intervention is the recognition and incorporation of social systems perspective into efforts to optimize the developmental outcomes of children with or at risk for developmental disabilities. This perspective includes, but is not limited to, the use of instructional and noninstructional (e.g., environmental arrangements and material availability) practices and the use of different kinds of learning opportunities and settings that enhance and promote children's acquisition of interactive competencies. It also includes the recognition that the effects of early cognitive interventions (as well as other types of interventions) are optimized when caregivers have the necessary time and energy and knowledge and skills to carry out caregiver responsibilities in ways that result in experiences that have competency-enhancing effects. Still further, a social systems perspective recognizes the fact that early intervention should be couched in a family-centered framework if cognitive-based early intervention practices are to be responsive to the individualized needs of children and their parents. This position translates into the following principle and corollaries:

PRINCIPLE 10. The effects of early cognitive intervention are likely to be maximized if they are conducted in ways that employ a range of social systems determinants for influencing child development.

COROLLARY 10.1. Social systems interventions should aim to provide a broad range of learning experiences and opportunities that promote and enhance interactive competence.

COROLLARY 10.2. Social systems interventions should be family centered so as to place parents in pivotal roles in deciding the targets, contexts, and so on, of early cognitive intervention practices (FP 21, FP 24, I 20).

A social systems perspective of early intervention acknowledges the fact that development is multiply determined (Bronfenbrenner, 1979, 1986). Such an approach not only necessitates but demands a broad-based definition of and approach to early intervention (Dunst, 1985). Social systems determinants both directly and indirectly influence behavior and development (Cochran & Brassard, 1979), and structuring early cognitive intervention practices in ways that take advantage of these determinants cannot but have a greater positive impact on a child's acquisition of interactive competencies.

A family-centered systems approach to early cognitive intervention goes one step further. It places a child's parents and other caregivers in important roles in determining both the goals of intervention and the strategies best suited for promoting and enhancing early cognitive competencies. This decision-making role is especially important in terms of the conditions that fit a family's lifestyle and desires. This approach means that instructional and noninstructional practices used to influence the acquisition of cognitive interactive competencies should differ according to both child and family needs and concerns. For instance, it may mean an emphasis on use of instructionally based intervention practices for one child, but the use of more naturally occurring learning opportunities and experiences as a means for promoting the competencies of another child.

Fashioning early cognitive intervention practices in both social systems and family-centered frameworks places such practices in a broader based ecological perspective. Doing so increases the likelihood that interventions aimed at influencing child behavior and development will be optimally effective because they become functionally relevant and meaningful to both children and their parents and other caregivers.

CLOSING

This chapter includes the description of 10 principles and 20 corollaries for structuring assessment and intervention practices aimed at enhancing and promoting early cognitive interactive competencies. Collectively, the material provides a framework for defining the goals of cognitive intervention and for employing a range of intervention factors (settings, child-initiated learning, engagement, instructional strategies, child–caregiver interactions, assistive technology, social systems determinants) for promoting early cognitive learning and development. The guidelines, taken together, provide a unified framework for conceptualizing, developing, and implementing cognitive interventions in ways that are consistent with current knowledge about the development of interactive competencies of young children with or at risk for disabilities.

Comparisons indicate that the principles and corollaries described in this chapter parallel what the National Association for the Education of

Young Children (NAEYC) has endorsed as developmentally appropriate practices (Bredekamp, 1987). The commonalities found in NAEYC's developmentally appropriate practices document and those described in this chapter suggest it is both feasible and practical to employ relatively similar kinds of early intervention practices for promoting the cognitive development of young children with and without disabilities. An integration of our own recommendations and those of NAEYC reveals that three themes common to both with regard to those conditions that seem crucial for early cognitive intervention are optimally effective: strengths-based practices, routine-based practices, and family-supportive practices.

Strengths-Based Practices

This chapter includes the description of a number of practices indicating that early cognitive intervention should include instructional procedures that reinforce and encourage children's current and emerging interactive competencies. The guidelines concerning the selection of intervention targets, child-initiated learning, and children's engagement each reflect the view that interventions should encourage existing interactive competencies and elaborate on a child's emerging developmental and behavioral capabilities. Moreover, the social–ecological framework for the recommended practices described here indicates a need to use instructional practices that focus less on deficits and delays associated with disabilities and more on a range of factors that support and encourage developmentally appropriate interactive behavior. Our recommendations are based on the assertion that practitioners and caregivers can best achieve such focus by responding to and encouraging children's activity and by guiding children's learning using experiences that lead to new levels of cognitive awareness and understanding. Consequently, intervention procedures should emphasize the preferences and interests of a developing child and deemphasize adherence to predetermined curricular objectives and activities as the basis for promoting the acquisition of early cognitive competence.

Routine-Based Practices

Guidelines regarding the meaning of development, assessment practices, environmental settings, engagement, and assistive technology each converge on the following: Interventions should be embedded in daily and developmentally appropriate activities and routines for the purpose of optimally promoting children's adaptive interactive competencies with people, objects, and activities. This approach is consistent with the social-ecological perspective of development from which most recommendations proposed in this chapter were derived and complements contemporary emphasis in early childhood education which calls for embedding instruction in daily routines and activities. It contrasts with the practice of conducting interventions in instructional or clinical contexts, which bear little or no resemblance to the activities that normally take place in children's lives (see especially Dunst, Wortman Lowe, & Bartholomew, 1990).

Family-Supportive Practices

The guidelines recommended here regarding the child–parent dyad as a primary context for learning, responsive instructional procedures, and family-centered practices reflect an approach that is intended to be supportive of parents' efforts to rear their young child in a competency-enhancing manner. Not only does this approach demand that early cognitive interventions be based on a closer collaboration between practitioners and families, but it also reflects the view that early intervention should develop and support the kinds of interactive relationships that are known to be an important context for development. Additionally, the view that family-centered interventions should support families is an acknowledgement of the critical role that parents and other caregivers play in the growth and development of young children.

Collectively, the guidelines described in this chapter reflect a view of early cognitive intervention that in many instances differs dramatically from prevailing, contemporary practices. The challenge confronting early intervention practitioners is to examine their practices in light of these guidelines and to identify strategies and procedures that will help them shift focus in the direction outlined here. Doing so cannot but have optimally beneficial outcomes for children with or at risk for developmental disabilities.

> The principles described in this chapter were initially developed as a result of discussions at the Intervention for Cognitive Skills Strand, DEC Best Practices Project. The members included Stephen Bagnato, Carl Dunst, Patti Huttinger, Mary Beth Kavacs, Toni Linder, Gerald Mahoney, Rune Simeonsson, Scott Snyder, Char Ward, Georgia Woodward, and Peggy Yousel. Appreciation is extended to Mary Brown, who typed various versions of the paper, and Carol Whitacre, for assistance in verifying the references.

REFERENCES

Appleton, T., Clifton, R., & Goldberg, S. (1975). The development of behavior competence. In F. Horowitz (Ed.), *Review of child development* (Vol. 4, pp. 101–186). Chicago: University of Chicago Press.

Baltes, P., Resse, H. M., & Nesselroade, J. (1977). *Life-span developmental psychology.* Belmont, CA: Wadsworth.

Bates, E. (1976). *Language and context.* New York: Academic Press.

Beeghly, M., & Cicchetti, D. (1985, October). *Early language development of children with Down syndrome: A longitudinal study.* Paper presented at the 11th Annual Boston University Conference on Language Development, Boston.

Beeghly, M., Weiss-Perry, B., & Cicchetti, D. (1990). Beyond sensorimotor functioning: Early communicative and play development of children with Down syndrome. In D. Cicchetti & M. Beeghly (Eds.), *Children with Down syndrome: A developmental perspective* (pp. 329–368). New York: Cambridge University Press.

Behrmann, M., Jones, J. K., & Wilds, M. L. (1989). Technology intervention for very young children with disabilities. *Infants and Young Children, 1,* 66–77.

Behrmann, M., & Lahm, E. (1984). Babies and robots: Technology-assisted learning. *Rehabilitation Literature, 45,* 194–201.

Boukydis, C. F. (Ed.). (1987). *Research on support for parents and infants in the postnatal period.* Norwood, NJ: Ablex.

Bredekamp, S. (1987). *Developmentally appropriate practice in early childhood programs serving children birth through age 8* (Rev. ed.). Washington, DC: National Association for the Education of Young Children.

Bricker, D., & Cripe, J. (1992). *An activity-based approach to early intervention.* Baltimore: Brookes.

Brinker, R., & Lewis, M. (1982). Discovering the competent handicapped infant: A process approach to assessment and intervention. *Topics in Early Childhood Special Education, 2*(2), 1–16.

Bronfenbrenner, U. (1979). *The ecology of human development.* Cambridge, MA: Harvard University Press.

Bronfenbrenner, U. (1986). Ecology of the family as a context for human development: Research perspectives. *Developmental Psychology, 22,* 723–742.

Brooks-Gunn, J., & Lewis, M. (1982). Development of play behavior in handicapped and normal infants. *Topics in Early Childhood Special Education, 2*(3), 14–27.

Brophy, K., & Stone-Zukowski, D. (1984). Social needs of special needs and nonspecial needs toddlers. *Early Child Development and Care, 13,* 137–154.

Burkhart, L. J. (1980). *Homemade battery devices for severely handicapped children with suggested activities.* College Park, MD: Author. (Available from Linda J. Burkhart, 8503 Rhode Island Avenue, College Park, MD 20740)

Burkhart, L. J. (1982). *More homemade battery devices for severely handicapped children with suggested activities.* College Park, MD: Author. (Available from Linda J. Burkhart, 8502 Rhode Island Avenue, College Park, MD 20740)

Butler, C. (1988). High tech tots: Technology for mobility, manipulation, communicating, and learning in early childhood. *Infants and Young Children, 1,* 66–73.

Case, R. (1985). *Intellectual development: Birth to adulthood.* Orlando, FL: Academic Press.

Cochran, M., & Brassard, J. (1979). Child development and personal social networks. *Child Development, 50,* 601–606.

Correa, V. I., Poulson, C. L., & Salzberg, C. L. (1984). Training and generalization of reach-grasp behavior in blind, retarded young children. *Journal of Applied Behavior Analysis, 17,* 57–70.

Crawley, S., & Chan, K. (1982). Developmental changes in free-play behavior of mildly and moderately retarded preschool-aged children. *Preschool Play, 8,* 235–239.
Crnic, K., Greenberg, M., & Slough, N. (1986). Early stress and social support influences on mothers' and high-risk infants' functioning in late infancy. *Infant Mental Health Journal, 7,* 19–48
Davidson, J., & Sternberg, R. (1985). Competence and performance in intellectual development. In E. Neimark, R. DeLisa, & J. Newman (Eds.), *Moderators of competence* (pp. 43–76). Hillsdale, NJ: Erlbaum.
Division for Early Childhood Task Force on Recommended Practices (Eds.). (1993). *DEC recommended practices: Indicators of quality in programs for infants and young children with special needs and their families.* Reston, VA: Council for Exceptional Children, Division for Early Childhood.
Douglas, J., Reeson, B., & Ryan, M. (1988). Computer microtechnology for a severely disabled preschool child. *Child: Care, Health, and Development, 14,* 93–104.
Dunst, C. J. (1980). *A clinical and educational manual for use with the Uzgiris and Hunt scales of infant psychological development.* Austin, TX: PRO-ED.
Dunst, C. J. (1981). *Infant learning.* Allen, TX: DLM Teaching Resources.
Dunst, C. J. (1984). Toward a social–ecological perspective of sensorimotor development among the mentally retarded. In P. Brooks, R. Sperber, & C. McCauley (Eds.), *Learning and cognition in the mentally retarded* (pp. 359–387). Hillsdale, NJ: Erlbaum.
Dunst, C. J. (1985). Rethinking early intervention. *Analysis and Intervention in Developmental Disabilities, 5,* 165–201.
Dunst, C. J. (1990). Sensorimotor development of infants with Down syndrome. In D. Cicchetti & M. Beeghly (Eds.), *Down syndrome: The developmental perspective* (pp. 180–230). New York: Cambridge University Press.
Dunst, C. J. (1993). Interventions to promote cognitive skills. In Division for Early Childhood Task Force on Recommended Practices (Eds.), *DEC recommended practices: Indicators of quality in programs for infants and young children with special needs and their families* (pp. 61–67). Reston, VA: Council for Exceptional Children.
Dunst, C. J. (in press). Sensorimotor development and developmental disabilities. In B. Hodapp, E. Zigler, & J. Burack (Eds.), *Handbook of mental retardation and development.* New York: Cambridge University Press.
Dunst, C. J., Holbert, K., & Wilson, L. (1990). Strategies for assessing infant sensorimotor competencies. In E. Gibbs & D. Teti (Eds.), *Interdisciplinary assessment of infants: A guide for early intervention practitioners* (pp. 91–112). Baltimore: Brookes.
Dunst, C. J., & Lesko, J. (1988). Promoting the active learning capabilities of young children with handicaps. *Early Childhood Intervention Monograph, 1* (No. 1). Morganton, NC: Family, Infant and Preschool Program, Western Carolina Center.
Dunst, C. J., Lesko, J., Holbert, K., Wilson, L., Sharpe, K., & Liles, R. (1987). A systemic approach to infant intervention. *Topics in Early Childhood Special Education, 7*(2), 19–37.
Dunst, C. J., & Lingerfelt, B. (1985). Maternal ratings of temperament and operant learning in two- to three-month-old infants. *Child Development, 56,* 555–563.
Dunst, C. J., & McWilliam, R. A. (1988). Cognitive assessment of multiply handicapped young children. In T. D. Wachs & R. Sheehan (Eds.), *Assessment of developmentally disabled children* (pp. 213–238). New York: Plenum Press.
Dunst, C. J., Snyder, S., & Mankinen, M. (1988). Efficacy of early intervention. In M. Wang, M. Reynolds, & H. Walberg (Eds.), *Handbook of special education: Research and practice (Vol. 3). Low incidence conditions* (pp. 259–294). Oxford, England: Pergamon Press.
Dunst, C. J., & Trivette, C. M. (1988). Determinants of parent and child interactive behavior. In K. Marfo (Ed.), *Parent–child interaction and developmental disabilities* (pp. 3–31). New York: Praeger.

Dunst, C. J., Trivette, C. M., Hamby, D., & Pollock, B. (1990). Family systems correlates of the behavior of young children with handicaps. *Journal of Early Intervention, 14,* 204–218.

Dunst, C. J., Vance, S. D., & Hamby, D. W. (1988). Supporting and strengthening pregnant teenagers and adolescent mothers: Principles, strategies and outcomes. *Family Systems Intervention Monograph, 1* (No. 2). Morganton, NC: Family, Infant and Preschool Program, Western Carolina Center.

Dunst, C. J., Vance, S. D., & Hamby, D. W. (1994, June). *Patterns and rates of sensorimotor development among children with developmental disabilities and delays.* Paper presented at the Ninth International Conference on Infant Studies, Paris, France.

Dunst, C. J., Wortman, L., & Bartholomew, P. (1990). Contingent social responsiveness, family ecology, and infant communicative competence. *NSSLHA (National Student Speech Language Hearing Association) Journal, 17,* 39–49.

Fazio, B. B., & Reith, H. J. (1986). Characteristics of preschool children's microcomputers use during free-choice periods. *Journal of the Division for Early Childhood, 10,* 247–254.

Field, T. M. (1977). Effects of early separation, interactive deficits, and experimental manipulation on infant–mother face-to-face interaction. *Child Development, 48,* 763–772.

Field, T. M. (1978). The three Rs of infant–adult interaction: Rhythms, repertoires, and responsivity. *Journal of Pediatric Psychology, 3,* 131–136.

Field, T. M. (1979a). Games parents play with normal and high-risk infants. *Child Psychiatry and Human Development, 10,* 41–48.

Field, T. M. (1979b). Interaction patterns of preterm and term infants. In T. Field, A. Sostk, S. Goldberg, & H. Shuman (Eds.), *Infants born at risk* (pp. 333–356). New York: SP Medical & Scientific Books.

Field, T. M., McCabe, P., & Schneiderman, N. (Eds.). (1988). *Stress and coping across development.* Hillsdale, NJ: Erlbaum.

Fischer, K. (1980). A theory of cognitive development: The control and construction of hierarchies of skills. *Psychological Review, 87,* 477–531.

Flanagan, K. (1982). Computer needs of severely mentally retarded persons. *Journal of Special Education Technology, 5*(4), 47–50.

Friedlander, B., McCarthy, J., & Soforonko, A. (1967). Automated psychological evaluation with severely retarded institutionalized infants. *American Journal of Mental Deficiency, 71,* 909–919.

Friedman, S., & Vietze, P. (1972). The competent infant. *Peabody Journal of Education, 4,* 1–8.

Goldberg, S. (1977). Social competence in infancy: A model of parent–infant interaction. *Merrill-Palmer Quarterly, 23,* 163–177.

Gowen, J., Goldman, B., Johnson-Martin, N., & Hussey, B. (1989). Object play and exploration of handicapped and nonhandicapped infants. *Journal of Applied Developmental Psychology, 10,* 53–72.

Hanzlik, J. (1986, May). *Mother–developmentally disabled infant interactions and intervention.* Paper presented at the annual meeting of the American Association on Mental Deficiency, Denver, CO.

Hanzlik, J. (1989). The effects of intervention on the freeplay experience for mothers and their infants with developmental delay and cerebral palsy. *Physical and Occupational Therapy in Pediatrics, 9,* 33–50.

Harding, C. G. (1983). Setting the stage for language acquisition: Communication development in the first year. In R. M. Golinkoff (Ed), *The transition from prelinguistic to linguistic communication* (pp. 93–113). Hillsdale, NJ: Erlbaum.

Harris, P. L. (1983). Infant cognition. In M. Haith & J. Campos (Eds.), *Handbook of child psychology: Vol. 2: Infancy and developmental psychobiology* (pp. 689–782). New York: Wiley.

Hart, B., & Risley, T. (1980). In vivo language training: Unanticipated and general effects. *Journal of Applied Behavior Analysis, 12,* 407–432.

Harter, S. (1978). Effectance motivation reconsidered: Toward a developmental model. *Human Development, 21,* 34–64.

Herbert-Jackson, E., O'Brien, M., Porterfield, J., & Risley, T. (1977). *The infant center.* Baltimore: University Park Press.

Hill, P., & McCune-Nicholich, L. (1981). Pretend play and patterns of cognition in Down syndrome children. *Child Development, 52,* 611–617.

Holdgrafer, G., & Dunst, C. J. (1986). Communicative competence: From research to practice. *Topics in Early Childhood Special Education, 6*(3), 1–22.

Horowitz, F. D. (1987). *Exploring developmental theories: Toward a structural/behavioral model of development.* Hillsdale, NJ: Erlbaum.

Hulsebus, R. (1973). Operant conditioning of infant behavior: A review. In H. Reese (Ed.), *Advances in child development and behavior* (Vol. 8, pp. 111–158). New York: Academic Press.

Hunt, J. McV. (1971). Intrinsic motivation and psychological development. In H. Schroder & P. Suefeld (Eds.), *Personality theory and information processing* (pp. 131–177). New York: Ronald Press.

Hunt, J. McV. (1987). The effects of differing kinds of experience in early rearing conditions. In I. Uzgiris & J. McV. Hunt (Eds.), *Infant performance and experience* (pp. 39–97). Urbana: University of Illinois Press.

Hunt, J. McV., Mohandessi, K., Ghodssi, M., & Akiyama, M. (1976). The psychological development of orphanage reared infants: Interventions with outcomes. *Genetic Psychology Monographs, 94,* 177–226.

Huttinger, P. (1984). Activating children through technology: Notes on using microcomputers with very young children. In M. Gergen & D. Hagen (Eds.), *Closing the Gap conference proceedings* (pp. 168–174). Henderson, MN: Closing the Gap Conference.

Huttinger, P. (1987). Computers and young handicapped children: More on communication. *Closing the Gap* (June–July), 16, 17, 19, 20.

Jennings, K., Connors, R., & Stegman, C. (1988). Does a physical handicap alter the development of mastery motivation during the preschool years? *American Academy of Child and Adolescent Psychiatry, 27*(3), 312–317.

Lamb, M. (1981). The development of expectancies in the first year of life. In M. Lamb & L. Sherrod (Eds.), *Infant social cognition* (pp. 155–175). Hillsdale, NJ: Erlbaum.

Lamb, M., & Easterbrooks, M. A. (1981). Individual differences in parental sensitivity. In M. Lamb & L. Sherrod (Eds.), *Infant social cognition* (pp. 127–153). Hillsdale, NJ: Erlbaum.

Langley, M. B. (1990). A developmental approach to the use of toys for facilitation of environmental control. In G. Hedman (Ed.), *Rehabilitation Technology* (pp. 69–91). New York: Haworth Press.

Lerner, R., & Busch-Rossnagel, N. (Eds.). (1981). *Individuals as producers of their own development.* New York: Academic Press.

Li, A. (1985). Toward more elaborate pretend play. *Mental Retardation, 23*(3), 131–136.

Linder, T. (1993). *Transdisciplinary play-based assessment: A functional approach to working with young children* (rev. ed.). Baltimore: Brookes.

Lipsitt, L. (1969). Learning capabilities of the human infant. In R. Robinson (Ed.), *Brain and early behavior* (pp. 227–249). New York: Academic Press.

Lipsitt, L. (1970). The experimental origins of human behavior. In L. Goulet & P. Baltes (Eds.), *Life span development psychology: Research and commentary* (pp. 285–303). New York: Academic Press.

Lipsitt, L., & Werner, J. (1981). The infancy of human learning processes. In E. Gollin (Ed.), *Developmental plasticity* (pp. 101–133). New York: Academic Press.

Mahoney, G. (1988a). Enhancing the developmental competence of handicapped infants. In K. Marfo (Ed.), *Parent–child interaction and developmental disabilities* (pp. 203–219). New York: Praeger.

Mahoney, G. (1988b). Maternal communication style with mentally retarded children. *American Journal on Mental Retardation, 92,* 352–359.

Mahoney, G. (1995). Developmental changes in the spontaneous play behavior of young children with disabilities: Implications for play-based interventions. In G. Mahoney (Ed.), *Family Child Development Reports* (Vol. 1, pp. 13–20). Tallmadge, OH: Family Child Learning Center.

Mahoney, G., Powell, A., Finnegan, C., Fors, S., & Wood, S. (1986). *The transactional intervention program: Theory, procedures and evaluation.* Ann Arbor: University of Michigan, Department of Special Education.

Maisto, A., & German, M. (1981). Maternal locus-of-control and developmental gains demonstrated by high risk infants: A longitudinal analysis. *Journal of Psychology, 109,* 213–221.

Marfo, K. (Ed.). (1988). *Parent–child interaction and developmental disabilities.* New York: Praeger.

McGonigel, M. J. (1991). Philosophy and conceptual framework. In M. J. McGonigel, R. Kaufmann, & B. Johnson (Eds.), *Guidelines and recommended practices for the individualized family service plan* (2nd ed., pp. 7–17). Bethesda, MD: Association for the Care of Children's Health.

McWilliam, R. A., Trivette, C. M., & Dunst, C. J. (1985). Behavior engagement as a measure of the efficacy of early intervention. *Analysis and Intervention in Developmental Disabilities, 5,* 59–71.

Millar, W. S. (1976). Operant acquisition of social behaviors in infancy: Basic problems and constraints. In H. Reese (Ed.), *Advances in child development and behavior* (Vol. 11, pp. 107–140). New York: Academic Press.

Motti, F., Cicchetti, D., & Stroufe, L. A. (1983). From infant affect expression to symbolic play: The coherence of development in Down syndrome children. *Child Development, 54,* 1168–1175.

National Council on Disability. (1993). *Study on the financing of assistive technology devices and services for individuals with diabilities.* A Report to the President and the Congress of the United States. Washington, DC.

O'Brein, M., Porterfield, J., Herbert-Jackson, E., & Risley, T. (1979). *The toddler center.* Baltimore: University Park Press.

Olds, A. (1979). A play center for handicapped infants and toddlers. In T. Field (Ed.), *Infants born at risk* (pp. 413–423). New York: SP Medical & Scientific Books.

Parsons, S. (1986). Function of play in low vision children: Part 2: Emerging patterns of behavior. *Journal of Visual Impairment and Blindness, 80,* 777–784.

Piaget, J. (1951). *Plays, dreams and imitation in childhood* (C. Gattegno & F. Hodgson, Trans.). New York: Norton. (Original work published 1945).

Piaget, J. (1952). *The origins of intelligence in children* (M. Cook, Trans.). New York: International Universities Press. (Original work published 1936).

Piaget, J. (1954). *The construction of reality in the child* (M. Cook, Trans.). New York: Basic Books. (Original work published 1937).

Piaget, J. (1970). Piaget's theory. In P. Mussen (Ed.), *Carmichael's manual of child psychology* (Vol. 1, pp. 703–732). New York: Wiley.
Power, T., & Radcliff, J. (1989). The relationship of play behavior to cognitive ability in developmentally disabled preschoolers. *Journal of Autism and Developmental Disorders, 19*, 97–107.
Raab, M. M., Wortman Lowe, L., & Dunst, C. J. (1991). Magic seven steps to responsive teaching. *Early Childhood Intervention Monograph, 4,* (No. 1). Morganton, NC: Family, Infant and Preschool Program.
Rowland, G., & McGuire, J. (1971). *The mind of man.* Englewood Cliffs, NJ: Prentice-Hall.
Sameroff, A., & Cavanagh, P. (1979). Learning in infancy: A developmental perspective. In J. Osofsky (Ed.), *Handbook of infant development* (pp. 344–392). New York: Wiley.
Schaefer, E., & Edgerton, M. (1985). Parent and child correlates of parental modernity. In I. Sigel (Ed.), *Parent belief systems* (pp. 287–318). Hillsdale, NJ: Erlbaum.
Schoville, R. (1984). Development of the intention to communicate: The eye of the beholder. In L. Feagans, C. Garvey, & R. Golinkoff (Eds.), *The origins and growth of communication* (pp. 109–122). Norwood, NJ: Ablex.
Segal, M. (1985). A study of maternal beliefs and values within the context of an intervention program. In I. Sigel (Ed.), *Parent belief systems* (pp. 271–286). Hillsdale, NJ: Erlbaum.
Sigel, I. (Ed.). (1985). *Parental belief systems: The psychological consequences for children.* Hillsdale, NJ: Erlbaum.
Trevarthen, C., & Hubley, P. (1978). Secondary intersubjectivity: Confidence, confiding and act of meaning in the first year. In A. Lock (Ed.), *Action, gesture and symbol* (pp. 183–229). New York: Academic Press.
Tronick, E. (Ed.). (1982). *Social interchange in infancy.* Baltimore: University Park Press.
Turner, I., & Small, J. (1985). Similarities and differences in behavior between mentally handicapped and normal preschool children during play. *Child: Care, Health and Development, 11*, 391–401.
Twardosz, S. (1984). Environmental organization: The physical, social, and programmatic context of behavior. In M. Hersen, R. M. Eisler, & P. M. Miller (Eds.), *Progress in behavior modification* (Vol. 18, pp. 123–161). New York: Plenum.
Twardosz, S., & Risley, T. (1982). Behavioral–ecological consultation to day care centers. In A. Jeger & R. Slotnick (Eds.), *Community mental health and behavioral ecology* (pp. 147–159). New York: Plenum Press.
Uzgiris, I. (1986a, May). *Interaction as the context for early intervention.* Paper presented at the Third Annual Eric Denhoff Memorial Symposium on Child Development, Brown University, Providence, RI.
Uzgiris, I. (1986b). Organization of sensorimotor intelligence. In M. Lewis (Eds.), *Origins of intelligence* (2nd ed., pp. 135–189). New York: Plenum Press.
Uzgiris, I., & Hunt, J. McV. (1975). *Assessment in infancy.* Urbana: University of Illinois Press.
Wachs, T., & Sheehan, R. (Eds.). (1988). *Assessment of young developmentally disabled children.* New York: Plenum Press.
Wacker, D. P., Wiggins, B., Fowler, M., & Berg, W. K. (1988). Training students with profound or multiple handicaps to make requests via microswitches. *Journal of Applied Behavior Analysis, 21*(4), 331–343.
Warren, S. F., & Kaiser, A. P. (1986). Incidental language teaching: A critical review. *Journal of Speech and Hearing Disorders, 51,* 291–298.
Watson, J. S. (1966). The development and generalization of "contingency awareness" in early infancy: Some hypotheses. *Merrill–Palmer Quarterly, 12,* 123–136.

Watson, J. S. (1972). Smiling, cooing, and the "Game." *Merrill–Palmer Quarterly, 18,* 323–339.

Weinstein, C., & David, T. (Eds.). (1987). *Spaces for children: The built environment and child development.* New York: Plenum Press.

Wenar, C. (1972). Executive competence and spontaneous social behavior in one-year-olds. *Child Development, 43,* 256–260.

White, B. (1971). *Human infants: Experience and psychological development.* Englewood Cliffs, NJ: Prentice–Hall.

White, B., & Watts, J. (1973). *Experience and environment.* Englewood Cliffs, NJ: Prentice–Hall.

Yarrow, L., Rubenstein, J. M., & Pederson, F. (1975). *Infant and environment: Early cognitive and motivational development.* Washington, DC: Hemisphere.

CHAPTER 8

Indicators of Quality in Communication Intervention

Howard Goldstein
Louise A. Kaczmarek
Nancy H. Hepting

The indicators of quality in communication intervention stem from the premise that intervention agents should be actively involved in teaching young children with special needs to communicate more effectively. Active involvement entails strategies for assessing communication performance, strategies for selecting appropriate intervention goals, as well as strategies for teaching those communication goals. The indicators of quality are meant to be as inclusive as possible with respect to (a) what constitutes communication and (b) what places and people are involved in communication intervention.

Communication entails transmission of all kinds of messages, such as information related to needs, desires, perceptions, knowledge, or feelings. One may transmit information to others, and one may receive information. However, because language also may be used to mediate one's own actions and thoughts, communication does not always imply social interaction. Furthermore, we have chosen not to refer to "speakers" and "listeners," because these roles seem to implicate intentional, verbal communication. Communication need not be intentional or conventional to affect people's interactions and behavior. Nonlinguistic forms, for example, pointing, facial expressions, body language, and whining, also are considered part of the communication system. Nor does communication need to be verbal. Oral and nonoral modes of communication, such as gestural, graphic, or written systems, are subsumed by our definition of communication. As one can see, early interventionists must maintain a broad conception of what constitutes communication.

Effective communication intervention requires a broad representation of individuals with knowledge of and familiarity with the child, the child's family, and their larger community or culture. Assessment, goal selection, and intervention processes call upon expertise and collaboration of professionals as well as other interested parties. Individuals who might be involved in these processes include teachers; paraprofessionals; speech–language pathologists and other related service personnel; parents and other immediate family members; extended family members and caretakers; advocates, interpreters, or other community members; and peers. Communication assessment and intervention should be implemented in multiple communicative contexts, sampling (if not including) all those settings in which the child normally has opportunities to communicate.

We propose that communication intervention should be considered for all young children with special needs. Others have suggested that "cognitive referencing" (i.e., whether communication development is delayed with respect to general cognitive functioning) be considered when setting priorities or eligibility criteria for speech–language pathology services (e.g., Fey, 1986; Lyngaas, Nyberg, Hoekenga, & Gruenewald, 1983; Miller, 1981; Owens & House, 1984). The underlying assumption that such children would profit more from treatment has not been borne out in the research literature (see Notari, Cole, & Mills, 1992). Indeed, children with developmental disabilities typically have ample room for improvement in the effectiveness and efficiency of their communication. One must keep in mind that language skills are integrally related to a myriad of academic and life-support skills. Thus, it is unlikely that individuals are apt to fulfill their potential unless efforts to maximize their communication skills are taken.

ASSESSMENT

Recommended practice in communication assessment stresses the broad sampling of communication skills. Assessments should include examination of the adequacy of modes of communication that are evidenced or plausible and take into consideration the comprehension and production of communicative content, forms, and functions (COM 1). In order to obtain a comprehensive picture of a child's communication abilities, team members should explore a variety of assessment methods.

Prior to the actual assessment, team members collaboratively develop an overall plan for the assessment of a child's communication skills. In keeping with a transdisciplinary approach to assessment, the plan for communication assessment can be at least partially interwoven with plans to assess other developmental areas so as to tap into communication skills as they interface with skills needed in various activities. The collaborative development of an assessment plan should benefit from the sampling of information as efficiently and as naturally as possible (COM 2). During planning, team members (including parents or other family members) might consider the following questions:

- What types of communication assessment methods will be used?

- What type of information will each method yield and how does the information fit into the comprehensive picture of the child's communication skills?
- In what order will the assessments be conducted? For example, will assessments in natural environments be conducted first, followed by more formal assessment measures, or vice versa?
- Who will conduct the various aspects of the assessment? For example, which parts will be conducted jointly with other team members? Which parts will be administered by the speech–language pathologist using more conventional assessment formats?

To maximize efficiency in the development of assessment plans, teams might wish to consider the development of a menu of assessment methods from which to draw during planning for individual children. Some methods, such as gathering information from parents, might be considered a standard part of every communication assessment, and other methods might be selected on the basis of the needs of a particular child. Many of the methods that might be included in such a menu are described next and are summarized in Table 8.1. One might consider many of the following practices as "under development," however, for lack of well-established protocols. Note the multiple sources of assessment information in the methods described.

Parents are one critical source of information because they provide accounts of their child's communication abilities and needs as well as their concerns and priorities. Input from parents might be obtained through interviews or questionnaires or both. In keeping with a collaborative approach to assessment, questions about communication should become a part of a more comprehensive questionnaire or interview that addresses other developmental areas. This approach is considered preferable to having families complete a stack of questionnaires or series of interviews given by a variety of professionals from different disciplines.

Interviews and surveys of teachers and other professionals might gather developmental information about some of the same communication skills based on different contexts. Information about previous communication intervention efforts and activities should also be gathered. Unfortunately, the literature has not focused extensively on this source of information (see Klein et al., 1981, for one example of a teacher questionnaire).

Formal and informal testing represent more traditional assessment options. The tools used for testing typically compare a child's performance to age norms that reflect an average course of communication development. Analysis of the results identify those developmental milestones that a child has and has not yet acquired. Standardized, norm-referenced assessment tools may be exclusively devoted to communication (e.g., *Sequenced Inventory of Communication Development*, Hedrick, Prather, & Tobin, 1984; *Test of Early Language Development*, Hresko, Reid, & Hammill,

Table 8.1. Types of Communicative Assessments and Their Purposes

Type	Purpose
Parent Questionnaires and Interviews	Gather information about a child's communication from parents and other family members; determine family concerns and priorities
Teacher/Other Professional Questionnaires	Gather information about a child's communication from teachers and other professionals; determine concerns, priorities, and previous intervention efforts by other professionals
Formal Testing	Determine how a child's language development compares with that of the "average" child; yields standard scores, percentiles, and age-equivalent scores
Informal Testing	Determine the specific developmental milestones that a child has and has not acquired; may yield developmental ages
Probes	Determine whether children display specific communication forms, meanings, and functions by designing environmental arrangements in natural and/or special environments intended to stimulate them
Dynamic Assessment	Examine the ease of facilitating more advanced communicative performance
Communication Samples	Analyze a corpus of a child's utterances collected in a facilitative communication environment to determine the range of forms, meanings, and functions a child displays and to calculate such quantitative measures as MLU, type-token ratios
Observational Coding	Assess the communicative interaction between a child and other persons with whom he or she regularly interacts in natural or contrived settings
Communication Environment Assessment	Assess the supportiveness of a child's communication environment
Functional Analyses	Determine the antecedents that predict certain communicative behaviors and the functional relationships between a communication behavior and its consequences
Ecological Inventories	Examine the skills necessary to function in given settings including how certain communicative skills interface with other skills

1981; *Peabody Picture Vocabulary Test*, Dunn & Dunn, 1981) or may be a part of a comprehensive developmental assessment instrument (e.g., *Battelle Developmental Inventory*, Newborg, Stock, Wnek, Guidubaldi, & Svinicki, 1984). Unfortunately, few well-accepted, thoroughly standardized, rigorously tested assessment instruments in the communication area are available (see McCauley & Demetras, 1990; McCauley & Swisher, 1984). Some relatively new tools hold promise (e.g., *Communication and Symbolic Behavior Scales*, Wetherby & Prizant, 1990; *McArthur Communicative Development Inventories*, Fenson et al., 1991). Formal test instruments also might be used as resources for the development of adapted measures. For example, adaptations might involve the use of parent presentation, reinforcers, longer response times, more breaks, or objects instead of pictures. Tests can be adapted to be administered in less intimidating contexts or to tap the communication abilities of children with specific physical disabilities.

Nonstandardized testing also may be conducted. These assessments might sample certain skill areas more extensively. A number of commercially available tests are devoted exclusively to communication skills but have not been standardized (e.g., *Environmental Prelanguage Battery*, Horstmeister & MacDonald, 1978; *Environmental Language Intervention Program*, J. MacDonald, 1978). A number of more global assessments include communication segments (e.g., *Assessment, Evaluation, & Programming System for Infants and Children*, Bricker, 1992; *Transdisciplinary Play-Based Assessment*, Linder, 1992).

One may design one's own test items and construct nonstandardized probes to determine whether a child can comprehend or produce a specific communicative form, meaning, or function (Miller, 1981). Probes present repeated opportunities for a certain behavior to be demonstrated with the use of somewhat different materials for each opportunity. For example, the evaluator might arrange for 10 different opportunities to request objects (e.g., giving the child a puzzle with only one piece; eating crackers in front of a hungry child without offering any; handing the child a desired toy that is sealed in a jar). Probes also can be embedded into everyday activities (e.g., "forgetting" to distribute one of the items needed for a classroom activity to see if a child requests the missing item). Because probes of this sort embody modifications in the way natural environments are arranged, they are referred to as a *naturalistic* assessment method. Such probes require evaluators to be "good actors," emphasizing "naturalness" but giving up some of the efficiency inherent in more traditional testing situations.

Evaluators may determine the ease of facilitating more advanced communicative performance to assess learning potential. In particular, with dynamic assessment procedures, evaluators systematically introduce prompts or teaching episodes into the assessment to determine how a child's performance is enhanced through instruction (Olswang, Bain, & Johnson, 1992). Specific attention is paid to identifying processes that enable a child to move toward more advanced functioning. Dynamic assessment is helpful in deriving information about (1) the child's potential for learning, (2) the factors that may influence the child's success or failure on particular tasks, and (3) strategies for facilitating the child's development or functioning (Minick, 1987). Olswang et al. (1992), for example, provide an application of Feuerstein's (1979) *Learning Potential Assessment Device* to the dynamic assessment of two-word semantic relations.

Gathering and analyzing communication samples is a method of assessment that can yield information about many aspects of a child's language development. Communication samples are generally collected in special environments that have been set up to facilitate rich communicative interaction (Miller, 1981). Because contextual factors influence communicative performance, careful consideration should be paid to the contexts in which samples are collected (Bain, Olswang, & Johnson, 1992). Some of these factors include the setting (e.g., home, clinic, classroom), interactors (e.g., parent, teachers, clinicians), situation (e.g., structured, unstructured, predictable, unpredictable), and materials (e.g., familiar, unfamiliar). Audiotapes are made of the interactions, and the child's utterances are then transcribed and analyzed with attention paid to adopting standard, replicable transcription procedures (Klee, 1992b). Computerized systems (e.g., Miller & Chapman, 1986) can assist evaluators in summarizing qualitative and quantitative information about a child's language development (e.g., mean length of utterance, type–token ratios, percentages of initiations vs. responses, frequency of specific forms, content, and functions). Additional research efforts are needed, however, to provide a better understanding of the developmental and diagnostic significance of many of these measures (Klee, 1992a).

Observational coding represents a way of assessing communicative interaction between a target child and other people. Observational coding may take place in the natural environment (e.g., snack time during a weekly toddler group) or may be used to assess interactions that occur in more contrived situations (e.g., a playtime with a parent, sibling, or peer within an arena assessment). This assessment method should yield representative information about the ways the child communicates with significant others and the ways that others facilitate the child's communication. Evaluators can use the information to assist significant others in expanding their use of facilitation strategies by building on their existing repertoires. For example, the data might reveal that a mother provides occasional models of phrases at her child's communicative level. A program for the mother might focus on increasing the frequency of her models and targeting a specific communicative structure. Many coding protocols have been developed for research purposes (e.g., Mahoney & Powell, 1988; Rice, Sell, & Hadley, 1990) but can also be adapted for practical use.

An alternative to observational coding is the administration of rating scales or checklists that focus on the communicative supportiveness of a communication environment. With these instruments, evaluators attempt to identify strategies that are thought to facilitate communication development. The *Communication Environment Checklist* (Rainforth, York, & Macdonald, 1992) and the *Teacher–Child Communication Scale* (Bailey & Roberts, 1987) are two such instruments that focus on classroom environments specifically.

Functional analyses (O'Neill, Horner, Albin, Storey, & Sprague, 1990; Reichle & Wacker, 1993) assist practitioners in specifying antecedents that predict certain behaviors and in identifying the consequences that maintain specific behaviors. Functional analyses have proven especially useful in helping interventionists design effective interventions for challenging behavior (e.g., Carr & Durand, 1985; Donnellan, Miranda, Mesaros, & Fassbender, 1984; Reichle & Wacker, 1993). In a functional analysis, the interventionist writes down the events and circumstances that precede and follow specifically defined behaviors. Analysis of this information may reveal that some behaviors that are not ordinarily thought of as communicative are in fact functioning successfully as unconventional communication strategies for a particular child. For example, a child may frequently approach other children and put her face unusually close to theirs. Functional analysis of this behavior may reveal that it occurs only in play settings and appears to be the way that the child enters into the ongoing play of the other children and results in the other children's generally responding negatively by pushing the child away. As a result of this analysis, one could decide to teach the child more appropriate play-entry behaviors (e.g., offering a toy to share; saying "Can I play too?"). Once a child starts using these new behaviors (with teacher prompting at first), the other children would respond positively to these play-entry skills, and the invasive behavior would stop occurring (e.g., Gallagher & Craig, 1984).

Ecological inventories (Brownier, 1991; Falvey, 1989; Rainforth et al., 1992) may be conducted to analyze the demands and supports for child communication in everyday settings and in future settings. Ecological inventories reveal the skills necessary for functioning in given settings (e.g., arrival or dismissal at school, bedtime or dinnertime at home, shopping at the mall, or taking swimming lessons at the community center). They also reveal how communication skills interface with other skills in the execution of specific tasks, activities, and routines (e.g., entering the classroom and greeting teachers and peers; listening to a story and saying "good night," requesting to ride the train and handing the ticket to the conductor). In an ecological inventory, the behaviors displayed by nondisabled children when functioning in a given setting are delineated. These behaviors, which include communicative behaviors, can be determined by observing other children of similar age to the target child as they function in the particular setting. Then the evaluator observes the target child in the same setting to determine the discrepancies in the skills used by the target child and those of nondisabled peers. Adaptations and instructional objectives can then be identified on the basis of this analysis. Figure 8.1 represents a completed ecological inventory. An *Assessment of Student Participation in General Education Classes* (C. Macdonald & York, 1992) lists many of the social and communication skills that assist children in functioning in many school settings. Although written for school-aged children, the instrument could be adapted for preschool and kindergarten children.

Two other general assessment issues are discussed in the chapter on assessment (Neisworth & Bagnato, Chapter 2) that are worthy of reiteration. Gathering and interpreting assessment information must reflect sensitivity

Ecological Inventory

Name: Jerome P. Date: 11/4/93

Setting: Cafeteria routine for kindergarten classroom

Legend
+ = displays skill
+/− = emerging skill
− = not displayed

Skills of Persons Without Disabilities	Student Inventory & Discrepancy Analysis	Teaching Targets & Adaptations
Get in line	+ when directed, follows classmates	
Get tray, silverware, etc.	+/− gets tray; not other things	Have buddy give cue
*Communicate drink selection to staff	+/− looks at items; doesn't indicate choice	Train buddy to point out choices and provide cue
Push tray along rail	+ without prompting	
Carry tray without spilling	+ independently	
*Find seat with friends	− wanders around	Train buddy to provide cue
*Engage in conversation	− eats without saying anything	Train buddy to initiate conversation

Figure 8.1. Example of an ecological inventory with communication skills asterisked.

to linguistic and social norms represented by the child's cultural, ethnic, community, and family contexts. Keeping this in mind, the interventionist must convey the explanations and discussions of assessment results in clear and meaningful ways to parents and other team members (COM 2).

GOAL SELECTION

Goal selection follows from the assessment process and is guided by many of the same principles. It is important that goal selection be a collaborative, family-centered process. Parents and other family members as part of a team are pivotal to the process through their identification of the kinds of communication skills they would like a child to learn. Family members assist other members of the team in understanding how different communication skills fit into their values, culture, and lifestyle.

By design, the assessment practices themselves should provide useful information pertaining to the many factors that must be considered in goal selection. Teams must consider *both* the developmental appropriateness of possible goals as well as their functionality in home, educational, and community settings. Team members need to think of more than the short-term benefits though. They should consider the potential of these goals to enhance participation not only in present settings but also in other likely mainstream settings in the future (COM 4). The extent to which specific goals will lead to increases in a child's social integration, including interaction with peers, and the preferences and interests of the children themselves must be deliberated. Team members also analyze the opportunities for effective use of communication goals and modes of communication in the child's present circumstances. They need to ensure that adequate support for maintained use of these communication skills are in place. Hence, they may need to consider the realistic potential for rearranging communication environments and for modifying communication partners' behaviors as well (COM 6).

Teams might find it helpful when prioritizing goals to conduct direct discussions of the these factors in order to consider the perspectives of different team members and the extent to which families consider specific factors important. Such discussions are critical if communication is to be interwoven into children's lives. Thus, recommended practice is indicated largely by the frequency and quality of the contexts that set the occasion for communication learning and use (COM 7).

INTERVENTION

Perhaps the most potent way to encourage the use and learning of communication skills is to arrange the environment to ensure that there are plenty of opportunities to communicate (COM 8). A number of environmental arrangement strategies have been designed specifically for increasing the number and saliency of teaching opportunities (Halle, 1988). These strategies include putting items in view but out of reach, delivering inadequate portions, sabotaging an activity or toy, creating a need for assistance, creating a need for protesting, violating routine expectations, and sparking a child's interest in a toy or activity (see Table 8.2). All of these events are expected to occur naturally within the child's environment but typically not with enough frequency or saliency to ensure learning. Therefore, structuring or "arranging" the environment provides multiple opportunities for teaching language throughout the day, across activities, and across communication partners.

Intervention environments should provide frequent opportunities to learn receptive as well as expressive language. It is important that these opportunities encompass the full range of communicative functions and content that are typical of children. For example, there may be an overemphasis on getting children to respond to questions and directions verbally and nonverbally. In fact, an emphasis on initiating may spark the realization that communication is an effective means of exerting control over one's environment more readily than does an emphasis on responding. Initiating pertains to multiple functions, including questioning, commenting, requesting attention or action, and rejecting.

Communication intervention should take place in the context of *interactions* with a variety of the adults and children. Comprehensive communication intervention involves multiple communication partners not only as interaction partners but also as potential intervention agents. Although the bulk of the intervention research has employed speech–language pathologists and teachers as intervention agents, a growing database indicates that parents, paraprofessionals, and typical peers can readily be taught to promote communication development in children with special needs (e.g., Campbell, Stremel-Campbell, & Rogers-Warren, 1985; Girolametto, 1988; Goldstein & Cisar, 1992; Goldstein & Ferrell, 1987; Goldstein & Kaczmarek, 1991; Goldstein, Kaczmarek, Pennington, & Shafer, 1992; J. MacDonald, Blott, Gordon, Spiegel, & Hartmann, 1974; Paul, 1985; Weistuch & Lewis, 1985). Communication intervention can be incorporated into daily routines in the home, in the community, and in the classroom. Playtime and mealtimes, for example, may provide as rich a context for intervention as time set aside for a language lesson. In fact, these more naturalistic contexts may have the advantage of enhancing motivation and of avoiding generalization problems because relevant antecedent stimuli and functional consequent stimuli that are present in the everyday environment are being manipulated (COM 7).

The use of multiple individuals in facilitating the communication development of children with special needs requires coordinated efforts and preferably collaborative efforts. Coordination, a concept embodied in an

Table 8.2. Suggestions for Facilitating Specific Communicative Functions Through Environmental Arrangements

Communicative Function	Technique	Examples
Comments	Sparking interest in toys or activities	Blow some bubbles then stop.
	Sabotage an activity	Give the child a car whose wheel falls off when pushed.
	Violate expectations	Turn all the pictures on the walls upside down.
Questions	Sparking interest in toys or activities	Peek into a brown paper bag, quickly close it, and look at child.
	Sabotage an activity	Show the child how to do a puzzle; when you walk away, palm one of the pieces.
Requests	Out of reach but in view	Put the toy that child always goes for at the front of a high but visible position on a shelf.
	Inadequate portions	At snack, pour only a drop of juice in a cup.
	Need for assistance	Put a favorite toy in a clear plastic container with the lid on very tight.
Protests	Out of reach but in view	Tell the child to *hurry up* and get her lunch after you have put it out of reach.
	Inadequate portions	Give another child two cookies and the targeted child a crumb.
	Sabotage an activity	Give one child a working race car and the targeted child a broken one and have them race.
	Need for protest	Hold on to the child's shirttail as he tries to walk past you.

interdisciplinary service delivery model, implies that relevant team members (e.g., teacher, speech–language pathologist) plan the communication intervention strategies for their settings within the general structure agreed on in the child's educational plan. Team members may regularly update each other so that all contributions to the communication program remain compatible and consistent. On the other hand, collaboration, which is suggestive of a transdisciplinary approach to service delivery, goes beyond coordination to include *joint planning and implementation by all* members of a child's team. This approach requires more frequent communication among team members. Intervention plans, including those for monitoring child progress, are developed within the team. Team members develop role-release strategies so that individuals with greater expertise in an area can enhance the knowledge and skills of other team members. Team members actively support each other in the implementation of the communication intervention program, making adjustments in the intervention as necessary. The active involvement of families on the team is helpful in extending the benefits of a collaborative communication program to home and community settings. Families should receive maximal opportunities for direct involvement in the intervention program, permitting them to determine the roles they wish to assume in these efforts (COM 6, COM 10).

The efforts of the team should facilitate the integration of intervention strategies into a variety of instructional contexts with minimal imposition on any one individual's routines or daily activities. Effective teams share responsibility for teaching communication skills; the speech–language pathologist should not be viewed as the individual solely responsible for teaching communication skills. This integrated approach contrasts with the traditional model in which speech–language pathologists take children out of their natural environments to deliver therapy. An integrated approach, however, does not preclude the use of more traditional language intervention services nor does it suggest that speech–language pathologists should never deliver services directly. Rather, an integrated approach implies a shift in what might be considered the "default intervention" model. In other words, an integrated approach should be provided as a given for every child receiving language intervention services with the addition of a more traditional pull-out model only if specifically justified. Thus, speech–language pathologists shift the primary site of their hands-on direct service delivery from special rooms to more natural environments and provide consultation to other team members (indirect therapy) in conjunction with transdisciplinary team participation. The balance between direct and indirect therapy should be determined for individual children on the basis of their particular needs (COM 11).

Teaching Procedures

A variety of intervention techniques have been shown to be effective in teaching communication skills. The relative effectiveness of different intervention techniques is difficult to discern, because most communication intervention studies have evaluated treatment packages composed of numerous intervention techniques. Communication interventions are likely to continue undergoing considerable change as investigators and practitioners evaluate refinements in specific techniques and the packaging and repackaging of multiple techniques. Many of the *commonly* used intervention techniques are identified in Table 8.3 (adapted from Goldstein, Kaczmarek, & Hepting, 1994).

Goldstein et al. (1994) attempted to review studies of language intervention that had been characterized as "naturalistic interventions" to evaluate similarities and differences among these treatment approaches. They analyzed 29 studies that utilized an experimental design and included at least one child 6 years old or younger. The main focus was on the specific procedures incorporated into the intervention plan of each study. Approximately 35 different procedures were initially identified as language training components. The list was narrowed to 11 when definitions could not be extracted from research reports to clearly or consistently distinguish procedures from one another. One such problem was the distinction between expansion and repetition. Expansion involves repeating a child's utterance but also expanding it into a more complex or more appropriate form. Authors often were not explicit about their definition of repetition as exact repetition, and Goldstein et al. had difficulty discerning whether expansion was prohibited. Therefore, expansions and repetitions were collapsed into a single category. This process of collapsing ambiguous or related procedures resulted in 11 categories that could be coded reliably. The studies were reanalyzed once the final 11 procedures were derived. Eight teaching techniques that emphasized manipulation of antecedent stimuli and three sets of consequences were identified. The review revealed that these procedures were regularly incorporated into a variety of naturalistic communication interventions.

Furthermore, intervention practices differed considerably even though they were sometimes called the same thing. For example, "incidental teaching" as described by McGee, Krantz, and McClannahan (1985) and by Hart and Risley (1968) differ substantially. Similarly, interventions may bear striking similarity even though they are called different things; for example, "environmental language intervention" (J. MacDonald et al., 1974) and "embedded instruction" (Neef, Walters, & Egel, 1984) are procedurally similar.

Regardless of the specific intervention techniques included in a treatment package, communicative interventions need to be applied systematically to be effective. Implementation needs to be individualized for children, and specific instructional techniques must be applied with sufficient consistency and frequency to facilitate the acquisition of the selected communication goals (COM 10).

As the data in Table 8.3 show, the first eight techniques involve the manipulation of antecedent stimuli or the setting generally. *Prompting imitation* involves an intervention agent's delivering a prompt that obligates

Table 8.3. Summary of the Teaching Techniques Used in Studies of Naturalistic Communication Interventions

Intervention Approaches	\multicolumn{29}{c}{Study Number (see citations below)}

Intervention Approaches	1	2	3	4	5	6	7	8	9	10	11	12	13	14	15	16	17	18	19	20	21	22	23	24	25	26	27	28	29
Manipulations of Antecedents																													
Prompting Imitation	x	x	x	x	x	x	x	x	x	x	x		x	x	x		x		x		x		x		x		x		
Manding verbalization	x	x	x	x	x	x	x		x	x	x	x	x	x	x	x	x	x	x	x	x	x	x	x	x		x		
Waiting for initiation or response								x	x	x	x	x	x	x	x	x	x	x		x		x	x	x	x	x			
Requesting clarification or elaboration				x	x	x																							
Modeling										x		x		x		x		x	x	x		x	x	x	x				x
Descriptive Talking			x			x		x	x	x			x		x	x	x	x	x	x	x	x			x	x	x		x
Repeating, Expanding, etc.		x	x		x	x	x	x	x	x	x		x	x	x	x	x	x	x	x	x		x	x	x	x	x	x	x
Arranging the Environment	x	x	x	x	x	x	x	x	x	x	x	x	x	x	x	x	x	x	x	x	x	x	x		x				x
Manipulations of Consequences																													
Praising	x	x		x	x	x	x				x				x	x							x	x					x
Using Minimal Encouragers				x														x						x				x	
Delivering Desired Consequences	x	x	x	x	x	x	x	x	x	x	x	x	x	x	x	x	x	x	x	x	x		x		x		x	x	x

(continues)

Table 8.3. *Continued*

1. Hunt et al., 1986
2. J. MacDonald et al., 1974
3. Neef et al., 1984
4. Warren et al., 1984
5. Rogers-Warren & Warren, 1980
6. McGee et al., 1985
7. Cavallaro & Bambara, 1982
8. Gobbi et al., 1986
9. Oliver & Halle, 1982
10. Angelo & Goldstein, 1990
11. Haring et al., 1987
12. Charlop et al., 1985
13. Halle et al., 1981
14. Yoder et al., 1991
15. Hart & Risley, 1974
16. Hart & Risely, 1975
17. Warren & Bambara, 1989
18. Warren & Gazdag, 1990
19. Warren, 1992
20. Girolametto, 1988
21. Wiestuch & Lewis, 1985
22. McLean & Vincent, 1984
23. Hart & Risley, 1968
24. Schwartz et al., 1985
25. Cavallaro & Bambara, 1982
26. Mahoney & Powel, 1988
27. Weiss, 1981
28. Cole & Dale, 1986
29. Wilcox et al., 1991

Note. From "Communication Interventions: The Challenges of Across-the-Day Implementation," by H. Goldstein, L. Kaczmarek, and N. Hepting, in *Behavior Analysis in Education* (p. 105), edited by R. Gardner III, D. Sainato, J. Cooper, T. Heron, W. Heward, J. Eshleman, and T. Grossi, 1994, Pacific Grove, CA: Brooks/Cole. Copyright 1994 by Brooks/Cole Publishing. Adapted with permission.

the child to imitate (e.g., "Say cookie"). A *mand* is a question or an imperative that obligates the child to request or respond (e.g., "Tell me what you want"). *Time delay* occurs when the adult provides a specific amount of time for the child to initiate in the presence of nonverbal or environmental cues. The obligation of a response is implicit, and if a response is not emitted during the delay period then a more explicit prompt typically follows. *Requesting clarification or elaboration* is a type of mand following a child's initiation or response. Its function is to evoke additional information, clarification, or a more appropriate linguistic form (e.g., "What did you say?"). *Modeling* is the presentation of an example to illustrate the use of a specific or general language target, with no obligation for the child to imitate. In *descriptive talking,* an intervention agent comments or talks about ongoing activities without obligating the child to respond. *Repeating, expanding, and recasting* all occur in response to a child's utterance. Repeating involves the adult's repeating the child's utterance; expanding involves the adult's repeating the child's utterance and elaborating on the structure; recasting involves the adult's taking the child's ungrammatical or incorrect utterance and recasting it into a grammatical form. The last category involves a number of general strategies for manipulating antecedent stimuli: *Environmental arrangement* includes specific strategies used to set the occasion for language use and to provide multiple opportunities for training (see Table 8.2). Procedures, such as putting objects in view and out of reach and violating expectations, provide opportunities for the child to demonstrate interest in acquiring something or to initiate communication independently, but communication is not obligated.

The final three techniques in Table 8.3 involve different types of consequences. *Praise* refers to verbal reinforcement for children's correct usage of language goals. *Minimal encouragers* are forms of acknowledgement for verbal performance, (e.g., "yes," "okay"). Minimal encouragers do not provide explicit feedback on the quality of the content or form of the child's communication. *Delivering desired consequences* is prevalent when children are being taught to produce requests. The natural consequence for requesting is to receive the requested item, action, or attention. Delivering desired consequences may be instituted for the child's correct performance regardless of whether that performance is imitative, responsive, or self-initiated. Some interventions allow for the delivery of assumed desired consequences when the adult completes a series of training procedures, regardless of whether the child actually performs the targeted goal.

Table 8.4 presents scripts of two teaching episodes to illustrate how these various intervention techniques may be used together to address specific target behaviors. In the first script, the child is being taught to request using an action–object form. In the second script, the target behavior is not so obvious, but it appears to focus on the use of adjectives in simple sentences. These examples illustrate how intervention techniques can be incor-

Table 8.4. Two Scripts Illustrating the Use of Intervention Techniques

	Action/Communication	Technique
Script 1		
Teacher	(holds up juice and looks at child)	Time Delay
Child	(unintelligible)	
Teacher	"What do you want me to do?"	Mand
Child	"Jute"	
Teacher	"What did you say?"	Request Clarification
Child	"Jute, please"	
Teacher	"Say 'pour juice'."	Prompt Imitation
Child	"Pour jute."	
Teacher	"Say 'pour juice'."	Prompt Imitation
Child	"Pour juice."	
Teacher	"Thanks for asking. (pours juice) I'm pouring the juice."	Praise, Deliver Desired Consequence, Expand
Script 2		
Teacher	"You're painting a beautiful house."	Descriptive Talking
Child	(shows teacher paint on her hand)	
Teacher	"I see."	Minimal Encourager
	(waits with expectant look)	Time Delay
	"Red paint on your hand."	Modeling
Child	"More paint, please."	
Teacher	"You need more paint."	Recast
	"That was nice asking, Emma."	Praise
	(adds to red paint, but leaves green paint empty)	Environmental Arrangement
Child	"I need green paint."	
Teacher	"Oh, you need green paint." (adds to green paint)	Repeat, Deliver Desired Consequences

porated readily into teaching episodes. Numerous variations are possible, based on the materials present, the child's linguistic sophistication, the level of specificity of the goals being targeted, the time available for teaching episodes, and other variables. Most treatment packages provide varying amounts of support for providing teaching materials, assessing children's communication skills, selecting specific or general goals; and they specify different regimens that constrain the use of the intervention techniques and their sequencing. We suspect that the effectiveness of communication intervention programs is related to (a) the extent to which communication goals selected are functional and developmentally appropriate for the child; (b) the number of opportunities for the child to practice receptive and expressive communication skills; and (c) the efficiency of the use of modeling, prompting, and fading procedures. Although these predictions make sense from a learning theory or instructional technology perspective, comparative studies of communication interventions have not been conducted to confirm these assumptions.

Adapting to the Needs of Children with Special Needs

Competent communicators are quite skilled at adapting their communication on the basis of the person with whom they are communicating. Indeed, even young children will modify their language according to whether they are interacting with an adult, an older child, a younger child, or a child with special needs (Guralnick & Paul-Brown, 1977, 1980, 1984, 1986). It is not clear, however, whether this code switching is associated reliably with comprehension levels, expressive language abilities, or other perceptible characteristics of the communication partner. Furthermore, many interaction partners may not be sensitive to the particular adaptations that are required for certain individuals. For example, most communicators need to make a conscious effort to ensure that their face is clearly visible when speaking to a child with a hearing impairment. Great care is needed to optimize the chances that communication is comprehensible to a child with special needs.

Many children have adaptive and prosthetic devices that are unique to their receptive and expressive modes of communication. One must regularly check proper functioning of assistive devices such as hearing aids, glasses, communication boards, and other mechanical or electronic adaptive and prosthetic devices (COM 12; English, 1991; Education of All Handicapped Children Act, §121, 1975). A variety of professionals and parents may need special training to ensure that assistive devices are maintained in proper working order.

Because middle-ear infections are commonplace among young children, one should recognize the need for listening environments that are relatively free of noise and reverberation for all children, not just for children with hearing impairments (COM 13; Berg, 1987; Finitzo, 1988). Early interventionists should try to optimize listening conditions in their setting. They can provide acoustical treatments to the environment that will reduce reverberation, for example, by installing carpet, drapes, and acoustical ceiling tiles. They also should monitor and control for excessive external and internal noise sources. Instruction should be presented from +20 to +30 dB above the ambient noise levels in the setting. Noise levels easily can be monitored with an inexpensive sound-level meter found in most establishments featuring audio equipment. However, consulting an educational audiologist is the most efficient and effective way to get ideas on improving the classroom sound environment (COM 13).

Evaluation

Finally, we should reemphasize that the effectiveness of intervention efforts must be the subject of continual scrutiny. The implementation of intervention efforts as well as their effects must be monitored systematically and regularly. Generally, the effects of intervention efforts need to be scrutinized at two levels. First, one needs to monitor change in the development of the specific communication goals that are being targeted. These data may be gathered during intervention or probes administered intermittently to assess a variety of exemplars of the target behaviors and the extent of spontaneous, generalized usage. Second, one needs to monitor overall changes in communication development. Studies of communication interventions have not revealed particular treatment programs that are robust enough to produce pervasive developmental improvements in communication consistently. Indeed, no one instrument provides detailed information about the multiple aspects of this developmental domain. Nonetheless, a broader perspective is needed to evaluate whether intervention efforts are having the desired effect for the child. This evaluation information should inspire periodic discussion about whether adjustments in intervention plans are needed to accommodate changes in the child's development and the child's everyday communication situations.

CLOSING

In sum, indicators of quality specify the various ways by which early intervention ensures that children with special needs attain socially effective communication repertoires. Early intervention practices and education systems generally are undergoing profound changes. Early childhood special education, in particular, has served as a fertile testing ground for new approaches to equipping all children to function productively in society. Indeed, early intervention is well positioned as a continuing impetus for educational reform and restructuring. We have attempted to highlight how general principles inform the interrelated processes of assessing communication skills in a comprehensive fashion, selecting appropriate goals, and teaching communication skills effectively and efficiently.

Readers should note that no particular assessment tools or curriculum packages are recommended. Two reasons underlie this lack of specificity. First, even the thought of developing such tools or packages is overwhelming, if not inappropriate. Communication is a far-reaching developmental domain that is integrally related to other developmental domains. Consequently, one should expect that early interventionists will differ in their opinions of what constitutes the more critical aspects of language and communication. Furthermore, any realistic attempts to address communication assessment, goal selection, or intervention will necessarily emphasize certain areas at the expense of others. At this point, we hope that individuals approach these tasks with conscious deliberation about the nature of communication and broad-minded discussions about how best to facilitate communication development in individual children.

Second, an extensive empirical basis for communication intervention is still under development (see Goldstein & Hockenberger, 1991). In many ways, broader conceptions of the nature of communication and the advent of more varied service delivery models are liberating to researchers. On the other hand, the shifting sands of theory and practice may paralyze some individuals in the research community, as they are overwhelmed with the myriad of difficult research questions that need to be addressed. Clearly, the research community is not big enough or supported well enough to resolve the issues of how best to assess communication, select goals, and teach communication skills to various populations of children with special needs. The point is not to downplay the tremendous value of the basic and applied research that has enabled interventionists to serve children more effectively now than in the past. Rather, we hope and expect that significant developments will continue to be evidenced.

New developments are expected on a variety of fronts. For example, technological advancements and research on behavior programming are likely to produce more effective techniques that use errorless prompting procedures to teach basic concepts and complex discriminations that underlie much of language content. A great amount of work is needed to determine how to maximize the potential uses of augmentative and alterative communication systems (Goldstein & Hochenberger, 1991). General case programming and other strategies are likely to continue to be developed for promoting generalized use of functional communication skills (e.g., Chadsey-Rusch & Halle, 1992; Chadsey-Rusch, Drasgow, Reinoehl, Halle, & Collet-Klingenberg, 1993). Innovative strategies may well increase the involvement of family members and peers in communication programming. It is our hope that this review spurs the use and improvement of recommended practices to address the communication needs of young children with special needs.

> Preparation of this manuscript was supported by Grants H024P0003 and H023C0053 from the U.S. Department of Education awarded to the University of Pittsburgh.

REFERENCES

Angelo, D. H., & Goldstein, H. (1990). Effects of a pragmatic teaching strategy for requesting information by communication board users. *Journal of Speech and Hearing Disorders, 55,* 231–243.

Bailey, D., & Roberts, J. E. (1987). *Teacher–Child Communication Scale.* Chapel Hill: University of North Carolina.

Bain, B., Olswang, L. B., & Johnson, G. A. (1992). *Topics in Language Disorders, 12*(2), 13–27.

Berg, F. (1987). *Facilitating classroom listening: A handbook for teachers of normal and hard of hearing students.* Austin, TX: PRO-ED.

Bricker, D. (1992). *Assessment, evaluation, and programming system (AEPS) for infants and children: Vol. 1. AEPS measurement for birth to three years.* Baltimore: Brookes.

Brownier, D. (1991). *Assessment of individuals with severe disabilities: An applied behavior approach to life skills assessment* (2nd Ed.). Baltimore: Brookes.

Campbell, C. R., Stremel-Campbell, K., & Rogers-Warren, A. (1985). Programming teacher support for functional language. In S. F. Warren & A. K. Rogers-Warren (Eds.), *Teaching functional language* (pp. 309–339). Austin, TX: PRO-ED.

Carr, E. G., & Durand, V. M. (1985). Reducing behavior problems through functional communication training. *Journal of Applied Behavior Analysis, 18,* 111–126.

Cavallaro, C. C., & Bambara, L. M. (1982). Two strategies for teaching language during free play. *Journal of the Association for Persons with Severe Handicaps, 7,* 80–92.

Chadsey-Rusch, J., Drasgow, E., Reinoehl, B., Halle, J., & Collet-Klingenberg, L. (1993). Using general-case instruction to teach spontaneous and generalized requests for assistance to learners with severe disabilities. *Journal of the Association for Persons with Severe Handicaps, 18,* 177–187.

Chadsey-Rusch, J., & Halle, J. (1992). The application of general-case instruction to the requesting repertoires of learners with severe disabilities. *Journal of the Association for Persons with Severe Handicaps, 17,* 121–132.

Charlop, M. H., Schreibman, L., & Thibodeau, M. G. (1985). Increasing spontaneous verbal responding in autistic children using a time delay procedure. *Journal of Applied Behavior Analysis, 18,* 155–166.

Cole, K. N., & Dale, P. S. (1986). Direct language instruction and interactive language instruction with language delayed preschool children: A comparison study. *Journal of Speech and Hearing Research, 29,* 206–217.

Donnellan, A. M., Miranda, P. L., Mesaros, R. A., & Fassbender, L. L. (1984). Analyzing the communicative functions of aberrant behavior. *Journal of the Association for Persons with Severe Handicaps, 9,* 201–212.

Dunn L., & Dunn, L. (1981). *Peabody Picture Vocabulary Test–Revised.* Circle Pines, MN: American Guidance Service.

Education for All Handicapped Children Act of 1975, 20 U.S.C. § 1400 *et seq.*

English, K. (1991). Best practices in educational audiology. *Language, Speech and Hearing Services in the Schools, 21,* 283–286.

Falvey, M. (1989). *Community-based curriculum: Instructional strategies for students with severe handicaps* (2nd ed.). Baltimore: Brookes.

Fenson, L., Dale, P., Reznick, S., Thal, D., Bates, E., Hartung, J., Pethick, S., & Reilly, J. (1991). *Technical manual for the MacArthur Communicative Development Inventories.* San Diego, CA: San Diego State University.

Feuerstein, R. (1979). *The dynamic assessment of retarded performers.* Baltimore: University Park Press.

Fey, M. E. (1986). *Language intervention with young children.* San Diego, CA: College-Hill Press.

Finitzo, T. (1988). Classroom acoustics. In R. Roeser & M. Downs (Eds.), *Auditory disorders in school children* (2nd ed., pp. 221–233). New York: Thieme Medical.

Gallagher, T. M., & Craig, H. K. (1984). Pragmatic assessment: Analysis of a highly frequent repeated utterance. *Journal of Speech and Hearing Disorders, 49,* 368–377.

Girolametto, L. (1988). Improving the social-conversational skills of developmentally delayed children: An intervention study. *Journal of Speech and Hearing Disorders, 53,* 156–167.

Gobbi, L., Cipani, E., Hudson, C., & Lapenta-Neudeck, R. (1986). Developing spontaneous requesting among children with severe mental retardation. *Mental Retardation, 24,* 357–363.

Goldstein, H., & Cisar, C. L. (1992). Promoting interaction during sociodramatic play: Teaching scripts to typical preschoolers and classmates with handicaps. *Journal of Applied Behavior Analysis, 25,* 265–280.

Goldstein, H., & Ferrell, D. R. (1987). Augmenting communicative interaction between handicapped and nonhandicapped preschool children. *Journal of Speech and Hearing Disorders, 52,* 200–219.

Goldstein, H., & Hockenberger, E. H. (1991). Significant progress in child language intervention: An 11-year retrospective. *Research in Developmental Disabilities, 12,* 401–424.

Goldstein, H., & Kaczmarek, L. (1991). Promoting communicative interaction among children in integrated intervention settings. In S. Warren & J. Reichle (Eds.), *Causes and effects in communication and language intervention* (pp. 81–112). Baltimore: Brookes.

Goldstein, H., Kaczmarek, L., & Hepting, N. (1994). Communication interventions: The challenges of across-the-day implementation. In R. Gardner III, D. Sainato, J. Cooper, T. Heron, W. Heward, J. Eshleman, & T. Grossi (Eds.), *Behavior analysis in education* (pp. 101–113). Pacific Grove, CA. Brooks/Cole.

Goldstein, H., Kaczmarek, L, Pennington, R., & Shafer, K. (1992). Peer-mediated intervention: Attending to, commenting on, and acknowledging the behavior of preschoolers with autism. *Journal of Applied Behavior Analysis, 25,* 289–305.

Guralnick, M. J., & Paul-Brown, D. (1977). The nature of verbal interactions among handicapped and nonhandicapped preschool children. *Child Development, 48,* 254–260.

Guralnick, M. J., & Paul-Brown, D. (1980). Functional and discourse analyses of nonhandicapped preschool children's speech to handicapped children. *American Journal of Mental Deficiency, 84,* 444–454.

Guralnick, M. J., & Paul-Brown, D. (1984). Communicative adjustments during behavior request episodes among children at different developmental levels. *Child Development, 55,* 911–919.

Guralnick, M. J., & Paul-Brown, D. (1986). Communicative interactions of mildly delayed and normally developing preschool children: Effects of listener's developmental level. *Journal of Speech and Hearing Research, 29,* 2–10.

Halle, J. W. (1988). Adopting the natural environment as the context of training. In S. N. Calculator & J. L Bedrosian (Eds.), *Communication assessment and intervention for adults with mental retardation* (pp. 155–185). Boston: Little, Brown.

Halle, J. W., Baer, D. M., & Spradlin, J. E. (1981). Teachers' generalized use of delay as a stimulus control procedure to increase language use in handicapped children. *Journal of Applied Behavior Analysis, 4,* 389–409.

Haring, T. G., Neetz, J. K, Lovinger, L., Peck, C., & Semmel, M. I. (1987). Effects of four modified incidental teaching procedures to create opportunities for communication. *Journal of the Association for the Severely Handicapped, 12,* 218–226.

Hart, B. M., & Risley, T. R. (1968). Establishing use of descriptive adjectives in the spontaneous speech of disadvantaged preschool children. *Journal of Applied Behavior Analysis, 1,* 109–120.

Hart, B. M., & Risley, T. R. (1974). Using preschool materials to modify the language of disadvantaged children. *Journal of Applied Behavior Analysis, 7,* 243–256.

Hart, B. M., & Risley, T. R. (1975). Incidental teaching of language in the preschool. *Journal of Applied Behavior Analysis, 8,* 411–420.

Hedrick, D., Prather, E., & Tobin, A. (1984). *Sequenced Inventory of Communicative Development–Revised.* Seattle: University of Washington Press.

Horstmeister, D. S., & MacDonald, J. M. (1978). *Environmental Prelanguage Battery.* Columbus, OH: Merrill.

Hresko, W. P., Reid, D. K., & Hammill, D. (1981). *Test of Early Language Development,* Austin, TX: PRO-ED.

Hunt, P., Goetz, L., Alwell, M., & Sailor, W. (1986). Using an interrupted behavior chain strategy to teach generalized communication responses. *Journal of the Association for the Severely Handicapped, 11,* 196–204.

Klee, T. (1992a). Developmental and diagnostic characteristics of quantitative measures of children's language production. *Topics in Language Disorders, 12*(2), 28–41.

Klee, T. (1992b). Measuring children's conversational language. In S. F. Warren & J. Reichle (Eds.), *Causes and effects in communication and language intervention* (pp. 315–330). Baltimore: Brookes.

Klein, M. D., Wulz, S. V., Hall, M., Waldo, L., Carpenter, S., Lathan, D., Myers, S., Fox, T., & Marshall, A. (1981). *Comprehensive communication curriculum guide.* Lawrence: University of Kansas, Early Childhood Institute.

Linder, T. (1992). *Transdisciplinary play-based assessment: A functional approach to working with young children.* Baltimore: Brookes.

Lyngaas, K., Nyberg, B., Hoekenga, R., & Gruenewald, L. (1983). Language intervention in the multiple contexts of the public school setting (ASHA Report 12). In J. Miller,

K. Yoder, & R. Schiefelbusch (Eds.), *Contemporary issues in language intervention* (pp. 239–252). Rockville, MD: American Speech-Language and Hearing Association.

Macdonald, C., & York, J. (1992). An assessment of student participation in general education classes. In B. Rainforth, J. York, & C. Macdonald (Eds.), *Collaborative teams for students with severe disabilities* (pp. 256–257). Baltimore: Brookes.

MacDonald, J. (1978). *Environmental language intervention program.* Columbus, OH: Merrill.

MacDonald, J. D., Blott, J. P., Gordon, K., Spiegel, B., & Hartmann, M. (1974). An experimental parent-assisted treatment program for preschool language-delayed children. *Journal of Speech and Hearing Disorders, 39,* 395–415.

Mahoney, G., & Powell, A. (1988). Modifying parent–child interaction: Enhancing the development of handicapped children. *Journal of Special Education, 21,* 82–96.

McCauley, R. J., & Demetras, M. J. (1990). The identification of language impairment in the selection of specifically language-impaired subjects. *Journal of Speech and Hearing Disorders, 55,* 468–475.

McCauley, R. J., & Swisher, L. (1984). Psychometric review of language and articulation tests for preschool children. *Journal of Speech and Hearing Disorders, 49,* 34–42.

McGee, G. G., Krantz, P. J., & McClannahan, L. E. (1985). The facilitative effects of incidental teaching on preposition use by autistic children. *Journal of Applied Behavior Analysis, 18,* 17–31.

McLean, M., & Vincent, L. (1984). The use of expansions as a language intervention technique in the natural environment. *Journal of the Division for Early Childhood, 9,* 57–66.

Miller, J. (1981). *Assessing language production in children: Experimental procedures.* Austin, TX: PRO-ED.

Miller, J., & Chapman, R. (1986). *Systematic analysis of language transcripts (SALT1)* [Computer software]. Madison: University of Wisconsin, Language Analysis Lab.

Minick, N. (1987). Implications of Vygotsky's theories for dynamic assessment. In C. Lidz (Ed.), *Dynamic assessment: An interactional approach to evaluating learning potential* (pp. 116–140). New York: Guilford Press.

Neef, N. A., Walters, J., & Egel, A. L. (1984). Establishing generative yes/no responses in developmentally disabled children. *Journal of Applied Behavior Analysis, 17,* 453–460.

Newborg, J., Stock, J. R., Wnek, L., Guidubaldi, J., & Svinicki, J. (1984). *Battelle Developmental Inventory.* Allen, TX: DLM Teaching Resources.

Notari, A. R., Cole, K. N., & Mills, P. E. (1992). Cognitive referencing: The (non)relationship between theory and application. *Topics in Early Childhood Special Education, 11*(4), 22–38.

Oliver, C. B., & Halle, J. W. (1982). Language training in the everyday environment: Teaching functional sign use to a retarded child. *Journal of the Association for Persons with Severe Handicaps, 8,* 50–62.

Olswang, L. B., Bain, B. A., & Johnson, G. A. (1992). Using dynamic assessment with children with language disorders. In S. F. Warren & J. Reichle (Eds.), *Causes and effects in communication and language intervention* (pp. 187–215). Baltimore: Brookes.

O'Neill, R., Horner, R., Albin, R., Storey, K., & Sprague, J. (1990). *Functional analysis of problem behavior: A practical assessment guide.* Sycamore, IL: Sycamore.

Owens, R., & House, L. (1984). Decision-making processes in augmentative communication. *Journal of Speech and Hearing Disorders, 49,* 18–25.

Paul, L. (1985). Programming peer support for functional language. In S. F. Warren & A. K. Rogers-Warren (Eds.), *Teaching functional language* (pp. 289–307). Austin, TX: PRO-ED.

Rainforth, B., York, J., & Macdonald, C. (1992). *Collaborative teams for students with severe disabilities.* Baltimore: Brookes.

Reichle, J., & Wacker, D. (Eds.). (1993). *Communicative alternatives to challenging behavior: Integrating functional assessment and intervention strategies.* Baltimore: Brookes.

Rice, M. L., Sell, M. A., & Hadley, P. E. (1990). The social-interactive coding system (SICS): An on-line clinically relevant descriptive tool. *Language, Speech, and Hearing Services in Schools, 21,* 2–14.

Rogers-Warren, A. K., & Warren, S. F. (1980). Mands for verbalization: Facilitating the generalization of newly trained language in children. *Behavior Modification, 4,* 230–245.

Schwartz, R. G., Chapman, K., Terrell, B. Y., Prelock, P., & Rowan, L. (1985). Facilitating word combination in language-impaired children through discourse structure. *Journal of Speech and Hearing Disorders, 50,* 31–39.

Warren, S. F. (1992). Facilitating basic vocabulary acquisition with milieu teaching procedures. *Journal of Early Intervention, 16,* 235–251.

Warren, S. F., & Bambara, L. M. (1989). An experimental analysis of milieu language intervention: Teaching the action–object form. *Journal of Speech and Hearing Disorders, 54,* 448–461.

Warren, S. F., & Gazdag, G. (1990). Facilitating early language development with milieu intervention procedures. *Journal of Early Intervention, 14,* 62–86.

Warren, S. F., McQuarter, R. J., & Rogers-Warren, A. K. (1984). The effects of mands and models on the speech of unresponsive language-delayed preschool children. *Journal of Speech and Hearing Disorders, 49,* 43–52.

Weiss, R. S. (1981). INREAL Intervention for language handicapped and bilingual children. *Journal of the Division for Early Childhood, 4,* 40–51.

Weistuch, L., & Lewis, M. (1985). The language interaction intervention project. *Analysis and Intervention in Developmental Disabilities, 5,* 97–106.

Wetherby, A., & Prizant, B. (1990). *Communication and Symbolic Behavior Scales–Research edition.* Chicago: Riverside.

Wilcox, M. J., Kouri, T. A., & Caswell, S. B. (1991). Early language intervention: A comparison of classroom and individual treatment. *American Journal of Speech-Language Pathology, 1,* 49–62.

Yoder, P. J., Kaiser, A. P., & Alpert, C. L. (1991). An exploratory study of the interaction between language teaching methods and child characteristics. *Journal of Speech and Hearing Research, 34,* 155–167.

CHAPTER 9

Strategies for Promoting Social Interaction and Emotional Development of Infants and Young Children with Disabilities and Their Families

Mary A. McEvoy
Samuel L. Odom

From birth, humans are social beings. Infants come equipped with the "hardware" (i.e., neurological system) to selectively attend to the social responses of their caregivers and, unconsciously at first, engage in behaviors (e.g., crying and smiling) that generate human responses. As infants' neurological systems develop, the caregivers' social responses begin to shape "software" (i.e., cognitive processes) in ways that allow the infants to perceive and learn about the predictable nature of social behavior. Such predictability may, in turn, lead to feelings of security and attachment to primary caregivers that eventually allow infants to participate in the world when the caregiver is not present. Also, very early in this developmental process, infants and caregivers exert a dynamic and reciprocal influence on each other's behavior, and infants' social development proceeds in a transactional manner (Sameroff & Chandler, 1975; Yoder, Warren, Kim, & Gazdag, 1994).

As children grow older, their interactions become more complex and varied. Both the quality and quantity of interactions change, with a greater emphasis given to interactions with peers and the development of peer relationships (Howes, 1988). These interactions are a critical part of child development. During the preschool years the nature of attachment with caregivers changes to allow children to function in settings in which they are separated from their parents. Moreover, apparently children who are socially competent and have secure attachment relationships with their caregivers often develop more advanced cognitive, communication, and social skills (Guralnick, 1981; Odom, McConnell, & McEvoy, 1992; Hartup & Sancilio, 1986). Professional organizations, such as the National Association for the Education of Young Children (NAEYC) and the Division for

Early Childhood (DEC), have identified social development as being critically important for young children.

For most children, learning to interact with their adult caregivers and to play with and enjoy interacting with peers is a typical part of child development. However, for some children with disabilities, social interaction skills do not develop independently (Odom, McConnell, & Chandler, 1994). Professionals and family members must often look for ways to enhance their children's social competence. In fact, promoting social competence is often seen as a critical dimension of early intervention and early childhood special education programs (Guralnick, 1994; McCollum & Bair, 1994).

The purpose of this chapter is twofold. First, we provide a description of typical infant and preschool social development in order to establish a context for planning interventions to support social development. Second, we describe interventions that help infants and parents engage in positive social interactions and that assist young children with disabilities in acquiring the skills necessary for peer social interaction.

SOCIAL AND EMOTIONAL DEVELOPMENT OF INFANTS

Most theorists believe social and emotional development is shaped through a learning process (Cairns, 1979). According to Sameroff and Chandler (1975), infants' social and emotional development is based on the transactional and reciprocal nature of interactions among infants and caregivers. Obviously, in early development, parents or other adults play a critical role. Skilled parents tend to be sensitive to social cues that signal when their infants are ready to engage in interaction. For example, before beginning an interaction, a parent may wait until the infant is alert and attentive, is looking at the parent, or is looking at a toy to which they are both attending. Such sensitivity and responsiveness to infants' cues and social behavior may well lay the foundation for infants' understanding of the ways their behavior effects change in the environment (Bornstein & Lamb, 1992). Such "contingent responsiveness" (i.e., caregivers' behavior being contingent on infants' behavior or social cues) directly affects the degree to which infants engage in positive social interaction with caregivers (Lussier, Crimmins, & Alberti, 1994). Maternal responsivity to infants' behavior appears across cultures and is proposed as a universal principle of early child development (Bornstein et al., 1992). However, socioeconomic and demographic variables (e.g., maternal education level) influence the degree to which maternal responsivity occurs, and the specific expression of responsivity (e.g., motor responses, vocal responses) differs across cultures (Dixon, Tronick, Keefer, & Brazelton, 1981; Richman, Miller, & LeVine, 1992).

In light of the transactional nature of social development, the infant also plays a critical role in influencing ongoing and subsequent interactions. Infants are born with relatively identifiable temperaments, which predispose them to respond to their environment in certain ways (Thomas & Chess, 1977). Parents with several children will often describe how their children were different "from day one" and how the difference maintained even though the children had relatively similar upbringing. Many researchers (e.g., Bates, 1980) describe ways in which child temperament influences adult interaction and vice versa. For example, parents are less likely to respond positively to infants who are consistently irritable than to infants who are easily engaged (van den Boom & Hoeksma, 1994). Infant–adult compatibility also influences reciprocal interactions (Grotevant & McRoy, 1988). Parents must be able to adapt to an infant's mood, individual characteristics, and development. In turn, infants usually learn to adapt to adults' styles and attitudes. In discussing these and other reciprocal influences on interaction, Bell and Harper (1977) noted, "If parents are effective they must in turn be affected by the products of their tutelage" (p. 83).

Maternal sensitivity to infants' social cues and responsiveness may well lay the foundation for the development of attachment relationships in the first year of life (van Ijzendoorn, Juffer, & Duyvesteyn, 1995). Infants usually form an attachment relationship with a primary caregiver, who in mainstream U.S. culture is often, but not always, the mother. Bowlby (1982) proposed that such a relationship serves as a basis for personal security and that during much of the first year of life attachment behaviors, such as smiling and crying, serve to bring the adult caregiver in closer proximity to the infant. As the development of motor skills and language skills converge in the second year of life, the infant is able to physically move away from or separate from the adult, while still "checking in" vocally. As cognitive skills develop in the second year and on through the preschool years, young children are able to "represent" or remember the caregiver when they are separated and have confidence that she will return. In an extensive body of research, Ainsworth and colleagues (Ainsworth, Bell, & Stayton, 1972; Ainsworth, Blehar, Waters, & Wall, 1978), followed by other researchers (Bretherton & Waters, 1985; Egeland & Farber, 1984; Sroufe & Waters, 1977), have documented multiple forms of attachment, ranging from secure forms to disorganized or disrupted forms. A secure attachment relationship appears to be related to the development of many social behaviors that appear later in childhood and to the formation of relationships during the preschool years (e.g., Lyons-Ruth, Alpern, & Repacholi, 1993; Youngblade, 1993).

Infants with Disabilities

For some infants with disabilities or at risk for disabilities and their caregivers, participation in positive and mutually satisfying social interaction is difficult. At times, characteristics related to a specific condition or disability may lead to difficulties. For example, infants with visual impairments may have muted smiles and provide different signals that indicate their interest in interacting with parents (Fraiberg, 1977). Similarly, infants with Down syndrome may have smiles that are less engaging for parents than the smiles of nondisabled infants (Emde, Katz, & Thorpe, 1978). Infants with cerebral palsy may feel stiff or unresponsive to parents because of high muscle tone and may not be able to respond quickly to parents' attempts to engage them in play (Wasserman, Lennon, Allen, & Shilansky, 1987). Infants who are premature and low in birthweight and have other medical problems, such as bronchopulmonary dysplasia, may be irritable and may tire easily during play (Gottwald & Thurman, 1990). Prenatal exposure to drugs may cause infants to be irritable and to display irregular sleep patterns (Gottwald & Thurman, 1994).

All of these characteristics may cause parents to respond in ways that either support or disrupt interactions. Because they may have difficulty reading the social cues of infants with disabilities, parents may withdraw from or become passive in interaction with infants (Yoder, 1987). Conversely, when an infant is not responsive, some parents become directive in interactions, possibly overstimulating their infant (Tannock, 1988). When either of these patterns is present, playful and mutually satisfying interactions often do not occur, a situation that may lead to frustration for the parent and for the infant.

Social Development of Preschoolers

As children grow older, their interactions with peers increase dramatically (Howes, 1988; Odom, 1992). At the same time, children's reliance on adults for fulfillment of emotional and social needs decreases somewhat (McEvoy & McConnell, 1995). The importance of participation in peer interaction for the development of social competence is well documented (see Hartup, 1983).

Clearly there are as many different definitions of social competence as there are theorists. However, the importance of increased affiliation with peers in effective and appropriate ways seems to be a common theme across theories of social and emotional development (Guralnick, 1992). In fact, an increased affiliation with peers and a decreased reliance on adults appear to be major components of healthy social and emotional development in the preschool years (McEvoy & McConnell, 1995). According to

Odom, McConnell, & McEvoy (1992), social competence is the "central organizing theme for development, and essentially for life" (p. 3).

During the preschool years, play becomes an important vehicle that supports peer interactions. Children's interactions often occur within the context of games and activities; a child's ability to interact influences his or her participation in these activities. Hartup, Glazer, and Charlesworth (1967) found that children who are effective interactors are chosen more often as playmates by peers. During play, children learn social behaviors that effectively initiate and maintain reciprocal interactions. For example, Tremblay, Strain, Hendrickson, and Shores (1981) found that children who shared, helped others, requested assistance, organized play activities, were affectionate, or engaged in "rough and tumble" play had a greater than 50% chance of being involved in interactions with peers. In their review of observational research on preschool children's social behavior, Odom and Ogawa (1992) found that social behaviors most often associated with relative measures of social competence were (a) effective in initiating interaction or responding to others, (b) positive or prosocial in nature, (c) often verbal in nature, and (d) effective in supporting play themes or the actions of others.

The skills that children learn in order to engage others in interactions vary as a function of cultural norms, beliefs, and patterns of interaction (Mallory & New, 1994). In fact, numerous factors contribute to the ongoing development of a preschooler's social interaction skills. These factors may include socioeconomic status, gender, or disability (Carta, Sainato, & Greenwood, 1988). On a more individual level, the social competence of a child's peers will likely influence both the quantity and quality of the child's interactions (Guralnick, 1994; Strain, 1983).

As the vehicles for and participants in social interaction expand (i.e., play and peers), preschool children experience opportunities for interaction in an increasing variety of settings and situations. Unlike their early years when they were cared for by a few primary caregivers, the preschool years are when children encounter new play partners such as peers in childcare centers; older neighborhood children; young, extended-family members; and other adults. These new partners are found in locations such as preschools, churches, and playgrounds. McEvoy and McConnell (1995) have pointed out that this variety of social partners and settings increases the expectations for child behavior and provides many opportunities for children to develop and shape their social interaction skills.

Preschool Children with Disabilities

Some children with disabilities may have difficulty engaging in effective and appropriate social interaction with peers. In a survey conducted by Odom and colleagues (1994), early childhood special education teachers reported that, on average, 75% of the children in their classes would benefit from learning age-appropriate social interaction skills. When observing preschool children with developmental delays and nondisabled peers in structured play settings, Kopp, Baker, and Brown (1992) found that children with disabilities engaged in more solitary and less social play than did their nondisabled peers. Across several studies in laboratory-based, mainstreamed play groups, Guralnick and his colleagues (Guralnick, Connor, Hammond, Gottman, & Kinnish, in press; Guralnick & Groom, 1988) have found that children with mild developmental delays engage in social interaction less frequently than do their nondisabled peers and that attempts to interact with those peers are often rebuffed. Using a multimethod assessment of social competence, Odom and McConnell (in press) found that children with disabilities performed significantly lower than did nondisabled peers. Concerns about peer social skills exist not only for children with general developmental delays but also for young children with other types of disabilities such as hearing impairments (Antia & Kreimeyer, 1992), visual impairments (Skellenger, Hill, & Hill, 1992), autism (Stone & LaGreca, 1986), behavior disorders (Quay, 1993), and communication disorders (Goldstein & Gallagher, 1992).

Children's peer social interactions may well affect the types of peer relationships that develop for young children with disabilities. In Buysee's (1993) study of children's friendships in mainstreamed settings, teachers and parents reported that children with disabilities have both mutual and unilateral friendships, although children with the most severe disabilities engaged in fewer friendships than did other children. Other investigators have found that children with disabilities who engage in less competent interactions with peers receive lower peer-rating scores than do the more competent interactors (Guralnick & Groom, 1988; Strain, 1983). Although some children with disabilities may have unique competence in social interaction (Salisbury, Britzman, & Kang, 1989) and may develop positive social relationships with peers, for many children with disabilities, active participation in positive interactions (especially with nondisabled peers) and the formation of positive social relationships are difficult. These difficulties are especially a concern because the development of peer social relationships is a major developmental task of the preschool years (Hartup & Moore, 1990). Concerns about the peer relationships of young children with disabilities have led researchers to recommend that early intervention and early childhood special education programs emphasize the development of social competence as a major goal (Guralnick, 1990; Strain, 1990).

INTERVENTIONS TO PROMOTE SOCIAL COMPETENCE

Given the importance of social competence and emotional development for the lives of young children with disabilities and their families, researchers and program developers have developed a range of practices for use in intervention settings. For infants and toddlers, these interventions have focused on supporting positive social interaction between children and caregivers and the development of attachment relationships. For preschool children, intervention strategies have supported children's participation in social interaction with peers, acquisition of specific social skills, and development of peer relationships.

Intervention Practices for Infants and Toddlers and Their Caregivers

Many early intervention programs establish practices that support positive and playful interactions between caregivers and infants with disabilities. Factors that guide these practices may include decision making about when to intervene, determining participants involved in the intervention, recognizing that values of the family should influence the intervention, arranging the environment, using triadic interaction strategies, interpreting interactions as meaningful, responding contingently, supporting mutual enjoyment, and supporting the attachment relationship.

Decision To Intervene

The decision to establish parent–infant interaction as a goal on an IFSP is probably more value laden than other types of goals that might be listed. IFSP teams, which include the parents, routinely establish goals for children and families (see Turbiville, Turnbull, Garland, & Lee, Chapter 4). However, if a professional proposes that parent–infant interaction (or attachment) become a goal without the caregiver's having first expressed a concern, the caregiver may perceive that their skills are inadequate—or that they are doing something wrong. This decision may be the most sensitive and reactive part of the intervention process for some families. Having caregivers present during the assessment of an infant's social skills (SE 6) and interpreting the information for the caregivers (SE 7) may help families understand the nature of social interaction and its importance. Responding to concerns or frustrations of family members or showing how interacting in a certain way will "help their baby learn to talk" (i.e., promote prelinguistic skills) may reduce the possibility that parents will "feel the blame" in such situations.

Participants in the Intervention Process

When infants are very young, it is critical that they establish a close, positive, and interactive relationship (i.e., attachment) with at least one caregiver. In U.S. society, the primary caregiver is often the mother, so most intervention programs supporting caregiver–infant interaction have been designed for mothers to be the adult participant. However, the father or other adult caregiver may also participate. In addition to the central attachment figure(s), other examples of significant individuals in an infant's social life may include siblings, grandparents, aunts or uncles, neighbors, childcare providers, and the home health care nurse. If these individuals spend significant portions of the day with the infant, it will be extremely important to discuss with them the social strategies being followed in the intervention program.

Family and Cultural Values

Intervention practices should not conflict with the family's personal and cultural values (DeGangi, Wietlisbach, Poisson, Stein, & Royeen, 1994). As noted previously, maternal responsivity appears to occur across cultures, but the specific expression of this responsiveness may vary. It is important for early interventionists to understand the style in which caregivers interact with their infant and make a judgment about its form (e.g., motoric, vocal) and its function (i.e., successfully engages the infant in positive social interchange). Shaping the intervention to fit the family is an essential element in supporting caregiver–infant interaction, as it is for promoting other types of skills (FP 24).

Arranging the Environment

Caregivers usually have opportunities to interact with their infants in many different activities during the day. However, when beginning an intervention, it is important for the interventionist and caregivers to set aside "playtimes" to practice and review interaction strategies. Together, they may also plan ways to support playful, positive interactions during other naturally occurring opportunities in the day (e.g., feeding, diapering, bathing, dressing).

The arrangement of the play setting will affect the degree to which children and caregivers are able to interact playfully. For example, infants need to be positioned so that they can see the caregiver and can reach (or see) toys and materials (SE 5). To the extent possible, caregivers should try to reduce sound or noises in the setting that might be disruptive or distracting. For example, the caregiver might make sure the television is turned off, the telephone is unplugged, or the answering machine is on during playtimes.

Social Interaction Coaching and Triadic Interaction

A primary strategy for promoting positive caregiver–infant interaction has been to coach the caregivers in ways they can engage their infants in playful interactions (Field, 1978). For example, Seifer, Clark, and Sameroff (1991) reported the positive effects of a coaching intervention in which mothers and infants were videotaped during interactive play sessions. The coach watched the videotape with the mother and pointed out examples of reciprocal interaction. With infants and parents in the home, McCollum and Yates (1994) have employed a similar "triadic" interaction approach. The components of this strategy included (a) establishing a positive context; (b) acknowledging the parents' competence; (c) focusing attention on the interaction; (d) providing the parents information about engaging their infant; (e) when necessary, modeling appropriate ways to interact with the infant; (f) making suggestions for the parent. A key feature of this intervention approach is the parent's enlistment in observing and hypothesizing about what the child is experiencing.

Interpreting Interactions as Meaningful

One feature of a facilitative interaction style is for caregivers to interpret infants' behavior as meaningful (SE 1). For nondisabled infants, parents naturally do this type of interpretation, and it eventually may lead to positive and playful interactions. Such interpretation requires that caregivers attend closely to the infants' social cues. These cues might be visual orientation and eye contact, motor activity, smiling, state of alertness, gaze aversion, fussiness, and so forth. As noted previously, the social cues of some infants with disabilities may not be easily interpreted. In her classic intervention work with parents, Fraiberg (1971) showed mothers how their infants who were blind used their hands to explore the mothers' faces as an alternative to visual exploration. Similarly, in a parent–infant intervention program designed by MacDonald and Gillette (1989), parents were taught to guide their responses by observing closely the infant's cues. Thus, a central feature of intervention practice for supporting caregiver–infant interaction is to assist caregivers in identifying social cues displayed by their infants and interpreting the meaning of those cues (Widerstrom, Mowder, & Sandall, 1991).

Responsiveness

Another aspect of a facilitative interaction style is the caregiver's responsiveness to the infant (SE 1). Responsiveness is important for several reasons. When social interaction between caregivers and infants is not fun, the caregiver may become passive and unresponsive. The infant, in turn, may not attempt to engage the caregiver. Conversely, some parents may be so active in their interactions with an infant that (a) the infant does not have time to respond, (b) the infant becomes overstimulated and withdraws, or (c) the infant never has an opportunity to respond (Marfo, 1991).

Intervention programs have been designed to assist parents of infants with disabilities in learning to become more responsive to their infant. Mahoney and Powell (1988) designed a program in which parents learned turn-taking strategies (e.g., waiting for a child to act, imitating an infant's behavior) and interactive matching (e.g., "fine-tuning" the interaction to match the child's pace and tempo). The program resulted in parents' being less directive in their interactions and also appeared to have positive effects on the children's development. For a program in which they used somewhat similar strategies to promote mother–infant communication, Haney and Klein (1993) reported similar developmental gains. Teaching parents to be responsive appears to be a standard component of interventions that support caregiver–infant interaction. The caregiver strategies that appear to be most effective are to (a) establish a joint focus of attention through materials or actions, (b) observe and wait until the infant makes a response, (c) respond in a way that fits the behavior of the infant, and (d) allow the infant an opportunity to engage in another response. Following the infant's interest in an activity or interaction appears to be essential for the responsive strategies to be successful.

A controversial issue in this form of intervention is whether the caregiver should always be responsive or whether there are times when the caregiver should initiate or start an interaction (McCollum, 1991). When an infant remains unfocused and inactive for a long period of time, it is appropriate for the adult to attempt to engage the infant in a social activity (SE 3). Such adult behaviors should match the infant's interests and understanding. Similarly, when an infant is unsuccessfully attempting to do something slightly beyond his or her ability, the adult might suggest or demonstrate how to do what the child is attempting (SE 2). Such "scaffolding" might well promote both learning and ongoing positive interactions. Girolametto, Verbey, and Tannock (1994) found increases in parents' and infants' joint playful interaction after the parents had learned to use interaction prompting, language modeling, and child-oriented strategies (e.g., responding to the child's communication, following the child's lead). Shifting the adult role in the social interaction from responder to initiator as the demands of the social context change may be an effective form of intervention practice (Marfo, 1991; McCollum & Bair, 1994).

Mutual Enjoyment

If the effects of intervention practices are to endure across time and to generalize across individuals, they must produce results that are beneficial or rewarding to infants and adults. One of the primary rewards of social interactions for parents and infants is the mutual enjoyment they experience. In her early intervention program, Bromwich (1981) established a progression of objectives that guided her interventions, the first objective being "The parent enjoys her infant" (p. 341). Subitems included "Pleasure in watching infant," "Pleasure in proximity—including physical contact," and "Pleasure in interaction." Before the more skill-directed phases (e.g., teaching parents to be observers of infants' cues) of the intervention began, the intervention plans created activities that were rewarding to parents and infants. It is not clear whether this mutual enjoyment objective must always precede work on specific skills. However, an emphasis on creating activities that will lead the parent and the infant to enjoy their interactions with one another (if that is not happening) appears to be critical if participation in positive social interactions is to continue beyond the formal intervention sessions.

Attachment Interventions

As noted previously, establishing an attachment relationship with a caregiver is a critical component of early development. Early intervention programs have focused specifically on such an objective. The specific practices followed by these attachment-related interventions are similar to the more skill-oriented intervention practices discussed earlier. For example, Carmen (1994) proposed that attachment interventions begin with assessment of both the infant (e.g., health, neurophysiology, development) and the caregiver (e.g., style of interaction, caregiving knowledge, beliefs). The intervention might emphasize parents' sensitivity to social cues, reciprocity, and parents' enhancement of infants' quiet states. In their meta-analysis of attachment interventions, van Ijzendoorn et al. (1995) found that interventions focusing on attachment-related behaviors were more effective in promoting maternal sensitivity to infants' behaviors and, in turn, in supporting attachment than were more broad-based, comprehensive interventions. The intervention designed by Bromwich (1981), mentioned previously, is one example of a set of practices that could ultimately effect attachment. Other interventions that have directly (and significantly) affected the formation of secure attachment relationships have included (a) providing soft baby carriers that increase the amount of direct physical contact between the mother and infant (Anisfeld, Casper, Nozyce, & Cunningham, 1990), (b) providing a volunteer coach to prepare the mother for the birth and postnatal caregiving as well as to plan activities appropriate for the infant (Jacobson & Frye, 1991), (c) providing home visitors to increase the family's ability to access resources for basic needs and to reinforce positive, interactive exchanges between the infant and mother (Lyons-Ruth, Connell, Grunebaum, & Botein, 1990), and (d) providing home visitors who help the mother understand the infant's unique social cues as well as support playful interactions (van den Boom, 1991). Although these studies all occurred with infants who were at risk for disabilities, such procedures may well be effective for infants with identifiable disabilities and their mothers.

SOCIAL INTERACTION INTERVENTIONS FOR PRESCHOOL CHILDREN WITH DISABILITIES

For over 25 years, intervention practices that have proven effective in helping children learn how to interact with their friends have steadily increased (McEvoy, Odom, & McConnell, 1992). The practices range in intensity, some requiring little teacher involvement and others requiring significant time and effort by the teacher. Teachers base their selection of intervention practices on children's needs for intervention, as well as on the availability of teacher or parent time for implementation.

Intervention practices can be divided into two major categories. First, some interventions simply provide opportunities for children to interact. Guralnick (1978) has noted that for some children, simple inclusion may be a sufficient intervention for promoting peer interaction. A second group of interventions combines opportunities to interact with specific adult- or peer-directed prompts for interaction.

Regardless of the type of interventions selected, three major indicators of quality are critical. First, interventions must include children who are good interactors. This inclusion will help children with disabilities learn patterns of interaction that are similar to those of typically developing children (SE 8; McEvoy & Brady, 1988). Second, when necessary, adults must be prepared to intervene to support and encourage appropriate interactions (SE 9). Adults play a critical role in choosing and implementing practices that address social development (Nourot & Van Hoorn, 1991). Third, there must be an emphasis on identifying activities that allow children to participate in social interactions across multiple settings and people (SE 15). These settings may include the early childhood classroom, home, or community playground.

Providing opportunities to interact, implementing adult-directed interventions if necessary, and planning for generalization and maintenance are all major components of effective intervention. Each of these components is reflected in the DEC-recommended practices on interventions to promote social skill development. A review of interventions that address each of these three major components and other critical issues follows.

Providing Opportunities to Interact

For some children, the lack of appropriate social skills may be the result of a lack of opportunities to be around and play with children who are good interactors. For these children, simple inclusion or access to situations where peer–peer interaction is reinforced naturally may be a simple and effective intervention (Odom & Brown, 1993). Providing opportunities for children to play together is an important first step in promoting social interaction. Sainato and Carta (1992) noted that the characteristics of a setting (e.g., presence of socially competent peers, specific play materials that promote interaction, and classroom activities) can enhance peer–peer interaction. In fact, research indicates that teachers or parents can change the physical aspects of a setting and thus increase opportunities for interaction, particularly for children with mild delays (Shores, Hester, & Strain, 1976). For example, activities that encourage sociodramatic theme play (e.g., dress-up, kitchen, cars and roads) increase the frequency of children's interactions (DeKlyen & Odom, 1989). Social toys, such as balls and blocks, may also set the stage for children to play together. Areas for play should be large enough to conduct an activity but small enough to assure that the children are in proximity to each other (Brown, Fox, & Brady, 1987). Finally, teachers may encourage children to play together in activities by selecting buddies (Goldstein, Kaczmarek, & Hepting, 1994). Clearly, a setting that is organized to promote interactions is a necessary, albeit perhaps not always sufficient, condition that sets the stage for interactions to occur.

Support Initiations and Responses

A variety of interventions have been developed to increase appropriate initiations for and responses to interactions (SE 9). In many instances, teachers have provided direct prompts and feedback to children with disabilities to encourage interaction (McConnell, Sisson, Cort, & Strain, 1991); in other instances, peers have been encouraged to include children with disabilities in play activities (Odom, Hoyson, Jamieson, & Strain, 1985; Strain & Odom, 1986). McEvoy, Shores, Wehby, Johnson, and Fox (1990) have noted the important role that adults and socially competent peers play in supporting and encouraging child–child interaction. Rogoff, Mistry, Goncu, and Mosier (1993) referred to the role of adults or peers as "guided participation": Children with disabilities are equal partners in the interaction but may need extra assistance in order to be successful interactors. Similarly, a typically developing child may need to be taught to recognize and respond to the social interaction attempts of a young child with disabilities.

A number of successful interventions have been developed that rely heavily on adults for effective implementation. Odom and Strain (1986) classified these interventions generally into two groups: adult mediated and peer mediated. During adult-mediated interventions, the teacher or parent plays a critical role in both prompting interactions and reinforcing successful initiations and responses that result in child–child interaction. For example, investigators in the Vanderbilt–Minnesota Social Interaction

Project (1993) developed a series of activities that teachers may use to show children how to share, assist others, and organize play. After the children practiced these skills, they participated in a free-play activity designed by the teacher to promote interaction. During the activity, the teacher prompted children to interact (e.g. "Scott, share the toy with Judy") if interaction did not occur on a consistent basis. Teachers acknowledged successful interactions by providing children with feedback (e.g. happy faces, thumbs up, etc.). Finally, teachers systematically faded the use of prompts and feedback as child–child interaction increased. This play-based intervention, although including an extensive amount of adult direction, was successful in increasing and maintaining peer social interaction (Odom & McConnell, in press). In addition, teachers became more sensitive to (and reinforced) subtle forms of initiations like handing a child a toy or waving to a peer.

Intensive teacher involvement is not always necessary. For example, McEvoy et al. (1988) used "Friendship Activities" to increase the social interaction rates of children with disabilities. Children with and without disabilities participated daily in a 10-minute activity that encouraged them to interact. The activities were typical preschool games, songs, and activities that had been modified to include prompts for interaction (see Brown, Ragland, & Bishop, 1989; McEvoy, Twardosz, & Bishop, 1990; Twardosz, Nordquist, Simon, & Botkin, 1983). For example, children were encouraged to sing "If you are happy and you know it, give your friend a (smile, pat on the back, high five, etc.)." Prompts for interaction can be included in almost any game or song. Children typically enjoy the activity, and research has shown that children use the skills they learn in the Friendship Activities during other times of the day (McEvoy et al., 1988).

Promoting Interactions Outside of the Preschool Classroom (SE 15)

Although the immediate effects of an intervention may be apparent in the setting in which it was implemented, it is important that children learn to use social skills in a number of settings and with a number of different peers and adults. Unfortunately, very few interventions have addressed this issue specifically (Chandler, Lubek, & Fowler, 1992). With the ever-growing need for culturally competent processes and methods of service delivery, this issue has become even more critical (Hanson & Lynch, 1992). By working collaboratively with the parents and others from the child's community to understand the different social expectations that the child may face, professionals can play a major role in helping a child learn to respond to different social situations. In addition, parents and professionals should work together to design interventions that are implemented easily in home and community settings. Professionals may need to observe the child in a number of settings in order to determine what type of interventions might be most effective. Finally, professionals should provide many opportunities in preschool activities for all children to be involved. In this way, acceptance of individual differences is facilitated.

Foster Interactions That Are Happy and Fun

When discussing parent–infant interactions, we noted that a goal of intervention programs should be to support interactions that both partners enjoy. The same principle applies for peer interactions. Professionals should foster social interactions with other children that are happy and fun (SE 12). One assumption in social-skills training is that participation in social interaction with peers will have rewarding qualities for children with disabilities that support the new social skills that they learn (McConnell, 1987). These rewarding qualities will come, in part, from participating in activities that the children find enjoyable. So, one "bottom-line" measure of successful intervention practices should be that the children are having fun. For example, Odom, Ostrosky, Favazza, and Keetz (1992) conducted an intervention in which preschool children with and without disabilities participated in social-skills training and structured play groups. In addition to measuring increases in social interaction with peers, they assessed the quality of the social interactions and found that ratings of "child appears to have fun" and "child smiles at others" increased substantially when the intervention was implemented. For practitioners, remaining aware of the need to make social activities fun as well as effective learning settings is critically important.

Acceptance and Social Relationships

In addition to promoting social skills and emotional development, practices in early intervention and early childhood special education programs should serve as settings in which young children with disabilities are accepted by and develop positive relationships with peers (SE 13; Haring, 1992). As the field moves to placing children with disabilities in inclusive early childhood settings, emphasizing acceptance and the development of relationships becomes even more important because many children with disabilities are not readily accepted by their nondisabled peers. Teaching skills that lead to positive social interactions may be one important step in supporting acceptance, but it may well be that social-skills intervention practices alone are not enough. Other intervention practices may need to directly address attitude formation of young children without disabilities who are peers in inclusive settings. Few studies have addressed this issue. In working with typically developing kindergarten children, Favazza and Odom (1995) employed a multicomponent package that included (a) teachers reading stories about children with different types of disabilities in early childhood settings and making friends, (b) teachers leading discussions about the stories, (c) parents reading and discussing the stories with the children at home, and (d) structured play activities that involved children with and without disabilities. Participation in this intervention package led to significantly more positive attitudes toward individuals with disabilities, as compared to a group of children not participating in the activities. The group friendship activities (McEvoy et al., 1990) described earlier may also promote acceptance and the development of social relationships, although this outcome has not been assessed directly. Clearly, intervention research should examine strategies and intervention practices that support the development of acceptance and positive social relationships among young children with disabilities and their peers.

CLOSING

Learning to participate effectively and appropriately in social interactions with caregivers and peers is a fundamental aspect of early childhood. Such participation may well lead to positive social relationships, and for infants it may support the necessary development of attachment with significant caregivers. Recognizing the importance of social skills and relationships, early intervention and early childhood special education professionals and researchers have identified social competence as a major programmatic goal. Although continued research on the interventions that promote both skills and relationships is necessary, a range of practices currently exist for designing programs for infants and young children with disabilities, their caregivers, and their peers. These practices provide children with disabilities a foundation upon which they may build more advanced social skills and lead them to become more socially effective and accepted members of society.

REFERENCES

Ainsworth, M. D. S., Bell, S. M., & Stayton, D. J. (1972). Individual differences in the development of some attachment behaviors. *Merrill–Palmer Quarterly, 18,* 123–143.

Ainsworth, M. D. S., Blehar, M. C., Waters, E., & Wall, S. (1978). *Patterns of attachment: A psychological study of the strange situation.* Hillsdale, NJ: Erlbaum.

Anisfeld, E., Casper, V., Nozyce, M., & Cunningham, N. (1990). Does infant carrying promote attachment? An experimental study of the effects of increased physical contact on the development of attachment. *Child Development, 61,* 1617–1627.

Antia, S. D., & Kreimeyer, K. H. (1992). Social competence intervention for young children with hearing impairments. In S. Odom, S. McConnell, & M. McEvoy (Eds.), *Social competence of young children with disabilities* (pp. 135–164). Baltimore: Brookes.

Bates, J. E. (1980). The concept of difficult temperament. *Merrill-Palmer Quarterly, 26,* 299–319.

Bell, R. Q., & Harper, L. V. (1977). *Child effects on adults.* New York: Wiley.

Bornstein, M. H., & Lamb, M. E. (1992). *Development in infancy: An introduction.* New York: McGraw-Hill.

Bornstein, M. H., Tamis-Lemonda, C. S., Tal, J., Ludeman, P., Toda, S., Rahn, C. W., Pecheux, M., Azuma, H., & Vardi, D. (1992). Maternal responsiveness to infants in three societies: The United States, France, and Japan. *Child Development, 63,* 808–831.

Bowlby, J. (1982). *Attachment and loss: Vol 1. Attachment* (2nd ed.). New York: Basic Books.

Bretherton, I., & Waters, E. (Eds.). (1985). Growing points of attachment theory and research. *Monographs of the Society for Research in Child Development, 50* (1–2, Serial No. 209).

Bromwich, R. (1981). *Working with parents and infants: An interactional approach.* Austin, TX: PRO-ED.

Brown, W. H., Fox, J. J., & Brady, M. (1987). Effects of spatial density on 3- and 4-year-old children's socially directed behavior during freeplay: An investigation of a setting factor. *Education and Treatment of Children, 10,* 247–258.

Brown, W. H., Ragland, E. U., & Bishop, N. (1989). *A socialization curriculum for preschool programs that integrate children with handicaps.* Nashville, TN: Vanderbilt University, John F. Kennedy Center.

Buysee, V. (1993). Friendship of preschoolers with disabilities in community-based child care settings. *Journal of Early Intervention, 17,* 380–395.

Cairns, R. B. (1979). *Social development: The origins and plasticity of interchanges.* San Francisco: Freeman.

Carmen, S. (1994). Attachment intervention. *Infants and Young Children, 7*(1), 34–41.

Carta, J., Sainato, D. M., & Greenwood, C. R. (1988). Advances in the ecological assessment of classroom instruction for young children with handicaps. In S. L. Odom & M. B. Karnes (Eds.), *Early intervention for infants and children with handicaps* (pp. 217–239). Baltimore: Brookes.

Chandler, L. K., Lubek, R. C., & Fowler, S. A. (1992). Generalization and maintenance of preschool children's social skills: A critical review and analysis. *Journal of Applied Behavior Analysis, 25,* 415–428.

DeGangi, G. A., Wietlisbach, S., Poisson, S., Stein, E., & Royeen, C. (1994). The impact of culture and socioeconomic status on family–professional collaboration: Challenges and solutions. *Topics in Early Childhood Special Education, 14,* 503–520.

DeKlyen, M., & Odom, S. L. (1989). Activity structure and social interaction with peers in developmentally integrated play groups. *Journal of Early Intervention, 13,* 342–351.

Dixon, S. D., Tronick, E. Z., Keefer, C., & Brazelton, T. B. (1981). Mother–infant interaction among Gusii of Kenya. In T. Fields, A. Sostek, P. Vietze, & P. Leiderman (Eds.), *Culture and early interactions* (pp. 63–94). Hillsdale, NJ: Erlbaum.

Egeland, B., & Farber, E. A. (1984). Infant–mother attachment: Factors related to its development and change over time. *Child Development, 55,* 753–771.

Emde, R. N., Katz, E. L., & Thorpe, J. K. (1978). Emotional expression in infancy: II. Early deviation in Down's syndrome. In M. Lewis & L. Rosenblum (Eds.), *The development of affect* (pp. 351–360). New York: Plenum Press.

Favazza, P. C., & Odom, S. L. (1995). *Promoting positive attitudes toward children with disabilities.* Manuscript submitted for publication.

Field, T. M. (1978). The three Rs of infant–adult interactions: Rhythms, repertoires, and responsivity. *Journal of Pediatric Psychology, 3,* 131–136.

Fraiberg, S. (1971). Intervention in infancy: A program for blind infants. *Journal of the American Academy of Child Psychiatry, 10,* 315–335.

Fraiberg, S. (1977). *Insight from the blind: Comparative studies of blind and sighted infants.* New York: Basic Books.

Girolametto, L., Verbey, M., & Tannock, R. (1994). Improving joint engagement in parent–child interaction: An intervention study. *Journal of Early Intervention, 18,* 155–167.

Goldstein, H., & Gallagher, T. M. (1992). Strategies for promoting the social-communicative competence of young children with specific learning disabilities. In S. Odom, S. McConnell, & M. McEvoy (Eds.), *Social competence of young children with disabilities* (pp. 165–188). Baltimore: Brookes.

Goldstein, H., Kaczmarek, L., & Hepting, N. (1994). Communication interventions: The challenges of across-the-day implementation. In R. Gardner, D. Sainato, J. Cooper, T. Heron, W. Heward, H. Eshleman, & T. Grossi (Eds.), *Behavior analysis in education: Focus on measurably superior instruction* (pp. 101–113). Belmont, CA: Brooks/Cole.

Gottwald, S. R., & Thurman, S. K. (1990). Parent–infant interaction in neonatal intensive care units: Implications for research and service delivery. *Infants and Young Children, 2*(3), 1–9.

Gottwald, S. R., & Thurman, S. K. (1994). The effect of prenatal cocaine exposure on mother–infant interaction and infant arousal in the newborn period. *Topics in Early Childhood Special Education, 14,* 217–231.

Grotevant, H., & McRoy, R. (1988). Emotionally disturbed adopted adolescents: Early patterns of family adaptation. *Family Process, 27,* 439–457.

Guralnick, M. J. (1978). Integrated preschools as educational and therapeutic environments: Concepts, design, and analysis. In M. Guralnick (Ed.), *Early intervention and the integration of handicapped and nonhandicapped children* (pp. 115–145). Balitmore: University Park Press.

Guralnick, M. J. (1981). Peer influences on development of communicative competence. In P. Strain (Ed.), *The utilization of peers as behavior chance agents* (pp. 31–68). New York: Plenum Press.

Guralnick, M. J. (1990). Social competence and early intervention. *Journal of Early Intervention, 14,* 3–14.

Guralnick, M. J. (1992). A hierarchical model for understanding children's social competence. In S. L. Odom, S. R. McConnell, & M. A. McEvoy (Eds.), *Social competence of young children with disabilities: Issues and strategies for intervention* (pp. 37–64). Baltimore: Brookes.

Guralnick, M. J. (1994). Social competence with peers: Outcome and process in early childhood special education. In P. L. Safford, (Ed.), *Early childhood special education.* New York: Teachers College Press.

Guralnick, M. J., Conner, R., Hammond, M., Gottman, J. M., & Kinnish, K. (in press). Immediate effects of mainstreamed settings on the social interactions and social integration of preschool children. *American Journal on Mental Retardation.*

Guralnick, M. J., & Groom, J. M. (1988). Friendships of preschool children in mainstream playgroups. *Developmental Psychology, 24*, 595–604.
Haney, M., & Klein, D. M. (1993). Impact of a program to facilitate mother–infant communication in high-risk families of high-risk infants. *Journal of Communication Disorders, 15*, 15–22.
Hanson, M. J., & Lynch, E. W. (1992). Family diversity: Implications for policy and practice. *Topics in Early Childhood Special Education, 12*, 283–306.
Haring, T. G. (1992). The context of social competence: Relations, relationships, and generalization. In S. Odom, S. McConnell, M. McEvoy (Eds.), *Social competence of young children with disabilities* (pp. 307–320). Baltimore: Brookes.
Hartup, W. W. (1983). Peer relations. In M. Hetherington (Ed.), *Handbook of child psychology* (Vol. 4, pp. 103–196). New York: Wiley.
Hartup, W. W., Glazer, J., & Charlesworth, R. (1967). Peer reinforcement and sociometric status. *Child Development, 38*, 1017–1024.
Hartup, W. W., & Moore, S. G. (1990). Early peer relations: Developmental significance and prognostic implications. *Early Childhood Research Journal, 5*, 1–17.
Hartup, W. W., & Sancilio, M. F. (1986). Children's friendships. In E. Schopler & G. Mesibov (Eds.), *Social behavior in autism* (pp. 61–80). New York: Plenum Press.
Howes, C. (1988). Peer interaction of young children. *Monographs of the Society for Research in Child Development*, No. 217, Chicago: University of Chicago Press.
Jacobson, S. W., & Frye, K. F. (1991). Effect of maternal social support on attachment: Experimental evidence. *Child Development, 62*, 572–582.
Kopp, C. B., Baker, B. L., & Brown, K. W. (1992). Social skills and their correlates: Preschoolers with developmental delays. *American Journal on Mental Retardation, 96*, 357–367.
Lussier, B. J., Crimmins, D. B., & Alberti, D. (1994). Effects of three adult interaction styles on infant engagement. *Journal of Early Intervention, 18*, 12–24.
Lyons-Ruth, K., Alpern, L., & Repacholi, B. (1993). Disorganized infant attachment classification and maternal psychosocial problems as predictors of hostile-aggressive behavior in preschool children. *Child Development, 64*, 572–585.
Lyons-Ruth, K., Connell, D. B., Grunebaum, H. U., & Botein, S. (1990). Infants at social risks: Maternal depression and family support services as mediators of infant development and security of attachment. *Child Development, 61*, 85–98.
MacDonald, J. D., & Gillette, Y. (1989). *Eco: A partnership program*. San Antonio, TX: Special Press.
Mahoney, G., & Powell, A. (1988). Modifying parent–child interaction: Enhancing the development of handicapped children. *Journal of Special Education, 22*, 82–96.
Mallory, B. L., & New, R. S. (1994). Social constructivist theory and principles of inclusion: Challenges for early childhood special education. *Journal of Special Education, 28*, 322–337.
Marfo, K. (1991). The maternal directiveness theme in mother-child interaction research: Implications for early intervention. In K. Marfo (Ed.), *Early intervention in transition: Current perspectives on programs for handicapped infants* (pp. 177–203). New York: Praeger.
McCollum, J. A. (1991). At a crossroads: Reviewing and rethinking interaction coaching. In K. Marfo (Ed.), *Early intervention in transition: Current perspectives on programs for handicapped infants* (pp. 137–176). New York: Praeger.
McCollum, J. A., & Bair, H. (1994). Research in parent–child interaction: Guidance to developmentally appropriate practice for young children with disabilities. In B. Mallory & R. New (Eds.), *Diversity and developmentally appropriate practices* (pp. 84–106). New York: Teachers College Press.

McCollum, J., & Yates, T. J. (1994). Dyads as a focus, triad as a means: A family-centered approach to supporting parent–child interactions. *Infants and Young Children, 6*(4), 54–63.

McConnell, S. R. (1987). Entrapment effects and the generalization and maintenance of social skills training for elementary school students with behavior disorders. *Behavior Disorders, 12,* 252–263.

McConnell, S. R., Sisson, L. A., Cort, C. A., & Strain, P. S. (1991). Effects of social skills training and contingency management on reciprocal interaction of preschool children with behavioral handicaps. *Journal of Special Education, 24,* 473–495.

McEvoy, M. A., & Brady, M. P. (1988). Effects of contingent access to play materials as an academic motivator for autistic and behavior disordered children. *Education and Treatment of Children, 11,* 5–18.

McEvoy, M. A., & McConnell, S. R. (1995). Understanding the emotional and behavioral development of young children: 3–6 years. In T. Zirpoli (Ed.), *Understanding and affecting the behavior of young children* (pp. 60–81). Columbus, OH: Merrill.

McEvoy, M. A., Nordquist, V. M., Twardosz, S., Heckaman, K. A., Wehby, J. H., & Denny, R. K. (1988). Promoting autistic children's peer interaction in an integrated setting using affection activities. *Journal of Applied Behavior Analysis, 21,* 193–200.

McEvoy, M. A., Odom, S. L., & McConnell, S. R. (1992). Peer social competence intervention for young children with disabilities. In S. Odom, S. McConnell, & M. McEvoy (Eds.), *Social competence of young children with disabilities* (pp. 3–36). Baltimore: Brookes.

McEvoy, M. A., Shores, R. E., Wehby, J. H., Johnson, S. M., & Fox, J. J. (1990). Special education teachers' implementation procedures to promote social interaction among children in integrated settings. *Education and Training in Mental Retardation, 25,* 267–276.

McEvoy, M. A., Twardosz, S., & Bishop, N. (1990). Affection activities: Procedures for encouraging young children with handicaps to interact with their peers. *Education and Treatment of Children, 13,* 159–167.

Nourot, P. M., & Van Hoorn, J. L. (1991). Symbolic play in preschool and primary settings. *Young Children, 46,* 40–50.

Odom, S. L., & Brown, W. H. (1993). Social interaction skills interventions for young children with disabilities in integrated settings. In C. Peck, S. Odom, & D. Bricker (Eds.), *Integrating young children with disabilities into community programs* (pp. 39–64). Baltimore: Brookes.

Odom, S. L., Hoyson, M., Jamieson, B., & Strain, P. S. (1985). Increasing handicapped preschoolers' peer interactions: Cross-setting and component analysis. *Journal of Applied Behavior Analysis, 18,* 3–16.

Odom, S. L., & McConnell, S. R. (in press). Promoting peer-related social competence of young children with disabilities. In M. Bambring, H. Rauh, & A. Beelman (Eds.), *Early child intervention: Theory, evaluation, and practice.* Berlin/New York: deGruyter.

Odom, S. L., McConnell, S. R., & Chandler, L. K. (1994). Acceptability and feasibility of classroom-based social interaction interventions for young children with disabilities. *Exceptional Children, 60,* 226–237.

Odom, S. L., McConnell, S. R., & McEvoy, M. A. (1992). Peer-related social competence and its significance for young children with disabilities. In S. Odom, S. McConnell, M. McEvoy (Eds.), *Social competence of young children with disabilities* (pp. 3–36). Baltimore: Brookes.

Odom, S. L., & Ogawa, I. (1992). Direct observation of young children's social interaction: A review of methodology. *Behavioral Assessment, 3/4,* 407–442.

Odom, S. L., Ostrosky, M., Favazza, P., & Keetz, A. (1992, May). *Inducing cross-setting generalization in a comprehensive social interaction intervention for young children with disabilities.* Paper presented at the Annual Conference of the Association for Behavior Analysis, San Francisco, CA.

Odom, S. L., & Strain, P. S. (1986). A comparison of peer initiation and teacher-antecedent interventions for promoting reciprocal social interaction of autistic preschoolers. *Journal of Applied Behavioral Analysis, 19,* 59–72.

Quay, L. (1993). Social competence in nonhandicapped, low interacting, and five handicapped groups of preschoolers. *Early Education and Development, 4,* 89–98.

Richman, A. L., Miller, P. M., & LeVine, R. A. (1992). Cultural and educational variations in maternal responsiveness. *Developmental Psychology, 28,* 614–621.

Rogoff, B., Mistry, J., Goncu, A., & Mosier, C. (1993). Guided participation in cultural activity by toddlers and caregivers. *Monographs of the Society for Research in Child Development, 58* (8, Serial No. 236).

Sainato, D., & Carta, J. (1992). Classroom influences on the development of social competence on young children with disabilities. In S. Odom, S. McConnell, & M. McEvoy (Eds.), *Social competence of young children with disabilities* (pp. 93–112). Baltimore: Brookes.

Salisbury, C., Britzman, D., & Kang, J. (1989). Using qualitative methods to assess the social–communicative competence of young handicapped children. *Journal of Early Intervention, 13,* 153–165.

Sameroff, A., & Chandler, M. (1975). Reproductive risk and the continuum of caretaking casualty. In F. Horowitz, M. Hetherington, S. Scarr-Salapatek, & G. Siegel (Eds.), *Review of child development research* (Vol. 4, pp. 187–244). Chicago: University of Chicago Press.

Seifer, R., Clark, G. N., & Sameroff, A. J. (1991). Positive effects of interaction coaching on infants with developmental disabilities and their mothers. *American Journal on Mental Retardation, 96,* 1–11.

Shores, R. E., Hester, P., & Strain, P. S. (1976). The effects of the amount and type of teacher-child interaction on child-child interaction during free-play. *Psychology in the Schools, 13,* 171–175.

Skellenger, A. C., Hill, M. M., & Hill, E. (1992). The social functioning of children with visual impairments. In S. Odom, S. McConnell, & M. McEvoy (Eds.), *Social competence of young children with disabilities* (pp. 165–188). Baltimore: Brookes.

Sroufe, L. A., & Waters, E. (1977). Attachment as an organizational construct. *Child Development, 48,* 1184–1199.

Stone, W. L., & LaGreca, A. M. (1986). The development of social skills in children. In E. Schopler & G. Mesibov (Eds.), *Social behavior in autism* (pp. 35–60). New York: Plenum Press.

Strain, P. S. (1983). Generalization of autistic children's social behavior change: Effects of developmentally integrated and segregated settings. *Analysis and Intervention in Developmental Disabilities, 3,* 23–34.

Strain, P. S. (1990). LRE for preschool children with handicaps: What we know, what we should be doing. *Journal of Early Intervention, 14,* 291–296.

Strain, P. S., & Odom, S. L. (1986). Peer social initiations: Effective intervention for social skills development of exceptional children. *Exceptional Children, 52,* 543–552.

Tannock, R. (1988). Mothers' directiveness in their interaction with their children with and without Down syndrome. *American Journal on Mental Retardation, 93,* 154–165.

Thomas, A., & Chess, S. (1977). *Temperament and development.* New York: Brunner/Mazel.

Tremblay, A., Strain, P. S., Hendrickson, J. M., & Shores, R. E. (1981). Social interactions of normally developing preschool children: Using normative data for subject selection and target behavior selection. *Behavior Modification, 5,* 237–253.

Twardosz, S., Nordquist, V. M., Simon, R., & Botkin, D. (1983). The effects of group affection activities on the interaction of socially isolate children. *Analysis and Intervention in Developmental Disabilities, 3,* 311–338.

van den Boom, D. C. (1991). Preventative intervention and the quality of mother–infant interaction and infant exploration in irritable infants. In W. Koops, H. Soope, J. van der Linden, P. Molenaar, & J. Schroots (Eds.), *Developmental psychology behind the dykes: An outline of developmental psychological research in the Netherlands* (pp. 249–269). Delft, The Netherlands: Eburon.

van den Boom, D. C., & Hoeksma, J. B. (1994). The effects of infant irritability on mother–infant interaction: A growth curve analysis. *Developmental Psychology, 30,* 581–590.

van Ijzendoorn, M. H., Juffer, R., & Duyvesteyn, M. G. (1995). Breaking the intergenerational cycle of insecure attachment: A review of the effects of attachment-based interventions on maternal sensitivity and infant security. *Journal of Child Psychology and Psychiatry, 36,* 225–248.

Vanderbilt–Minnesota Social Interaction Project. (1993). *Play time/social time.* Tucson, AZ: Communication Skills Builders.

Wasserman, G. A., Lennon, M. C., Allen, R., & Shilansky, M. (1987). Contributors to attachment in normal and physically handicapped infants. *Journal of the American Academy of Child and Adolescent Psychiatry, 26*(1), 9–15.

Widerstrom, A. H., Mowder, B. A., & Sandall, S. R. (1991). *At-risk and handicapped newborns and infants: Development, assessment, and intervention.* Englewood Cliffs, NY: Prentice–Hall.

Yoder, P. J. (1987). Relationship between degree of infant handicap and clarity of infant cues. *American Journal of Mental Deficiency, 91,* 639–641.

Yoder, P. J., Warren, S. F., Kim, K., Gazdag, G. (1994). Facilitating prelinguistic communication skills in young children with developmental delays II: Systematic replication and extension. *Journal of Speech and Hearing Research, 37,* 841–851.

Youngblade, L. M. (1993). *Association between infant–parent attachment security, conceptions of friendship, and behavioral characteristics of friendships in 5-year-olds.* Paper presented at the Biennial Meeting of the Society for Research in Child Development.

CHAPTER 10

Intervention Strategies to Promote Motor Skills

Rebecca Fewell

Long before birth, neonates are moving. The birth process is simply another stage in what might be viewed as a movement process. What becomes apparent when newborns are observed is the linkage between movement and learning. Head movements in search of a voice, hand movements to explore a bright toy, and later, the full body movement of walking that opens the wonderful world of independence, are all ways in which motor development contributes to the foundation and acquisition of all learning. Through physical growth, observations of others, needs and desires, most children acquire movement skills. These skills emerge in a timely manner within the context of a nurturing environment. For some children, events during the course of development create delays or interfere with the acquisition of motor skills. When this happens, a range of early interventions can facilitate the acquisition of the motor skills. This chapter describes recommendations for motor skill intervention. In addition, the chapter provides a brief overview of the roles of persons who take responsibility for implementing motor intervention and an overview of research investigating the various practices.

THEORETICAL CONSTRUCTS FOR MOTOR SKILL DEVELOPMENT

For professionals, motor intervention strategies based on sound theoretical constructs are viewed as optimal for supporting children's progress or for alleviating problems (M 1). In this section, I review the major theoretical models that teachers, physical educators, and therapists favor in the design and implementation of their intervention practices.

Physical Developmental Model

Theorists who support a physical developmental model view motor skill development as a natural unfolding process in which skills emerge in a predictable, orderly sequence but are affected by growth, maturation, environment, and cultural practices. This view is often associated with physicians such as Arnold Gesell (Gesell & Amatruda, 1947), who described from detailed observations the motor skills of children of different ages. Others whose contributions have been based on this model are Bayley (1935, 1969), McGraw (1943), and Wickstrom (1970). More recent advocates of this model are Folio and Fewell (1983), Werder and Bruininks (1991), and Karnes (1992).

Neurodevelopmental Model

The neurodevelopmental model is a treatment approach, developed in England by Bobath and Bobath (1964) for the treatment of children with cerebral palsy. The approach has been used with children with other disabilities and delays (Harris, 1981; Palmer et al., 1988). This model is based on the premise that muscle tone must first be normalized in order to facilitate automatic reactions such as righting, equilibrium, and protective extension responses and to inhibit abnormal tone and reflex patterns. These actions are prerequisite to the achievement of developmental motor milestones such as sitting, creeping, and walking.

Perceptual Motor Model

Perceptual motor theory is based on the premise that the sensory information received affects the quality of the motor response. This approach is frequently used with children who experience learning difficulties, as their problems are often linked to sensory information deficits. Perceptual–motor theorists such as Kephart (1971), Frostig and Horne (1964), Getman (1965), Barsch (1968), and Cratty (1980) were among the early proponents who developed intervention techniques to use with children with learning disabilities and others thought to have perceptual deficit disorders. Because of the association of this program with academic learning, it is rarely used with infants and toddlers but is often included in programs for children in kindergarten and the early elementary years.

Sensory Integration Model

Sensory integrative therapy, described originally by Jean Ayres (1972b), is based on the theory that certain learning deficits are caused by dysfunction in sensory integrative processes within the brain. To remedy these deficits, interventionists engage the child in a series of tactile, vestibular, and proprioceptive inputs aimed at achieving sensory integration at the lower brain-stem levels. This therapeutic approach is widely used by occupational therapists, particularly those working with a pediatric population (Ottenbacher, 1982).

Other Models

A number of other theoretical models for motor skill development are used in therapy and educational instruction in other countries but are less known or less used in the United States. Among these models are both conductive education and the Vojta method. The conductive education theory, originated by Andras Peto in Hungary, is a comprehensive system of intervention practices for persons with movement disorders. It is viewed as a learning process as opposed to a treatment process. Those who have movement disorders are taught to move their bodies in order to gain maximum independence. The teaching is done by conductors, who use reinforcement strategies, rhythmic intention, and adaptive equipment such as plinths, ladderback chairs, ladder frames, and modified canes (Finn, Campbell, & Fewell, 1990). The Vojta method, developed in Germany, is specifically used with children with cerebral palsy. The method is based on the premise that a set of systematic exercises, carried out daily by family members, following the identification of cerebral palsy and before the child is 6 months of age, will prevent the extensive problems frequently associated with cerebral palsy.

IDENTIFICATION AND ASSESSMENT OF MOTOR SKILL DEVELOPMENT

In the previous section I described a number of theoretical constructs that undergird how intervention is approached. These constructs are also apparent in how children are examined to determine whether motor problems exist and to measure the extent of the problem. In this section, I provide a brief overview of some of the major ways motor dysfunction is identified and assessed. Every quality intervention or therapy program must begin with a competent examination to identify the nature of the problem and to assess the extent of the problem (for best practices, see Chapter 2). These data are essential for determining what is to be done in intervention or therapy.

Informal Observations

In many cases, the first persons to notice a child's motor problems are parents or family members. They may notice these during diaper changing, movement observations, or interactions with an infant. These observations are then shared with physicians or others, playing an important role in the first major step that leads to intervention services.

Medical Identification and Assessment

In some states, a physician, dentist, or chiropractor must write a medical prescription declaring that a child needs occupational or physical therapy treatment before the child can receive services. This medical professional may actually specify the type of treatment or state the need in very general terms and leave the determination of the details to the therapist who will provide a program of motor therapy that has written criteria, standards, and guidelines for the intervention (M 4). In other states, therapy needs can be determined by licensed therapists, who also determine the conditions of the therapy.

Motor Skill Assessment

Not all children have motor needs that require therapy intervention. Many have motor delays that do need the kind of intervention that school or program teaching staffs address in the context of early intervention. Before any intervention can be planned, a first step in the process is the assessment of the child's developmental level. Many options for performing this assessment are available, including the use of curriculum-referenced motor tests such as the *Hawaii Early Learning Profile* (Furuno et al., 1988) or standardized tests with programs such as the *Peabody Developmental Motor Scales and Activity Cards* (Folio & Fewell, 1983). This assessment information, required on the IEP or IFSP, serves as a measure of child progress as well as a means of identifying appropriate instructional targets. DEC Recommended Practices (DEC Task Force on Recommended Practices, 1993) include the use of assessment information for designing programs for infants and young children.

Follow-Up Assessment and Evaluation

All quality intervention programs follow initial assessment and intervention with subsequent assessments to measure change and to determine the need for programmatic changes. Follow-up assessment is normally done at both micro and macro levels. At the micro level, daily charts that record a child's acquisition of program objectives represent follow-up or follow-through assessment. At the macro level, on a quarterly or semiannual basis, children are reassessed to determine behavioral and developmental changes. Both micro- and macro-level assessment are a necessary component of quality motor instruction.

PROMOTING MOTOR SKILLS

Motor skills are acquired when needs are identified, programs are planned to address the needs, environments are modified to accommodate instruction, skills are generalized, and significant persons work with the child and with each other to ensure that the needed skills are facilitated in an effective, successful manner. Although some program staff members may be specifically trained to address the motor needs of children, many of these skills are promoted by all members of the transdisciplinary team. Sometimes the especially trained professionals consult directly with classroom teachers, including the teachers of children who are served in inclusive settings. In addition, service providers draw upon what has been stated in a child's IFSP and his or her own knowledge of motor development to ensure that motor needs are being met within the context of other learning experiences. In this section, I address each of these important variables. For each variable, there are indicators of quality intervention that deserve attention.

Adult Facilitators

The implementation of a child's early intervention or therapy program is the responsibility of early education intervention staff, therapy staff, family members, and any other caregivers who play a significant role in the daily lives of children with motor problems (M 2). Professional staff members need the training, experience, and certification or licensure to perform their assigned tasks (M 3). These roles and responsibilities are briefly described.

Physical therapists focus on the child's motor movements and the therapeutic exercises that facilitate movements, particularly those associated with the large muscles of the body. Occupational therapists focus on the psychosocial needs of the child, particularly those that are essential for life tasks such as activities of daily living (Effgen, 1988). These therapies involve a corrective medical approach to intervention (Folio, 1986). Both therapists assess skills, facilitate movement skills in response to and coordinated with sensory input, and interact with family members, teachers, and other staff (M 5). Physical and occupational therapists must receive certification through an approved college or university program and be licensed by the state in which they practice or through a national program (Harris & Tada, 1983). There are also 2-year college programs for the preparation of certified physical and occupational assistants. Under preferred conditions, a physical therapist working with infants, toddlers, and very young children has been specifically trained as a pediatric or developmental therapist; however, such an endorsement is not a prerequisite to working with young children. Optimal programs provide therapy services either in conjunction with other early intervention services or in collaboration with other agencies responsible for these services.

Physical educators and adaptive physical educators also play important roles in the education of young children with special motor needs. These educators focus on physical and motor fitness, fundamental motor skills, motor development, movement education, individual and group sports, aquatics, and dance. Physical education is a curricula requirement of special education; therefore, children who qualify for special services must also receive physical education. Physical educators have a minimum of a bachelor's degree and are certified by the state to teach physical education. Some states have separate certification requirements for adaptive physical educators. These persons have had special courses that focus on individuals with special needs and stress modifications in the environment that enable individuals to move effectively and efficiently in their environments. Physical educators are more prevalent in elementary and high schools than in programs of early intervention. Nevertheless, these professionals play an important role in early intervention, and optimal programs include these staff members.

Classroom teachers and other staff members also have a responsible role in promoting motor skills in children (M 3). They may set motor objectives on IEPs or IFSPS, and they have a responsibility to engage children in instructional programs to accomplish these objectives.

Environments for Skill Development

Classroom staff are in an excellent position to implement motor skill intervention in the context of normal activities in the class (M 7). These activities include opportunities for organized physical activities on playgrounds with peers without special needs (M 13). Likewise, caregivers have a similar responsibility for the carry through and instruction of motor interventions in the home and community, integrating these skills into the daily routines of the child and family (M 7). This responsibility includes adapting motor activities, materials, equipment, environments, and intervention strategies as needed to accommodate the individual child's ability to function as easily as possible with peers—in environments with and in interactions with peers without special needs (M 8). In addition, professionals and caregivers position children in ways that facilitate appropriate social and instructional interactions (e.g., children sit at eye level with other seated children, movement and positions are done efficiently so that children do not miss parts of activities) (M 11). Children are repositioned frequently when they are unable to do so independently (M 12).

For some children, specialized environments are needed and in optimal programs, these are provided (M 10). These environments may be special rooms in which equipment is available that cannot be easily accommodated in natural environments. For example, a therapy room might include ceiling swings or an enclosure with numerous small balls for tactile stimulation. A hydrotherapy or water environment is another example.

CURRICULA AND THERAPY GOALS AND STRATEGIES

Both public laws and quality practices require intervention to be planned on the basis of specified goals and objectives. Objectives must be quantifiable, and data must be kept so that progress can be measured. Once objectives are achieved, new objectives are set, and this process continues until the child's motor skills are within the normal range and special intervention strategies are no longer needed.

Curricula may be from a commercial program such as *Fit for Me* (Karnes, 1992) or the *Peabody Developmental Motor Scales and Activity Cards* (Folio & Fewell, 1983). These programs were designed to be implemented by all intervention staff members and do not require training outside of that normally given to teachers or therapists. A typical example of how physical or occupational therapists design and implement a curriculum is found in Rainforth and Salisbury's (1988) article, "Functional Home Programs: A Model for Therapists." These authors described the early intervention program for the child "Matthew." The program is based on the family daily routine model (Vincent, Salisbury, Laten, & Baumgart 1979). Within the context of this model, "the occupational and physical therapists identified several goals they thought important to address in Matthew's home program: 1. Increase range of motion in shoulders and hips. 2. Establish symmetry and head control in sitting. 3. Establish cooperation in reaching patterns. . . . 4. Increase phasic flexion, extension, and rotation for segmental rolling. . . . 5. Establish controlled jaw closure and tongue lateralization during eating. . . . 6. Indicate choices by gazing at desired objects" (p. 39). Although these goals convey the behavior to be changed, they are less specific than the curricula goals in the Peabody program. The Peabody program states objectives that provide a measurable criteria, for example, "Places 10 candies in a bottle within 30 seconds" (Folio & Fewell, 1983, p. 91). These examples may reflect the differences in theoretical perspectives, in the training and curricula preferred by different professionals, or possibly the severity of a child's disability, with more specificity needed when changes come in very small increments (M 6).

Equipment and Materials

A wheelchair for mobility, a curved spoon for scooping, a bolster, and a chair strap are just a few examples of the many pieces of equipment and materials that are needed to instruct children in motor skills or to adapt their environment to meet their needs (M 8). Quality programs have these materials available, and they employ them in instruction and therapy, with adaptations based on the specific needs of individual children.

Evaluations

Caregivers and program staff want to know whether interventions are responsible for changes in a child's behavior. This information helps the program on two levels. First, the results are used by staff in formative evaluations. That is, the results enable staff to make daily, weekly, or monthly programmatic changes. For example, if the data indicate that the child's behavior is not changing, then a change can be made in some aspect of the program and this change can thus be tested. Second, the results are used in summative evaluations by staff to determine long-term changes. These changes, often measured with standardized tests, can partial out gains that are expected through maturation alone, so that motor gains, as a result of specific interventions or therapy, can be determined. These data are essential if early intervention services are to be viewed as effective and are to gain the fiscal support that will be needed in the future. Quality programs evaluate child change through formative and summative methods.

INTEGRATION AND GENERALIZATION

Motor skills are a means to an end, and the ends should always govern how skills are taught. This goal can best be met through multiple-skills instruction and generalization of skills from the context of initial instruction. Motor skill instruction is very broad and addresses many components of motor development such as strength, fitness, postural control, eye–hand coordination, spatial awareness, and interactions in physical activities with others (M 6).

Multiple-Skills Instruction

Children need to move independently in their environments and are taught to do so through walking, through walking with the assistance of a walker, or perhaps through using a wheelchair (M 10). They are taught the important skill of independent mobility in the context of language learning (e.g., the parts of the wheelchair are given as new vocabulary); fine motor skills are developed in the operation of the wheelchair's electronics; social skills are developed as the adult and child dialogue and exchange information; cognitive problem-solving skills are taught as the child learns to sequence the tasks and to decide how to manipulate new environs. These techniques are examples of the concept of integrated learning. Motor skills are taught in conjunction with skills in other domains.

Generalization of Motor Skills

Just as important as multiple-skills instruction is the generalization of skills beyond the instructional environment. A child may learn a protective reaction within a therapy room, but the most important use of the skill may be in the bedroom, living room, or car. Quality motor programs ensure that motor skills are in a child's repertoire and are used across multiple environments and across many different times of the day and are available whenever they are needed (M 7, M 9).

SUPPORT FROM RESEARCH

A number of investigators have examined the effectiveness of motor programs and have published results that are helpful to early intervention specialists. This short review includes individual studies and meta-analyses.

Individual Studies

First, I review some of the group studies reported in the literature. DuBose and Folio (1977) examined the effectiveness of the developmental activities program of the *Peabody Developmental Motor Scales* (Folio & DuBose, 1974) with 56 preschool children aged 2 through 6 years with delays and with no delays. Children were randomly assigned to experimental and control groups. The intervention program consisted of 30 minutes of training in the experimental program 4 days a week for a period of 12 weeks. A station model was used with children rotating between balance locomotion, receipt and propulsion of objects, and propulsion of body in space. The control participants received each of the three center's current motor curriculum. Results indicated that both experimental and control group scores increased significantly. For the nondelayed groups, results indicated that score gains across testing occasions significantly favored the experimental group. This finding was not the case when the delayed groups were examined separately. The authors concluded that the findings support the general maturation of motor skills and the effectiveness of the program with normally developing children (M 13). They believed the brief intervention period was not sufficient to produce differences between the experimental and control programs.

DePauw (1978), Montgomery and Richter (1977), and Ottenbacher, Short, and Watson (1981) compared sensory integration therapy with physical education or motor programming approaches. All three studies reported results suggesting the relative efficacy of a sensory integrative approach over more traditional approaches. Unfortunately, these studies also had serious methodological flaws.

Jenkins, Fewell, and Harris (1983) designed a study to overcome the flaws in the previously cited studies. These researchers compared the same Peabody program used by DuBose and Folio (1977) to a sensory integration program. This study involved the random assignment of 44 children aged 3 through 5 years, with mild and moderate delays. The Peabody program was provided to small groups of 3–4 children for 25 minutes, four times weekly by teachers or graduate students. The sensory integration program was a one-to-one treatment program for 25 minutes twice weekly by therapists certified in sensory integration. The intervention program lasted 17 weeks. Results indicated that both groups gained on the two dependent measures; however, for both groups there were no main effects nor interaction effects. Neither treatment, need, nor the interaction produced reliable differences. Though their scores did not differ statistically, children in the therapy group had relatively larger gains on the Peabody, and children in the motor program group had larger gains on the *Assessment of Sensorimotor Integration* (Ayres, 1972a).

Harris (1981) examined the effects of the neurodevelopmental therapy (NDT) approach on the motor performance of 20 infants with Down syndrome. Infants were pretested and posttested on the *Bayley Scales of Infant Development* (Bayley, 1969) and the *Peabody Developmental Motor Scales* (Folio & Dubose, 1974). After pretesting, four individualized therapy objectives were written for each infant. These objectives were based on the infant's developmental scores and were congruent with the goals of the neurodevelopmental therapy program. Infants were randomly assigned to experimental and control groups. Control group infants continued in their regular early intervention program, and experimental group infants received 3 sessions of 40 minutes of NDT therapy weekly for 9 weeks. No differences were found on the two standardized measures, when given by examiners blind to group assignment. However, a significant difference in favor of the experimental group was noted on attainment of the therapy objectives.

Lydic, Windsor, Short, and Ellis (1985) studied the effects of a controlled rotary vestibular stimulation program on the motor performance of 18 infants with Down syndrome over a 12-week period. Children in the control group received their regular intervention program whereas infants in the treatment group received the rotary vestibular stimulation program in their homes, 3 times weekly for 12 weeks. Effects were measured on the Peabody scales and the *Movement Assessment of Infants* (Chandler, Andrews, & Swanson, 1980). Analysis of variance indicated no significant between-group differences on either instrument; both groups made equivalent changes according to both instruments. The study did indicate that infants with Down syndrome are capable of significantly enhancing their motor scores over a 12-week period.

With regard to single-participant research designs, this methodology is much more likely to be useful in the evaluation of children with cerebral palsy (Harris, 1987; Horn, 1991; Martin & Epstein, 1976). MacLean and Baumeister (1982) investigated the effects of semicircular canal stimulation via rotation in a motor-driven chair in a semidarkened room. The intervention occurred in 10 sessions of 10 minutes over a 2-week period; an ABA design was used. Three of the four infants showed improvement in motor performance at posttreatment and one-month follow up. Three of the four infants showed increase in maturity of reflex behavior.

Filler and Kasari (1981) conducted a study of children with severe impairments to train reach and grasp (fine and group motor skills). They used a combination of positioning, verbal prompting, physical prompting, contingent social praise, and toy manipulation.

Similarly, Horn and Warren (1987) conducted a study targeting very specific motor skills. Results from both of these studies indicate that these techniques were effective.

Grouped Studies

Horn (1991) examined a group of 28 studies on the effectiveness of basic motor skills instruction for children with neuromotor delays. Studies were grouped into four kinds of treatment programs: neuromotor interventions, sensory integration techniques, behavioral programming, and naturalistic programming. The neuromotor studies were found to be based on a plausible theoretical framework, but very little empirical data were found either to refute or to support their value. The studies of sensory stimulation techniques produced mixed results; most explored only isolated applications of the techniques, and most failed to employ adequate measure of maintenance and generalization. Studies of behavioral programming intervention appear to have results that offer more precise findings. These studies offer support that a variety of basic motor skills can be isolated and then taught through behavioral techniques and that these skills can be accelerated or decelerated through the use of reinforcement. Natural context studies are very rare; because none of these was experimental, no conclusions could be drawn. Horn (1991) lamented the lack of conclusive results on program effects but suggested that motor interventionists engage in more behavioral programming because this technique has been widely used in other domains and, in the few studies in which it has been used with motor skills, results have been positive.

Parette, Hendricks, and Rock (1991) examined the efficacy of therapeutic intervention intensity with infants and young children with cerebral palsy across 13 studies that met their specified criteria. The authors found some support for the efficacy of interventions; however, they failed to find any consensus relating to the delineation of intensity of intervention, a critical element when programs grapple with cost issues today.

Ottenbacher et al. (1986) investigated the effectiveness of NDT when used alone or in combination with other developmental therapies as reported in previous studies that met the criteria established for their meta-analysis. These authors concluded that evidence existed, albeit small, to support the use of NDT or NDT in combination with other treatments. These results appear to be related to some specific research design and study characteristics.

CLOSING

This chapter provides some explanations and examples of the DEC-recommended practices to promote motor skills while children are receiving early intervention services. Although practioners and families view instruction and therapy in motor skill development as an important part of intervention services, far more research is needed to determine precisely the best practices, the frequency and duration of practices, and the competencies needed by those who provide instruction. Given the added cost of therapy services, I recommend that this area be a topic of careful research in the future.

REFERENCES

Ayres, A. J. (1972a). Improving academic scores through sensory integration. *Journal of Learning Disabilities, 5,* 338–342.
Ayres, A. J. (1972b). *Sensory integration and learning disorders.* Los Angeles: Western Psychological Services.
Barsch, R. H. (1968). *Achieving perceptual-motor efficiency.* Seattle, WA: Special Child Publications.
Bayley, N. A. (1935). The development of motor abilities during the first three years. *Monograph of the Society for Research in Child Development, 1,* 1–26.
Bayley, N. A. (1969). *Bayley Scales of Infant Development.* New York: The Psychological Corp.
Bobath, K., & Bobath, B. (1964). The facilitation of normal postural reactions and movements in the treatment of cerebral palsy. *Physiotherapy, 80,* 246–262.
Chandler, L., Andrews, M., & Swanson, M. (1980). *Movement assessment of infants.* Rolling Bay, WA: AM Larson.
Cratty, B. J. (1980). *Adapted physical education for handicapped children and youth.* Denver, CO: Love.
DEC Task Force on Recommended Practices. (1993). *DEC recommended practices: Indicators of quality in programs for infants and young children with special needs and their families.* Reston, VA: Council for Exceptional Children.
DePauw, K. P. (1978). Enhancing sensory integration of aphasic students. *Journal of Learning Disabilities, 1978, 2,* 29–33.
DuBose, R. R., & Folio, R. (1977). Investigation of short-term gains in motor skill achievement in delayed and non-delayed preschool children. *Peabody Journal of Education,* 181–184.
Effgen, S. K. (1988). Preparation of physical therapists and occupational therapists to work in early childhood special education settings. *Topics in Early Childhood Special Education 7*(4), 10–19.
Filler, J., & Kasari, C. (1981). Acquisition, maintenance, and generalization of parent taught skills with two severely handicapped infants. *Journal of the Association of Persons with Severe Handicaps, 6*(1), 30–38.
Finn, D. M., Campbell, P. H., & Fewell, R. R. (1990). Conductive education: An intervention strategy for children who have cerebral palsy. *Networker, 3*(3), 7–9.
Folio, M. R. (1986). *Physical education programming for exceptional learners.* Rockville, MD: Aspen.
Folio, M. R., & DuBose, R. F. (1974). *Peabody Developmental Motor Scales,* IMRID Behavioral Science Monograph No. 25. Nashville, TN: George Peabody College.
Folio, M. R., & Fewell, R. R. (1983). *Peabody Developmental Motor Scales and Activity Cards.* Chicago: Riverside.
Frostig, M. A., & Horne, D. (1964). *The Frostig Program for the Development of Visual Perception.* Chicago: Follett.
Furuno, S., O'Reilly, K. A., Hosaka, C. M., Inatsuka, T. T., Zeisloft-Falbey, B., Allman, T. (1988). *Hawaii Early Learning Profile.* Palo Alto, CA: Vort.
Gesell, A., & Amatruda C. (1947). *Developmental diagnosis* (2nd ed.). New York: Noeber.
Getman, G. N. (1965). *Visuomotor complex in the acquisition of learning skills.* Seattle, WA: Special Child Publications.
Harris, S. R. (1981). Effects of neurodevelopmental therapy on motor performance of infants with Down's syndrome. *Developmental Medicine and Child Neurology, 23,* 477–483.

Harris, S. R. (1987). Early intervention for children with motor handicaps. In M. Guralnick & F. C. Bennett (Eds.), *The effectiveness of early intervention for at-risk handicapped children* (pp. 175–211). New York: Academic Press.

Harris, S. R., & Tada, W. L. (1983). Providing developmental therapy services. In S. G. Garwood & R. R. Fewell (Eds.), *Educating handicapped infants* (pp. 343–368). Rockville, MD: Aspen.

Horn, E. M. (1991). Basic motor skills instruction for children with neuromotor delays: A critical review. *The Journal of Special Education, 25*(2), 168–197.

Horn, E. M., & Warren, S. F. (1987). Facilitating the acquisition of sensorimotor behavior with a microcomputer mediated teaching system: An experimental analysis. *Journal of the Association for Persons with Severe Handicaps, 12*, 205–215.

Jenkins, J. R., Fewell, R. R., & Harris, S. R. (1983). Comparison of sensory integrative therapy and motor programming. *American Journal of Mental Retardation, 88*(2), 221–224.

Karnes, M. B. (1992). *Fit for me: Activities for building motor skills in young children*. Circle Pines, MN: American Guidance Service.

Kephart, N. C. (1971). *The slow learner in the classroom* (2nd ed.). Columbus, OH: Merrill.

Lydic, J. S., Windsor, M. M., Short, M. A., & Ellis, T. A. (1985). Effects of controlled rotary vestibular stimulation on the motor performance of infants with Down syndrome. *Physical and Occupational Therapy in Pediatrics, 5*(2 & 3), 93–118.

MacLean, W. E., & Baumeister, A. A. (1982). Effects of vestibular stimulation on motor development and stereotyped behavior of developmentally delayed children. *Journal of Abnormal Child Psychology, 10*, 229–245.

Martin, J. E., & Epstein, L. H. (1976). Evaluating treatment effectiveness in cerebral palsy: Single-subject designs. *Physical Therapy, 53*, 285–294.

McGraw, M. B. (1943) *The neuromuscular motivation of the human infant.* New York: Columbia University Press.

Montgomery, P., & Richter, E. (1977). Effects of sensory integrative therapy on the neuromotor development of retarded children. *Physical Therapy, 57*, 799–806.

Ottenbacher, K. (1982). Sensory Integration therapy: Affect or effect. *The American Journal of Occupational Therapy, 36*(9), 571–578.

Ottenbacher, K. J., Biocca, Z., DeCremer, G., Gavelinger, M., Jedlovec, K. B., & Johnson, M. B. (1986). Quantitative analysis of the effectiveness of pediatric therapy. *Physical Therapy, 66*(7), 1098–1101.

Ottenbacher, K., Short, M. A., & Watson, P. J. (1981). The effects of a clinically applied program of vestibular stimulation on the neuromotor performance on children with severe developmental disability. *Physical and Occupational Therapy in Pediatrics, 1*(3), 1–11.

Palmer, F. B., Shapiro, P. K., Wachtel, R. C., Allen, M. C., Hiller, J. F., Harryman, S. E., Mosher, B. S., Meinert, C. L., & Caputo, A. J. (1988). The effects of physical therapy on diplegia. *New England Journal of Medicine, 318*, 803–808.

Parette, H. P., Hendricks, M. D., & Rock, S. L. (1991). *Infants and Young Children, 4*(2), 1–19.

Rainforth, B., & Salisbury, C. L. (1988). Functional home programs: A model for therapists. *Topics in Early Childhood Education, 7*(4), 33–45.

Vincent, L. J., Salisbury, C., Laten, S., & Baumgart, D. (1979). *Designing home programs for families with handicapped children.* Unpublished manuscript, University of Wisconsin, Department of Rehabilitation Psychology and Special Education, Madison.

Werder, J. K., & Bruininks, R. H. (1991). *Bodyskills.* Circle Pines, MN: American Guidance Service.

Wickstrom, R. L. (1970). *Fundamental motor patterns.* Philadelphia: Lea & Febiger.

CHAPTER 11

Interventions to Promote Adaptive Behavior Skills

Eva M. Horn

Independent functioning as an adult typically means that an individual can live on his or her own and provide for his or her basic needs such as food, clothing, and shelter. Competent adults can do these tasks without regular supervision or help from others. Further, competent adults can interact with others in a variety of social contexts including employee–employer relationships, casual acquaintances, and friendships. They can organize and use their time for a variety of activities. Competence, in this sense, means having the skills to take care of oneself and to do things needed and valued in everyday life. This vision of a competent, independently functioning adult is a normal expectation. The intermediate steps toward this vision can be described as adaptive behavior. It is this vision that provides the philosophical foundation for the indicators of recommended practices to promote adaptive behavior skills.

The recommended practice indicators (see the Appendix for a complete listing) specify a number of issues to be addressed when intervening to promote children's adaptive behaviors. The indicators can be grouped into related subsets. These are (a) context for intervention (AB 2, AB 6, AB 8), (b) intervention planning related to the scope and sequence of curricular planning (AB 1, AB 7, AB 3), and (c) intervention issues including child characteristics (AB 4, AB 5) and modifications (AB 9). These subsets are discussed after a definition of adaptive development and a rationale for promoting adaptive development in early childhood programs are offered.

DEFINING ADAPTIVE BEHAVIOR IN EARLY CHILDHOOD

Adaptive behavior is a dynamic construct, influenced by cultural norms and age-related expectations (Horn & Fuchs, 1987). The construct emphasizes the individual's capacity to respond to demands of the immediate environment and community. A person judged as "adaptive" in one setting (community) may not necessarily be evaluated similarly in another

259

setting. The nature of these demands also changes as an individual progresses through the life cycle. For the young child, adaptive behavior encompasses skills such as walking, talking, and basic self-care. For the school-aged child, it reflects the capacity to understand and respond appropriately to the social rules of various settings, which include school, community, and home. For the adult, adaptive behavior includes the ability to hold a job, maintain a residence, contribute to family life, and so forth. Adaptive behaviors at one developmental level are qualitatively different from those at another level. In short, adaptive behavior is relative and dynamic, rather than absolute and static (Horn & Fuchs, 1987).

The recommended practice indicators thus begin with a definition that addresses the construct from an early childhood perspective, not as a single entity, but as a composite of a wide range of abilities that are dependent on one's age, environment, and cultural group at any moment. Three assumptions are basic to the definition offered: (a) Demonstration of competence in adaptive behavior is linked to the context of community environments typical of the individuals's age peers; (b) adaptive behavior curriculum should include skills that reflect chronological age-appropriate skills for meeting the demands of the child's multiple, unique environments; (c) instruction requires accommodating and adapting to support the specific strengths of individual children; and (d) comprehensive intervention should address the subdomains of self-care, community self-sufficiency, personal–social responsibility, and social adjustment.

RATIONALE FOR INCLUSION OF ADAPTIVE BEHAVIOR INTERVENTIONS

Adaptive behavior is a concept that has played a critical role in intervention for persons with disabilities for many years (Harrison, 1987). This role is particularly evident in the area of eligibility evaluation. An assessment of adaptive behavior is generally necessary before individuals are classified as mentally retarded and, increasingly, before other disabilities are diagnosed (Frankenberger, 1984). In this context, adaptive behavior has been defined as the degree to which individuals meet standards of personal independence and social responsibility appropriate for their chronological age and cultural subgroup (Grossman, 1983). It refers to the capacity to use one's physical abilities (whatever they may be) to achieve the greatest degree of independence in self-care (e.g., sleeping, eating, bathing, toileting), safety skills (e.g., avoiding danger and injury), self-direction, use of the community, work, and leisure (Luckasson et al., 1992). In addition, the person must demonstrate competence in understanding social expectations and the behavior of others and judging appropriately how to conduct oneself in social situations.

In early childhood special education programs, the broader concept of adaptive behavior has been less evident, particularly in program planning. Narrower definitions and terminology, such as self-care or self-help skills, are typically used. For example, most curricula (e.g., *Hawaii Early Learning Profile and Activities,* Furuno et al., 1979; *The Carolina Curriculum for Preschoolers with Special Needs,* Johnson-Martin, Attermeier, & Hacker, 1990) and texts (e.g., Allen & Hart, 1984; Bailey & Wolery, 1992) in early intervention and early childhood include a self-care domain rather than an adaptive behavior domain. Under Part H (the Infant/Toddler Programs) of the Education of the Handicapped Act Amendments of 1986 (P.L. 99-457), self-help was included as an area of development for both assessment and intervention. With the Individuals with Disabilities Education Act Amendments of 1991 (P.L. 102-119), the term was changed to adaptive development. A broad definition should be applied. Adaptive behavior as a curriculum domain should include skills that reflect chronologically age-appropriate skills for meeting the demands of the child's multiple, unique environments.

Several rationales for including adaptive behavior in early childhood curricula can be offered. First and foremost, independent participation in normal environments is an anticipated outcome of early intervention (Bailey & Wolery, 1992; Peterson, 1987). Children who can dress, feed, and toilet are more independent than children who cannot. Similarly, children's attainment of these skills should decrease caregiving demands on parents. All children require caregiving, but a child with disabilities may have more intense and enduring caretaking demands (Dyson & Fewell, 1986). Further, many of the behaviors defined as adaptive, such as social adjustment and personal–social responsibility, address important socially acceptable behaviors. Attainment of these skills results in the child's appearing more normal and thus promotes his or her meaningful inclusion within community settings.

Specific characteristics of adaptive behaviors provide logical support for their inclusion in early childhood curriculum. First, many adaptive behaviors are acquired during early childhood. Mastery of these skills are part of daily routines for all children with or without disabilities. In addition, the development of these skills requires a long time and reflects a hierarchial sequence from simple to complex. For example, the skill area of dressing may proceed as follows: cooperating with the adult, anticipating the next step when being dressed by pushing a leg through a pants leg, taking off and putting on simple articles of clothing, managing fasteners, and then selecting appropriate clothing based on the context.

The acquisition of adaptive behaviors may also appear to have a more immediate, concrete impact, particularly from the family's perspective. Many adaptive behaviors are visible skills (e.g., using the toilet, feeding self, independent play) that provide obvious evidence of accomplishment.

Others are tied to safety issues, such as appropriate behaviors on supervised community trips (e.g., holding the adult's hand before walking across the street). A few skills may even have an immediate economic benefit. For example, toileting and eating regular food eliminates the need for expensive infant diapers and foods.

A final rationale for the inclusion of the adaptive behavior domain is the impact of independent functioning on the child's sense of competence and self-concept. One need only remember the toddler who proudly proclaimed, "I did it!" upon pulling off her shoe, to recognize the tremendous impact that the mastery of these skills can have on the child's sense of self-worth. Conversely, a lack of independence surely breeds learned helplessness and passivity.

CONTEXT FOR INTERVENTION

The conceptual framework that drives intervention across the subdomains of adaptive behavior is a functional–ecological approach (DeStefano, Howe, Horn, Smith, 1991; McDonnell & Hardman, 1988). Several themes are commonly identified with this approach: (a) Content is referenced to the unique needs and lifestyle of the child, family, peers, and community; (b) curriculum content should increase the child's ability to interact with his or her world; (c) content emphasizes skills that are useful to the child immediately and in the future; and (d) planning should provide for instruction that can be implemented naturally in multiple, daily family and child routines and activities (AB 2, AB 6, AB 8).

The major goal of a functional–ecological curriculum approach is to increase the young child's control, participation, and interaction in natural social and physical environments (Cook, Tessier, & Klein, 1992). The approach is viewed as a process for deriving content (what to teach) rather than as a predetermined set of sequenced skills to be taught. The content is derived through environmental analysis. The goals are developed individually and reflect the skill demands of natural, age-appropriate environments (McDonnell & Hardman, 1988). The content "grows with the child" and responds to the increasing requirements of the settings in which the child participates as he or she gets older. Furthermore, the uniqueness of each child and family's environment is valued. The curriculum is responsive to the unique characteristics and needs associated with a variety of social environments.

The characteristics of adaptive behavior readily allow the application of this model. As noted previously, adaptive behaviors relate to the "fit" of the child within and across settings. The specific behaviors at any given developmental stage that determine competence in adaptive behavior are identified from an analysis of the unique needs and lifestyle of the child, family, peers, and community, much as the content for instruction is determined for a functional-ecological curriculum approach.

Families tend to be the primary facilitator of learning in many of the environments and activities in which young children participate on a daily basis (e.g. home, community, mealtimes, bathing, dressing; Shelton, Jeppson, & Johnson, 1987). Further, they are usually the most consistent support across time. It follows, then, that families should know best their children's strengths and needs and their impact on the child's fit within and across settings, because they have the broadest and most continuous picture. Thus, they should be the primary source for identification of skills, priorities, and contexts for intervention.

Similarly, adaptive behaviors are typically a part of regularly occurring events that focus on socially prescribed behaviors (e.g., which food requires the use of utensils in eating and which utensil). This prescription requires that the child learn the cultural expectations of self-care and self-sufficiency necessary in group settings inside and outside the home. Exactly what skills are learned is determined by the culture of the sub-settings in which the family and child participate on a regular basis. Finally, there is significant variance in normal developmental sequences with heavy cultural influence. For example, the child's movement from breast milk or formula to solid food has varied across generations, regions, and nationalities from as early as 6 weeks to as late as 2 years. All of these characteristics provide support for the appropriateness of utilizing a functional–ecological orientation for identifying curriculum content and context when intervening to promote adaptive behaviors.

INTERVENTION PLANNING

As early interventionists begin to plan adaptive behavior interventions collaboratively with families, the scope and sequence of curricular content must be addressed. In the definition, noted previously, the importance of addressing all subdomains (i.e., self-care, community self-sufficiency, personal–social responsibility, and social adjustment) was emphasized. Each of these subdomains has multiple areas of concern (AB 1, AB 7). Attaining skills within these subdomains is based on the child's developmental and chronological age (AB 3). In the remainder of this section, each subdomain is described along with the multiple areas within the continuum of training to be addressed.

Self-Care

In early childhood, self-care refers to dressing/undressing, eating/feeding, toileting, and grooming (e.g., hand washing, face washing, toothbrushing) (AB 1). These sets of skills are needed for independence in meeting basic needs such as food and warmth. By the age of 5, most children have learned basic self-care skills (Johnson-Martin, et al., 1990). Opportunities to practice these skills are a regular aspect of most preschool programs. A child's early years may be the best time for acquiring basic self-care skills. Young children often assert their independence by wanting to do things for themselves. They are also avid imitators who enjoy watching and mimicking others and seeing others attempting to model their movements and actions. By understanding these characteristics, teachers can capitalize on them in teaching self-care skills. Finally, it must be noted that all of the discrete behaviors in this subdomain are related to other areas of development. For example, dressing is more than putting on a shirt. It requires discriminating the front from the back, determining the appropriateness of the shirt for the weather, and controlling a range of refined motor abilities.

Table 11.1 provides a list of potential skills and suggested sequences across the major areas of self-care. This list is not intended to be comprehensive, nor does it break the skills down into their smallest components.

Dressing/Undressing and Grooming

It is important that young children learn that being clean and properly groomed feels good. Early instruction (before age 2 years) focuses on the child's cooperation with the caregiver. When the adult is helping a young child with dressing or grooming, it is important for the adult to talk to the child about what is occurring. The adult might comment on the child's clothing, encourage the child to help in selecting the clothing for a particular day, and discuss the implication of the choice in terms of appearance and climate. Children should feel that someone is engaging them in an important activity that has positive outcomes for them.

All the skills in this subdomain require a degree of motor proficiency. Caregivers should encourage children to be as independent as possible even if initially slow. Adults might start with simple clothing and adaptive supplies (e.g., bathing-mitts, lever handles on sinks, velcro closures) to encourage the child to use his or her current motor abilities. With the child's demonstrated success and confidence, caregivers might introduce more difficult articles (e.g., buttons) and skills (e.g., toothbrushing).

In a preschool setting, as at home, these skills are best practiced within daily routines (e.g., before and after eating, after toileting, before bedtime, when coming and going, after engaging in messy activities). Mealtimes, for examples, offer a chance for practicing a variety of grooming skills. Children can wash their hands before and after eating and brush their teeth after meals. After nap time is an excellent time to naturally embed a variety of dressing and grooming skills, such as putting on socks and

Table 11.1. Example Skills Across Major Self-Care Skill Areas

Skill Area	Examples
Dressing/Undressing	Cooperates in dressing/undressing (e.g., holds arm out for sleeve, foot out for shoe)
	Removes loose clothing (e.g., mitten, hat, untied shoes)
	Unfastens clothing zipper that has a large pull tab
	Puts on sock, loose shoes, and "stretch pants"
	Puts on all clothes unaided, except for fasteners
	Undoes fasteners (e.g., large buttons, snaps, shoelaces)
	Zips front-opening clothing such as jacket
	Selects and matches clothing appropriate for weather conditions and specific activities
Grooming	Enjoys playing in water
	Cooperates in hand washing and drying
	Wipes nose, if given tissue
	Washes and dries hands and face without assistance
	Brushes teeth
	Runs brush or comb through hair
	Bathes self
Toileting	Usually indicates need to toilet; rarely has bowel accident
	Urinates in toilet
	Has bowel movement in toilet
	Anticipates need to toilet
	Cares for self at toilet (may need assistance wiping after bowel movement)
	Wipes and flushes after toileting
	Cares for clothing before and after toileting
Eating/Feeding	Smoothly sucks from nipple
	Munches food, chewing up and down

(continues)

Table 11.1. *Continued*

Skill Area	Examples
	Pulls food off spoon with lips
	Chews with rotary and side-to-side actions
	Feeds self with fingers
	Brings spoon to mouth and eats food off it
	Holds and drinks from cup
	Scoops food from dish with spoon
	Uses fork
	Gets drink unassisted (e.g., turns tap on and off)
	Spreads with knife
	Uses napkin to wipe fingers and mouth
	Uses appropriate mealtime behaviors, including social graces

Note. From "Assessment of adaptive behavior development," by E. M. Horn & A. Childre, 1996, in M. E. McLean, D. B. Bailey, and M. Wolery (Eds.), *Assessing infants and preschoolers with special needs* (pp. 462–490). Columbus, OH: Merrill/Prentice Hall. Reprinted with permission.

shoes, washing hands and face, combing hair, and even brushing teeth. Many of these skills can also be effectively embedded into planned activities and play. Teachers can provide a variety of types of clothing (e.g., work clothes, glamorous clothes, beachwear, shoes, boots, hats) and grooming items (e.g., combs, brushes, hairpins) for dress-up and pretend play. Dressing and undressing is more motivating when the replaced garment represents a "fun" activity, such as bath time, swimming, painting, or sand play.

To become proficient in grooming and dressing skills, young children need many opportunities to experience the natural consequences of planned and routine activities. Many functional and motivating opportunities can be created and provided throughout the day. Initially adults should address these skills as partnerships, allowing the child to do as much as possible and decreasing their assistance as the child acquires skills. Physical support and guidance are not the only teaching tools. Adults and peer models, verbal cues, and prompts can also be powerful teaching supports.

Toileting

The typical time line for accomplishing toilet training is highly variable, with some children being trained well before 2 years while others are 3 or even 4 years old. Training can be viewed as a three-level process: (a) When taken to the toilet, the child will urinate or have a bowel movement or both in the toilet; (b) the child indicates the need to void and requests assistance or goes independently to the toilet; and (c) the child recognizes his or her need to void, goes alone, removes and replaces clothing, cleans self and flushes the toilet. Although the third level is the ultimate goal, each level represents a number of complex skills, and success depends on the child's physical and social maturity.

Muscle control is obviously needed to control elimination. In addition, the behavioral control to stop an interesting activity to attend to toileting needs may be difficult for the young child. Snell (1993) suggested the following three criteria for initiating toilet training: (a) the child has a relatively stable pattern of urination and bowel elimination rather than a random pattern throughout the day; (b) the child has periods of 1½–2 hours of dryness; and (c) the child is chronologically 2½ years old or older. As with many other adaptive behaviors, toileting is learned in a logical, developmental sequence, building on certain earlier skills. Toilet training may begin with the child's indicating an awareness of wet or soiled pants. The child may experience discomfort in wearing the soiled clothes, which can be a motivation for beginning toileting. If the child expresses discomfort, immediately reinforce this by changing the soiled pants.

As the child matures, the time between eliminations increases, and the child can begin to learn to "hold it" between adult-initiated trips. It is important at this time of "training" for the adult to be aware of subtle signals that the child needs to void. By taking the child to the toilet at these times, the child will begin to associate the physical sensation with the need to use the toilet. Taking the child at regular intervals and rewarding successes are very important at this time. Often in group care settings, there are logically occurring times for children to use the toilet, such as after snacks or meals and before and after naps. The modeling effect of other children's using or beginning to use the toilet can be powerful.

Once the child is having some success on a regular basis, allowing them to wear training pants can be a positive reward. At this time, the caregiver may begin encouraging the child to assist in pulling down his or her pants. After using the toilet, the child should begin to assist in wiping and pulling their pants on, with the caregiver gradually fading assistance. Children often enjoy flushing the toilet, and this activity can be incorporated early into the full toilet routine.

Several "rapid toilet training" methods have been reported in the literature (e.g., Foxx & Azrin, 1974; Mahoney, Van Wagenen, & Meyerson, 1971; Richmonds, 1983). These are referred to as rapid because the method is implemented with high intensity, and empirical research has demonstrated rapid changes in the child's performance. The intensity of the methods, however, can conflict with accepted practices in the field today (Snell, 1993). The majority of approaches use one or more of the following practices:

(a) increased fluid intake, (b) removing the child from all or most other activities, and (c) punishment. The use of increased fluid intake as a method to promote urination, thereby increasing opportunities for bladder training must be implemented with caution. Overhydration can lead to hyponatremia, which is associated with nausea, vomiting, muscular twitching, grand mal seizures, and eventually coma (Thompson & Hanson, 1983).

Usually, the intensive nature of these approaches has required sitting on the toilet far more often than is naturally needed. Teachers provide extensive hands-on assistance and reinforcement, which may pull the child and teacher away from the ongoing activities of the day. These methods may also mean that mistakes are followed by punishing consequences (e.g., excessive clean-up, repetition of the behavioral chain being taught, removal of food). Current recommended practices support methods more suited to community-based programs, respect the child's right to privacy and protection from harm, are individually designed, and promote generalized learning of skills in response to natural routines (Snell, 1993).

Eating

Eating is much more than a means for ingesting adequate nutrition in a safe manner. Eating can be a pleasant and naturally reinforcing event. Pleasant mealtimes can enhance the maintenance and generalization of eating skills and the other social and communication skills naturally embedded into mealtime routines. Unfortunately, young children with disabilities may experience problems that interfere with appropriate nutritional intake and that result in excessive demands on the caregiver's effort and time (Eicher, 1992). These problems may set the stage for highly negative interactions and stress between the child and the parent around feeding routines. Therefore, eating, self-feeding, and mealtimes may be seen as high priorities for families of children with disabilities.

Ultimately, children should be able to eat unassisted in a range of settings (e.g., home, school cafeteria, restaurants). Eating interventions should address the following aspects: (a) caregivers' understanding of strategies for assessing and ensuring adequate nutritional intake, (b) the abilities and skills of the infant and young child related to food and liquid intake, (c) the skills for teaching children to feed themselves independently, (d) eating preparation (e.g., serving one's plate), (e) table manners, (f) maintaining conversation, and (g) clean-up activities (e.g., clearing one's plate, wiping the table clean).

Feeding. Adequate nutritional intake can be problematic for young children with disabilities, particularly those with physical disabilities or other chronic health impairments (Eicher, 1992). These potential problems may be related to the child's particular diagnosis (e.g., metabolic disorders, inadequate food intake due to oral motor impairments), the side effect of a medication, specialized diets, or behavioral factors (Brizee, Sophos, & McLaughlin, 1990; O'Brien, Repp, Williams, & Christopherson, 1991; Sobsey, 1983). These threats to nutritional intake can lead to malnutrition, obesity, constipation, and other problems. Professionals should be aware of nutritional screening procedures and be able to recognize indications of need for further nutritional assessment. Brizee and her colleagues provided a helpful guide for collecting relevant dietary information (Brizee et al., 1990). Information germane to nutritional screening includes (a) interviews with caregivers; (b) recordings of changes in height or weight and in appearance of gums, teeth, hair, and skin; and (c) reviews of health and medical records. Before beginning eating or feeding programming, young children should be seen by a physician to rule out possible organic causes for the eating problems (O'Brien et al., 1991). Further, if there are any indicators of threats to the child's nutritional status, a nutritionist should be included in the team.

Effective eating depends on the following steps: (a) the ability to take in food, form a bolus, and swallow; (b) the absence of aspiration into the airway; (c) the lack of reflux of food once it enters the stomach; and (d) the normal digestion and movement of food through the intestines (Eicher, 1992). Problems can occur at one or more of these steps.

Transdisciplinary teamwork is required to assess and plan for interventions. Professionals from different disciplines (e.g., educators, occupational therapists, physical therapists, speech pathologists, and nurses) have expertise that should be considered in mealtime assessment and planning. Parents and other primary caregivers must be included because they typically know the child and history of interventions better than any other team member and because they generally participate in feeding the child the majority of the time. Assessment requires a determination of both the child's current skills and the skills critical to improving the child's oral motor functioning. Setting objectives is a key step in program planning (Campbell, 1982). Vague goals such as "to improve nutritional status" or "will chew better" defy evaluation and may make training extremely difficult.

The feeding difficulties may result from the interaction of multiple problems and thus require multiple methods of intervention (Crane, 1987). A large number of intervention techniques have been proposed to improve oral motor skills for eating. Entire books (e.g., Campbell, 1982; Gallendar, 1979; Morris & Klein, 1987) have focused on this topic and are available to practitioners. Nine general categories of intervention can be addressed: (a) adjusting the position of the child, (b) adjusting foods, (c) adapting utensils, (d) altering feeding schedules, (e) changing the feeding environment, (f) modifying food presentation, (g) providing physical assistance, (h) enhancing sensory stimulation, and (i) providing specific instruction (Eicher, 1992; Morris & Klein, 1987; Orelove & Sobsey, 1991).

Feeding is a motor activity that requires more coordination between muscle groups than does any other motor activity. The importance of positioning for performance of eating skills cannot be overemphasized (Nwaobi & Smith, 1986). The optimal position will vary from child to child, but three principles remain constant: (a) The child should have firm support through the hips and trunk to provide a stable base; (b) the child should be as upright as possible; and (c) the child's head and neck should be aligned in a neutral position, which decreases extension through the oral musculature while maintaining an open airway.

Food textures can be manipulated to facilitate safe, controlled swallowing (Gisel, 1991). Although some literature has suggested using soft or pureed foods with children with feeding disabilities (e.g., Blockley & Miller, 1971), more recent empirical studies have demonstrated that children given pureed foods would do as well or better with whole or more coarsely textured foods (Gisel, 1991; T. Jones, 1983; Sobsey, 1983). Many normal oral motor skills (e.g., chewing) require the stimulation of having solid food in the mouth to allow for their development. Further, pureed food can lead to constipation, dental caries, weakened and deformed oral structures, and vitamin deficiencies (Gisel, 1991; Sobsey, 1983).

Modified utensils (e.g., spoons and cups) can be extremely useful for many young children with feeding disabilities when used in combination with other interventions. For example, "cutaway" cups allow drinking without hyperextension of the neck and allow a controlled flow from the cup to the mouth (Morris, 1977). Trefler, Westmoreland, and Burlingame (1977) found that a spatula spoon minimized stimulation within the mouth for individuals with extreme oral hypersensitivity. Further, this type of spoon worked well in combination with modified placement to the sides of the mouth and physical pressure down on the tongue to facilitate appropriate tongue movements.

Some children have little appetite or are unable to communicate that they are hungry. Caregiviers can try feeding the child at different times of the day to find out which hour he or she eats best. The child may eat his or her largest meal at breakfast or lunch rather than at dinner. Also, caregivers might pair food the child likes with less favored ones (Iwata, Riordan, Wohl, & Finney, 1982).

Food presentation for the child is extremely important. Caregivers should present food or drink from the center and slightly below chin level to encourage flexion patterns and symmetry of the neck and head. The pace and cues provided can enhance relaxation and coordination of eating and drinking with breathing patterns (Stainback, Stainback, Healy, & Healy, 1980). Similar attention must be given to the placement of utensils. Caregivers should place eating utensils only partially into the mouth to prevent gagging and to promote the removal of the food with lips rather than by scraping off with teeth. Spoon placement with gentle pressure on the midtongue region can help remind the child to keep the tongue inside the mouth and promote more normalized tongue movement during swallowing (Trefler et al., 1977). Chewing may be enhanced by placing food between the upper and lower back teeth. This placement encourages the child to move the jaw and to use the tongue in lateral patterns in an effort to dislodge the food. The rim of the cup should be placed on the child's lower lip; this positioning encourages good lip seal and avoids stimulation of the bite reflex (Morris, 1977).

If changes in position, food texture, and feeding utensils do not elicit desired oral movement, direct physical assistance or oral control can be provided by the feeder (Alexander, 1991). Oral control can be used to stimulate lip closure, coordinate swallowing, and influence graded jaw movements while reducing the influence of tongue and jaw thrusting. Methods must be selected according to a child's pattern of eating or drinking difficulty and are described in detail in a number of eating skill program readings (e.g., Alexander, 1991; Morris, 1977; Stainback et al., 1980; Utley, Holvoet, & Barnes, 1977).

Programs to promote feeding for a young child with a disability may often require a number of creative approaches and the involvement of several different professionals and family members. When effective, these methods enable the child to receive the necessary combination of nutrients, fluids, and oral motor stimulation to help them grow, remain healthy, and develop new skills.

Self-Feeding. More has been written about the specialized training of oral motor skills in feeding than about training self-feeding skills (Orelove & Sobsey, 1991). Basic self-feeding includes handling finger foods, drinking from a self-held cup, and eating with a spoon. The primary procedures for teaching these basic skills include physical prompting of targeted behaviors followed by fading or delaying prompts and by shaping. Each of these skills involves a fairly long chain of discrete responses by the child. A task analysis may be useful in determining exactly what step in the sequence needs work and support.

The first level in moving to independence in self-feeding is the predictably messy stage of eating finger foods. It provides the child opportunities to practice skills necessary for utensil use and simultaneously to continue to refine oral motor skills. The young child picks up food and thus practices and refines his or her grasp and hand-to-mouth movement in combination with gumming, sucking, chewing, and swallowing of many soft foods. In planning intervention, a teacher or caregiver must determine which piece of the "eating finger food chain" is missing or weak—finding the food, grasping, lifting to mouth, opening mouth at the appropriate time, leaving food in mouth, chewing, or swallowing. Furthermore, the teacher or caregiver may determine how the child handles larger food (tears it into smaller bites or bites off smaller pieces), how messy the child is, and what causes the messiness (e.g., too much food in the mouth). The determination of missing or weak skills or links in the chain allows the identification of training skills.

Once the child can move food from a table into the mouth, the teacher or caregiver can provide self-feeding or drinking opportunities with utensils and a cup. For most children, only the caregiver's willingness to provide ample opportunities is needed. For others, coordinating arm, hand, head, and mouth movements is a challenge. For a child who cannot acquire independence in cup drinking, drinking liquids with a straw from a stabilized cup is a good alternative means to independence. Using utensils and drinking from cups and glasses can be taught simultaneously. Spoon use is the simplest of the utensil skills, followed in difficulty by eating with a fork, using a knife for spreading, and using a knife and fork for cutting.

The teacher's first priority for young children is to develop instruction that is normalized and developmentally appropriate. The least intrusive procedures should be selected. Teachers and caregivers should expect young children to be messy while they learn to eat. Spilling and messiness are typical well into the latter part of early childhood. If excessive spilling and messiness continue as the child becomes more proficient in eating, observation can assist in determining when the "error" occurs (e.g., while scooping something out of the bowl) and why (e.g., poor lip closure around the spoon in removing food). Once the problem is identified, adjustments in the equipment or instruction can occur.

Eating and mealtimes, as previously noted, include more than just getting the food to one's mouth and consuming it. Preschool children can participate in mealtime preparation (e.g., serving one's plate), using appropriate table manners (e.g., discriminating between finger food and utensil food, using a napkin), maintaining a conversation (e.g., turn taking, appropriate volume, not talking with food in the mouth), and clean-up activities (e.g., clearing one's plate, wiping the table clean). These activities are best taught within the natural flow of the mealtime settings in which the child participates (e.g., home, visiting relatives or friends, preschool, restaurant, fast food).

Summary of Self-Care

An individually defined self-care curriculum is important for children with developmental delays if they are to maintain good health, increase their personal independence, and enjoy acceptance in a broad array of community settings. Direct observation and interviews with significant adults can determine if instruction is indicated in a given area at a specific point in time. When it is, then it can also provide important information on what to teach. Teachers must carefully match the skills and instructional procedures to the individual child and to the settings where the skills will be used. Decisions must be made about procedures, times for teaching, and teaching materials. Procedures should be socially and developmentally appropriate. Caregivers should strive to avoid approaches that violate privacy, disrespect age-group practices, are unnecessarily intrusive, and separate children by ability.

Community Self-Sufficiency

Previously, instruction in the area of community self-sufficiency for individuals with disabilities focused on helping them acquire readiness skills for community placement as adults (Browder & Snell, 1993). Research supports the conclusion that skill acquisition is only one of many factors that affects successful and continued inclusion in the community (Nisbet, Clark, & Covert, 1991). Providing individualized supports either to the child with disabilities or to the child's family improves the chance of success. Supports may include advocacy, financial assistance, instructional planning, caregiving, respite, and companionship (Luckasson et al., 1992). Although this chapter focuses on instructional support or intervention, it is important to view instruction as a form of support that, like the other areas of support, may enhance the child's success.

From a life-span perspective, appropriate use of community resources includes skills such as traveling in the community; grocery and general shopping at stores; obtaining services from other community businesses such as doctor and dentist's offices, clinics, restaurants, and repair shops; using public transportation; using public facilities such as schools, libraries, post offices, parks, and recreational areas; attending church or synagogue; and attending theaters and other recreational events (Ford et al., 1989). Related skills include communication of choices and needs, social interaction and behavior in the community, and use of functional academics.

An instructional emphasis on these skills is appropriate during the early childhood years. However, the degree of independence, the range of settings, and the complexity (e.g., purchasing may involve making a choice between a chicken nugget or hamburger "kid's" meal) are adjusted to reflect developmental, age, and cultural expectations. Thus, community self-sufficiency within an early childhood curriculum includes skills that promote age and culturally appropriate functioning *with adult supervision* within community environments such as restaurants, neighborhoods, and recreational areas. The primary method for addressing these skills, as it is with typically developing children, is through regular and repeated exposure to an array of community settings.

Skills related to "use of the community" overlap with other subdomains of adaptive behavior (e.g., eating, toileting), as well as with other domains such as cognitive (e.g., problem solving), motor (e.g., mobility), social, and communication. Although this overlap is obvious, the distinction of community self-sufficiency as a subdomain is important in terms of measuring competency in a given skill based on the demands of the setting (e.g., eating in a restaurant). That is, competence requires the ability to change behavior to suit the demands of the setting (Evans, 1991). Thus, content must be determined by evaluating these community environments of the young child, the child's access to them, and the demands for appropriate participation.

Most nondisabled infants are in the hospital for a short time, and at home with at least one caregiver at least part of the time. They may regularly journey into the community to visit doctor's offices or clinics, grocery stores, drug stores, neighbor's yard, house of worship, parks, theaters, and other settings. In addition, many infants and toddlers attend childcare, parents' day out, preschool, or other group care or play settings. They encounter all of these environments before they attend kindergarten, and each environment presents an array of opportunities for the child to begin learning community self-sufficiency skills. It is an examination of these "instructional" opportunities in typical environments in which nondisabled infants, toddlers, and preschoolers function that provides the foundation for "what" to teach.

The actual as well as the future community environments that the infant or toddler is apt to encounter must first be indexed. Then specific areas of each environment, the age-appropriate activities that occur there, and the specific skills needed to participate in those activities must be outlined (Brown et al., 1979). For example, eating is an activity in which an infant regularly engages at home and in the community. While at home or in the community with the mother, the infant may be breast-fed, but while at the childcare program, the infant might be fed from a bottle. The component motor movements required to suck from a bottle constitute an important instructional objective because it is immediately useful. Drinking from a bottle could be exhibited in multiple community environments (e.g., doctor's office, grocery store, riding in the car). Thus, for this infant, bottle drinking is an adaptive, community activity. This approach is highly individualized and specific to each child and family. It requires establishing goals through consensus of the family and the interventionists, not by referring solely to a developmental list.

Teachers need to be cautious in providing instruction for community self-sufficiency. Typical infants, toddlers, and young children do not have constant instruction at home or in public. Professionals must respect the child's and family's desire to have times alone and times with friends and family. Sometimes it is better to bypass instruction to create more time for the family and child to enjoy each other and leisure activities. In planning instructional opportunities, teachers and caregivers should devise subtle cues that are still discernible in order to avoid stigmatizing the child. Teachers should not draw attention to the instruction (e.g., carry clipboards; provide loud, unnatural praise like "Good talking!"). Finally, normative comparisons can assist in assessing mastery of goals by noting if the child performs the skill in a manner that is developmentally appropriate for a chronologically same-aged peer.

Personal–Social Responsibility

Personal–social responsibility includes basic environmental interactions, self-directed behaviors, independent play or self-occupation, peer cooperation and interaction, and assumption of responsibility.

Self-Directed Behaviors

More specifically, self-directed behaviors include skills such as making choices, learning and following a schedule, initiating context-appropriate activities, completing necessary or required tasks, seeking assistance as needed, problem solving in familiar and novel situations, and demonstrating appropriate assertive and self-advocacy skills. For the young child between 12 and 24 months, it becomes increasingly important to be allowed to initiate and direct activities. Toddlers begin to "strike out on their own." That is, they will move away from the primary caregiver and initiate an interaction with another adult or child. They will explore their immediate environments and begin resisting having things done for them (e.g., resist attempts from others to feed them and attempt to do it themselves). They begin to make simple choices (e.g., have preferred toys, foods, clothes, books). While simultaneously encouraging independence, curiosity, and exploring, adults should provide clear limits with firm consequences for violating the rules.

Independent Play or Self-Occupation

This skill area is related to the long-range goal of developing a variety of leisure and recreational interests that reflect individual preferences and choices, and, if applicable, that are appropriate to age and cultural norms. Skills include choosing and self-initiating interests and using and enjoying home and community play activities. The child must learn to extend his or her duration of participation in play activities and to expand his or her repertoire of interests, awareness, and skills. For young children, these skills are directly related to the concept of engagement or the amount of time spent appropriately interacting with the environment (McWilliams, 1991).

Child engagement levels have been shown to be influenced by specific characteristics of the environment (Doke & Risley, 1972; Dunlap & Koegel,

1980; Dunst, McWilliams, & Holbert, 1986; LeLaurin & Risley, 1972). The least intrusive approach for enhancing engagement is to provide space, materials, and activities that stimulate a child's attention and reinforce engagement (McGee, Daly, Izeman, Mann, & Risley, 1991). The adult's primary role is that of organizing the environment and providing selective attention. This role may include providing materials that are appealing, providing intermittent positive attention when the child is engaged, providing systematic commenting (i.e., making observations about the child's play behaviors), and interacting with the child to keep her or him going. Materials should be developmentally appropriate and promote a variety of play behaviors. Children will be more engaged if materials and toys are challenging and offer a variety of play opportunities. These and other strategies for promoting engagement are described by others (e.g., H. Jones & Warren, 1991; McGee et al., 1991; McWilliams & Bailey, 1992; Whaley & Bennett, 1991) as well as in other chapters of this volume.

Peer Cooperation and Interaction

Getting along with other people involves knowing how to join, share, help, and negotiate. It also involves a recognition of the rights, feelings, and needs of others. Specifically, peer cooperation and interaction include such social play skills as initiating a social interchange, learning to take turns, learning to end an interaction appropriately, increasing the duration of social interaction, and appropriately refusing a social interchange. Recommended practices for interventions to promote these behaviors are discussed at length in Chapter 9 of this volume.

Assuming Responsibility

An important part of growing up is assuming responsibility for one's own behaviors and actions. In fact, many children demand the right to take responsibility (e.g., "I want to do it myself!"). Intervention in this area addresses not only controlling one's behavior but also learning the rules of safety, caring for property, and functioning in the community. The amount of responsibility one gives to a child depends on his or her understanding of the potential consequences of various actions and the potential for physical or emotional harm. However, it is very important to avoid limiting the child by overprotecting rather than by teaching. Caregivers should talk to the child about the potential dangers as they engage in activities together. For example, as the adult and child come to a street, the adult might say, "We need to make sure no cars are going. Let's look carefully in both directions. No, there aren't any cars. We can go across." Caregivers should give reasons for rules (e.g., "I want you to hold my hand in the parking lot because I'm taller and cars can see me easier"). If the child starts to do something dangerous, caregivers should calmly but firmly stop her or him and explain why she or he must not do that. Also, adults need to communicate to the child the expectation of being responsible, to let the child know that they notice, and to applaud when the child is acting responsibly. At times, when it is appropriate, the caregiver might delay before intervening to see if the child will respond appropriately. Eventually children will assume more responsibility, but continued praise for their following the rules and for being responsible is important.

Social Adjustment

Social adjustment includes behaviors such as the ability to adjust to new situations, regularity of behavior patterns, general disposition, tendency to stick to tasks despite obstacles, attention span and degree of distractibility, and amount of stimulation necessary to evoke a response. Positive adjustment reflects an integration and display of these attributes as well as other developmental skills in the context of the demands of the environment and personal needs (Zeitlin & Williamson, 1994). Effective adjustment fosters the acquisition of developmental skills, the development of a positive self-concept, and the ability to develop meaningful social relationships (Williamson, 1994).

For young children, coping behaviors focus on nutrition, security, and a combination of activity and rest, combined with an opportunity to pursue interests and motivations and to satisfy the drive to achieve mastery. The cluster of attributes, skills, and behaviors identified with coping in infants and toddlers can be divided into three descriptive categories: sensorimotor organization, reactive behaviors, and self-initiated behaviors (Zeitlin, Williamson, & Szczepanski, 1988). Sensorimotor organization behaviors reflect to some degree the neurobiological state of the child. They include the child's ability to attend, to self-comfort, to control activity level, to manage the intensity and variety of sensory stimuli, and to adapt to handling. Reactive behaviors are responses to external demands from the physical and social environment. They include the ability to adjust to daily routines, to accept warmth and comfort from a familiar person, to respond to vocal and gestural directions, and to adjust to changes in the environment. Self-initiated behaviors are more spontaneous and intrinsically motivated. They include the ability to express likes and dislikes, to initiate action for communicating a need, to persist during activities, and to generalize skills to new situations.

A thorough understanding of the child's current coping style and strategies is necessary before initiating intervention. Observing the child in a variety of situations is the most effective assessment strategy (Zeitlin & Williamson, 1994). Assessment of the child's coping behaviors may include identifying behaviors across the three areas of sensorimotor organization, reactive behaviors, and self-initiated behaviors (all noted previously). In addition, the assessor must note flexibility in the use of the behaviors, circumstances under which they are applied, their success in managing specific stressors, and the child's feelings about the effectiveness of his or her efforts. Based on this information, interventions can be planned to enhance the effectiveness of the child's coping strategies.

Three primary intervention options have been identified: (a) modifying the demands and expectations to match the child's abilities (e.g., adapting the pace of the interaction to match the child's attention span and energy level); (b) enhancing the child's coping skills (e.g., teaching awareness of when and how to request adult help by pointing, verbal appropriate vocalizations, and words rather than by crying or whining); and (c) providing supportive, contingent feedback to the child's demonstration of positive coping (e.g., reinforcing gradual approximations of desired coping behaviors in new contexts; Zeitlin & Williamson, 1994). Intervention activities should be developed and prioritized by professionals and families to address coping-related difficulties (e.g., separation problems, inability to manage the range and expression of emotions, low frustration tolerance). The emphasis should be on ways to decrease maladaptive or ineffective strategies and to increase the development and generalization of effective strategies. Finally, it is important to support child-initiated activity that encourages exploration, problem solving, and development of coping strategies.

INTERVENTION ISSUES

The goal of any early intervention team is to promote the child's development and independence. Even when the child must be taught alternative methods to complete a task, such as self-catheterization for toileting (Neef, Parish, Hannigan, Page, & Iwata, 1989), the goal remains the highest level of independence possible. Plans for interventions in the adaptive behaviors domain must consider the child's characteristics, strengths, and limitations (AB 4, AB 5) as well as instructional modification and adaptations (AB 9).

Child Characteristics

Each child has a unique approach to learning. Learning is enhanced when activities are structured in ways that make the most of the child's strengths and minimize the child's vulnerabilities. Two critical aspects of early learning styles are behavioral state (the level of arousal or responsiveness to stimulation) and temperament (the behavioral style).

The processing of sensory information forms the foundation for the child's attention, self-regulation, and engagement (Simeonsson, Huntington, & Parse, 1980). Young children vary in ability to control their states of arousal and to habituate to changes in the environment. Some children are hyporeactive and need active stimulation to become attentive and engaged. Others are hyperreactive, easily becoming overloaded and developing exaggerated responses to specific sensory stimuli (i.e., hypersensitivity to touch, movement, or sound; DeGangi, Craft, & Castellan, 1991). Adults need to be alert for signs that the child is becoming overloaded. Behavioral indicators include active withdrawal (e.g., running away), tuning out (e.g., staring into space), rejection (e.g., pushing away), or signaling distress (e.g., crying). The intervention challenge is to base the choice, intensity, and variety of environmental demands upon the child's changing ability to process information and his or her behavioral responses. Table 11.2 offers some suggestions for accommodating individual child styles.

Instructional Modifications

Professionals should not eliminate skills from the adaptive behaviors domain merely on the basis of perceived difficulty or child characteristics. Partial participation (Baumgart et al., 1982) and modifications may allow the child to actively take part to some degree and to attain a level of self-accomplishment and independence. Baumgart and colleagues identified four categories of adaptations and modifications: (a) providing personal assistance—using aides, peer tutors, or buddy system to accomplish components of a task; (b) modifying skills or activities—rearranging the order of steps in the skill sequence or changing other aspects of the task such as amount of time allowed or the number of repetitions; (c) using an adaptive device—using special handles, communication devices, lifts, adaptive seating; and (d) modifying the physical and social environment—changing the assumptions and beliefs of family, friends, professionals, and community members. Table 11.3 provides examples of instructional adaptations across the four categories for a variety of adaptive behavior skills for young children with developmental disabilities.

Caregivers should reevaluate adaptations regularly to assess whether they can be faded or eliminated. The general rules to follow in considering the use of modifications and adaptations include (a) using no modification or equipment unless it is appropriate and specific to the child's current needs, (b) having the child and family assist in defining the needs and actual modification, (c) selecting a device or modification that makes the child appear the least different from peers who are nondisabled, (d) selecting adaptations that can be modified as the child grows or as skill levels

Table 11.2. Suggestions for Accommodating Individual Child Processing Styles

Behavior	Techniques
Early Signs of Distress	Stop activity and provide time to recover
	Slow pace rather than stopping the activity
Calming	Apply firm pressure on the skull (avoid light touch that tickles and is excitatory)
	Provide nonnutritive sucking
	Slow repetitive rocking or other rhythmic movement (swing, car ride, stroller)
	Massage for relaxation
	Provide soft melodic music or music boxes
Self-Comforting	Mouthing
	Cuddling a soft toy
	Snuggling in a quiet corner
	Using transitional objects
Reducing Complexity	Provide only one sensory modality at a time (i.e., looking, listening, feeling, or moving)
	Provide specific combinations of two or more sensory modalities
	Provide high-interest activities (sensory tolerance higher when child enjoys task)
	Grade environmental stimulation (e.g., avoid overcrowding, loud noises, glaring light)
Adjusting to Transitions	Provide reasonably consistent, predictable, and structured routines

change, and (e) assisting the child in developing skills that will make her or him no longer dependent on the adaptation.

CLOSING

In general, interventions in adaptive behavior for young children with disabilities should reflect typical practices and expectations for the child's

Table 11.3. Examples of Instruction Adaptations

Adaptation Category	Child Need	Activity	Adaptation
Providing Personal Assistance	Uses ileostomy bag for bowel and bladder elimination	Toileting	Adult assists with changing bag due to bag leakage. Adult provides instruction in emptying bag.
Modifying Skills or Activities	Has difficulty maintaining standing balance	Toileting	Child sits on toilet, then removes pants
	Has difficulty eating quickly	Self-feeding meals	Provide extra time by letting child begin before others or letting child stay longer
Using an Adaptive Device	Has weak grasp	Self-feeding	Use large-handle utensils or velcro-strap grips
Modifying the Physical and Social Environments	Not independent in toileting	Criteria for "moving up" to next class in toilet training	General discussion and information sharing about the normal variability in attainment of independent toileting, "brain storming" about how to accommodate the nontrained child

age, although adjustments must be made for movement and sensory disabilities. The manner in which peers perform the task are important for determining skills for instruction. Research indicates that the attitudes of typical peers toward children with disabilities are better when children with disabilities are viewed by their peers as being similar to them (Bak & Siperstein, 1987). Peers may be better models than age-inappropriate teachers.

As teachers begin implementing instruction, it becomes important that the child is presented opportunities to learn and master skills that meet social expectations. Although adaptive behavior skills are critical and should be taught when they are needed, they are used at a relatively low frequency. Related to this characteristic is the fact that skills must become habitual to be truly functional. They must be performed fluently in response to natural cues, maintained by natural consequences, and performed in varied settings and circumstances. These parameters imply that interventionists may need to change traditional instructional settings to reflect the diversity of settings in which the skills naturally occur (e.g., home, community, and preschool). In addition, the intervention team may need to make adaptations to schedules to increase the opportunities for practicing these skills within the context of routines. Children must be given real-life opportunities to practice and thus to establish habitual responses to natural cues provided across multiple, current and future environments.

Many self-care skills are based on physiological maturity and learned behavior (e.g., feeding skills, toilet skills). These skills are not discrete behaviors but rather are a sequence of behaviors that result in accomplishing a complex function. The implication of these characteristics is that early interventionists must be skilled in analyzing the component parts of the complex skills and in appropriately assessing each child's current developmental and physiological status in relation to each of these component parts.

In conclusion, the adaptive behaviors domain is an important part of the early intervention endeavor. Providing instruction requires that professionals and caregivers accommodate and adapt in order to support the specific strengths of individual children and their families. Competent, independent functioning is the long-term goal.

REFERENCES

Alexander, R. (1991). Prespeech and feeding. In J. L. Bigge (Ed.), *Teaching individuals with physical and multiple disabilities* (3rd ed., pp. 175–198). New York: Macmillan.

Allen, K. E., & Hart, B. (1984). *The early years: Arrangements for learning.* Englewood Cliffs, NJ: Prentice-Hall.

Bailey, D. B., & Wolery, M. (1992). *Teaching infants and preschoolers with disabilities* (2nd ed.). New York: Merrill.

Bak, J. J., & Siperstein, G. N. (1987). Similarity as a factor effecting change in children's attitudes toward mentally retarded peers. *American Journal of Mental Deficiency, 91,* 524–531.

Baumgart, D., Brown, L., Pumpian, I., Nisbet, J., Ford, A., Sweet, M., Messina, R., & Schroeder, J. (1982). Principle of partial participation and individualized adaptations in educational programs for severely handicapped students. *Journal for the Association for Persons with Severe Handicaps, 7,* 17–27.

Blockley, J., & Miller, G. (1971). Feeding techniques with cerebral palsied children. *Physiotherapy, 57,* 300–308.

Brizee, L. S., Sophos, C. M., & McLaughlin, J. F. (1990). Nutrition issues in developmental disabilities. *Infants and Young Children, 2*(3), 10–21.

Browder, D., & Snell, M. E. (1993). Daily living and community skills. In M. E. Snell (Ed.), *Instruction of students with severe disabilities: Fourth Edition*, pp. 480–525.

Brown, L., Branston, M. B., Hamre-Nietupski, S., Pumpian, I., Certo, N., & Gruenwald, L. (1979). A strategy for developing chronological-age-appropriate and functional curricular content for severely handicapped adolescents and young adults. *Journal of Special Education, 13*(1), 81–90.

Campbell, P. (1982). *Problem-oriented approaches to feeding the handicapped child* (rev). Akron, OH: Children's Hospital Medical Center. (ERIC Document Reproduction Service No. ED 231 127).

Cook, R. E., Tessier, A., & Klein, M. D. (1992). *Adapting early childhood curriculum for children with special needs* (3rd ed.). New York: Merrill.

Crane, S. (1987). Feeding the handicapped child—A review of intervention strategies. *Nutrition and Health, 5*, 109–118.

DeGangi, G. A., Craft, P., & Castellan, J. (1991). Treatment of sensory, emotional, and attentional problems in regulatory disordered infants: Part 2. *Infants and Young Children, 3*, 9–19.

DeStefano, D. M., Howe, A. G., Horn, E. M., & Smith, B. A. (1991). *Best practices: Evaluating early childhood special education programs*. Tucson, AZ: Communication Skill Builders.

Doke, L., & Risley, T. R. (1972). The organization of daycare environments: Required vs. optional activities. *Journal of Applied Behavior Analysis, 5*, 405–420.

Dunlap, G., & Koegel, R. L. (1980). Motivating autistic children through stimulus variation. *Journal of Applied Behavior Analysis, 13*, 619–627.

Dunst, C. J., McWilliams, R. A., & Holbert, K. (1986). Assessment of preschool classroom environments. *Diaqnostique, 11*, 212–232.

Dyson, L., & Fewell, R. R. (1986). Stress and adaptation in parents of young handicapped and nonhandicapped children: A comparative study. *Journal of the Division of Early Childhood, 10*(1), 25–34.

Education of the Handicapped Act Amendments of 1986, 20 U.S.C. §1400 *et seq.*

Eicher, P. M. (1992). Feeding the child with disabilities. In M. L. Batshaw & Y. M. Perret (Eds.), *Children with disabilities: A medical primer* (pp. 197–211). Baltimore: Brookes.

Evans, I. M. (1991). Testing and diagnosis: A review and evaluation. In L. H. Meyer, C. A. Peck, & L. Brown (Eds.), *Critical issues in the lives of people with severe disabilities* (pp. 25–44). Baltimore: Brookes.

Ford, A., Schnorr, R., Meyer, L., Davern, L., Black, J., & Dempsey, P. (1989). *The Syracuse community-referenced curriculum guide*. Baltimore: Brookes.

Foxx, R. M., & Azrin, N. H. (1974). *Toilet training in less than a day*. New York: Simon & Schuster.

Frankenberger, W. (1984). A survey of state guidelines for identification of mental retardation. *Mental Retardation, 22*, 17–20.

Furuno, S., O'Rielly, K. A., Hosaka, C. M., Inatsuka, T. T., Allman, T. L., & Zeisloft, B. (1979). *Hawaii Early Learning Profile and Activities*. Palo Alto, CA: Vort.

Gallendar, D. (1979). *Eating handicaps*. Springfield, IL: Thomas.

Gisel, E. G. (1991). Effect of food texture on the development of chewing of children between 6 months and 2 years of age. *Developmental Medicine and Child Neurology, 33*, 69–79.

Grossman, H. J. (Ed.). (1983). *Classification in mental retardation* (rev. ed.). Washington, DC: American Association on Mental Deficiency.

Harrison, P. L. (1987). Research with adaptive behavior scales. *Journal of Special Education, 21*(1), 37–68.

Horn, E., & Fuchs, D. (1987). Using adaptive behavior in assessment and intervention: An overview. *Journal of Special Education, 21*(1), 11–26.

Individuals with Disabilities Education Act Amendments of 1991, 20 U.S.C. §1400 *et seq.*

Iwata, B. A., Riordan, M. M., Wohl, M. K., & Finney, J. W. (1982). Pediatric feeding disorders: Behavioral analysis and treatment. In P. J. Accardo (Ed.), *Failure to thrive in infancy and early childhood* (pp. 297–329). Baltimore: University Park Press.

Johnson-Martin, N. M., Attermeier, S. M., & Hacker, B. (1990). *The Carolina curriculum for preschoolers with special needs.* Baltimore: Brookes.

Jones, H. A., & Warren, S. F. (1991). Enhancing engagement in early language teaching. *Teaching Exceptional Children, 23*(4), 48–50.

Jones, T. W. (1983). Remediation of behavior-related eating problems: A preliminary investigation. *Journal of the Association for Persons with Severe Handicaps, 8*(4), 62–71.

LeLaurin, K., & Risley, T. R. (1972). The organization of day care environments: "Zone" versus "man-to-man" staff assignments. *Journal of Applied Behavior Analysis, 5,* 225–232.

Luckasson, R., Schalock, R. L., Coulter, D. L., Snell, M. E., Polloway, E. A., Spitalnik, D. M., Reiss, S., & Stark, J. A. (1992). *Mental retardation: Definition, classification, and systems of support* (9th ed.). Washington, DC: American Association on Mental Retardation.

Mahoney, K., Van Wagenen, R. K., & Meyerson, L. (1971). Toilet training of normal and retarded children. *Journal of Applied Behavior Analysis, 4,* 173–181.

McDonnell, A., & Hardman, M. (1988). A synthesis of "best practice" guidelines for early childhood services. *Journal of the Division for Early Childhood, 12,* 328–341.

McGee, G. G., Daly, T., Izeman, S. G., Mann, L. H., & Risley, T. R. (1991). Use of classroom materials to promote preschool engagement. *Teaching Exceptional Children, 23*(4), 44–47.

McWilliams, R. A. (1991). Targeting teaching at children's use of time: Perspectives on preschoolers' engagement. *Teaching Exceptional Children, 23*(4), 42–43.

McWilliams, R. A., & Bailey, D. (1992). Promoting engagement and mastery. In D. B. Bailey & M. Wolery (Eds.), *Teaching infants and preschoolers with disabilities* (2nd ed., pp. 229–255). New York: Merrill.

Morris, S. (1977). *Program guidelines for children with feeding problems.* Edison, NJ: Childcraft.

Morris, S.E., & Klein, M. D. (1987). *Pre-feeding skills.* Tucson, AZ: Communication Skills Builders.

Neef, N. A., Parish, J. M., Hannigan, K. F., Page, T. J., & Iwata, B. (1989). Teaching self-catheterization skills to children with neurogenic bladder complications. *Journal of Applied Behavioral Analysis, 22,* 237–243.

Nisbet, J., Clark, M., & Covert, S. (1991). Living it up! An analysis of research on community living. In L. H. Meyers, C. A. Peck, & L. Brown (Eds.), *Critical issues in the lives of people with severe disabilities* (pp. 115–144). Baltimore: Brookes.

Nwaobi, O. M., & Smith, P. D. (1986). Effect of adaptive seating on pulmonary function of children with cerebral palsy. *Developmental Medicine and Child Neurology, 28,* 351–354.

O'Brien, S., Repp, A., Williams, G. E., & Christopherson, E. R. (1991). Pediatric feeding disorders. *Behavior Modification, 15,* 394–418.

Orelove, F. P., & Sobsey, D. (1991). *Educating children with multiple disabilities: A transdisciplinary approach* (2nd ed.). Baltimore: Brookes.

Peterson, N. (1987). *Early intervention for handicapped and at-risk children.* Denver, CO: Love.

Richmonds, G. (1983). Shaping bladder and bowel continence in developmentally retarded preschool children. *Journal of Autism and Developmental Disorders, 13,* 197–205.

Shelton,T. L., Jeppson, E. S., & Johnson, B. H. (1987). *Family-centered care for children with special health care needs.* Washington, DC: Association for the Care of Children's Health.

Simeonsson, R. J., Huntington, G. S., & Parse, S. A. (1980). Expanding the developmental assessment of young children. In J. Gallagher (Ed.), *New directions for exceptional children* (pp. 51–74). Washington, DC: Jossey-Bass.

Snell, M. E. (1993). *Instruction of students with severe disabilities* (4th ed.). New York: Merrill.

Sobsey, R. J. (1983). Nutrition of children with severely handicapping conditions. *Journal of the Association for Persons with Severe Handicaps, 8*(4), 14–17.

Stainback, S., Stainback, W., Healy, H., & Healy, J. (1980). Basic eating skills. In J. Umbriet & P. J. Cardullias (Eds.), *Educating the severely physically handicapped: Basic principles and techniques* (Vol. 1, pp. 16–30). Reston, VA: Council for Exceptional Children, Division for Physically Handicapped.

Thompson, T., & Hanson, R. (1983). Overhydration: Precautions when treating urinary incontinence. *Mental Retardation, 21,* 139–143.

Trefler, E., Westmoreland, D., & Burlingame, D. (1977). A feeding spatula for cerebralpalsied children. *American Journal of Occupational Therapy, 31,* 260–261.

Utley, B. L., Holvoet, J. F., & Barnes, K. (1977). Handling, positioning and feeding the physically handicapped. In E. Sontag, J. Smith, & N. Certo (Eds.), *Educational programming for the severely and profoundly handicapped* (pp. 279–299). Reston, VA: Council for Exceptional Children.

Whaley, K. T., & Bennett, T. C. (1991). Promoting engagement in early childhood special education. *Teaching Exceptional Children, 23*(4), 51–54.

Williamson, G. G. (1994). Assessment of adaptive competence. *Zero to Three, 14*(6), 28–33.

Zeitlin, S., & Williamson, G. G. (1994). *Coping in young children: Early intervention practices to enhance adaptive behavior and resilience.* Baltimore: Brookes.

Zeitlin, S., Williamson, G. G., & Szczepanski, M. (1988). *Early Coping Inventory.* Bensenville, IL: Scholastic Testing Service.

CHAPTER 12

Transition

Mary Beth Bruder
Lynette Chandler

Transition has been defined as an outcome-oriented process (Will, 1985), the key elements of which are planning and cooperation. A successful transition is a series of well-planned steps that result in the smooth placement and subsequent adjustment of the child and family into another setting (Hutinger, 1981).

Successful transitions are a primary goal of early intervention and early childhood special education (Fowler, 1982; McCormick & Kawate, 1982; Salisbury & Vincent, 1990). The importance of transition has been addressed in state and federal legislation, federal funding initiatives, and professional literature. Transition presents children and families with new opportunities for growth and development. Well-planned transitions can be an enabling and satisfying experience, and positive experiences with early transitions can set the pattern for future transitions (Diamond, Spiegel-McGill, & Hanrahan, 1988; Edgar, McNulty, & Goetz, 1984). However, transitions also present challenges and can create stress for both children and families. Poorly planned or unplanned transitions can be a time of vulnerability and uncertainty for children and families and may not result in a successful move to the new program. Needless to say, the type of planning and practices that are employed can influence the success of transition as well as the satisfaction with the transition process. In this chapter we present indicators of recommended practice that will help program administrators, program providers, and families prepare for transition. The practices that are described apply to the variety of transitions that may occur during the early childhood years.

TYPES OF TRANSITION

Within the field of early intervention and early childhood special education, transition can be defined as the process of moving from one program

---

Authorship of this chapter reflects alphabetical order as both authors contributed equally to the chapter.

to another, or from one service delivery mode to another (Chandler, 1992). Others have emphasized the dynamic process of transition. Children with disabilities in an education-sponsored program may also be enrolled in a childcare program or a community program such as Head Start or other preschool program, and transition may be a daily occurrence. Each of these programs may differ on a number of dimensions, and these differences only add to the potential for confusion, miscommunication, and lapses in service.

Unfortunately, many preservice training programs for those preparing to be service providers for young children with disabilities neglect to teach collaboration or team-process skills (Bailey, Palsha, & Huntington, 1990; Courtnage & Smith-Davis, 1987). As a result, the personnel who provide services to young children and their families may be operating independently of each other and thus creating additional transition points for families. These personnel may each represent different professional disciplines, service philosophies, and training requirements. For example, hospital and health professionals view early intervention very differently than do community-oriented agencies and professionals (Gilkerson, 1990). These differences can result in a lack of joint philosophy and teamwork in the transition of a child from a medical setting to home and community services. Families must be prepared to receive isolated information and assistance from a number of different staff. It seems reasonable to suggest that the effectiveness of any early childhood services depends on the ability of agencies, programs, and personnel to commit themselves to a collaborative model of service delivery in which transition points are mutually planned, implemented, and evaluated with the family.

INDICATORS OF RECOMMENDED PRACTICE

According to Wolery (1989), the transition process should fulfill four goals: (a) to ensure continuity of services, (b) to minimize disruptions to the family system by facilitating adaptation to change, (c) to ensure that children are prepared to function in the receiving program, and (d) to fulfill the legal requirements of federal legislation. In order for these goals to be achieved, it is necessary to plan for transition. The responsibility for transition planning should be shared across the sending and receiving programs and involve families. Transition procedures should assist families and their children. They should promote collaboration between members of the transition team: program staff and related personnel and families. Unfortunately, many programs and services have not adopted formal procedures to facilitate the transition of families and children either into or out of their programs, and programs that do address transition often focus on only one aspect or component of transition, such as the family, child preparation, or administrative issues. A primary assumption of this chapter is that transition efforts must be comprehensive, addressing multiple components during planning, implementation, and follow-up activities. In order to develop comprehensive, formal transition procedures, interventionists must address several components that influence the success of transition. These are (a) state and local agencies, (b) families and other caregivers, (c) sending and receiving programs, and (d) the children.

State and Local Agencies

Clearly few agencies have the resources to provide a total continuum of services that encompasses all the issues that may impinge upon a young child with disabilities and his or her family (Swan & Morgan, 1993). Therefore, agencies, programs, and staff must be prepared to cooperate and collaborate for the benefit of families, especially during service transitions. Effective transitions rely on proactive planning to ensure a smooth process. This planning must be comprehensive, and it must occur prior to a child's and his or her family's actually moving into or out of a new program. Planning for transition should occur both within (*intra*) and between (*inter*) agencies. A number of indicators have been identified as recommended practices during agency transition.

Interagency Agreements (T 1)

The development of cooperative arrangements among agencies (e.g., early intervention and community early childhood programs) is a common strategy that has been used to improve the existing service delivery structure (Shenet, 1982). Cooperative arrangements are required by many federal laws. The desired outcome of such arrangements is often the development of an interagency cooperative agreement. However, cooperative arrangements rarely result in improved services (Melaville & Blank, 1991). The reason is that cooperating agencies maintain their own autonomy as well as their own philosophy and service goals, and not all may be appropriate for the target population. Additional barriers have been identified that may impinge further on the successes of interagency models (Bruder & Bologna, 1993). Unfortunately, this model tends to drive most initial attempts to cooperatively provide services from more than one agency for young children with disabilities and their families.

In order to improve this situation, some have suggested that the focus of interagency agreements should shift from cooperative arrangements among agencies to collaborations focused on joint service delivery (Melaville & Blank, 1991). This collaboration requires the involved agencies to agree on a common philosophy and service goal that can be achieved only by joint agency activities. Thorough interagency planning will involve the development of interagency agreements that specify the roles and responsibilities of each agency, the composition of the transition team, the policies and procedures related to transition, and time lines for initiating and completing transition tasks. Interagency agreements will promote interagency cooperation and communication and should ensure the continuity of a child's program and the implementation of transition procedures as planned (Hains, Fowler, & Chandler, 1988). Effective interagency agreements must jointly address the needs of administrators, service providers, and families and ensure the coordination of services across and within agencies.

Formal Communication Mechanisms (T 2)

Communication has been described as both the giving and receiving of information through a variety of modes. Both aspects are important to facilitate effective transitions for children with disabilities and their families. Ongoing communication across and within agencies is inherent in any effective service delivery system (Swan & Morgan, 1993). Each agency involved in service delivery for young children with disabilities and their families should specify its lines of communication, both within the agency and with other agencies.

Agencies should be prepared to formally recognize the importance of communication by structuring meetings for staff and families on all aspects of transition. These meetings should focus on policy formation as well as on dissemination. Likewise, a variety of written communication strategies should be utilized both to give and to receive information. For example, brochures can be used to communicate the parameters of the agency's service model. Likewise, written satisfaction inventories can be used to recruit information to improve the agencies' services that affect transition. Transition inventories can also be available both to recruit and to give information to service providers and families on all aspects of service transitions. A common transition planning tool (across agencies) may be one mechanism to assure effective transitions for families and their children. Care should also be taken to ensure that both oral and written communication is available in a family's preferred language.

Time for Planning and Preparation (T 3)

Planning within and across agencies can help assure that program providers and families will have adequate time and resources to plan for transition and to complete transition tasks. It is a well-known fact that planning time is an elusive commodity for many in early intervention and early childhood special education. Yet, planning is an integral component of successful transitions. The time commitment for transition planning is essential to the process, and the commitment must encompass both the pre- and posttransition period.

Because it is acknowledged that time is such a premium, it is strongly recommended that time be used efficiently. This requirement usually means that time is structured by someone on the transition team to efficiently address transition planning, implementation, and evaluation tasks. The time commitment may vary from child to child and from service circumstance to service circumstance. The important variable is that time be adequate to address child and family needs. Time lines should be used to structure planning time, and all involved should be held accountable for utilizing planning time to ensure the child's and family's smooth transition.

Families and Other Caregivers

Parents of young children with disabilities rarely take on this parenting role with any amount of preparation for the special challenges they will face. Rather, the early days, weeks, and months of parental responsibility may be spent in a blur of visits to the hospital, physician's office, and special clinics, with little or no opportunity to adapt to the significant change that has taken place in their lives. Although most parents report an increase in the level of stress they perceive as a result of the birth of a child, the parents of a young child with multiple or severe disabilities must deal with unanticipated pressures and responsibilities that can make the parenting role appear to be overwhelming.

Just as the population of children who are considered to have special needs is not a homogeneous group, neither are the children's families. The early intervention professional serving young children with disabilities will no doubt work with a diversity of families who vary by cultural and economic conditions as well as by family structure (Lynch & Hanson, 1992; Vincent & Salisbury, 1988; Vincent, Salisbury, Strain, McCormick, & Tessier, 1990). Each family will bring unique resources to the task of parenting their child with special needs, and each family will identify unique needs that must be addressed through early intervention and early childhood special education.

An expanded focus on family systems theory has resulted in the recommendation that early intervention and early childhood special education programs move away from a narrow focus on the child and encompass the broader and self-identified needs of the enrolled parents (Blacher, 1984; Turnbull, Turnbull, Summers, Brotherson, & Benson, 1986). It has been suggested that the primary goal of early intervention and early childhood special education should be to facilitate the parents' awareness of and adaptation to the primary role of parenting a child with disabilities. Service delivery systems should focus on helping the family address the needs of the child through the continuum of service models and staffing patterns. This perspective represents a family-centered approach to intervention, which is based on the premise that the family is the enduring and central force in the life of the child and serves as the primary support for the child as he or she adapts to the demands of the environment. Transitions play a key role in the ability of families to adapt to the service delivery system. Therefore, a number of practices will facilitate their success with the system during times of transition.

Families Are Informed Early About Anticipated Transitions (T 4)

Families are rarely prepared for the birth of a child with a disability. Even when the child receives a diagnosis or lags in development after the newborn period, the news of the child's disability often takes a family by surprise. Compounding this surprise is the need for families to quickly adapt to an expanding definition of caregiving that includes a variety of new services and staff. Families often lack knowledge about service options and may lack knowledge about the service requirements of the various programs with which they may be involved (Rubin & Quinn-Curran, 1983). Both result in undue anxiety and stress on parents.

One way to ease a family's entry into and through the service delivery system is to provide information to the family as early as possible on the service system and the fluctuations within the system that will affect their child's service delivery (Lazzari, 1991). Parents will have more time to accommodate to the transitions required of them if practitioners include them in the planning process as early as possible (Hanline, 1988). This requirement also means that service agencies and staff are also aware of possible transitions as early as possible.

Families Can Initiate Transitions (T 5)

A family-centered approach ensures that services revolve around the families' priorities, resources, and concerns. Families may choose to alter the type, frequency, and duration of various services their child may be receiving, at any time. Families should be made aware of their right to request changes in service delivery, and they should be encouraged to feel comfortable in initiating any changes that result in a transition to another service model or staffing pattern.

Families Should Receive Comprehensive Information About the Transition Process (T 6)

The transition process demands that parents be given a great amount of information throughout the early intervention years. Parents need to be told in advance about the transitions their child will be participating in, what steps are involved, what their options are for involvement, and what time lines exist for the actual transition (Lazzari & Kilgo, 1989). Many parents will want to be the decision makers in terms of placement options and time lines. It is imperative that programs provide an abundance of information to parents, and this information should be distributed often to parents and in many different communication modes (e.g., brochures, workbooks, large meetings, individual home visits) in the families' preferred language (Lazzari, 1991).

Families Have Opportunities To Visit Program Options (T 7)

The selection and subsequent adjustment to a new service model is enhanced when families are encouraged to visit and learn about the service options (Chandler, 1992). Visits should allow time for the family to observe services adequately and to talk to the service providers. Parent-to-parent contact should also be facilitated as other parents often have unique insight into the drawbacks and benefits of program models (Bruder & Cole, 1991). Visits should be arranged at the convenience of the family, and transportation should be provided.

Families Jointly Meet with Sending and Receiving Providers (T 8)

In any transition, all involved persons must periodically meet to jointly plan, implement, and evaluate the process. Families must be a part of this process and be an integral component of any joint planning that occurs. The meetings that are used to structure this process must be available and accessible to the family and should revolve around the family's agenda, time lines, and priorities.

Program Providers Receive Adequate Training on Transitions and Families (T 9)

The family-centered approach requires interventionists to operate within a system that expands their usual method of practicing within their discipline's boundaries. In order to work with young children with disabilities, interventionists must be able to examine the resources, concerns, and priorities of a family; work with the child within the context of the family; communicate effectively with the family in order to establish collaborative goals for the child; and provide services to the entire family (which often involves service coordination skills). Along with these demands, family-centered service implies that parents and professionals have parallel positions on a team, with all parties bringing their expertise together to solve problems. Successful implementation of the family-centered approach to service delivery depends on a commitment to the family as the decision maker and a partner in the transition process (Hains et al., 1988).

Many service providers must redesign their perspective on the family's role in early intervention and early childhood special education. To accommodate this perspective, staff must have training and support by which they learn the skills required to collaborate effectively with families.

Single Point of Contact (T 10)

Historically, families have had to assume the role of service coordinators for their child (Hazel et al., 1988). Services have often been fragmented, disorganized, and difficult to access; and many families have been extremely frustrated by this situation. This frustration can be exacerbated during a transition point.

A strong recommendation, which is required by early intervention legislation, is the designation of a service coordinator to assist the family through the service maze. This person is key to effective transitions. A service coordinator, or single point of contact, during times of transition can help ensure that the family is able to participate actively in a productive collaborative process that views the child from the family's perspective (Bruder & Bologna, 1993). This coordination should alleviate confusion for the family and assist in the coordination of all aspects of the transition process.

Sending and Receiving Program Providers

"Sending" program providers work in the program the child is leaving; "receiving" providers work in the program to which the child is moving. In order for transition to be successful and for planning to be comprehensive, all team members must participate. The team includes program providers; the child, when applicable; and the child's family. The program providers' component includes individuals within programs and agencies that provide services to the child and family. Program providers may include home-based or classroom-based teachers and aides, physical and occupational therapists, speech and language pathologists, doctors, nurses, medical technicians and therapists, social workers, administrators, case managers or service coordinators, and parent coordinators.

Providers in both programs can facilitate the transition process by (a) preparing the child for transition and providing environmental supports to meet the child's needs during the transition process, (b) involving families and other caregivers in transition planning to the extent that families desire, (c) providing information concerning community resources and options for transition to families, and (d) working cooperatively as members of the transition team. Four indicators of recommended practice serve as guidelines to assist program providers in planning the types of tasks and activities that will maximize their participation in the transition process.

Service Providers Are Familiar with the Interagency Transition Agreement and Related Procedures (T 11)

Typically staff within the sending program are responsible for initiating the transition process and preparing the child and family for transition. Staff within the receiving program are responsible for providing supports to promote the child's adjustment and to assist the child's family when they enter the new program or services. Both sending and receiving program providers are responsible for assisting families in making decisions concerning transition (e.g., selecting program placement and child and family goals; identification of family concerns, priorities, and resources).

Many of the tasks that service providers are expected to complete will be identified on the interagency agreement and transition time line. Familiarity with the interagency agreement and timeline promotes cooperation and will ensure that program providers know the roles and tasks for which they and other providers are responsible. This knowledge should enable providers to anticipate transition-related activities and tasks that must be accomplished throughout the transition period. This will further help providers plan sufficient time in their schedules to design and implement transition-related activities.

Service Providers Are Familiar with Service Options and Resources (T 12)

An important function of service providers is to assist families and the transition team in making decisions about transition. The types of decisions that families and teams make will vary across different types of transitions (e.g., hospital to home, preschool to kindergarten). For example, some families may make decisions concerning the type and location of the program their child will attend (e.g., segregated or inclusive programs; home-based or center-based services). Other families may make decisions concerning the use of community resources, the frequency and type of intervention or educational service provided, their level of involvement in the program, and child and family goals. Regardless of the type of decisions to be made, providers can make the decision-making process easier if they are able to inform team members of the range of options and to identify positive features of each option (Fowler, 1982). This information will promote decisions that take into consideration the concerns and priorities of the family and that best meet the needs of the child.

In addition to being familiar with community and service or program options, providers also can provide information that will help families and other providers become informed members of the transition team. For example, service providers can inform families about child and family rights afforded under state and federal laws, discuss the terms *least restrictive* and *natural* environments, describe IEPs and IFSPs, discuss differences that may occur across programs, and share information concerning the transition process and transition time line.

Service Providers Visit Each Other's Programs and Share Observations (T 13)

One of the keys to collaboration is information sharing. Several types of information may be shared among team members, including child strengths and needs; family concerns, resources, and priorities; assessment results and previous program plans; program curricula and teaching practices, typical activities, and routines; physical layout of the environment (e.g., home or classroom setting); parent involvement opportunities; and expectations for skill development.

Sharing information and observing each other's programs can help providers identify the similarities and differences across programs. This approach has been termed "criterion of the next environment" (Vincent et al., 1980). With this approach, program providers and other team members observe each other's programs to identify differences in a variety of areas. For example, programs may differ in behavioral and developmental skill expectations, environmental supports, teaching strategies, rules and behavior management techniques, activities and routines, developmental philosophy, IEP or IFSP formats, and parent involvement options or expectations. Program providers then seek to minimize the differences between programs when possible and to prepare children to negotiate the differences in order to increase the probability that children will generalize adaptive behaviors across settings and function well during the transition period (Fowler, 1982; Salisbury & Vincent, 1990).

Knowledge of the differences between programs also can help families and other team members plan for some of the changes that will occur as a result of transition (Bruder & Walker, 1990; Johnson, Chandler, Kerns & Fowler, 1986). For example, parents can anticipate reduced (or increased) levels of parent–teacher contact and increased child–teacher ratios, prepare for different styles of caregiving, arrange for transportation and childcare, and inform other team members of concerns that may arise from the differences across programs that need to be addressed in planning (e.g., the child has never been on a bus before; the parents need to learn to use medical equipment, such as a ventilator).

Knowledge of each other's programs will help providers in the sending program identify transition skills that will facilitate the child's adjustment to the new program. These skills may be placed on the IEP or IFSP during the last year in the sending program as intervention focuses on the types of experiences and instruction that will promote child adjustment and successful functioning in the new program. When a child enters the receiving program, service providers may adjust expectations to reflect the requirements of the sending program; use familiar materials, teaching strategies, activities, and routines; and alter the physical environment to accommodate the child's adjustment during transition.

Team members can learn about each other's programs in several ways. They can visit each other's programs, observe each other's program when they are in session, share curricula and program plans, and exchange information through teacher interviews. An important part of learning about each other's programs is the sharing of information. Program providers should discuss their observations, impressions, and concerns and ask questions to clarify potential misconceptions. This interchange will promote collaboration and cooperation in planning, implementing, and evaluating the transition process.

Service Providers in the Receiving Programs Prepare Other Individuals for a Child's Transition (T 14)

One of the goals of early childhood special education is to prepare children for the next least restrictive environment (Vincent et al., 1980; Walter & Vincent, 1982). For many children, transition to a new program often involves placement in settings that include children of varying abilities. For example, a child may attend an inclusive preschool or kindergarten classroom, a community day-care center, or a reverse mainstreaming program that contains children with and without disabilities. An important part of transition is preparing children in the receiving program for the entrance of children with varying abilities into the program. This preparation can reduce the often noted lack of interaction that occurs between children of differing abilities. Activities to prepare children for transition generally have produced positive interaction and social acceptance among children (Odom & McEvoy, 1988).

Preparation activities may include (a) providing simulation activities (Raab, Nordquist, Cunningham, & Bleim, 1986); (b) providing information concerning children with disabilities, while emphasizing similarities between all children (Donder & York, 1984); (c) providing information about specific children entering a program, emphasizing strengths and abilities (Turnbull, Winton, Blacher, & Salkind, 1982); and (d) arranging the environment to promote cooperative social and academic activities (McEvoy et al., 1988; Sainato, Maheady, & Shook, 1986). Program providers must consider the developmental level of children when selecting and implementing preparation activities. Preparation activities will be most successful when they match the developmental level of children in the program. For example, simulation activities and group discussion may be appropriate for preschool and kindergarten children but may not be appropriate for infants and toddlers.

Preparation of other individuals in the receiving program also includes preparing family members (e.g., brothers and sisters, grandparents), caregivers (e.g., baby-sitter, home health care nurse) who may care for the child, and program staff who are not familiar with the child and family. In addition to the activities previously identified, receiving program providers may share information concerning the child's disability and the child's strengths, abilities, and needs; share information about the family's concerns, resources, and priorities; and train other individuals to conduct specific medical and caretaking tasks and developmental or educational activities.

The Child Component

The final component in the transition process is the child. Simply moving an infant or young child from one program to another will not guarantee success in the new program (Noonan & Kilgo, 1987). The success of transition is influenced by the skills and behaviors the child exhibits during transition and the match between child skills and behaviors and the expectations and requirements of the receiving program. This match depends, in part, on the preparation for transition provided by sending and receiving program providers, the family and other caregivers, and the environmental supports provided in the receiving program.

An important part of child preparation is the development of transition skills and the generalization of transition skills from the sending program to the receiving program (Chandler, 1992; Fowler, 1982). Transition skills are skills and behaviors that facilitate transition between programs by helping a child function well in and adjust to the next environment. Transition skills may include social behaviors and self-help skills, motivation and problem-solving skills, preacademic or academic support skills and task-related behaviors, conduct behaviors, and communication skills. Child preparation should focus on (a) the assessment of transition skills that are needed in the receiving program, (b) the development and implementation of methods to promote acquisition of these skills, (c) methods to promote the maintenance and generalization of transition skills as well as other skills and behaviors (e.g., academic skills, child strengths) to the new program, and (d) environmental arrangements or supports in the receiving program and methods to address difficulties when they occur.

The recommended practice indicators associated with child preparation can be divided into two phases: an assessment phase and a planning and intervention phase.

Assessment Phase Indicators (T 15, T 16)

The first step in assessment is to identify the transition skills that will facilitate the child's adjustment to the new program. Although children typically participate in a comprehensive evaluation prior to entrance into a new program, transition skills often are not assessed as part of this evaluation. For example, many of the transition skills identified as important for the transition from preschool to kindergarten are not included on traditional readiness tests or norm-referenced developmental assessments (Hains et al., 1988; McCormick & Kawate, 1982). Therefore, team members will need to identify the type of skills that will help the child cope with the demands of the new program and function well in a new setting.

The type of transition skills needed in receiving programs will vary across the type of program the child is entering (e.g., early intervention program, preschool, kindergarten). Transition skills that the child may need in the new program can be identified in several ways. Team members may consult professional literature for an indication of skills that have been identified as critical to transition (e.g., Chandler, 1993; Hains, Fowler, Schwartz, Kottwitz, & Rosenkoetter, 1989; Murphy & Vincent, 1989; Thompson, 1979). For example, Carden-Smith and Fowler (1983) and Walter and Vincent (1982) recommended that transition preparation focus on increasing skills that promote independence and on-task behaviors and decreasing inappropriate behaviors.

Team members also can observe each other's programs; share information; exchange curricula, program goals, and daily lesson plans; and identify the differences between programs in terms of environmental supports, teaching strategies, teacher requirements and expectations, and activities and routines. These activities will result in a list of transition skills that may be used in evaluating individual children and in developing individualized transition preparation goals.

The second step in assessment involves child evaluation. The team should identify, from the transition skills list, those skills that the child currently exhibits and those that the child does not exhibit or that may be partially mastered. They also may assess the conditions under which the child demonstrates transition skills (e.g., Does the child exhibit a skill in therapy but not in the classroom or at home?). The transition team may ask three questions when assessing transition skills: What will be different for the child in the new program? What skills does the child have that will be useful in the receiving program? What skills should the child learn before entering the new program? Answering these questions will help the team identify strengths that should be maintained and skills that should be addressed as part of the child's program plan (e.g., IEP or IFSP). It must be emphasized that transition skills lists are not to be used as "readiness criteria" to exclude children from placement. The purpose of identifying and assessing transition skills is to help prepare the child for transition; the lack of transition skills should not preclude placement in least restrictive or inclusive programs (Hains, 1992; Salisbury & Vincent, 1990).

Planning and Intervention Phase Indicators (T 17–T 22)

Once important transition skills have been identified, team members incorporate needed training and experiences into the child's program plan. All members of the team are responsible for preparing the child for transition. Child preparation may involve numerous activities: (a) teaching transition skills through adult-directed and child-directed activities or activity-based interventions (Bricker & Cripe, 1992); (b) arranging or adapting the sending and receiving classroom or other environments; (c) developing environmental and social supports in the sending and receiving programs; (d) adjusting expectations and requirements within programs; (e) arranging activities and routines to provide new experiences and opportunities; and (f) talking with the child about transition, identifying child preferences and opinions, and helping the child anticipate the transition.

Part H of IDEA requires early intervention programs to address transition as part of the IFSP when a child moves to preschool or other services. Transition preparation must include (a) procedures to prepare the child for transition, including strategies to help the child adjust to and function in the receiving program; (b) discussions with and training of families on issues related to transition; and (c) with parent consent, the transmission of information between agencies. Transition plans must be added to the IFSP at least 3 months prior to the child's third birthday.

The model provided by IDEA should be adopted by all sending and receiving programs. Transition planning should begin during the child's final year in the sending program and address child preparation, family involvement, and information sharing. The time needed to plan for and address child preparation will vary across programs and with the age of the child. For example, investigators have recommended that providers address preschool-to-kindergarten transitions 9–12 months prior to transition (Conn-Powers, Ross-Allen, & Holburn, 1990; Lazzari & Kilgo, 1989). This extended planning time may not be possible, however, when an infant moves from the hospital to home. These transitions often occur over shorter periods of time (e.g., several days or weeks, depending on the health of the child; Odom & Chandler, 1990). The critical factor in planning for transition is adequate time for the transition team to assess and address transition skill needs and to evaluate the child's adjustment to the new program.

Critical Issues to Enhance Transitions

The purpose of transition planning is to support the movement of children and families as they move from program to program or from service to service. In order to facilitate transitions, service providers and the agencies they work for must also address a number of other issues. These issues include administrative support for planning and implementation of transition activities, personnel training at the preservice and inservice level, and evaluation of the transition process.

Administrative Support for Planning

The success of transition planning largely depends on the support provided by program administrators. Administrators can influence the attitudes and commitment of transition team members by demonstrating their interest in and commitment to the transition process. They can coordinate interagency transition agreements, recognize the efforts of transition team members, provide inservice training, and promote interagency communication and cooperation (Chandler, 1991). Administrators also must support the efforts of staff by allocating time and resources necessary to conduct transition-related activities (Hains et al., 1988). For example, as part of planning for the transition, staff should be encouraged to visit both the sending and receiving programs in order to share information about similarities and differences between programs and to familiarize themselves with the requirements of each program. Time and resources for staff to visit programs and collaboratively plan for transition must be provided through administrative support and documented on interagency and intraagency transition plans.

Personnel Training

In order to address the need for comprehensive, successful transitions, personnel must be prepared to include transition as part of the intervention plan. Transition must be seen as a continuation of a child's intervention plan, and the intervention team must be able to develop, implement, and evaluate any transition involving the child and family. Staff must be skilled at curriculum development and adaptation, and they must be able to collaborate across programs and other disciplines.

These competencies should be incorporated into personnel training programs at both the preservice and inservice levels and within discipline-specific training (e.g., for nurses and speech and language pathologists). Training at an inservice level (i.e., within an agency or between sending and receiving programs) should focus on general issues related to transition planning as well as on the specific skills, tasks, and processes that staff will be expected to employ. Administrators may determine inservice topics by identifying the skills needed to conduct transition activities and by assessing the skill level, interests, and needs of transition team members (Stephens, 1991).

At a preservice level, personnel training should focus on general issues and recommended practices related to all types of transition as well as on models and options for transitions that may occur at various points in a child's life and across a variety of programs. This training becomes especially important when programs differ with respect to educational environments, parent involvement, intervention practices, service options, and regulations concerning eligibility for services (Fowler, Hains, & Rosenkoetter, 1990). Preservice students should be familiar with issues that are important in making a transition (a) from hospital services to the home, early intervention program, and community services; (b) from early intervention programs to preschool or other services; and (c) from preschool to kindergarten programs and other services. They should also be familiar with issues surrounding other types of transition that may occur during the early childhood years (e.g., between service providers within a program).

Evaluation of the Transition Process

Evaluation of the effectiveness of the transition process is often the weakest part of the transition plan. Yet, evaluation of the transition process has been recognized as one of the most important measures in early childhood special education programs (Noonan & Kilgo, 1987). Evaluation should occur within each transition component and should include both formative (continuous) and summative (summary) measures. All members of the transition team, including administrators, should be involved in transition evaluation.

Evaluation should include a follow-up component in which the team reviews the child's and family's adjustment after the child has moved to the receiving program. This review should occur within the first few weeks or months of the child's movement to the next program. During follow-up evaluation, the transition team should determine whether or not transition is progressing smoothly, and if it is not, they can provide support to address problems that are occurring. Follow-up evaluation supports the efforts of the transition team to prepare the child for transition and continues to address the goal of promoting successful transitions.

Evaluation should include objective as well as subjective measures. Objective measures may include information such as the number of transition skills exhibited by the child, the supports provided in the receiving program, and maintenance of the child and family in the receiving program. Evaluation also should include subjective measures such as parent and teacher satisfaction with and perception of the transition process. The success of transition usually is indicated when the transition team agrees that the child and family have adjusted well to the new program. The specific beginning and end points of transition may differ for each child and family (Odom & Chandler, 1990). Subjective information from transition participants will complement objective information concerning transition and provide social validation of the transition process from the perspective of program consumers (Schwartz & Baer, 1991).

Evaluation also should be multidimensional, addressing all aspects of the transition process within and between agencies, within and between sending and receiving programs, and within and across individual children and families. Information obtained from evaluation may be used to revise transition time lines, interagency agreements, child preparation activities, and other aspects or components of the transition plan.

FUTURE DIRECTIONS: COLLABORATIVE SERVICE MODELS

Part H of IDEA mandates that many agencies work together to develop joint activities focused on the development of collaborative early intervention services (Trohanis, 1989). A logical extension of this mandate is the adoption of such service requirements for all children, regardless of disability (Kagan, 1991), and through the early childhood years. This extension would require communities to coalesce around early childhood service delivery. The challenge would be to identify the various agencies, professionals, and payment sources currently involved in the provision of early childhood services. Although interagency and cross-disciplinary collaboration would be the first step toward alleviating formal transition points for children and families, the ultimate goal would be a seamless system of service delivery that fluctuates around a family and child's needs rather than a system of artificially imposed transitions reflective of agency jurisdiction.

There are many benefits to collaborative service delivery models (Elder & Magrab, 1980). Most important is an improvement in service delivery to the target population. Improvement occurs as a result of more efficient and effective use of services, providers, and funding streams across agencies (Audette, 1980; Bailey, 1984). These models also result in a reduction in service duplication (Garland & Linder, 1988; Healy, Keesee, & Smith, 1989). Collaborative models enable parents and service providers to efficiently locate and manage the necessary services required by the family (Bailey, 1989; Dunst, Trivette, & Deal, 1988). Last, collaborative models eliminate the need for formal transitions, because services are integrated, comprehensive, and longitudinal.

Unfortunately, the development of collaborative early childhood service systems remains an elusive goal for many states. This situation is not surprising because the service delivery system is composed of independent agencies, institutions, and organizations, each providing a specific service or function. As a result, each participating service agency provider has its own orientation toward the service system; these orientations thus create the need for transition points for families and their children.

A collaborative model would not, however, negate the need for the recommended practices cited in this chapter. Many of the practices reflect effective service delivery principles that will, in fact, facilitate the movement of children and families within a seamless, collaborative service model. The challenge facing the field is to redefine service priorities to support families and their children as they make choices in service delivery reflective of their needs.

CLOSING

Transition is a passage from one program or service to another. Transition is a process. It is not meant to be a quick, short act; rather it should be a series of steps across time that require planning, implementation, and evaluation (Bruder, 1988; Lazzari & Kilgo, 1989; Stephens, 1991). A successful transition requires time and effort and depends on the commitment of team members to the process and to the children and families. A comprehensive plan for transition should encompass the following four components: state and local agencies, sending and receiving program providers, family and other caregivers, and the child. In addition, a comprehensive plan should address issues related to program evaluation, personnel training, and administrative support.

REFERENCES

Audette, R. H. (1980). Interagency collaboration. In J. Elder & P. Magrab (Eds.), *Coordinating services to handicapped children* (pp. 25–45). Baltimore: Brookes.

Bailey, D. (1984). A triaxial model of the interdisciplinary team and group process. *Exceptional Children, 51*(1), 17–25.

Bailey, D. (1989). Issues and directions in preparing professionals to work with young handicapped children and their families. In J. Gallagher, P. Trohanis, & R. Clifford (Eds.), *Policy implementation and P.L. 99-457: Planning for young children with special needs* (pp. 97–132). Baltimore: Brookes.

Bailey, D., Palsha, S., & Huntington, G. (1990). Preservice preparation of special education to serve infants with handicaps and their families: Current status and training needs. *Journal of Early Intervention, 14*(1), 43–54.

Blacher, J. (1984). *Severely handicapped young children and their families.* Orlando, FL: Academic Press.

Bricker, D., & Cripe, J. (1992). *An activity-based approach to early intervention.* Baltimore: Brookes.

Bruder, M. B. (Ed.). (1988). *Transition practices in early childhood for Connecticut.* Farmington, CT: Author.

Bruder, M., & Bologna, T. (1993). Collaboration and service coordination for effective early intervention. In W. Brown, S. K. Thurman, & L. Pearl (Eds.), *Family-centered early intervention with infants and toddlers: Innovative crossdiscipline approaches* (pp. 103–127). Baltimore: Brookes.

Bruder, M., & Cole, M. (1991). Critical elements of transition from NICU to home and follow-up. *Children's Health Care, 20*(1), 40–49.

Bruder, M., & Walker, L. (1990). Discharge planning: Hospital to home transitions for infants. *Topics in Early Childhood Special Education, 9*(4), 26–42.

Carden-Smith, L., & Fowler, S. A. (1983). An assessment of student and teacher behavior in treatment and mainstreamed classes for preschool and kindergarten. *Analysis and Intervention in Developmental Disabilities, 3,* 35–57.

Chandler, L. K. (1991). Strategies to promote physical, social, and academic integration in mainstream kindergarten programs. In G. Stoner, M. R. Shinn, & H. M. Walker (Eds.), *Interventions for achievement and behavior problems* (pp. 305–331). Washington, DC: National Association of School Psychologists.

Chandler, L. K. (1992). Promoting young children's social competence as a strategy for transition to mainstreamed kindergarten program. In S. L. Odom, S. R. McConnell, & M. A. McEvoy (Eds.), *Social competence of young children with disabilities* (pp. 245–276). Baltimore: Brookes.

Chandler, L. K. (1993). Steps in preparing for transition: Preschool to kindergarten. *Teaching Exceptional Children, 25,* 52–55.

Conn-Powers, M. C., Ross-Allen, J., & Holburn, S. (1990). Transition of young children into the elementary education mainstream. *Topics in Early Childhood Special Education, 9*(4), 92–105.

Courtnage, L., & Smith-Davis, J. (1987). Interdisciplinary team training: A national survey of special education teacher training programs. *Exceptional Children, 53*(5), 451–458.

Diamond, K., Spiegel-McGill, P., & Hanrahan, P. (1988). Planning for school transition. An ecological–developmental approach. *Journal of the Division for Early Childhood, 12,* 245–252.

Donder, D. D., & York, R. (1984). Integration of students with severe handicaps. In N. Certo, N. Haring, & R. York (Eds.), *Public school integration of severely handicapped students: Rationale, issues and progressive alternatives* (pp. 1–14). Baltimore: Brookes.

Dunst, C., Trivette, C., Davis, M., & Weeldreyer, J. (1988). Enabling and empowering families of children with health impairments. *Children's Health Care, 17,* 71–81.

Dunst, C., Trivette, C., & Deal, A. (1988). *Enabling and empowering families: Principles and guidelines for practice.* Cambridge: Brookline Books.

Edgar, E., McNulty, B., & Goetz, J. (1984). Educational placement of graduates of preschool programs for handicapped children. *Topics in Early Childhood Special Education, 4*(3), 19–29.

Elder, J., & Magrab, P. (1980). *Coordinating services to handicapped children: A handbook for interagency collaboration.* Baltimore: Brookes.

Fowler, S. A. (1982). Transition from preschool to kindergarten for children with special needs. In K. E. Allen & E. M. Goetz (Eds.), *Early childhood education: Special problems, special solutions* (pp. 309–330). Rockville, MD: Aspen.

Fowler, S. A., Hains, A.H., & Rosenkoetter, S. (1990). The transition between early intervention services and preschool services: Administrative and policy issues. *Topics in Early Childhood Special Education, 9*(4), 55–65.

Garland, C., & Linder, T. (1988). Administrative challenges in early intervention. In J. Jordan, J. Gallagher, P. Hutinger, & M. Kames (Eds.), *Early childhood special education: Birth to three* (pp. 5–27). Reston, VA: Council for Exceptional Children.

Gilkerson, L. (1990). Understanding institutional functioning style: A resource for hospital and early intervention collaboration. *Infants and Young Children, 2*(3), 22–30.

Hains, A. H. (1992). Strategies for preparing preschool children with special needs for the kindergarten mainstream. *Journal of Early Intervention, 16,* 320–333.

Hains, A. H., Fowler, S. A., & Chandler, L. K. (1988). Planning school transitions: Family and professional collaboration. *Journal of the Division of Early Childhood, 12*(2), 108–115.

Hains, A., Fowler, S. A., Schwartz, I., Kottwitz, E., & Rosenkoetter, S. (1989). A comparison of preschool and kindergarten teacher expectations for school readiness. *Early Childhood Research Quarterly, 4,* 75–88.

Hanline, M. F. (1988). Making the transition to preschool: Identification of parents' needs. *Journal of the Division for Early Childhood, 12,* 98–107.

Hazel, R., Barber, P. A., Roberts, S., Behr, S., Helmsetter, E., & Guess, D. (1988). *A community approach to an integrated service system for children with special needs.* Baltimore: Brookes.

Healy, A., Keesee, P. D., & Smith, B. S. (1989). *Early services for children with special needs: Transactions for family support.* Baltimore: Brookes.

Hutinger, P. L. (1981). Transition practices for handicapped young children: What the experts say. *Journal of the Division for Early Childhood, 2,* 8–14.

Johnson, R. J., Chandler, L. K., Kerns, G., & Fowler, S. A. (1986). What are parents saying about family involvement in school transitions? A retrospective transition interview. *Journal of the Division for Early Childhood, 11,* 10–17.

Kagan, S. (1991). *United we stand: Collaboration for child care and early intervention and education services.* New York: Teachers' College Press.

Lazzari, A. M. (1991). *The transition sourcebook: A practical guide for intervention programs.* Tucson, AZ: Communication Skill Builders.

Lazzari, A. M., & Kilgo, J. L. (1989). Practical methods for supporting parents in early transitions. *Teaching Exceptional Children, 22*(1), 40–43.

Lynch, E., & Hanson, M. (1992). *Developing cross-cultural competence: A guide for working with young children and their families.* Baltimore: Brookes.

McCormick, L., & Kawate, J. (1982). Kindergarten survival skills: New directions for preschool special education. *Educating and Training the Mentally Retarded, 17,* 247–252.

McEvoy, M. A., Nordquist, V. M., Twardosz, S., Heckaman, K. A., Wehby, J. H., & Denny, R. K. (1988). Promoting autistic children's peer interaction in an integrated early childhood setting using affection activities. *Journal of Applied Behavior Analysis, 21,* 193–200.

Melaville, A. I., & Blank, M. J. (1991). *What it takes: Structuring interagency partnerships to connect children and families with comprehensive services.* Washington, DC: Education and Human Services Consortium.

Murphy, M., & Vincent, L. J. (1989). Identification of critical skills for success in day care. *Journal of Early Intervention, 13*(3), 221–229.

Noonan, M., & Kilgo, J. (1987). Transition services for early age individuals with severe mental retardation. In R. Ianacone & R. Stodden (Eds.), *Transition issues and directions* (pp. 25–37). Reston, VA: The Council for Exceptional Children.

Odom, S. L., & Chandler, L. K. (1990). Transition to parenthood for parents of infants with chronic health care needs. *Topics in Early Childhood Special Education, 9*(4), 43–54.

Odom, S. L., & McEvoy, M. A. (1988). Integration of young children with handicaps and normally developing children. In S. L. Odom & M. B. Kames (Eds.), *Early intervention for infants and children with handicaps* (pp. 241–267). Baltimore: Brookes.

Raab, M. M., Nordquist, V. M., Cunningham, J. L., & Bleim, C. D. (1986). Promoting peer regard of an autistic child in a mainstreamed preschool using pre-enrollment activities. *Child Study Journal, 16*(4), 265–284.

Rubin, S., & Quinn-Curran, N. (1983). Lost, then found: Parents' journey through the community service maze. In M. Seligman (Ed.), *The family with a handicapped child: Understanding and treatment* (pp. 63–94). New York: Grune & Stratton.

Sainato, D. M., Maheady, L., & Shook, G. L. (1986). The effects of a classroom manager role on the social interaction patterns and social status of withdrawn kindergarten students. *Journal of Applied Behavior Analysis, 19*, 187–195.

Salisbury, C. L., & Vincent, L. J. (1990). Criterion of the next environment and best practices: Mainstreaming and integration 10 years later. *Topics in Early Childhood Special Education, 10*(2), 78–79.

Schwartz, I. L., & Baer, D. M. (1991). Social validity assessments: Is current practice state of the art? *Journal of Applied Behavior Analysis, 24*(2), 189–204.

Shenet, M. A. (1982). *State education coordination efforts: Summary* (Project Report No. 1449). Washington, DC: Urban Institute.

Stephens, P. (1991). *Early childhood transition*. Lexington: University of Kentucky, Interdisciplinary Human Development Institute.

Swan, W. W., & Morgan, J. L. (1993). *Collaborating for comprehensive services for young children and their families*. Baltimore: Brookes.

Thompson, B. (1979). *Out of the nest: Instructional strategies to prepare young exceptional children for the mainstream*. Madison, WI: Department of Public Instruction.

Trohanis, P. L. (1989). An introduction to P.L. 99-457 and the national policy agenda for services to young children with special needs and their families. In J. J. Gallagher, P. L. Trohanis, & R. M. Clifford (Eds.), *Policy implementation and P.L. 99-457* (pp. 1–18). Baltimore: Brookes.

Turnbull, A., Turnbull, H., Summers, J., Brotherson, M., & Benson, H. (1986). *Families, professionals, and exceptionality: A special partnership*. Columbus, OH: Merrill.

Turnbull, A. P., Winton, P. J., Blacher, J., & Salkind, N. (1982). Mainstreaming in the kindergarten classroom: Perspectives of parents of handicapped and nonhandicapped children. *Journal of the Division for Early Childhood, 6*, 14–20.

Vincent, L., & Salisbury, C. (1988). Changing economic and social influences on family involvement. *Topics in Early Childhood Special Education, 8*(1), 48–59.

Vincent, L., Salisbury, C., Strain, P., McCormick, K., & Tessier, A. (1990). A behavioral–ecological approach to early intervention: Focus on cultural diversity. In S. Meisels & J. Shonkoff (Eds.), *Handbook of early intervention* (pp. 173–195). London, England: Cambridge University Press.

Vincent, L. J., Salisbury, C., Walter, G., Brown, P., Grunewald, L. J., & Powers (1980). Program evaluation and curriculum development in early childhood special education. In W. Sailor, B. Wilcox, & L. Brown (Eds.), *Methods of instruction for severely handicapped students* (pp. 303–328). Baltimore: Brookes.

Walter, G., & Vincent, L. J. (1982). The handicapped child in the regular kindergarten program. *Journal of the Division for Early Childhood, 6*, 82–95.

Will, M. (1985). Transitioning: Linking disabled youth to a productive future. *OSERS, News in Print, 51*, 11–16.

Wolery, M. (1989). Transition in early childhood special education: Issues and procedures. *Focus on Exceptional Children, 22*, 1–16.

CHAPTER 13

Early Childhood Education of Children Who Are Gifted

Stephen W. Stile

According to Gallagher (1988), one of the first priorities in a national agenda to counter American ambivalence toward addressing the educational needs of gifted students should be provision of services to various subgroups of gifted children who are presently underserved. In his words,

> The *underserved gifted* [italics added] are those students receiving limited or no special services in the schools, such as the underachievers, gifted handicapped students, culturally diverse students, very young gifted children, and gifted girls. The potential of such students may often be lost to themselves, and to us all, and we will probably need special policy initiatives beyond current efforts to find these special students and to provide quality educational programs for them. (p. 113)

Gallagher's identification of young gifted children as an underserved subgroup was recently validated in a national survey conducted by Stile, Kitano, Kelley, and LeCrone (1993). In this study, only 51 gifted preschool programs were reported by early childhood coordinators in 14 states and Guam. Although small, this number *does* represent an increase since 1981, when 18 gifted preschool programs were identified (Karnes, Shwedel, & Linnemeyer, 1981). Although over 2,655 kindergarten programs for gifted children were reported by the respondents in the Stile et al. (1993) survey, no gifted kindergarten programs were reported in 21 states. Again, Guam was the only territory that reported a kindergarten-level program.

What explains this lack of services for young children who are gifted? According to Kitano and Kirby (1986), opponents of identification and programming for these children have argued that (a) "hurrying" young children is potentially damaging, (b) standardized intelligence measures have lower reliability for these children, and (c) a potential exists for misidentification of children who are "early bloomers" rather than "truly gifted." As a result of such opposition, many school districts systematically delay identification and services until as late as the third or fourth grade. This delay is unfortunate because many gifted children can be identified at the preschool level (Silverman, 1988). According to Shaklee (1992), the practice of relatively late identification appears to have been maintained in school districts despite substantial research evidence that the optimal years for child development in such areas as self-esteem and self-image, social competence, specific cognitive abilities, and achievement motivation are birth through 8 years. Shaklee (1992) summarized the problem: "While it is not clear how many young gifted students we never identify or appropriately serve, it is clear that schools often fail to motivate and develop the talents of many young children who could benefit from alternative instructional or environmental plans" (p. 135).

However, despite opposition, a number of authorities in the field of gifted education have recently emphasized the *benefits* of early intervention. First, early recognition can provide opportunities for professionals and parents to interact on issues of development and advocacy (Karnes et al., 1981). Second, enriched preschool programs provide opportunities for young children to nurture their high potential and to demonstrate strengths (Kitano, 1990). Third, early recognition and nurturance of talents may foster children's mental health (Karnes & Johnson, 1991). Fourth, early childhood programs have been viewed as the best policy initiative for disadvantaged youth (VanTassel-Baska, Patton, & Prillaman, 1989). Fifth, prevention of underachievement among students who are gifted may be accomplished in part by early identification and placement in challenging preschool and kindergarten programs (Kitano & Kirby, 1986).

Although other chapters in this book describe recommended practices in 13 domains across disability groupings, this chapter provides recommended practices for working with young children with giftedness across the 13 domains. Therefore, this chapter includes the following sections: assessment, IFSPs and IEPS, service delivery model and environment, general curriculum and intervention strategies, interventions to promote communication development, interventions to promote motor development, interventions to promote cognitive development, interventions to promote social–emotional development, interventions to promote adaptive behavior and independence, transition, personnel competence, program evaluation, and family participation.

RECOMMENDED PRACTICES

Assessment

According to Bailey and Wolery (1989), "assessment may be defined as the process of gathering information for the purpose of making a decision" (p. 2). Bailey and Wolery provided the following guidelines for effective assessment programs for young exceptional children: "An effective assessment component (a) covers important domains, (b) involves parents as significant partners in the assessment process, (c) incorporates multiple sources and multiple measures, (d) involves multiple disciplines in an interdisciplinary fashion, (e) is ecologically valid, (f) is non-discriminatory, and (g) evaluates child progress on a regular basis" (1989, p. 8).

As Gregory (1984–1985) traced it, sole dependence on individual intelligence testing to identify giftedness has yielded over time to a call for multiple criteria. Among additional instruments and approaches described in the early childhood gifted literature reflecting this trend are naturalistic observations (e.g., videotaped) of sample behaviors at regular intervals; questionnaires and checklists used singly or in combination; anecdotal reports on the child's development compiled by parents; nominations from significant others in the community including peers, teachers, and parents; standardized tests of achievement, perceptual–motor functioning, creativity, and critical thinking; and curriculum placement as a means to observe and assess skills and abilities (Davis & Rimm, 1994; Karnes & Johnson, 1989, 1991); Karnes, Shwedel, & Kemp, 1985; Kitano & Kirby, 1986; Shaklee, 1992; Stile & Kitano, 1991; Wolfle, 1989).

Overreliance on single standardized IQ measures has seriously underidentified giftedness in young children from disadvantaged and minority backgrounds (Feldhusen, 1989; Hardman, Drew, Egan, & Wolf, 1990; Karnes, 1988; Karnes & Johnson, 1989; Shaklee, 1992). Promising practices for identifying young children from culturally diverse and economically disadvantaged backgrounds include the developmental curriculum (Richert, 1985); portfolio assessment (Barbour, 1992; Shaklee, 1992); assessment of learning potential, or *dynamic assessment* (Lidz, 1983); approaches that apply Gardner's (1983) theory of multiple/semiautonomous intelligences (Kitano, 1990); and adaptive behavior assessments (Hardman et al., 1990).

Upon completion of his research on early signs of giftedness, Tannenbaum (1992) concluded, "Giftedness in young children is a treasure waiting to be fully uncovered. The probes made thus far promise an abundance of riches, if more efforts are invested in this enterprise. One can only hope that past probers will usher in future uncoverers, because the prizes which still lie hidden may well prove to be priceless" (p. 129).

IFSPs and IEPs

Once children are found eligible and are placed, ongoing assessment may be conducted to determine strengths, weaknesses, and interests to achieve a *differentiated curriculum* (Karnes et al., 1985; Karnes, Shwedel, & Williams, 1983). Wolfle (1989) suggested the use of a combination of checklists that describe specific characteristics of young children for this purpose. As Khatena (1992) has observed, individualizing programs is a long-standing tradition in gifted education. However, Silverman (1988) has pointed out that this level of assessment is still relatively rare in programs for the gifted: "The potential exists within the identification process for assessing specific needs of these students but unfortunately the information gathered in the identification process is commonly ignored in future programming" (p. 272).

With passage of such legislation as the Education of All Handicapped Children Act of 1975 (EHA) amended by the Individuals with Disabilities Education Act of 1990 (IDEA), the process of individualizing has become more systematic. These laws require IEPS and individualized transition plans (ITPs) for school-aged children and youth. Although gifted students are not covered by these laws, state regulations that derive from them often recommend or require IEPs for gifted students (Kitano & Kirby, 1986). The Education of the Handicapped Act Amendments of 1986 (P.L. 99-457) extends the mandates of EHA and IDEA to infants and toddlers (ages birth through 2 years) with disabilities and their families and requires development of IFSPs. IFSPs are now an option in preschool programs serving students with disabilities.

Several advantages of developing IEPs or IFSPs for gifted students have been identified in the literature (Feldhusen, 1989; Khatena, 1992; Kitano & Kirby, 1986; Seeley, 1989; Strom, Johnson, Strom, & Strom, 1992; Turbiville, Turnbull, Garland, & Lee, 1993). According to these writers, the IEP or IFSP process treats children as total persons because it requires observations by interdisciplinary teams across multiple domains; serves the community better by involving families in the decision-making process; gives families an opportunity to choose their level of decision making; allows for programmatic reflection of family cultural, linguistic, and religious diversity; and provides for different learning outcomes based on individual needs (e.g., upgrading the level and pace of instruction, using strengths to compensate for weak areas).

However, Khatena (1992) and Kitano and Kirby (1986) expressed concern that some educators may mistake individualization of learning for unnecessary structure. As Kitano and Kirby (1986) stated,

> IEP guidelines developed for the handicapped are appropriate, with modifications, to gifted students. The major modification concerns the amount of flexibility in the stated instructional objectives. Educating handicapped learners requires specific, precise, quantitatively stated objectives (for example, "Given a nickel, a dime, a quarter, and a penny, the student will identify the nickel with 100% accuracy over four consecutive trials"). In contrast, appropriate objectives for gifted learners are open-ended and flexible to allow for the spontaneous changes and developments that

should occur continuously throughout the year (for example, "The student will identify and pursue one interest area in depth"). (p. 159)

Service Delivery Model and Environment

Davis and Rimm (1994) have organized service delivery models into three categories of grouping options within which activities may be enriched (e.g., field trips) or accelerated (e.g., early admission to kindergarten)—to fit the needs and characteristics of children. The categories and options are as follows:

1. Full-time homogeneous classes
    Magnet schools
    Special schools for the gifted
    Private schools
    School-within-a-school plans
    Special classes in the elementary school

2. Full-time heterogeneous classes
    Combined grades in a regular class
    Cluster groups of gifted students placed with regular students
    Mainstreaming in the regular class

3. Part-time or temporary groups
    Pullout programs
    Resource room plans
    Special classes
    Activity clubs
    Honors programs (pp. 136–137)

Although several of these options may be inappropriate for very young children, others, such as private schools, have been used successfully. Whatever option is chosen, the learning environment should be made as rich and as stimulating as possible to take advantage of the critical periods of the first 4 through 5 years of life during which development is most rapid. Barbara Clark (1992) has described this period:

> The personality established *and* the type of learning opportunities available will facilitate or inhibit the development of inherited intellectual capacity. Again we have the choice. We may either plan to provide the most nourishing environment that is possible within our current knowledge, or we may allow this important interaction to occur by chance. Regardless of how we choose to approach these formative years, interaction will occur and intelligence will develop. Whether that development leads to actualization or loss of human potential depends on us. (p. 73)

DEC-recommended practices to foster such an environment include well-defined areas (G 16); use of a large variety of developmentally appropriate activities and materials (G 17); clear, consistent cues (G 18); and child-sized furniture (G 19).

General Curriculum and Intervention Strategies

In their discussion of curriculum for gifted education programs, Kitano and Kirby (1986) defined curriculum as "a comprehensive educational plan designed to maximize instructional interactions in achieving and potentiating behavior change" (p. 128). This definition implies that curriculum development for young gifted children is a long-term process of planning experiences that address unique needs of this population, not merely listings of specific, identified program elements such as daily lesson plans. The New Mexico State University (NMSU) Preschool for the Gifted, for example, attempts to capitalize on student characteristics, such as precocious thinking and advanced interests, by selecting broad social studies topics such as ecology around which enjoyable, high-interest activities may be organized. For example, divergent thinking may be encouraged by asking children to name different ways (as suggested by Gallagher & Gallagher, 1994) empty egg cartons, paper bags, crayon stubs, and pencil shavings can be reused.

Because structured, homogeneous groupings such as NMSU's preschool program are the exception rather than the rule, the present discussion of curriculum for young gifted children must also include curricular adaptations for heterogeneous groupings such as day care and kindergarten programs in which gifted children are included. For example, Karnes and Johnson (1991) suggested that staff members can accommodate gifted students in such programs by employing strategies such as (a) teacher questioning to help explore additional facets of an issue, (b) use of specific projects to provide increased focus, (c) providing differentiated instruction within curriculum units (e.g., exploring *unusual* aspects), and (d) providing access to microcomputers to enable gifted students to create their own stories or to engage in problem solving.

Parents of young gifted children can also become involved in instruction. This involvement might take place for children before they enter an early childhood program or after they begin a program in order to complement school-based curricular activities. Davis and Rimm (1994) have recently pointed out that research clearly supports early language experience at home as the most critical type of involvement: "Talking to children, reading and telling stories, rhyming and imitation, word games, children's records, and even simply listening to children all increase the children's opportunities to learn communication and attention skills" (p. 385).

Interventions to Promote Communication Development

Communication is the transfer of messages between senders and receivers. Although the primary method for communication in our society is oral, other processes are also employed. For example, messages may be transmitted via (a) nonverbal signals such as flicking lights to achieve attention; (b) vocal (speech) symbols; (c) written symbols (e.g., letters of the alphabet); and (d) sign language, which employs gestural symbols (Smith & Luckasson, 1992). Language may be thought of as the rules that govern use of these signals and symbols.

In his *Creative Child and Adult*, Torrance (1979) held that creative individuals need opportunities to communicate in acceptable ways: "The curriculum at any educational level or in any subject has possibilities for providing creative persons exciting and rewarding outlets. The need to communicate creative ideas and discoveries seems to be a natural and strong need and is especially powerful in creative children and adults" (p. 370).

According to Kitano and Kirby (1986), "effective communication requires several different skills: articulating orally and in writing one's feelings and ideas, recognizing and interpreting the feelings and expressions of others, and understanding visual cues" (p. 258). They suggested inclusion of these skills in a curriculum designed to enhance leadership development. In their words, "all gifted and talented students, not just those with obvious leadership potential, should receive leadership training because all fields of human endeavor require effective leaders" (p. 256). Communication skills may also be used to foster development in other domains. For example, Meador (1992) identified several experiments conducted with gifted preschoolers that successfully employed language to facilitate creativity.

Feldhusen and VanTassel-Baska (1989) have noted that gifted children are often described as children who communicate well. Among common identifiers of giftedness are "early word recognition and reading, rapid and easy learning, large vocabulary, ability to deal with complex and abstract concepts, verbal expressiveness, voracious reading, and precocious reading comprehension" (Feldhusen & VanTassel-Baska, 1989, p. 219). Similarly, Silverman (1988) has noted that "advanced language development is the most frequently mentioned characteristic in young gifted children" (p. 269). In her view, young gifted children need opportunities to develop *strengths* (e.g., in the communication domain) rather than participating in programs where they are required to learn in the same manner as others their age. However, according to Feldhusen and Van Tassel-Baska (1989), the clear orientation of gifted education toward verbal giftedness might have led to a perception that gifted education programs overemphasize language arts while neglecting mathematics and science areas of the curriculum.

Communication interventions for young children who are gifted involve professionals who participate with children as "colearners" in activities (G 39). These interactions are designed to foster exploration of different ways of communicating (e.g., signing; G 37); encourage communication among peers and classmates with typical or atypical development throughout the day (G 38); and provide opportunities to exchange ideas, express opinions, and tell about feelings (G 33).

Interventions to Promote Motor Development

Motor development refers to the process of acquiring the necessary postural control and movement components to perform purposeful volitional movements (Bailey & Wolery, 1989). Motor advances appear to follow an orderly plan. As described by Shirley (1959), during the first 2 years, infants and toddlers first gain control of the upper trunk. Later, control moves downward to involve the entire trunk region. Still later, locomotion is observed, postural control of the entire body is completed, and standing and walking emerge. Development in the motor domain can be assessed beginning in infancy. In turn, motor interventions based on careful assessments can result in achievement of motor milestones such as sitting or running, which are results of combining and recombining components.

According to Clark (1988), although gifted children typically excel in such areas as verbal abilities, physical abilities are more problematic for them. Clark (1992) has offered the following explanation for a somewhat slower rate of development in the motor domain among gifted children:

> For many [gifted youngsters], body coordination does not keep pace with their accelerated mental development, thereby frustrating their expectations of performance. The patience required to drill and practice assures average youngsters of adequate physical performance in games and competitive activities. Youngsters more accustomed to moving rapidly through new ideas and challenges often lack that patience. When their physical performance falls short of the standards they set for themselves, when their opportunities for improvement come from repetitive activity, they often choose other alternatives. (p. 340)

Douthitt (1992), for example, in her study of 296 gifted and nongifted children aged 2.67 through 16 years, found significant positive relationships between communication, socialization, and daily living skill domain subscores on the *Vineland Adaptive Behavior Scale* (VABS; Sparrow, Balla, & Cicchetti, 1984) and *Stanford–Binet L–M* (Terman & Merrill, 1972) IQ scores. However, the relationship for the fourth VABS domain (motor skills) and IQ was not statistically significant. Similarly, motor skills was the only VABS domain in which a significant difference between the two groups was not exhibited. In support of Douthitt's findings, Milne (1994) found no significant difference ($p = .05$) in motor development as measured by the short form of the *Bruininks–Oseretsky Test of Motor Proficiency* (BOT–S; Bruininks, 1978) between 78 gifted children (mean age 4.96 years) from the NMSU Preschool for the Gifted and 78 nongifted preschoolers (mean age = 4.97 years) from three regular preschools.

Therefore, it seems appropriate that opportunities should be provided for young children who are gifted to use large and fine motor skills and to explore alternative ways of movement (G 40, G 42, G 43). In NMSU's Preschool for the Gifted, motor activities are treated as an integral part of the curriculum for all children. Typical classroom gross motor activities include negotiating pretend obstacle courses, walking on balance beams, and throwing and catching bean bags and balloons in games in which children make up their own rules. Outdoor gross motor activities (G 41) during the daily free-play period include running, skipping, hopping, riding, sliding, digging, climbing, and swinging. Nonstructured fine motor activities are a mainstay of NMSU's daily *self-select* period in which materials for cutting, beading, writing, lacing, molding, and miscellaneous art activities are provided. When needs arise, motor skills should be addressed in IFSPs and IEPS. In this regard, occupational and physical therapy support staff should also participate in planning and carrying out intervention activities (G 44).

Interventions to Promote Cognitive Development

Some controversy exists regarding cognitive development of young gifted children. Using Piaget's stages of cognitive development as a template, Carter (1984) found that although the sequence stays the same, children who are gifted progress within and through subsequent stages of cognitive development at a faster rate than do nongifted children. However, Kitano and Kirby's (1986) more recent synthesis of research on this topic suggests that although very young gifted children may progress within stages at a quicker rate, transitions to advanced stages may come at about the same time as for nongifted age mates.

It is generally agreed, however, that "by definition, children who are gifted exhibit advanced cognitive skills" (Shey & Bauer, 1994, p. 418). Because precociousness in this area is acknowledged, it follows that environments be structured in such ways that young children who are gifted have opportunities to perform at the very highest levels of operation within their present stages of cognitive development. Structuring should begin with an assessment of present levels of cognitive development with an instrument such as the *Uzgiris–Hunt Ordinal Scales of Psychological Development* (Uzgiris & Hunt, 1975) and proceed to development of objectives and identification of appropriate experiences and activities. Such practices may not only optimize cognitive development but also prevent boredom and frustration as well. Similarly, the Bloom *Taxonomy* (cited in VanTassel-Baska, 1994) is a handy tool for teachers who wish to address the cognitive domain during planning activities. Keeping in mind individual characteristics of children, teachers can arrange opportunities and experiences for young gifted children that correspond to Bloom's six levels of cognitive behavior arranged on a continuum from *knowledge* (Level 1) to *evaluation* (Level 6). For example, preschool children involved in decision making regarding a field trip would be working at Level 6 (evaluation). Experiences directed at recognizing examples of primary colors would be tapping Level 1 (knowledge).

Clark (1992) suggested that rather than merely providing exposure to stimulating environments in order to promote cognitive development, teachers should provide young children with ongoing opportunities to *interact* and cope with people and things. In addition to creating such environments for young gifted children, school personnel can promote thinking skills in at least three ways (Davis & Rimm, 1994). First, they can indirectly teach thinking by infusing *why, what if,* and *how* questions into all content areas. Thinking can also be directly taught within a preschool curriculum by treating it as a curricular content area. Davis and Rimm (1994) stated, "Critical thinking can be taught by helping students deliberately evaluate biases, qualifications, and ability to observe; to examine whether a statement is an assumption or an opinion; and to evaluate whether particular conclusions necessarily follow" (p. 228).

A third way to teach children to think is by teaching them how to think *metacognitively* (i.e., teaching them to think about how they think). For example, master teachers in the NMSU Preschool for the Gifted routinely assist children in identification and understanding of sources for their values and attitudes.

Davis and Rimm (1994) have summarized teaching thinking skills in the following way: "In the classroom, the indirect, direct, and metacognition approaches to teaching thinking may not be so neatly divided. The teaching of thinking skills often will include a combination of exercising underlying abilities; helping students to consciously analyze problems and plan steps for solving them; and helping them to metacognitively understand the reasons for these steps and for their own thinking and the thinking of others" (p. 230).

Interventions to Promote Social–Emotional Development

As Clark (1992) traced it, "in the 1920s people assumed that gifted children were emotionally borderline neurotics or even psychotics.... Parents who found their preschoolers reading would discourage such activities and encourage 'playing with little friends' as an antidote. The fear that a neighbor, or worst yet a teacher, would discover precocious behavior in their child led many parents to adopt drastic and punitive actions when they observed any advanced behavior" (p. 117).

In turn, recognition of this climate led to Terman's well-known longitudinal study of emotional and social characteristics of children identified as gifted. According to Clark (1992), Terman's findings did not validate the prevalent thinking of the 1920s. Instead, as adults these children became community leaders who were more capable of adjusting socially than were their nongifted peers.

Today, Clark (1992) has asserted that the previous climate of suspicion and rejection has given way to a feeling among professionals and others that "for the most part, given the opportunity for healthy development, the social–emotional adjustment of gifted children tends to proceed better than among the more typical population" (p. 119).

In this newer climate, interventions to promote development of social–emotional competence in young gifted children have two interrelated thrusts. First, personnel working in such programs attempt to foster normal development by engaging in such practices as recognizing and respecting children's feelings and personality traits (G 52), encouraging children to identify and verbalize their feelings (G 53), arranging curriculum activities that are fun and that encourage laughter (G 56), providing small-group activities in order to bring about cooperative learning (G 54), and assuring children that their contributions are important and valued (G 55).

A second thrust is that of managing inappropriate behaviors. These behaviors may come about for several reasons in young gifted children. Some may be simply due to imitating aggressive and other types of inappropriate behaviors from television, playgrounds, or homes. Others may be the direct result of lowered self-esteem brought about by placing gifted children in homogeneous groups where they are no longer "stars." However, with regard to this last point, Maddox, Scheiber, and Bass (1982) did not find a relationship between type of placement and level of self-esteem. Instead, their findings supported those of others who found that self-esteem of children who are gifted tends to be higher than for nongifted peers regardless of type of placement option chosen. Interventions to address problem behaviors in young gifted children include dealing with inappropriate behavior firmly but with discretion and flexibility (G 60) and using related service personnel such as school psychologists and counselors when needed (G 57).

Interventions to Promote Adaptive Behavior and Independence

As viewed by Pendarvis, Howley, and Howley (1990), one of the broadest measures of intelligence is *adaptation* to one's environment. Although adaptive behavior per se is one of three major themes in classification and placement of persons with mental retardation, it is rarely diagnosed at present with respect to eligibility for gifted programs, including those for very young children. However, current practice in programs for young gifted children does include careful assessment of the extent of children's independent functioning (i.e., adaptive behavior) across domains such as cognition, play, social skills, and self-care. This practice permits development of individualized programs (IFSPs/IEPs; G 51) and, therefore, appropriate adaptive behavior interventions.

Cognitive adaptation, for example, "consists of two complementary processes: (a) assimilation, or the incorporating of features of the environment into the child's existing structures, and (b) accommodation, the modifying of one's structures in response to environmental demands" (Kitano & Kirby, 1986, pp. 48–49). As illustrated by these authors, "when an infant encounters a mobile dangling from the crib, the infant must *accommodate* his or her vision and movements to the distance. The infant also *assimilates* the mobile into already existing patterns of behavior—that is, structures for reaching and grasping" (Kitano & Kirby, 1986, p. 49).

In the social domain it should be noted that adaptive behavior is often more difficult for young children with high levels of intelligence due to a lack of *true peers*. According to Silverman (1989), true peers are mental equals who demonstrate similar interests, perspectives, and understandings. Silverman (1989) illustrated this issue in the following way: "A 5-year old who plays checkers, chess, Scrabble, and Monopoly will be unable to play those games with average or more modestly gifted 5-year-olds. Most 5-year-olds do not have a conception of rules. They make up the rules as they go along and then declare, 'I win!' The highly gifted child is likely to say, 'He cheats!' and refuse to play with age mates" (p. 76).

As discussed earlier in the section on assessment, measurement of adaptive behavior is considered a *promising practice* in identification of children who are gifted from culturally diverse and economically disadvantaged backgrounds. This topic seems especially ripe for research.

Transition

As defined by Hutinger (1981), early childhood transition practices are "strategies and procedures . . . planned and employed to insure the smooth placement and subsequent adjustment of the child as he or she moves from one program into another" (p. 6). Structured activities to accomplish efficacious transition between programs (e.g., from special education preschool to regular public kindergarten) have been employed increasingly in early intervention and preschool programs for infants, toddlers, and preschoolers with disabilities and their families during the past decade due to the growing realization that caregivers and children need such assistance and in response to EHA amendments (P.L. 99-457) transition plan mandates.

One example of structured transition programming to accommodate children with disabilities as they near kindergarten transition is the *survival skills* approach (Rule, Fiechtl, & Innocenti, 1990; Salisbury & Vincent, 1990). In this approach, ecological assessment of local public kindergarten programs or literature reviews or both are employed to yield critical student competencies thought necessary to avoid kindergarten retention or referral to special education. Rule et al. (1990) determined through ecological assessment that successful inclusion in kindergarten requires that

> children must (a) work independently, (b) participate in groups, (c) follow varied directions, and (d) use varied materials. Thus, a functional survival skills curriculum should teach these skills. The authors developed such a curriculum. . . . [Their] Skills for School Success curriculum . . . addresses nine activities: (a) entry routines (hanging up coat, selecting toy, and playing until the teacher signals the next activity); (b) sequence tasks (individually completing a series of tasks announced daily); Pledge of Allegiance; (d) group circle activities (discussion of calendar, weather, etc.); (e) individual tasks; (f) large-group activities using commercially available curricula; (g) workbook tasks; (h) quiet time activities (child-selected, child-guided activity); and (i) transition activities (getting coat and materials to take home, lining up, and walking in line through the building). (p. 81)

Although programs for young gifted children do not fall under EHA amendments transition plan mandates, they nevertheless address transition in order to assist children and their families and caregivers. For example, preschools for the gifted routinely address the majority of Rule et al.'s (1990) survival skills because they are traditional early childhood activities cognitively appropriate for 3- and 4-year-old gifted children. In addition, preschools for the gifted conduct field trips to local kindergarten programs for children and caregivers (G 63), include discussion of kindergarten as part of a life-cycle unit, invite early childhood and gifted education coordinators to parent meetings, provide assessment information to private and public schools upon request (G 62), and invite former preschool graduates to class or parent meetings to discuss their experiences after graduation from the preschool.

Personnel Competence

Among desirable traits and abilities of effective teachers of gifted children previously identified in the literature are the ability to develop flexible programs, respect for individuality and creativity, innovativeness, focus on process as well as on product, ability to guide rather than to coerce, knowledge and proficiency in disciplines at students' levels, ability to teach problem-solving and metacognitive strategies, ability to model some expert or artist behavior, knowledge of theories of learning, superior intellectual ability, ability to model inquiry in search for new knowledge, enthusiasm to seek new ideas, and the quality of being inspirational (Davis & Rimm, 1994; Feldhusen, 1985; Gallagher & Gallagher, 1994; Lindsey, 1980; VanTassel-Baska, 1994). In contrast, Gowan, Demos, and Torrance (cited in Clark, 1992) found the following traits in teachers who could *not* encourage development in gifted children: "Authoritarian, defensive, dominated by time, insensitive to their pupils' intellectual and emotional needs, lacking in energy, preoccupied with their information-giving functions, intellectually inert, disinterested in promoting initiative and self-reliance in their pupils, preoccupied with disciplinary matters and unwilling to give much of themselves in the teaching–learning compact" (p. 162).

The positive abilities and traits of effective teachers just listed represent a baseline for preparation of teachers of young gifted children. Although many of these characteristics are innate and may be recognized as present or lacking in trainees, others can be addressed in a training program. Taken together with the DEC-recommended practices identified in this chapter, a strong foundation for preparation of personnel for programs for young gifted children is presently available. As suggested by Clark (1992), personnel can gain the necessary abilities through traditional or competency-based course work and practice at universities (i.e., preservice training) or through inservice training provided at state-sponsored conferences and workshops, demonstration classes, and regional consortiums and service centers. Weiner and Shea (cited in Clark, 1992) have found that "attitudes of teachers are influenced favorably toward gifted learners if they have had even one course in education of the gifted" (p. 487). This finding suggests the importance of providing at least one course on gifted education in the teacher training curriculum when a more complete set of offerings is not feasible due to lack of resources.

According to J. Parker (personal communication, September 30, 1993), 114 U.S. and 8 Canadian colleges and universities in 39 states and 6 provinces currently offer at least a master's degree with a major or an emphasis in the area of gifted and talented education. This number represents a decrease since 1990–1991, when Parker and Karnes (1990) found graduate programs in 135 colleges and universities in 40 states and 6 provinces. Despite the decrease in the overall number of graduate programs indicated by Parker's longitudinal data, I predict a steady growth in preservice and inservice training programs directed at early intervention with children who are gifted. This prediction is based on such factors as Gallagher's (1988) identification of educational services for young gifted children as a first priority on his national agenda; DEC's recognition of young gifted children as a population in need of services as witnessed by inclusion of the present chapter; interest and continued expansion of the Jacob Javits grant program, which includes early childhood programs among its funded demonstration projects; and Stile et al.'s (1993) finding of a steady increase in the number of programs providing educational services to young gifted children in the United States and its territories during the last decade.

Program Evaluation

Bailey and Wolery (1989) have identified program evaluation as one of five important levels of assessment conducted in programs for young children with exceptionalities for *decision-making* purposes. Gallagher and Gallagher (1994) have found that evaluation plans for gifted education programs employ two patterns of evaluation strategy. First, ongoing data collection, or *formative* evaluation, is conducted to systematically improve programs while they operate. With this method, informal comments and suggestions by families and staff are recorded, and this information is then used as a basis for revision (G 69). An example of a more specific type of formative evaluation in gifted education has been described by Callahan, Covert, Aylesworth, and Vanco (cited in Gallagher & Gallagher, 1994). These authors described activities of a formative evaluation team who visited a program midyear to gather information regarding a *specific* program component (the application of Bloom's taxonomy within the cognitive domain). This team maintained contact with the program after its visit and subsequently visited with program staff to present recommendations. Among program revisions based on the team's recommendations was development of 24 new content units.

A second pattern of evaluation strategy in gifted programs is *summative* evaluation. Gallagher and Gallagher (1994) described summative evaluation as the gathering of information that can be used by outside decision makers regarding continuance or discontinuance of a program. They described the effects of such an evaluation: "Naturally, summative evaluation substantially increases the anxiety level of people in education. An unfavorable result can lead to dismemberment of the program itself. It would be advisable for teachers and principals not to make any unusual requests of the school administration within a week of a forthcoming summative evaluation, because the school atmosphere is likely to be charged with doubt, anxiety, and naked fear" (Gallagher & Gallagher, 1994, p. 377).

Kitano and Kirby (1986) identified several issues unique to gifted education that professionals should consider when developing evaluation plans for programs for young gifted children. First, institutions that support gifted programs may require written annual reports of student progress. In contrast, it may be more appropriate to expect long-term gains. Second, valid and reliable standardized instruments to measure student change are lacking. Third, gifted programs that address individual interests of children cannot be expected to demonstrate uniform gains. Fourth, use of behavioral objectives to measure change is often inappropriate due to the unique content of the programs (e.g., higher levels of cognitive development versus simple academic tasks).

Additional recommended practices for evaluation of programs for young gifted children are providing written reports on progress at the end of the year to parents (G 70), soliciting information from multiple sources (G 71), gathering qualitative in addition to quantitative data (G 72), and employing third-party evaluators (G 73).

Family Participation

Use of IEPs and IFSPs is viewed as best practice in school programs for young gifted children. Therefore, families should be involved in much of the decision making at various levels of assessment (e.g., helping school personnel pinpoint types of classroom activities that promote self-esteem in their children and formative evaluation). Also, and of equal importance, they can be directly involved in interventions designed to promote optimal levels of performance across important domains described elsewhere in this chapter. For example, weekend family activities such as a trip to the beach can complement a concurrent school unit on geography by expanding vocabulary and understanding.

In addition to welcoming family members in the classroom at any time (G 77) and encouraging them to become involved at their current comfort level (e.g., working as a teaching assistant; G 74), DEC-recommended practices include making resources such as books available (G 75) and organizing parent group meetings (G 76). In the NMSU Preschool for the Gifted, for example, an annual parent needs assessment is conducted to determine areas in which parents perceive needs for further knowledge or skill. In turn, parent "inservice" sessions based on needs-assessment data have addressed such topics as normal development and prereading skills (Stile, 1992).

Prior to school, family members can enrich home environments in ways that maximize development and performance in such areas as language and cognition. Cognitive development can be enhanced by asking children to classify and compare objects during daily routines (e.g., Which one tastes sweet? Which one tastes bitter?). Similarly, language development can be enhanced by playing board and card games with children and by reading and acting out stories together. The following statement by Clark (1992) captures best my attitude regarding family or parent participation: "I am firmly convinced that the home is the true cradle of eminence. Whatever we find in our world that we would like to change, we must begin at the starting place with parenting. Some have tried to show that other influences are equally or even more important; however, they have yet to account for the powerful effects of motivation, self-image, and attitudes toward self and others—the factors that find their definition in the home" (pp. 502–503).

CLOSING

This chapter began with a rationale for early childhood education of children who are gifted. The chapter emphasized interventions to promote development in several important domains. Assessment, IFSPs/IEPs, service delivery model and environment, general curriculum and intervention strategies, transition, personnel competence, program evaluation, and family participation were also discussed. The 77 DEC-recommended practices solicited from and validated by early childhood gifted educators are included in the Appendix.

REFERENCES

Bailey, D. B., & Wolery, M. (1989). *Assessing infants and preschoolers with handicaps*. New York: Merrill.

Barbour, N. B. (1992). Early childhood gifted education: A collaborative perspective. *Journal for the Education of the Gifted, 15*, 145–162.

Bruininks, R. H. (1978). *Bruininks–Oseretsky Test of Motor Proficiency*. Circle Pines, MN: American Guidance Service.

Carter, K. R. (1984). Cognitive development in intellectually gifted: A Piagetian perspective. *Roeper Review, 1*(3), 180–184.

Clark, B. (1988). *Growing up gifted* (3rd ed.). Columbus, OH: Merrill.
Clark, B. (1992). *Growing up gifted* (4th ed.). New York: Merrill.
Davis, G. A., & Rimm, S. B. (1994). *Education of the gifted and talented* (3rd ed.). Boston: Allyn & Bacon.
Douthitt, V. L. (1992). A comparison of adaptive behavior in gifted and nongifted children. *Roeper Review, 14*(3), 149–151.
Education of All Handicapped Children Act of 1975, 20 U.S.C. §1400 *et seq.*
Feldhusen, J. F. (1985). The teacher of gifted students. *Gifted Education International, 3*(2), 87–93.
Feldhusen, J. F. (1989). Synthesis of research on gifted youth. *Educational Leadership, 46,* 6–11.
Feldhusen, J. F., & VanTassel-Baska, J. (1989). Social studies and language arts for the gifted. In Feldhusen, J. F., VanTassel-Baska, J., & Seeley, K. (Eds.), *Excellence in educating the gifted* (pp. 213–228). Denver: Love.
Gallagher, J. J. (1988). National agenda for educating gifted students: Statement of policies. *Exceptional Children, 55,* 107–114.
Gallagher, J. J., & Gallagher, S.A. (1994). Teaching the gifted child (4th ed.). Boston: Allyn & Bacon.
Gardner, H. (1983). *Frames of mind. The theory of multiple intelligences.* New York: Basic Books.
Gregory, D. A., (1984–1985). Assessment of the gifted [monograph]. *Diagnostique, 10*(1–4), 88–77.
Hardman, M. L., Drew, C. J., Egan, M. W., & Wolf, B. (1990). *Human exceptionality: Society, school, and family* (3rd ed.). Boston: Allyn & Bacon.
Hutinger, P. L. (1981). Transition practices for handicapped young children: What the experts say. *Journal of the Division for Early Childhood, 2,* 8–14.
Individuals with Disabilities Education Act of 1990, 20 U.S.C. §1400 *et seq.*
Karnes, M. B. (1988). Issues in educating young gifted children: Promising practices. *Resources in Education, 25*(7), 75. (ERIC Document Reproduction Service No. 315 946)
Karnes, M. B., & Johnson, L. J. (1989). Training for staff, parents, and volunteers working with gifted young children, especially those with disabilities and from low-income homes. *Young Children, 44*(3), 49–56.
Karnes, M. B., & Johnson, L. J. (1991). The preschool/primary gifted child. *Journal for the Education of the Gifted, 14,* 267–283.
Karnes, M. B., Shwedel, A. M., & Kemp, P. B. (1985). Preschool: Programming for the young gifted child. *Roeper Review, 7,* 204–209.
Karnes, M. B., Shwedel, A. M., & Linnemeyer, S. A. (1981). *Survey of programs for the gifted.* Unpublished manuscript, University of Illinois.
Karnes, M. B., Shwedel, A. M., & Williams, M. (1983). Combining instructional models for young gifted children. *Teaching Exceptional Children, 15,* 128–135.
Khatena, J. (1992). *Gifted: Challenge and response for education.* Itasca, IL: F. E. Peacock.
Kitano, M. K. (1990). A developmental model for identifying and serving young gifted children. *Early Childhood Development and Care, 63,* 19–31.
Kitano, M. K., & Kirby, D. F. (1986). *Gifted education: A comprehensive view.* Boston: Little, Brown.
Lidz, C. S. (1983). Dynamic assessment and the preschool child. *Journal of Psychoeducational Assessment, 1,* 59–72.
Lindsey, M. (1980). *Training teachers of the gifted and talented.* New York: Teachers College Press.
Maddox, C. D., Scheiber, L. M., & Bass, J. E. (1982). Self-concept and social distance in gifted children. *Gifted Child Quarterly, 26*(2), 77–81.

Meador, K. S. (1992). Emerging rainbows: A review of the literature on creativity in preschoolers. *Journal for the Education of the Gifted, 15,* 163–181.

Milne, C. (1994, April). *Motor proficiency comparisons of young children from gifted and regular classrooms.* Paper presented at the meeting of the American Association for Health, Physical Education and Dance, Denver, CO.

Parker, J. P., & Karnes, F. A. (1990). *The 1990–1991 directory of graduate degree programs in gifted and talented education.* Circle Pines, MN: National Association for Gifted Children.

Pendarvis, E. D., Howley, A. A., & Howley, C. B. (1990). *The abilities of gifted children.* Englewood Cliffs, N.J.: Prentice–Hall.

Richert, E. S. (1985). Identification of gifted children in the United States: The need for pluralistic assessment. *Roeper Review, 8*(2), 68–72.

Rule, S., Fiechtl, B. J., & Innocenti, M. S. (1990). Preparation for transition to mainstreamed post-preschool environments: Development of a survival skills curriculum. *Topics in Early Childhood Special Education, 9*(4), 78–90.

Salisbury, C. L., & Vincent, L. J. (1990). Criterion of the next environment and best practices: Mainstreaming and integration 10 years later. *Topics in Early Childhood Special Education, 10*(2), 78–89.

Seeley, K. (1989). Underachieving and handicapped gifted. In J. Feldhusen, J. VanTassel-Baska, & K. Seeley (Eds.), *Excellence in educating the gifted* (pp. 29–37). Denver: Love.

Shaklee, B. D. (1992). Identification of young gifted children. *Journal for the Education of the Gifted, 15,* 134–144.

Shey, T. M., & Bauer, A. M. (1994). *Learners with disabilities.* Dubuque, IA: WCB Brown & Benchmark.

Shirley, M. (1959). *The first two years: A study of 25 babies.* Minneapolis: University of Minnesota Press.

Silverman, L. K. (1988). Gifted and talented. In E. L. Meyen & T. M. Skrtic (Eds.), *Exceptional children and youth.* Denver: Love.

Silverman, L. K. (1989). The highly gifted. In J. Feldhusen, J. VanTassel-Baska, & K. Seeley (Eds.), *Excellence in educating the gifted* (pp. 71–83). Denver: Love.

Smith, D. D., & Luckasson, R. (1992). *Introduction to special education: Teaching in an age of challenge.* Needham Heights, MA: Allyn & Bacon.

Sparrow, S. S., Balla, D. A., & Cicchetti, D. V. (1984). *Vineland Adaptive Behavior Scales.* Circle Pines, MN: American Guidance Service.

Stile, S. W. (1992, April). *Perceived needs of parents of preschool-aged gifted students.* Paper presented at the meeting of the Council for Exceptional Children, Baltimore, MD.

Stile, S. W., & Kitano, M. K. (1991). Research forum: Preschool-age gifted children. *DEC Communicator, 17*(3), 4.

Stile, S. W., Kitano, M. K., Kelley, P., & LeCrone, J. (1993). Early intervention with gifted children: A national survey. *Journal of Early Intervention, 17*(1), 30–35.

Strom, R., Johnson, A., Strom, S., & Strom, P. (1992). Designing curriculum for parents of gifted children. *Journal for the Education of the Gifted, 15,* 182–200.

Tannenbaum, A. (1992). Early signs of giftedness: Research and commentary. *Journal for Education of the Gifted, 15,* 104–133.

Terman, L. M., & Merrill, M. A. (1972). *Stanford–Binet Intelligence Scale, Third Revision (Form L–M).* Iowa City, IA: Houghton–Mifflin.

Torrance, E. P. (1979). Unique needs of the creative child and adult. In A. H. Passow (Ed.), *The gifted and talented: Their education and development (78th Yearbook of the National Society for the Study of Education)* (pp. 352–371). Chicago: University of Chicago Press.

Turbiville, V., Turnbull, A., Garland, C., & Lee, I. (1993). IFSPs and IEPS. In *DEC-recommended practices: Indicators of quality in programs for infants and young children with special needs and their families* (pp. 30–39). Reston, VA: Council for Exceptional Children.

Uzgiris, I., & Hunt, J. (1975). *Assessment in infancy: Ordinal scales of psychological development.* Champaign: University of Illinois Press.

VanTassel-Baska, J. (1994). *Comprehensive curriculum for gifted learners* (2nd ed.). Needham Heights, MA: Allyn & Bacon.

VanTassel-Baska, J., Patton, J., & Prillaman, D. (1989). Disadvantaged gifted learners at-risk for education attention. *Focus on Exceptional Children, 22*(3), 1–15.

Wolfle, J. (1989). The gifted preschooler: Developmentally different, but still 3 or 4 years old. *Young Children, 44*(3), 41–48.

CHAPTER 14

Personnel Preparation in Early Education and Intervention: Recommended Preservice and Inservice Practices

Patricia S. Miller
Vicki D. Stayton

Essential to the provision of quality services to young children with special needs and their families is the availability of qualified personnel. Qualified personnel for early education and intervention are those who work with infants, toddlers, and preschoolers in inclusive settings. A qualified workforce in early education and intervention should reflect a consensus about professional standards regarding knowledge and skills required across disciplines. The greatest challenge to states confronted with critical personnel shortages in early intervention, for children from birth through 5 years, is to prepare adequate numbers of personnel while ensuring that those personnel meet professional standards of quality (McCollum & Maude, 1993). Our purpose in this chapter is to explore issues related to preparing personnel to work with children birth through 5 years with disabilities and their families and to describe current understandings about preservice and inservice practices.

Personnel shortages in early intervention and early childhood special education cited in early literature as critical (McLaughlin, Smith-Davis, & Burke, 1986; Meisels, Harbin, Modigliani, & Olson, 1988; U.S. Department of Education, 1992) are growing as a result of intensive efforts to identify more children and families (Yoder, Coleman, & Gallagher, 1990). The U.S. Department of Labor Bureau of Labor Statistics (1988) has estimated employment growth rates of 36% for preschool teachers and 42% for health professionals by the year 2000. With all 50 states mandating services for children aged 3 through 5 years with disabilities in the 1991–92 school year, 49 states providing comprehensive or partial services to infants and toddlers under Part H (Hamilton, 1994), this need is likely to continue. At the same time, the pool of qualified personnel is likely to decrease rapidly (Gilkerson, Hilliard, Schrag, Shonkoff, 1987; U.S. Department of Education, 1992).

Compounding the personnel shortages across disciplines involved in early childhood is the specialized training required to provide services to infants, toddlers, and preschoolers with disabilities and their families (Bruder, Klosowski, & Daguio, 1991). Skills to work within the field of early education and intervention are qualitatively different from skills typically included in programs that train professionals in physical therapy, occupational therapy, communication disorders, and other related disciplines (Bailey, 1989; Bricker & Slentz, 1988; McCollum & Thorp, 1988).

Particular knowledge and skills required of early intervention professionals have been described in the federal legislation under the Individuals with Disabilities Education Act of 1990 (IDEA). The law emphasizes the need for training in family-centered intervention, service coordination, interdisciplinary teaming, and interagency collaboration (Bailey, Simeonsson, Yoder, & Huntington, 1990). The unique nature of infancy as a developmental period and the literature describing quality services for infants, toddlers, and families support the position that discrete kinds of knowledge and skills are needed by professionals (McCollum & Bailey, 1991). Professional associations have delineated specific competencies required to work with infants, toddlers, and preschoolers with disabilities. Documents from these associations include the disciplines of early childhood special education (McCollum, McLean, McCartan, & Kaiser, 1989; McCollum & Thorp, 1988), nursing, (Consensus Committee, 1993), nutrition (Kaufman, 1989), occupational therapy (Dunn, Campbell, Detter, Hall, & Berger, 1989), physical therapy (Effgen, Bjorson, Chiarello, Sinzer, & Phillips, 1991), speech and language (American Speech-Language-Hearing Association, 1991), social work (Nover & Timberlake, 1989), and psychology (Drotar & Sturm, 1989).

CONSIDERATIONS FOR PLANNING

Legal Framework for Licensing and Credentialing

Two of the 14 components of Part H of IDEA require the development of personnel standards and a comprehensive system of personnel development (CSPD) that includes both preservice and inservice training. States, however, have been slow to develop policy in this area (Gallagher, 1989). The complexity of personnel development in early intervention may be due in part to the requirement that policy include multiple professional disciplines. State agencies, professional associations, and institutions of higher education have been working to develop personnel preparation and credentialing plans that meet the requirements in the law and that reflect the professional standards of individual disciplines. Joint planning across agencies and disciplines is essential.

To facilitate joint planning and to address personnel needs across the age range of birth through 5 years, the CSPD of each state under Part H must be consistent with the state's CSPD under Part B (*Federal Register*, 1993). Federal regulations require that the Part B CSPD include an annual needs assessment to determine the need for both new and retrained personnel. Based on the need for qualified personnel, the CSPD must also include strategies for providing training through both preservice and inservice activities (*Federal Register*, 1977).

Many states, however, have reported a scarcity of training programs to prepare personnel to serve infants, toddlers, and preschoolers in compliance with IDEA. Shortages of specialists exist in each of the 10 disciplines initially named under Part H (audiology, nursing, nutrition, occupational therapy, physical therapy, special education, speech therapy, social work, psychology, and medicine; Gallagher, Harbin, Thomas, Clifford, & Wenger, 1988). These disciplines have not typically emphasized working with very young children and families in their inservice and preservice training programs. State regulatory standards for meeting the needs for increased numbers of personnel, while maintaining standards of excellence, are critical to the success of the laws regarding early childhood and in providing guidance to universities and colleges in the development of personnel preparation programs.

State Standards

Federal law requires that personnel in early intervention services meet the "highest entry-level standard" according to state regulations in each relevant discipline (*Federal Register*, 1993). State standards across disciplines in early education and intervention should reflect the uniqueness of infants, toddlers, and preschoolers and their families, and be derived from national professional standards. The CSPD requirements of both Parts B and H of IDEA address components that must be incorporated into state planning: qualified personnel across disciplines, preservice preparation, inservice preparation, and technical assistance in personnel development. Part H further stipulates that the preservice and inservice preparation should be conducted on an interdisciplinary basis to the greatest extent appropriate (*Federal Register*, 1993).

To adequately address IDEA's requirements specific to personnel, state personnel systems must be conceptualized from an interdisciplinary and interagency perspective with credentialing and certification systems developed in tandem with state CSPDs. Cooperation and collaboration in both the planning and delivery of training, particularly between higher education and state agencies, are essential (Bruder & McLean, 1988; Rooney, Gallagher, Fullagher, Eckland, & Huntington, 1992). Both inservice and preservice training and education should be available to and inclusive of professionals from diverse disciplines who provide services in early childhood. Once appropriate standards and credentialing processes are defined, short-term and long-range plans should be developed for personnel development across the state. McCollum and Bailey (1991) described a number of issues to be faced by states in both short-term and long-range planning. Those issues include the following:

- credentialing currently employed personnel,
- establishing a statewide system of preservice programs that will address both personnel shortages and quality concerns across disciplines,
- building an ongoing system for professional development and continuing education, and
- developing a state system of information collection regarding supply and demand for personnel across disciplines.

Although many states are moving toward competency-based licensure and certification plans, a recent study reported that most states rely more on completed course work than on competencies in the credentialing process (Bruder et al., 1991). The licensure and certification standards for entry-level skills vary from discipline to discipline, and for some disciplines, from state to state. Some disciplines require a master's degree whereas others offer an entry-level credential at the undergraduate level. Bailey (1989) suggested that this difference may create problems among professionals who are expected to serve on interdisciplinary teams and to share expertise equally. Issues related to credentialing include those specific to individual states and others that are common across states.

A number of guidelines are available to states as issues regarding credentialing standards arise. Examination of the literature and review of state plans that have been adopted or proposed suggest that the following components should be incorporated in state-level personnel preparation systems:

- integration of early childhood education (Association for Teacher Education [ATE] & National Association for the Education of Young Children [NAEYC], 1991) and early childhood special education (McCollum et al., 1989) professional standards for entry-level early educators who are uniquely trained to meet the needs of infants, toddlers, and preschoolers in integrated settings (Bredekamp, 1992; Burton, Hains, Hanline, McLean, & McCormick, 1992; McCollum & Bailey, 1991; Miller, 1992);

- sequenced field experiences and clinical work with graduated responsibility and contact hours with infants, toddlers, preschoolers, and families in a variety of programs and settings (Bailey, Simeonsson, et al., 1990);
- interdisciplinary inservice and preservice curricula developed by teams that include disciplines represented in the legislation for early intervention (McCollum & Thorp, 1988; Miller, 1992) as well as family members (Bailey, McWilliam, & Winton, 1992; Winton, 1990);
- articulation between state licensure and certification standards and preservice preparation programs (Bruder et al., 1991);
- a preparation and credentialing framework and model that sets an expectation for professional teaming and collaboration (Bailey, Simeonsson, et al., 1990; Miller, 1992; Rooney, Fullagher, & Gallagher, 1993);
- competencies for the early education teacher and early interventionist as a professional who is a change agent and advocate for inclusion, a reflective and analytic decision maker, a person who is grounded in theories of typical and atypical development of infants and young children and in curriculum and methods for infants, toddlers, and preschool children with disabilities, and who is a person who can access current knowledge and skills in making decisions about children and families (McCollum & Bailey, 1991; Smith & Powers, 1987);
- a plan for horizontal and vertical career advancement and credentialing of degreed and nondegreed personnel (Bredekamp & Willer, 1993);
- a plan that meets the needs for increased numbers for and affordable entry-level professionals (Stedman, 1990);
- the inclusion of core competencies for professionals in early intervention (Stayton & Miller, 1993b; McCollum Maude, 1992);
- content specifically related to infants, toddlers, and families (Bricker & Slentz, 1988; McCollum & Bailey, 1991);
- plans that reflect a family-centered orientation, especially with infants and toddlers (Dunst & Deal, 1990; McCollum & Maude, 1993); and
- plans that address the need for continuing education (Bailey, 1989; Joyce & Showers, 1980; Korinek, Schmid, & McAdams, 1985).

Interdisciplinary Focus

Public Law 99-457 requires systems of services to infants, toddlers, and preschoolers with disabilities that are coordinated, comprehensive, interagency, and interdisciplinary in nature (Hanson & Lovett, 1992). The law also mandates that the professional disciplines provide those services in the least restrictive, most natural settings. That is, services rendered by professionals across disciplines should be provided in settings that fully integrate each child as a member of a naturally inclusive environment. Additionally, services should be integrated throughout the curriculum and daily routines (Miller & McDowelle, 1993). The ethical, legal, and developmental benefits of integration for children with and without disabilities have been documented over time (Bricker, 1978; Esposito, 1987; Odom & McEvoy, 1988; Strain, 1990; Turnbull, 1982). The concept of integration is equally important in personnel preparation.

Early childhood education (ECE) professionals are beginning to recognize that full inclusion of infants, toddlers, and preschoolers with disabilities and full integration of services will be more likely to happen if personnel preparation programs are also integrated (Bredekamp, 1992; Burton et al., 1992; Miller, 1992; Odom & McEvoy, 1990). Genuine efforts to provide interdisciplinary personnel preparation can produce the attitudes, knowledge, and skills required for delivery of services representing the desired expectation for integration and inclusion of professionals, children, and families. Interdisciplinary practices in early childhood personnel preparation programs can be justified from philosophical, economic, and moral standpoints (Miller, 1992).

Interdisciplinary planning and delivery of personnel preparation programs are perceived as different from multidisciplinary personnel preparation efforts (Stayton & Miller, 1993a). Multidisciplinary programs may be defined as those that include more than one academic professional discipline in the degree program. Students take courses from different departments that are related to the course of study, in this case, early education and intervention. Department chairs may agree to allow students to enroll in the particular courses if seats are available after departmental majors have registered. Courses are already in existence, and the planning of the early education program depends on the availability of appropriate areas of study. Program faculty and department chairs may rarely, if ever, meet to discuss the multidisciplinary program and the students in that program. Program standards for the program may have to adhere to a variety of expectations regarding such things as field experiences, course requirements, and grading procedures that might have been designed for majors in the "host" departments. Content across the various courses required in the new program in early education may be fragmented and require special professional seminars to "knit" together a whole.

The concept of interdisciplinary program planning suggests a greater degree of collaboration (Stayton & Miller, 1993a). The interdisciplinary curriculum can be defined as one that is actually derived from several related disciplines. The core of the curriculum is new. The required course content is designed specifically for the new degree program and is derived from the different disciplines jointly. The faculty representing the development of the program may consist of a planning team that meets regularly to share in decision making, planning of curriculum experiences, and monitoring and revising the program. Decisions about student involvement may also be made by this group. For instance, the decision regarding courses that will be required of all related discipline majors should be made by the team. Each faculty member may have additional responsibilities in her or his home department but is assigned responsibility as a contributor to the interdisciplinary program. Courses may be taught independently of any one department or may be offered within specific departments as part of the interdisciplinary core or full degree program. Such a program requires that deans of the various related colleges and chairs of the discipline-specific programs provide informed support and approval prior to any planning meetings. Developing a new curriculum, or an interdisciplinary core including several discipline-specific degree programs, may require that each department delete some existing courses or field experiences in order to receive approval from the administration.

From an advocacy point of view, professional unification through interdisciplinary personnel preparation in early childhood education and early intervention can strengthen the emerging reality of professionalism in early education. The two primary national early childhood organizations, the Division for Early Childhood (DEC) of the Council for Exceptional Children and NAEYC, along with other discipline-specific associations, are actively working to achieve consensus about standards for teachers and other service providers in programs for very young children with and without disabilities (Bredekamp, 1992).

The Association for Teacher Education and the National Association for the Education of Young Children (1991) issued a position paper calling for all states to offer specialized early childhood certification that incorporates standards for working with young children who have disabilities. In addition, ATE, DEC, and NAEYC have begun a collaborative effort to review personnel standards specific to early educators across a variety of organizations and to implement a process for cooperation on the development of a position regarding personnel standards. This joint effort toward the definition of professionalism in early childhood education and early intervention should lead to a broader definition of a new interdisciplinary field of study and of services to children and families.

Research Base

Research into models and practices regarding personnel preparation in early childhood is meager. Although descriptions of preservice and inservice programs contain much relevant and instructive information, little comparative research or validated practice data are available. The relatively new field of early intervention personnel preparation requires innovation in planning and implementing training programs. The efforts by professional teams to examine standards and recommend training content and processes specific to infants, toddlers, and preschoolers and their families are currently viewed as an essential priority for this new field. The length of time to establish preservice training programs can be from 2 to 4 years (Gallagher, 1989).

Some empirical data are available to program planners, however. Several studies have examined the nature of content in training programs across disciplines. Findings suggest that students receive little specific training and practice with infants and families (Bailey, Palsha, & Huntington, 1990; Bailey, Simeonsson, et al., 1990). These studies found considerable variability in the kind and amount of early intervention content regarding typical and atypical development, assessment, and services to infants and families. The results further suggested that programs are not likely to increase the extent of content for infants from birth through 2 years. In an extensive study of preservice programs across early intervention disciplines in California, Hanson and Lovett (1992) supported the finding that few graduates receive specialized training in content related to infants and families. In addition, they reported that few programs represented an interdisciplinary perspective and that the program graduates were typically white and, thus, not representative of a range of cultural and ethnic diversity.

There seems to be general agreement in the field that some roles of personnel in birth-through-2 and 3-through-5 programs differ whereas other roles are similar. Little research is available, however, to guide the development of personnel programs. McCollum (1987) examined the preservice training needs for Illinois personnel in birth-through-2 and 3-through-5 programs, finding some similarities in needs of the two groups and some differences based on the age range served. No significant difference was found in training needs related to (a) assessment, (b) developing individual programs, (c) implementing activities with individual children, (d) communicating with parents, (e) planning family involvement, (f) training other professionals, and (g) participating in professional development. Results suggested that more emphasis should be placed on training preschool early educators who are qualified to (a) plan learning activities, (b) implement group activities, (c) organize the learning environment, (d) collect and analyze progress data, (e) work with paraprofessionals and volunteers, and (f) conduct program evaluation. Data indicated that training for infant interventionists should place more emphasis on (a) communicating with families about their needs, (b) participating in team meetings, (c) finding and coordinating services, and (d) record keeping. This differentiation of content may vary in training programs across states or even within states, however, according to the expected roles of early interventionists and early educators.

The comprehensive service delivery system called for by law requires a multidisciplinary work force of personnel qualified to perform early childhood services (Bailey, Simeonsson, et al., 1990). Although the current work force providing early intervention services is generally highly educated (Brown, Mesich, & Hames, 1990; Hanson, 1990), fewer than half may have specialized training in early intervention (Kontos & Dunn, 1989). Because specialized training and education, not experience alone, are the best predictors of competent early childhood staff, states' comprehensive systems of personnel development must adequately address both preservice and inservice training needs of these professionals (Kontos & File, 1992).

The following sections of this chapter provide descriptions of the content, processes, and field experiences judged by early education and intervention professionals and parents to be essential practices in preservice personnel preparation programs. The sections on inservice and preservice practices also incorporate existing literature or empirical evidence to support and expand current professional thinking. Specific practices and indicators of quality in personnel development for early intervention and early childhood special education may be found in the Appendix.

PRESERVICE PREPARATION

Cooperation, especially between higher education and state agencies, was identified by Bruder et al. (1991) as a critical factor in states' progress toward planning for personnel preparation. Standards for training, credentialing, and employment should be collaboratively developed across traditional boundaries of power and autonomy. Preservice programs designed to meet entry-level requirements in each discipline may include 2-year, 4-year, and graduate-level preservice preparation. Rooney et al. (1992)

described characteristics of states exemplifying successful collaboration between higher education and state agencies. Those characteristics of states were (a) a mission traditionally inclusive of education in general, and early intervention specifically; (b) value placed on the phenomenon of progress and systematic planning; (c) consistency of leadership in either higher education, state agencies, or both; (d) active professional organizations; (e) support from high-level policy makers; (f) availability of resources including funds, time, and expertise; (g) "bias for action" as part of the state's culture; and (h) key individuals in leadership roles.

Preservice education programs to prepare personnel to serve infants, toddlers, and preschoolers with disabilities and their families have most often been provided at the graduate level. As more undergraduate and associate degree programs are developed, the need to identify appropriate entry-level curriculum content, desired outcomes, and strategies for delivering the content will intensify. Although some graduate programs may continue to prepare entry-level personnel, others will target the development of specialization and leadership or administrative skills. Interdisciplinary graduate-level preparation programs may offer specializations in infancy, family study, consultation and collaboration, administration, or low-incidence disabilities. Prerequisites for admission to these programs should include some level of experience and formal training in working with children birth through 5 years who have varying abilities and their families. Undergraduate programs are needed to train large numbers of entry-level early education professionals. Associate degree programs are essential to prepare early childhood personnel who work with children and families under the supervision of degreed personnel.

Many states are approaching personnel development in early childhood education and early intervention as a three-tiered effort with articulation between associate, bachelor's, and master's degree programs providing the foundation for a state career-development system in early education. This three-tiered development system may be more attractive to policy makers and deans of colleges if existing curricula, disciplines, and theories in early childhood education and development are specifically delineated and integrated across degree programs.

Collaborative development of curricula across degree programs necessitates a merger of personnel competencies and standards and coordinated training efforts. Merging professional standards and coordination across preparation programs in early education and intervention is consistent with the philosophy of inclusive services for infants, toddlers, and preschoolers with disabilities and their families (Miller, 1992).

The extant literature on teacher education at the preservice level comes largely from general education. Although little research in teacher education for the field of early intervention exists, the available research in general education can be applied in other areas of teacher education (McCollum &

McCartan, 1988). Outcomes in the teacher education literature that have particular relevance to early childhood education and intervention are discussed here in terms of four different aspects of preservice teacher education programs: content, process, clinical or field experiences, and faculty. Each of these aspects is discussed in relationship to the recent findings in the validation of recommended practices conducted by DEC; Stayton & Miller, 1993b). Whenever possible, the quality indicators provided by early education and intervention professionals in response to the survey are tied to research in teacher education. When discussed, the indicators are referenced according to the Personnel Competence listing in the Appendix. For example, discussion of the theory to practice orientation is referenced as "PC 5."

Preservice Content

Personnel preparation programs in early childhood education and early intervention prepare professionals who assume a variety of roles in a wide range of service settings (PC 11). Curricula should reflect a "theory-to-practice" orientation with course work and knowledge content sequentially linked to practica, internships, and all clinical components (PC 5). Interdisciplinary courses and field experiences may offer the opportunities for students from related disciplines to build necessary knowledge competencies and to train collaboratively in the areas of interdisciplinary planning and implementation of early childhood education and early intervention programs (PC 19; McCollum & Bailey, 1991).

The content of preservice curricula in teacher education should reflect current and emerging professional thought regarding the nature of teaching and learning as it applies to very young children with and without disabilities. The literature has consistently described the knowledge and skills needed by early childhood special educators (McCollum et al., 1989; Shearer & Mori, 1987) and the content typically included in personnel preparation programs (Bailey, Palsha, & Huntington, 1990; Bricker & Slentz, 1988; Bruder & McLean, 1988; Smith & Powers, 1987; Stayton & Miller, 1993b). These needs for training have recently been validated as noted in the listing of competency indicators (see Appendix) and apply also to other related disciplines. The needs include (a) foundations and philosophies in early childhood and early childhood special education, (b) typical and atypical child development, (c) assessment and individual program development, (d) designing and managing learning environments, (e) intervention strategies, (f) family involvement and family-focused services, (g) teaming and communication, and (h) professional values and ethics.

The current literature supports the need for intentional planning of a curriculum that offers more than superficial content in working with infants and their families (Bricker & Slentz, 1988; McCollum & Bailey,

1991). Content that prepares teachers to design learning experiences that are sensitive, responsive, and celebratory of diversity has also been identified as weak in many preparation programs (Mitchell & Modigliani, 1989).

Students must be grounded in both typical and atypical developmental patterns and characteristics in infants, toddlers, and preschoolers (PC 2). The study of early child development should be the cornerstone of the curriculum. Although professional standards may support one approach to early education over another, students should be knowledgeable of various theories of development and how to use specific aspects of different theories when needed with individual children (Berkeley & Ludlow, 1992).

Preservice personnel preparation programs that involve families in planning, implementing, and evaluating the core knowledge and application phases of the program demonstrate adherence to the standards and philosophy of family-centered early education and intervention (PC 1). The study of families as systems operating within particular cultural and ethnic influences has been included as an indicator of good teacher education curricula (PC 3, PC 6).

The content of preservice curricula should infuse the expectation that the early educator is a reflective and analytic decision maker who has a current professional base of knowledge and who can intentionally access that knowledge base in making decisions (PC 29). Students need many opportunities to exercise reflective problem-solving skills and processes (i.e., class discussions, journals, case-study methods). Otherwise, the students may enter the final internship or student teaching experience with no capability to reject, accept, or modify what they observe in the supervising professionals. Research supports the conclusion that when students have not been prepared to reflect, analyze, and use knowledge according to contextual situations, they tend to mimic the current, prevailing practice (Lanier, 1986).

The content of the curriculum should set expectations for continued professional development in a field of rapidly growing knowledge and understanding (PC 9). Course work and experiences should acquaint and familiarize students with professional associations, agencies, and resources. Accessing and using research data and current professional literature should guide the work of all curricular activities. Student chapters of professional associations within each discipline can be established. Joint meetings of early-childhood-related association chapters can foster attitudes of interdisciplinary collaboration. Interdisciplinary courses, practica, and professional meetings will also enhance students' abilities to enter jobs with greater flexibility and expectations for collegiality.

Despite general agreement that roles of personnel differ for the birth-through-2 and 3-through-5 populations, little differentiation has been noted in the content of personnel preparation curricula (Bailey, Simeonsson, et al., 1990). The need for greater emphasis on content related to infancy has been noted repeatedly in the literature. This is an area that requires further research to determine how preservice curricula should be designed to meet the training needs of personnel.

Preservice Processes

How preservice programs transmit knowledge and how they engage students in activities designed to produce specific, desired outcomes can be thought of as the processes of learning and teaching. Bricker and Slentz (1988) reported that 92% of the programs surveyed in their study were competency based. Most national professional associations related to early intervention have described their professional standards in competency-based statements of knowledge and performance (PC 35). Although early childhood education standards traditionally have not been expressed as performance competencies, the standards may easily be transformed into competency statements and objectively measured. Preservice programs may provide opportunities for developing professional competencies in a variety of ways (PC 20).

The theory-to-practice approach to training ought to evidence early and continuous linkages between course work and practice and should foster data-based decision making (PC 7). Sequentially ordered practica and other field experiences should move from observation and reflection to greater degrees of responsibility for planning and decision making in actual service settings (PC 22; e.g., classrooms, homes, hospitals, clinics). Student learning experiences should involve engagement in guided reflection incorporating observations, readings, and specific case-study problems related to the knowledge base acquired in courses and other data-based activities. Application of recommended practices for intervention in authentic, real-world settings and culturally diverse situations should be fully integrated with all theory (PC 23, PC 26, PC 27, PC 28).

Curricular processes must match students' experiences, interests, and needs with expectations for outcomes (PC 17). Selection of students for admission to preservice programs may involve personal interviews designed to assess these and other variables such as personality, attitudes, and professional goals. Student admissions criteria may include specific cutoff scores on standard tests of aptitude and achievement.

Field Experiences

McCollum and McCartan (1988), in their comprehensive review of research in teacher education, suggested a number of implications for personnel preparation in early education and intervention. The literature supports the conclusions that field experiences are typically isolated from the pedagogical and knowledge bases in the curriculum and that what is learned in field experiences can negate the other aspects of curriculum. The result of the absence of coherence is that students may graduate from the program with less than adequate ability to function as knowledgeable, reflective professionals. The full integration of course content and field experiences throughout the curriculum, with student activity focused on analyzing alternative models of teaching and therapy, deliberating about real problems encountered in service provision, and debating the whys of contextually based decisions will better approach the desired outcomes for teacher education.

Within the context of a family-centered preservice curriculum, field experiences with families in different settings ought to be sequenced and clearly structured. They might build toward a comprehensive family project, one that allows a student to participate in the life of a single family over an extended period of time (PC 4). The valuative feedback from families concerning their experiences with a student should be considered as important as other valuative data.

Field experiences should take place in settings that demonstrate standards of quality services to infants, toddlers, and preschoolers with and without disabilities (PC 24). Checklists that record indicators of quality for field placements can be used in the selection process. When field sites need assistance in developing exemplary practices, university faculty may participate in an agreement of reciprocal resource exchange, which may involve training and individualized support of site-based personnel.

Bonar (1985) discussed components of quality field experiences that can be applied across disciplines in early education and intervention. Those components include (a) ensuring that field experiences serve as natural extensions of the curriculum; (b) targeting specific skills and behavior in students for evaluation; (c) ensuring that content from course to course and from field experience to field experience is integrated; (d) organizing field experiences around highly structured tasks and activities on the basis of targeted skills and behaviors; (e) training cooperating site personnel, students, and university supervisors in the roles and expectations related to field experiences; and (f) having frequent conferences and debriefing seminars in which university faculty facilitate student reflection on experiences.

Supervision in field experiences should be conducted by faculty with formal training and experiences with infants, toddlers, and preschoolers with varying abilities (PC 13). Supervision requires knowledge of communication skills, supervision skills, and the specific field in which the supervisor operates. Students who are new to field experience activities and inexperienced with self-initiation and independence may initially prefer a more directive style of supervision. As students gain experience, faculty supervisors can assess the degree of support and direction required and modify their style of supervision.

Preservice Faculty

Qualified university faculty should supervise all field experiences (PC 21). That is, supervising faculty should demonstrate the knowledge and be able to model and coach practices offered in the preparation program. Program faculty have formal training and experiences with infants, toddlers, and preschoolers with varying abilities and their families. Many states require faculty who teach methods courses or who supervise field experiences to be eligible for or hold certification in early education and intervention. Summer institutes designed for training of faculty in early intervention content and practice may be funded by private, state, or federal funds. Faculty should represent the diverse ethnic and cultural groups served in this field (PC 31). Program faculty should provide feedback, both formal and informal, that is frequent, clear, and precise (PC 8). Whenever possible, the faculty members who teach the courses should also supervise the field experiences and assess the performance of competencies (PC 30).

Graduate Preparation

It is likely that students in graduate-level preservice programs may have degrees in child development, early childhood education, early childhood special education, nursing, or other related disciplines. Requirements for prerequisites should be based on prior experience and training. Many graduate programs require entering students to have the entry-level certification or license in the area. Current professional standards support the specialist role in graduate preparation (PC 16; Klein & Campbell, 1990). The age span in early education, birth through age 8 years, presents complex issues in personnel preparation. Students may choose to specialize according to age range (birth through 2, 3 through 5, 6 through 8), by low-incidence categories of disability, or in areas of family studies or consultation. In addition to a common core of knowledge and skills, the area of specialization would require special content and areas of application.

Content in the infant–toddler area of specialization must provide more than an introduction to infant development, family systems, family functioning, and family support. Content must also focus on interdisciplinary collaboration with families, development of the IFSP, and interagency cooperation in service delivery. Students should become skilled in participating in and leading interdisciplinary planning teams (PC 19). This function requires intense study and practice of effective communication skills. Students will become knowledgeable in developing and evaluating learning environments for individual or group settings and in providing consultation services.

Content in graduate-level specialization in preschool (ages 3 through 5) early education and intervention should emphasize child development for children from birth through 8, influence of disabilities on developmental patterns, working in inclusive settings, and early childhood education. At the graduate level, students should become competent in analyzing and applying various theories of learning and development and should be very familiar with professional literature and research. Additionally, students in this area should be competent in initiating and facilitating interdisciplinary collaborative teams, which, as with the infancy specialization, requires study and practice of communication skills. Curriculum development, teaching, and self-evaluation are components within the preschool program. Integrating therapies, throughout the daily routines, consulting with professionals from related disciplines, and working with personnel in special programs and in mainstream settings are essential content areas as well.

Graduate-level programs prepare professionals who will evaluate programs and deliver staff development and inservice training activities. Roles for which graduate-level students may be prepared include master teacher, mentor, consultant, agency planner, program coordinator, and administrator. Early childhood educators who perform leadership functions need specialized training and experience that have been described in the literature (PC 15; Miller & McDowelle, 1993).

INSERVICE PREPARATION

Inservice can be defined as "the process by which practicing professionals participate in experiences designed to improve or change professional practice" (Bailey, 1989, p. 24). Trohanis (1985) emphasized that this process is ongoing and systematic and the changes in professional practice may result from training that supports either organizational or individual goals (PC 36, PC 50).

With the emphasis in educational reform efforts on learning as a lifelong process, inservice should be considered an integral component of early childhood program planning. Inservice is critical in the organizational and individual professional growth process for three major reasons:

- Preservice preparation may provide only entry level knowledge and skills for a profession. The acquisition of advanced skills and increased competence develops over time (Bailey, 1989; Joyce & Showers, 1980; Korinek et al., 1985).
- Education is a dynamic profession. As new information and practices are implemented, others may become obsolete. Inservice programs serve as a vehicle for professionals to keep abreast of a changing field (Bailey, 1989; Joyce & Showers, 1980; Korinek et al., 1985).
- A relatively new field, such as early education and early intervention, that has a shortage of qualified personnel may consider strategies in addi-

tion to preservice preparation to provide initial training for the profession. Inservice is one viable strategy (Bailey, 1989).

Preceding sections of this chapter have highlighted the projected shortages in both early education and early intervention. These shortages are not likely to be addressed through traditional preservice programs. Many states have not yet developed personnel standards and certification guidelines for personnel who work with children ages birth through 5 years (Bruder et al., 1991). Special education is one of the disciplines least likely to have standards beginning at birth. Compounding this problem is the fact that many institutions of higher education do not have preservice programs that focus on the birth-through-5 age range (Bailey, Palsha, & Huntington, 1990) and specifically do not plan to increase coverage of birth-through-2 content (Bailey, Simeonsson, et al., 1990).

Another factor having an impact on inservice training needs is the large number of early childhood personnel who are employed in educational roles but who do not have training specific to early education and intervention. A national survey of 34 federally funded projects that serve children birth through 2 years with disabilities and their families reported that only 94 of approximately 300 staff are infant interventionists (Stayton & Karnes, in press) and that only 13 of those infant interventionists have formal training in early childhood special education.

Changing practices in early childhood education that result in changing roles are yet another factor with implications for inservice training. Major changes in the organization and delivery of services (e.g., family-centered services, interdisciplinary or transdisciplinary teaming, inclusion) result in new roles for individual staff as well as systemic changes. Although Bricker and Slentz (1988) reported that the majority of university and college programs prepare early childhood special educators for multiple roles (e.g., teacher, infant specialist, team collaborator, facilitator or consultant), there is no guarantee that all personnel have such comprehensive training. Some personnel may not have any early education and intervention training, and others, because of the dearth of programs and qualified university faculty, may have completed programs that are weak in addressing recommended practices in the field.

In view of these factors, it is imperative that state agencies, institutions of higher education, and local early childhood programs work collaboratively to develop inservice plans (a) that provide current personnel with new knowledge and skills and (b) that are integral components of both the Part H and the Part B CSPDs in addressing the shortage of qualified entry-level personnel in early education and early intervention. As states develop or modify personnel standards and certification and licensing guidelines, comprehensive inservice activities should be integrated as one of the vehicles by which outcomes can be obtained. From this perspective, inservice must be viewed as one strategy in an ongoing systems-change process with underlying assumptions about the change process incorporated into inservice plans (Bailey et al., 1992; Fullan, 1982; Hall & Hord, 1987; Havelock & Havelock, 1973; Winton, 1990). These assumptions suggest that change (a) be based on a comprehensive, long-term, systematic approach; (b) require consumers of training to recognize the gap between their current knowledge and skills and the knowledge and skills for which they are being trained; (c) require individuals within a social organization to be trained together to develop shared knowledge and values for changing roles; and (d) empower consumers of training to become competent team members in decision making about their own training needs and strategies for addressing those needs (PC 38, PC 49, PC 50).

As with preservice preparation, little literature is available regarding inservice preparation specific to early education and early intervention. The available literature tends to be descriptive in nature. Therefore, the following discussion of inservice content, processes, and context is based primarily on the general education inservice literature specific to elementary and secondary education. Each of these aspects of inservice preparation are discussed in relation to the DEC-recommended practices.

Hutson (1981), in a discussion of inservice best practices, stressed that inservice content, or the *what* of inservice, should be based on assessed needs and should focus on changing educators' behaviors rather than children's behaviors (PC 38). For an effective needs-based approach to be implemented, the characteristics of adult learners must be considered. Knowles (1980, 1984) characterized four concepts of the adult learner that are applicable to the inservice process:

- Adult learners have a need to be self-directed. Adults have an increasing psychological need to move from dependency to self-directedness. Adults, therefore, have a need to take responsibility for their own learning in terms of individual style and pacing.
- Adult learners enter any educational activity with a wealth of personal and professional experiences. Adult learners are a rich resource of information for themselves and for others. Therefore, the content and process of inservice should be designed to facilitate sharing of experiences and application to life situations. Because experiences vary across participants, however, individualization of content is also essential. In addition, previous experiences may result in some adults being "set in their way" of thinking and doing things, and they must be assisted in recognizing the gap between current thinking and practices before changes can be made.
- Adult learners demonstrate a readiness to learn when they experience a need to know or perform more effectively. Content should be based on the adult learner's readiness level, which seems to be motivated by the need to cope with real-life tasks or situations. Learning can then be viewed as a process by which the learner progresses toward a greater degree of competence.

- Adult learners are oriented toward performance-based learning. Adults desire to acquire knowledge and skills that can be applied in their daily work setting. Therefore, inservice content should focus on topics that adults confront on a day-to-day basis.

Application of the adult learning literature to a needs-based approach suggests that inservice content should be derived from assessed needs of the participants, with the needs assessment addressing competencies that the learner must demonstrate in his or her employment setting (PC 36, PC 38). Needs-based inservice lends itself to activities that acknowledge the experiences of participants and builds upon those experiences that are relevant to the learner's situation and that emphasize the learner's own goals as the primary incentive for participation.

Competencies may be assessed via a variety of strategies (PC 47; Trohanis, 1985). These include (a) written self-reports of needs, (b) observations of participants' performance with recommendations of needs, (c) written pretests, (d) recommendations from an inservice planning committee, and (e) interviews with participants.

The actual competencies incorporated into needs-assessment activities should be based on current recommended practices and new roles required of early educators due to legislative mandates and changing practices in the field. The eight competency areas identified in the preservice content section of this chapter should also serve as a foundation for inservice competencies. The literature reports that all related-discipline professionals should receive specific training in providing family-centered services, in collaborating as team members, and in providing consultant or direct services in inclusive settings (Bailey, Simeonsson, et al., 1990; McCollum & Thorp, 1988; Bailey, Palsha, & Huntington, 1990; Fenichel & Eggbeer, 1991; Bailey, Palsha, & Simeonsson, 1991). Some recipients of inservice may be focusing on refining knowledge and skills, others on acquiring new skills to fulfill changing roles, and yet others on obtaining entry-level competencies in early education and intervention. Needs assessments, therefore, should be individualized to address variability in knowledge, skills, and roles.

Inservice Processes

Decision Making and Planning

The first step in determining *how* the content of inservice is determined and implemented is the development of an inservice plan. Those who develop inservice plans should consider the following steps as guidelines:

1. Identify an inservice coordinator.

2. Obtain support from all the key players (e.g., administrators, parents, staff).
3. Plan and implement a needs assessment.
4. Prioritize competencies based on assessed needs.
5. Develop specific goals and objectives.
6. Develop a philosophy regarding adult learners and the change process.
7. Identify characteristics of the participants, children and families whom they serve, and the community.
8. Incorporate a variety of delivery methods including active strategies such as demonstration and supervised practice and feedback.
9. Relate learning to the workplace and plan for transfer activities.
10. Include follow-up activities.
11. Integrate evaluation throughout the plan (Korinek et al., 1985; Trohanis, 1985).

Section 303.360 of P.L. 99-457 (Part H of early intervention legislation; *Federal Register,* 1993) includes the requirement that inservice be provided on an interdisciplinary basis when appropriate and provided to a variety of personnel. This provision has been interpreted as meaning that inservice planning should be a team effort involving family members as consumers, professionals from a variety of disciplines, and paraprofessionals (PC 37, PC 39, PC 40). This contention is supported by the adult learning (Knowles, 1980; 1984) and the inservice best practices literature (Hutson, 1981; Korinek et al., 1985), which reports that decision making specific to inservice should be a collaborative effort between the recipients, the provider, and other constituencies. Winton (1990) stressed that if the inservice process is to result in systemic changes, individuals with power and authority must be involved in the planning process (PC 43). These would include (a) program administrators who can ensure that such things as program procedures and salaries are modified, (b) leaders from all disciplines identified in P.L. 99-457 to ensure that practices that may differ from traditional practices are implemented, and (c) individuals who are viewed as innovative and influential in using and disseminating practice. Hutson (1981) reported that such a collaborative effort should result in higher quality inservice because of the multiple perspectives in planning, greater ownership of the participants, and decision making based on competence rather than on position.

Support Factors

Successful implementation of inservice depends, in part, on the consideration of certain logistical and support factors (PC 46; Hutson, 1981; Korinek et al., 1985). First, inservice should be financially and geographically accessible to participants, with local sites most desirable. On-site training has several advantages in that it (a) requires less time away from work, (b) requires fewer travel expenses, (c) allows administrators to be more involved, (d) encourages participants in a geographical area to network, (e) facilitates evaluation in the context of service delivery, and (f) provides the context to individualize training (Bennett, Watson, & Raab, 1991). Second, inservice should be scheduled at times that are convenient for participants to avoid interfering with job requirements. Third, inservice should have explicit administrative support (PC 43). This support may be evidenced by facilitating staff participation in inservice (e.g., released time), providing incentives for completing activities (e. g., salary increases), and allowing for change in direct service practices. Fourth, incentives for participation should be an integral part of the inservice plan. Wade (1984/1985), in her meta-analysis of 91 inservice studies, found significantly greater effect sizes if the individuals were chosen as participants instead of being required to participate. She also reported moderately positive effect sizes for college credit, followed by released time. Fifth, inservice is most successful if coworkers support the inservice by participating as team members in the actual inservice activities; by participating in work-site activities, such as team meetings, to discuss the application of skills; or by working in teams or pairs to provide each other with immediate feedback (PC 44). To facilitate the change process, this team should include collegial support across disciplines (Fenichel & Eggbeer, 1991) and families (Winton, 1990). And finally, outside agencies should be included, as appropriate, to provide consultant services and links with certification and required training activities.

Delivery of Inservice

Inservice has more long-lasting benefits if it is conducted as a comprehensive, ongoing, systematic process rather than as a "one-shot" activity (PC 50; Hutson, 1981; Korinek et al., 1985). Through a review of over 100 articles related to inservice, Korinek et al. (1985) identified the three most common types of in-service: information transmission, skill acquisition, and behavior change. A meta-analysis of inservice studies by Showers, Joyce, and Bennett (1987) divided the most common inservice outcomes into three categories: the outcomes of knowledge, enhanced or new skills, and transfer of concepts to the work situation. The results of these two studies suggest a relationship between common in-service types and outcomes:

- Information transmission is related to the outcome of knowledge. This seems to be the most common type of inservice but the most unpopular with educators. The inservice is typically a 1- to 3-hour presentation including more passive strategies such as lecture, panel discussions, and videos (PC 49). It is held at a local site or as part of a conference. Content seems to be unrelated, self-contained topics that are evaluated by ratings of usefulness and satisfaction (PC 47). In earlier work, Joyce and Showers (1980) divided this outcome area into (1) awareness and (2) concepts and organized knowledge. If the outcome is awareness, participants realize the importance of a topic or issue and begin to focus on it. If the outcome is concepts and organized knowledge, however, the relevant information is understood and organized for use.
- Skill acquisition is related to the outcome of enhanced or new skills. This type of inservice typically includes multiple sessions of 2–3 hours over several days that are held at a local site. The content is based on sequential presentation of a topic, with more active strategies such as demonstration, practice, feedback (PC 49). Evaluation is based on demonstration of the skill (PC 47).
- Behavior change is related to the outcome of transfer of concepts and skills to the work situation. This inservice type is the most costly, is the most time consuming, requires the greatest commitment, and is the least used. Multiple sessions of varying length are held with interdependent presentations connected by common concepts and practice. A variety of strategies, both passive and active, are employed, with evaluation based on the degree to which goals and objectives are achieved (PC 49). Local sites are utilized.

The outcome achieved (i.e., knowledge, skills, behavior change) seems to be affected by the actual structure and format of the inservice program. Researchers have described various components that are essential to the overall design of the inservice program. Each of these researchers offered a comprehensive set of components designed to result in behavior change (PC 41).

Joyce and Showers (1980) identified five components of effective staff-development programs: (a) presentation of theory or of the new skill or strategy, (b) demonstration or modeling of the new skill or strategy, (c) practice in simulated or real-life settings, (d) structured and open-ended feedback regarding performance in the practice situation, and (e) follow-up coaching for implementation of the new skill. These authors suggested that each of the five components is critical for effective inservice, but that modeling and feedback result in the greatest transfer of learning.

Stallings (1982) presented a similar model with the four components: (a) pretest (observe and assess what the needs are), (b) inform (present content with an integration of theory and practice while honoring participants' experiences), (c) organize and guide practice (demonstrate new skills, observe participants using the new skills, and provide feedback in a simulated setting), and (d) posttest (observe participants after the inservice activities as follow-up and provide feedback).

More recently, Bailey et al. (1992) studied a four-component, team-based model for facilitating change. This model was designed for local early intervention teams, who progress through the following components:

1. Presentation in which information and issues related to key questions about a specific topic(s) are presented.

2. Case study in which information and issues are applied to a family and an early intervention program through a case study that involves guided small-group discussion and problem solving.

3. Team discussion and decision making in which participants individually identify changes specific to each question addressed in the first component and rank those changes. Then, local teams discuss the changes and individual rankings and reach consensus on incorporating these into an action plan for the team.

4. Follow-up in which the action plan is implemented at the work site with follow-up through regular team meetings, peers working in pairs and providing feedback to each other, skills practice through on-site role plays and simulations, and self-assessment via videotapes of work activities (PC 45).

Each of these researchers presented similar components. The three models emphasize an ongoing, systematic approach to move participants from initial awareness and knowledge of concepts and skills to the transfer of knowledge and skills to the actual work situation, a process which facilitates long-term behavior change (PC 48). The meta-analysis by Showers et al. (1987) supported the inclusion of some combination of four components in an inservice model designed to result in behavior change in the workplace. These components are presentation of theory, modeling and demonstration, practice in simulated and actual settings, and structured and open-ended feedback. It is estimated that for a person to effectively perform a new complex skill, 25 uses of the new strategy are needed before transfer occurs. The Showers et al. (1987) study reported that practice with some type of peer or expert coaching resulted in higher effect sizes than when practice was not accompanied by coaching. A model that includes these components facilitates the active involvement of participants in a problem-centered rather than subject-centered approach, which is consistent with the adult-learning literature (PC 51).

A model with the components just described lends itself to a variety of activities that are selected on the basis of the components being implemented. Harris (1980) described delivery methods as being on a continuum from passive to active and suggested that the selection of methods be based on the goals and objectives for the inservice component (PC 49). He asserted that more passive methods (e.g., lecture, discussion, panels, demonstrations) are most effective for knowledge acquisition whereas more active methods (e.g, microteaching, role plays, simulations) are more effective for skill acquisition. In her meta-analysis of inservice studies, Wade (1984/1985) reported the highest effect sizes for observation of classroom practices, microteaching, video or audio feedback, and practice. Lower effect sizes were found for discussion, lecture, games or simulations, and guided field trips. Wade, however, did not relate these strategies to desired outcomes. It would be extremely difficult to present new information through microteaching, for example. Hutson (1981), in his report of inservice best practices, stressed that methods should model good teaching and encourage the active involvement of participants.

To ensure that inservice delivery is effective, providers must conduct an evaluation (PC 47, PC 48). The literature (Hutson, 1981; Korinek et al., 1985) suggests that evaluation should be a collaborative process and an integral component in both planning and implementing inservice. Evaluation plans and processes should address both long-term and short-term effects, thus providing for both formative and summative measures of change. Evaluation strategies should be matched with the goals and objectives of each component with a variety of strategies implemented (e.g., satisfaction questionnaires, pre- and posttests, observation, completed products).

Inservice Context

Inservice Participants

Section 303.360 of P.L. 99-457 has been interpreted as meaning that inservice audiences should represent the variety of disciplines providing services within the participating programs. This practice should ensure that individuals within programs develop a shared knowledge, attitude, and skill base, and a sense of responsibility for implementing changes in service delivery (PC 52) . Family members are essential participants on the inservice team for four primary reasons: (1) Family involvement increases the degree of acceptability of decisions for families; (2) family involvement is consistent with a family-centered philosophy; (3) family involvement establishes the precedent of families as decision makers; and (4) family involvement may influence professionals to recognize the need for change (PC 37; Bailey, et al., 1992).

Inservice Facilitators

Section 303.360 of P.L. 99-457 (*Federal Register*, 1993) is also interpreted to mean that in-service should be conducted by interdisciplinary teams, including family members, to the extent appropriate (PC 40). Each team member must be competent in the inservice process by being able to (a) plan and organize inservice, (b) work with adults, (c) match content with appropriate training strategies, and (d) evaluate training effectiveness. The effectiveness of a good trainer is not role related but, instead, is based on having a good inservice design and knowing how to implement it (Showers et al., 1987). Although the role of inservice facilitators may vary according to the component of the inservice (e.g., informer, demonstrator), the literature indicates that successful inservice is characterized by facilitators who (a) are knowledgeable about the inservice content (Bailey et al., 1992; Sharp, 1988); (b) integrate participants' experiences and priorities for training into the inservice (Bailey et al., 1992; Edwards & Barnes, 1985; Griffin & Barnes, 1986; Sharp, 1988); (c) allow for interaction through activities that encourage reflection and analysis (Edwards & Barnes, 1985; Griffin & Barnes, 1986); (d) employ effective questioning skills and allow time for questions (Bailey et al., 1992; Sharp, 1988); (e) give specific directions for small-group activities (Sharp, 1988); (f) provide feedback that is concrete, objective, and focused (Edwards & Barnes, 1985); (g) demonstrate flexibility and can "think on their feet" (Bailey et al., 1992); and (h) are exciting, motivating, and inspiring (Sharp, 1988) (PC 42).

CLOSING

Personnel preparation in early education and intervention is at a critical stage. If preservice and inservice programs are to adequately address personnel shortages and the need to prepare both entry-level and practicing professionals for new roles in a rapidly changing field, then changes must occur in preservice and inservice practices. First, personnel preparation must be recognized as an interdisciplinary activity in all phases of program planning, implementation, and evaluation. This requirement suggests cross-disciplinary programs with the active involvement of families as team members. Second, personnel preparation must be viewed as a collaborative effort between state agencies, institutions of higher education, and local programs. This requirement suggests collaboration in developing personnel standards and licensing and certification guidelines, in developing and implementing the comprehensive system of personnel development (CSPD) for both Part H and Part B, and in pooling resources to ensure that training is accessible to consumers and that efforts are not duplicated. Third, performance-based training practices must be developed that recognize both formal and informal training activities as well as professional experience as viable means for obtaining knowledge and skills. Finally, professional organizations must take a leadership role in providing guidelines for state agencies and institutions of higher education that adhere to recommended practices in the field.

REFERENCES

American Speech-Language-Hearing Association. (1991). Guidelines for speech pathologists serving persons with language, socio-communicative and/or cognitive communication impairments. *ASHA, 33*(5), 21–28.

Association for Teacher Education & National Association for the Education of Young Children. (1991). Early childhood teacher certification. *Young Children, 47*(1), 16–21.

Bailey, D. B. (1989). Issues and directions in preparing professionals to work with young handicapped children and their families. In J. Gallagher, P. Trohanis, & R. Clifford (Eds.), *Policy implementation and P.L. 99-457: Planning for young children with special needs* (pp. 97–132). Baltimore: Brookes.

Bailey, D. B., McWilliam, P. J., & Winton, P. J. (1992). Building family-centered practices in early intervention: A team-based model for change. *Infants and Young Children, 5*(1), 73–82.

Bailey, D. B., Palsha, S. A., Huntington, G. S. (1990). Preservice preparation of special educators to serve infants with handicaps and their families. Current status and training needs. *Journal of Early Intervention, 14*(1), 43–54.

Bailey, D. B., Palsha, S. A., & Simeonsson, R. J. (1991). Professional skills, concerns, and perceived importance of work with families in early intervention. *Exceptional Children, 58*(2), 156–165.

Bailey, D. B., Simeonsson, R. S., Yoder, D. E., & Huntington, G. S. (1990). Infant personnel preparation across eight disciplines: An integrative analysis. *Exceptional Children, 57*(6), 26–35.

Bennett, T., Watson, A. L., & Raab, M. (1991). Ensuring competence in early intervention personnel through personnel standards and high-quality training. *Infants and Young Children, 3*(3) 49–58.

Berkeley, T. R., & Ludlow, B. L. (1992). Developmental domains: The mother of all interventions; or the subterranean early development blues. *Topics in Early Childhood Special Education, 11*(4), 13–21.

Bonar, B. (1985). Needed: Structured activities in early field experience programs. *Action in Teacher Education, 7*(3), 43–47.

Bredekamp, S. (1992). The early childhood profession coming together. *Young Children, 47*(6), 36–39.

Bredekamp, S., & Willer, B. (1993). Professionalizing the field of early childhood education: Pros and cons. *Young Children, 48*(3), 82–84.

Bricker, D. D. (1978). A rationale for the integration of handicapped and nonhandicapped preschool children. In M. Guralnick (Ed.), *Early intervention and the integration of handicapped and nonhandicapped children* (pp. 3–26). Baltimore: University Park Press.

Bricker, D. D., & Slentz, K. (1988). Personnel preparation: Handicapped infants. In M. Wang, M. C. Reynolds, & H. J. Walberg (Eds.), *Handbook of special education: Research and practice* (Vol. 3, pp. 319–345). Elmsford, NY: Pergamon Books.

Brown, L. J., Mesich, C. R., & Hames, G. (1990). Early intervention in Washington State: Personnel and training needs. Olympia, WA: Birth to Six State Planning Grant.

Bruder, M., Klosowski, S., & Daguio, C. (1991) A review of personnel standards for Part H of P.L. 99-457. *Journal of Early Intervention, 15*(1), 66–79.

Bruder, M. B., & McLean, M. (1988). Personnel preparation for infant interventionists: A review of federally funded projects. *Journal of the Division for Early Childhood, 12,* 299–305.

Burton, C. B., Hains, A. H., Hanline, M. F., McLean, M., & McCormick, K. (1992). Early childhood intervention and education: The urgency of professional unification. *Topics in Early Childhood Special Education, 11*(4), 53–69.

Consensus Committee. (1993) *National standards of nursing practice for early intervention services.* Lexington: University of Kentucky, College of Nursing.

Drotar, D., & Sturm, L. (1989). Training psychologists as infant specialists. *Infants and Young Children, 2*(2), 58–66.

Dunn, W., Campbell, P. H., Detter, P. L., Hall, S., & Berger, E. (1989). *Guidelines for occupational services in early intervention and preschool services.* Rockville, MD: American Occupational Therapy Association.

Dunst, C., & Deal, A. (1990). Individualized family support plans: Model, methods and strategies. *Family Systems Intervention Monograph, 2* (No. 1). Morganton, NC: Western Carolina Center, Family, Infant, and Preschool Program.

Edwards, S., & Barnes, S. (1985). A research-based staff development model that works. *Education Leadership, 42*(7), 54–56.

Effgen, S., Bjorson, K., Chiarello, L., Sinzer, L., & Phillips, W. (1991). Competencies for physical therapists in early intervention. *Pediatric Physical Therapy, 4,* 77–80.

Esposito, B. (1987). The effects of preschool integration on the development of nonhandicapped children. *Journal of the Division for Early Childhood, 12*(1), 31–46.

Federal Register. 42, p. 163 (August 23, 1977).

Federal Register. 58, p. 145 (July 30, 1993).

Fenichel, E. S., & Eggbeer, L. (1991) Preparing practitioners to work with infants, toddlers, and their families: Four essential elements of training. *Infants and Young Children, 4*(2), 56–62.

Fullan, M. (1982). *The meaning of educational change.* New York: Teachers College Press.

Gallagher, J. (1989). *Planning for personnel preparation: A policy alert.* Chapel Hill: University of North Carolina, Carolina Policy Studies Program.

Gallagher, J., Harbin, G., Thomas, D., Clifford, R., & Wenger, M. (1988). *Major policy issues in implementing Part H–P.L. 99-457 (infants and toddlers).* Chapel Hill: University of North Carolina, Carolina Policy Studies Program.

Gilkerson, L., Hilliard, A. G., Schrag, E., & Shonkoff, J. P. (1987). Point of view: Commenting on P.L. 99-457. *Zero to Three, 7*(3), 13–17.

Griffin, G. A., & Barnes, S. (1986). Using research to change school and classroom practices: Results of an experimental study. *American Educational Research Journal, 23*(4), 572–586.

Hall, G. E., & Hord, S. (1987). *Change in schools: Facilitating the process*. Albany: State University of New York Press.

Hamilton, J. (1994, January). *EEPCD projects' business meeting*. Paper presented at the meeting of the National Technical Assistance Conference, Washington, DC.

Hanson, M. J. (1990). *Final report: California early intervention personnel model, personnel standards, and personnel preparation plan*. San Francisco: San Francisco State University, Department of Special Education, California Early Intervention Personnel Study Project.

Hanson, M. J., & Lovett, D. (1992). Personnel preparation for early interventionists: A cross-disciplinary study. *Journal of Early Intervention, 16*(2), 123–135.

Harris, B. (1980). *Improving staff performance through in-service education*. Boston: Allyn & Bacon.

Havelock, R., & Havelock, M. C. (1973). *Training for change agents*. Ann Arbor: University of Michigan.

Hutson, H. M. (1981). In-service best practices: The learnings of general education. *Journal of Research and Development in Education, 14*(2), 1–10.

Individuals with Disabilities Education Act of 1990, 20 U.S.C. §1400 et seq.

Joyce, B., & Showers, B. (1980). Improving in-service training: The messages of research. *Educational Leadership, 37*, 379–385.

Kaufman, M. (1989). Are dieticians prepared to work with handicapped infants? P.L. 99-457 offers new opportunities. *Journal of the American Dietetic Association, 89*(11), 1602–1605.

Klein, N., & Campbell, P. (1990). Preparing personnel to serve at-risk and disabled infants, toddlers, and preschoolers. In S. Meisels & J. Shonkoff (Eds.), *Handbook of early childhood intervention* (pp. 679–699). Cambridge: Cambridge University Press.

Knowles, M. S. (1980). *The modern practice of adult education* (rev. ed.). Cambridge, MA: Adult Education Company.

Knowles, M. (1984). *The adult learner: A neglected species* (3rd ed.). Houston, TX: Gulf.

Kontos, S., & Dunn, L. (1989). Characteristics of the early intervention workforce: An Indiana perspective. *Early Education and Development, 1*, 141–157.

Kontos, S., & File, N. (1992) Conditions of employment, job satisfaction, and job commitment among early intervention personnel. *Journal of Early Intervention, 16*(2), 155–165.

Korinek, L., Schmid, R., & McAdams, M. (1985). In-service types and best practices. *Journal of Research and Development in Education, 18*(2), 33–38.

Lanier, J. (1986). Teacher education: Needed research and practice for the preparation of teaching professionals. In D. C. Corrigan, D. Palmer, & P. Alexander (Eds.), *The future of teacher education: Needed research and practice* (pp. 13–35). Denton: Texas A & M University, College of Education.

McCollum, J. (1987). Early interventionists in infant and early childhood programs: A comparison of preservice training needs. *Topics in Early Childhood Special Education, 7*(3), 24–35.

McCollum, J., & Bailey, D. (1991) Developing comprehensive personnel systems: Issues and alternatives. *Journal of Early Intervention, 15*(1), 51–56.

McCollum, J., McLean, M., McCartan, K., & Kaiser, C. (1989). Recommendations for certification of early childhood special educators. *Journal of Early Intervention, 12*(3), 195–211.

McCollum, J., & Maude, S. (1992). *Compilation of professional competencies for early intervention personnel*. Reston, VA: Division for Early Childhood, Council for Exceptional Children.

McCollum, J., & Maude, S. (1994). Early childhood special educators as early interventionists: Issues and emerging practices in personnel preparation. In P. Safford (Ed.), *Yearbook of early childhood education* (pp. 263–270). New York: Longman.

McCollum, J., & McCartan, K. (1988). Research in teacher education: Issues and future directions for early childhood special education. In S. L. Odom & M. B. Karnes (Eds.), *Early intervention for infants and children with handicaps: An empirical base* (pp. 269–286), Baltimore: Brookes.

McCollum, J. A., & Thorp, E. K. (1988). Training of infant specialists: A look to the future. *Infants and Young Children, 1*(2), 55–65.

McLaughlin, M. J., Smith-Davis, J., & Burke, P. J. (1986). *Personnel to educate the handicapped: A status report.* College Park: University of Maryland.

Meisels, S. J., Harbin, G., Modigliani, K., & Olson, K. (1988) Formulating optimal state early childhood intervention policies. *Exceptional Children, 55*(2), 159–165.

Miller, P. S. (1992). Segregated programs of teacher education in early childhood: Immoral and inefficient practice. *Topics in Early Childhood Special Education, 11*(4), 39–52.

Miller, P. S., & McDowelle, J. (1993) *Administering preschool programs in public schools.* San Diego, CA: Singular Publishing Group.

Mitchell, A., & Modigliani, K. (1989). Young children in public schools? *Young Children, 44*(6), 56–61.

Nover, A., & Timberlake, E. (1989). Meeting the challenge: The educational preparation of social workers for practice with at-risk children (0–3) and their families. *Infants and Young Children, 2*(1), 59–65.

Odom, S. L., & McEvoy, M. A. (1988). Integration of young children with handicaps and normally developing children. In S. L. Odom & M. B. Karnes (Eds.), *Early intervention for infants and children with handicaps: An empirical base* (pp. 241–267). Baltimore: Brookes.

Odom, S. L., & McEvoy, M. A. (1990). Mainstreaming at the preschool level: Potential barriers and tasks for the field. *Topics in Early Childhood Special Education, 10*(2), 48–61.

Rooney, R., Fullagher, P., & Gallagher, J. (1993). *Distinctive personnel preparation models for Part H: Three case studies.* Chapel Hill: University of North Carolina, Carolina Policy Studies Program.

Rooney, R., Gallagher, J., Fullagher, P., Eckland, J., Huntington, G. (1992). *Higher education and state agency cooperation for Part H personnel preparation.* Chapel Hill: University of North Carolina, Carolina Policy Studies Program.

Sharp, P. A. (1988). Planning for better presentations. *Journal of Staff Development, 9*(3), 38–43.

Shearer, M., & Mori, A. (1987). Administration of preschool special education programs: Strategies for effectiveness. *Journal of the Division for Early Childhood, 11*, 161–180.

Showers, B., Joyce, B., & Bennett, B. (1987). Synthesis of research on staff development: A framework for future study and a state-of-the art analysis. *Educational Leadership, 45*(3), 77–87.

Smith, B., & Powers, C. (1987). Issues related to developing state certification policies. *Topics in Early Childhood Special Education, 7*(3), 12–23.

Stallings, J. (1982.) *What is effective staff development for basic skills instruction?* Palo Alto, CA: Stallings Teaching and Learning Institute.

Stayton, V. D., & Karnes, M. B. (in press). Model programs for infants and toddlers with disabilities and their families. In L. J. Johnson, R. J. Gallagher, M. J. LaMontagne, J. Jordan, J. J. Gallagher, P. L. Hutinger, & M. B. Karnes, (Eds.), *Early intervention for children and their families: Providing services from birth to three* (2nd ed.). Baltimore: Brookes.

Stayton, V., & Miller, P. (1993a). Combining early childhood and early childhood special education standards in personnel preparation programs: Experiences from two states. *Topics in Early Childhood Special Education, 13*(3), 372–387.

Stayton, V., & Miller, P. (1993b). Personnel competence. In *DEC Task Force on Recommended Practices: Indicators of quality in programs for infants and young children with special needs and their families* (pp. 107–113). Reston, VA: Council for Exceptional Children.

Stedman, D. (1990, January). *The professional preparation of teachers and early childhood educators: Changes in the wind.* Paper presented at the South Pacific International Conference on Special Education, Auckland, New Zealand.

Strain, P. S. (1990). LRE for preschool children with handicaps: What we know, what we should be doing. *Journal of Early Intervention, 14*(4), 291–296.

Trohanis, P. L. (1985). Designing a plan for in-service education. *Topics in Early Childhood Special Education, 5*(1), 63–82.

Turnbull, A. P. (1982). Preschool mainstreaming: A policy and implementation analysis. *Educational Evaluation and Policy Analysis, 4*, 281–291.

U.S. Department of Education. (1992). *Fourteenth annual report to Congress on the implementation of the Individuals with Disabilities Education Act.* Washington, DC: Author.

U.S. Department of Labor, Bureau of Labor Statistics (1988). *Projections 2000.* Washington, DC: U.S. Government Printing Office.

Wade, R. K. (1984/1985). What makes the difference in in-service teacher education? A meta-analysis of research. *Educational Leadership, 42*, 48–54.

Winton, P. J. (1990). A systemic approach for planning in-service training related to Public Law 99-457. *Infants and Young Children, 3*(1), 51–60.

Yoder, D. E., Coleman, P. P., & Gallagher, J. J. (1990). *Personnel needs: Allied health personnel meeting the demands of Part H, P.L. 99-457.* Chapel Hill: University of North Carolina, Carolina Policy Studies Program.

CHAPTER 15

Program Evaluation

Scott Snyder
Robert Sheehan

Program evaluation in early intervention and early childhood special education (EI/ECSE) settings consists of systematically collecting, synthesizing, and interpreting information about programs for the purpose of assisting with decision making. Within the parameters of this definition lies substantial diversity in the possible (a) program evaluation questions and decisions; (b) sources of evaluation questions; (c) aspects of the programs to be evaluated; (d) evaluation methodologies (e.g., procedures for gathering, organizing, analyzing, and interpreting information); (e) sources of evaluation information; (f) groups who will receive, act upon, or be affected by the results of the evaluations; and (g) resources available for conducting the evaluations.

There is also substantial diversity in the characteristics of early intervention programs, children and families served by such programs, and the contexts of such programs. Practices appropriate for program evaluation in early intervention will vary according to the nature of the evaluation and the characteristics of the program.

The knowledge base concerning program evaluation in early intervention is not derived from specific and comprehensive practice guidelines that have been established as valid and reliable in each possible evaluation situation. Therefore, rather than attempting to present specific best practice recommendations in each possible aspect of program evaluation in early intervention we address fundamental standards that can be broadly applied within the field. The purpose of this chapter is to introduce and describe the standards.

A FRAMEWORK FOR DISCUSSING RECOMMENDED PRACTICES FOR PROGRAM EVALUATION

The framework for discussing recommended practices of program evaluation follows the outline of the *Program Evaluation Standards* prepared by the Joint Committee on Standards for Educational Evaluation (1994). The framework categorizes the practices according to four fundamental attributes of evaluation: utility, feasibility, propriety, and technical adequacy. These attributes include the following:

- *utility*—those practices that support the ability of an evaluation to serve the needs of evaluation stakeholders (program staff, administrators, parents, funding agents) in a manner that is credible, informative, timely, and influential;
- *feasibility*—those practices that support the conduct of program evaluation within the constraints imposed by limited resources, time, and the political subtext of early intervention programs;
- *propriety*—the ethical and constitutional rights of participants in and audiences of program evaluation and the responsibilities of evaluators to protect such rights;
- *technical adequacy*—those practices that support the gathering, analysis, and interpretation of information in ways that are valid, reliable, accurate, fair, and replicable.

When evaluations are conducted in early intervention settings, we suggest that a four-step process be followed. First, before conducting an evaluation, those undertaking the task need to be certain that the findings will be useful. Second, if the evaluation is expected to be useful, they must determine whether conducting the evaluation is feasible and efficient, given the nature of the task and the logistical constraints. Third, if the evaluation is determined to be feasible, possible obstacles to conducting the evaluation within the bounds of propriety must be addressed. Fourth, if it is determined that the evaluation can be conducted ethically, legally, and responsibly, attention and efforts should be focused on the technical adequacy of the evaluation.

When any program evaluation is conducted, a number of evaluation models are available. These include the context, input, process, and product (CIPP) model of Stufflebeam (1983), the goal free evaluation model of Scriven (1972), the responsive evaluation model proposed by Stake (1983), the illuminative evaluation model suggested by Parlett (1974), and the discrepancy evaluation model proposed by Provus (1971). In our experience, the evaluation model chosen as a paradigm for any evaluation reflects an evaluator's assumptions about the nature of educational change, the role of objectivity in data collection, and the use of hypotheses to guide an evaluation study. In this chapter, we do not attempt to identify a particular model of program evaluation as most appropriate for early intervention settings. Instead, we address the recommended practices that are applicable to any evaluation model.

We hope that this chapter will provide stakeholders in local programs (administrators, staff, parents, etc.) with broad guidelines for (a) planning and conducting their own internal evaluations and (b) being better informed consumers of and partners in external evaluations of their programs.

RECOMMENDED PRACTICES

This chapter synthesizes recommended practices relative to program evaluation that were validated by the membership of the Division for Early Childhood of the Council for Exceptional Children as described in Chapter 1. We extend our appreciation to members of the program evaluation task force for their assistance in proposing recommended practices. We discuss the implementation of these practices (listed in the Appendix) in early childhood evaluation settings.

Utility

Useful practices are those that support the ability of an evaluation to serve the needs of evaluation stakeholders (program staff, administrators, parents, funding agents) in a manner that is credible, informative, timely, and influential. Evaluations are made more useful when the evaluator is qualified, stakeholders are actively involved, evaluation questions are clearly articulated to assist with decision making, appropriate information is gathered, the results are disseminated in a manner that maximizes opportunities for successful decision making, and program evaluation is an integral part of service delivery (PE 1–PE 8).

A distinction should be made between internal and external evaluators for programs serving young children with special needs. Internal evaluators are typically program staff assigned the responsibility for conducting an evaluation. External evaluators are persons from outside the program with specific training and experience in program evaluation and early intervention. The costs for hiring external evaluators may be prohibitive in light of the limited budgets of most early intervention programs.

Many needs for program evaluation (e.g., improving program operations) can be adequately served by qualified internal evaluators. However, if high-cost decisions are to be made as a result of the evaluation (e.g., renewing or terminating a program serving children and families in a geographically isolated area; continuing federal funding for a grant-based project in which the quality of evaluation design and outcome information influence funding decisions), external evaluators are typically viewed as having greater objectivity.

According to Snyder and Sheehan (1993), if an internal evaluator (or an internal evaluation team) is to be used, such individuals should "have some training in program evaluation, limit their efforts according to their own level of qualification, have the authority to facilitate data collection, and not have a direct investment in the outcome of the evaluation" (p. 271). Readers interested in a discussion of the roles and responsibilities of internal evaluations are referred to Love (1991).

An evaluator must identify four groups of individuals prior to initiating a program evaluation in an early childhood setting: (1) those persons who will decide about the focus of the evaluation, (2) those who will be making decisions based on the evaluation information, (3) those who might be affected by decisions resulting from the evaluation, and (4) those who will have primary roles in the conduct and outcome of the evaluation (e.g., children, family members, or professionals from whom information will be collected; staff and others who will be involved as data collectors). Individuals who must make decisions, individuals who must implement decisions, and individuals who are directly and indirectly affected by decisions are *stakeholders* in a program evaluation. Identifying stakeholders and involving them in all phases of evaluation (from planning to dissemination) is critically important to maximizing utilization of program evaluation results (Smith, 1988).

Consistent with the intent of the Individuals with Disabilities Education Act Amendments of 1991 and with the value of parent–program partnership is the recommendation that parents routinely participate in the identification of program evaluation purposes. Lobosco and Newman (1992) concluded that stakeholder groups in early intervention programs have differing perspectives and differing information needs and that the involvement of stakeholders in evaluation planning facilitates the use of evaluation results.

Although input and involvement from all stakeholders is important to the planning and conduct of program evaluations, the evaluator must be especially focused on securing the commitment and involvement of persons who will be making decisions or using evaluation findings. The people who *want* information because they *want* to make informed decisions are the people most likely to ensure that evaluation results are used. Patton (1978) reminded practitioners that "formal position and authority are only partial guides for determining decision makers and information users. Evaluators must find the strategically located person or persons who are enthusiastic, commited, competent, interested, and aggressive" (p. 71). Within early intervention settings, these key players include (but are not limited to) teachers, team leaders, supervisors, parents or parent liaisons, and related service providers.

When the decision maker has clear and well-defined questions that he or she wants addressed in order to facilitate decision making and therefore does not wish to solicit recommendations from other stakeholders, it is important that all stakeholders are informed about the evaluation and, to the extent possible, that they are engaged in the planning. Harrison (1989) encouraged decision makers and evaluators to ensure that program staff have the opportunity to contribute to or review the management plan for a program evaluation. The greater the sense of shared commitment to program evaluation in general and to the focus of the targeted evaluation in particular is, and the lower the level of personal threat (e.g., employment termination) perceived from the evaluation is, the greater are the levels of cooperation and application of evaluation results a decision maker might expect.

To a substantial degree, we define utility of program evaluation efforts as the extent to which such efforts facilitate decision making. At least three general types of decisions are served by program evaluation:

- Front-end decisions—Are there are any unmet needs within a community that a program might be able to meet? If so, how might the program succeed in doing so?
- Program-process decisions—To what extent is the program functioning in a manner congruent with internal or external standards or expectations? What are the reasons for departures, and what, if any, changes need to be made to correct or improve program operations?
- Impact decisions—In which ways is and is not a program successful, and what modifications are needed to make it successful?

To the extent possible, evaluations should be designed to serve the priority needs of a diverse group of stakeholders. For example, when individuals representing one or more groups of stakeholders (intervenors, supervisors, parents, representatives of the local education agency, outside agency personnel, community representatives, etc.) attempt to identify a manageable set of evaluation questions, the evaluator should work with the group to prioritize evaluation questions by (a) level of consensus (within and between groups); (b) importance of the question in serving the program mission; (c) feasibility of gathering data to answer the question given logistical constraints (e.g., time, money, and personnel); (d) the importance decision makers assign to answering the question; (e) likelihood that the answer to the question will be tied to decisions or actions; and (f) the immediacy of the need for the information, decision, and action. According to Snyder and Sheehan (1993), "the evaluator should not impose an evaluation agenda on decision makers or stakeholders, but should instead facilitate the identification of relevant objectives to meet the decision making needs of the program" (p. 272). Program evaluation questions that are clear, prioritized, embraced by decisionmakers, and overtly formulated to aid decision making and action planning are most likely to be useful for stakeholders.

When conducting program evaluations in early childhood settings, evaluators should be on constant guard against competing pressures. They do not want to overlook gathering useful information that aids decision making, and, at the same time, they do not want to collect any data that prove to be unnecessary or unrelated to the purposes of the evaluation. To help resolve these pressures, even before an evaluation is conducted, they ask stakeholders to identify the decisions they might make if the data are already gathered and ready for use. They ask, What if the data indicate that children are not receiving services recommended on their IEPs? Or they ask, What will you do if the evaluation indicates that a staff-development program has had no discernible impact? If administrators cannot imagine a realistic decision emanating from such results, evaluators should advise against conducting that part of the evaluation.

We have argued elsewhere (Snyder & Sheehan, 1993) that it is necessary for program evaluation to be tied to decisions for two primary reasons. First, important and defensible decisions help to justify the costs, inconveniences, and disruptions of services associated with systematic program evaluation. Second, the nature of the decision influences the selection of methodology. Most often program evaluation results will not be the sole influence on decision making. Rather, program evaluation findings will impact on decisions by supplementing the overall knowledge and belief base of decision makers. The impact of program evaluation results on decision making is maximized when issues of dissemination and application are considered during evaluated planning. For example, the decision maker should see how the program evaluation plans will directly and logically aid with decision making. The evaluation plan should include concrete ideas for disseminating evaluation findings and facilitating their use.

The evaluator must determine (a) what information is essential for making the decision, (b) from whom or where trustworthy (valid and reliable) information can be gathered, and (c) the amount of information that is needed to make a decision without being redundant or wasteful of time and resources. The answers will vary according to the nature of the questions being asked (and therefore decisions that are being made) and the resources that are available for conducting the evaluation.

Credible sources for aiding front-end decisions in early intervention include parents of children with disabilities, community service providers, demographic data, incidence figures, population projections, and usage rates for existing programs. Program-process decisions may be aided by collecting information concerning program-process standards from one or more important sources (contracts, state and federal guidelines, documented program standards and expectations [e.g., policy, procedure, and service delivery manuals, job descriptions], best practice standards for a field, and/or administrators) and comparing such expectations with evidence or perceptions of actual program function. For any specific standard, there may be one or more credible sources of information. Often, the evaluator will conduct observations of program content and function as a primary source of information, or the evaluator will use the information to supplement data from records, program staff, administrators, families, or community service providers. Credible information concerning impact decisions must derive from the target (child, family, program, or community) or from a source sufficiently familiar with the target to provide an informed estimate of status or change (e.g., a parent may provide information about achievement of developmental milestones). The reader is referred to Snyder and Sheehan (1993) for more discussion concerning sources of evaluation information.

For program evaluation to be effective in aiding decision making, the evaluator must work closely with the decision maker to identify (a) the extent of information the decision maker needs to guide her or his actions and (b) the sources of information the decision maker deems credible and influential for the decision. The evaluator should serve in an educative role to ensure fair, representative, and valid information.

We note here the important distinction between basic research and program evaluation. Basic research is conducted for purposes of developing and testing theories of education whereas evaluation research is conducted for purposes of aiding in decision making. When a basic researcher is unsure whether a particular type of data should be collected, the researcher usually proceeds in collecting the data just in case the data might be useful at some later time. If a program evaluator is unsure whether a particular type of data should be collected, the evaluator typically does not collect the data, recognizing that decision making is unlikely to be served by collection of too much data or irrelevant data.

Recall that real-world decisions affecting children, parents, and staff of early childhood programs are affected by program evaluations. In light of the potential impact of program evaluation on practice, evaluators must be very clear about their assumptions, their evaluation questions, their evaluation procedures, and the rationale for their recommendations. For example, an evaluator who simply averages the performance of children in an intervention program and concludes that average developmental growth in a program is zero may overlook the possibility that some children in an early childhood program have progressive diseases that intervention personnel are seeking to mitigate (thus a reduction in developmental decline may be a goal for these children). In contrast, other children may be expected by intervention program staff to progress, but not at a normal rate. Program evaluators who measure children's progress must be very clear about their developmental assumptions for each subgroup of children.

Different audiences will have different needs in terms of program evaluation results. Individuals and audiences vary in terms of previous experience with program evaluation, level of awareness of or involvement in the program evaluation, reasons for being interested in the evaluation results, learning modes, and language abilities (e.g., English language proficiency reading level). Program evaluation findings must be prepared and presented in such a way as to be understandable by target audiences. This requirement often will mean that evaluation results are developed in more than one form.

The reporting of the program evaluation findings presents a dilemma for evaluators due to two competing demands—trustworthiness and responsiveness. The trustworthiness of evaluation findings are enhanced by evidence of high research quality (Weiss & Bucuvalas, 1980) and completeness of documentation. Unfortunately, many decision makers have neither the expertise nor the time to read extensive technical reports. Although technical reports provide important records of evaluations, they are not responsive to the needs of most consumers. Responsive reporting involves presenting evaluation findings in language and format (e.g., executive summaries) appropriate to the needs of the audience. Feedback should be congruent with the vocabulary and reading abilities of consumers. For example, reports should be written at an appropriate reading level, should be as free from jargon as possible, and should explain any necessary technical terms. Utilization is also supported when reports are brief, concern specific program evaluation questions, and reflect concrete needs of specific stakeholder groups.

There are several reporting recommendations that apply to both technical reports and executive summaries. First, audiences should have access to information that may have affected the results of an evaluation. All reports or presentations should provide sufficient information (consistent with needs of the audience) describing and justifying the purposes, assumptions, methods, results, and recommendations. Second, regardless of the audience, the use of pictorial aids (graphs and charts) and illustrative anecdotes is recommended to facilitate understanding and application of results. Third, we recommend that in order to facilitate understanding, findings be reported for each specific evaluation question. Furthermore, if questions, results, or recommendations can be prioritized in terms of their importance or immediacy, we recommend that findings be reported or summarized in order of importance. Fourth, the evaluator can facilitate use of evaluation results by providing concrete recommendations that logically tied to evaluation data. Fifth, we suggest that any recommendations for change be offered in small stages rather than as major shifts. Siegel and

Tuckel (1985) argued that focusing on manageable incremental changes rather than on global changes reduces resistance to utilization. Worthen and Sanders (1987) presented a number of other very useful suggestions for preparing evaluation reports.

There are two primary reasons for encouraging the timely dissemination of program evaluation information to stakeholders. First, delays in the provision of program evaluation findings will delay decision making and responsive actions. As evaluation objectives are typically selected due to their importance and immediacy, delays in decision making and action are not acceptable. Second, program evaluation typically requires stakeholders to invest time on program evaluation tasks such as planning the evaluation, managing the evaluation, collecting information, and providing information. If administrators hope to institutionalize program evaluation as a routine and an influential component of intervention, stakeholders should receive fairly frequent evidence that their efforts are contributing to program improvement. Interim communication of the progress of evaluation does not need to be limited to formal reports. Active involvement of stakeholders and periodic informal feedback concerning findings may increase the perceived compatibility of findings with the beliefs of stakeholders. Utilization increases when findings conform to stakeholder (user) expectations (Weiss & Bucuvalas, 1980).

Finally, the timely presentation of findings is important. Although basic research findings can be delayed for 1–2 years, program evaluation results, to be effective, must be released within weeks of being concluded.

Research shows that program evaluation is, to date, not an integral, valued, or influential component of most special education programs (George, George, & Grosenick, 1990). Much of the "program evaluation" that is being conducted is simply compliance monitoring for federal and state mandates. Evidence, however, suggests that programs can and do benefit when program evaluation is made a routine component of operations (Sechrest & Figueredo, 1993; George et al., 1990).

Although a number of evaluation models reflect a common belief in the importance of ongoing formative feedback for the sake of improving a program, Tharp and Gallimore's (1979) evaluation succession model may prove to be particularly valuable for early intervention programs. These authors suggested that social and educational programs mature in stages until reaching a point of stability. Because an iterative process in which impact data (qualitative and quantitative) were used to modify program functions (learning as much from mistakes as from successes), a substantial improvement in a Hawaiian educational program was demonstrated. Similarly, if services for young children with special needs and their families are to achieve their full potential, programs (and school districts) must recognize and value the need for routine (frequent) process- and impact-data collection, feedback, and corrections in order to promote quality service provision.

The program evaluator can assist in making evaluation an influential component of early intervention by encouraging utilization even after the evaluation has been completed. If the program evaluator is to come back at some later date to solicit participation of stakeholders in another evaluation, he or she is more likely to get cooperation if previous evaluation efforts have been productive.

Feasibility

Evaluation practices are feasible when they support the conduct of program evaluation within the constraints imposed by limited resources, time demands, and politics. Evaluations are most feasible when they minimize disruptions to stakeholders (PE 9, PE 10).

Program evaluators should never lose sight of the fact that the success of a program evaluation is frequently determined by the goodwill and support of staff and families of early childhood programs. Staff and families are correct in asserting that an evaluation should not disrupt delivery of early intervention services.

Program evaluators should also acknowledge the diversity of families who participate in early childhood programs, respecting the values, cultures, coping styles, and priorities of all families. This requirement means that program evaluators should carefully review their data-collection tools to ensure that language usage is respectful of families. Program evaluations that are not sensitive to diversity in respondents and stakeholders cause unintended frustrations for participants. Program evaluators should also seek to identify the strengths of parents and families as well as their needs (McGonigel, 1988).

By involving staff and families in the planning of a program evaluation, evaluators can minimize disruptions. Using extant data (assessment results, IEPs, staff logs, minutes of meetings, memos, budget expenditures, enrollments, placement records, census, etc.) or gathering data that can also be used to assist individual intervention planning (supplemental assessment data, etc.) can also reduce disruptions. We strongly recommend that to minimize unintended disruptions the evaluator pilot data-collection procedures or measures if he or she is uncertain about their practicality or time and resource requirements.

This principle essentially is a call for undertaking *evaluability assessment* as an integral component of an evaluation. Essentially evaluability assessment is a determination of whether the anticipated benefits of the evaluation (plans and efforts to improve staff performance, service delivery, parent satisfaction, etc.) are likely to substantially outweigh the expected costs (staff time, expense, loss of service delivery time). A "shotgun" approach to impact evaluations, in which a wide spectrum of outcomes are addressed simultaneously, is likely to be too costly or cursory to provide information sufficient to accurately inform evaluation decisions (Snyder & Sheehan, 1993).

Program evaluators must realize that effort directed toward an evaluation is effort taken away from some other early childhood program activity. It is effort taken away from speech therapy, effort taken away from parent education, and effort taken away from staff development. Once this realization occurs, program evaluators and decision makers become committed to planning and conducting an evaluation that outweighs its costs.

Propriety

Evaluation practices are proprietary when they protect the ethical and constitutional rights of participants in and audiences of program evaluation (PE 11).

There are ethical and constitutional standards that must be respected during the conduct of an evaluation. These standards apply to treatment of families, staff, and children as data sources; treatment of data that have been gathered; and reporting of data once they have been gathered.

Before data are gathered, families and staff should be allowed opportunities to ask about the kind of information they will share. Families, staff, and even children should also be reassured that their participation is confidential and voluntary and can cease, with no recrimination, at the request of the family member, staff member, or child.

Once data have been gathered, the data should be coded in such a way that informants' identity is protected. Data gathered for one purpose, with permission of informants, should not be used for any other purpose, unless all identifying information is stripped from the data. We also note that even the removal of identifying information from data is often not enough to prevent informants from feeling anger and resentment if data gathered for one purpose (i.e., to evaluate a program) is used for another totally different purpose without permission.

Once data have been gathered and reported back to the agency, evaluators should make it a policy to keep a copy of all obtained data for 7 years. This practice allows the retrieval of the data, upon request, and the performance of follow-up analyses or reanalyses for the program being evaluated.

Ownership of data is an issue that has arisen in almost every program evaluation that we have conducted. When working under contract, as either internal or external evaluators, we prefer to take a stance that data gathered during a program evaluation are actually the property of the agency paying for the evaluation. In most cases, this agency is the program being evaluated. We do not publish or make public presentations on the results of the evaluation without the express permission of the agency funding the evaluation.

We have, upon request, conducted an evaluation gratis, to provide an experience for one of our students or simply to provide a service to the program. Under these circumstances we have always clarified the issue of ownership of data and any use of data other than providing results back to the agency that requested the evaluation.

Technical Adequacy

Evaluation practices are technically adequate when they support the gathering, analysis, and interpretation of information in ways that are reliable, valid, accurate, representative, fair, and replicable. Evaluations are made more technically adequate when descriptions of programs and contexts are precise; when methodology and analyses are clearly described, justified, systematically monitored, and understood by decision makers; when multiple appropriate sources of information are accessed; when instruments and measurement procedures are appropriate for the respondents and generate information that is reliable and valid for decision making; and when objective findings are clearly reported (PE 12–PE 23).

According to Snyder and Sheehan (1993), "many evaluations of the past have given inadequate attention to the description of the programs under investigation. The lack of adequate documentation reduces what is known about program variations and about how such variations effect program outcomes" (p. 278). Detailed descriptions of specific aspects of programs are essential for a program to be adequately understood and replicated. Thorough descriptions also facilitate high-quality process decisions (program monitoring) and high-quality impact decisions.

Program monitoring involves the ongoing assessment of program operation for the purpose of assessing compliance with expectations (external standards, program-level policies, recommended practice guidelines). Although decisions based on program monitoring may influence allocation of funds or the accreditation/approval of a program, decisions are more likely to concern the nature of or needs for staff development, technical assistance, and program improvement. Service components that can be described and compared with expectations include public awareness and child-find efforts, service delivery, coordination of services and resources, family involvement, assessment, case management, transitioning, IFSP/IEP development and review, and record keeping. Administrative components that can be described and compared with expectations include program management, supervision of personnel, budget management, staff development, program funding, and due process. Because service and administrative components of programs are dynamic rather than static, periodic evaluations are necessary.

The description of program components is also an essential component of impact evaluation. Snyder and Sheehan (1993) have argued for applying impact evaluation primarily as a formative tool for improving program effectiveness. For evaluations to serve such a function, evaluators must seek not only to document program outcomes but also to describe the factors that seem to account for variability in such outcomes. Snyder and Sheehan argued that adequate description of program components is essential for such investigation.

To have sufficient information to make process decisions and impact decisions and to facilitate program replication, evaluators must describe not only characteristics of the program but also characteristics of the context within which the program is nested. Factors such as the availability, proximity, and rates of usage of services and resources in the community; cultural diversity within the community; demographic information; population projections; community support for children with special needs; medical trends in the area; and size and geographic distribution of a catchment area (high-density urban area, large low-density rural catchment area) influence the program goals, program operations, and the evaluation plan. Such descriptions are central to needs assessments. They also provide information important for understanding the results of program monitoring (i.e., the context may affect the extent to which program processes are congruent with standards) and for explaining differences in program impact.

Planning should result in a written description of the evaluation design, sources of information, methods for selecting and sampling such sources, measurement procedures to be used, data analysis procedures, reporting procedures, and an overall system for managing the evaluation. Program evaluators should describe and monitor the purposes, designs, and procedures of an evaluation in enough depth and precision to permit adequate critique, management, or replication of the evaluation (PE 14).

Although good evaluation is dynamic and responsive, it should be based on a clearly articulated plan. Such a plan is designed (a) to ensure that the components of the evaluation (design and procedures) are congruent with the purpose of the evaluation and (b) to provide some assurance that evaluation tasks can be achieved in a timely and cost-effective manner with minimal disruptions to service delivery and program administration. The research plan provides a mechanism for describing the integrity of the evaluation while serving as a document for assessing the adequacy and defensibility of information. According to Snyder and Sheehan (1993),

> such a management plan defines the relationship between: 1) each of the major tasks required to answer an evaluation question, 2) timelines

(beginning and end dates) estimated for completing each task, 3) the personnel used to complete each task (and the individual responsible for insuring its completion), 4) the resources needed to complete each task (including staff time) and their costs, and 5) potential disruptions in services that may result. Supplemental detail should be provided on specific data collection procedures and dates, data entry and storage plans, and individuals responsible for ensuring the timeliness and quality of each task. (p. 298)

The reader is referred to Worthen and Sanders (1987) and Suarez (1980) for examples of management plans.

Whether conducting needs assessment, process evaluation, or impact evaluation, the evaluator should, to the extent possible, access various sources of information to answer questions. In determining whether (and how) to implement a new or expanded program to serve young children with special needs and their families (i.e., needs assessment), the evaluator can collect information and perceptions concerning unmet, undermet, and projected needs from a variety of sources including parents of children with special needs, community service providers, and existing records concerning population projections, health data, and usage rates for existing programs. When deciding if and how program operations must be modified to comply with expectations (program monitoring), evaluators can collect information concerning the actual status of activities, services, and materials from mandated records (e.g., number of children served by age, program setting, number of service delivery personnel by discipline, etc.); evaluator(s) (e.g., observations using rating scales or checklists); existing records (such as logs of phone and written communications, referrals, attendance, and travel); and parents, staff, and administrators having knowledge of (and experience with) program processes. Such information can then be compared to expectations and standards, which may also be derived from a variety of sources (mandates, internal policies and procedures, guidelines for recommended conditions and practice).

Evaluators who prefer naturalistic inquiry (e.g., Lincoln & Guba, 1985) will typically gather information from multiple sources concerning actual program functions prior to examining intended policies, procedures, and models. The benefit of this approach is that the description of program processes is relatively free of bias. As internal evaluators are not naive about the internal expectations, such naturalistic methods may not be appropriate for program-monitoring decisions.

In determining the ways a program is and is not successful and what can be done to improve the program's effectiveness, evaluators need information concerning intended and unintended impacts of a program and factors that mediate such impacts. Effectiveness can be defined in terms of changes in child outcomes, peer interactions and relations, parent–child interactions, parent and family outcomes, social support outcomes, teacher attitudes (e.g., in inclusive settings), and community outcomes. Child-outcome information can be provided by the child (e.g., through observations and testing), parents (from perceptions and reports), existing records (IFSPs/IEPs), and intervenors. Interaction outcomes can be gathered from observations of interactions, parent reports, and staff reports. Family outcomes are typically provided by individual family members or existing records (parent communications, minutes of parent-advisory meetings). Teacher attitudes can be gathered from the teacher (self-report or observation) or from parents (perceptions). Community-outcome information is gathered from advisory boards and a variety of community agencies (health, social, and educational) involved with or affected by the program. The specific nature of outcome data to be collected, and therefore the most appropriate source of outcome information, is influenced by the definition of program success. Typically, the more narrowly a program defines success, the fewer sources of information will be needed to evaluate impact.

As with needs assessment and program monitoring, the gathering of information from multiple sources should improve the quality of evidence available to make informed decisions. Also, if periodic collection of information is important to the evaluation (as it is with much process and impact evaluation), accessibility and cooperation should be considered when sources are identified and accessed.

We recommend that, in addition to using multiple sources of information, the evaluator apply multiple methods to the extent possible and appropriate. Different data-gathering procedures have unique strengths and limitations. The use of more than one method helps to provide a balanced perspective.

Instruments and data-collection procedures must be selected and applied in a manner that is sensitive and responsive to the diversity and special needs of the children, adults, and families from whom program evaluation data are gathered. The validity and reliability of program evaluation decisions are tied to the appropriateness of measurement. Instruments that are not adaptive to disabilities or assessors who are not skilled in working with young children with special needs are at risk of yielding data that are not accurate, representative, or useful.

Standardized measures used with young children with severe impairments are not likely to be sufficiently sensitive to document change. Assessments that are not conducted in the respondents' native language may not generate complete, replicable, or accurate information. Instruments for stakeholders may be written at reading levels that are too high for a substantial portion of respondents. Hanson, Lynch, and Wayman (1990) argued that the successful gathering and interpreting of information from non-White, non-Anglo families require the evaluator to recognize, value, and respond to the cultural differences. The fields of assessment and program evaluation in early intervention are clearly challenged to improve the appropriateness of their measures and the approaches they use for collecting information.

A discussion of the range of issues surrounding validity and reliability of measurement is beyond the scope of this chapter. Evidence of acceptable levels of the types of validity and reliability essential for judgments based on evaluation information is vital for successful evaluations. Well-constructed evaluation designs are quickly compromised by the use of procedures that are invalid or unreliable for their intended uses.

The lack of available measures, the high cost of existing measures, and the desire for fidelity between evaluation goals and measurement procedures may lead programs to develop their own surveys, checklists, rating scales, or interviews. Although there is often good reason for developing local measures, there are also a number of problems that may be overlooked by program personnel. For example, when developing surveys concerning beliefs and attitudes of parents and other stakeholders, the evaluator must consider (a) the reading level of questions and directions; (b) the appropriateness, completeness, and clarity of directions, questions, and response formats; (c) the extent to which the format of the survey encourages or discourages completion of the survey; (d) the placement of sensitive items within the survey; (e) the appropriateness of the rating scales or checklists used; (f) methods for gathering information about factors that might account for differences in responses; and (g) the way in which responses can be summarized (e.g., Can the rating scale scores be added to reflect a summary score?).

Before any locally developed instrument or procedure is used for program evaluation, it should be pilot tested with a smaller group who are similar to the targeted recipients. Such groups should complete the measures and also provide feedback to the developer(s) about concerns and suggestions for improving the measure. The scope of this chapter does not allow for a thorough discussion of procedures for developing measures or for conducting review panels and pilot studies. Individuals interested in developing their own instruments are referred to sources on instrument development including Neilson and Buchanan (1991) and Sudman and Bradburn (1982).

The purpose of an evaluation is not for the evaluator to dazzle and amaze audiences with his or her statistical and methodological sophistication (they'll be irritated rather than impressed) but rather for the evaluator to facilitate good decision making. The decision maker should be able to explain how the program evaluation method and data analysis approaches serve the targeted questions and enhance decision making. The decision maker needs to understand where the results and recommendations come from if they are to be invested in taking action and explaining the results to other audiences.

Needs-assessment and process evaluations typically require only descriptive analysis (narrative descriptions, frequencies, measures of central tendency and range, comparisons of expected and actual events). Impact evaluations involve documenting the rate or extent of change across time, establishing that the program had at least some impact on the change, and identifying factors that account for differences in program impact. As a result, impact evaluation involves more complex problems, requires more complex methods, and often requires more complex data analysis.

We have argued elsewhere (Snyder & Sheehan, 1993) that documenting changes across time that are, at least in part, due to experiences in the program can be accomplished in three major ways. First, changes in outcomes that are sensitive to intervention but that are not likely to be influenced by maturation can be documented (e.g., progress toward IEP objectives, parental satisfaction, community outcomes). Goal attainment scaling (Kiresuk & Lund, 1976), which produces a standardized metric, may be a particularly valuable application of this method (e.g., Simeonsson, Huntington, & Short, 1982). Indexes that describe the rate of developmental change during a program based on performance on standardized tests (e.g., developmental quotients) have been criticized for a number of reasons. For example, they describe the rate of change *during* intervention rather than *due to* intervention (Rosenberg, Robinson, Finkler, & Rose, 1987; Snyder & Sheehan, 1993).

The second approach involves repeated administrations of one or more outcome measures to two equivalent groups of children (one group who receives the program and one group who receives an alternative treatment or no program) prior to and following the beginning of intervention. When groups are equivalent and substantial differences in gains are evident, statistical evidence may not be necessary to inform decision making. Alternatively, differences in gains between the two groups can be standardized (translated into standard deviation units). If such *effect sizes* exceed an established criterion (e.g., 0.5), the treatment is deemed educationally significant (e.g., Tallmadge, 1977). A range of more complex statistical procedures are also available for analyzing this type of design (e.g., analysis of variance with multiple factors, repeated measures, and multiple outcomes). A potential problem with such analyses is overreliance on statistical significance. Snyder and Sheehan (1993) cautioned evaluators about the limitations of interpreting statistical significance without considering educational significance. McConnell (1990) discussed a number of cautions relating to the logistics, ethics, and analyses of control-group comparison-group designs.

The third approach involves frequent collection of outcome information prior to, during, and (perhaps) after an intervention. If the evaluator gathers sufficient data prior to starting or modifying an intervention and modifies the general design or data-collection context, participants are able to serve as their own comparisons. Although complex strategies are available for summarizing the results of such designs, the strength of the method for most evaluators is found in the graphing of results (time along the horizontal axis and degree of outcome along the vertical axis) and the comparisons of graphs between individuals and groups.

Each of these basic designs is complicated when the evaluator examines factors that mediate outcomes. In one common approach, prior to data collection, the evaluator identifies (on the basis of the literature, theory, experience, or suggestion by stakeholders) factors that might account for differences in outcome; gathers data on the hypothesized factors and outcomes; and then determines whether such differences do exist. Often, simple graphic comparisons (e.g., bar charts or scatter plots) of outcomes between groups or between outcomes and levels of a factor (e.g., level of treatment acceptability) will suffice. The standardized metrics generated from goal attainment scaling (Kiresuk & Lund, 1976; Simeonsson et al., 1982) and effect sizes are particularly appropriate for such purposes. Single-participant behavioral graphs can be simply sorted by grouping factors and examining for variability within and between groups. More rigorous analytical procedures are available and are discussed in texts on evaluation methods and educational statistics.

A considerable number of alternative approaches for analyzing qualitative and quantitative information are available. The appropriateness of a particular approach depends on a number of factors such as the congruence of the approach with evaluation questions being addressed, the familiarity of the evaluator with the program under consideration, time constraints on data collection, and the availability of valid and reliable measures for gathering information. Evaluators should apply only those analytical procedures that (a) are consistent with the purposes of the evaluation, (b) provide the type of information that will be most helpful to the decision maker, (c) are within the evaluator's repertoire, and (d) are logically consistent with the designs and measures used in service to the evaluation. Regardless of the analytical approach used, the evaluator should be able to clearly describe the analytical method and to defend its appropriateness in light of the purpose and design of the evaluation. A study by Lobosco and Newman (1992) has indicated that although stakeholders tended to perceive quantitative information as more technically adequate, more convincing, and more objective, such preferences are not overwhelming. These authors recommended incorporating both quantitative and qualitative approaches in conducting and reporting of program evaluation in early intervention and early childhood special education.

CLOSING

The practices recommended in this chapter are consistent with general guidelines for evaluating educational or intervention programs. We recognize the difficulties of implementing any, far less all, of these recommendations. The challenge of implementing appropriate evaluation practice is made complex in early intervention due to charactersitics of the field including the great diversity of response repertoires of children being served, the cultural diversity of families being served, competing demands for limited program resources and external funding, ambiguities (in some programs) about program goals and service models, shortages of valid and reliable measures of program impact, and ethical and logistic constraints on evaluation designs.

Program evaluators in early intervention and early childhood special education, whether an individual classroom teacher addressing an isolated question or an external evaluation team examining a comprehensive service delivery system, must negotiate and compromise in order to generate the most technically sound and useful information. We hope that these recommended practices can help stakeholders and evaluators plan and conduct the best evaluations possible, given the needs, constraints, and compromises unique to a specific evaluation.

We believe that the inclusion of a chapter on program evaluation in this book on recommended practices in early intervention is evidence of the field's recognition of the contribution of program evaluation to improving service delivery and decision making. We hope to see in the next several years the examination and refinement of and elaboration on these recommended practices.

REFERENCES

George, M. P., George, N. L., & Grosenick, J. K. (1990). Features of program evaluation in special education. *Remedial and Special Education, 11,* 23–30.

Hanson, M. J., Lynch, E. W., & Wayman, K. (1990). Honoring the cultural diversity of families when gathering data. *Topics in Early Childhood Special Education, 10,* 112–131.

Harrison, P. J. (1989). Evaluating programs. In M. Hanson & E. Lynch (Eds.), *Early intervention: Implementing child and family services for infants and toddlers who are at-risk or disabled* (pp. 360–397). Austin, TX: PRO-ED.

Horn, E., & Childre, A. (1996). Assessment of adaptive behavior development. In M. McLean, D. Bailey, & M. Wolery (Eds.), *Assessing infants and preschoolers with special needs* (pp. 462–490). Columbus, OH: Merrill/Prentice-Hall.

Individuals with Disabilities Education Act Amendments of 1991, 20 U.S.C. § 1400 *et seq.*

Joint Committee on Standards for Educational Evaluation. (1994). *The program evaluation standards: How to assess evaluations of educational programs.* Thousand Oaks, CA: Sage.

Kiresuk, T., & Lund, S. (1976). Process and measurement using goal attainment scaling. In G. Glass (Ed.), *Evaluation studies review manual* (Vol. 1, pp. 389–399). Beverly Hills, CA: Sage.

Lincoln, Y. S., & Guba, G. G. (1985). *Naturalistic inquiry.* Newbury Park, CA: Sage.

Lobosco, A., & Newman, D. (1992). Stakeholder information needs: Implications for evaluation and practice and policy development in early childhood special education. *Evaluation Review, 16*(5), 443–463.

Love, A. J. (1991). *Internal evaluation: Building organizations from within.* Newbury Park, CA: Sage.

McConnell, S. R. (1990). Best practices in evaluating educational programs. In A. Thomas & G. Grimes (Eds.), *Best practices in school psychology* (Vol. 2, pp. 357–370). Washington, DC: National Association of School Psychologists.

McGonigel, M. (1988). *Guidelines for family-centered research.* Washington, DC: Association for the Care of Children's Health.

Neilsen, M. E., & Buchanan, N. K. (1991). Evaluating gifted programs with locally constructed instruments. In N. K. Buchanan & J. F. Feldhusen (Eds.), *Conducting research and evaluation in gifted education: A handbook of methods and applications* (pp. 275–310). New York: Teacher's College Press.

Parlett, M. (1974). The new evaluation. *Trends in Education, 34,* 13–18.

Patton, M. A. (1978). *Utilization-focused evaluation.* Newbury Park: CA. Sage.

Provus, M. M. (1971). *Discrepancy evaluation.* Berkeley, CA: McCutchan.

Rosenberg, S. A., Robinson, C. C., Finkler, D., & Rose, J. S. (1987). An empirical comparison of formulas evaluating early intervention program impact on development. *Exceptional Children, 54,* 213–219.

Scriven, M. (1972). Prose and cons about goal-free evaluation. *Evaluation Comment, 3,* 1–7.

Sechrest, L., & Figueredo, A. J. (1993). Program evaluation. *Annual Review of Psychology, 44,* 645–674.

Siegel, K., & Tuckel, P. (1985). The utilization of evaluation research: A case analysis. *Evaluation Review, 9*(3), 307–328.

Simeonsson, R. J., Huntington, G. S., & Short, R. J. (1982). Individual differences and goals: An approach to the evaluation of child progress. *Topics in Early Childhood Special Education, 1*(4), 71–80.

Smith, M. F. (1988). Evaluation utilization revisited. In J. A. McLaughlin, L. Weber, R. Covert, & R. Ingle (Eds.), *Evaluation utilization* (pp. 7–19). San Francisco: Jossey-Bass.

Snyder, S., & Sheehan, R. (1993). Program evaluation and early intervention. In W. Brown, K. Thurman, & L. Pearl (Eds.), *Family-centered early intervention with infants and toddlers: Innovative cross-disciplinary approaches* (pp. 269–302). Baltimore: Brookes.

Stake, R.E. (1983). Program evaluation, particularly responsive evaluation. In G. Madaus, M. Scriven, & D. Stufflebeam (Eds.), *Evaluation models: Viewpoints of educational and human services evaluation* (pp. 287–310). Boston: Kluwer-Nijhoff.

Stufflebeam, D. L. (1983). The CIPP model for program evaluation. In G. Madaus, M. Scriven, & D. Stufflebeam (Eds.), *Evaluation models: Viewpoints of educational and human services evaluation* (pp. 117–141). Boston: Kluwer-Nijhoff.

Suarez, T. M. (1980). *A planning guide for the evaluation of educational programs for young children and families.* Chapel Hill: Technical Assistance Development System. University of North Carolina.

Sudman, S., & Bradburn, N. M. (1982). *Asking questions.* San Francisco: Jossey-Bass.

Tallmadge, G. K. (1977). *The joint dissemination review panel ideabook.* Mountain View, CA: RMC Research Corporation. (ERIC Document Reproduction Service No. ED 148 329)

Tharp, R. G., & Gallimore, R. (1979). The ecology of program research and evalaution: A model of evaluation succession. In L. Sechrest, S. West, M. Phillips, R. Redner, & W. Yeaton (Eds.), *Evaluation studies review annual* (pp. 39–60). Beverly Hills, CA: Sage.

Weiss, C. H., & Bucuvalas, M. J. (1980). Truth tests and utility tests: Decision-makers' frames of reference for social science research. *American Sociological Review, 45,* 302–313.

Worthen, B. R., & Sanders, J. R. (1987). *Educational evaluation: Alternative approaches and practical guidelines.* New York: Longman.

APPENDIX

DEC Recommended Practices

ASSESSMENT

Assessment in early intervention refers to the systematic collection of information about children, families, and environments to assist in making decisions regarding identification, screening, eligibility, program planning, monitoring, and evaluation.

Preassessment Activities

A1   Professionals contact families and share information about the assessment process.

A2   Professionals solicit and review existing information from families and agencies.

A3   Professionals and families identify the questions and concerns that will drive the choice of assessment materials and procedures.

A4   Professionals and families identify pertinent agencies, team members, and team approaches to be employed (e.g., inter-, multi-, transdisciplinary approach).

A5   Professionals and families identify a mode of teaming that fits individual children's needs and families' desires to collaborate.

Procedures for Determining Eligibility, Program Placement, Program Planning and Monitoring

A6   Professionals gather information from multiple sources (e.g., families, other professionals, paraprofessionals, and previous service providers) and use multiple measures (e.g., norm-referenced, interviews, etc.).

A7   Professionals gather information on multiple occasions.

A8   Team members discuss qualitative and quantitative information and negotiate consensus in a collaborative decision-making process.

A 9   Team members select assessment instruments and procedures that have been field tested with children similar to those assessed for the purposes intended.

A 10 Assessment approaches and instruments are culturally appropriate and nonbiased.

A 11 Professionals employ individualized, developmentally compatible assessment procedures and materials that capitalize on children's interests, interactions, and communication styles.

A 12 Materials and procedures, or their adaptations, accommodate the child's sensory and response capacities.

A 13 Professionals assess strengths as well as problems across developmental or functional areas.

A 14 Measures and procedures facilitate education and treatment (i.e., intervention or curriculum objectives) rather than only diagnosis and classification.

A 15 Measures are sensitive to child and family change.

A 16 Professionals assess not only skill acquisition but also fluency, generalization, and quality of progress.

A 17 Professionals maintain confidentiality and discretion when sharing information.

A 18 Curriculum-based assessment procedures are the foundation or "mutual language" for team assessment.

Assessment Reports

A 19 Professionals report assessment results in a manner that is immediately useful for planning program goals and objectives.

A 20 Professionals report assessment results so that they are understandable to and useful for families.

A 21 Professionals report strengths as well as priorities for promoting optimal development.

A 22 Professionals report limitations of assessments (e.g., questions of rapport, cultural bias, and sensory/response requirements).

A 23 Reports contain findings and interpretations regarding the interrelatedness of developmental areas (e.g., how the child's limitations have affected development; how the child has learned to compensate).

A24 Professionals organize reports by developmental/functional domains or concerns rather than by assessment device.

FAMILY PARTICIPATION

Families are equal members in and can take part in all aspects of early intervention systems. This includes participation in all aspects of their child's care and all levels of decision making.

Program Advising/Policy Making

FP 1 Family members receive payment for their expertise, time, and expenses while participating on councils, committees, and other aspects of early intervention policy/planning.

FP 2 Meetings occur at times and locations that allow family members to participate.

FP 3 Programs specify in writing, in an understandable manner, the roles of family members in program advising.

FP 4 Program advising and policy-making activities include members from more than one family.

FP 5 Family members participate in the entire policy and procedures development process (from conceptualization through public comment and revision).

FP 6 Families have the opportunity to develop policy-making skills if they choose through mentoring and/or training.

FP 7 When it is necessary to use terminology (words or phrases) that are not familiar to family members, professionals explain the meaning of the terms in family-friendly language and provide written descriptions.

Staff Hiring, Training, Evaluation

FP 8 Family members participate in and, if they choose, are paid for: developing job descriptions, advertising for positions, reviewing applications, interviewing candidates, selecting person for the job, conducting orientation activities for new staff, and evaluating staff.

FP 9 Families may participate in a variety of roles in staff training: planner, needs assessor, deliverer, participant, and evaluator.

FP 10 Programs involve family members in gathering evaluative data and input from other families.

FP 11 Evaluative feedback from and decision making with family members produces program changes, development, and expansion.

FP 12 Family members help develop evaluation tools.

FP 13 Family members have a role in the process of formulating conclusions and implications of evaluation data and in disseminating the results.

Family-to-Family Support

FP 14 Family support services (respite, advocacy, parent-to-parent networking) are available as requested by the family.

FP 15 Program personnel/staff introduce new families to other families in the program.

FP 16 Family-to-family support services create an atmosphere which supports exchange of information among families.

FP 17 Linkages to natural community supports for families are built and encouraged.

FP 18 Support groups can include extended family members and other family support network members if a family chooses.

Intervention

FP 19 Natural community settings are developed and accessible as an option for early intervention.

FP 20 Family concerns, priorities, and preferred resources have priority in the determination of the instructional setting.

FP 21 Program staff provide information to families about using intervention strategies across settings.

FP 22 Families receive information when they ask for it in a way that is meaningful to them.

FP 23 Families determine the pace of service delivery (e.g., to change intensity of child and family participation as needed to meet the family's needs).

FP 24 Dreams and visions for the future expressed by families are encouraged and supported.

FP 25 Families can initiate program monitoring activities if they choose.

FP 26 Program staff explain methods of monitoring progress to families and offer options for modes of monitoring.

FP 27 Families are asked to monitor progress and satisfaction to the extent they feel comfortable.

FP 28 Essential supports such as child care and transportation are available so that families can participate in all levels of early intervention.

Interagency Collaboration—Meetings, Evaluation, Implementation

FP 29 Families are included on all interagency teams and groups, throughout all phases of the effort.

FP 30 Families are provided the opportunity and support to develop a handbook which helps them and subsequent parents through the "agency process."

FP 31 Families are asked on an ongoing and systematic basis to provide feedback on the interagency collaboration process.

FP 32 Agencies, with the help of families, develop one form which will be acceptable to all for intake, the IFSP/IEP, and monitoring.

FP 33 Public awareness efforts are targeted at typical community settings to expand their availability to families of children with disabilities.

Legislative Issues

FP 34 A mechanism exists to inform families about the importance of legislative involvement.

FP 35 Families receive information in language they prefer and understand about the laws that support services to their children and themselves.

FP 36 Professionals respect family members' decisions to become involved, or not involved, in political action.

Advocacy

FP 37 Advocacy groups to support regular early childhood services include the concerns of children with special needs and their families.

FP 38 Families participate equally (with professionals) in determining issues that are targeted for advocacy efforts by a program.

FP 39 Professionals or agencies inform family members when they cannot advocate for issues identified by families because of professional conflict.

FP 40 Programs provide families with information on their state's advocacy services and organizations.

FP 41 Veteran families support new families as they begin advocacy efforts.

Procedural Safeguard Development

FP 42 Programs have clearly specified procedures for recourse/redress of grievances.

FP 43 A mediator, independent from the program, participates in grievance procedures if they cannot be settled by the family members and the program.

FP 44 Families may make decisions to use alternative services, programs, and methods unless they jeopardize their child's life.

Leadership Training Opportunities for Parents

FP 45 Intervention programs coordinate training opportunities for families with parent training groups funded to provide such training as well as with other community training opportunities.

FP 46 Families receive parent-directed newsletters and literature.

FP 47 Programs provide support, financially if necessary, for families to attend local, state, and national level meetings.

FP 48 The program provides families with options for training opportunities, times, and methods from which to choose.

FP 49 State lead agencies and ICCs fund an annual, formal leadership training for family members.

IFSPS/IEPS

Best practice indicators are based on the assumption that parents or legal guardians have the ultimate responsibility for decisions regarding the IFSP/IEP process.

IFSP/IEP Process

I 1   The IFSP/IEP process is ongoing, dynamic, and individualized.

I 2   As an initial step, the person(s) responsible for the development of the IFSP/IEP clearly describe to families the IFSP/IEP process, the rights that families have during the process, and the role of the service coordinator in the process.

I 3   A supportive and mutually respectful relationship with families occurs from the time of initial contact with families.

I 4   Each family has the opportunity to select from among the pool of available service coordinators the person whose skills and resources most closely match the needs and preferences of the family.

I 5   Families have the option to have a family member serve as the service coordinator or co-service coordinator and to receive adequate pay for that work.

I 6   In initial IFSPs/IEPs when families are not familiar with any of the people who are available to serve as service coordinator, they may ask professional team members to recommend the service coordinator.

I 7   Families may request a change in the service coordinator at any time and have that request honored if resources allow.

I 8   State and local agencies provide competency-based training to ensure that the service coordinator appropriately fulfills roles.

I 9   A system for training service coordinators also includes training family members if they want to participate.

I 10   Training in service coordination includes methods to help family members identify informal supports.

I 11   The person responsible for coordinating the development of the IFSP/IEP determines with the family the persons to be included on the IFSP/IEP team and, with family authorization, ensures participation of all relevant team members.

I 12 Families may select as other team members persons who provide emotional support and practical assistance to the family, including service providers, friends, and families of other children with disabilities.

I 13 With the consent of the family, the team may also include representatives of agencies and community programs that have previously served, or are likely to serve, the child or family.

I 14 Families may choose: a family-directed process in which they have a leadership role; a collaborative process in which the family shares equal decision-making responsibility with other team members; or a process that delegates decision making to other members of the team.

I 15 Each family will have the opportunity to select or change the nature of their role in decision making for each issue in question.

I 16 Families receive individualized support and information so that they can participate in the process in the ways they have chosen. Other team members adjust their roles in response to family preferences.

I 17 Families are invited to participate in any team discussion of their child or family.

I 18 Families receive complete copies of all reports concerning them and their children, and team members offer assistance, when appropriate, in interpreting those reports.

I 19 Families decide what information they wish to share with the team.

I 20 Team members base decisions pertaining to updating and revising IFSPs/IEPs on family preferences, assessment results, and newly emerging child information.

I 21 All communications, actions, and written statements of team members reflect their respect for one another.

I 22 All team members are honest with each other.

I 23 All team members recognize the critical role of emotional support and provide this support to other team members.

I 24 The IFSP/IEP meetings and documents contain jargon-free communication and include explanation of technical information when necessary.

I 25 The IFSP/IEP document includes only and all the information the family wants included.

I 26 Professional members of the team are knowledgeable about laws, policies, and recommended practice for the development, implementation, and monitoring of IFSPs/IEPs.

I 27 Families are given the opportunity to receive information about current recommended practices related to the IFSP/IEP.

I 28 Professional members of the team actively advocate for the full rights of the child and family.

I 29 Team members keep policy makers informed of gaps in community services.

I 30 Agencies allow sufficient time for their team members to work in ways that are consistent with recommended practice.

I 31 Team members should ensure that meeting times and locations are convenient for, and accessible to, the family members of the team.

I 32 Team members individualize criteria for assessing progress toward outcomes.

I 33 Family-initiated outcomes, goals, and objectives are given priority in the development of the IFSP/IEP.

I 34 Persons responsible for coordinating the development of the IFSP/IEP discuss with families all options for the range of service settings and assist families in considering the advantages and disadvantages of each.

I 35 Families choose the setting for each service that is consistent with their preferences.

State and Local Monitoring

I 36 State and local monitoring teams determine the degree to which outcomes for children and families have been achieved.

I 37 State and local monitoring teams determine the degree to which families are satisfied with the IFSP/IEP process and document.

I 38 State and local teams obtain information from families whose children are in early intervention programs, from professionals providing those services, and from professionals providing other services to these families and their children as a part of the monitoring process.

I 39 State and local monitoring teams are made up of equal numbers of family members and professionals.

I 40 Monitoring practices protect family confidentiality.

I 41 State and local monitoring teams clearly document and report service gaps and scarce resources.

SERVICE DELIVERY MODELS

Service delivery models consist of the overall pattern and location of interventions for young children with disabilities or at risk for disabilities and their families.

Indicators Across All Models of Service Delivery

SDM 1   Program staff coordinate early intervention services with all other modes of service delivery available to and needed by the child and family.

SDM 2   Services include a measure of effectiveness, and results should be communicated in a timely fashion to the family.

SDM 3   The nature of services provided are based upon families' informed selection from an array of viable options.

SDM 4   The early intervention program frequently monitors delivery of services to insure that agreed upon procedures and outcomes are achieved in a timely fashion.

SDM 5   Programs are staffed by personnel who have received competency-based training with children of the age being served.

SDM 6   Someone in the program or immediately available to the program speaks the family's preferred language.

SDM 7   Program staff individualize services in response to children's characteristics, preferences, interests, abilities, and health status.

SDM 8   Staff monitor interventions frequently and make changes in programming as needed.

SDM 9   Staff employ a variety of strategies and interventions to address individual child and family needs.

SDM 10 Staff design services to allay children's fears and anxieties regarding separation, medical interventions, and other intervention-related issues.

Home-Based

SDM 11 Staff base the nature, delivery, and scope of intervention upon activities of daily living (e.g., bathing, feeding, play, bedtime, etc.).

SDM 12 Intervention includes all family members (family members being defined by the family) who wish to be involved.

SDM 13 The level of intensity and range of services match the level of need identified by the family.

SDM 14 Staff base their communication with family members upon principles of mutual respect, caring, and sensitivity.

Center-Based

SDM 15 Environments are safe and clean.

SDM 16 The setting is physically accessible to families (i.e., within a short distance to allow for regular contact).

SDM 17 Services insure an unbiased, nondiscriminatory curriculum around issues of disability, sex, race, religion, and ethnic/cultural origin.

SDM 18 Service programs are well integrated within the administrative unit with which they are affiliated.

SDM 19 The ratio of adult staff to children maximizes safety, health, and promotion of identified goals.

SDM 20 Programs employ pull-out services (e.g., for ECSE, OT, PT, Speech) only when routine, activity-based options for services have failed to meet identified needs.

SDM 21 Services for children with disabilities are noncategorical.

SDM 22 Environments are barrier free.

SDM 23 Environments include an adequate quantity and variety of toys and materials suitable for ages and needs of children enrolled.

SDM 24 Environments are fun: They stimulate children's initiations, choices, and engagement with the social and material ecology.

SDM 25 Staff arrange environments to promote high levels of engagement for children with diverse abilities.

SDM 26 Personnel delivering related or consulting services (OT, PT, Speech, ECSE) communicate regularly with teaching staff and families.

Clinic-Based

SDM 27 Programs employ clinic-based services *only* when they are identified as the least restrictive option.

SDM 28 Professionals encourage and provide support for families to be with children during interventions/procedures.

SDM 29 Services in clinics continue only as long as it takes to reach prearranged goals.

SDM 30 Clinics include comfortable care for family members (e.g., on-site daycare, sleep-in options).

SDM 31 Clinic services prepare children for the next, less restrictive environment.

SDM 32 All clinic services are available regardless of family income.

SDM 33 Professionals keep appointments in a timely fashion.

Hospital-Based

SDM 34 Neonatal intensive care units provide environments (stimulation levels, schedules, etc.) appropriate for the neurological status and developmental level of the child.

SDM 35 Hospital-based services provide ongoing opportunities for family participation.

SDM 36 Hospital-based services include opportunities for the family to have access to medical decision makers.

SDM 37 Program staff delineate and communicate to families the roles of decision makers in hospital-based services.

SDM 38 Medical personnel in hospital-based services understand recommended practices in early intervention.

SDM 39 Hospital-based services include referrals appropriate for individualized child and family outcomes.

GENERAL CURRICULUM AND INTERVENTION STRATEGIES

Curriculum and intervention strategies are derived from and based on (a) the individual abilities and needs of infants/children, families' preferences, and the cultural context; (b) information obtained from a comprehensive assessment process; and (c) the philosophy of the program.

Curriculum and intervention strategies result in:

GC 1   No harm to infants/children, families, or their relationship.

GC 2   Active engagement of infants/children with objects, people, and events.

GC 3   Increased initiative, independence, and autonomy by infants/children across domains.

GC 4   Increased ability to function/participate in diverse and less restrictive environments.

GC 5   Independent (unprompted) performance of age-appropriate, prosocial behaviors, skills, and interaction patterns.

GC 6   Supported or partial participation in routines/activities when independent performance is not possible.

GC 7   Acquisition (initial learning) of important values, behaviors, skills, and interaction patterns across domains.

GC 8   Generalization, adaptability, application, and utilization of important behaviors, skills, and interaction patterns across relevant contexts.

GC 9   Efficient learning (most rapid acquisition) of important goals (behaviors, skills, patterns of interaction).

Curriculum and intervention strategies are developed, selected, and implemented in a manner which:

GC 10   Supports and promotes family values and participation.

GC 11   Is responsive to infants'/children's interests, preferences, motivation, interactional styles, developmental status, learning histories, cultural variables, and levels of participation.

GC 12   Integrates information and strategies from different disciplines.

GC 13   Structures learning activities in all relevant environments.

GC 14   Establishes a balance between child- and adult-initiated/directed activities.

GC 15 Integrates skills from various domains within routine activities in the classroom (i.e., is activity-based).

GC 16 Promotes acquisition (initial learning), fluency (proficiency), maintenance (retention), and generalization (application, utilization) of important goals (behaviors, skills, and patterns of interaction).

GC 17 Is most natural, normalized, and/or least intrusive, given that the benefits to individual infants'/children's learning are equal.

GC 18 Is most parsimonious (simpler/simplest) given that the benefits to individual infants'/children's learning are equal.

Curriculum and intervention strategies are modified and adjusted as needed and in a timely manner based upon:

GC 19 The changing needs of individual infants/children and their families.

GC 20 Observed and documented performance of infants/children.

GC 21 Concerns, opinions, and needs expressed by the family.

Effective curriculum and intervention strategies include:

GC 22 Use of materials that have multiple purposes, are adaptable, are varied, and reflect functional skills.

GC 23 Milieu strategies (i.e., incidental teaching, mand–model procedure, modeling, and naturalistic time delay) that involve brief interactions between adults and children.

GC 24 Peer-mediated strategies (e.g., social interaction training, peer initiation training, peer modeling, peer prompting and reinforcement).

GC 25 Adult imitation of infants'/children's play and other behavior.

GC 26 Elaboration of infants'/children's behavior by providing models, restating the child's vocalizations, suggesting alternatives, and open-ended adult questions.

GC 27 Prompting strategies (e.g., constant and progressive time delay, system of least prompts, simultaneous prompting, most to least prompting, graduated guidance) that provide learning opportunities, adult assistance, reinforcement for correct performance, and fading prompt assistance.

GC 28 Differential reinforcement that provides children with feedback for desired performance and withholding feedback (e.g., planned ignoring) when desired performance does not occur.

GC 29 Response shaping that provides positive reinforcement for progressively more complex performance.

GC 30 Self-management procedures that involve teaching children to identify appropriate behavior, evaluate their own performance, direct their performance verbally, and select reinforcement based on an evaluation of their performance.

GC 31 Correspondence training, which involves providing children with positive reinforcement for matching what they say they will do (say–do strategy) or have done (do–say strategy) with their actual performance.

INTERVENTIONS TO PROMOTE COGNITIVE SKILLS

Cognitive interventions and curricula are based upon theories and models that specify the progressive changes in children's knowledge, cognitive skill acquisition, and skill use. Cognitive skills cover such diverse capacities as attention, memory, purposeful planning, decision making, communication, discrimination, and idea/competence generation. Intervention practices enhance the acquisition and use of knowledge and cognitive skills that permit social adaptation to a broad range of demands and challenges involving a range of objects, persons, and events.

COG 1 Cognitive assessment procedures focus on the identification of persons and environmental factors that promote children's acquisition of cognitive skills and competencies with other people, objects, and events.

COG 2 Cognitively based curricula are based upon processes of human learning that progress from awareness to exploration to inquiry to utilization.

COG 3 Cognitively based curricula enhance children's knowledge about their own capacities as they relate to objects and people in different settings.

COG 4 Interventions encourage child-initiated and child-directed learning and mastery of skills in social and nonsocial environments.

COG 5 Intervention practices emphasize children's integration of previously and newly acquired knowledge and skills.

COG 6 Professionals use a broad range of teaching methods and instructional strategies to enhance engagement in daily routines and activities that match children's developmental abilities and interests.

COG 7 Teaching methods emphasize reciprocity and joint-action within the child–caregiver dyad as a primary social context for children to learn cognitive skills.

COG 8 Professionals use adaptive and augmentative devices and equipment (when appropriate) to promote acquisition of cognitive skills and competencies by allowing children to actively participate in the environment or learning activity.

INTERVENTIONS TO PROMOTE COMMUNICATION SKILLS

Practices that change or enhance the ability of young children with special needs: (a) to receive information from others, (b) to share information with other individuals, and (c) to use language to mediate their actions and cognition and to control their environment. The purpose of communication intervention is to facilitate improvement in the effectiveness and efficiency of communication (however it is demonstrated) in young children with special needs. Communication is broadly conceived: it may be intentional or nonintentional; it may involve conventional or nonconventional signals; it may be expressed through linguistic or nonlinguistic forms; and it may be conveyed through oral or non-oral (gestural, graphic, and written) modes. It should be noted that communication development need *not* be delayed with respect to other developmental areas in order to justify communicative intervention that involves the services of speech–language pathologists.

Assessment Practices

COM 1 Assessment samples the comprehension and production of content, form, and social functions of communication.

COM 2 The professional samples communicative performance in a variety of the situations and with a variety of communicative partners represented in the child's everyday life, including peers without disabilities.

COM 3　The professional examines the adequacy of current mode of communication and the potential of alternative/augmentative mode(s) of communication if the need for such mode(s) is/are indicated.

Goal Selection Practices

COM 4　Functional, oral use in the child's present social settings (and the potential for enhancing participation in mainstream settings) guide the selection and prioritization of goals.

COM 5　Goals reflect assessment results regarding children's comprehension and production of various forms, content, functions, and modes of communication, and how these abilities may vary given different social situations.

COM 6　The selection of communication goals focuses on potential modifications in environments and partners' behavior (e.g., expectations, opportunities, responsiveness of environments) as well as the child's communicative skills.

Intervention Practices

COM 7　Intervention environments provide opportunities for communication involving (a) multiple functions and content, (b) multiple partners, and (c) multiple communicative contexts (e.g., home, classroom, community).

COM 8　Communication partners (a) recognize and respond positively to communicative attempts and (b) build on children's interests, topics, leads, requests, and comments.

COM 9　Team members integrate communicative intervention strategies into a variety of instructional contexts by providing information about objectives/strategies, relevant training, and giving periodic feedback to other team members.

COM 10　Communication interventions include a range of techniques (e.g., milieu teaching, responsive interaction, didactic teaching, direct instruction, etc.) that professionals and/or parents employ with sufficient intensity and duration to result in the acquisition of the child's goals.

COM 11　Communication partners individualize/adapt their communication to the child's linguistic sophistication and disability status (e.g., hearing impairment) to ensure that communication directed to the child is understandable.

COM 12 Professionals design environments to enable and accommodate children's unique receptive and expressive modes of communicating (i.e., include properly functioning assistive devices such as hearing aids, glasses, communication boards, and other mechanical or electronic adaptive and prosthetic devices) and provide specific training in maintaining such devices.

COM 13 Early intervention settings maintain optimal listening/acoustical conditions (i.e., a +30 Db signal-to-noise ratio).

INTERVENTIONS TO PROMOTE SOCIAL SKILLS AND EMOTIONAL DEVELOPMENT

Best practices in social/emotional development include opportunities for young children with disabilities to develop social competence across a variety of settings with parents, grandparents, brothers and sisters, other family members, peers with and without disabilities, or others, and when necessary, provide intervention to enhance this development. It is assumed that adults are the primary, though not exclusive, social partners who foster social development in the early years. From approximately three years of age and beyond, peers assume a greater role in fostering social development.

Parent–Infant Interaction (Birth Through Two Years)

Unless it conflicts with the values of the primary caregivers, professionals encourage and support parents and other primary caregivers of a child to use the facilitative interaction style described in Items SE 1–SE 5.

SE 1 During interactions, adults (a) interpret infant's/children's behavior as meaningful, (b) respond contingently in positive ways, (c) allow children to withdraw briefly for the purposes of re-orienting to social interaction, (d) are nonintrusive, and (e) expect developmentally appropriate object manipulation and social interaction.

SE 2 When infants/children struggle to do something slightly beyond their ability, adults suggest or demonstrate how to do what the child is attempting.

SE 3   When infants/children remain unfocused and inactive for a sustained period, adults attempt to get children to interact with the adult or adult-selected object.

SE 4   Adults and infants/children show mostly positive and/or neutral affect during facilitative interactions.

SE 5   Professionals or parents appropriately position infants/children for easy access to objects and the adult interactor.

SE 6   Family members (parents) are present for and, if appropriate, participate directly in the assessment of infants'/children's social/emotional development.

SE 7   Professionals interpret assessment information on caregiver–child interaction as the result of the historical and immediate influence of caregiver and infants/children on each other.

Peer Social Interaction (Three to Five Years)

SE 8   Professionals design play activities in which children participate in social interaction with other children and, at times, adults.

SE 9   Professionals support children's appropriate initiations and/or responses that indicate their wish to play with other children or adults.

SE 10 Professionals provide opportunities for children to develop social skills such as turn-taking, sharing, cooperation.

SE 11 Adults provide a positive, nurturing social environment that encourages individual participation and responds to individual social and emotional needs of children.

SE 12 Professionals foster social interactions with other children that are happy and fun.

SE 13 Professionals facilitate acceptance of children by peers.

SE 14 Professionals assist children in learning to respond to (cope with) difficult social situations (e.g., physical aggression from another child, toy conflicts, multiple demands from peers) in an appropriate manner.

SE 15 Professionals plan program activities to allow children to participate in social activities with the same children in multiple settings.

INTERVENTIONS TO PROMOTE MOTOR SKILLS

Motor intervention facilitates control of one's own body, including large and small muscle groups, in order to interact with and move within the environment. The assumptions underlying motor development interventions are that (a) motor development is a key component for the foundation and acquisition of all learning and (b) motor intervention is a necessary component for all children eligible for early intervention.

M 1   Professionals base motor development interventions on theoretical constructs accepted by the field.

M 2   All caregivers for individual children participate in the interventions that enhance motor development.

M 3   All persons providing motor development interventions receive the necessary education and training for conducting the interventions.

M 4   The intervention program establishes written criteria, standards, and guidelines for making decisions about the service format for motor interventions.

M 5   Professionals facilitate movement skills in response to and coordinated with sensory input.

M 6   Motor skills intervention addresses all components of motor development including but not limited to: strength, physical and motor fitness, postural control, eye–hand coordination, object manipulation, positioning, mobility, adaptation, generalization, parent education, technology, sensory motor integration, and spatial awareness.

M 7   Professionals and/or caregivers implement motor skills interventions in the context of normal activities and routines (i.e., that are activity-based).

M 8   Professionals and/or caregivers adapt motor activities, materials, equipment, environments, and intervention strategies as needed to accommodate the abilities of individual children.

M 9   Professionals and/or caregivers facilitate motor skills in a way that promotes use in multiple environments.

M 10 Professionals provide children with methods for independent mobility.

M 11 Professionals and/or caregivers position children in ways that facilitate appropriate social and instructional interactions (e.g., children sit at eye level with other seated children, movement and positioning are done efficiently so that children do not miss parts of activities).

M 12 Professionals and/or caregivers change the position of children frequently for children who are unable to reposition themselves.

M 13 Programming for all children includes opportunities for organized gross motor activity.

INTERVENTIONS TO PROMOTE ADAPTIVE BEHAVIOR SKILLS

Adaptive behavior consists of changes in children's behavior as a consequence of maturation, development, and learning to meet increasing demands of multiple environments. Independent functioning in these environments is the long-term goal. Instruction requires accommodating and adapting to support the specific strengths of individual children. Comprehensive intervention should address the following subdomains: self-care, community self-sufficiency, personal–social responsibility, and social adjustment.

AB 1 Adaptive behavior instruction addresses all areas of self-care such as dressing/undressing, eating/feeding, toileting, and grooming.

AB 2 Instruction occurs within the context of daily routines in the home, school, and community settings, and results in the independent use of adaptive behavior skills in multiple environments.

AB 3 Adaptive behavior instruction reflects a continuum of skill training that ranges from cooperation with others who are assisting with a task to making choices independently that are appropriate for the social context and setting.

AB 4 Professionals collect assessment information on children's temperament—the underlying style of children's behavior that sets the stage for their reactions to the world—and adjust intervention procedures to accommodate styles of temperament.

AB 5 Instructional strategies consider infants'/children's state of alertness and responsiveness to stimulation prior to interactions and make necessary accommodations.

AB 6 Instruction promotes functioning in age-appropriate ways, with adult supervision, within community environments such as restaurants, neighborhoods, churches, and recreational areas.

AB 7 Adaptive behavior instruction addresses basic skills in personal–social responsibility, such as basic environmental interactions, self-directed behaviors, independent play/self-occupation, cooperation and interaction in play, and the assumption of responsibility.

AB 8 Adaptive behavior activities, materials, and training strategies are concrete and relevant to the lives of young children and their families.

AB 9 Adaptive behavior activities, materials, and training strategies are modified as needed to accommodate children's developmental level, specific sensory impairment, specific physical impairments, or special health conditions (that may require medical equipment).

TRANSITION

Transition is the process of change within or between services that involves children, families, other caregivers, and service providers. The transition process should fulfill the following four goals: (a) ensure continuity of services; (b) minimize disruption of the family system; (c) promote child functioning in the natural environment or the least restrictive environment (e.g., home, mainstreamed preschool program, Head Start, day care, etc.); and (d) involve planning, preparation, implementation, and evaluation within and between programs and with the family. Transition may occur when there is a change in agencies, programs, location or type of services, personnel, program philosophy, regulations, or funding sources.

State and Local Interagency Systems

T 1 Administrators, sending and receiving providers, and family and other caregivers develop written interagency agreements.

T 2 Formal mechanisms are in place for ongoing communication, within and between agencies.

T 3 Program providers, administrators, and families have adequate time to plan and prepare for transition.

Families and Other Caregivers

T 4 Program staff inform families about anticipated transition as early as possible.

T 5 Families can initiate transition when they believe it is necessary.

T 6 Families receive information about the transition process, the components and steps in transition, the child and family's options for future services, and options for participation in the transition process.

T 7 Families have opportunities to visit future program options and to talk to other families as well as service providers about future programs.

T 8 Families have the opportunity to jointly meet with sending and receiving providers.

T 9 Program providers have or receive adequate training to address issues of transition and to work with families during transition.

T 10 Families have a single point of contact (i.e., one individual) concerning transition.

Sending and Receiving Providers

T 11 Service providers are familiar with the tasks, time lines, roles, and responsibilities of all providers as designated on the interagency transition agreement and related procedures.

T 12 Service providers are familiar with service options and resources within the community and are able to make resource referrals.

T 13 Service providers visit each other's programs and share observations in planning for transition.

T 14 Service providers in the receiving programs prepare other individuals (i.e., children, staff members) for a child's transition into that program.

Child

T 15 Service providers and family members determine the transition skills the child needs in the next or receiving program.

T 16 Service providers, family members, and other caregivers assess transition skills in order to determine those skills that a child currently exhibits and those that a child will need in the next or receiving program.

T 17 Service providers, the child's family, and other caregivers develop plans to help a child acquire transition skills.

T 18 Service providers, the child's family, and other caregivers arrange or adapt the environment and use adaptive or assistive devices as methods to facilitate the development of transition skills as needed.

T 19 When possible, service providers assess and incorporate child preferences and opinions.

T 20 Service providers, the child's family, and other caregivers build supports to anticipate and address difficulties children may have in making transitions (e.g., visits to receiving program, gradual increase in attendance in receiving program).

T 21 Service providers, the child's family, and other caregivers plan for or allow adequate time for the child's adjustment to the new service or program.

T 22 Service providers, the child's family, and other caregivers have access to supervision, training, and support necessary to carry out the roles and responsibilities associated with preparing a child for transition.

PROGRAMS FOR CHILDREN WHO ARE GIFTED

Assessment

G 1 Assessment occurs through an interdisciplinary team effort.

G 2 Professionals consider the value families place on "giftedness" when conducting assessments of children.

G 3 Professionals conduct assessments of children in warm, friendly environments.

G 4 Licensed school psychologists/diagnosticians participate on the assessment team.

G 5 Assessment is an ongoing process.

G 6 Children's levels of development are considered within and across multiple domains (e.g., cognitive, motor, communication, social).

G 7 Professionals use a variety of sources and methods, such as naturalistic observations, family interviews, and standardized assessment in the assessment process.

G 8 Professionals may use parent nomination as one form of information when assessing children for eligibility purposes.

G 9 Professionals use assessment instruments and techniques that are sensitive to the child's and family's cultural values and primary language spoken in the home.

IEP/IFSP

G 10 The IEP/IFSP process actively involves members of multiple disciplines (inter- or transdisciplinary) as well as family members.

G 11 IEPs/IFSPs reflect children's strengths as well as their needs.

G 12 The IEP/IFSP objectives reflect the cultural, linguistic, and religious diversity of families and children in the program.

G 13 The IEP/IFSP addresses multiple domains (e.g., cognition, communication, social skills).

G 14 Elementary-level academic goals/objectives are developed only at the request of the families or in response to demonstrated readiness of the child.

Service Delivery Model/Environment

G 15 Professionals provide a warm, positive, stimulating (e.g., bright, colorful) environment.

G 16 Professionals organize classrooms into well-defined areas for specific activities.

G 17 Professionals change activities and materials often.

G 18 Professionals provide clear and consistent cues about transitions within activities or routines in the schedule.

G 19 Environments contain child-sized furniture and equipment appropriate for developmental age ranges.

G 20 Environments allow for ample use of imagination and opportunities to create with a variety of hands-on activities.

G 21 Children who are not gifted (normally developing, developmentally delayed) participate in the program all or part of the time.

General Curriculum/Intervention Strategies

G 22 The curriculum integrates the social science disciplines by focusing on social problems or broad themes (such as technology or ecology).

G 23 Professionals employ thematic units as a routine aspect of the curriculum.

G 24 The time allotted to curriculum units is flexible in order to take advantage of children's interests and spontaneous ideas.

G 25 The program provides frequent and appropriate field trips.

G 26 Curriculum activities encourage critical thinking, creativity, curiosity, and problem solving.

G 27 Professionals use games and activities (e.g., calendar) to teach preschool forms of academics, such as letter and number recognition.

G 28 Professionals give children opportunities to learn through engagement in activities they enjoy.

G 29 Curriculum activities allow exploration of the beginning (e.g., awareness) stages of career development.

G 30 Professionals integrate learning opportunities into natural activities rather than artificially structured activities (e.g., putting 10 toy people in a bus and taking them for a ride rather than counting while putting 10 pegs in a pegboard).

G 31 Professionals vary the settings, materials, personnel, cues, and consequences in order to promote generalization.

G 32 The program provides guest speakers when appropriate (e.g., a chemist visits the program and provides a demonstration of various chemical reactions during an energy unit.)

Communication Interventions

G 33 Professionals encourage children to exchange ideas, express their opinions, and talk about their feelings.

G 34 Professionals encourage children to listen to others without interrupting them.

G 35 Professionals encourage children to solve disputes by discussions and compromise.

G 36 Professionals use open-ended questions.

G 37 Curriculum activities foster (on a daily basis) children's exploration of different ways of communicating (e.g., Spanish, sign language).

G 38 Curriculum activities encourage communication among peers throughout the day.

G 39 Professionals participate with children as "co-learners" in activities.

Physical/Motor Interventions

G 40 Children have opportunities to use large-motor skills (e.g., swinging, climbing, dancing).

G 41 The program provides supervised outdoor playground activities daily.

G 42 Children explore alternative ways of movement indoors and outdoors (e.g., children can scoot to circle time).

G 43 Active manipulative activities provide opportunities for children to develop fine-motor skills.

G 44 Occupational and physical therapy support staff participate in planning intervention activities when children's needs dictate.

Cognitive Skills Interventions

G 45 Professionals enlist families to support at home the use of open-ended questioning, alternative thinking, problem solving, and higher order thinking skills such as synthesis and evaluation.

G 46 Professionals employ a holistic approach to learning.

G 47 Preschool-level books are available to children in the classroom.

G 48 Professionals encourage group problem solving.

G 49 Professionals praise and encourage children for their ideas and solutions.

G 50 Professionals respond to children's questions with appropriate levels of interest and understanding.

Adaptive Behavior Interventions

G 51 Professionals base adaptive behavior interventions (e.g., self-care, independence, etc.) on children's individual characteristics and needs as reflected in the IEP/IFSP.

Social–Emotional Interventions

G 52 Professionals acknowledge and respect children's feelings and personality traits.

G 53 Professionals encourage children to identify and verbalize their feelings.

G 54 Children participate in small group activities designed to foster cooperative learning.

G 55 Professionals make children feel their contributions are important and valued.

G 56 Curriculum activities are fun and encourage laughter.

G 57 Counselors and psychologists serve as support staff when needed.

G 58 Professionals may reorganize ongoing group activities to achieve ethnic/gender mix.

G 59 Professionals encourage children to interact with peers but do not force interaction if children express a preference for being alone.

G 60 Professionals deal with inappropriate behavior firmly but with discretion and flexibility.

Transition

G 61 The program provides parents/family members with an orientation about what to expect in public school kindergarten.

G 62 The program provides assessment information to public schools if requested by parents.

G 63 The program organizes field trips to public school kindergartens for children and parents.

G 64 Professionals develop preschool–public school transition plans.

G 65 Private preschool and public-school kindergarten eligibility criteria are consistent in order to achieve continuity.

Personnel Competence

G 66 Professionals have coursework, training, and experience in gifted education.

G 67 Professionals have knowledge of gifted research findings.

G 68 Professionals engage in ongoing upgrading of skills and knowledge through inservice training and participation in professional organizations.

Program Evaluation

G 69 Program evaluation includes an ongoing record of informal comments and suggestions by families and staff.

G 70 Families provide a formal written evaluation at the end of the year of their child's participation.

G 71 Program evaluation includes information solicited from multiple sources.

G 72 Program evaluation information is both qualitative and quantitative in nature.

G 73 Professionals from outside the program are employed as program evaluators.

Family Participation

G 74 Programs allow families to participate at their level of choice (e.g., acquire information, work as teaching assistant).

G 75 The program makes available to families a resource library of books, audiotapes, films, and other materials.

G 76 The program organizes and provides periodic parent group meetings, if the parents express a desire for the meetings.

G 77 Professionals welcome family members in the preschool program at anytime.

PERSONNEL COMPETENCE

Personnel development includes inservice and preservice efforts to recruit, prepare, and retain degree and nondegree personnel from all early intervention (B–5) and related disciplines.

Preservice Best Practice Indicators

PC 1 Family members are involved in planning, implementing, and evaluating preservice curriculum.

PC 2 Content provides a strong foundation in typical and atypical child development.

PC 3 Content includes study of cultural diversity.

PC 4 Experiences ensure participation with families that develops an awareness of families' daily lives.

PC 5 Content and process reflect a "theory to practice" orientation.

PC 6 Content emphasizes families as systems.

PC 7 Students develop and implement intervention plans based on knowledge of developmental/learning theories.

PC 8 Students receive feedback from professors, supervisors, and parents on a regular basis through both formal and informal means.

PC 9 Educational content and activities promote a commitment to continuing professional development.

PC 10 Content reflects a life-span perspective that promotes smooth transitions for children and families.

PC 11 The program prepares students to assume a variety of roles with families and young children (e.g., service coordinator, direct service provider, consultant, program manager).

PC 12 Instructors model the values and behavior expected of professionals in the field.

PC 13 Instructors have both experience and professional training related to children birth through five with special needs and their families.

PC 14 Content and process in graduate training develops skills in advocacy, policy development, and analysis.

PC 15 Content and process in graduate training includes work in program development and administration.

PC 16 Content and process at the graduate level focuses on a specialization area in early intervention (B–5).

PC 17 Instructors match field experiences to students' prior experiences, interests, and needs.

PC 18 Field experiences provide opportunities with infants, toddlers, preschoolers, with and without disabilities, and their families.

PC 19 Field experiences include experience as an interagency and intragency team member.

PC 20 Field experiences provide opportunities to demonstrate performance competencies identified by the discipline's professional association.

PC 21 Qualified university personnel supervise all field experiences.

PC 22 Field experiences include a variety of settings that represent potential employment models.

PC 23 Field experiences provide opportunities to work with children both with and without disabilities who represent diverse cultural and ethnic backgrounds.

PC 24 Field experience sites and personnel reflect recommended practice competence.

PC 25 Field experiences include substantial work with families, which is closely supervised.

PC 26 Students learn and practice assessment that is culturally unbiased and includes diagnosis for placement, assessment for developing IEP/IFSP goals and for planning individualized curriculum, performance monitoring, and evaluation of program effectiveness.

PC 27 Students learn and practice a variety of interventions with children ages birth through five with disabilities and their families, including (a) direct instructional techniques, (b) activity-based techniques, (c) developmentally appropriate practices, (d) incidental learning strategies, and (e) strategies for promoting effective adult–child and child–child interactions.

PC 28 Students learn and practice strategies that foster children's engagement with appropriate tasks and activities, and strategies to maintain children's engagement.

PC 29 Students learn to access, read, and understand current literature and research related to young children with disabilities and their families.

PC 30 The preparation program includes a comprehensive examination, written thesis, and/or field study as culminating experiences, carried out under the supervision of program faculty.

PC 31 The preparation program's full-time faculty, part-time instructors, and field supervisors represent the diverse ethnic and cultural groups served in programs for young children with disabilities and their families.

PC 32 The preparation program's faculty and staff make efforts to recruit and retain members of ethnic and cultural minorities as students.

PC 33 Students become aware of, discuss, and apply their profession's code of ethics.

PC 34 Students learn and practice strategies to incorporate technology to support children's learning.

PC 35 Preparation programs base course work on performance competencies as identified by the discipline's professional associations.

Inservice Indicators

PC 36 Personnel development addresses competencies that individuals must demonstrate in their job.

PC 37 Families participate in delivery of inservice training.

PC 38 Program staff base inservice training on assessed needs of participants.

PC 39 Inservice is developed with input from persons representing multiple disciplines.

PC 40 Team members representing multiple disciplines deliver inservice training.

PC 41 Inservice training adheres to the following four-step model: (a) presentation, (b) opportunities to observe, (c) opportunities to practice, and (d) feedback about practice.

PC 42 Persons delivering inservice are qualified, enthusiastic, knowledgeable, well prepared, and empathetic.

PC 43 Administrators facilitate staff participation in inservice training (e.g., reimbursement of expenses, release time), support/accommodate change in practice based on training, and provide incentives for participation (e.g., salary, career ladder).

PC 44 Colleagues at the work site support inservice training (i.e., team participation, on-site support for implementation).

PC 45 Inservice training includes follow-up.

PC 46 Inservice is accessible and planned according to participants' schedules, geographic locations, and financial resources.

PC 47 Evaluation of inservice training includes a variety of methods (e.g, satisfaction, demonstration of competency, change in roles).

PC 48 Evaluation addresses long-term effects as well as short-term effects.

PC 49 Goals and objectives of the inservice training serve as the basis for selecting the type and intensity of inservice activities.

PC 50 Inservice training is multiphased, sequential, and ongoing.

PC 51 Inservice training includes training and practice in using a problem-solving approach to decision making for all team members.

PC 52 Training includes practice in promoting a sense of shared responsibility for planning and intervention among family members, paraprofessionals, and professionals.

PC 53 Team members receive training in conflict resolution, mediation, and expressing differences of opinion in positive ways.

PROGRAM EVALUATION

Program evaluation consists of collecting and reporting information to answer significant questions about aspects of programs. Examples of such program aspects include child or family functioning, staff performance, educational materials, transition, classroom environments, parent participation, curriculum, program expenditures, and community programming needs. Answers to such evaluation questions might serve: a) to make decisions within a classroom; b) to formalize policy; c) to determine the viability of implementing a new program; d) to modify and improve program practices; e) to determine how funds should be allocated; f) to support the continuation, expansion, or discontinuation of a program; and g) to demonstrate accountability or cost-effectiveness.

Many of the following best practice indicators are congruent with standards presented by the Evaluation Research Society (Rossi, 1982) and by the Joint Committee on Standards for Educational Evaluation (Joint Committee, 1981; Worthen & Sanders, 1987). As there is substantial overlap between the two sets of standards and recommendations of task force members, individual citations for the recommended practice indicators are not provided. The framework for grouping these indicators according to four attributes of evaluation (utility, feasibility, propriety, and technical adequacy) approximates the approach used by the Joint Committee (1981).

Utility

PE 1 Program evaluators or staff identify audiences involved in or affected by the evaluation so their needs and expectations can be addressed and their cooperation obtained.

PE 2 The evaluator(s) must be competent (i.e., received training) to perform the desired evaluation and must be trustworthy.

PE 3 Information collected is sufficient in scope, and derived from sources sufficient in credibility, to address pertinent evaluation questions.

PE 4 Program evaluators describe thoroughly their assumptions, perspectives, methods, and rationale used to generate and interpret findings so that the audience can judge the basis for decisions.

PE 5 Evaluation reports clearly describe the purpose and rationale of the evaluation, the specific evaluation questions addressed, the program aspects being evaluated (materials, program components, staff performance, parent participation), the programmatic context, the evaluation procedures (design, data collection, analysis, etc.), findings, conclusions, and recommendations.

PE 6 Program evaluators present their findings clearly, completely, and fairly in language the audiences understand.

PE 7 Program evaluators present multiple findings or recommendations in order of relative importance.

PE 8 Program evaluators disseminate their findings in a timely manner so that audiences can best use the information.

Feasibility

PE 9 Program evaluators conduct evaluations with minimal disruptions to the program, staff, and families.

PE 10 Before beginning data collection, program evaluators, adminstrators, and/or staff determine that the evaluation plan is an effective, ethical, legal, and fiscally responsible use of resources.

Propriety

PE 11 Program evaluators report findings in a legal and ethical manner that is in due regard for the rights and welfare of participants and audiences.

Technical Adequacy

PE 12 Program evaluators describe the focus of an evaluation (e.g., program, materials) as precisely as possible.

PE 13 Program evaluators describe and examine precisely the context in which the object of the evaluation exists to determine the influences of the context on the object.

PE 14 Program evaluators describe and monitor the purposes, designs, and procedures of an evaluation in enough depth and precision to permit adequate critique, management, and/or replication of the evaluation.

PE 15 Whenever appropriate, program evaluators assess multiple sources of information.

PE 16 Program evaluators describe and justify sources of information and sampling procedures so that the adequacy and defensibility of information can be assessed.

PE 17 Measurement instruments and procedures are appropriate for the characteristics of the respondent (e.g., handicapping condition, gender, language, culture, developmental level).

PE 18 Program evaluators select, develop, and use measurement instruments and procedures in ways that assure that the interpretation of the information is reliable and valid for the intended use.

PE 19 Program evaluators pilot test locally developed instruments/procedures to insure technical adequacy, validity, and reliability.

PE 20 Program evaluators systematically review and correct (if necessary) the collection, storage, management, analysis, and reporting of program evaluation data.

PE 21 Program evaluators use for data analysis the simplest systematic procedures that are appropriate, given the purposes and design of the evaluation and the nature of the data.

PE 22 Program evaluators describe and justify procedures for analyzing qualitative or quantitative information.

PE 23 In assessment reports, program evaluators distinguish between objective findings (e.g., statistical and practical interpretations of information), opinions, judgments, and recommendations.

REFERENCES

Joint Committee on Standards for Educational Evaluation. (1981). *Standards for evaluation of educational programs, projects, and materials.* New York: McGraw–Hill.

Rossi, P. H. (1982). *Standards for educational practice.* San Francisco: Jossey–Bass.

Worthen, B. R., & Sanders, J. R. (1987). *Educational evaluation: Alternative approaches and practical guidelines.* New York: Longman.

Author Index

Able-Boone, H., 69, 82, 84, 85, 87
Acton, S. J., 81
Ainsworth, M. D. S., 225
Akiyama, M., 166
Alberti, D., 224
Albin, R., 203
Alexander, R., 271
Allen, K. E., 129, 261
Allen, R., 226
Allred, K., 88, 90
Alpern, L., 225
Amado, R., 83
Amatruda, C., 246
American Speech and Hearing Association, 28
American Speech-Language-Hearing Association, 330
Anastasi, A., 40
Anastasiow, N. J., 132
Anderson, P. P., 10
Andrellos, P., 51
Andrews, J. R., 96
Andrews, M., 255
Andrews, M. A., 96
Angelo, D. H., 211
Anisfeld, E., 233
Antia, S. D., 228
Appleton, T., 160, 180
Apter, D. S., 71
Arizona State Department of Education, 5
Arndorfer, R., 40
Arter, J. A., 40
Artis, N. E., 70
Association for Teacher Education, 332, 335
Attermeier, S. M., 33, 261
Atwater, J. B., 3, 24, 127, 128, 130, 131, 137
Audette, R. H., 303
Ault, M. J., 146
Ausubel, D. P., 27
Ayers, B. J., 5
Aylesworth, 323
Ayres, A. J., 246, 254
Azrin, N. H., 267

Baer, D. M., 132, 143, 144, 303

Baer, R. A., 142
Bagnato, S. J., 10, 11, 16, 25, 26, 27, 28, 29, 30, 31, 39, 43, 45, 49, 126, 204
Bailey, D., 4, 9, 12, 28, 35, 36, 37, 41, 45, 59, 60, 68–69, 71, 81, 87, 90, 91, 95, 102, 126, 127, 128, 129, 131, 136, 137, 138, 141, 146, 149, 203, 261, 266, 276, 288, 303, 310, 316, 323, 330, 332, 333, 336, 337, 339, 340, 344, 345, 346, 347, 351, 353
Bailey, E. J., 65
Bain, B., 201, 202
Bair, H., 224, 232
Bak, J. J., 281
Baker, B. L., 228
Balla, D. A., 316
Baltes, P., 174
Bambara, L. M., 211
Banach, W. J., 115, 117, 120
Barbour, N. B., 311
Barnes, K., 271
Barnes, S., 353
Barnett, D., 28, 128, 149
Barringer, K., 27
Barsch, R. H., 246
Bartholomew, P., 139, 165, 189
Bass, J. E., 319
Bates, E., 170
Bates, J. E., 225
Bauer, A. M., 317
Baumeister, A. A., 255
Baumgart, D., 61, 251, 279
Bayley, N. A., 246, 254
Beckett, J., 7
Beckman, P. J., 65
Beeghly, M., 163
Behr, S. K., 67
Behrmann, M., 185
Belfiore, P., 141
Bell, R. Q., 225
Bell, S. M., 225
Benner, S., 39, 126
Bennett, B., 349
Bennett, T., 276, 349
Benowitz, S., 27
Benson, H., 291
Berg, F., 215

415

Berg, W. K., 185
Berger, E., 330
Berger, M., 102
Berkeley, T. R., 340
Bijou, S. W., 132
Billings, S. S., 146
Billingsley, F. F., 146
Bishop, B., 85
Bishop, N., 144, 236
Bjorson, K., 330
Blacher, J., 91, 291, 297
Blacher-Dixon, J., 42
Blank, M. J., 289
Blasco, P. M., 87
Blehar, M. C., 225
Bleim, C. D., 297
Blockley, J., 270
Bloom, 318, 323
Blott, J. P., 207
Bobath, B., 246
Bobath, K., 246
Bologna, T., 65–66, 70, 129, 289, 294
Bonar, B., 342
Bornstein, M. H., 224
Botein, S., 233
Botkin, D., 236
Boukydis, C. F., 166
Bowlby, J., 225
Bracken, B., 26, 28, 33
Bradburn, N. M., 374
Brady, M., 138, 141, 234, 235
Brassard, J., 167, 187
Brault, L., 82, 83
Brazelton, T. B., 225
Bredekamp, S., 2, 4, 11, 12, 28, 32, 35, 38, 105, 130, 131, 135, 188, 332, 333, 334, 335
Bretherton, I., 225
Brewer, E. J., 8
Bricker, D., 25, 33, 43, 51, 64–65, 83, 128, 131, 149, 176, 201, 300
Bricker, D. B., 9
Bricker, D. D., 65, 90, 330, 333, 334, 339, 341, 345
Brickman, P., 67
Brinckerhoff, J. L., 66
Brinker, R., 65, 186
Bristol, M. M., 65
Britzman, D., 228

Brizee, L. S., 269
Bromwich, R., 232, 233
Bronfenbrenner, U., 159, 164, 166, 167, 169, 170, 180, 187
Brooks-Gunn, J., 163
Broome, K., 65
Brophy, K., 163
Brotherson, M., 291
Browder, D., 273
Brown, C., 92
Brown, K. W., 228
Brown, L., 3, 12, 274
Brown, L. J., 337
Brown, P., 3, 61
Brown, W., 83
Brown, W. H., 142, 144, 234, 235, 236
Brownier, D., 203
Bruder, M., 3, 7, 11, 19, 35, 65–66, 70, 129, 289, 293, 294, 296, 304, 330, 331, 332, 333, 337, 339, 345
Bruininks, R. H., 66, 246, 317
Brunk, G., 78
Bryant, D., 50, 65
Buchan, K., 18
Buchanan, N. K., 374
Bucuvalas, M. J., 366, 367
Burgio, L. D., 143
Burke, P. J., 329
Burkhart, L. J., 185
Burlingame, D., 270
Burton, C. B., 332, 334
Burton, S., 44
Busch-Rossnagel, N., 165, 178
Butler, C., 185
Buysee, V., 81, 228
Buysse, J., 68–69
Buysse, V., 126, 129

Cairns, R. B., 224
Callahan, 323
Campbell, C. R., 207
Campbell, D. T., 38
Campbell, M., 81
Campbell, P., 84, 89, 91, 269, 343
Campbell, P. H., 247, 330
Carden-Smith, L., 299
Cardillo, J. E., 37
Carey, K. T., 28, 128, 149

Carlson, P., 90–91
Carmen, S., 233
Carr, E. G., 203
Carta, J., 3, 24, 36, 38, 127, 128, 130, 131, 137, 143, 227, 235
Carter, K. R., 317
Case, R., 161, 168
Casper, V., 233
Castellan, J., 279
Catron, T., 67
Cavallaro, C. C., 211
Cavanagh, P., 178, 180
Chadsey-Rusch, J., 217
Champlin, J., 115, 117, 118
Chan, K., 163
Chandler, L., 19, 137, 143, 255
Chandler, L. C., 36
Chandler, L. K., 7, 224, 236, 288, 290, 293, 296, 298, 299, 300, 301, 302
Chandler, M., 223, 224
Chapman, R., 202
Charlesworth, R., 227
Charlop, M. H., 211
Chess, S., 225
Chiarello, L., 330
Child Development Resources, 96
Christensen, C. M., 83
Christopherson, E. R., 269
Christy, D. S., 88
Cicchetti, D., 163, 316
Cisar, C. L., 207
Clark, B., 313, 316, 318, 319, 322, 325
Clark, G. N., 231
Clark, M., 273
Clifford, R., 331
Clifton, R., 160
Cloninger, C., 48
Cochran, M., 78, 167, 187
Cohen, D. S., 66
Cole, K. N., 198, 211
Cole, M., 27, 293
Cole, N. S., 40
Cole, S., 27
Coleman, P. O., 103
Coleman, P. P., 329
Collet-Klingenberg, L., 217
Collins, A., 25
Collins, B. C., 146

Connell, D. B., 233
Connell, M. C., 143
Connor, R., 228
Connors, R., 163
Conn-Powers, M. C., 300
Consensus Committee, 330
Cook, R. E., 262
Cooper, C. S., 88, 90
Cooper, J. O., 141, 144
Copple, C., 131
Cornwell, J. C., 127
Correa, V. I., 186
Cort, C. A., 235
Coster, W., 30, 35, 51
Courtnage, L., 288
Covert, S., 273, 323
Craft, P., 279
Craig, H. K., 203
Craig, J. H., 79
Craig, M., 79
Crane, S., 269
Cratty, B. J., 246
Crawley, S., 163
Crimmins, D. B., 224
Cripe, J., 176, 300
Cripe, J. J. W., 131, 149
Crnic, K., 167
Crocker, A. C., 126
Cronbach, L., 25, 40
Cunningham, J. L., 297
Cunningham, N., 233
Curry, L., 84
Cybriwsky, C. A., 146

Daguio, C., 330
Dale, P. S., 211
Daly, T., 138, 276
Darling, R., 82, 85
David, T., 166
Davidson, J., 171
Davis, C. A., 141
Davis, G. A., 311, 313, 314, 318, 322
Davis, M., 82, 127
Deal, A., 9, 67, 126, 127, 129, 303, 333
Dean, C., 78
Dechillo, N., 60
DeGangi, G. A., 230, 279
DeHaas-Warner, S. J., 143

Deiner, P., 24
DeKlyen, M., 235
Demchak, M., 83
Demetras, M. J., 201
Demos, 322
Dennebaum, J., 84
DePauw, K. P., 254
DeStefano, D. M., 4, 262
Detter, P. L., 330
Diamond, K., 41, 42, 287
Division for Early Childhood, 82
Division for Early Childhood Task Force on Recommended Practices, 13, 28, 168, 248
Dixon, S. D., 225
Dobbins, N. J., 70
Doke, L., 275
Dokecki, P. R., 59, 78, 79, 87
Donder, D. D., 297
Donnellan, A. M., 203
Douglas, J., 185
Douthitt, V. L., 316, 317
Doyle, P., 66, 146
Dragow, E., 217
Drew, C. J., 311
Drinkwater, S., 83
Drotar, D., 330
DuBose, R. F., 253, 254
DuBose, R. R., 253, 254
Dunlap, G., 275
Dunn, L., 201, 337
Dunn, W., 330
Dunst, C., 7, 9, 18, 45, 67, 70, 81, 94, 125, 126, 127, 129, 136, 139, 159, 160, 162, 163, 165, 167, 168, 169, 170, 171, 173, 175, 176, 177, 179, 180, 183, 187, 189, 276, 303, 333
Durand, V. M., 203
Duwa, S. M., 9
Duyvesteyn, M. G., 225
Dyson, L., 261

Easterbrooks, M. A., 180
Eckland, J., 331
Edgar, E., 24, 287
Edgerton, M., 165
Edmondson, R., 81
Edmonson, R., 68–69

Edwards, S., 353
Effgen, S., 249, 330
Egan, M. W., 311
Egel, A. L., 209
Egeland, B., 225
Eggbeer, L., 347, 349
Eichenger, J., 5
Eicher, P. M., 268, 269
Eisner, E. W., 121
Elder, J., 303
Elkind, D., 36
Elliott, M., 128
Elliott, S., 33, 36, 37
Ellis, T. A., 255
Emde, R. N., 226
English, K., 214
Epstein, L. H., 255
Erevelles, N., 5
Esposito, B., 334
Evans, I. M., 274

Failey, R., 81
Falvey, M., 203
Farber, E. A., 225
Fassbender, L. L., 203
Favazza, P., 237, 238
Fazio, B. B., 185
Feldhusen, J. F., 311, 312, 315, 322
Feldman, H., 45
Fellows, M., 115
Fenichel, E. S., 10, 347, 349
Fenson, L., 201
Fernie, D. E., 138
Ferrell, D. R., 207
Feuerstein, R., 31, 202
Fewell, R., 7, 18, 34, 37, 66, 85, 89, 246, 247, 248, 251, 252, 254, 261
Fey, M. E., 198
Fialka, J., 66
Fiechtl, B. J., 321
Field, T., 139–140, 165, 181, 231
Fifield, B., 25
Figueredo, A. J., 367
File, N., 131, 337
Filler, J., 255
Fine, M. J., 70
Finitzo, T., 215
Finkler, D., 375

Finn, C., 115
Finn, D. M., 247
Finnegan, C., 179
Finney, J. W., 270
Fischer, K., 161
Fiske, D. W., 38
Flanagan, K., 186
Fleming, L. A., 125, 131, 146
Flynn, L., 5
Foley, G., 10, 25
Folio, M. R., 246, 248, 249, 251, 252, 253, 254
Folio, R., 253, 254
Ford, A., 273
Forest, M., 85
Fors, S., 179
Foster, M., 102
Fowler, M., 185
Fowler, S., 6, 143, 236, 287, 290, 295, 296, 298, 299, 302
Fox, J. J., 235
Fox, L., 131, 146
Fox, T. J., 121
Foxx, R. M., 267
Fraiberg, S., 226, 231
Frankenberger, W., 260
Frederiksen, J. R., 25
Fredrick, L., 69, 85
Friedlander, B., 186
Friedman, S., 170, 178, 181
Friedrich, W. N., 66
Frostig, M. A., 246
Frye, K. F., 233
Fuchs, D., 27, 29, 259, 260
Fuchs, L. S., 27
Fullagher, P., 331, 333
Fullan, M., 346
Fullen, M. G., 115, 120, 121
Furman, G. C., 70
Furuno, S., 248, 261

Gallagher, J., 103, 309, 314, 322, 323, 324, 329, 330, 331, 333, 336
Gallagher, P. A., 85
Gallagher, S. A., 314, 322, 323, 324
Gallagher, T. M., 203, 228
Gallendar, D., 269
Gallimore, R., 367

Gardner, H., 311
Garland, C., 7, 17, 59, 79, 81, 82, 86, 94, 115, 120, 229, 303, 312
Garshelis, J. A., 66–67
Garwood, S. G., 30, 59, 66, 70
Gaschnig, M. A., 60
Gast, D. L., 146
Gazdag, G., 211, 223
George, M. P., 367
George, N. L., 367
German, M., 165
Gesell, A., 246
Getman, G. N., 246
Getz-Sheftel, M., 3
Ghodssi, M., 166
Giangreco, M., 48
Gilkerson, L., 68, 69, 288, 329
Gillette, Y., 140, 231
Girolametto, L., 207, 211, 232
Gisel, E. G., 270
Glascoe, F., 42
Glazer, J., 227
Glovinsky, I., 50
Gobbi, L., 211
Goetz, J., 287
Goldberg, S., 160, 170, 180, 184
Goldman, B., 163
Goldstein, H., 7, 18, 142, 207, 209, 211, 216, 228, 235
Goldstein, S., 84
Goncu, A., 235
Goodwin, L. D., 69
Gordon, K., 207
Gordon, N., 67, 69
Gottman, J. M., 228
Gottwald, S. R., 226
Gowan, 322
Gowen, J., 163
Gowen, J. W., 88, 90
Gradel, K., 42
Graham, M., 50
Green, A. L., 91
Greenberg, M., 167
Greene, J. W., 25
Greenwood, C. R., 137, 227
Gregory, D. A., 311
Gresham, F., 33, 36, 37
Griffen, A. K., 146

Griffin, G. A., 353
Groom, J. M., 228
Grosenick, J. K., 367
Grossman, H. J., 260
Grotevant, H., 225
Gruenewald, L., 198
Gruenwald, L. J., 3
Grunebaum, H. U., 233
Guba, E. G., 36
Guba, G. G., 372
Guetzloe, E. C., 117
Guidubaldi, J., 43, 201
Guralnick, M. J., 65, 67, 90, 91, 128, 214, 223, 224, 226, 227, 228, 234

Hacker, B., 33, 261
Hadley, P. E., 202
Hains, A., 69, 290, 293, 299, 301, 302, 332
Haley, S., 51
Haley, S. M., 30, 35
Hall, G. E., 346
Hall, S., 330
Halle, J., 144, 206, 211, 217
Hamby, D., 9, 165
Hamby, D. W., 162, 167
Hames, G., 337
Hamilton, J., 9, 329
Hammill, D., 201
Hammond, M., 228
Handen, B. L., 146
Haney, M., 232
Hanline, M., 65, 131, 146, 292, 332
Hannigan, K. F., 278
Hanrahan, P., 287
Hanson, M., 4, 10, 65, 135, 236, 291, 334, 336, 337, 373
Hanson, R., 268
Hanzlik, J., 165, 179, 181
Harbin, G., 329, 331
Harding, C. G., 170
Hardman, M., 3, 262, 311
Haring, T. G., 128, 211, 237
Harper, L. V., 225
Harper-Whalen, S., 60, 67
Harris, B., 352
Harris, P. L., 161
Harris, S. R., 11, 246, 250, 254, 255
Harrison, P. J., 363

Harrison, P. L., 260
Hart, B., 144, 182, 209, 211, 261
Harter, S., 178, 184
Hartmann, M., 207
Hartup, W. W., 223, 226, 227, 228
Havelock, M. C., 346
Havelock, R., 346
Hayes, S. C., 28
Hazel, R., 116, 117, 119, 294
Healy, A., 303
Healy, H., 270
Healy, J., 270
Hedrick, D., 199
Heflinger, L. A., 59
Helmstetter, E., 70, 90–91
Hemby, D., 81
Hendricks, M. D., 256
Hendrickson, J. M., 227
Hepting, N., 18, 209, 211, 235
Herbert-Jackson, E., 166
Heron, T. E., 3, 141
Hester, P., 235
Heward, W. L., 141
Higgins-Hains, A., 143
Hill, B. K., 66
Hill, E., 228
Hill, M. M., 228
Hill, P., 163
Hilliard, A. G., 329
Hockenberger, E. H., 216
Hockless, M. F., 89
Hoekenga, R., 198
Hoeksma, J. B., 225
Holbert, K., 171, 173, 276
Holburn, S., 300
Holcombe, A., 128, 131, 146
Holcombe-Ligon, A., 146
Holdgrafer, G., 170
Holm, V. A., 129
Holtiwanger, J., 51
Holvoet, J. F., 271
Hord, S., 346
Horn, E., 7, 259, 260
Horn, E. M., 4, 18, 255, 256, 262, 266
Horne, D., 246
Horner, R., 203
Horowitz, F. D., 161, 168, 178
Horstmeister, D. S., 201

House, L., 198
Howe, A. G., 4, 262
Howes, C., 223, 226
Howley, A. A., 320
Howley, C. B., 320
Hoyson, M., 235
Hresko, W., 44, 201
Hubley, P., 170
Hulsebus, R., 180
Hunt, J., 318
Hunt, J. McV., 161, 162, 166, 178
Hunt, P., 211
Huntington, G., 37, 59, 129, 279, 288, 330, 331, 336, 339, 345, 347, 375
Hussey, B., 163
Hutchins, V. L., 8
Hutinger, P. L., 287, 321
Hutson, H. M., 346, 348, 349, 352
Huttinger, P., 185

Ilott, B., 90
Innocenti, M. S., 321
Irvin, L. K., 66
Iscoe, I., 34, 42
Iverson, V., 48
Iwata, B., 270, 278
Izeman, S. G., 138, 276

Jacobson, S. W., 233
Jamieson, B., 235
Jarrett, R. B., 28
Jenkins, J. R., 254
Jennings, K., 163
Jens, K. G., 33
Jeppson, E. S., 81, 263
Johanson, C., 9
Johnson, A., 312
Johnson, B. H., 4, 70, 81, 93, 263
Johnson, C., 81
Johnson, G. A., 201, 202
Johnson, J. E., 130, 131
Johnson, K. M., 130, 131
Johnson, L., 6, 49
Johnson, L. J., 13, 64, 310, 311, 314
Johnson, M. R., 143
Johnson, R. J., 296
Johnson, S. M., 235
Johnson-Martin, N., 33, 163, 261, 264

Johnston, R. G., 81
Johs, J., 60
Joint Committee on Standards for Educational Evaluation, 360, 411
Jones, H. A., 276
Jones, J. K., 185
Jones, T. W., 270
Joyce, B., 333, 344, 349, 350
Juffer, R., 225

Kaczmarek, L., 18, 207, 209, 211, 235
Kagan, S., 303
Kaiser, A., 144, 146, 181
Kaiser, C., 330
Kaluzny, A. D., 117, 118
Kalyanpur, M., 78, 87
Kang, J., 228
Karnes, F. A., 323
Karnes, M. B., 246, 251, 309, 310, 311, 314, 345
Kasari, C., 255
Katims, D. S., 150
Katz, E. L., 226
Kauffman, C., 88
Kaufman, M., 330
Kaufmann, R. K., 4, 70, 93
Kawate, J., 287, 299
Kazdin, A. E., 35
Keefer, C., 225
Keesee, P. D., 303
Keetz, A., 146, 237
Kelley, P., 309
Kelly, D., 115
Kemp, P. B., 311
Kephart, N. C., 246
Kerns, G., 296
Khatena, J., 312
Kieffer, C. H., 78
Kilgo, J., 293, 298, 300, 302, 304
Killoran, J., 117
Kim, K., 223
Kinnish, K., 228
Kirby, D. F., 309, 310, 311, 312, 314, 315, 317, 320, 324
Kiresuk, T., 37, 375, 376
Kitano, M. K., 309, 310, 311, 312, 314, 315, 317, 320, 324
Kjerland, L., 86, 89

Klee, T., 202
Klein, D. M., 232
Klein, M. D., 199, 262, 269
Klein, N., 343
Klosowski, S., 330
Knoll, J. A., 67
Knowles, M. S., 346, 348
Koegel, R., 275
Kontos, S., 131, 337
Kopp, C. B., 228
Koren, P. E., 60
Korinek, L., 333, 344, 348, 349, 352
Kottwitz, E., 299
Kovach, J., 86, 89
Kozloff, M., 126
Krantz, P., 137
Krantz, P. J., 209
Kreimeyer, K. H., 228
Kurth-Schai, R., 49

La Forme, C., 84
LaGreca, A. M., 228
Lahm, E., 185
Lakin, K. C., 66
Lalinde, P., 9
Lamb, M., 170, 178, 180, 183, 184, 224
Lambour, G., 117, 120
LaMontagne, M., 13, 49, 64
Lamorey, S., 83
Langley, M. B., 185
Lanier, J., 340
Laten, S., 61, 251
Lazzari, A. M., 292, 293, 300, 304
LeCrone, J., 309
Lee, I., 17, 59, 78, 81, 229, 312
Lefebvre, D., 143
Lehr, S., 67
LeLaurin, K., 83, 103, 137, 276
Lennon, M. C., 226
Lennox, D., 40
Lerner, E., 85
Lerner, R., 165, 178
Lesko, J., 162, 180
Levine, J., 84
LeVine, R. A., 225
Leviton, A., 88
Lewin, K., 40
Lewis, M., 163, 186, 207, 211

Li, A., 163
Lidz, C. S., 31, 51, 311
Lincoln, Y. S., 36, 372
Linder, T., 11, 81, 162, 201, 303
Lindsey, M., 322
Lingerfelt, B., 165
Linnemeyer, S. A., 309
Linstone, H., 48
Lipsitt, L., 180
Lobosco, A., 362, 376
Long, C. E., 70
Losardo, A., 131
Loughry, A., 69
Love, A. J., 362
Lovett, D., 334, 336
Lowe, L. W., 139
Lu, C. H., 42
Lubeck, R., 137
Lubek, R. C., 236
Luckasson, R., 260, 273, 315
Ludlow, B. L., 340
Ludlow, L., 51
Lund, S., 375, 376
Lund, S. H., 37
Lussier, B. J., 224
Lydic, J. S., 255
Lynch, E., 4, 65, 135, 236, 291, 373
Lyngaas, K., 198
Lyon, G., 11
Lyon, S., 11
Lyons-Ruth, K., 225, 233

MacDonald, C., 65, 203, 204
MacDonald, J., 201
MacDonald, J. D., 140, 207, 209, 211, 231
MacDonald, J. M., 201
Mace, F. C., 141
MacLean, W., 42
MacLean, W. E., 255
Maddox, C. D., 319
Maeroff, G. I., 115
Magrab, P., 303
Magrab, P. R., 8
Maheady, L., 297
Mahoney, G., 18, 84, 138, 139, 165, 171, 172, 179, 181, 202, 211, 232
Mahoney, K., 267
Maisto, A., 165

Mallory, B. L., 227
Mankinen, M., 160
Mann, L. H., 138, 276
Marfo, K., 165, 231, 232
Marquis, J., 85
Martin, D. G., 69
Martin, J. E., 255
Martin, S. S., 138
Maude, S., 329, 333
McAdams, M., 333
McBride, S., 69
McCabe, P., 165
McCartan, K., 330, 338–339, 341
McCarthy, J., 186
McCauley, R. J., 201
McClannahan, L. E., 209
McCollum, J., 231, 329, 330, 332, 333, 336, 338–339, 339, 341
McCollum, J. A., 60, 224, 232, 330, 333, 347
McConnell, S., 3, 24, 36, 66–67, 127, 128, 130, 137, 142, 143, 223, 224, 226, 227, 228, 234, 235, 236, 237, 375
McCormick, K., 291, 332
McCormick, L., 12, 65, 138, 287, 299
McCubbin, H. I., 66
McCune-Nicholich, L., 163
McDonnell, A., 3, 262
McDowelle, J., 334, 344
McEvoy, M., 6, 7, 18, 67, 128, 129, 131, 137, 142, 144, 223, 226, 227, 234, 235, 236, 238, 297, 334
McGee, G. G., 138, 209, 211, 276
McGonigel, M., 4, 10, 45, 70, 79, 82, 86, 93, 94, 95, 160, 368
McGraw, M. B., 246
McGuire, J., 161
McLaughlin, J. F., 269
McLaughlin, M. J., 329
McLean, M., 6, 28, 38, 65, 102, 211, 330, 331, 332, 339
McLean, M. E., 13, 17, 49, 64, 130, 131, 266
McNulty, B., 71, 118, 120, 287
McPherson, M., 8
McQuarter, R. J., 144
McRoy, R., 225
McWilliam, P. J., 69, 71, 102, 333

McWilliam, R., 7, 12, 17, 67, 69, 127, 129, 130, 136, 138, 159, 162, 169, 171, 173, 175, 176, 183
McWilliams, R. A., 83, 275, 276
Meador, K. S., 315
Meehl, P., 28
Meisels, S., 38, 40
Meisels, S. J., 117, 149, 329
Melaville, A. I., 289
Merrill, M. A., 316
Mesaros, R. A., 203
Mesich, C. R., 337
Messick, S., 25, 26
Meyer, C. A., 40
Meyer, D. J., 85
Meyer, L. H., 5
Meyerson, L., 267
Miguel, S., 44
Miles, M. B., 115, 120, 121
Millar, W. S., 180
Miller, G., 270
Miller, J., 198, 201, 202
Miller, P., 7, 333, 334, 335, 339
Miller, P. A., 137
Miller, P. M., 225
Miller, P. S., 19, 332, 333, 334, 338, 344
Mills, P. E., 198
Milne, C., 317
Miltenberger, R., 36, 40
Minick, N., 202
Miranda, P. L., 203
Mistry, J., 235
Mitchell, A., 340
Modigliani, K., 329, 340
Mohandessi, K., 166
Montgomery, P., 254
Moore, K. J., 25, 45
Moore, S. G., 228
Morgan, J. L., 117, 120, 289, 290
Mori, A., 339
Morningstar, M. E., 85
Morris, S., 270, 271
Morris, S. E., 269
Mosier, C., 235
Moss, P., 25, 38, 40
Motti, F., 163
Mowder, B. A., 231
Mueller, M., 88

Munson, S. M., 28, 30
Murphy, J., 121
Murphy, M., 299
Myers, M., 50

Nash, J. K., 81
National Association for the Education of Young Children, 28, 29, 332, 335
National Association of Early Childhood Specialists in State Departments of Education, 29
National Council on Disability, 185
Neef, N. A., 209, 211, 278
Neilson, M. E., 374
Neisworth, J., 7, 10, 11, 16, 25, 26, 27, 28, 29, 30, 31, 34, 37, 39, 42, 43, 49, 50, 126, 204
Nelson, R. O., 28
Nesselroade, J., 174
Nevin, A., 79
New Mexico State Department of Education, 118
New, R. S., 227
Newborg, J., 43, 201
Newman, D., 362, 376
Newmann, F. M., 25, 38
Nirje, B., 12
Nisbet, J., 273
Noonan, M., 298, 302
Noonan, M. J., 12, 138
Nordquist, V. M., 137, 236, 297
Norris, J. A., 130
Notari, A. R., 198
Nourot, P. M., 234
Nover, A., 330
Nozyce, M., 233
Nuttall, D., 39
Nwaobi, O. M., 270
Nyberg, B., 198

O'Brien, M., 166
O'Brien, S., 269
Odom, S., 6, 13, 14, 18, 24, 28, 36, 38, 49, 64, 67, 83, 90, 128, 129, 130, 131, 137, 142, 143, 223, 224, 226, 227, 228, 234, 235, 236, 237, 238, 297, 300, 302, 334
Ogawa, I., 227
Olds, A., 166

Oliver, C. B., 211
Olson, J., 117, 119
Olson, K., 329
Olswang, L. B., 201, 202
O'Neill, R., 203
Orelove, F. P., 269, 271
Orth-Lopes, L., 128
Ostrosky, M., 137, 143, 237
O'Sullivan, P., 84
Ottenbacher, K., 247, 254, 256
Owens, R., 198

Page, T. J., 278
Paget, K. D., 61, 66, 70
Palmer, F. B., 246
Palsha, S., 59, 288
Palsha, S. A., 129, 336, 339, 345, 347
Paniagua, F. A., 142
Paolucci-Whitcomb, P., 79
Parette, H. P., 256
Parish, J. M., 278
Parker, J., 323
Park-Lee, S., 5
Parks, S., 33
Parlett, M., 360
Parse, S. A., 279
Parsons, S., 163
Patton, J., 310
Patton, M. A., 362
Paul, L., 207
Paul-Brown, D., 214
Payne, S., 34, 42
Peck, C. A., 70, 90–91, 128, 136
Pederson, F., 181
Pendarvis, E. D., 320
Pennington, R., 207
Perrett, S., 6, 68
Perrone, V., 32
Peters, M. T., 3
Peterson, C., 137
Peterson, C. A., 67
Peterson, N., 261
Peterson, N. L., 10, 71
Peto, A., 247
Phillips, W., 330
Phyfe-Perkins, E., 137
Piaget, J., 17, 132, 161, 169, 178, 317
Pletcher, L. L., 67

Ploof, D., 45
Poisson, S., 230
Pollock, B., 165
Porterfield, J., 166
Poulson, C. L., 186
Powell, A., 138, 139, 179, 202, 211, 232
Powell, T. H., 85
Power, T., 163
Powers, C., 333, 339
Powers, M., 3
Prather, E., 199
Prillaman, D., 310
Prizant, B., 201
Provus, M. M., 360

Quay, L., 228
Quinn-Curran, N., 292
Quinters, M., 117
Quirk, J. P., 70

Raab, M., 82, 179, 297, 349
Radcliff, J., 163
Ragland, E. U., 236
Rainforth, B., 65, 203, 251
Ramey, C. T., 65
Rao, S. S., 78, 87
Rapp, N., 143
Raver, S. A., 103
Reaney, S., 143
Reese, H. M., 174
Reeson, B., 185
Reichle, J., 203
Reid, D. K., 201
Reinoehl, B., 217
Reith, H. J., 185
Repacholi, B., 225
Repp, A., 269
Reynolds, C. R., 29, 30
Rhyner, P., 50
Rice, M. L., 202
Richert, E. S., 311
Richman, A. L., 225
Richmonds, G., 267
Richter, E., 254
Rimm, S. B., 311, 313, 314, 318, 322
Riordan, M. M., 270
Risley, T., 137, 138, 144, 166, 182, 209, 211, 275, 276

Roberts, J. E., 203
Roberts, L., 70
Robinson, C. C., 375
Rock, S. L., 256
Rogers-Warren, A., 144, 207, 211
Rogoff, B., 235
Romer, L., 146
Rooney, R., 331, 333, 337
Rose, D. F., 106, 107, 108, 109, 115, 117, 118, 119, 120
Rose, J. S., 375
Rosegrant, T., 4, 11, 12, 32, 35, 38, 130
Rosenberg, S. A., 375
Rosenfield, S., 29, 30
Rosenkoetter, S., 299, 302
Ross-Allen, J., 300
Rossi, P. H., 411
Rostetter, D., 117
Roszmann-Millican, M., 10
Rounds, K., 93
Rowan, L. R., 60
Rowland, G., 161
Royeen, C., 230
Rubenstein, J. M., 181
Rubin, S., 292
Rule, S., 321
Rundall, D., 3
Ryan, M., 185

Safer, N. D., 9
Safford, P. L., 128
Sainato, D., 17, 65, 137, 142, 143, 179, 182, 227, 235, 297
Salisbury, C., 3, 6, 61, 65, 228, 251, 291
Salisbury, C. L., 65, 251, 287, 296, 299, 321
Salkind, N., 91, 297
Salzberg, C. L., 186
Sameroff, A., 178, 180, 223, 224, 231
Sancilio, M. F., 223
Sandall, S., 69, 85, 231
Sanders, J. R., 367, 372, 411
Santa Cruze County Office of Education, 33
Santelli, B., 85, 90
Sapir, S. G., 117
Sava, S., 118
Scarlato, M., 25
Schaefer, E., 165

Scheiber, L. M., 319
Schiefelbusch, R. L., 129
Schmid, R., 333
Schneider, L. A., 50
Schneiderman, N., 165
Schon, D. A., 78
Schoville, R., 170
Schrag, E., 329
Schuster, J. W., 146
Schwartz, I., 24, 299
Schwartz, I. L., 303
Schwartz, I. S., 3, 127, 128, 130, 137
Schwartz, R. G., 211
Scott, S., 66
Scriven, M., 360
Sechrest, L., 367
Seeley, K., 312
Segal, M., 165
Seifer, R., 231
Seligman, M., 82, 85
Sell, M. A., 202
Servatius, J. D., 115, 117, 118, 120
Sexton, D., 89
Shafer, K., 207
Shakel, J., 28
Shaklee, B. D., 310, 311
Sharp, L., 69
Sharp, P. A., 353
Shea, 322
Shearer, M., 339
Sheehan, R., 19, 34, 42, 59, 66, 70, 173, 362, 363, 364, 365, 369, 370, 371–372, 375
Shelton, T. L., 81, 263
Shenet, M. A., 289
Sherbenov, R., 44
Shey, T. M., 317
Shilansky, M., 226
Shirley, M., 316
Shonkoff, J. P., 149, 329
Shook, G. L., 297
Shores, R. E., 227, 235
Short, M. A., 254, 255
Short, R., 37
Short, R. J., 375
Showers, B., 333, 344, 349, 350, 351, 353
Shuster, S., 36
Shwedel, A. M., 309, 311

Siegel, K., 366–367
Sigel, I., 165
Silverman, L. K., 310, 312, 315, 320
Silverstein, R., 86
Simeonsson, R. J., 35, 36, 37, 42, 71, 87, 129, 279, 347, 375, 376
Simeonsson, R. S., 330, 333, 336, 337, 340, 345, 347
Simon, R., 236
Simpson, S. L., 146
Singer, G. S., 66
Sinzer, L., 330
Siperstein, G. N., 281
Sisson, L. A., 235
Skellenger, A. C., 228
Slentz, K., 330, 333, 339, 341, 345
Slentz, K. L., 9, 64–65, 83
Slough, N., 167
Small, J., 163
Smith, A., 37
Smith, B., 6, 70, 333, 339
Smith, B. A., 4, 262
Smith, B. J., 17, 106, 107, 108, 109, 115, 117, 118, 119, 120
Smith, B. S., 303
Smith, D. D., 315
Smith, M. F., 362
Smith, P. D., 270
Smith, P. M., 85
Smith, S. L., 3
Smith, T., 81
Smith, T. M., 68–69
Smith-Davis, J., 288, 329
Snell, M. E., 267, 268, 273
Snyder, P., 89
Snyder, S., 7, 19, 160, 362, 363, 364, 365, 369, 370, 371–372, 375
Sobsey, D., 269, 271
Sobsey, R. J., 269, 270
Soforonko, A., 186
Sokoly, M. S., 78, 79, 87
Sontag, J., 69
Sophos, C. M., 269
Spandel, V., 40
Sparling, J., 65, 88
Sparrow, S. S., 316
Speigel-McGill, P., 287
Spiegel, B., 207

Spiegel, J., 60, 67, 69
Spira, D. A., 25
Spradlin, J. E., 144
Sprague, J., 78, 203
Squires, J., 41, 42
Sroufe, L. A., 225
Stagg, V., 67
Stainback, S., 270, 271
Stainback, W., 270
Stake, R. E., 360
Stallings, J., 351
Stayton, D. J., 225
Stayton, V., 6, 7, 333, 334, 335, 339
Stayton, V. D., 19, 345
Stedman, D., 333
Stegman, C., 163
Stein, E., 230
Stephens, P., 301, 304
Sternberg, R., 171
Stevens, E., 85
Stiggins, R. J., 38
Stile, S., 7, 18, 309, 311, 323, 325
Stineman, R. M., 85
Stock, J., 43
Stock, J. R., 201
Stone, W., 42
Stone, W. L., 228
Stoneman, Z., 91, 117, 118, 120
Stonestreet, R. H., 81
Stone-Zukowski, D., 163
Storey, K., 203
Strain, P., 4, 7, 17, 65, 67, 106, 120, 129, 130, 131, 142, 143, 227, 228, 235, 291, 334
Stremel-Campbell, K., 207
Strickland, B., 84, 89
Striefel, S., 117
Strom, P., 312
Strom, R., 312
Strom, S., 312
Stroufe, L. A., 163
Stufflebeam, D. L., 360
Sturm, L., 330
Suarez, T. M., 372
Sudman, S., 374
Suen, H. K., 42
Sugai, G. M., 136
Sullivan, E. V., 27
Summers, J., 291

Summers, J. A., 67, 69, 83, 88
Svinicki, J., 43, 201
Swan, W. W., 117, 289, 290
Swanson, M., 255
Swisher, L., 201
Szczepanski, M., 277

Tada, W. L., 11, 250
Taha, A. H., 117
Tallmadge, G. K., 375
Tannen, D., 86
Tannenbaum, A., 311
Tannock, R., 226, 232
Taylor, S. J., 67, 69
Terman, L. M., 316, 319
Tessier, A., 65, 262, 291
Tharp, R. G., 367
Thomas, A., 225
Thomas, D., 6, 331
Thompson, B., 299
Thompson, M., 42
Thompson, T., 268
Thorp, E. K., 60, 330, 333, 347
Thorpe, J. K., 226
Thousand, J., 79
Thurman, S. K., 226
Timberlake, E., 330
Tobin, A., 199
Torrance, 322
Torrance, E. P., 315
Trefler, E., 270, 271
Tremblay, A., 227
Trepanier, A., 82
Trevarthen, C., 170
Trivette, C., 9, 303
Trivette, C. M., 9, 67, 81, 94, 126, 127, 129, 165, 167, 183
Trohanis, P. L., 70, 303, 344, 347, 348
Tronick, E., 165
Tronick, E. Z., 225
Tuckel, P., 366–367
Turbiville, V., 312
Turbiville, V. P., 17, 59, 77, 229
Turnbull, A., 7, 17, 36, 45, 59, 61, 67, 69, 70, 78, 81, 83, 84, 85, 89, 91, 135, 229, 291, 297, 312, 334
Turnbull, H., 45, 61, 69, 70, 85, 291
Turnbull, R., 78, 81, 83

Turner, I., 163
Turoff, M., 48
Twardosz, S., 137, 166, 236

U.S. Bureau of Labor Statistics, 329
U.S. Department of Education, 329
U.S. General Accounting Office, 115, 117
Utley, B. L., 271
Uzgiris, I., 161, 162, 168, 179, 181, 318

Vadasy, P. F., 66, 85
Van den Boom, D. C., 225, 233
Van den Pol, R., 69
Van Hoorn, J. L., 234
Van Ijzendoorn, M. H., 225, 233
Van Wagenen, R. K., 267
Vance, S. D., 162, 167
Vanco, 323
Vandercook, T., 85
VanTassel-Baska, J., 310, 315, 318, 322
Vassilaros, M. A., 146
Venn, M. L., 129, 131, 146
Venuto, C., 59
Verbey, M., 232
Vietze, P., 170, 178, 181
Villa, R., 79
Vincent, L., 3, 7, 17, 59, 61, 65, 66, 67, 68, 70, 211, 251, 287, 291, 296, 297, 299, 321
Vygotsky, L., 17, 132

Wachs, T., 173
Wacker, D., 203
Wacker, D. P., 185
Wade, R. K., 349, 352
Walker, B., 64–65, 66
Walker, L., 296
Walker, L. S., 25
Walker, P. M., 67
Wall, S., 225
Walter, G., 3, 297, 299
Walters, J., 209
Warren, F., 61, 69, 70
Warren, S. F., 61, 69, 70, 144, 181, 211, 223, 255, 276
Wasik, B. H., 65
Wasserman, G. A., 226
Waters, E., 225
Watson, A. L., 349

Watson, J. S., 170, 179, 184
Watson, P. J., 254
Watts, E., 142
Watts, J., 165, 179, 180, 181
Wayman, K., 373
Weaver, P., 60
Wehby, J. H., 235
Weil, M., 93
Weiner, 322
Weinstein, C., 166
Weiss, C. H., 366, 367
Weiss, R. S., 211
Weiss-Perry, B., 163
Weistuch, L., 207
Wells, C., 9
Wenar, C., 179, 181
Wenger, M., 331
Werder, J. K., 246
Werner, J., 180
Werts, M. G., 131, 146
Wesley, P. W., 126, 129
Westmoreland, D., 270
Wetherby, A., 201
Whaley, K. T., 276
White, B., 161, 165, 166, 179, 180, 181
Whitehead, A., 69
Whitman, L., 143
Wickstrom, R. L., 246
Widerstrom, A. H., 231
Wiestuch, L., 211
Wietlisbach, S., 230
Wiggins, B., 185
Wilbers, J. S., 128, 131, 134, 140
Wilcox, M. J., 211
Wilds, M. L., 185
Will, M., 287
Willer, B., 333
Williams, G. E., 269
Williams, M., 311
Williams, R. E., 138
Williams, W., 121
Williamson, G. G., 277, 278
Wilson, L., 171, 173
Wilturner, L. J., 66
Windsor, M. M., 255
Winton, P., 36, 59, 69, 71, 90, 91, 102, 135, 297, 333, 346, 348, 349
Wnek, L., 43, 201

Wohl, M. K., 270
Wolery, M., 2, 4, 7, 17, 28, 41, 65, 125, 126, 128, 129, 131, 134, 136, 137, 138, 140, 141, 146, 149, 150, 179, 182, 261, 266, 288, 310, 316, 323
Wolf, B., 311
Wolf, M. M., 29, 34, 35
Wolfle, J., 311
Wood, S., 179
Woodruff, G., 10, 45
Worthen, B. R., 367, 372, 411
Wortman Lowe, L., 165, 179, 189

Yarrow, L., 181
Yates, T. J., 231
Yoder, D. E., 103, 129, 329, 330
Yoder, P., 7, 146, 211, 223, 226
York, J., 65, 85, 203, 204
York, R., 297
Youngblade, L. M., 225

Zane, T., 146
Zeitlin, S., 277, 278
Ziegler, M., 59, 66
Zipper, I. N., 93

Subject Index

Acceptance, and social interaction, 237–238
Accommodation, 320
Action planning, and systems change model, 118–120
Adapting behaviors, 176
Adaptive behavior skills
  assessment of, 260
  assuming responsibility, 276–277
  child characteristics and, 278–280
  community self-sufficiency, 273–275
  context for intervention, 262–263
  family participation and, 261–263
  gifted children and, 320
  independent play, 275–276
  instructional modifications and, 279–281
  intervention issues and, 278–280
  interventions promoting, 259–282, 320
  peer interactions and, 276, 281
  personal-social responsibility, 275–277
  rationale for inclusion of, 260–262
  recommended practices and, 18–19, 263–278, 399–400
  self-care and, 263–273
  self-directed behaviors, 275
  self-occupation, 275–276
  social adjustment and, 277–278
  transition and, 296
  young children and, 259–260
Adaptive devices, 184–186, 214, 264, 279
Adaptive physical educators, 250
Administrative support for planning, 301
Adult facilitators, and motor skills promotion, 249–250
Adult learners, characteristics of, 346–347
Adult-mediated interventions, 235
Advances in Family-Centered Care, 61
Advocacy
  family participation and, 69–70
  of inclusion, 90–91
  service coordination and, 93
  of team members, 89–91

AEPS. *See Assessment, Evaluation, and Programming System for Infants and Children* (AEPS)
American Speech and Hearing Association (ASHA), 28
Arizona Department of Education, 5
ASHA. *See* American Speech and Hearing Association (ASHA)
Assessment
  of adaptive behavior skills, 260
  behavioral differences and, 26–27
  cognitive competency and, 171–174
  collaborative decision-making formats and, 51
  communication intervention and, 198–205
  concerns and perspectives, 23–27
  consensual validity and, 44–49
  convergent assessment and, 38–44
  cultural differences and, 26–27
  curriculum-based assessment, 32–33, 39, 43, 47–48, 51
  developmentally appropriate practice and, 35, 36, 38, 40
  Division for Early Childhood and, 28, 49
  dynamic assessment, 311
  ecological definition of, 174
  evaluability assessment, 368–369
  evaluation and, 248–249
  family participation and, 40–45, 88
  follow-up assessment, 248–249
  functional assessment approaches and, 40, 51
  future trends in, 49–51
  of gifted children, 310–311
  intelligence tests and, 31–32
  legislation and, 24, 34, 38
  medical identification and, 248
  of motor skill development, 247–249
  National Association for the Education of Young Children and, 28, 29
  naturalistic assessment methods, 201
  observation and, 24–26
  professional assessment practices, 24–26

431

432 Subject Index

recommended practices and, 16–17, 32, 37–38, 43–44, 47–48, 248, 379–381
of self-care skills, 269
service coordination and, 93
service-based eligibility and, 50
sharing information and, 88
social validity of, 34–38
societal context and, 23–24
standards for, 28–49
technology use and, 50–51
transition and, 298–299
treatment utility and, 28–33
of young children, 26–27
Assessment, Evaluation, and Programming System for Infants and Children (AEPS), 33, 43, 201
Assessment of Sensorimotor Integration, 254
Assessment of Student Participation in General Education Classes, 204
Assimilation, 320
Assistive technology, 184–186
Association for Teacher Education (ATE), 332, 335–336
Assuming responsibility, 276–277
ATE. *See* Association for Teacher Education (ATE)
Attachment interventions, 233
Attitudinal issues
  awareness and, 108
  communication/collaboration/respect, 108
  social change and, 106–109
  "Someone will lose" attitudes, 108–109
  systems change model and, 118, 120
  teacher preparedness attitudes, 107–108
  turf attitudes, 107

Balance of power, 159–160
Battelle Developmental Inventory, 43, 201
Bayley Scales of Infant Development, 254
Beach Center on Families and Disability, 92
Behavior functions, 175–176
Behavioral differences, and assessment, 26–27

Behavioral momentum, and general curriculum and intervention strategies, 141–142
Behavioral programming, 255
Best practices, and recommended practices, 2–3
BOT-S (*Bruininks-Oseretsky Test of Motor Proficiency*), 317
Bracken Basic Concepts Scale, 33
Bruininks-Oseretsky Test of Motor Proficiency (BOT-S), 317

Caregivers. *See also* Family participation; Mothers
  attachment with, 223
  child-caregiver interactions, 183–184, 225, 232
  cognitive competence and, 165
  dressing/undressing and, 264
  feeding and, 269
  infant-caregiver interactions, 224, 229–230, 232
  instructional modifications and, 279
  social competence interventions for, 229–233
  transition and, 291–294
The Carolina Curriculum for Infants and Toddlers with Special Needs, 33
The Carolina Curriculum for Preschoolers with Special Needs, 33, 261
Carolina Institute for Research on Infant Personnel Preparation, 4
CBA. *See* Curriculum-based assessment (CBA)
Change, social significance of, 36–37
Checklists, 203
Child characteristics, and adaptive behavior intervention, 278–280
Child component, of transition, 298–300
Child-caregiver interactions, 183–184, 225, 232
Child Development Resources, 91
Child-engagement, 182–183
Child-environment interactions, 132
Child-initiated learning, 178–179
Children with disabilities
  cognitive competence of, 162–164

infants and, 226
play of, 162, 172
preschool children and, 227–228, 234–238
social interaction interventions for, 234–238
Children with special needs, and communication intervention, 214–215
Choosing Options and Accommodations for Children (COACH), 48
Chronologically age appropriate, and recommended practices, 11–12
Clarification, 212
COACH. *See* Choosing Options and Accommodations for Children (COACH)
Coaching, and social interaction, 181, 230–231
Cognitive competence
  adaptive devices and, 184–186
  assessment and, 171–174
  assistive technology and, 184–186
  child engagement, 182–183
  child-caregiver interactions and, 183–184, 225
  child-initiated learning, 178–179
  of children with disabilities, 162–164
  cognitive development theories and models, 168–171
  communication and, 198
  community self-sufficiency and, 274
  conceptual and procedural considerations, 160–168
  environmental determinants and, 166
  family determinants, 165
  family participation and, 187
  family-centered practices, 189
  gifted children and, 317–318
  instructional strategies, 179–182
  interactional determinants, 165
  intervention and, 174–187, 317–318
  intervention settings, 176–178
  intervention targets, 174–176
  motor skills and, 253
  National Association for the Education of Young Children and, 187–188
  nature of, 160–162
  principles for cognitive intervention, 168–187
  recommended practices and, 17–18, 168, 174–187, 393–394
  routine-based practices, 188–189
  social systems context of development, 186–187
  social-ecological perspective in, 164–167
  strengths-based practices, 188
  systems determinants and, 166–167
Cognitive development theories, 168–171
Collaboration
  assessment and, 51
  as attitudinal issue, 108
  communication intervention and, 207–208
  decision-making formats and, 51
  personnel preparation and, 335
  preservice training programs and, 288
  service delivery and, 10–11, 288, 289–290, 303–304
  of team members, 79–82, 88, 92
Commitment, and systems change model, 117
Communication
  as attitudinal issue, 108
  cognitive referencing and, 198
  community self-sufficiency and, 274
  definition of, 197
  formal communication mechanisms, 290
  motor skills and, 225
  personnel preparation in, 330
  samples of, 202
  social interaction and, 197
  state and local agencies, 290
Communication and Symbolic Behavior Scales, 201
Communication Environment Checklist, 203
Communication intervention
  adaptive devices and, 214
  assessment and, 198–205
  children with special needs and, 214–215

collaboration and, 207–208
communication samples and, 202
cultural differences and, 205
environmental arrangements and, 206–207, 212
evaluation and, 215
family participation and, 199, 205, 208
gifted children and, 315–316
goal selection and, 205
natural environment and, 208, 210–211
new developments in, 216–217
recommended practices and, 18, 205–215, 394–396
scripts illustrating, 213
teaching procedures and, 208–214
team members and, 198–199, 207–208
Community Resource Parents Program, 96
Community self-sufficiency, 273–275
Competence, definition of, 170–171
Competence motivation, 184
Comprehensive system of personnel development (CSPD), 330–331, 345
Computers, and assessment, 51. *See also* Technology use
Conductive education, and motor skills, 247
Consensual validity
  assessment and, 44–49
  recommended practices and, 47–48
  team member consensus and, 44–47
Contingent responsiveness, 224
Controlled rotary vestibular stimulation program, 255
Conventionalization, 159
Convergent assessment
  assessment materials and, 39–40
  legislation and, 38
  multiple occasions and, 42–43
  multiple sources and, 40–43
  recommended practices and, 43–44
Correspondence training, 142
Credentialing, 330–332
Cross-disciplinary collaboration, 10–11
Cross-disciplinary service delivery, 102–103

CSPD (Comprehensive system of personnel development), 330–331, 345
Cultural differences
  assessment and, 26–27
  caregiver-infant interactions and, 230
  communication intervention and, 205
  general curriculum and intervention strategies and, 130
  gifted children and, 311
  IFSP/IEP process and, 83
  maternal responsivity and, 224–225
  peer interactions and, 227
  preservice training programs and, 340
  recommended practices and, 9–10
  service delivery systems and, 105
  strategy selection and, 135–136
Current use ratings, and recommended practices, 13–16
Curriculum. *See also* General curriculum and intervention strategies
  definition of, 125–127
  differentiated, 311
  motor skills and, 251–252
Curriculum-based assessment (CBA)
  consensual validity and, 47–48
  convergent assessment and, 39, 43
  treatment utility and, 32–33
  trends in, 51

Daily routines and situations. *See* Routine-based practices
DAP. *See* Developmentally appropriate practice (DAP)
DEC. *See* Division for Early Childhood (DEC) of the Council for Exceptional Children
Decision making
  assessment and, 51
  collaboration and, 51
  family participation and, 81–82, 293, 312
  impact decisions and, 363, 365
  inservice training programs and, 347–348

program evaluation and, 323, 363–365, 374, 375
team members and, 89
Default intervention, 208
Delivering desired consequences, 212
Delphi technique, 48–49
Descriptive talking, 212
Determinants
  cognitive competencies and, 164–165
  environmental, 166
  family, 165
  interactional, 165
  systems, 166–167
Development. *See also* Social development
  competency and, 160
  development discontinuity, 27
  meaning of, 169–170
  milestones of, 34–35
  social systems context of, 186–187
  transition and, 27
Developmental Observation Checklist System, 44
Developmentally appropriate practice (DAP)
  assessment and, 35, 36, 38, 40
  general curriculum and intervention strategies and, 130–132
  recommended practices and, 11–12, 104
  service delivery systems and, 104–105
Differential reinforcement strategies, 140–142
Differentiated curriculum, 311
Diversity. *See* Cultural differences
Division for Early Childhood (DEC) of the Council for Exceptional Children
  assessment and, 28, 49
  attitudinal issues and, 106
  developmentally appropriate practice, 104
  general curriculum and intervention strategies outcomes and, 127
  IFSP/IEP process and, 84
  inclusion and, 12, 82
  personnel preparation and, 335–336
  program evaluation and, 361

recommended practices and, 2, 6, 17
social development and, 223–224
Task Force on Recommended Practices, 6, 11, 13
Dressing/undressing, 264, 266
Dynamic assessment, 311
Dynamic variable, 164

Early childhood education (ECE), and personnel preparation, 334
Early Education Program for Children with Disabilities (EECPD), 5
Early Intervention/Early Childhood Special Education (EI/ECSE)
  adaptive behavior skills and, 259–282
  assessment and, 23–52
  cognitive competence and, 159–189
  communication intervention and, 197–217
  contexts of, 129–132
  developmentally appropriate practice and, 105
  emotional development and, 223–238
  empowerment and, 77–97
  family participation and, 59–72, 129, 160
  general curriculum and intervention strategies, 125–150
  gifted children and, 309–325
  goals and objectives of, 127–128
  history of, 1
  IFSP/IEP process and, 77–97
  motor skills and, 245–256
  personnel preparation and, 329–354
  personnel shortages in, 329
  program evaluation and, 359–377
  recommended practices and, 2–16
  service delivery systems and, 101–122
  social interaction and, 223–238
  transition and, 287–304
Eating, 268–272
ECE. *See* Early childhood education (ECE)
Ecological assessment, 39, 40–41, 174
Ecological inventories, 203–204
Ecological-functional approach, 262–263

Ecological-social perspective, 164–167, 169, 171
Education. *See* Inservice training programs; Personnel preparation; Preservice training programs
Education of All Handicapped Children Act of 1975 (P.L. 94-142), 65, 312
Education of the Handicapped Act Amendments (P.L. 99-457)
  family participation and, 9, 59, 78, 86
  gifted students and, 312
  inservice training programs and, 348, 352
  interdisciplinary personnel preparation and, 334
  self-help skills and, 261
  transition and, 321
EECPD (Early Education Program for Children with Disabilities), 5
Effect sizes, 375–376
EHA. *See* Education of All Handicapped Children Act of 1975 (P.L. 94-142)
EI/ECSE. *See* Early Intervention/Early Childhood Special Education (EI/ECSE)
Elaboration, 212
Embedded instruction, 209
Emotional development. *See also* Peer interaction; Social development; Social interaction
  gifted children and, 319–320
  recommended practices and, 18, 228–233, 396–397
Empowerment
  balance of power and, 159–160
  of family, 78–82
  IEP plans and, 77
  IFSP/IEP process and, 77, 78–83
  inclusion and, 82–83
  recommended practices and, 79–96
  of team members, 78–80, 87
Engagement, 182–183
Engaging behaviors, 175
Environmental arrangements
  communication intervention and, 206–207, 212

  general curriculum and intervention strategies and, 136–137
  for motor skill development, 250–251
  social development and, 230
Environmental determinants, and cognitive competence, 166
Environmental language intervention, 209
Environmental Language Intervention Program, 201
Environmental Prelanguage Battery, 201
Equipment, for motor skills development, 252
Evaluability assessment, 368–369
Evaluation. *See also* Program evaluation
  assessment and, 248–249
  communication intervention and, 215
  family participation and, 67–69
  formative evaluation, 323
  gifted children and, 323–324
  of inservice training programs, 352
  motor skills and, 248–249, 252
  needs-assessment, 374–375
  process evaluations, 374–375
  service coordination and, 93
  summative evaluation, 324
  systems change model and, 120–121
  transition and, 299, 302–303
  treament utility and, 31–32
Expanding, 212
Expert opinion, and recommended practices, 3–4

Faculty, of preservice training programs, 343
Family-centered services. *See also* Family participation
  cognitive competence and, 189
  Individuals with Disabilities Education Act of 1990 and, 102
  recommended practices and, 8–9
Family Concerns Committee, 6–7
Family determinants, 165
Family-Focused Early Intervention System (FFEIS), 113
Family Needs Survey, 37
Family participation
  adaptive behavior skills and, 261–263

advocacy and, 69–70
anticipated transitions and, 292
assessment and, 40–45, 88
caregiver-infant interactions and, 229
cognitive competence and, 187
communication intervention and, 199, 205, 208
community self-sufficiency and, 274
decision-making and, 81–82, 293, 312
definition and values, 62–63
Education of the Handicapped Act Amendments and, 9, 59, 78, 86
empowerment and, 78–82
evaluation and, 67–69
family determinants, 165
family support and, 66–67
gifted children and, 314, 324–325
IFSP/IEP development and, 77
IFSP/IEP process and, 9, 81–82, 90
IFSP/IEP process outcomes and, 78–79
inclusion and, 83
Individuals with Disabilities Education Act Amendments of 1991 and, 9
initiating transitions, 292
inservice training programs and, 60–62, 69, 348, 352–353
interagency collaborations and, 70–71
intervention and, 64–67, 126, 127, 229–230
leadership and, 69–71
legislation and, 70
monitoring and, 96
motor skill development and, 248, 249
policy making and, 67–69
preservice training programs and, 59–60, 68–69
procedural safeguards and, 64–67
program advising and, 67–69
program evaluation and, 362
receiving providers and, 293, 297–298
recommended practices and, 17, 63–71, 79–82, 381–387
sending providers and, 293
service delivery systems and, 291–292
staff hiring, training, and evaluation, 67–69

strategy selection and, 135
team member collaboration and, 79–82, 88
transition and, 291–294
validation and, 63–64
visiting program options, 293
Family support services, 66–67
Feasibility, and program evaluation, 360, 368–369
Feeding, 268–271
FFEIS (Family-Focused Early Intervention System), 113
Field experiences, of preservice training programs, 341–342
Fiscal issues, of service delivery systems, 109–112
Fit for Me, 251
Focal Point, 60
Follow-up assessment, 248–249
Forging Partnerships with Families, 60–61
Formal communication mechanisms, 290
Formative evaluation, 323
Free-play activity, 236
Friendship activities, 236
Front-end decisions, 363, 364
Functional analyses, 203
Functional assessment, 40, 51
Functional capabilities, 185
Functional-ecological approach, 262–263

GAS. *See* Goal Attainment Scaling (GAS)
General curriculum and intervention strategies. *See also* Curriculum; Intervention
contexts of, 129–132
continuum of, 133–136
correspondence training, 142
developmentally appropriate practice and, 130–132
differential reinforcement strategies and, 140–142
effective strategies, 136–146
environmental arrangements, 136–137
foundational assumptions of, 132–133
future trends in, 149–150
gifted children and, 314
goals and outcomes of, 127–128

milieu strategies and, 144
peer-mediated strategies, 142–143
recommended practices and, 17, 136–146, 390–393
response shaping, 144–145
response-prompting strategies, 145–149
responsive elaboration and, 138–140
self-management strategies, 143–144
specialized materials, 137–138
strategy list, 133–135
strategy modification and adjustment, 146, 149
strategy selection, 135–136
Generalization, of motor skills, 252–253
Gifted children
adaptive behavior skills and, 320
assessment of, 310–311
cognitive competence and, 317–318
communication intervention and, 315–316
cultural differences and, 311
differentiated curriculum for, 311
evaluations and, 323–324
family participation and, 314, 324–325
general curriculum and intervention strategies, 314
IFSP/IEP process and, 311–313, 320, 324
motor skills and, 316–317
personnel preparation and, 322–323
program evaluation and, 323–324
recommended practices for, 19, 310–325, 402–407
service delivery model and environment, 313–314
social-emotional development and, 319–320
transition and, 321–322
Goal Attainment Scaling (GAS), 37–38
Goals and objectives
action planning and, 118–119
for caregiver-infant interactions, 229
communication intervention and, 205
of Early Intervention/Early Childhood Special Education, 127–128
of general curriculum and intervention strategies, 127–128

for motor skill development, 251–252
routines-based, 83
social validity and, 34–35
team members and, 81
treatment utility and, 29–30
Grooming, 264, 266
Guided participation, 235

Hawaii Early Learning Profile, 248
Hawaii Early Learning Profile and Activities, 261
Hawaii Early Learning Profile-Inside Help, 33
Head Start, 107, 108, 110, 117, 288
Help for Special Preschoolers, 33
Human ecology, and cognitive competence, 164

ICCs. *See* Interagency coordinating councils (ICCs)
IDEA. *See* Individuals with Disabilities Education Act of 1990 (IDEA)
IEP. *See* IFSP/IEP process
IFSP/IEP process. *See also* IFSP/IEP team members and teamwork
attitudinal issues and, 109
caregiver-infant interaction and, 229
development of, 81
empowerment indicators and, 77, 78–83
family participation and, 9, 81–82, 90
gifted children and, 311–313, 320, 324
IFSP/IEP document and, 91–92
monitoring of, 95–96
motor skills and, 248, 249, 250
natural environment and, 82
outcome of, 78–79
program providers' awareness of, 296
recommended practices for, 17, 79–96, 385–387
service coordination and, 92–95
team member responsibilities, 86–91
team member selection, 84–86
transition and, 85, 300
IFSP/IEP team members and teamwork. *See also* IFSP/IEP process
advocacy of, 89–91
collaboration of, 79–82, 88, 92

communication intervention and, 198–199, 207–208
consensual validity and, 44–47
developing outcomes, 89
empowerment of, 78–80, 87
feeding and, 269
goals and objectives, 81
IFSP/IEP development and, 81
inclusion and, 82–83, 92
information sharing and, 87–89, 297
inservice training programs and, 345
interdisciplinary teams, 10–11
measuring progress, 89
motor skills promotion and, 249
multidisciplinary teams, 10–11
need for, 129
preservice training programs and, 288
problems and solutions in, 46–47
providing supportive, informal relationships, 86–87
recommended practices and, 84–96
responsibilities of, 86–91
selection of, 84–86
transdisciplinary teams, 10–11, 129
Impact decisions, 363, 365
Impinging factors, and systems change model, 121
Incidental teaching, 181–182, 209
Inclusion
advocacy of, 90–91
attitudinal issues and, 106–109
Division for Early Childhood of the Council for Exceptional Children, 12, 82
empowerment and, 82–83
family participation and, 83
inservice training programs and, 345
peer interactions and, 234–235
recommended practices and, 82–83
systems change model for preschool inclusion, 116
teacher preparedness attitudes, 107–108
team members and, 82–83, 92
turf attitudes and, 107
Independent play, 275–276
Individual education program. *See* IFSP/IEP process

Individual family service plan. *See* IFSP/IEP process
Individualized transition plans (ITPs), 312
Individuals with Disabilities Education Act Amendments of 1991 (P.L. 102-119)
adaptive behavior skills and, 261
family participation and, 9
program evaluation and, 362
Individuals with Disabilities Education Act of 1990 (IDEA)
collaboration and, 303–304
comprehensive system of personnel development and, 331
family-centered service and, 102
gifted children and, 312
IFSP/IEP monitoring and, 96
least restrictive environment and, 101
multidisciplinary collaboration and, 10–11
personnel preparation and, 330–331
services coordination and, 92–94
transition and, 300
Infants
with disabilities, 226
emotional development of, 223–238
infant-caregiver interactions and, 224, 229–230, 232
motor skills of, 225, 254–255
preservice training programs and, 340–341
social and emotional development of, 224–225
social competence interventions for, 229–233
social interaction of, 223–238
special educators and, 345
Informal observations, 248
Information
program evaluation and, 372–373
program providers and, 296–297
team members and, 87–89, 297
transitions and, 292–293
Initiating behaviors, 175
Initiations, support of, 235–236

440 Subject Index

Inservice training programs
  comprehensive system of personnel development and, 330–331
  context of, 352–353
  decision making, 347–348
  delivery of, 349–352
  evaluation of, 352
  facilitators of, 353
  family participation and, 60–62, 69, 348, 352–353
  gifted children and, 322–323
  inclusion and, 345
  needs-based approach, 346–347
  participants of, 352–353
  personnel preparation and, 112–113, 344–353
  planning and, 347–348
  processes of, 347–352
  recommended practices and, 344–353
  state standards for, 331–332
  support factors, 349
  teamwork and, 345
  transition and, 301–302
Institute for Family-Centered Care, 61
Instruction
  communication intervention and, 208–214
  embedded instruction, 209
  incidental teaching, 181–182, 209
  inclusion and, 107–108
  modifications of, 279–281
  motor skills promotion and, 250
  multiple-skills instruction, 253
  responsive teaching, 179
  strategies of, 179–182
  teacher preparedness attitudes, 107–108
  treatment utility and, 30–31
Integration, of motor skills, 252–253
Intelligence tests, and assessment, 31–32
Interactional determinants, and cognitive competence, 165
Interactions, and communication intervention, 207. *See also* Social interaction
Interactive coaching, 181, 230–231

Interactive competency. *See also* Social interaction
  children's acquisition of, 161
  definition of, 159
  devleopmental competency and, 160
  play and, 162
Interagency agreements, 289–290, 295
Interagency collaboration, 70–71
Interagency coordinating councils (ICCs), 68
Interdisciplinary focus, of personnel preparation, 334–336
Interdisciplinary teams, 10–11
Intervention. *See also* Communication intervention; General curriculum and intervention strategies
  adaptive behavior skills and, 259–282, 320
  adaptive devices and, 184–186
  adult-mediated, 235
  assistive technology and, 184–186
  attachment interventions, 233
  child characteristics and, 278–279
  child engagement, 182–183
  child-caregiver interactions, 183–184, 232
  child-initiated learning and, 178–179
  cognitive competence and, 174–187, 317–318
  context of, 262–263
  default intervention, 208
  definition of, 125–127
  family participation and, 64–67, 126, 127, 229–230
  instructional modifications and, 279–281
  instructional strategies and, 179–182
  intervention settings, 176–178
  intervention targets, 174–176
  motor skills and, 245–256, 316–317
  peer-mediated, 235
  planning of, 263–278
  routine-based intervention, 177
  social competence and, 228–233, 319–320
  social interaction, 228–238, 319–320

social systems context of development, 186–187
transition and, 300
ITPs (Individualized transition plans), 312

JBA. *See* Judgment-based assessment (JBA)
Joint committee on Standards for Educational Evaluation, 360
Journal of Early Intervention, 2
Judgment-based assessment (JBA), 39

Language skills. *See* Communication
Laws. *See* Legislation; and specific laws
Leadership, and family participation, 69–71
Learning, child-initiated, 178–179
Learning Potential Assessment Device, 202
Least restrictive environment
  Education of the Handicapped Act Amendments and, 334
  general curriculum and intervention strategies and, 130
  Individuals with Disabilities Education Act of 1990 and, 101
  program providers' awareness of, 295–296
Legislation. *See also* names of specific laws
  and assessment, 24, 34, 38
  early intervention and, 9
  family participation and, 70
  licensing and credentialing, 330–332
  transition and, 288
Licensing, 330–332

Mand-model technique, 144, 212
Maternal responsivity, 224–225
McArthur Communicative Development Inventories, 201
Medical identification, and assessment, 248
Medical needs, and service coordination, 94
Metacognition, 318
Middle-ear infections, 215
Milieu strategies, 144

Minimal encouragers, 212
Modeling, 212
Modulating behaviors, 176
Monitoring, 95–96, 370–371
Mothers, 84, 224–225, 229. *See also* Family participation
Motor programming, 254
Motor skills
  adult facilitators and, 249–250
  assessment of, 247–249
  cognitive competence and, 253
  communication and, 225
  community self-sufficiency and, 274
  conductive education and, 247
  curricula for, 251–252
  environmental arrangements, 250–251
  equipment and materials, 252
  evaluation and, 248–249, 252
  family participation and, 248, 249
  generalization of, 252–253
  gifted children and, 316–317
  goals and objectives for, 251–252
  grouped studies, 255–256
  IFSP/IEP process and, 248, 249, 250
  individual studies on, 253–255
  of infants, 225, 254–255
  informal observations and, 248
  integration of, 252–253
  intervention and, 245–256, 316–317
  medical identification and assessment, 248
  multiple-skills instruction, 253
  neurodevelopmental model, 246
  perceptual motor model, 246
  physical developmental model, 246
  promotion of, 249–251
  recommended practices and, 18, 249–251, 397–398
  research on, 253–256
  self-care and, 264, 269–270
  sensory integration model, 246–247
  social interaction and, 253
  theoretical constructs for development of, 245–247
  therapy goals and strategies, 251–252
  Vojta method and, 247
Movement Assessment of Infants, 255

Multicultural differences. *See* Cultural differences
Multidisciplinary teams, 10–11. *See also* Cross-disciplinary collaboration
Multiple-skills instruction, 253
Mutual enjoyment, 232–233

NAEYC. *See* National Association for the Education of Young Children (NAEYC)
National Academy of Early Childhood Program Accreditation, 5
National Association for the Education of Young Children (NAEYC)
  assessment and, 28, 29
  cognitive competence and, 187–188
  developmentally appropriate practice and, 11, 104–105
  personnel preparation and, 332, 335–336
  recommended practices and, 4, 5
  social development and, 223–224
National Association of Early Childhood Specialists in State Departments of Education, 29
National Association of School Psychologists, 28
National Council on Disability, 185
National validation, and recommended practices, 5–6
Natural environment
  communication intervention and, 208, 210–211
  Education of the Handicapped Act Amendments and, 334
  general curriculum and intervention strategies and, 130
  IEP/IFSP process and, 82
  program providers' awareness of, 296
Naturalistic assessment, 201
Naturalistic programming, 256
NBA. *See* Norm-based assessment (NBA)
NDT. *See* Neurodevelopmental theory (NDT)
Needs assessment evaluation, 374–375
Needs-based approach, to inservice training programs, 346–347

Neurodevelopmental motor skills model, 246
Neurodevelopmental theory (NDT), 254–256
New Mexico State University (NMSU) Preschool for the Gifted, 314, 317, 318, 325
Nonlinear progression, 27
Nonsocial behaviors, 176
Normalization, and recommended practices, 12, 101–102
Norm-based assessment (NBA), 39, 43

Observation
  assessment and, 24–26
  informal, 248
  observation coding, 202
Occupational therapists
  motor skills promotion and, 249–250, 251
  training of, 330

P.L. 94-142. *See* Education of All Handicapped Children Act of 1975 (P.L. 94-142)
P.L. 99-457. *See* Education of the Handicapped Act Amendments (P.L. 99-457)
P.L. 102-119. *See* Individuals with Disabilities Education Act Amendments of 1991 (P.L. 102-119)
Parent trainer, 69
Parent Training and Information Center, 90
Parents. *See* Caregivers; Family participation; Mothers
Parent-to-Parent programs, 90
Peabody Developmental Motor Scales, 253–254
Peabody Developmental Motor Scales and Activity Cards, 248, 251–252
Peabody Picture Vocabulary Test, 201
Peer interactions
  adaptive behavior skills and, 276, 281
  inclusion and, 234–235
  play and, 227, 228, 235
  preschool children and, 226, 234–238
  true peers, 320

Subject Index   443

Peer-mediated intervention, 235
Peer-mediated strategies, 142–143
Perceptual motor model, 246
Performance, definition of, 171
Personal-social responsibility, 275–277
Personnel competence. *See* Inservice training programs; Personnel preparation; Preservice training programs
Personnel preparation. *See also* Inservice training programs; Preservice training programs
  collaboration and, 335
  communication and, 330
  gifted children and, 322–323
  Individuals with Disabilities Education Act of 1990 and, 330–331
  interdisciplinary focus, 334–336
  legal framework for, 330–331
  licensing and credentialing, 330–332
  planning considerations, 330–337
  recommended practices and, 19, 337–353, 407–411
  research base and, 336–337
  service delivery systems and, 112–113
  state standards for, 331–333
  transition and, 293–294, 301
Physical developmental motor skills model, 246
Physical differences, and assessment, 26–27
Physical education, 250, 254
Physical therapists
  motor skills promotion and, 249–250, 251
  training of, 330
Planning
  action planning, 118–120
  administrative support for, 301
  inservice training programs and, 347–348
  of interventions, 263–278
  for personnel preparation, 330–337
  program evaluation and, 371–372
  transition and, 290–291, 300
Play
  caregiver-infant interactions and, 230
  of children with disabilities, 162, 172

free-play activity, 236
  independent play, 275–276
  interactive competencies and, 162
  peer interactions and, 227, 228, 235
Policy barriers, and systems change model, 118, 119, 120
Policy making, and family participation, 67–69
Potential social consequences, 25
Power. *See* Empowerment
Praise, 212
Preparation time, 290–291
Preschool children
  with disabilities, 227–228, 234–238
  social development of, 226–228
  social interaction interventions for, 234–238
Preservice training programs
  attitudinal issues and, 107–108
  collaboration and, 288
  comprehensive system of personnel development and, 330–331
  content of, 339–341
  cultural differences and, 340
  faculty of, 343
  family participation and, 59–60, 68–69
  field experiences of, 341–342
  gifted children and, 322–323
  graduate preparation, 343–344
  infants and, 340–341
  personnel preparation and, 112–113, 337–344
  processes of, 341
  recommended practices, 337–344
  state standards for, 332
  teamwork and, 288
  transition and, 301
Procedural safeguards, and family participation, 64–67
Process evaluation, 374–375
Professional assessment practices, 24–26
Professional organizations. *See* names of specific organizations
Professional training. *See* Inservice training programs; Personnel preparation; Preservice training programs

Program advising, and family
    participation, 67–69
Program evaluation
    decision making and, 323, 363–365, 374, 375
    family participation and, 362
    feasibility and, 360, 368–369
    framework for, 359–361
    gifted children and, 323–324
    models of, 360
    multiple sources of information and, 372–373
    propriety and, 360, 369–370
    recommended practices and, 19, 361–376, 411–413
    reporting of, 366–367
    standardized measures and, 373–374
    technical adequacy and, 360, 370–376
    utility and, 360, 361–368
Program-level issues, 114–115
Program monitoring, 95–96, 370–371
Program options, 293
Program-process decisions, 363, 364–365
Program providers. *See also* Inservice training programs; Personnel preparation; Preservice training programs
    information sharing, 296–297
    interagency transition agreements and, 295
    sending and receiving, 293, 294–298
    service options and resources, 295–296
    transition training, 293–294
Project Dakota, 89, 91
Prompting imitation, 209, 212
Prompting procedures. *See* Response-prompting strategies
Propriety, and program evaluation, 360, 369–370
Prosthetic devices, 214
Public schools, special education programs of, 70, 109

Rapid toilet training, 267–268
Rating scales, 203
Ratings of current use, and recommended practices, 13–16
Recasting, 212

Receiving program providers
    family participation and, 293, 297–298
    transition and, 294–298
    transition preparation and, 297–298
Recommended practices
    adaptive behavior skills and, 18–19, 263–278, 399–400
    assessment and, 16–17, 32, 37–38, 43–44, 47–48, 248, 379–381
    best practices and, 2–3
    chronologically age appropriate, 11–12
    cognitive competency and, 17–18, 168, 174–187, 393–394
    communication skills and, 18, 204–217, 394–396
    cross-disciplinary collaboration, 10–11
    cultural differences and, 9–10
    developmentally appropriate practice and, 11–12, 104
    Division for Early Childhood (DEC) of the Council for Exceptional Children, 2, 6, 11, 13, 17
    emotional development and, 18, 228–233, 396–397
    empirically and value-driven practices, 103–104
    empowerment indicators, 79–96
    establishment of, 2–16
    expert opinion and, 3–4
    family participation and, 17, 63–71, 79–82, 381–387
    family-centered services, 8–9, 102
    general curriculum and intervention strategies and, 17, 136–146, 390–393
    for gifted children, 19, 310–325, 402–407
    identification of, 3–6
    for IFSP/IEP process, 17, 79–96, 385–387
    inclusion and, 82–83
    inservice training programs and, 344–353
    motor skills and, 18, 249–251, 397–398
    national validation, 5–6
    normalization and, 12, 101–102
    personnel preparation and, 19, 337–353, 407–411

philosophical criteria and, 8
preservice training programs and, 337–344
procedures for identifying and validating, 6–12
professional consensus and, 4
program evaluation and, 19, 361–376, 411–413
ratings of current use, 13–16
research and, 8
service delivery systems and, 17, 92–95, 101–105, 387–390
social change and, 105–115
social interaction and, 18, 228–233, 396–397
state-level consensus building, 5
strands within, 7
team members and, 84–96
transition and, 19, 288–303, 400–402
validation and, 5–6, 13
value based, 8
Regulating behaviors, 176
Regulatory issues, of service delivery systems, 109–112
Reinforcement strategies, 140–142
Repeating, 212
Requesting clarification or elaboration, 212
Research
  on motor skills, 253–256
  for personnel preparation, 336–337
  recommended practices and, 8
Research Institute on Preschool Mainstreaming, 115
Resource allocation, 120
Respect, as attitudinal issue, 108
Response-prompting strategies, 145–149
Response shaping, 144–145
Responses, support of, 235–236
Responsibility, assumption of, 276–277
Responsiveness
  contingent responsiveness, 224
  maternal, 224–225
  responsive elaboration, 138–140
  responsive teaching, 179
  of social interaction, 231–232
Role acceptance, 103

Role release, 11, 103, 208
Routine-based practices, 83, 176, 177, 188–189, 264

Safe environment recommendation, 109–111
Scaffolding, 232
Self-care
  adaptive behavior skills and, 263–275
  assessment of, 269
  cognitive competence and, 274
  communication and, 274
  dressing/undressing and grooming, 264, 266
  eating, 268–272
  example skills, 265–266
  family participation and, 274
  feeding, 268–271
  intervention planning for, 263–275
  motor skills and, 264, 269–270, 274
  self-feeding, 271–272
  social development and, 274
  summary of, 272–275
  toileting, 266–268
Self-directed behaviors, 275
Self-feeding, 271–272
Self-help skills, 261
Self-management strategies, 143–144
Self-occupation, 275–276
Self-select, 317
Self-sufficiency, 273–275
Senate's Committee on Disability Policy, 86
Sending program providers
  family participation and, 293
  transition and, 294–298
Sensitivity, and assessment, 31
Sensory integration motor skills model, 246–247
Sensory integration therapy, 254–255
Sequenced Inventory of Communication Development, 199
Service coordinator, 294
Service delivery systems
  attitudinal issues and, 106–109
  collaboration and, 10–11, 288, 289–290, 303–304
  coordination of, 92–95

cross-disciplinary service delivery, 102–103
developmentally appropriate practice, 104–105
empirically and value-driven practices, 103–104
family participation and, 291–292
family-centered service and, 8–9, 102
fiscal and regulatory issues, 109–112
for gifted children, 313–314
inservice training programs and, 345
monitoring of, 95–96
normalization and, 101–102
options and resources, 295–296
personnel preparation issues, 112–113
program-level issues, 114–115
recommended practices and, 17, 92–95, 101–105, 387–390
social change and, 105–115
systems change model, 115–121
transition and, 93
Service-based eligibility, 50
SHARE Center for Excellence in Early Intervention, 92
Single point of contact, 294
Social adjustment, and adaptive behavior skills, 277–278
Social behaviors, 176
Social change
attitudinal issues and, 106–109
fiscal and regulatory issues and, 109–112
personnel preparation issues, 112–113
program-level issues, 114–115
recommended practices and, 105–115
Social development
community self-sufficiency and, 274
environmental arrangements and, 230
of gifted children, 319–320
of infants, 224–225
National Association for the Education of Young Children and, 223–224
of preschool children, 226–228
Social-ecological perspective, and cognitive competence, 164–167

Social interaction
acceptance and, 237–238
attachment interventions, 233
caregivers and, 229–233
coaching and, 230–231
communication and, 197
foster fun interactions, 237
infants and, 223–238
interpreting as meaningful, 231
interventions promoting competence, 228–233, 319–320
motor skills and, 253
mutual enjoyment of, 232–233
for preschool children with disabilities, 234–238
promoting interactions outside classroom, 236–237
providing opportunities to interact, 234–235
recommended practices and, 18, 228–233, 396–397
responsiveness and, 231–232
support initiations and responses, 235–236
triadic interaction and, 230–231
Social-personal responsibility, 275–277
Social Skills Rating System (SSRS), and assessment, 33, 37, 43
Social systems context of development, 186–187
Social validity
of assessment, 34–38
assessment methods and, 35–36
goals and objectives, 34–35
recommended practices and, 37–38
social significance of change, 36–37
Societal context, and assessment, 23–24
"Someone will lose" attitudes, 108–109
Special educators. *See also* Inservice training programs; Personnel preparation; Preservice training programs
infants and, 345
preschool children with disabilities and, 227
in public schools, 109
roles of, 129
Specialized materials, 137–138

Subject Index 447

SPECS. *See System to Plan Early Childhood Services* (SPECS)
Speech-language pathology services, 198, 208
SSRS. *See Social Skills Rating System* (SSRS)
Staff hiring, and family participation, 67–69
Stakeholder team, 117, 362
Standards
 for assessment, 28–49
 for personnel preparation, 331–333
Stanford-Binet L-M, 316
State and local agencies
 formal communication mechanisms, 290
 interagency agreements, 289–290
 planning and preparation time, 290–291
 transition and, 289–291
State-level consensus building, and recommended practices, 5
State standards, for personnel preparation, 331–333
Static variable, 164
Strands, 6–7
Strategies. *See also* General curriculum and intervention strategies
 differential reinforcement, 140–142
 effectiveness of, 136–146
 environmental arrangement strategies, 206–207
 instructional, 179–182
 list of, 133–135
 milieu, 144
 modification and adjustment of, 146, 149
 peer-mediated, 142–143
 reinforcement, 140–142
 response-prompting, 145–149
 selection of, 135–136
 self-management, 143–144
Strengths-based practices, 188
Summative evaluation, 324
Supportive relationships, 86–87
Survival skills, 321
Sustaining behaviors, 175
Synergistic power, 79, 87, 88

System to Plan Early Childhood Services (SPECS), 49
Systems change model
 action planning and, 118–120
 attitudinal issues, 118, 120
 cautionary notes, 121
 commitment and, 117
 evaluation and, 120–121
 impinging factors, 121
 implementation and, 120
 inclusion and, 116
 maintaining change and, 121
 policy barriers and, 118, 119, 120
 resource allocation and technical assistance, 120
 service delivery systems and, 115–121
 stakeholder team and, 117
 vision setting and, 118
Systems determinants, and cognitive competence, 166–167

Task Force on Recommended Practices (DEC), 6, 11, 13
Taxonomy, 318
Teacher-Child Communication Scale, 203
Teacher education and training. *See* Inservice training programs; Personnel preparation; Preservice training programs
Teacher preparedness attitudes, 107–108
Teaching. *See* Instruction; Special educators
Team members. *See* IFSP/IEP process; IFSP/IEP team members and teamwork
Technical adequacy, and program evaluation, 360, 370–376
Technical assistance, and systems change model, 120
Technology use
 assessment and, 50–51
 assistive technology, 184–186
Test of Early Language Development, 199
Time delay, 212
Toddlers. *See also* Infants; Preschool children; Young children
 self-directed behaviors and, 275

social competence interventions for, 229–233
Toileting, 266–268
Topics in Early Childhood Special Education, 2
Training. *See* Inservice training programs; Personnel preparation; Preservice training programs
Transdisciplinary Play-Based Assessment, 201
Transdisciplinary teams, 10–11, 129
Transition
 adaptive behavior skills and, 296
 administrative support for planning, 301
 anticipation of, 292
 assessment phase indicators, 298–299
 caregivers and, 291–294
 child component of, 298–300
 collaborative service models and, 303–304
 critical issues to enhance, 300–303
 developmental, 27
 evaluation of, 299, 302–303
 family participation and, 291–294
 gifted children and, 321–322
 IFSP/IEP process and, 85, 300
 individualized transition plans, 312
 Individuals with Disabilities Education Act of 1990 and, 300
 information about, 292–293
 initiation of, 292
 intervention phase, 300
 legislation and, 288
 personnel preparation and, 293–294, 301
 planning phase, 290–291, 300
 receiving program providers and, 294–298
 recommended practices and, 19, 288–303, 400–402
 sending program providers and, 294–298
 service coordination and, 93
 single point of contact, 294
 state and local agencies, 289–291
 types of, 287–288

Treatment utility
 assessment and, 28–33
 curriculum-based assessment and, 32–33
 evaluation and, 31–32
 goals and objectives identification and, 29–30
 instructional methods and, 30–31
 recommended practices and, 32
Triadic interaction, 230–231
True peers, 320
Turf attitudes, 107

United States Air Force, 48
Utility, and program evaluation, 360, 361–368
Uzgiris-Hunt Ordinal Scales of Psychological Development, 318

Validation
 family participation and, 63–64
 recommended practices and, 5–6, 13
Validity, consensual validity, 44–49
Value based, and recommended practices, 8
Vanderbilt-Minnesota Social Interaction Project, 235–236
Variable, dynamic, 164
Videotaping, 50–51, 231, 311
Vineland Adaptive Behavior Scale, 316–317
Vision setting, and systems change model, 118
Vojta method, motor skills and, 247

Work Sampling System, 40

Young children. *See also* Children with Disabilities; Children with special needs; Infants; Preschool children
 adaptive behavior and, 259–260
 assessment of, 26–27
 caregiver styles and, 165
 cognitive competence of, 159–189
 emotional development of, 223–238
 middle-ear infections of, 215
 public educational responsibility and, 70
 social interaction of, 223–238

LC 4031 .E27 1996

Early intervention/early childhood special education

CALLAHAN LIBRARY
ST. JOSEPH'S COLLEGE
25 Audubon Avenue
Patchogue, NY 11772-2399